Mastering the Chess Openings

Volume 2

John Watson

First published in the UK by Gambit Publications Ltd 2007

ISBN-13: 978-1-904600-69-5
ISBN-10: 1-904600-69-7

DISTRIBUTION:
Worldwide (except USA): Central Books Ltd, 99 Wallis Rd, London E9 5LN, England.
Tel +44 (0)20 8986 4854 Fax +44 (0)20 8533 5821. E-mail: orders@Centralbooks.com

Gambit Publications Ltd, 99 Wallis Rd, London E9 5LN, England.
E-mail: info@gambitbooks.com
Website (regularly updated): www.gambitbooks.com

Edited by Graham Burgess
Typeset by Petra Nunn
Cover image by Wolff Morrow
Printed in Great Britain by The Cromwell Press, Trowbridge, Wilts.

10 9 8 7 6 5 4 3 2 1

Gambit Publications Ltd
Managing Director: Murray Chandler GM
Chess Director: Dr John Nunn GM
Editorial Director: Graham Burgess FM
German Editor: Petra Nunn WFM
Webmaster: Dr Helen Milligan WFM

Contents

Symbols   5
Bibliography   6

Introduction   8

Section 1: Closed Games

1   **Introduction to 1 d4 and the Closed Games**   9

2   **Queen's Gambit Declined**   11
    Declining the Gambit: Other 2nd Moves   12
    Early Commitment   23
    Classical Variations   25
        Lasker Defence   25
        Orthodox/Capablanca Defence   29
        Tartakower Variation   35
        Alatortsev Variation   42
    Exchange Variation   46
        Carlsbad Variation   53
        Modern Exchange   61
    Move-Orders in the Queen's Gambit Declined   66

3   **Slav and Semi-Slav**   70
    Slav Main Line   74
        Dutch Variation: 6 e3   76
        Modern Line with 6 ♘e5   86
    Exchange Slav   94
    Semi-Slav   97
        The Meran   102
        Anti-Meran (6 ♕c2)   110

Section 2: Indian Systems

4   **Introduction to the Indian Defences**   114

5   **Nimzo-Indian Defence**   116
    Sämisch and Related Lines   118
        Lines with ...d6 and ...e5   120
        Lines with ...d5 and the Botvinnik Approach   122
        Sämisch Main Line with ...c5 and ...♗a6   131
    4 e3 and the Hübner Variation   135
        Early Castling   135

	4...c5 and the Hübner Proper	138
	Classical Nimzo-Indian: 4 ♕c2	143
	Central Counter-Attack: 4...d5	143
	Classical with 4...0-0	154
6	**Queen's Indian Defence**	**164**
	Introduction to 3 ♘f3	164
	Fianchetto Variation	165
	The Classical 4...♗b7	166
	The Modern 4...♗a6	169
	Petrosian System (4 a3)	173
7	**King's Indian Defence**	**183**
	Four Pawns Attack	188
	Central Break	191
	6...♘a6 vs the Four Pawns	201
	Classical King's Indian	204
	Exchange Variation	205
	Strongpoint Variation	208
	The Classical Main Line with 7...♘c6	216
	9 ♘e1	218
	9 ♘d2	231
	The Bayonet Variation	236
	Averbakh Variation	238
	Sämisch Variation	240
	Sämisch with ...e5	241
	Sämisch with ...c5	244
8	**Grünfeld Defence**	**248**
	Exchange Variation	249
	7 ♗e3 with 8 ♕d2	249
	7 ♗c4 and the Classical Exchange	253
	Modern 7 ♘f3 System	268
	Modern Main Line with ♖b1	272
	Russian System	280
9	**Modern Benoni**	**290**
	Classical Main Line	294
	Pawn-Storm Systems	301
	Mikenas Attack	302
	Taimanov Attack	303
	Fianchetto System	309
	Index of Players	316
	Index of Openings	319

Symbols

+	check
++	double check
#	checkmate
!!	brilliant move
!	good move
!?	interesting move
?!	dubious move
?	bad move
??	blunder
Ch	championship
Cht	team championship
Wch	world championship
Wcht	world team championship
Ech	European championship
Echt	European team championship
Ct	Candidates event
IZ	interzonal
Z	zonal
ECC	European Clubs Cup
OL	olympiad
jr	junior event
tt	team event
1-0	the game ends in a win for White
½-½	the game ends in a draw
0-1	the game ends in a win for Black
(n)	nth match game
(D)	see next diagram

Bibliography

Periodical Publications
ChessBase Magazine (up to no. 113); ChessBase
New in Chess Magazine; New in Chess
Informator (up to no. 96); Šahovski Informator

Websites
ChessPublishing; Kosten, A.; http://www.chesspublishing.com
The Week in Chess (up to no. 608); Crowther, M.; http://www.chesscenter.com/twic/twic.html
Jeremysilman.com; Silman, J.; http://www.jeremysilman.com
ChessCafe.com; Russell, H.; http://www.chesscafe.com

CDs and DVDs
Breutigam, M.; *King's Indian with h3*; ChessBase 2002
Breutigam, M.; *The Chigorin Defence*; ChessBase 2001
Corr Database 2006; ChessBase 2006
Dreev, A.; *Meran Variation*; ChessBase 2002
Henrichs, T.; *Queen's Gambit Orthodox Defence – Exchange Variation D31/D35-D36*;
    ChessBase 2005
Kasparov, G.; *How to Play the Queen's Gambit* (DVD); ChessBase 2005
Milov, V.; *Nimzo-Indian – 4 f3 and Sämisch Variation*; ChessBase 2002
Neven, K.; *The Grünfeld*; ChessBase 2004
Neven, K.; *Classical Nimzo-Indian – 4 ♕c2*; ChessBase 2005
Opening Encyclopaedia 2005; ChessBase 2005
Ripperger, R.; *How to Play the Nimzo-Indian?*; ChessBase 2002
Rogozenko, D.; *The Slav Defence*; ChessBase 2002

Books and Articles
Aagaard, J.; *Queen's Indian Defence*; Everyman 2002
Bosch, J.; *Secrets of Opening Surprises 1-5*; New in Chess 2003-6
Bronstein, D.; *Bronstein on the King's Indian*; Everyman 1999
Bronznik, V.; *The Chigorin Defence* (English version); Kania 2005
Burgess, G.; *The Slav*; Gambit 2001
Collins, S.; *Understanding the Chess Openings*; Gambit 2005
Cox, J.; *Starting Out: 1 d4!*; Everyman 2006
Emms, J.; *Starting Out: The Queen's Indian*; Everyman 2004
Emms, J.; *Easy Guide to the Nimzo-Indian*; Gambit/Cadogan 1998
Emms, J., Ward, C. & Palliser, R.; *Dangerous Weapons: The Nimzo-Indian*; Gloucester 2006
Fine, R.; *The Ideas Behind the Chess Openings* [3rd Edition]; McKay 1989
Gallagher, J.; *Starting Out: The King's Indian*; Everyman 2002
Gallagher, J.; *Play the King's Indian*; Everyman 2005
Gligorić, S.; *Play the Nimzo-Indian*; Pergamon 1985
Golubev, M.; *Understanding the King's Indian*; Gambit 2006
Hansen, Ca.; *The Nimzo-Indian: 4 e3*; Gambit 2002
Kallai, G.; *More Basic Chess Openings* [1 d4]; Cadogan 1997

Krnić, Z. (ed.); *ECO D – 3th Edition*; Šahovski Informator 1998
Krnić, Z. (ed.); *ECO E – 3th Edition*; Šahovski Informator 1998
Lalić, B.; *Queen's Gambit Declined: ♗g5 Systems*; Gambit/Everyman 2000
Nunn, J., Burgess, G., Emms, J. & Gallagher, J.; *Nunn's Chess Openings*; Gambit/Everyman 1999
Nunn, J.; *Grandmaster Chess Move by Move*; Gambit 2006
Nunn, J. & Burgess, G.; *New Classical King's Indian*; Batsford 1997
Nunn, J. & Burgess, G.; *Main Line King's Indian*; Batsford 1996
Palliser, R.; *Play 1 d4!*; Batsford 2005
Palliser, R.; *The Modern Benoni Revealed*; Batsford 2004
Panczyk, K. & Ilczuk, J.; *The Cambridge Springs*; Gambit 2002
Pedersen, S.; *The Meran System*; Gambit 2000
Rowson, J.; *Understanding the Grünfeld*; Gambit 1999
Sadler, M.; *Queen's Gambit Declined*; Everyman 2000
Shaw, J.; *Starting Out: The Queen's Gambit*; Everyman 2002
Vaïsser, A.; *Beating the King's Indian Defence and Benoni*; Batsford 1997
Ward, C.; *Starting Out: The Nimzo-Indian*; Everyman 2002
Ward, C.; *The Controversial Sämisch King's Indian*; Batsford 2004
Watson, J.; *Secrets of Modern Chess Strategy*; Gambit 1998
Watson, J.; *Chess Strategy in Action*; Gambit 2003
Watson, J. & Schiller, E.; *How to Succeed in the Queen Pawn Openings*; Trafford 2005
Watson, J.; *The Gambit Guide to the Modern Benoni*; Gambit 2001
Watson, J.; *The Unconventional King's Indian Defense*; Hypermodern 1999
Yakovich, Y.; *Play the 4 f3 Nimzo-Indian*; Gambit 2004
Yermolinsky, A.; *The Road to Chess Improvement*; Gambit 1999
Yrjölä, J. & Tella, J.; *The Queen's Indian*; Gambit 2003

Introduction

This second volume of *Mastering the Chess Openings* investigates openings in which White plays 1 d4. As in Volume 1, which examines 1 e4, I work from the ground up, starting with the very first moves of each opening to explain its elementary properties. Someone with only a modicum of playing experience should be able to master these fundamentals and use them as a basis for understanding the more sophisticated material that follows. For a primer on the rudimentary principles that apply to all opening play, please refer to Chapter 1 of Volume 1. The next two chapters of that volume may also be useful, since they identify the ideas and themes most often referred to in the book as a whole.

My philosophy is the same in both volumes, but a few points bear repeating. These books are not meant to cover all openings, much less all of their variations; such an undertaking would require scores of volumes. Instead, I have selected systems that I consider the most useful for the sake of explanation and instruction. In the main, these are the most 'important' openings, in that they have had a large following through the years and have a well-developed theoretical underpinning. Within these major openings I have picked a number of variations to study in some detail, based upon the belief that in-depth familiarity with several variations is better than superficial understanding of all. In order to place this selection in context, I leave signposts to indicate the direction in which alternatives may lead.

While some of the games and analysis are recent, many classic examples are used to illustrate general points.

This is not primarily a theoretical tome: some of the opinions that I venture about the value of hotly-contested individual lines will undoubtedly prove wrong or irrelevant. Instead, my goal is to provide a solid basis for the reader to play openings successfully, emphasizing positional features and techniques that extend to variations beyond those at hand. Notice that this differs from a full explanation of an opening using concepts specific to that opening. We shall see that individual moves themselves express ideas, whether or not they fit into a general scheme that has previously been set forth. Accordingly, a certain level of detail is absolutely necessary to understand both the consistent strategies and the anomalies that can render such strategies irrelevant.

On a practical level, I have subjected readers to recitations about the niceties of move-orders; the associated issues can be confusing but bear a direct relation to real-world results. Assessments of variations can evolve very rapidly, but how one best arrives at the desired starting points tends not to change much.

In the next chapter I examine the fundamental characteristics of 1 d4 and how it differs from 1 e4. You will find further comparisons between these moves in both volumes. The study of 1 d4 by itself will suffice to improve your chess understanding by leaps and bounds, but if you truly aspire to master the game you will want to know as much as possible about the e-pawn openings as well. I sincerely hope that these volumes will help you in both respects.

1 Introduction to 1 d4 and the Closed Games

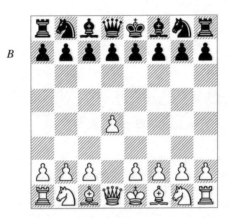

B

At the most basic level, 1 d4 might seem to resemble 1 e4. It brings a pawn to the fourth rank to occupy the centre and frees a bishop for action. Very much as the main 'goal' of 1 e4 is to enforce a successful d4, it may be said that after 1 d4 White's goal is to achieve e4. Nevertheless, even from this most primitive standpoint, we can see that 1 e4 only controls one central square (d5) and 1 d4 controls two (d4 and e5). This latter quality accounts for some immediate differences between opening with the queen's pawn and the king's pawn. For example, when we look at the defences to 1 e4, some of them attack e4 directly: the Alekhine Defence (1 e4 ♘f6) and the Scandinavian Defence (1 e4 d5). Others allow 2 d4 and then attack e4 on Black's 2nd move: the Caro-Kann Defence (1 e4 c6 2 d4 d5), the French Defence (1 e4 e6 2 d4 d5) and the Pirc Defence (1 e4 d6 2 d4 ♘f6). But versus 1 d4, none of Black's major defences attack the d4-pawn, and none even allow 2 e4, i.e., these defences all start with either 1...d5 or 1...♘f6, fighting for control of e4.

It doesn't take much thought to see how that difference arises: after 1 e4 White's e-pawn is unprotected, meaning that attacking it with

tempo can bring significant rewards, or at least a temporary initiative. Since White's d-pawn is already protected by his queen after 1 d4, the chances for Black to gain the initiative by targeting it are correspondingly low.

On the other hand, when he plays 1 d4, White has done nothing to contribute towards castling kingside. In fact, he often follows up with the moves 2 c4, 3 ♘c3 and in some cases moves such as 4 ♗f4, 4 ♗g5 or 4 ♕c2, none of which clear the way for kingside castling. One might argue that in such situations White's prospects of queenside castling are enhanced, since early moves by the knight, bishop, and queen clear the road for castling queenside. However, apart from a few attacking lines such as the Exchange Queen's Gambit and the Sämisch Variation of the King's Indian, White seldom avails himself of the opportunity to castle queenside. As is the case in most chess openings, queenside castling carries with it too many risks in terms of exposing White's king to quick attacks.

Then the question becomes whether Black can gain anything from White's delayed kingside castling. Can he put pressure on White that requires a degree of compromise in White's strategic plans? Before turning to 1 d4 d5, let's consider the Indian Defences that begin with 1 d4 ♘f6. The answer to our question changes with each opening and in each variation. In the main line of the King's Indian Defence, for example, Black puts very little pressure on White while he's getting castled, since his first five moves don't threaten anything or even directly challenge the centre. For example, the main line goes 1 d4 ♘f6 2 c4 g6 3 ♘c3 ♗g7 4 e4 d6 5 ♘f3 0-0 6 ♗e2 with 7 0-0 next. As in all major openings, Black's counterplay is based upon a central advance, normally the move ...e5. In that case White has great strategic leeway and delayed castling hasn't proved a decisive factor in the ensuing play. Furthermore, White can achieve positions in which his moves allow rapid castling anyway; e.g., 1 d4 ♘f6 2 c4 g6 3 ♘f3 ♗g7 4 g3 d6 5 ♗g2 and 6 0-0. But if White plays more ambitiously and delays 0-0 longer, he may run into other issues – for example, after 5 f4 0-0 6 ♘f3 c5 7 d5 e6 8 ♗e2 exd5 9 cxd5. In that case White has exposed his e4-pawn, which can't be supported by other pawns. Thus Black can play 9...♖e8, leaving White having to respond to the threat on his e-pawn before being able to castle.

White's e-pawn is not always Black's main target. For example, in the main line of the Exchange Grünfeld, 1 d4 ♘f6 2 c4 g6 3 ♘c3 d5 4 cxd5 ♘xd5 5 e4 ♘xc3 6 bxc3 ♗g7, White needs to set up his pieces having in mind Black's quick attack on his d4-pawn by ...c5 and ...♘c6. This means that White is confined to just a few ways of rearranging his pieces in order to bring his king to safety, placing them on what he may consider non-optimal squares; for instance, 7 ♗c4 c5 8 ♘e2 ♘c6 9 ♗e3. Or, in the process of shoring up his centre with pieces, White might allow Black to play ...cxd4 and ...♕a5+ on the move before he's managed to arrange 0-0; for example, 7 ♘f3 0-0 8 ♖b1 c5 9 ♗e2 cxd4 10 cxd4 ♕a5+. More obvious situations arise from variations in the same opening such as 1 d4 ♘f6 2 c4 g6 3 ♘c3 d5 4 ♗f4 and 4 ♗g5, in which Black can play ...c5 and White's necessary defensive moves relate directly to his delayed kingside development and inability to castle quickly.

In the Nimzo-Indian Defence, 1 d4 ♘f6 2 c4 e6 3 ♘c3 ♗b4, there are several situations in which Black can play ...♘e4 quickly in order to disturb White's plans on the kingside. Two examples are 4 ♘f3 b6 5 ♗g5 h6 6 ♗h4 ♗b7 7 e3 g5 8 ♗g3 ♘e4 and 4 ♘f3 c5 5 g3 ♘e4. If White plans to play ♗d3 and ♘ge2, he might run into, for example, 4 e3 b6 5 ♗d3 ♗b7, when White will normally play 6 ♘f3, because after 6 ♘e2 he can't castle in time to protect his g-pawn. Of course there are just as many variations in which delaying 0-0 doesn't affect White's plans, but in contrast to most 1 e4 openings he has to take into account the trade-offs involved in delaying his kingside development.

Openings beginning with 1 d4 d5 *(D)* are known as the 'Closed Games'. We shall begin our 1 d4 investigations in the next two chapters by examining those openings.

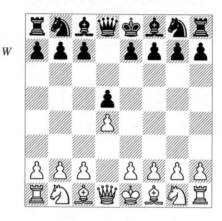

Black emphasizes prevention of e4, since that would ideally be White's next move. In fact, very seldom will you see a successful e4 on one of the first six or seven moves of a Queen's Gambit Declined (2 c4 e6) or a Slav (2 c4 c6), which are the most important Closed Games. This contrasts with both the King's Indian and Grünfeld Defences mentioned above. Still, the importance of the move e4 motivates both sides' play. White's predominant response to 1...d5 is 2 c4, clearly aimed at undermining d5 and thus shaking Black's control of e4. With the positional threat of 3 cxd5 ♕xd5 4 ♘c3 and 5 e4, Black usually feels compelled to prevent the key move e4 even at the cost of compromising his position. Thus we see the main lines 2...e6 and 2...c6. As explained in the next chapter about the Queen's Gambit Declined (2...e6), other second moves tend to give White a central majority in return for Black's lead in development. What we'll find is that although Black can cope with or prevent e4 in the Closed Games, he doesn't get away untouched in doing so. In the next two chapters, we'll discuss the ways in which White can try to exploit Black's concessions within the context of specific, selected opening variations. We shall also see how Black tries to combine pressure upon White's centre with maximum activity for his pieces. The Closed Games with 1 d4 d5 are rightly considered essential to the education of all developing players.

2 Queen's Gambit Declined

1 d4 d5 2 c4 *(D)*

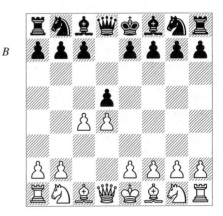

This is the venerable Queen's Gambit, the most popular response to 1...d5 by a huge margin (all the more so if you include 2 ♘f3 followed by 3 c4). White's immediate goal is to break down Black's control over d5, or otherwise gain concessions from him. This chapter is primarily about 2...e6, and includes short sections on other less important ways to decline the gambit.

Before moving on to more sophisticated analysis, I should stipulate that the Queen's Gambit is not a gambit in the sense of giving up a pawn for the sake of other compensating factors. White can recover his pawn almost immediately after 2...dxc4 3 e3 or 3 ♘f3 or even 3 e4. To show this, let's try the simple 3 e3, intending 4 ♗xc4 with easy development. At this point Black has a perfectly acceptable game by returning the pawn. He can play 3...♘f6 4 ♗xc4 e6, for example. But Black doesn't normally try to hang on to the pawn by 3...b5? because it leads to a disadvantage. White plays 4 a4! *(D)*.

Here Black needs to avoid 4...c6? 5 axb5 cxb5?? 6 ♕f3, attacking the rook on a8 and winning at least a piece. But other moves return the pawn under poor circumstances; for example, 4...bxa4 5 ♗xc4 ♗b7 6 ♘f3 e6 7 ♕xa4+, or 4...♗d7 5 axb5 ♗xb5 6 ♘c3 c6 7 b3! cxb3 8

♘xb5 cxb5 9 ♗xb5+ ♘d7 10 ♕xb3. In these positions White has the advantages of the central majority and pressure on Black's weakened queenside.

On the other hand, Black can't just sit around. The move 2 c4 attacks his d5-pawn, and if White were given a free move he would play 3 cxd5 ♕xd5 4 ♘c3, gaining a tempo on the queen, and play 5 e4 next. That would establish the classic ideal centre. How to respond? If Black doesn't want to accept the gambit, he can choose to defend his pawn by 2...e6 or 2...c6. Alternatively he can decline by counterattack with, for example, 2...e5, 2...♗f5 or 2...♘c6.

These latter moves are relatively less common, and we shall look at them shortly. But first I want to make some introductory comments about Black's main choice:

2...e6 *(D)*

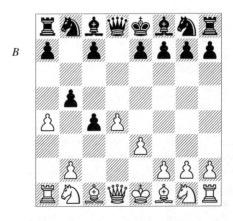

The position after 2...e6 introduces the classical Queen's Gambit Declined, an opening rivalling the Ruy Lopez as the greatest in chess history. For generations this move was almost obligatory at the highest levels. The greats such as Steinitz, Lasker, Capablanca, and Alekhine chose in it in the vast majority of the games in which they confronted 1 d4 d5 2 c4. The 1927 World Championship match between Alekhine and Capablanca featured no fewer than 32 out of 34 games with the Queen's Gambit Declined.

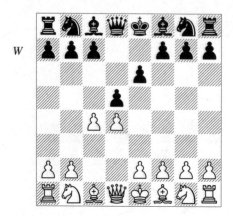

Although no longer holding such an exalted status, 2...e6 has remained the most important defence to the Queen's Gambit throughout the years and into the present. In some ways this is strange, because Black imprisons his bishop on c8 behind its own pawns. This is no trivial matter, since the bishop won't be able to participate in the struggle to control the centre nor in any active role. As usual, pieces condemned to staying on the first rank cause other problems, such as interfering with the connection of the rooks.

The struggle to free the light-squared bishop and find a good spot for it is arguably Black's main problem in the Queen's Gambit Declined (a.k.a. 'QGD'). As Kasparov indicates, the theme of finding a role for this bishop permeates the theory of the opening, and even complex ideas can often be reduced to it. The obvious question, then, is why Black would subject himself to a potentially arduous task. What happens if Black doesn't block off his bishop?

A superficial explanation concerns the two conventional alternatives. First, accepting the pawn by 2...dxc4 immediately cedes the centre to White. And in both Queen's Gambit Accepted theory and practice, it turns out that ...e6 is usually played within a few moves, before Black's c8-bishop is developed anyway! For example, the traditional main line of the Queen's Gambit Accepted is 1 d4 d5 2 c4 dxc4 3 ♘f3 ♘f6 4 e3 e6 5 ♗xc4 c5, when that bishop is left sitting on its original square behind the e6-pawn.

By contrast, the Slav Defence with 2...c6 keeps the c8-bishop open for development, but it takes away the best square for Black's queen's

knight. The move 2...c6 also foregoes ...c5, which is one of Black's most effective ways to attack White's centre. Furthermore, Black's two main lines in the Slav Defence are hardly perfect solutions to the light-squared bishop problem. After 2...c6 3 ♘f3, he can choose the extremely popular Semi-Slav by 3...♘f6 (or 3...e6) 4 ♘c3 e6, in which case the bishop on c8 is still hemmed in, even more so than after 2...e6. The most favourable variation in this respect is the old main line 3...♘f6 4 ♘c3 dxc4 5 a4 ♗f5. While this develops the bishop quite actively, it comes at the cost of giving White a central majority. These variations and associated issues will be discussed in detail in the next chapter.

Declining the Gambit: Other 2nd Moves

After 1 d4 d5 2 c4, the argument for playing 2...e6 gains force when one investigates less-played responses to 2 c4 which *don't* imprison Black's bishop on c8. This book is not encyclopaedic and I certainly won't analyse many side-variations in detail. But in this case it's extremely valuable to examine the ideas associated with those deviations from both 2...e6 and 2...c6, including their good points and the problems that accompany them. In each case, Black wants to keep the c8-bishop's path open and leave the c6-square free for his knight on b8. These lines are terribly instructive and hopefully useful.

Marshall Defence

1 d4 d5 2 c4 ♘f6 *(D)*

What could be simpler? Black develops a piece, defends the pawn on d5, and leaves the c8-bishop with a clear path to the outside world. It's interesting that if you show this position to even fairly experienced players and ask how they would proceed, many will react by suggesting 3 cxd5 ♘xd5 4 e4, which certainly is natural: White thereby forms the ideal centre with the gain of a tempo. Then if Black plays 4...♘f6, the obvious response is 5 ♘c3 (5 e5 ♘d5 leaves Black comfortably placed on the

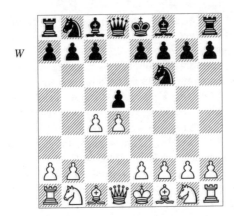

ideal blockading square in front of White's backward pawn). Up to this point, White has done everything logically and correctly, but Black can fight back with 5...e5! *(D)*.

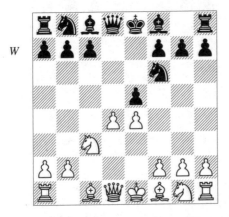

This changes the central equation, as every advanced player will recognize from similar positions in several openings. Play might continue, for example, 6 dxe5 (6 d5 ♗c5 allows free and easy development for Black's pieces) 6...♛xd1+ 7 ♚xd1 (7 ♘xd1 ♘xe4) 7...♘g4, threatening the pawns on f2 and e5 with a complex fight ahead in which Black has fully-fledged play. Also, for the record, 5 ♗d3 has a couple of drawbacks, the straightforward one being 5...♘c6 with pressure on the centre. Then Black is well developed following 6 d5 ♘e5 or 6 ♘f3 ♗g4. Also possible but less clear is the temporary pawn sacrifice 5...e5!? 6 dxe5 ♘g4.

So is 2...♘f6 the solution to the Queen's Gambit? Alas, it turns out that there is a better move than 4 e4. Simply 4 ♘f3! gains the advantage, since it stops ...e5 and truly threatens 5 e4.

Then the only efficient way for Black to prevent that move and still remain competitive in the centre is 4...♗f5 (the dubious move 4...f5?! creates a big outpost on e5 for White's pieces, at the same time restricting the range of that c8-bishop Black was trying so hard to free). But 4...♗f5 can be met by 5 ♛b3! and it is awkward for Black to defend b7; for example, 5...b6 (5...♘b6 allows 6 ♘c3 with e4 to come next) 6 ♘bd2. White has won the central battle. This time e4 cannot be stopped, as can be seen from an instructive line after 6...♘f6 *(D)*:

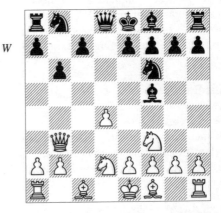

7 e4! ♘xe4 (7...♗xe4 8 ♘xe4 ♘xe4 9 ♘e5 not only threatens checkmate, but also ♗b5+ and sometimes ♛f3) 8 ♘e5! ♘d6 (the only real move, since 8...e6 9 ♗b5+ is too strong) 9 ♗b5+ (also good is 9 ♘xf7!? ♘xf7 10 ♛f3, but that is messier) 9...c6 10 ♘xc6 ♛d7 11 ♘xa7 ♘xb5 12 ♘xb5 and White has an extra pawn and good development.

What's the lesson behind the apparently lucky forcing moves at White's disposal (7 e4! and 8 ♘e5!) in this last variation? In the 1 d4 openings, a recurring theme is that an early move by Black's bishop from c8 may be met by attacking the squares that the bishop has just abandoned, usually by the move ♛b3 threatening the pawn on b7, and sometimes by ♛a4. This occurs, for example, in many Slav and Queen's Gambit Exchange variations (and we see it in many other openings, including some beginning with 1 e4). The situation with reversed colours can elicit the same response; for example, when White plays 1 d4 ♘f6 2 ♗g5 (the Trompowsky), Black often replies ...c5 to get ...♛b6 in. The same ...c5 (or, sometimes,

...c6) idea comes up in the Torre Attack (with ♗g5), London System (with ♗f4), the Veresov Attack (1 d4 d5 2 ♘c3 ♘f6 3 ♗g5), several variations of the King's Indian Defence, and a host of other openings.

The fact that 4 ♘f3 was clearly superior to 4 e4 in this simple example illustrates that White needs to refrain from occupying the centre with his pawns until he is sure that those pawns cannot be attacked to good effect. For instance, Black may be able to compel White's centre pawns to advance, or get the opportunity to exchange one or both of them. The problem is obvious enough, but often White's decision is not an easy one to make. This basic situation will arise throughout the openings that we are studying.

Baltic Defence

1 d4 d5 2 c4 ♗f5 (D)

Rather than defend d5, Black can directly develop with this bishop move, known as the Baltic Defence or sometimes the Keres Defence.

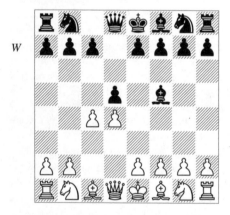

Black's idea is simple: he would like to play the move ...e6, but wants to get his bishop out in front of his own pawns first. We have emphasized that after 2...e6, the c8-bishop can be a passive piece. So why not develop it first, especially to a nice active post? Well and fine, but White still has his idea of cxd5, and if Black plays ...♕xd5, he wins a tempo against Black's queen by ♘c3 (perhaps followed by e4). Alternatively, we know already that early moves by Black's c8-bishop can sometimes be met by

♕b3 with an attack on the b7-square. Both of these themes arise after the following two moves:

a) 3 cxd5 (White chooses a gentle way to proceed, immediately establishing a central majority of pawns) 3...♗xb1 (this capture is Black's idea, so as to prevent White from achieving the powerful centre that would arise after 3...♕xd5 4 ♘c3, when e4 will follow, even after 4...♕e6 5 f3) 4 ♕a4+ (4 ♖xb1 ♕xd5 attacks White's pawn on a2, so White interpolates this check) 4...c6 (4...♕d7 5 ♕xd7+ ♘xd7 6 ♖xb1 leaves White with the bishop-pair and central majority; for example, 6...♘gf6 7 ♗d2 ♘xd5 8 e4 ♘5f6 9 f3) 5 ♖xb1 ♕xd5 6 f3 (D).

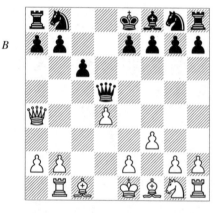

Without looking at the theory of this position in depth, we can see how powerful White's centre is about to become if Black waits a move and permits White to play e4. Then White's two bishops will rule the board. So let's briefly look over Black's most obvious continuation: 6...e5 (note that when playing against the two bishops and with no weaknesses in the position, Black usually wants to transform the pawn-structure and create opportunities for his knights; among several other variations favouring White are 6...♘d7 7 e4 ♘b6 8 exd5 ♘xa4 9 dxc6 bxc6 10 ♗d3! and 6...♘f6 7 e4 ♘xe4 8 ♗c4 ♕f5 9 fxe4 ♕xe4+ 10 ♘e2 ♕xb1 11 ♕b3! with various threats including 12 ♕xb7 and 12 ♗d3 ♕a1 13 0-0; in the latter case Black's queen won't escape) 7 dxe5 ♘d7 8 ♗f4 ♘c5?! (8...♘xe5 9 e4) 9 e4! ♕d7 10 ♕c4 ♖d8 11 ♗e2 with an extra pawn and the bishop-pair. The basic idea here is that unless some tactic by Black changes the overall dynamic of the game, White's centre and two bishops will grant him the long-term advantage.

b) Even though 3 cxd5 gave White the advantage, much more aggressive is 3 ♕b3! *(D)*, following the rule that when Black's bishop moves from c8, look at attacks on the queenside first.

B

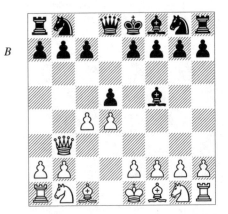

In fact 3 ♕b3 seems to be a virtual refutation of the Baltic (with the usual disclaimer that anything can change). Since the play that ensues is essentially tactical (and rather chaotic), it isn't particularly instructive to demonstrate all the details. Nevertheless, we have a situation in which capturing a pawn on b7 is followed by aggressive use of White's queen rather than a retreat to safety. This is a theme enunciated at various points in this book. So I shall show only the theoretically most critical move 3...e5!? (Black lashes out with aggressive intent; he has the usual problems that crop up when his early sortie by the c8-bishop is met by ♕b3; for example, 3...♘c6? 4 cxd5 ♘xd4?? loses to 5 ♕a4+; instead, 3...b6 4 cxd5 ♘f6 5 ♘c3 e6 6 ♗g5 keeps White a clear pawn ahead; and still worse is 3...♕c8? 4 cxd5 ♘f6 5 f3! with e4 next) 4 ♕xb7 ♘d7 5 ♘c3! exd4 (these moves are hard to improve upon; for example, 5...dxc4 6 e4 exd4 7 ♘d5 ♖b8 8 ♘xc7+ ♔e7 9 ♕c6) 6 ♘xd5 ♗d6 and now 7 ♘f3! *(D)* is simpler and more effective than 7 e4!?, although in my opinion both moves ultimately lead to winning games.

A critical variation goes 7...♘c5 8 ♘xc7+ ♕xc7 (8...♗xc7 9 ♕b5+) 9 ♕xa8+ ♔e7 10 ♕d5 ♗e6 11 ♕xd4 ♘f6 12 b4! and wins. Notice how keeping the queen in the enemy camp

B

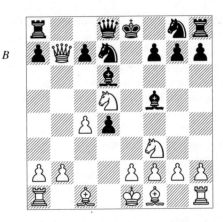

disturbed Black's development. I discussed this in Volume 1.

Albin Counter-Gambit

1 d4 d5 2 c4 e5!?

This is another counterattacking defence that refuses to acknowledge the need to defend against cxd5. It is a more serious challenge to the Queen's Gambit than the second moves of the preceding two variations. Black sacrifices a pawn following 3 dxe5 d4! and hopes that the cramping effect of his advanced pawn will limit White's pieces while giving him freer development. There normally follows 4 ♘f3 ♘c6 *(D)*.

W

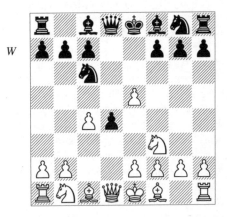

Unlike the 2nd-move variations seen above, White has neither an ideal centre nor tactical threats. But he does have an extra pawn and good development. White has a choice between 5 g3 and 5 ♘bd2 (moves like 5 a3 are also played but held in lesser regard). This is not a theoretical tome, but it's my opinion (and almost all theoreticians and players concur) that Black will not quite achieve full compensation. The reasons for this are concrete and explicable only by investigating the actual variations. But one way of thinking about it is that White, having the privilege of the first move and relatively logical places to put his pieces, is likely to achieve one advantage or another if and when Black takes time to regain his pawn, whereas White's position is sufficiently solid and free of weaknesses that he should be able to resist a brute-force attack. Nevertheless, this verdict is hardly etched in stone given the activity of Black's pieces. There is in fact no fundamental chess principle that ensures the superiority of either 2...e5 or 2...e6, in spite of their opposing characters.

What are each side's strategies in the Albin Counter-Gambit? In general (but not always) Black's chances lie with a direct kingside attack (versus 5 g3, for example, he can play ...♗e6/f5/g4, ...♕d7, ...0-0-0, ...♗h3 and ...h5-h4), or with a central initiative usually associated with ...0-0-0 and ...d3 or ...f6. Recently, Black's attention has turned to ...♘ge7-g6. For White, a variation that promises an advantage, albeit a limited one, begins with 5 ♘bd2, when White has ideas of attacking the d4-pawn by means such as ♘bd2-b3 and/or b4 and ♗b2; this is causing Black some problems at present. White's oldest and most popular plan is to develop by 5 g3 followed by 6 ♗g2 and 7 0-0. Then, after Black commits to ...0-0-0, White can attack via b4, often playing this as a pawn sacrifice to open queenside lines. One standard attacking idea for White involves moves like b5 and ♕a4. The move b4 may also support the simple idea of ♗b2 and ♘b3, attacking Black's d-pawn. Versus ...♗g4, ...♕d7 and ...0-0-0, White will often play the move ♕b3 (without b4) to gain threats against Black's vulnerable b7-square. All this is time-consuming, however, and the simple ...♘ge7-g6 plan challenges its effectiveness.

Naturally there are other strategies for both sides. In this sort of position featuring attacks and forcing moves, there is no substitute for careful study, which requires independent research. I won't be able to guide you through that maze, but here are a couple of excerpts,

beginning with the traditional 1 d4 d5 2 c4 e5 3 dxe5 d4 4 ♘f3 ♘c6 5 g3:

a) The old main line was 5...♗g4 6 ♗g2 ♕d7, as in Kozlovskaya-Mosionzhik, USSR 1971: 7 a3!? (7 0-0 ♗h3 8 ♕b3 prepares the standard trick 8...0-0-0? 9 e6! ♗xe6 10 ♘e5) 7...0-0-0 8 0-0 ♘ge7 9 ♕a4 ♔b8. This position isn't entirely clear, but the game went well for White following 10 ♘bd2 ♘g6 11 b4 h5 12 c5 ♗h3? (D).

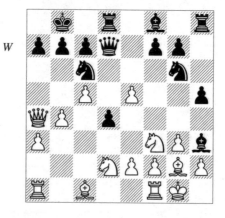

13 e6! (the same tactic) 13...♗xe6 (13...♕xe6 14 ♘g5) 14 b5 ♘ce5 15 c6 with a terrific attack.

b) Practice over the last five years has been dominated by 5...♘ge7; for example:

b1) 6 ♗g5 (depending upon the specifics, it can be favourable for White to exchange pieces, to reduce both Black's attacking chances and his ability to win his pawn back) 6...♕d7!? (6...h6 7 ♗xe7 ♗xe7 8 ♗g2 0-0 9 ♘bd2 with the idea ♘b3 is probably a tad better for White) 7 ♗xe7?! (7 h4! with the idea ♗h3 is promising; White will probably make the exchange on e7 later) 7...♗xe7 8 ♗g2 0-0 9 0-0 ♖d8! 10 ♘bd2 ♕e6 11 ♕c2 ♘xe5 12 ♖ad1 c5! 13 ♘xe5 ♕xe5, Kunte-Sales, Kuala Lumpur 2005. Black has recovered his pawn and has the two bishops. Although White's pieces are well-placed he stands a little worse.

b2) 6 ♘bd2 a5!? (a late addition to Black's arsenal, appropriate in several positions) 7 ♗g2 a4 8 ♘e4 ♘g6 9 ♗g5 ♗b4+ 10 ♔f1 ♗e7 11 ♗xe7 ♘gxe7 12 ♘c5 a3 13 bxa3?! (13 b4! ♘xb4 14 ♘xd4 leaves White with somewhat better prospects) 13...0-0 14 ♘b3 ♘g6 15 ♘bxd4 ♘cxe5 with equality, Asgeirsson-Kristjansson, Reykjavik 2005.

b3) 6 ♗g2 ♘g6 7 ♗g5 (there have been numerous games with 7 0-0 ♘gxe5 8 ♘xe5 ♘xe5 and Black has held his own; balanced play followed 7 ♕a4 ♗b4+ 8 ♘bd2 0-0 9 0-0 a5 10 a3 ♗e7 11 ♖d1 ♘cxe5 12 ♘xe5 ♘xe5 13 ♘f3 ♘xf3+ 14 ♗xf3 ♗f6 15 c5!? ♕e7 16 ♗f4? g5 17 ♗d2 c6 {17...g4!} 18 ♕c2 a4 in Khenkin-Morozevich, Mainz (rapid) 2005) 7...♕d7 8 0-0 h6 9 ♗f4 ♘xf4 10 gxf4, and now the typically dynamic idea 10...g5! *(D)*.

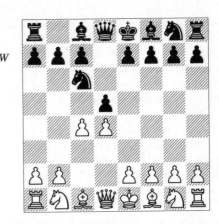

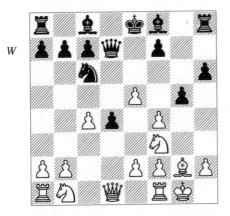

11 ♘bd2 (a later game Mlynek-Hasan, Brno 2005 saw 11 e3 gxf4 12 exd4 ♖g8 13 ♔h1 ♖xg2!? 14 e6! fxe6 15 ♔xg2 e5 16 ♘xe5 ♕h3+ 17 ♔h1 ♘xe5 18 dxe5 ♗d7 19 ♘c3 0-0-0 20 f3 ♗c5; then Black has definite attacking chances but he is a pawn and exchange down) 11...gxf4 12 ♘e4 ♗e7 13 ♕d2 ♕g4 14 ♔h1 ♗f5 15 ♘xd4? ♖d8 16 ♘xf5 ♖xd2 17 ♘xe7 ♔xe7 18 ♘xd2 ♕xe2 with a winning game for Black, Gelfand-Morozevich, Monte Carlo (Amber blindfold) 2004. Of course it's entirely unclear who was better after 10...g5 or, indeed, earlier in the game.

Needless to say, these examples are merely indicative of typical themes rather than best play.

Chigorin Defence

1 d4 d5 2 c4 ♘c6 *(D)*

The Chigorin Defence is increasingly popular and is currently considered a legitimate attempt to gain equality. It could even command its own section because the positional and strategic themes associated with it are so varied. Right away we can see that 2...♘c6 is unique in that it both develops a piece and attacks White's d-pawn. That means that the positional threat set up by 2 c4, that is, 3 cxd5 ♕xd5 4 ♘c3, doesn't work after 2...♘c6 3 cxd5 ♕xd5 4 ♘c3? because of 4...♕xd4. Black's 2nd move also sets up the advance 3...e5. A primary idea behind the Chigorin is rapid development: Black will rush his bishops to squares like g4 and b4, his king's knight to f6 or e7, and he will castle rapidly, either kingside or queenside. This is often necessary because White will have played cxd5 at some early point to gain a central majority and, given time to breathe, will march his centre pawns forward to drive away Black's pieces. In many lines Black needs to pin and/or capture knights on c3 and f3 in order to stop this expansion from taking place or at least delay it. For example, after 3 cxd5 ♕xd5 4 e3 e5 5 ♘c3, Black has given himself the opportunity for 5...♗b4 and can maintain the queen on d5. Or, after 3 ♘f3 (renewing the idea of 4 cxd5 ♕xd5 5 ♘c3), Black will play 3...♗g4, and if 4 cxd5, 4...♗xf3 5 gxf3 ♕xd5 follows, when again 6 ♘c3? loses the d-pawn. Therefore White might play 6 e3, threatening 7 ♘c3 for real, but after 6...e5, Black is once more ready for 7 ♘c3 ♗b4.

Such a strategy has two main problems. It often necessitates the exchange of one or both bishops for knights, thus presenting White with the bishop-pair. Moreover, as described, White will gain a central majority at some point; in combination with two bishops, mobile pawns can be devastating. For example, this pairing of two bishops and broad centre just about invalidates the Baltic Defence, as described above (of course the Baltic also has tactical problems).

The difference here is a matter of specifics and timing. In the Chigorin, Black is normally able to inflict weaknesses in White's position as the play develops. If not, his lead in development can sometimes produce attacking chances or force advantageous transformations of the pawn-structure.

Here are some game excerpts representing a small fraction of Chigorin Defence themes. As with any aggressive system, specific study of variations is necessary if you don't want to be rudely surprised.

We'll start with the classic Pillsbury-Chigorin, St Petersburg 1895, hardly the latest theory but with a few nice ideas from the man whose name the defence bears: 1 d4 d5 2 c4 ♘c6 3 ♘f3 ♗g4 4 cxd5 ♗xf3 5 dxc6 ♗xc6 6 ♘c3 e6 7 e4 ♗b4 8 f3 f5 (D).

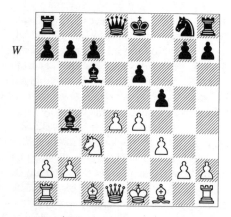

9 e5?! (in order to protect the pawn on e4 White concedes the d5 outpost to Black; White should play the dynamic counterattack 9 ♗c4! with some typical play going 9...♕h4+! 10 g3 ♕h3 11 ♕b3! ♗xc3+ 12 bxc3 ♕g2 13 ♖f1 fxe4 14 ♗xe6, when Breutigam suggests the equally dynamic 14...♘f6! 15 ♗f7+?! ♔d8 16 ♗g5?! e3! 17 ♗xe3 ♗xf3 18 ♗f2? ♖f8; Black seems to be doing quite well in this variation starting with 9...♕h4+ and 10...♕h3) 9...♘e7 10 a3 ♗a5 11 ♗c4 ♗d5 (Black keeps occupying the light squares, a colour-complex strategy that often occurs in the Chigorin) 12 ♕a4+ c6 13 ♗d3 ♕b6! (threatening ...♗b3!) 14 ♗c2 ♕a6 15 ♗d1 ♗c4 16 f4 0-0-0 17 ♗e3 ♘d5 (D).

The culmination of a typical Chigorin Defence light-square strategy. After 18 ♗d2 ♘b6

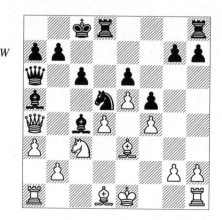

19 ♕c2 ♖xd4 20 ♖c1 ♗d3 21 ♕b3 ♘c4, Black went on to win.

Kasparov-Smyslov, Vilnius Ct (11) 1984 shows us the flip side. White's strategy is simple: take over the centre and attack with the bishops! 1 d4 d5 2 ♘f3 ♘c6 3 c4 ♗g4 4 cxd5 ♗xf3 5 gxf3 ♕xd5 6 e3 e5 7 ♘c3 ♗b4 8 ♗d2 ♗xc3 9 bxc3 ♕d6 10 ♖b1 b6 (D).

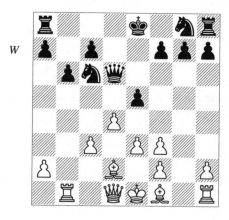

It looks as though White's centre can't advance but Kasparov found the idea 11 f4!? exf4 12 e4, establishing a powerful centre. White also has two very active bishops, but he is a pawn down. The game continued 12...♘ge7 13 ♕f3 0-0 14 ♗xf4 ♕a3?! (14...♕e6! is a typical attempt to grab the light squares: 15 d5 ♘xd5 16 ♗c4 ♖fe8, 15 ♗e2 f5 16 e5 ♕xa2 17 0-0 ♖ad8 18 ♗g5 ♕e6 or 15 ♗xc7 ♕xa2 16 ♖d1 ♖ac8 17 ♗g3 f5 18 ♗h3 ♕c4 19 e5?! ♘d5) 15 ♗e2 f5!? 16 0-0 fxe4? 17 ♕xe4 ♕xc3 18 ♗e3! ♕a3 (else ♖bc1) 19 ♗d3! ♕d6 (the bishop-pair are overwhelming Black's position; after

19...g6 20 ♗c4+ followed by d5 White wins a piece) 20 ♕xh7+ ♔f7 21 ♖b5 ♘xd4 22 ♕e4? (after some complications, 22 ♗xd4 ♕xd4 23 ♖g5! wins) 22...♖ad8! 23 ♗xd4 ♕xd4 *(D)*.

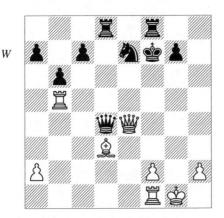

24 ♖f5+! ♘xf5 25 ♕xf5+ ♔g8 26 ♕h7+ ♔f7 ½-½. As shown in the notes, however, Black could probably have equalized before White achieved a winning position.

We get a slightly more up-to-date look in Flear-Miladinović, Athens 1999: 1 d4 d5 2 c4 ♘c6 3 cxd5 ♕xd5 4 e3 e5 5 ♘c3 ♗b4 6 ♗d2 ♗xc3 7 ♗xc3 exd4 8 ♘e2 (over the last few years, this position has occurred more than any other in the Chigorin) 8...♘f6 9 ♘xd4 0-0 10 ♘b5 ♕g5! *(D)*.

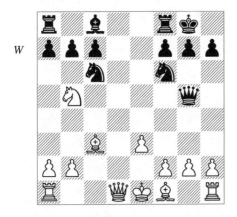

And this one! After scores of games no one seems to know what's happening in this fashionable line, although Black has his share of wins. The game went 11 ♘xc7 ♗g4 12 ♕b3 ♖ad8 13 h3 ♗c8! 14 ♕b5 ♕g6 15 ♗xf6 gxf6

16 ♖c1! ♕e4! with great complications. Another case of very rapid development on Black's part, in this instance in return for a pawn.

Don't forget the bishops and centre. Wells-Shannon, Hastings 1988/9 makes the point again: 1 d4 d5 2 c4 ♘c6 3 ♘f3 ♗g4 4 cxd5 ♗xf3 5 gxf3 ♕xd5 6 e3 e5 7 ♘c3 ♗b4 8 ♗d2 ♗xc3 9 bxc3 exd4 10 cxd4 ♘ge7 11 ♖g1 0-0? 12 f4 ♖fe8 13 ♗g2 *(D)*.

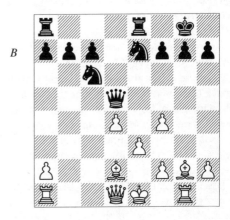

13...♕e6 14 d5! ♘xd5 15 ♗xd5 ♕xd5 16 ♖xg7+! ♔f8 17 ♗c3 with a strong attack.

After all that, let's return to the standard Queen's Gambit Declined, which is defined by 1 d4 d5 2 c4 e6. As an introduction to the main lines analysed in this chapter, we'll walk through the first moves.

3 ♘c3 *(D)*

This is White's most obvious and natural continuation, increasing his control over the key squares d5 and e4.

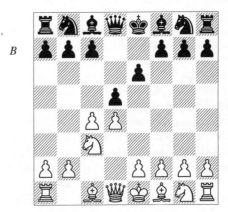

Move-order issues permeate the Queen's Gambit Declined. As I wrote this chapter, it got more and more cluttered with move-order subtleties. I felt that they shouldn't interfere too greatly with the presentation of the most important material, especially keeping in mind that many readers may be unfamiliar with the opening. Nevertheless I have to address a limited set of options over the next few moves, especially if they involve elementary moves that you should avoid if you want to play a particular variation that I've written about. I think that most moderately experienced players will appreciate having some guideposts as we move towards the actual systems that we'll be examining.

For a more thorough treatment, I have placed an extra section at the end of this chapter that deals with the more complex details. It talks about what transpositions and independent paths can result from playing one order of moves or another, even if they seem to be heading for the same position. Experienced players may wish to take a look at that section if they need clarification about this or that path through the jungle.

However, I want to emphasize that you can skip *all* of the explanations about move-orders and not worry about them until after you've read the meat of this chapter. They may not be so vital until you have played the Queen's Gambit Declined for a while as White or as Black. If it's a question of doing so or giving up on this wonderful and instructive opening, by all means jump ahead to the section 'Early Commitment' below, or even 'Classical Variations' below that.

All right, let's jump into some whys and wherefores. Many players like the Exchange Variation of the Queen's Gambit when they're playing White; in fact, it is the most popular choice of all against the Queen's Gambit. That variation normally begins with 3 ♘c3 ♘f6 4 cxd5 exd5. Is there any reason why White wouldn't want to play the immediate 3 cxd5 exd5 *(D)* instead? The answer is that from the resulting position White cannot *force* a transposition into that form of Exchange Variation.

This requires a fairly complicated digression. To repeat, the sequence actually called the Exchange Variation begins 1 d4 d5 2 c4 e6 3 ♘c3 ♘f6 4 cxd5 exd5 and has its own lengthy section in this chapter (in fact, the move 5 ♗g5

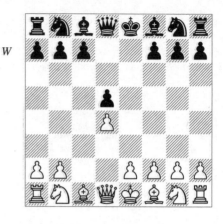

W

is also part of what some call the traditional Exchange Variation). But if White tries to get to that position by 3 cxd5 exd5 4 ♘c3, Black can choose moves other than 4...♘f6. The most useful of these is probably 4...c6. Then of course White cannot play 5 ♗g5?? without losing the bishop. But the alternate bishop move 5 ♗f4 hasn't much punch, because Black can oppose the bishop by 5...♗d6 if he wants to. Another perfectly satisfactory move for Black after 5 ♗f4 is 5...♗f5.

What if, after 3 cxd5 exd5 4 ♘c3 c6, White rejects 5 ♗f4 and plays the natural move 5 ♘f3? This still isn't ideal for someone who likes the white side of the main lines of the Exchange Variation, because after 5 ♘f3, Black has a good move in 5...♗f5, and then if White plays 6 ♕b3, Black can comfortably answer by 6...♕b6. By comparison, you might ask why 5...♗f5 isn't a good move in our 'real' Exchange Variation above (1 d4 d5 2 c4 e6 3 ♘c3 ♘f6 4 cxd5 exd5 5 ♗g5); the answer is that White can play 6 ♕b3 *(D)*:

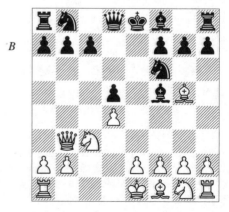

B

Then he attacks the pawn on b7 and threatens ♗xf6 to win the pawn on d5.

So it seems as though the best move to get to the Exchange Variation is to play 3 ♘c3. But about playing 3 ♘f3 *(D)*?

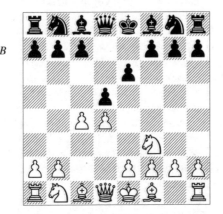

B

Players frequently get to this and related positions via other move-orders. For example, the opening might go 1 d4 ♘f6 2 c4 e6, and White may not want to play 3 ♘c3 because he'll have to go up against 3...♗b4, the Nimzo-Indian Defence. This is the feeling of many strong masters, whose solution is to play 3 ♘f3. Then Black in turn may want to play 3...d5, transposing to a form of the Queen's Gambit below. Notice that if you're playing Black and you like the Nimzo-Indian Defence, this can be an effective move-order, because it gets White to commit his knight to f3, a move which is generally less feared if Black now plays 3...d5. But is there any drawback to that strategy? Let's see. After 1 d4 d5 2 c4 e6 3 ♘f3, Black will play 3...♘f6 *(D)* here most of the time.

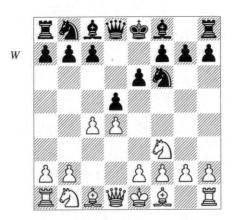

W

In the Move-Orders section at the end of this chapter, I've gone into a lot of detail about the differences between having played ♘c3 or ♘f3. The most important thing to understand is that if you get to the Exchange Variation, it would probably be in the following way: 4 ♘c3 ♗e7 5 cxd5 exd5 6 ♗g5 0-0 7 e3 c6 *(D)*.

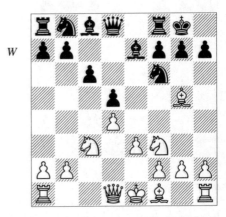

W

White's knight is committed to f3. I'll refer to this as the 'Carlsbad Variation' (the corresponding pawn-structure is called the 'Carlsbad pawn-structure' or 'Carlsbad formation'). There's nothing wrong with this position, as we'll see, but having the knight on f3 has limited White's freedom of choice. We'll look at this position at great length in the Exchange Variation section later on. Many players as White prefer to develop their king's knight from g1 to e2, and now they've lost that option.

There's more to think about when White plays the order 3 ♘f3 ♘f6 4 ♘c3; Black can even avoid the Exchange Variation altogether, without having to concede much. I've said a little about that below.

3...♘f6 *(D)*

This is the move that we shall look at first. It has easily been the most common choice for Black over the years. 19th-century practice of 1 d4 d5 by the world's best players usually led to this position, and in fact to the positions stemming from both sides' next few moves. The only other move that was employed fairly consistently was 3...c5 (the Tarrasch Variation), although it was put under a bit of a cloud for some time by 4 cxd5 exd5 5 ♘f3 ♘c6 and now Rubinstein's move 6 g3. That's still the line that most dissuades Black from the Tarrasch. Only much later, particularly since the 1960s, was 3...♘f6 challenged in terms of effectiveness by 3...♗e7, an important variation called the 'Alatortsev' which is examined in its own section.

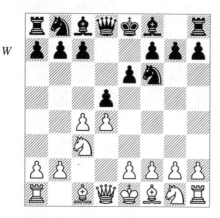

4 ♗g5

White heads for the traditional main line, which goes 4 ♗g5 ♗e7 5 e3 0-0 6 ♘f3. Instead 4 cxd5 exd5 5 ♗g5 is finally the 'real' Exchange Variation, which we'll be looking at carefully later.

As I described above, 4 ♘f3 (D) is an important move-order for a couple of reasons. First, it arises via 3 ♘f3 ♘f6 4 ♘c3 as well.

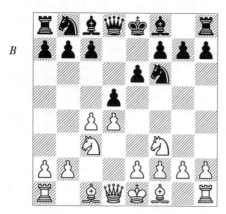

Again I'll refer you to the Move-Orders section at the end of this chapter for a lengthier discussion. But there are a couple of points that you might find useful:

a) After 4 ♘f3, Black can choose to play 4...dxc4. This introduces the Vienna Variation, which is a very complex opening. You may want to consider playing that as Black. As White,

you can't avoid the Vienna Variation if you play ♘f3 and ♘c3 on the 3rd and 4th moves. That probably means you'll want to put a little study time into it, as explained at the end of the chapter.

b) I should also point out that Black can still prevent White from getting into *any* kind of true Exchange Variation by fiddling with move-orders. For example, after 4 ♘f3, Black can play 4...♗e7, and if 5 cxd5 exd5 6 ♗g5, then Black plays 6...c6 with the idea 7 e3 ♗f5. That is probably easier for Black to play than the true Exchange Variation.

On the other hand, by using that order (1 d4 d5 2 c4 e6 3 ♘c3 ♘f6 4 ♘f3 ♗e7), Black does allow 5 ♗f4, an important variation that I won't be covering in detail but will touch upon at the end of the chapter.

So much for early move-orders. We can't avoid the transpositions from one line to another, but at least you've got the basics.

Now let's continue stepping through our main line – we return to 4 ♗g5 (D):

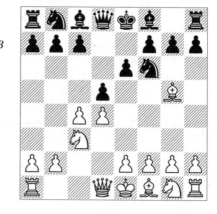

4...♗e7

Black unpins the knight. We'll look quickly at some weaker moves:

a) 4...h6? 5 ♗xf6 creates serious problems for Black, who must either accede to the isolated doubled pawns resulting from 5...gxf6 6 cxd5 exd5, or lose a pawn by 5...♕xf6 6 cxd5 exd5 (6...c6 7 dxc6 ♘xc6 8 ♘f3) 7 ♘xd5 ♕d6 8 e4, etc.

b) Also favouring White is 4...c5?! 5 cxd5 cxd4 (5...exd5 6 ♗xf6! gxf6 7 ♘f3 and Black's pawn-structure is shattered while he's behind in development) 6 ♕xd4 ♗e7 (6...♘c6 7 ♗xf6!

gxf6 8 ♕d2 exd5 9 e3 and again, Black's pawns are badly damaged) 7 e4! ♘c6 8 ♕d2! and White clearly has the better of it because of his pressure on Black's centre. If you're interested, you can work on this material by yourself or look up the relevant theory.

5 e3 (D)

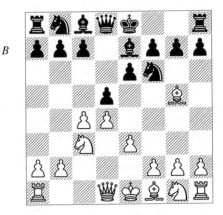

In the famous position after 5 e3 we have a split in material and shall look at two moves for Black.

Early Commitment

5...h6

This move is considered more accurate by some players and less so by others! It's true that 6 ♗xf6 is considered harmless at this point, so that it seems a good time to nudge White into committing to ♗h4. But one potentially important difference is that now White can skip or delay the move ♘f3, as he does in what follows.

6 ♗h4 0-0 7 ♖c1 (D)

This move-order is a Korchnoi speciality, delaying 7 ♘f3 (which would give us the main-line Classical Queen's Gambit Declined, seen below).

Finally we get to see a game!

Korchnoi – Short
Rotterdam 1988

7...b6!?

Black wants to play a fianchetto system. After 7...♘e4 8 ♗xe7 ♕xe7, 9 ♘xe4 dxe4 with

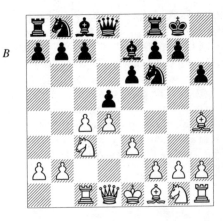

...e5 to come is OK for Black, but White can also play simply 9 ♘f3 and we're back in the main line of the Lasker Variation, something which we'll see in detail in just a moment. The problem is that Black may not like that line; a lot of players prefer not to initiate exchanges with ...♘e4 since they'd like to use a system with ...b6 instead.

8 cxd5 ♘xd5

After 8...exd5, 9 ♗d3 ♗b7 10 ♘ge2 ♖e8 11 0-0 and ♗g3 is a good follow-up; that's a bit awkward for Black because the b7-bishop is running into its own pawn. You will find that in many openings with ...b6, cxd5 is an effective move for White.

9 ♘xd5 exd5 10 ♗xe7 ♕xe7 11 ♗d3 (D)

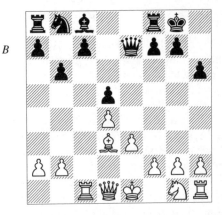

A funny position. This strongly resembles the Tartakower Variation that I shall discuss later, but with options for White that don't exist in that sequence, because he hasn't committed his knight to f3.

11...♗b7

Hjartarson-Vaganian, Bundesliga 1990/1 took an instructive course after Black played the logical 11...♗e6 12 ♘e2 c5 13 0-0 ♘d7. Then 14 ♘f4! grabbed a handy place for the knight, putting pressure on d5 but also retaining the option of ♘xe6. The game continued 14...♘f6 15 dxc5 bxc5. Black has hanging pawns on c5 and d5, which Hjartarson proceeds to 'fix' (discourage from advancing) by his next move: 16 b3 a5 17 ♕c2 ♖ac8 18 ♘xe6! fxe6 19 e4! d4 20 ♕e2 e5 21 g3 ♔h7 22 f4 (D).

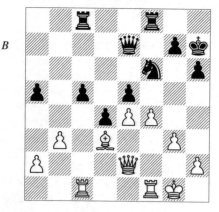

In this type of position, Black's central majority is completely blocked whereas White's on the kingside is potentially mobile and c4 is a handy outpost in front of a backward pawn. The upshot is that White has the better of it, although it takes a lot of work to make progress.

12 ♘e2

White's knight development to e2 (instead of f3) means that the knight can go to f4 to put pressure on the d-pawn or even to g3 to worry Black on the kingside.

12...c5 13 0-0 c4

Korchnoi-Spassky, Clermont-Ferrand 1989 went 13...♘d7 14 ♕a4 ♘f6 15 dxc5 bxc5 16 ♕a3. That presents a standard QGD motif: Black's c-pawn is pinned and White will pile up on it. If and when Black moves it to c4, White gains the d4-square for his pieces, in particular his knight. In practice, Black sometimes gets queenside pressure down the b-file. The game continued 16...♖fc8 17 ♖c3 ♘e4 18 ♗xe4 ♕xe4 19 ♘g3 ♕e5 20 ♖xc5 ♖xc5 21 ♕xc5 ♕xb2 22 ♘f5 (D).

White has emerged from the opening with a very strong knight on f5 versus a bad bishop.

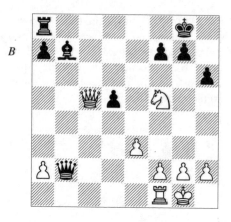

14 ♗b1 ♘c6 15 b3 cxb3 16 ♕xb3 ♕d6 17 ♘f4 ♖ad8 18 h4! f5

Not 18...♘xd4?? 19 ♕d3 with a double threat.

19 h5! ♘xd4 20 ♕a4 ♘e6 21 ♘xe6 ♕xe6 22 ♖c7 ♖f7 23 ♖xf7 ♔xf7 24 ♕f4! (D)

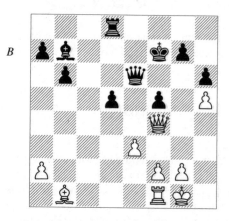

The position still isn't clear, but the difference in bishops is impressive.

24...♔g8!

After 24...♗c8, the reply 25 ♖c1 would be very strong.

25 ♗xf5 ♕f6 26 ♕c7 ♗a6 27 ♖d1 ♗c4?!

This was a good spot for 27...d4!.

28 ♖d4! ♖e8 29 ♗b1 ♕e7?! 30 ♕g3 ♕e6 31 ♖f4 b5 32 ♗g6! ♖f8? 33 ♗h7+ ♔xh7 34 ♖xf8 ♗e2 35 ♕g6+! ♕xg6 36 hxg6+ ♔xg6 37 ♖a8

and White won quickly. You can actually argue that Black's problems trace back to 5...h6. That is a good move in general, but it happens to work better in conjunction with ...b6 if White has already played ♘f3. We shall see better versions of the queenside fianchetto below.

Classical Variations

5...0-0 6 ♘f3

We are at the first great dividing point that the Old Masters faced when playing the Classical Queen's Gambit Declined. They generally chose between the Lasker Variation (6...h6 7 ♗h4 ♘e4) and the Capablanca/Orthodox Variation (6...♘bd7 and in most cases ...c6). Modern players have tended to switch to various other systems as both White and Black, and the one that truly stands out is the Tartakower Variation (6...h6 7 ♗h4 b6), a line that existed on the margins of play in early times but exploded into prominence some 40 years ago and has remained the most popular choice since.

Lasker Defence

6...h6 (D)

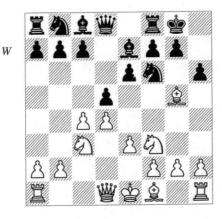

This move is a significant decision. Although it breaks the beginner's rule about moving a pawn in front of your king, 6...h6 has at least two advantages:

a) it provides an escape-square for Black's king on h7;

b) it means that if White lines up his bishop on d3 and his queen on c2, Black won't have to waste a tempo guarding his h-pawn.

On the flip side, Black makes a weakness when he plays ...h6 and you never know how that might end up hurting him. We shall see other examples in which Black avoids ...h6, with ambiguous results.

7 ♗h4

7 ♗xf6 gives up the two bishops but gains time. This exchange occurs with loss of time versus ...b6 systems (Tartakower), for reasons that we'll describe later. After 7...♗xf6 (D), we'll often see Black free his game at the cost of exchanging one of his bishops.

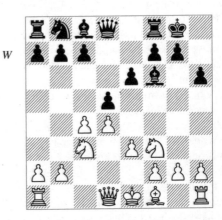

A high-level illustration went 8 ♕b3 c6 9 ♖d1 ♘d7 10 ♗d3 b6 11 cxd5 cxd5 12 e4 dxe4 13 ♗xe4 ♖b8 14 0-0 b5 15 ♖fe1 ♕b6 16 ♗b1 ♗b7 17 ♕c2 g6 18 d5 (initiating a mass liquidation before his IQP becomes a problem) 18...exd5 19 ♘xd5 ♗xd5 20 ♖xd5 ♖fd8 ½-½ Kasparov-Karpov, Moscow Wch (3) 1985.

7...♘e4 (D)

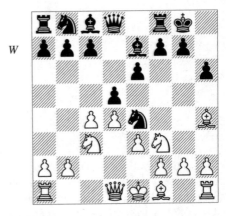

The first move of the Lasker Variation. Here we have one of the oldest defences in the Classical Queen's Gambit Declined complex. Study of such traditional lines is a great way to understand not just 1 d4 d5 ideas but chess in general.

With 7...♘e4, Black uses a tempo (moving the knight again) to transform his position by exchanging pieces. Normally you'd think that the resulting position would be much more cramped than the original – certainly Black hasn't done anything to solve his problem with the bishop on c8, while the bishop on e7 was a pretty good piece. But it turns out that the combination of a queen on e7 and knight on d7 can enforce the freeing advance ...e5, which will finally give that light-squared bishop some breathing room. The drawback to all this is that it takes time, and there's no reason why White can't mount an attack when there have been only two sets of minor pieces exchanged.

8 &xe7 &xe7 9 &c1

White develops his rook so as not to lose time with 9 &d3 &xc3 10 bxc3 dxc4 11 &xc4. This is only one of several moves.

a) For some time it was thought that White could gain some advantage after 9 cxd5 &xc3 10 bxc3 exd5 11 &b3, but his lead in development has vanished and his extra centre pawn is easily restrained. The main line goes 11...&d8 12 c4 (12 &e2 has several answers, including 12...&c6, eyeing the light squares via ...&a5, as in the game) 12...dxc4 13 &xc4 *(D)*.

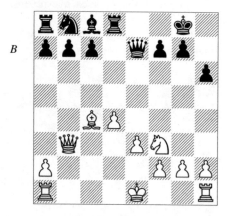

An instructive position, because White has two central pawns to Black's none, and even potential pressure down the c-file. But he hasn't castled yet, often an issue in openings stemming from 1 d4. Here Black will develop quickly to harass White's pieces before he can get organized: 13...&c6! (this threatens ...&a5; time is more important than structure) 14 &c3 (the old move, to cover a5 and keep the bishop on c4; not much better is 14 &e2!? b6! 15 0-0 &b7, or here 15...&e6 16 &c3 &d5 also has its points;

after that move Black can even think about challenging White's kingside by ...&d6-g6) 14...&g4 (rapid development!) 15 0-0 (15 &e2 &xf3 forces 16 gxf3 anyway in view of 16 &xf3? &xd4) 15...&xf3 16 gxf3 &f6 17 &e2 &ac8 18 &ab1 b6 19 &fc1 &e7! 20 &h1 &d5 and in Karpov-Yusupov, London Ct (5) 1989 Black had no problems and even a modest attack.

b) 9 &c2 is certainly natural, intending to stop ...e5 cold after 9...&xc3 10 &xc3, but then Black can play 10...dxc4 (10...&c6!? is worthy of consideration) 11 &xc4 c5!, his alternative freeing move. Then White finally catches up in development by 12 0-0, and Black has time to protect his centre by 12...&d7 with ...cxd4 and/or ...b6 to follow. Theory rates this as equal, but perhaps it's a place for White to investigate further in the hunt for a small advantage.

We now return to the position after 9 &c1 *(D)*:

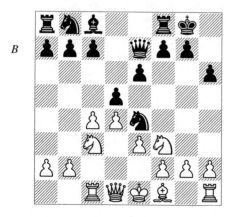

9...c6

It seems strange to put more pawns on light squares. But this time we can easily grasp the idea: Black wants to play ...e5, so he has to protect the pawn on d5 first. More important is the manner in which he does it. White must now try to find a useful move, and capturing the knight by 10 &xe4 dxe4 11 &d2 e5! has long been known to be equal. Instead, 9...&xc3 10 &xc3 dxc4? 11 &xc4 would leave White a valuable tempo ahead of the game.

10 &d3 &xc3 11 &xc3 dxc4 12 &xc4

12 &xc4 is sometimes played, but that's a different story.

12...♘d7 13 0-0 *(D)*

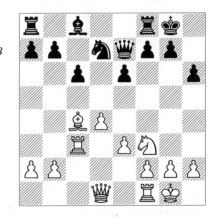

B

At this point we'll look at two games, one a well-known classic of attack (with Black playing 13...e5), and the other a typical old-style Queen's Gambit with positional manoeuvring (with Black playing 13...b6). Incidentally, Sadler suggests 13...c5!?. It's quite logical, and something to consider if Black's standard plans all come up short or you simply don't like them.

Karpov – Yusupov
London Ct (7) 1989

13...e5 14 ♗b3 *(D)*

A multi-purpose move. The obvious idea is to avoid the potential sequence of ...e4 and ...♘b6 with an attack on the valuable bishop on c4, followed by bringing out Black's c8-bishop, his problem piece. White also introduces a little threat. This can be seen by comparing the old line 14 dxe5 ♘xe5 15 ♘xe5 ♕xe5 16 f4 ♕e4, after which 17 ♗d3?! allows 17...♕xe3+; then lengthy analysis shows that Black can escape with his extra pawn. But with the bishop on b3, White threatens 15 dxe5 ♘xe5 16 ♘xe5 ♕xe5 17 f4, when 17...♕e4 could be answered by 18 ♗c2 followed by 19 e4 and to great effect, since White's central majority would be mobilized. Needless to say, Black won't wait around for that to happen.

14...exd4

There have been a few games since this one in which Black tried to delay opening up the position so quickly. These alternatives may be playable but they have led to some attractive wins for White:

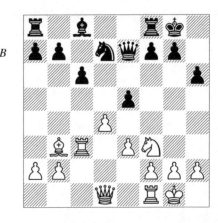

B

a) 14...e4 15 ♘d2 ♘f6 leaves White the possibility of ♖c5-e5, which might be exploited by starting with 16 ♕b1!?; for example, 16...♖e8 17 ♖c5 ♕c7 18 f3! exf3 19 ♘xf3 threatening ♘e5. The move ♕b1 should be remembered in any case – it's important in many variations to watch over e4.

b) 14...♖e8 15 ♕c2!? e4 16 ♘d2 ♘f6 17 ♖c5!? (17 f3! exf3 18 ♘xf3 ♘g4 {18...♘e4?? 19 ♘e5} 19 e4!) 17...♕d8?! 18 ♖e5! ♖xe5 19 dxe5 ♘g4 20 ♘xe4 ♘xe5? (the best try is 20...♕e7, but obviously White stands better) 21 ♕c5! *(D)*.

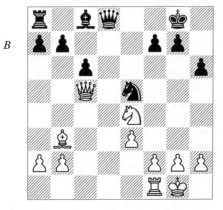

B

Remarkably, the game is resignable! Vyzhmanavin-Klovans, Berne 1993 finished 21...♕c7 22 ♘d6 ♕e7 23 f4 ♘g4 24 h3 b6 (24...♕xe3+ 25 ♕xe3 ♘xe3 26 ♖e1!) 25 ♕d4 c5 26 ♕d5 ♕xe3+ 27 ♔h1 1-0.

c) 14...♖d8 15 ♖e1 exd4 16 exd4 ♕d6 (an isolated queen's pawn position that is similar to the main game) 17 ♕e2! (17 ♖ce3 ♘f8!; in fact, ...♘f8! is the answer to almost every move!)

17...♘f8 18 ♕e7 ♘e6 19 ♕h4! ♕f4? 20 ♕xd8+! ♘xd8 21 ♖e8+ ♔h7 22 ♖xd8. Black can't defend this. Zakharevich-Biriukov, St Petersburg 2000 continued 22...♕c7 (or 22...b6 23 ♖f8) 23 ♖f8 ♖b8 (23...♕d6? loses to 24 ♗c2+ f5 25 ♖xc8!) 24 ♖xf7 ♕d6 25 ♖e3! ♗g4 26 ♖ee7 ♖g8 27 ♘e5 ♕xd4 (on 27...♗h5 the nicest win is 28 ♖e6!? ♕xd4 29 ♗c2+ ♔h8 30 ♖xh6+! gxh6 31 ♖h7#) 28 ♗c2+ ♔h8 29 ♖f4! 1-0.

15 exd4 ♘f6 16 ♖e1 (D)

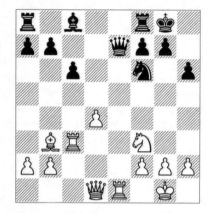

In this position we have the familiar isolated queen's pawn trade-off: White's weak d-pawn versus Black's activity. There has been some simplification, which is probably why Yusupov was ready to enter this position. But simplification shouldn't be one's only consideration; various situations arise in this book where exchanging pieces doesn't really hurt the owner of the IQP (see the Giuoco Piano chapter in Volume 1 for an excellent example). It's a matter of piece placement and, in this case, attack.

16...♕d6 17 ♘e5 ♘d5

A natural defensive move, blockading the isolani. 17...♗e6 18 ♗xe6 fxe6 19 ♖g3 is strong for White in view of 19...♖ad8 20 ♕b3! ♕xd4 21 ♕xb7; and worse is 17...♗f5? 18 ♘xf7 ♖xf7 19 ♗xf7+ ♔xf7 20 ♕b3+ ♔f8 21 ♕xb7, when Black is losing too much material while White's rooks are growing ever more active.

18 ♖g3 (D)

18...♗f5

18...♗e6 19 ♕d2! attacks the h6-pawn; there may follow 19...♗f5?! (but 19...♔h7 20 ♗c2+ is no good either) 20 ♗xd5 cxd5 21 ♕f4.

19 ♕h5! ♗h7 20 ♕g4 g5 21 h4! f6 22 hxg5 hxg5 23 f4!?

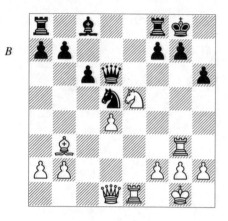

Also good are 23 ♕h5 and 23 ♖h3.
23...♖ae8 24 fxg5! (D)

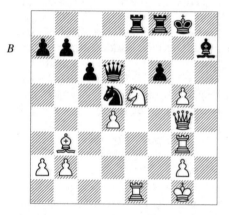

24...fxe5

A wonderful variation is given by Karpov: 24...♗f5 25 gxf6+!! ♗xg4 26 ♖xg4+ ♔h8 27 ♘f7+ ♖xf7 28 ♖xe8+ ♖f8 29 f7 ♘f6 30 ♖xf8+ ♕xf8 31 ♖g8+ ♘xg8 32 fxg8♕+ ♕xg8 33 ♗xg8 and White wins the pawn ending.

25 g6 ♗xg6 26 dxe5 ♕e6 27 ♗xd5 cxd5 28 ♕xg6+ ♕xg6 29 ♖xg6+ ♔h7 30 ♖d6

White will emerge with a couple of extra pawns, sufficient to win the day.

Kramnik – Kasparov
Las Palmas 1996

13...b6!? (D)

Oddly enough, after working so hard to play ...e5, it may be better to go in the other direction! Black calmly prepares ...♗b7 followed by ...c5.

14 ♗d3!

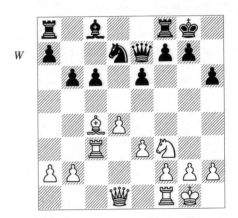

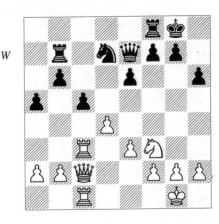

White unmasks the c3-rook and simultaneously prepares ♗e4. 14 ♕e2 has also been played and is worth looking at more closely.

14...c5! 15 ♗e4 (D)

Or 15 ♗b5 ♖d8 16 ♗c6 ♖b8 17 ♕c2 cxd4 18 ♘xd4 e5! 19 ♘f5 (control of this excellent square is only temporary) 19...♕f6 20 ♖d1 ♘c5 with equality, Smyslov-Kasparov, Vilnius Ct (6) 1984.

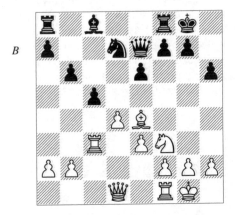

15...♖b8 16 ♕a4

Perhaps Karpov's move 16 ♕c2!?, played in the first major game with 14 ♗d3, is more effective (an aside: if the h-pawn were on h7, as in the Capablanca Variation below, this move would gain a tempo and White would definitely stand better). Black has trouble getting full equality in these lines; e.g., 16...a5?! (16...e5!?) 17 ♖c1 ♗b7 18 ♗xb7 ♖xb7 (D).

19 dxc5!? (19 a3! may be better; for example, 19...♖d8 20 dxc5 ♘xc5 21 ♘d4! ♕f6 22 b4 with advantage) 19...♘xc5 20 ♘e5 ♕f6 21 ♘d3 (21 f4!?) 21...♖d8 22 ♘xc5 bxc5 23 ♕e2

♖bd7 24 ♖3c2 a4 (24...c4! improved in Khalifman-Yusupov, Bundesliga 1992/3) 25 g3 ♖d5 26 ♔g2 g6 27 a3 h5 28 ♕f3 ♕e5 29 ♕f4 ♕xf4 30 gxf4 ♖b8 31 ♖xc5 ♖xc5 32 ♖xc5 ♖xb2 33 ♖c4 and Karpov went on to win versus Yusupov in Baden-Baden 1995. There's something irritating about White's small advantages in these lines: they don't seem to disappear completely.

16...♗b7

16...♘f6! looks like a good solution (so far!): 17 ♗c6 cxd4 18 exd4 a6 19 ♘e5 ♗b7 20 ♖fc1 ♘d5 21 ♗xd5 ♗xd5! 22 ♕xa6 ♖a8 23 ♕xb6 ♕g5 24 g3 ♖xa2 with equality, Zviagintsev-Bologan, Poikovsky 2003.

17 ♗xb7 ♖xb7 18 ♕c2! ♖c8 19 ♖c1 ♖bc7 20 b4 e5

In this position, instead of 21 dxc5?, Dolmatov suggests 21 bxc5! exd4 22 exd4 bxc5 23 ♖c4 with advantage. This theory will change, but the ideas are fundamental.

Orthodox/Capablanca Defence

1 d4 d5 2 c4 e6 3 ♘c3 ♘f6 4 ♗g5 ♗e7

It is obligatory here to point out one of the oldest traps in a d-pawn opening: 4...♘bd7 (D).

5 cxd5 exd5 6 ♘xd5?? ♘xd5! 7 ♗xd8 ♗b4+ 8 ♕d2 ♗xd2+ (or 8...♔xd8) 9 ♔xd2 ♔xd8 and Black has won a piece for a pawn.

There are some move-order issues involving 4...♘bd7, and one is really worth mentioning. If White continues 'normally' by 5 e3 c6 6 ♘f3 (or 5 ♘f3 c6 6 e3, which is the same position), then Black has the move 6...♕a5, introducing the Cambridge Springs Variation. It is considered sound and at worst only slightly

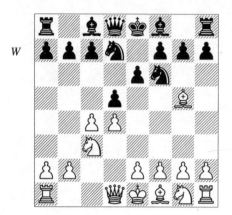

disadvantageous for Black. White can bypass the Cambridge Springs via 5 cxd5 exd5 6 e3 or 6 ♘f3, entering the Exchange Variation without the hassles of ...♗f5 variations.

But if White has played 4 ♘f3 (instead of 4 ♗g5), then after 4...♘bd7, 5 cxd5 exd5 6 ♗f4 is a promising order which can lead in several directions; e.g., 6...c6 7 e3 ♘h5!? (7...♗e7 8 h3! is a comfortable version of the Carlsbad Exchange Variation; refer to that section) 8 ♗e5!? (8 ♗g5 is the safer and rational course: 8...♗e7 9 ♗xe7 ♕xe7 10 ♗e2! with 0-0 and ♕c2 next should favour White; but watch out for 10 ♗d3?! ♘f4!) 8...♘xe5 9 ♘xe5 (hitting h5) 9...♘f6 10 ♗d3 ♗d6 11 f4! and White has a stereotyped attack on the kingside. Black may well want to avoid this line and not play 4...♘bd7 after 4 ♘f3.

5 e3 0-0 6 ♘f3 ♘bd7

This move-order contrasts with 6...h6 7 ♗h4 ♘e4 above, although the same ideas may still arise.

7 ♖c1 *(D)*

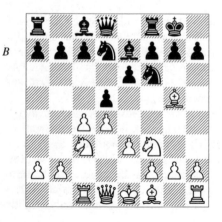

7...c6

Black's modest advance has an idea similar to the Lasker Variation. As befits Capablanca's style, 7...c6 creates no weakness, in contrast to a line with ...h6. However, we shall see in the examples below how the omission of ...h6 can also be a disadvantage for Black.

The move 7...a6 is still played from time to time, with the idea of ...b5 and ...c5, gaining space on the queenside and preventing piece incursions on b5. It may well be underrated. We'll follow the most famous game with 7...a6, Capablanca-Alekhine, Buenos Aires Wch (21) 1927: 8 a3 (White plays the waiting game, trying to avoid losing a tempo following 8 ♗d3 dxc4 9 ♗xc4, but this proves to be harmless; 8 c5 and 8 cxd5 exd5 9 ♗d3 are the main lines today – the latter isn't very threatening because in the Exchange Variation, which we shall examine in depth below, the moves ♖ab1 and ♖ae1 are generally more effective than ♖ac1; after 8 c5, one critical continuation is 8...c6 9 ♗d3 e5! 10 dxe5 ♘e8 11 h4! ♘xc5 12 ♗b1 ♘e6! 13 ♕c2 g6, when White has some initiative but with accurate defence, Black may be able to hold his own or at least emerge with only a modest disadvantage) 8...h6! 9 ♗h4 dxc4 10 ♗xc4 b5 11 ♗e2 ♗b7 12 0-0 c5 13 dxc5 ♘xc5 (with actively-placed pieces and control of e4, Black has equalized) 14 ♘d4 ♖c8 15 b4! ♘cd7 *(D)*.

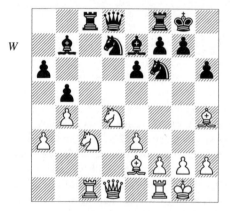

16 ♗g3!? (Black is bringing his pieces to c4 while White in turn looks to occupy c5; for these purposes, Black's bishop on b7 is more suited than White's on g3) 16...♘b6 17 ♕b3 ♘fd5?! (a natural move, but because of the specifics,

17...♘bd5, 17...♘c4 or 17...♕d7 holds out more chance for advantage) 18 ♗f3? (a key juncture: White is doubtless afraid to play 18 ♘e4! and leave his knight unprotected, but Black can't take advantage; e.g., 18...♘xb4 19 ♘xe6; thus the idea of ♘c5 causes Black some discomfort) 18...♖c4! 19 ♘e4 (or 19 ♗e2 ♖xc3 20 ♖xc3 ♘xc3 21 ♕xc3 ♕d7 with the idea ...♖c8, and Black's pieces will settle in on c4) 19...♕c8 20 ♖xc4 ♘xc4 21 ♖c1 ♕a8! (D).

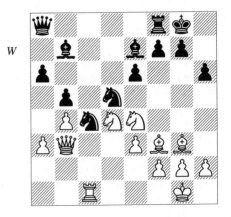

W

Black increases his control over the light-square colour-complex. This theme persists until the end of the game: 22 ♘c3 ♖c8 23 ♘xd5 ♗xd5 24 ♗xd5 ♕xd5 (with the exchange of White's bishop, the c4 outpost has become unassailable) 25 a4 ♗f6 26 ♘f3 ♗b2! 27 ♖e1 ♖d8 28 axb5 axb5 29 h3 e5 30 ♖b1 e4 31 ♘d4 ♗xd4 32 ♖d1 ♘xe3! 0-1, because 33 ♕xd5 ♖xd5 34 fxe3 ♗xe3+ wins the rook. A highly instructive game for players of the QGD.

8 ♗d3

The standard move, but sometimes White tries to save a tempo (which is lost after 8 ♗d3 dxc4 9 ♗xc4) by playing 8 ♕c2, also covering e4. Then a great old example was Alekhine-Rubinstein, Carlsbad 1923: 8...a6!? 9 a4!? (Alekhine tries to stop ...b5 directly, an unusual idea; both 9 ♗d3 dxc4 10 ♗xc4 b5 and 9 cxd5 are options) 9...♖e8 10 ♗d3 dxc4 11 ♗xc4 ♘d5 12 ♗f4!? ♘xf4 13 exf4 (D).

A modern-looking position! These d4/f4 structures, although still infrequent, have become accepted in a greater number of situations than was the case 20 years ago. If White's d-pawn disappears, he'll have a doubled f-pawn formation that typically arises in the Dutch

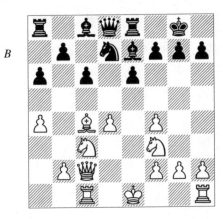

B

Defence Stonewall variation and in various openings where Black plays ...♗g4 (or ...♗b7) followed by ...♗xf3 and White recaptures with the e-pawn. From Black's point of view, we see the same structure occurring in the main-line Slav ♘h4xf5 variations, and the Nimzo-Indian with ...♕f5 and ♕xf5, among other openings.

One of the ideas of allowing ...♘xf4 is that White's central pawns will clamp down on the freeing move ...e5. So naturally, Rubinstein looks to his other central break and counts upon his bishop-pair: 13...c5 14 dxc5 (a key point for understanding the opening: White will either concentrate upon the centre or kingside, depending upon Black's reply) 14...♕c7!? (this is one of three ways to recover the pawn; by moving his queen, Black gets off the d-file, attacks the f4-pawn, and waits to see what White will do; other moves apparently fail to equalize; e.g., 14...♘xc5 15 0-0 ♕c7 16 ♘e5 f6 17 ♘d3 ♘xd3 18 ♗xd3 f5 19 ♘d5! or 14...♗xc5 15 0-0 ♘f6 16 ♘e5 ♕c7 17 ♗d3, threatening ♘e2) 15 0-0 ♕xf4 16 ♘e4 ♘xc5 17 ♘xc5 ♗xc5 18 ♗d3 b6? (18...♗e7! 19 ♗xh7+ ♔f8 20 ♖fe1 ♗d7 21 ♘e5 ♗xa4 22 ♕c7 is unclear) 19 ♗xh7+ ♔h8 20 ♗e4 ♖a7 21 b4! ♗f8 (21...♗xb4 22 ♕xc8!) 22 ♕c6 ♖d7 23 g3 ♕b8 24 ♘g5 ♖ed8 25 ♗g6! ♕e5 (25...fxg6 26 ♕e4 with mate shortly) 26 ♘xf7+ ♖xf7 27 ♗xf7 ♕f5 28 ♖fd1 ♖xd1+ 29 ♖xd1 ♕xf7 30 ♕xc8 ♔h7 31 ♕xa6 ♕f3 32 ♕d3+ 1-0. Nevertheless, Black has several alternatives and this line is as yet unresolved.

8...dxc4 9 ♗xc4 ♘d5 10 ♗xe7 ♕xe7 (D)

We have arrived at the Capablanca (or 'Orthodox') Variation. It is characterized by solidity and strongly resembles the Lasker Variation, because Black will aim for the freeing move

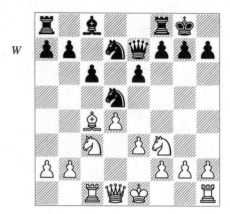

...e5. One motivation for Capablanca's Variation was to avoid certain orders in the Lasker Variation; for example, ones in which White exchanges on e4 after 6...h6 7 ♗h4 ♘e4, or the line in which White plays 8 ♗xe7 ♕xe7 9 cxd5 ♘xc3 10 bxc3 exd5 11 ♕b3. See the section on the Lasker Variation to make sense of that explanation. As it turns out, however, neither of those ideas is particularly effective for White, so the relevant difference between the two variations has to do with the h-pawn, which is either on h6 (in the Lasker Variation) or on h7 (in the Capablanca Variation). You'll see what I mean in the discussion about 11 0-0 below.

At this juncture I'll concentrate upon the unique move 11 ♘e4 (A), with a briefer look at 11 0-0 (B).

A)

11 ♘e4 (D)

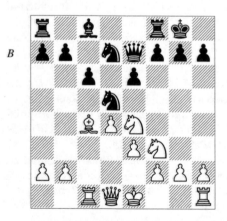

This was Alekhine's solution in his World Championship match versus Capablanca and

later in a famous game versus Lasker. White's idea is to keep the pieces on and mobilize his centre later. It still has promise.

11...♘5f6

Black retreats in order to challenge White's knight. He still intends ...e5 if possible. It is the best-known move. Black shouldn't play 11...e5?! immediately, if only because 12 0-0! (12 ♗xd5!? cxd5 13 ♘c3 e4 14 ♘xd5 ♕d6 15 ♘c7 exf3!) 12...exd4 13 ♕xd4 yields a position where he is struggling to equalize. Furthermore, 11...♕b4+ 12 ♕d2 ♕xd2+ 13 ♔xd2!, from Alekhine-Capablanca, Buenos Aires Wch (6) 1927, is a thankless position for Black. This queenless middlegame features White's centralized king and mobile centre pawns, whereas Black hasn't solved the problem of his queen's bishop. And of course, Black's weakness at d6 doesn't help matters.

Nevertheless, Black's position after 11 ♘e4 is fundamentally sound, so arguably he can keep things in hand by 11...b6 with the simple idea ...♗b7 and ...c5. Then the natural move is 12 0-0 ♗b7 13 ♘g3 (13 ♘e5! poses more problems; at least White stops ...c5) 13...c5 14 e4 ♘5f6!. This knight attacks the centre, which White can't maintain: 15 ♖e1 cxd4 16 ♗b5 ♖fc8 17 ♕xd4 ♖c5 18 ♗xd7 ♘xd7 19 b4 ♖xc1 20 ♖xc1 ♖c8 and Black had no problems in Alekhine-Maroczy, San Remo 1930.

After 11...♘5f6, we have two games.

Topalov – Yermolinsky
Erevan OL 1996

12 ♘g3 (D)

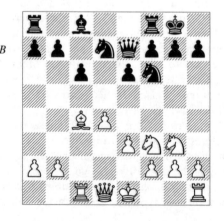

12...e5

In this instructive game, Black demonstrates how to neutralize White's pressure when faced with Alekhine's 12 ♘g3, reducing White's advantage to a bare minimum.

Another method is 12...♕b4+ 13 ♕d2 ♕xd2+ 14 ♔xd2 ♖d8 15 ♗d3!? (15 e4! is probably a better route) 15...e5! 16 dxe5 ♘g4 17 e6! ♘de5! 18 ♘xe5 ♘xe5 19 exf7+ ♔xf7 20 ♖c3 b5! (with the idea ...b4) 21 f4! b4 22 fxe5 bxc3+ 23 ♔xc3 ♔e6! 24 ♘e2! ♔xe5 25 ♘d4 ♗b7 26 ♗xh7 with only a tiny advantage for White because Black's king will prove a bit exposed and White's is better-placed, Alekhine-Capablanca, Buenos Aires Wch (20) 1927. An almost perfectly-played game up to this point; note the nice freeing idea for Black, 15...e5!.

13 0-0 exd4 14 ♘f5

Yermolinsky gives 14 ♘xd4 g6 15 ♖e1 ♖d8 with the idea ...c5.

14...♕d8 15 ♘5xd4

It seems as though every book shows the famous game Alekhine-Lasker, Zurich 1934 (it's short enough!): 15 ♘3xd4 ♘e5 16 ♗b3 ♗xf5 17 ♘xf5 ♕b6? (mistakenly removing the queen from defence) 18 ♕d6! (D).

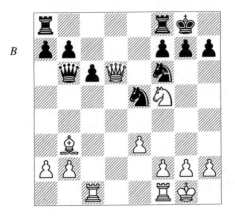

18...♘ed7 (Black is in big trouble) 19 ♖fd1 ♖ad8 20 ♕g3! g6 21 ♕g5! ♔h8? (but 21...♕b5! 22 ♘e7+ ♔g7 23 ♕xb5 cxb5 24 ♖c7 with the idea of f3 and e4 is still depressing for Black) 22 ♘d6 ♔g7 23 e4! ♘g8 24 ♖d3 f6 25 ♘f5+ ♔h8 26 ♕xg6! hxg6 1-0. It's mate after 27 ♖h3+ ♘h6 28 ♖xh6#.

Instead 17...g6! is correct: 18 ♘d6! (18 ♕d4 ♕xd4 19 ♘xd4 ½-½ Euwe-Flohr, Nottingham 1936) 18...♕e7 19 ♕d4 ♖fd8 20 ♖fd1 ♘e8 21

♖c5 (21 f4 ♘c4!? 22 ♗xc4 ♘xd6 equalizes due to the idea 23 ♗b3? ♘f5) 21...♘f3+! 22 gxf3 ♕xd6 with equality.

15...♘b6 16 ♗d3!? ♕e7 17 ♕c2 ♗g4 18 a3 ♖ad8 19 ♖fe1 (D)

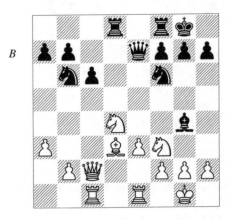

19...♘bd7!

Yermolinsky calls this equal. I've skipped the details of this contest, but you can see the general idea.

20 ♘g5 h6! 21 ♘h7 ♖fe8 22 h3 ♗e6 23 ♘xf6+ ♕xf6 24 ♗f1 ♗d5

with full equality. Even with best play it's unlikely that White can squeeze much out of 12 ♘g3.

Atalik – Zheliandinov
Podlehnik 2001

12 ♘xf6+

This seems the way to go if White wants real chances.

12...♕xf6 13 0-0 e5 (D)

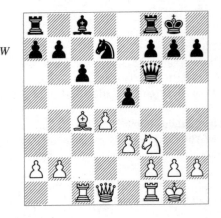

14 e4! exd4 15 ♕xd4 ♕xd4 16 ♘xd4 ♘e5 17 ♗b3 *(D)*

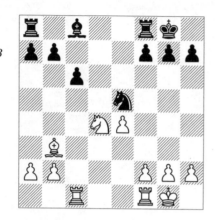

This is a difficult position for Black. White's kingside majority is about to march, and Black's bishop on c8 has no good squares.

17...♖d8!? 18 ♖fd1 ♗d7 19 f4 ♘g6 20 f5! ♘e5 21 ♖c5! ♘g4 *(D)*

21...♖e8 may be best, but White has the tactical shot 22 ♘e6! ♗xe6 23 fxe6 f6 24 ♖d7! with ongoing pressure.

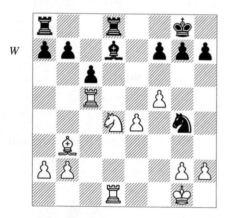

22 h3 b6!?

The alternative 22...♘f6 23 e5 ♘e4 24 ♖cc1 ♘g3 25 e6 isn't encouraging.

23 ♘xc6 ♗xc6 24 ♖xd8+ ♖xd8 25 ♖xc6 1-0

There might follow 25...♘e5 26 ♖c7 a5 27 ♖e7!. White exploited every advantage in the position.

B)

11 0-0 ♘xc3 12 ♖xc3 e5 *(D)*

Way back on move 6, Black could have implemented the Lasker Variation idea without the insertion of 6...h6 7 ♗h4 by means of 6...♘e4 7 ♗xe7 ♕xe7 8 ♖c1 c6 9 ♗d3 ♘xc3 10 ♖xc3 dxc4 11 ♗xc4 ♘d7 12 0-0 e5. Strange to say, this is exactly the position before us! Instead of 12...e5, however, 12...b6?! doesn't seem advisable because the pawn on h7 can be attacked with tempo by a queen on c2 and bishop on d3. In that case the pawn on c6 becomes more vulnerable.

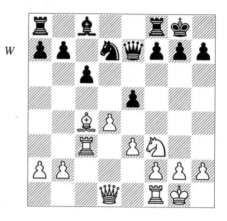

We shall now take a look at a practical example:

Khenkin – Sulskis
Koszalin 1998

13 ♗b3 exd4

Here 13...e4 14 ♘d2 ♖e8 15 f3! exf3 16 ♕xf3 (16 ♘xf3 also looks strong) 16...♘f6 17 e4 ♗e6! 18 ♗xe6 ♕xe6 19 e5 ♘d5 20 ♖b3 b6 21 ♘e4 favours White. The central majority again has its effect.

14 exd4 ♘f6 *(D)*

This position is also precisely the same one that arose in Lasker's variation, but without the move ...h6 as we saw there. It has been claimed that this is a favourable trade-off for Black because he has avoided the weakening move ...h6. Kasparov himself has stated this. But the pawn on h7 is also a target, and sometimes limits the mobility of Black's pieces.

15 ♖e1 ♕d6 16 ♘e5 ♗e6!

a) The natural 16...♘d5?! leaves Black's kingside undefended and allows the interesting line 17 ♖g3 ♗f5 (17...♗e6 18 ♕d2 ♔h8 19

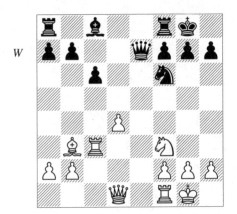

W

♕g5 ♖g8 20 ♖e4 is also difficult to defend) 18 ♕f3! ♗g6 19 h4! *(D)*.

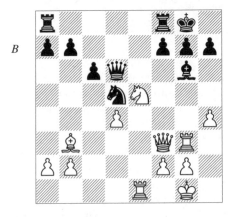

B

Notice that this only works because Black has omitted ...h6. 19...♘f6 20 ♖g5 ♕xd4? 21 h5 ♘xh5 22 ♖xg6 hxg6 23 ♗xf7+ ♔h7 24 ♗xg6+ ♔h6 25 ♕xh5#.

b) 16...♗f5?! has the same problem as in the Lasker Variation: 17 ♘xf7! ♖xf7 18 ♗xf7+ ♔xf7 19 ♕b3+ and 20 ♕xb7, etc., with the better game.

17 ♗xe6 fxe6 18 ♕b3

White obviously has the superior position due to his e-file pressure and e5 outpost.

18...♖ab8 19 ♘ce3 ♘d5 20 ♖e4 ♖f6 21 ♘d3 b6 22 g3 ♖c8 23 ♖1e2 ♖c7 24 h4 h5 25 a3 g6 26 ♕c4 c5?

But against slow moves White can play, e.g., b4, ♘e5, ♕c1 and g4.

27 dxc5 bxc5 28 ♕c2 ♔h7 29 ♖c4 ♖f5 30 ♖xc5 ♖xc5 31 ♕xc5 ♕xc5 32 ♘xc5

White is a clear pawn ahead and went on to win.

Tartakower Variation

1 d4 d5 2 c4 e6 3 ♘c3 ♘f6 4 ♗g5 ♗e7 5 e3 0-0 6 ♘f3 h6 7 ♗h4 b6 *(D)*

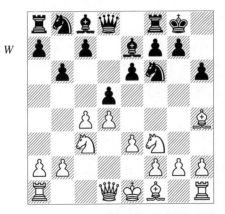

W

Now we are moving into a territory of more complex and usually more dynamic positions than we saw in the Lasker and Capablanca variations, which after all were aimed at exchanging pieces and reaching some kind of simplified equality. After 7...b6 pieces tend to stay on the board longer, and the resulting unbalanced situation creates difficult and double-sided play. What is Black doing? It's not so mysterious, at least not to begin with. He'll play ...♗b7, shoring up d5. That allows him to play for the freeing move ...c5, often prepared by ...♘bd7. Notice that the move 7...c5?! straightaway would expose the unprotected status of d5 after 8 dxc5 ♗xc5 9 cxd5 exd5 10 ♖c1 (for example), when Black will have to take up a passive position merely to hold on to his material. By playing ...b6 and ...♗b7 first, the move ...c5 will definitely be on the cards, and ...♘e4 at the right moment can also be effective.

White has a large number of strategies ranging from simple exchanges to exertion of long-term pressure by clamping down upon any freeing move by Black, especially ...c5. In almost all cases White restrains his own aggressiveness until Black's position is under control. It turns out that Black can answer this method of play in two very different ways. In many lines Black is the one trying to mix things up; he wants to do this before falling into some kind of static disadvantage. This can involve pawn sacrifices for activity and other tactical devices.

However, in a majority of variations he will gain the bishop-pair, so that gives him a choice: he can still look for energetic unbalancing moves but he also has the option of consolidating his position before slowly opening up the game on the bishops' behalf. In those cases it may be *White* who undertakes a vigorous advance before he loses the long-run battle. It is this unpredictability and potential dynamism that attracts players to the Tartakower Variation. In order to gain familiarity with the positions, and to achieve some depth of understanding, I'll concentrate on just a few of both players' set-ups by looking at a series of games. Fortunately, the ideas cross over into other lines of the Tartakower, and of the Queen's Gambit in general.

The Older Exchange Line

8 cxd5

This is the older move, which received a lot of attention before it began to appear that White might get better chances by complicating the situation instead. Nevertheless, some players still use 8 cxd5, and very rich positions can result.

8...♘xd5! *(D)*

Here is the move that helped to revive the Tartakower Defence. 8...exd5 is playable but more rigid; according to theory White keeps the better of it. Compare the Exchange Variation below, in which ...b6 isn't optimal.

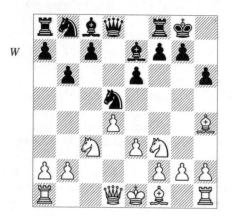

9 ♗xe7 ♕xe7 10 ♘xd5

10 ♖c1 ♗b7 has always been considered harmless because Black can assault White's central majority by ...c5 before it gets rolling; for example, 11 ♗d3 ♖c8 12 0-0 c5 13 ♕e2 ♘xc3 14 ♖xc3 ♘d7 with equality, Keres-Petrosian, Curaçao Ct 1962.

10...exd5 11 ♖c1 ♗e6! *(D)*

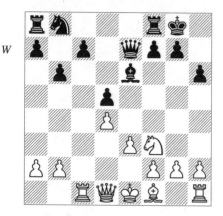

This is a major idea in the Tartakower. Once Black has a pawn fixed on d5 blocking the long diagonal, the bishop would usually be poorly placed on b7; therefore in many situations Black will put it on e6 where it has some open lines and doesn't get in the way of his queenside pieces. Specifically, after the advance ...c5, the bishop encourages rooks to come to b8 and c8 in support of the idea of ...c4 and ...b5; this makes use of Black's queenside majority. You will see a bishop heading for e6 in a great number of games with this defence. In fact, the re-routing manoeuvre ...♗b7-c8-e6 is a recurrent theme!

12 ♕a4

White delays castling in order to meet ...c5 with ♕a3, pinning the pawn. 12 ♕a4 also eyes the somewhat weakened light squares in Black's camp, namely a6 and c6. Notice that if White plays ♘e5 next, all four of his active pieces will be attacking one or both of those squares.

12...c5

We'll look at two games in the position after 12...c5:

Mamedyarov – Lputian
Tripoli FIDE KO 2004

13 dxc5 bxc5 14 ♕a3 ♖c8 *(D)*

Before moving on, let's take a quick look at this pawn-structure, which is characteristic of

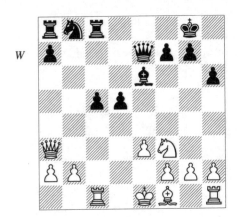

W

many Tartakower variations (although there are usually more pieces on the board). As we discussed in Chapter 3 of Volume 1, Black's c5- and d5-pawns are called 'hanging pawns'. Whether they are good or bad depends upon how well protected they are, how mobile they are, and what activity can be generated around them. In this kind of position White wants to restrain the advance of the pawns for the moment and then target them, much as one fights against an isolated pawn. For this purpose he has pinned Black's pawn on c5 and can increase the pressure on it down the c-file. The move ...d4 isn't on the cards (yet), and an important idea (executed in the Fischer-Spassky game below) will be to force one pawn to advance so as to blockade both.

Black's position has its own good points. The c5-square is well defended, and Black will normally play ...♘d7 to reinforce its protection. Then the b-file can be a real asset. Black can approach the situation in two ways:

a) he can try to attack White's b-pawn down the open file and provoke the move b3, after which ...a5-a4 or ...a5 and ...♕b7-b4 is possible; or

b) he can simply play ...c4 without provocation because, although that permanently gives up the d4-square, it also discourages the move b3 and facilitates an attack down the b-file.

You'll see these ideas in more than one line of the Tartakower Defence.

15 ♗e2 a5 16 ♘d4

Also a standard idea. The knight can go to b3 in order to put pressure on Black's c-pawn, or in some cases White will exchange the bishop on e6. Now Black plays a surprising move:

16...♘a6! 17 ♗xa6

Else the knight comes to b4.

17...♖xa6 18 0-0 ♗d7 19 ♘b3?!

Kregelin-Trost, corr. 1995 went 19 ♖fd1 ♖b6! 20 ♘e2 ♕g5 21 ♖d2? d4! *(D)*.

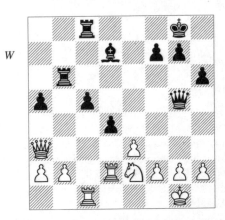

W

As explained in our discussion about hanging pawns, once Black can productively play ...d4 he will often stand better: 22 f4 ♕d5 23 exd4 ♖g6 24 ♘c3 ♕f3 25 ♘b1 ♕xf4 26 dxc5 ♗c6 with a very dangerous attack due to Black's unobstructed bishop.

19...♖g6! 20 ♔h1!

20 ♖xc5 is tempting, but Black doesn't need much material to attack: 20...♕e4 21 ♖xc8+ ♗xc8 22 f3 ♕xe3+ 23 ♔h1 (23 ♖f2 ♗h3) 23...♕e2 24 ♖g1 ♗h3 and mate follows.

20...♕e4 21 f3 ♕xe3 22 ♘xc5 ♕d2!? 23 g4! ♗e6

Here White would have been holding on after 24 ♖fd1, with near-equality, but instead there followed 24 ♕c3? ♕xc3 25 ♖xc3 d4 26 ♖cc1 ♗xa2, and Black was winning.

Timman – Geller
Hilversum 1973

13 ♕a3

Again this manoeuvre. White pins the pawn on c5 and threatens to win it, in the meantime preventing the pawn-majority advance by ...c4.

13...♖c8 *(D)*

14 ♗b5!?

This prophylactic move, Furman's invention, was favoured at the time this game was played. It discourages ...♘d7, while White can contemplate ♘e5-d3 increasing his pressure on

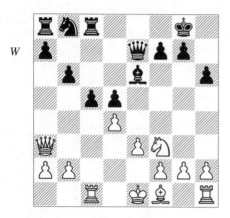

c5. A simple alternative is 14 ♗e2 ♔f8 (14...a5! is one of the better options here) 15 dxc5 bxc5 16 0-0 a5!? 17 ♖c3 ♘d7 18 ♖fc1 ♖cb8 with equality, Winants-Kasparov, Brussels 1987.

14...♕b7!

a) One of the most famous games in modern chess (as much because of the setting as the play itself) was Fischer-Spassky, Reykjavik Wch (6) 1972, which continued 14...a6 15 dxc5 bxc5 16 0-0 (D).

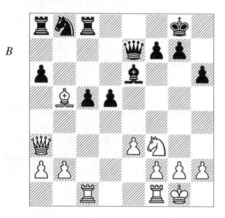

16...♖a7 (16...♕b7 17 ♗a4! ♕b6 18 ♘e5 with the idea ♘d3; this knight repositioning is what tips the scales in many of these lines; once Black has to play ...c4 in this particular position White will own all the dark squares – then Black needs immediate counterplay, which in this case isn't available) 17 ♗e2 ♘d7 (it's hard to believe that this was Spassky's preparation because it doesn't seem to improve upon the 17...a5 18 ♖c3 ♘d7 19 ♖fc1 ♖e8 20 ♗b5! of Furman-Geller, USSR Ch (Riga) 1970) 18 ♘d4 (now White threatens ♘b3) 18...♕f8?! 19 ♘xe6

fxe6 20 e4! (remember this characteristic move! It is used to attack this same structure in several different openings and associated middlegames) 20...d4?! 21 f4 (D).

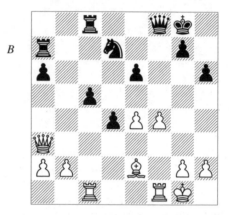

Now we have what should become a familiar picture in your chess databank: a mobile kingside majority versus a thoroughly blockaded central one. After 21...♕e7 22 e5 ♖b8 23 ♗c4 ♔h8 24 ♕h3 ♘f8 25 b3 a5 26 f5! exf5 27 ♖xf5 ♘h7 28 ♖cf1 ♕d8 29 ♕g3 ♖e7 30 h4 ♖bb7 31 e6! ♖bc7 32 ♕e5 Fischer went on to win this overwhelming position.

b) Another educational move is 14...♔f8 (preparing ...c4! followed by ...a6 and ...b5) 15 dxc5 ♖xc5! (15...bxc5 16 b3 and the hanging pawns are restrained) 16 ♖xc5 ♕xc5! 17 ♕xc5+ bxc5 18 ♔d2 ♔e7 with ...♘d7 and ...♔d6 to follow. This equalizes easily.

15 dxc5 bxc5 16 ♖xc5 ♖xc5 17 ♕xc5 (D)

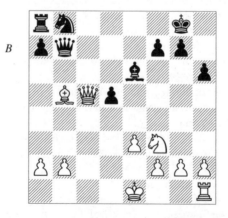

Probably Timman, who was very familiar with the games and analysis of the Fischer-Spassky match, was happy with this position. It's only natural for Black to recover his pawn by 17...a6, when he had analysed 18 ♗d3 ♕xb2, after which 19 0-0! ♘d7 (19...♕xa2?? 20 ♘d4 and the threat of ♘xe6 and ♕c8+ forces 20...♘d7 21 ♕c6 ♖d8 22 ♘xe6 fxe6 23 ♕c7) 20 ♕c6 ♖b8 21 ♘d4!? ♕b6 22 ♖c1 yields a small but lasting advantage. But Geller found something better:

17...♘a6! 18 ♗xa6

Now White can't castle, but he's trying to avoid 18 ♕c6 ♕xc6 19 ♗xc6 ♖b8! (19...♖c8 20 ♗a4), when the b-pawn falls in view of 20 b3? ♖c8.

18...♕xa6 19 ♕a3

The best move, defending against ...♖c8 while threatening to exchange queens.

19...♕c4 20 ♔d2!

This bold move looks best, intending ♘d4 and/or ♖c1.

20...♕g4 21 ♖g1 *(D)*

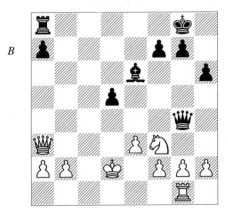

21...d4!

The first line-opening sacrifice. Black pitches another pawn to free his e6-bishop.

22 ♘xd4?!

Although this capture is perfectly logical, it seems that 22 exd4 was correct.

22...♕h4 23 ♖e1!? ♕xf2+

Or 23...♗c4!, which would preserve the bishop. Now White gets rid of it and reduces material even further, but Geller manages to keep an attack going and shows his brilliance in that regard. You can enjoy the rest of the game without notes:

24 ♖e2 ♕f1 25 ♘xe6 fxe6 26 ♕d6 ♔h8 27 e4 ♖c8 28 ♔e3 ♖f8 29 ♖d2!? e5! 30 ♕xe5??

The defence required in such a position is almost impossible to conduct properly. White was probably concerned with protecting f4.

30...♕e1+ 31 ♖e2 ♕g1+ 32 ♔d3 ♖d8+ 33 ♔c3 ♕d1 34 ♕b5 ♕d4+ 35 ♔c2 a6! 36 ♕xa6 ♕c5+ 0-1

The Newer Exchange Line with 8 ♗e2

1 d4 d5 2 c4 e6 3 ♘c3 ♘f6 4 ♗g5 ♗e7 5 e3 0-0 6 ♘f3 h6 7 ♗h4 b6 8 ♗e2 *(D)*

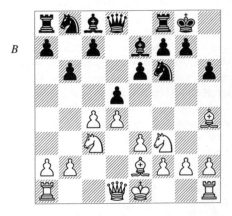

White's modest bishop move is considered the main line of the Tartakower. First, he waits until Black commits his bishop to b7.

8...♗b7 9 ♗xf6 ♗xf6 10 cxd5 exd5 *(D)*

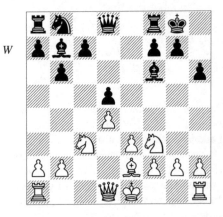

White's paradoxical idea is to take two moves (♗h4xf6) to capture Black's knight instead of one. This has been played in hundreds if not thousands of games, including many from the Karpov-Kasparov world championship matches, in which both played the position with each colour. What's the point? Essentially it's that Black's bishop is poorly placed for this pawn-structure. It was actually better on c8, so the reasoning goes. And as we mentioned above, Black's bishop very often retreats from b7 to c8 and then (usually) goes to e6. So White in that case has gained one move by taking two moves to capture the knight! In the meantime, why is White giving up the bishop-pair? Essentially, he feels that it's a sufficiently controlled position that he can use his well-placed knights to make progress, probably with a pawn advance before Black's bishops find good homes for themselves. Black on the other hand thinks that as long as his queenside pawn-structure can't be compromised by White (by means of b4-b5, for example), and as long as the advance e4 isn't effective, he will be able to open the game at his discretion and use the bishop-pair to his advantage. It's easiest to understand this by examples:

11 b4 *(D)*

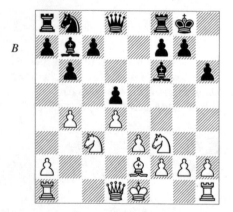

The main line, which is now used by a large majority of masters. White tries to hold down ...c5 and also prepares a minority attack by b5 in some positions. There are several fascinating alternatives (11 ♕b3, for example) that you may find it interesting to research for yourself. I think that it is more useful, however, to see 11 b4 in depth.

11...c6

Black tries the strategic approach; it is a more ambitious idea than 11...c5, which has been seen in many grandmaster games (including those Karpov-Kasparov encounters mentioned above) with a high drawing rate, especially in the main line 12 bxc5 bxc5 13 ♖b1 ♗c6 14 0-0 ♘d7 15 ♗b5 ♕c7 16 ♕d3 ♖fc8 (or 16...♖fd8), when the verdict ranges between equal and a bit better for White.

12 0-0 *(D)*

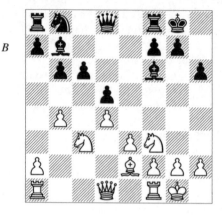

From this archetypal position we shall examine some games and excerpts.

Alterman – Pigusov
Beijing 1997

12...a5!?

Black could also develop more slowly than this; however, he wants to force White's hand and perhaps free his bishops in the meantime.

13 bxa5!?

13 b5 is met by 13...c5, when 14 ♘e5 exerts some pressure but not enough to worry Black.

The main alternative is 13 a3, when the game Speelman-Lputian, Kropotkin 1995 continued 13...♘d7 14 ♕b3 ♖e8 15 ♖ad1 axb4 16 axb4 b5 *(D)*.

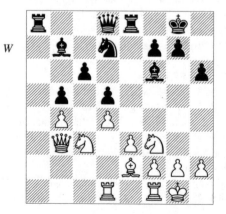

Setting up the pawns in this fashion is now a standard idea. You wouldn't think that Black would want to close up the position for his own bishops, but he does have the nice outpost on c4 in return for White's on c5, and he can bring his bad bishop around to f5. Perhaps most significantly, his weaknesses are masked and not likely to become a problem soon; remember that third-rank weaknesses are usually easier to defend than ones on the fourth rank. In this game it all works perfectly: 17 ♘e1?! ♘b6 18 ♘d3 ♗c8! 19 ♘c5 ♗f5 20 ♖a1 ♗e7! 21 ♖a2 ♖xa2 22 ♕xa2 ♗d6 (this is the same manoeuvre that seems to work in all of our Exchange Variation pawn-structures! Black gets some real chances on the kingside) 23 ♖a1 ♕h4 24 g3 ♕g5 25 ♗d3? (Scherbakov's line 25 ♕d2 ♘c4 26 ♗xc4 bxc4 leaves Black better, but with nothing concrete) 25...♗xd3 26 ♘xd3 ♖xe3! 27 fxe3 ♕xe3+ 28 ♕f2 ♕xd3 29 ♘e2 ♗xb4 30 ♖a7 ♕b1+ 31 ♔g2 ♕e4+ 32 ♕f3 ♕e8! and with three pawns and active pieces for the exchange, Black ultimately won the game.

13...♖xa5 14 a4

Now White's weak a-pawn is difficult to get at and he hopes to generate his own queenside pressure.

14...♗c8!

Again, Black gets the bishop off that horrible b7-square! Does anyone remember why he put it there in the first place? 14...c5, intending to block everything off by ...♘a6/c6-b4, is another way to play.

15 ♖b1 ♗e6 16 ♕c2 ♘d7 17 ♖fc1 ♕a8! *(D)*

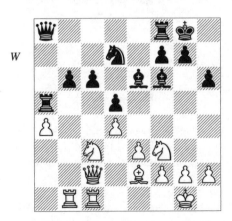

Perfect coordination. Black's pieces are well-placed and he has no trouble defending his

pawns. So he prepares ...c5, but after that it's still hard for either side to make progress.

18 ♗d3 c5 19 ♗h7+ ♔h8 20 ♗f5 ♕c6 21 h3 ♖c8 22 ♗xe6 fxe6?!

22...♕xe6! is more active and a better move. As it happens, Black's d-pawn won't be a problem in that situation.

23 ♕g6 ♖aa8 24 ♕h5! ♕d6 25 ♘b5 ♕e7 26 ♖a1 e5!? 27 ♖e1?!

27 ♕f5! would give White some chances. But it's fair to say that the whole variation is balanced.

27...♕e6 28 ♘h2 e4 29 ♖ed1 cxd4?! 30 ♘xd4 ♗xd4 31 ♖xd4 ♘f6 ½-½

Karpov – Ki. Georgiev
Tilburg 1994

12...♕d6 13 ♕b3 *(D)*

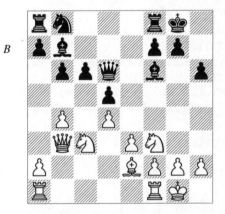

13...♘d7 14 ♖fe1

White makes a slow but useful move. Given time, he will play e4.

14...♗e7

Scherbakov offers the line 14...a5!? 15 bxa5 ♖xa5 16 a4 ♗d8! 17 ♗f1 ♘f6 18 g3 ♗c7 with a satisfactory game for Black. Moving Black's bishop to the b8-h2 diagonal is a relatively common theme in these positions. Again the pawn on a4 prevents White from using that square, although that doesn't hurt Karpov in the game that we're following:

15 ♖ab1 a5 16 bxa5 ♖xa5 17 a4 ♖e8 18 ♗f1

White seems to be doing nothing.

18...♗f8 19 ♕c2 g6 20 e4! dxe4 21 ♘xe4 ♕f4 22 ♗c4

Suddenly Karpov's pieces are getting active and aiming towards Black's king!

22...♗g7! 23 ♖e2 c5 24 d5

The attack is over for the moment. But no one can handle a passed d-pawn like Karpov.

24...♖aa8 25 ♖be1 ♖ad8 26 ♕b3 ♗a8 27 g3 ♕b8?! 28 d6! ♖f8 *(D)*

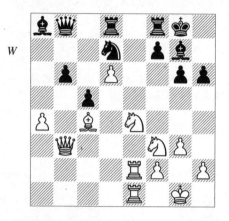

29 ♗xf7+!

A strong move that had to be precisely calculated. I'll skip the details.

29...♖xf7 30 ♘eg5 hxg5 31 ♘xg5 ♖df8 32 ♖e8! ♕xd6 33 ♕xf7+ ♔h8 34 ♘e6! 1-0

Alatortsev Variation

1 d4 d5 2 c4 e6 3 ♘c3 ♗e7 *(D)*

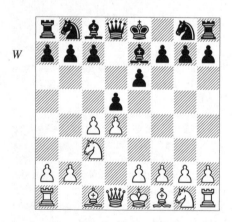

Black often chooses this move because he wants to avoid the Modern Exchange Variation (discussed forthwith). He still intends to play ...♘f6 and usually doesn't mind entering the Classical lines that we have been analysing via

3...♗e7 4 ♘f3 ♘f6 5 ♗g5 0-0 6 e3, etc. What's more, Black may be willing to go into the type of *classical* Exchange Variation that follows 1 d4 d5 2 c4 e6 3 ♘c3 ♗e7 4 ♘f3 ♘f6 5 cxd5 exd5 6 ♗g5. This line, with the knight committed to f3, is sometimes called the 'Carlsbad Variation'. As we shall see in the Exchange Variation section, White's modern set-up with ♗d3 and ♘ge2 is the one that many players fear most, and that is bypassed by the sequence 3...♗e7 4 ♘f3.

Originally this move-order 'trick' was only used by grandmasters, but now even moderately experienced players are familiar with it; the fact is that a lot of players who use the Queen's Gambit Declined as their regular defence don't like facing the Modern Exchange Variation.

Of course, White isn't forced to cooperate by playing 4 ♘f3. He can exchange on d5 and then develop his pieces independently thereafter, as more than one World Champion has done.

Kasparov – Short
Thessaloniki OL 1988

1 d4 d5 2 c4 e6 3 ♘c3 ♗e7 4 cxd5 exd5 5 ♗f4 *(D)*

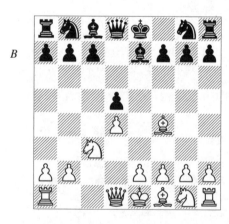

There could hardly be anything more natural than to place a bishop on f4, especially when ♗g5 isn't available. White wants to play e3 next and develop his pieces.

5...c6

Undoubtedly the most subtle reply, and considered best by theory. Black wants to get ...♗f5 in as soon as he can, but 5...♗f5? loses to our old friend 6 ♕b3.

6 ♕c2

In the next two games we shall see 6 e3 ♗f5. White sometimes develops the queen first in order to stop ...♗f5. In turn, Black wants to get that move in so that he can develop (and perhaps exchange) his bad bishop. Thus his next move.

6...g6

This has to come before White can play e3 and ♗d3, preventing ...♗f5.

7 e3 ♗f5 8 ♕d2!

White can exchange bishops by 8 ♗d3, but then Black has achieved his goal and isn't under the slightest risk of attack. The queen move intends to preserve White's good light-squared bishop and take advantage of the position of Black's on f5.

8...♘f6

Kasparov was on the other side of the board and played 8...♘d7 9 f3 ♘b6 10 e4 ♗e6 in Karpov-Kasparov, London/Leningrad Wch (7) 1986. After 11 e5 White had an excellent position with a lot of space, although Kasparov drew in the end.

9 f3 *(D)*

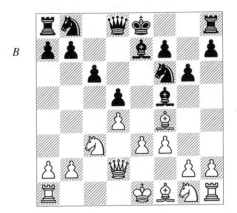

White doesn't want Black's knight settling in on e4. What's more, f3 prepares g4 in some cases so as to gain space and drive away Black's bishop.

9...c5?!

It's hard to believe that this move in combination with the next constitutes a positional mistake, but perhaps Black should be more patient. The straightforward 9...h5, stopping g4 (as well as ♗h6), was played ten years later in Topalov-Karpov, Wijk aan Zee 1998. That game

continued 10 ♗d3 ♗xd3 11 ♕xd3 ♘a6 12 ♘ge2 ♘c7 13 0-0 ♘e6 14 ♗e5 and it's fair to say that White has some advantage; Topalov went on to win. Needless to say there have been other games in this line before and since.

10 ♗h6! *(D)*

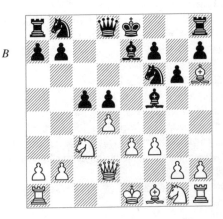

White ignores his development to stop castling, and he prevents ...h5.

10...cxd4?!

This exchange turns out to hurt Black badly, both on the e-file and on the kingside. Maybe moves such as dxc5 and ♗g7xf6 or g4-g5 were becoming problems, but probably not with White still undeveloped. Therefore Black could try 10...♘c6; e.g., 11 dxc5?! (11 ♗b5! a6 12 ♗xc6+ bxc6 13 ♘ge2 gives White some advantage due to Black's castling situation; 11 g4 is well answered by 11...♗e6) 11...♗xc5 (or 11...d4!?) 12 ♗g7 ♖g8 13 ♗xf6 ♕xf6 14 ♘xd5 ♕d6 15 e4 0-0-0 with a lot of open lines for a pawn.

11 exd4 *(D)*

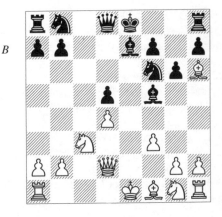

This doesn't look good for Black. For starters, White's queen protects his bishop on h6, so that it is ready to take over that square after a possible exchange. And in general White's development is easy, while Black needs to untangle his pieces.

11...a6

11...♘c6 12 ♗b5! opens all the right squares for White's pieces; for example, 12...♖c8 13 ♘ge2 a6 14 ♗xc6+ ♖xc6 15 ♘g3 ♗e6 16 0-0 and Black still cannot castle.

12 g4! ♗e6 13 ♘ge2 ♘bd7

Somehow Black can't get his pieces out or his king to safety. Kasparov has won another opening battle. An example is 13...♘c6 14 ♗g2 ♘a5 15 b3 ♖c8 16 0-0 and Black isn't getting anywhere. For the rest of the game I can't see what he should do.

14 ♗g2 ♘b6 15 b3 ♖c8 16 0-0 ♖c6 17 h3!? ♘fd7 18 ♘d1!?

Planning f4-f5.

18...♖g8 19 ♘f2 f5 20 ♖ae1 (D)

There's that e-file.

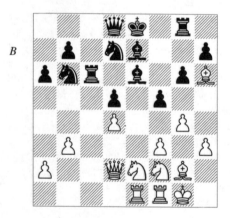

20...g5 21 gxf5 ♗f7

Probably not the objectively best move, but then again 21...♗xf5 22 ♘g3 ♗e6 23 f4! is unbearable.

22 ♘g4 ♗h5 23 ♘g3 1-0

A surprising game. The pawn-structure in particular bears notice. You will see it again.

Kasparov – Karpov
Moscow Wch (21) 1985

1 d4 d5 2 c4 e6 3 ♘c3 ♗e7 4 cxd5 exd5 5 ♗f4 c6 6 e3 ♗f5 7 g4! *(D)*

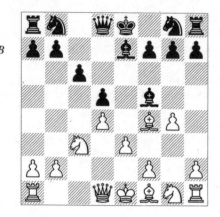

The stem game for this advance is Botvinnik-Petrosian, Moscow Wch (12) 1963. Gaining space is an enormous advantage in chess, so much so that in this case it more than balances out the resulting weaknesses.

7...♗e6 8 h4 ♘d7 9 h5 ♘h6! *(D)*

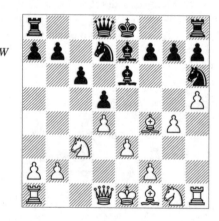

Kasparov's successful use of the g4/h4 attack (in contrast to g4/h3, as in the next game) inspired this ingenious solution. It's worth noting that Karpov had trouble countering the set-up with 5 ♗f4, losing games to Korchnoi (below) while getting into trouble in this game. Yet we saw in a note above that as White he got the better of Kasparov in the same line. In Linares 1989, he also used 7 g4 to defeat Portisch. Although it's not fair to speak of a forced advantage, Black has yet to prove that he can equalize completely against White's strategy. The games in this section show the love of space that the greatest players of the ex-Soviet Union had (and have).

10 ♗e2!

Not 10 ♗h3?! g5!; the most important point of 9...♘h6 is 10 f3 f5!.

10...♘b6 11 ♖c1 ♗d6

11...♘c4 would apparently have equalized, since Kasparov's 12 ♗xc4 dxc4 13 ♗xh6 gxh6 looks OK for Black. From here on out it's hard to suggest significant improvements.

12 ♘h3 ♗xf4 13 ♘xf4 ♗d7 14 ♖g1! g5

Kasparov gives the exotic line 14...♕h4 15 g5 ♘f5 16 ♖g4! ♕h2 (16...♕h1+ 17 ♔d2) 17 ♖g2 ♕h4 18 ♔d2 with advantage.

15 hxg6 hxg6 16 ♔d2!

The safest place for this piece!

16...♕e7 17 b3 g5 18 ♘d3 0-0-0 19 ♖h1 f6 20 ♕g1 ♘f7 21 ♕g3 ♕d6! 22 ♕xd6 ♘xd6 23 f3 (D)

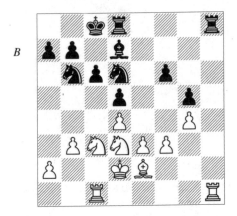

Notice how Black's knights are restricted by White's pawns.

23...♖dg8 24 ♘c5 ♔d8 25 ♗d3 ♗c8 26 ♘e2 ♘a8?!

This looks right, trying to bring his worst piece into play, but it allows White an attractive reorganization of his pieces.

27 ♗h7! ♖f8 28 ♖h6 ♘c7 29 ♘g3 ♘f7 30 ♖h2 ♘e6 31 ♘d3 ♘g7 32 ♖ch1

Kasparov has quite a large advantage, but in time pressure he failed to convert it into victory.

Korchnoi – Karpov
Merano Wch (13) 1981

1 c4 e6 2 ♘c3 d5 3 d4 ♗e7 4 cxd5 exd5 5 ♗f4 c6 6 e3 ♗f5 7 g4 ♗e6 8 h3 (D)

This is the more conservative move. Great players have gone back and forth between 8 h3 and 8 h4.

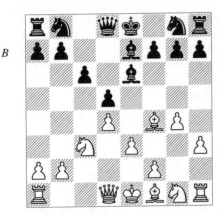

8...♘f6 9 ♘f3 0-0 10 ♗d3 c5 11 ♔f1!

Castling by hand. The problem with 11 0-0 is nothing dramatic like 11...h5!?, but simply 11...c4 12 ♗c2 ♘c6, when the f1-rook won't participate in a kingside attack.

11...♘c6 12 ♔g2 ♖c8

12...cxd4?! 13 ♘xd4 ♘xd4 14 exd4 was a poor choice in Botvinnik-Petrosian, Moscow Wch (14) 1963: 14...♘d7 15 ♕c2 ♘f6 16 f3 (D).

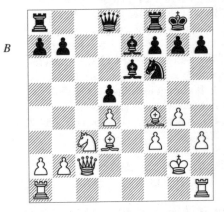

You should commit this pawn-structure to memory: it's almost always better for White! Even without the move g4, the pawns will usually frustrate Black, who has difficulty finding places to attack in White's position, whereas his opponent has multiple ways to make progress. The game continued 16...♖c8 17 ♗e5 ♗d6 18 ♖ae1 ♗xe5 19 ♖xe5. White's pieces are more active and his position is significantly better.

13 ♖c1 ♖e8 14 dxc5 ♗xc5 15 ♘b5 ♗f8 16 ♘fd4 ♘xd4?

Now we can see why this is such a mistake: it gives White the very favourable pawn-structure that we just saw! Unzicker suggests 16...♕b6! 17 ♘xe6 ♖xe6 (17...fxe6 18 g5 ♘e4) 18 g5 ♘e4.

17 ♖xc8 ♕xc8

Or 17...♗xc8 18 exd4! a6 19 ♘c7 ♖e7 20 ♕c2.

18 exd4! *(D)*

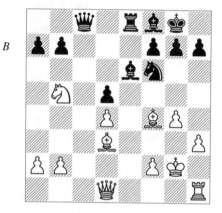

18...♕d7 19 ♘c7 ♖c8 20 ♘xe6 fxe6

Black loses material after 20...♕xe6? 21 ♗f5. But now his pawn-structure is weak and he's facing White's two active bishops.

21 ♖e1 a6 22 g5 ♘e4 23 ♕g4 ♗b4?!

Karpov launches a sort of desperate counter-attack. It's not quite sound, but Black's position was rather a wreck in any case.

24 ♖e2 ♖f8 25 f3 ♕f7 26 ♗e5 ♘d2 27 a3!
♘xf3 28 g6?

28 ♗g3! wins.

28...hxg6 29 ♗g3 ♗e7?

29...♘h4+! 30 ♔h2 ♘f3+ 31 ♔h1 ♘h4! draws.

30 ♖f2 ♘e1+ 31 ♔h1 ♕xf2 32 ♗xf2 ♘xd3
33 ♕xe6+ ♖f7 34 ♗g3 ♘xb2 35 ♕xd5 ♗f6 36
♗d6 g5 37 ♕b3 ♗xd4 38 ♕e6 g6 39 ♕e8+
♔g7 40 ♗e5+ ♗xe5 41 ♕xe5+ ♔h7 1-0

Exchange Variation

To introduce this extremely important topic, let me go over the beginning moves once more. There are multiple paths and obstacles for both sides to get to or avoid the main lines. Fortunately, most of these were already discussed in the introduction to this chapter. Here I'd like to fill out some variations that we've missed.

1 d4 d5 2 c4 e6 3 ♘c3

Here 3 ♘f3 ♘f6 4 ♘c3 ♗e7 5 cxd5 exd5 6 ♗g5 is a possible path to the Carlsbad Variation, which is one of our two main lines in this section, but Black is not forced to play that way (as explained there, 6...c6 and ...♗f5 may avoid it). All major issues with an early ♘f3 are gone over in the chapter introduction. There are more details at the end of the chapter.

3...♘f6 4 cxd5 *(D)*

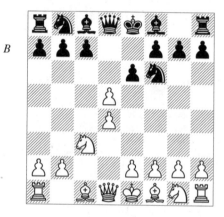

4...exd5

4...♘xd5 can transpose to a line of the Semi-Tarrasch (the standard sequence for which is 4 ♘f3 c5, when 5 cxd5 ♘xd5 6 e4 ♘xc3 7 bxc3 can follow). White's most aggressive approach (and Black's most confrontational reply) is 5 e4 ♘xc3 6 bxc3 c5 7 ♘f3 (this completes the transposition; 7 ♖b1!? is interesting, to prevent ...♗b4+ in some lines; by targeting b7, White hinders the development of Black's queen's bishop) 7...cxd4 8 cxd4 ♗b4+ 9 ♗d2 ♗xd2+ 10 ♕xd2 *(D)*.

We've arrived at the starting point of many a famous battle. Most lower-ranked players don't like to concede the ideal centre to White, who can advance his central pawns to make a passed pawn or aim his forces at Black's king. But Black has no weaknesses and can think about taking over queenside light squares as he does in the Grünfeld Defence. The variation as a whole is probably more difficult for Black to play than for White. I won't discuss the line except to show the famous example Polugaevsky-Tal, USSR Ch (Moscow) 1969, in which

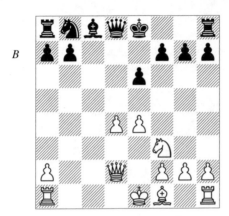

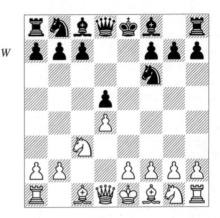

the main ideas show through: 10...0-0 11 ♗c4 ♘c6 12 0-0 b6 13 ♖ad1 ♗b7 14 ♖fe1 ♘a5 (14...♕d6!? would keep the knight in the centre and prevent ♕f4; that looks like a good way to play it) 15 ♗d3 ♖c8 *(D)*.

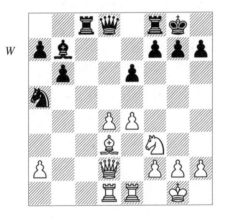

Here White initiates the key manoeuvre 16 d5! exd5 17 e5!. For a pawn, he has blocked Black's bishop and freed his own, winning the d4-square for a knight while targeting Black's king. The last factor proved decisive: 17...♘c4 18 ♕f4! ♘b2 19 ♗xh7+! ♔xh7 20 ♘g5+ ♔g6 21 h4! (the star move of White's attack) 21...♖c4 22 h5+ ♔h6 23 ♘xf7++ ♔h7 24 ♕f5+ ♔g8 25 e6 ♕f6 26 ♕xf6 gxf6 27 ♖d2 ♖c6 28 ♖xb2 ♖e8 29 ♘h6+! ♔h7 30 ♘f5 ♖exe6 31 ♖xe6 ♖xe6 32 ♖c2 ♖c6 33 ♖e2 ♗c8 34 ♖e7+ ♔h8 35 ♘h4 f5 36 ♘g6+ ♔g8 37 ♖xa7 1-0. The threat is ♘e7+ and if Black's rook strays, h6-h7 decides.

Let's return to 4...exd5 *(D)*:

We've reached the Exchange Variation of the Queen's Gambit, written about in great detail in countless books and articles. One reason for

this, perhaps even the main one, is that the important strategic ideas are so clear and definable, and thus easy to write about. They can be presented in a relatively simple fashion or with more detail, depending upon the level of sophistication the writer wants to indulge in. The particular version of queenside minority attack that arises from the Exchange Variation, for example, is the standard one given in almost every textbook, with a host of well-known set-ups for both sides. However, the more carefully that you scrutinize the Exchange Variation, the more you appreciate the subtleties that inform its execution in practice. Right off, we see that in most variations none or only one pair of minor pieces is exchanged up to the start of the middlegame. Ordinarily, any opening with such properties allows for complex and original play. Most Tartakower Defence lines in the Classical Queen's Gambit fit that description, and it is no coincidence that the Exchange and Tartakower are by far the two most popular QGD variations in modern grandmaster chess.

We should start with the basics. Why would White free Black's light-squared bishop, his problem piece in the variations that we have examined thus far? Doesn't this negate the whole point of playing 2 c4? White gets the c-file, to be sure, but Black gets the e-file, arguably a more important one. I think the answers to this question are more accidental than logical. It turns out that in this *precise* position Black normally has no particularly good square for his liberated queen's bishop and must be satisfied with the passive move ...♗e6 (or – often worse – ...b6 and ...♗b7). Why? In the first place White usually develops by ♗d3 and/or ♕c2 and prevents ...♗f5, whereas ...♗g4 is either impossible, because one of the moves f3 or h3 has already been played, or undesirable, because the move f3 is extremely valuable even if Black's bishop retreats to g6 via h5. The other strong point behind cxd5 is that now, if and when Black tries to attack White's centre via ...c5, he has to reckon with the idea of dxc5, isolating Black's d-pawn (this is especially true if White has occupied f3 with a knight and not a pawn). In most variations, the arrangement of Black's pieces is not such that the isolated pawn is compensated for by his activity, as it so often is in other openings (in the Exchange Variation, for example, you will see a knight on d7 rather than the more active c6). Thus variables not already inherent in the pawn-structure, i.e., the particularities of piece dispositions, happen to favour White's otherwise illogical exchange on d5. Note that these are exceptional characteristics that are not shared by other Exchange Variations, such as those in the French Defence (1 e4 e6 2 d4 d5 3 exd5 exd5) or the Slav (1 d4 d5 2 c4 c6 3 cxd5 cxd5).

5 ♗g5 (D)

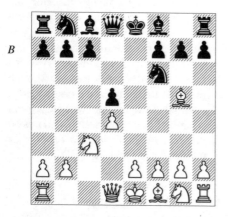

Actually, some writers call this the starting position of the Exchange Variation 'Proper', because ♗g5 is part of the standard set-up. At some point in the naming process, however, things become ambiguous and there's no point in fretting over subtleties.

5...♗e7

There are a number of other move-orders, but in this position the most significant alternatives tend to converge upon the positions and structures that follow. An important side-variation is

5...c6 6 e3 (6 ♕c2 prevents Black's next, but that's another move that is associated with numerous subvariations) 6...♗f5 7 ♕f3! ♗g6 8 ♗xf6 ♕xf6 9 ♕xf6 gxf6 (D).

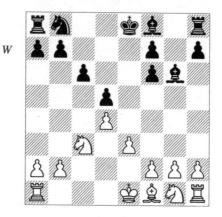

It looks ridiculous to allow White to get into an ending with Black having weak doubled pawns and no positive chances, but especially at master level there are players who don't necessarily mind playing with a slightly worse position if they think they can ultimately achieve a drawn result. Fortunately most of us aren't like that; and anyway, in a real game there are always plenty of chances to win. The variation which seems to have the most promise for White at this point in time is 10 ♘f3 ♘d7 11 ♘h4 (or 11 g3 followed by ♘h4) 11...♘b6 (Black intends to play ...♘c8-d6 to protect the vulnerable f5-square) 12 g3; for example, 12...♘c8 13 f3 ♘d6 14 ♔f2. This is a position in which Black will generally have to wait around while White can try several plans in order to make progress. An example with a different move-order but not radically different strategy is Van Wely-Short, Wijk aan Zee 2005: 10 ♘f3 ♘d7 11 ♘h4 ♗e7 12 g3 ♘b6 13 f3 a5 14 ♔f2 a4 15 ♖c1 ♘c8 16 ♗e2 ♘d6 17 ♖hd1 0-0 18 ♗d3 ♖fe8 19 g4 ♗f8 20 ♘e2 ♗h6 21 f4 ♗xd3 22 ♖xd3 ♗f8 23 ♘g3 ♖a5 24 ♖c2 ♖b5 25 ♘hf5 ♘c4 26 b3 axb3 27 ♖xb3 ♖xb3 28 axb3 ♘a5 29 ♘h5 ♖e6 30 ♖a2 b6 31 ♖a4 1-0. Impressive, although naturally Black has alternatives. If he wants to enter into the 7 ♕f3 ♗g6 line, Black should study what White's logical set-ups are and specifically how to respond to them. For his part, White has to decide whether to avoid the ending altogether in favour of more complex play.

We now return to the position after 5...♗e7 *(D)*:

6 e3

6 ♕c2 can be played here, perhaps to prevent an early ...♗f5. It's worth noting that in some variations with ♕c2 and 0-0-0 soon thereafter, Black's most dangerous idea is to play ...c5, hopefully quickly, in order to exert pressure down the c-file and in some cases to put his knight on c6, where it is a bit closer to White's king. And there are other problems for White when he plays an early ♕c2, particularly (but not limited to) situations in which he has developed his knight to f3: Black can play ...g6, with the idea of ...♗f5, gaining a tempo or exchanging a good bishop on d3. Also, Black's knight will sometimes develop via a6, irritating White because of the possibility of ...♘b4 but also leaving open the manoeuvre ...♘c7-e6, which has the same result as the conventional route ...♘bd7-f8-e6. For all that, Black can only try one plan at a time, and White has ways of trying to counter each one, so 6 ♕c2 is certainly playable.

The following game isn't the most pertinent example of ♕c2 ideas, but at least it begins that way. I present it for those of you who think that the Queen's Gambit Declined is boring. The actual move-order of this game is slightly different from the one we've been following.

Guseinov – Magomedov
Dushanbe 1999

1 d4 d5 2 c4 e6 3 ♘f3 ♘f6 4 ♘c3 ♗e7 5 cxd5 exd5 6 ♗g5 c6 7 ♕c2 *(D)*

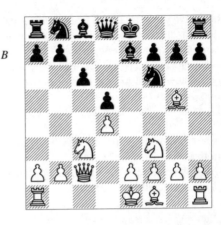

So far so normal: White plays ♕c2 so as to prevent ...♗f5. He has also delayed e3 in order to retain the possibility of playing e4 without wasting time.

7...♘a6

Black develops his knight to the side of the board. As noted, this combines the idea of ...♘b4 with that of ...♘c7-e6, a standard centralization in the Exchange Variation.

8 a3

Before undertaking central action, White anticipates Black's planned attack by ...g6, ...♘b4 and ...♗f5. By stopping ...♘b4, however, he uses up a precious tempo.

8...g6 9 e4 ♘xe4! 10 ♘xe4 ♘c7!! *(D)*

Amazing. Black remains a piece down for a moment in order to regain it favourably. This isn't just a clever move, but a necessity if Black wants to avoid the significant disadvantage that would follow both 10...♗f5 11 ♗xa6 ♗xe4 12 ♕c3 and 10...dxe4 11 ♕xe4.

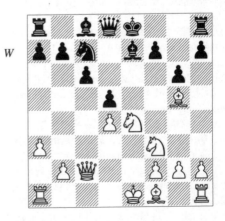

11 ♕c5!?

This move prevents Black from castling but works out badly. Both sides have options on almost every move, and strategy has to some extent been superseded by tactics. But there are a few points at which the game is informative in a positional sense.

11...dxe4 12 ♕e5 ♖f8 13 ♕xe4 ♗f5 14 ♕e3!?

It's not clear whether this is objectively best, but notice that 14 ♕xe7+ ♕xe7+ 15 ♗xe7 ♔xe7 *(D)* is the kind of position strong players will do almost anything to avoid:

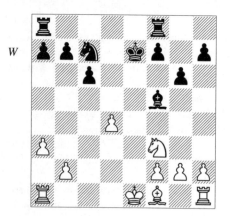

White's d-pawn will ultimately be lost (for example by exchanging off White's knight on f3), and with accurate play the game will end in Black's favour. Hence the retreat of the queen, which at least leads to complications.

14...♘d5 15 ♕d2 ♗e4!?

This is based upon a nice combinative idea, but Guseinov points out that Black could achieve a large and safe advantage following 15...♗xg5! 16 ♘xg5 (or 16 ♕xg5 ♕xg5 17 ♘xg5 f6 18 ♘f3 0-0-0) 16...f6 17 ♘f3 ♕d6! with a superiority based upon the moves ...♘f4 and ...0-0-0.

16 ♗h6?

White plays a natural move which fails tactically. He could keep his disadvantage to a minimum by 16 ♗xe7! ♕xe7 17 0-0-0 ♗xf3 (17...0-0-0 18 ♖e1) 18 ♖e1! ♗e4 19 f3 f5 20 ♗d3 0-0-0 21 fxe4 fxe4 22 ♗xe4 ♕d6 23 ♔b1.

16...♗xf3! 17 ♗xf8!?

After 17 gxf3 ♖g8 18 0-0-0 ♕d6, White's pawns are shattered while even ...g5 is a threat.

17...♗g5! *(D)*

This is Black's point. White's king is trapped in the centre.

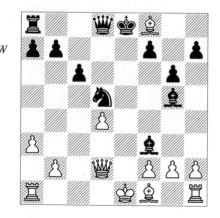

18 ♕c2

18 ♕d3 loses to 18...♕b6!; for example, 19 ♕xf3 ♗d2+! 20 ♔xd2 ♕xb2+ 21 ♔e1 ♕xa1+ 22 ♕d1 ♕xd1+ 23 ♔xd1 ♔xf8.

18...♔xf8 19 gxf3 ♕a5+

Black is an exchange down, but it's not even close. The rest is for your enjoyment:

20 ♔d1 ♖d8! 21 ♗e2 ♘f4!? 22 ♕c3 ♕e5! 23 ♕e3? ♖xd4+ 24 ♔c2 ♕f5+ 25 ♔b3 ♕d5+ 26 ♔c3 ♘xe2+ 27 ♕xe2 ♖d2 28 ♕e4 ♗f6+ 0-1

Fantastic. Now let's return to 6 e3 *(D)* and the sanity of 150 years of experience:

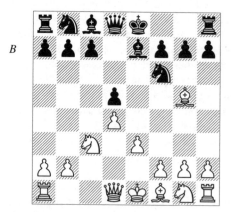

6...0-0

6...c6 usually transposes to the lines that we are exploring, but Black can try to delay it. See, for example, Kasparov-Short below. Also, watch out for the tactical mistake 6...♗f5? *(D)*.

7 ♗xf6! ♗xf6 8 ♕b3 and White picks off either the b- or d-pawn. I hate to bore you with the same advice for the umpteenth time, but the first thing to look for if a bishop moves from c1

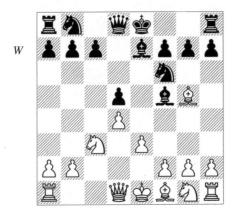

W

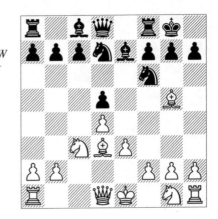

W

(or c8) is whether a queen move to attack the opponent's abandoned queenside can be effective. Even if it doesn't win a pawn, the necessity to defend b2 (or b7) can create a serious concession from your opponent. The corollary is always to watch out for such queenside attacks if you're about to move your bishop.

7 ♗d3

White plays the move that leads to the widest variety of Exchange Variation lines. For a number of reasons White may wish to play 7 ♕c2 here, but we'll leave that to study and experience.

7...c6

Black shores up his centre and delays the development of his pieces until he can decide where they want to go. He concedes that he's not going to play for ...c5 and accept an isolated pawn on d5. Let's look at a game in which Black delayed ...c6. It will be our first main-line Exchange Variation example, and contains a number of provocative ideas.

Kasparov – Short
London PCA Wch (15) 1993

1 d4 d5 2 c4 e6 3 ♘c3 ♘f6 4 cxd5 exd5 5 ♗g5 ♗e7 6 e3 0-0 7 ♗d3 ♘bd7 *(D)*

8 ♘ge2

White announces that he's going with the Modern Exchange Variation formation. 8 ♘f3 would be the Carlsbad Variation.

8...♖e8 9 0-0 ♘f8

Black skips ...c6. As you get used to Exchange Variation theory, you'll realize how nice it would be for Black to gain a tempo in order to beat White to the punch on the kingside.

10 b4! *(D)*

But he's not allowed to!

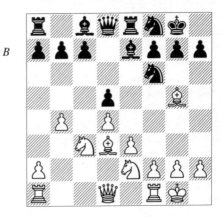

B

White exploits Black's omission of ...c6 to get his minority attack rolling early, without having to worry about preparatory moves such as a3 or ♖b1. Since ...c6 will only encourage b5, and ...c5 has been stopped, White stands better both on the queenside and in the centre. This all depends, of course, upon whether Black can't simply grab the unprotected b-pawn.

10...a6

Kasparov's tactical justification can be seen in the forced line 10...♗xb4? 11 ♗xf6 gxf6 (after 11...♕xf6?, 12 ♘xd5 ♕d6 13 ♕a4 attacks both b4 and e8) 12 ♘xd5! ♕xd5 13 ♕a4 (the same idea) 13...♗h3! (threatening mate while defending his rook) 14 ♘f4 ♕a5 15 ♕xa5 ♗xa5 16 ♘xh3 ♘e6! (stopping the powerful move ♘f4, although now the knight is poorly placed on e6) 17 ♖fd1! *(D)*.

White has a clear advantage because of Black's horrible f-pawns. He will stop Black's

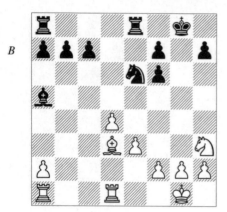

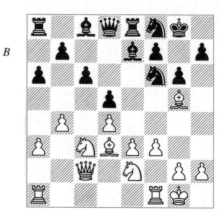

queenside pawns from advancing and then improve the positions of his pieces. If Black doesn't allow White's knight to f4, it may even make the journey ♘g1-e2-g3-f5 to Kasparov's favourite square for a knight. The key for White is not to exchange pieces. With the two rooks and two minor pieces each remaining, the opposite-coloured bishops will favour the side with the superior position.

Incidentally, there was no profound inconsistency or logical error in Black's strategy of gaining time by omitting ...c6. The specifics of the situation, expressed by the tactic 10 b4!, was an unfortunate accident of the position.

In the event, Black had to make an extra queenside pawn move after all (10...a6), and yet another follows:

11 a3 c6 12 ♕c2 g6

It's important to know that one of Black's standard freeing moves is ...♘e4, whether White's knight is on f3 or e2. Here the simplest answer to 12...♘e4 is 13 ♗f4!, keeping pieces on the board. This is a move that comes up in similar Queen's Gambit positions and should always be considered.

13 f3 (D)

With White's knight on e2, his plan is usually f3 and eventually e4. To counter this, Black normally plays ...c5, as we shall see in the Modern Exchange section. That move renders White's d-pawn (and d4-square) vulnerable should he play e4. Unfortunately, Short doesn't have ...c5 available here, so Kasparov has the best of both worlds: a queenside attack and the potential for a relatively problem-free central expansion.

13...♘e6 14 ♗h4 ♘h5

It's generally a good idea to get rid of White's dark-squared bishop, because the pawn on e3 is weak, and even if he plays the move e4, White will have an interior weakness on that square. Of course, e4 also carries with it the threat to bowl Black over!

15 ♗xe7

15 ♗f2 is sometimes played to protect e3 and d4 in preparation for e4. Kasparov decides that in this position it isn't necessary. See more examples of this as we go along.

15...♖xe7 16 ♕d2 b6?!

Black's queenside is weakened by this understandable attempt to develop and work up counterplay.

17 ♖ad1 ♗b7 18 ♗b1 ♘hg7 19 e4 (D)

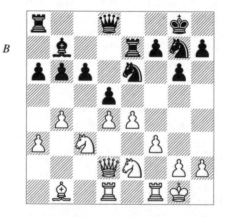

There it is. White has won the opening battle so I'll show the rest with minimal details, although of course it's never easy to win against a leading grandmaster.

19...♖c8 20 ♗a2 ♖d7 21 ♘f4!?

A perhaps unnecessary tactic.

21...♘xf4

21...dxe4 22 ♘xe6 ♘xe6 23 fxe4 ♘xd4 24 ♕f2 turns out in White's favour.

22 ♕xf4 ♘e6 23 ♕e5 ♖e7 24 ♕g3 ♕c7 25 ♕h4 ♘g7 26 ♖c1 ♕d8 27 ♖fd1 ♖cc7 28 ♘a4 dxe4 29 fxe4 ♕e8? 30 ♘c3 ♖cd7 31 ♕f2 ♘e6 32 e5 (D)

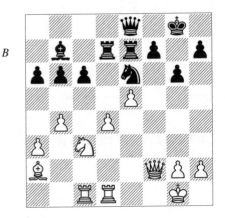

32...c5?

Desperation. White's 2:0 central majority now asserts itself.

33 bxc5 bxc5 34 d5 ♘d4 35 ♘e4 ♕d8 36 ♘f6+ ♔g7 37 ♘xd7 ♖xd7 38 ♖xc5 ♘e6 39 ♖cc1 1-0

A highly instructive game, if only because it wasn't too muddied by tactics in the late opening stage.

We return to **7...c6** (D):

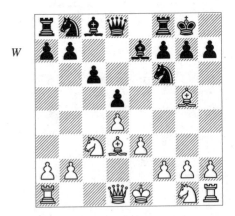

8 ♕c2

White delays a commitment of his knight on g1 and hints at the possibility of queenside

castling. The queen also covers e4 and prevents Black's f6-knight from moving to h5 or e8 due to ♗xh7+. 8 ♘ge2 is also played and will usually transpose.

8...♘bd7 (D)

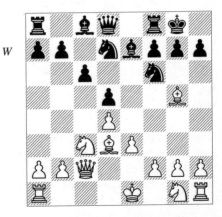

In this position, still following the main line of the Exchange Variation, White makes a consequential decision. Where he puts his king's knight will determine the nature of further play. First, we look at putting it on f3 (the Carlsbad Variation), and then on e2 (the Modern Exchange Variation).

Carlsbad Variation

9 ♘f3 (D)

As explained more than once, the move ♘f3 may not actually be a decision now, but one already made at an earlier stage. Because so many players use move-orders with an early ♘f3, even 1 d4 d5 2 ♘f3, the Carlsbad Variation is more important in practice than the Modern Exchange Variation. It is as strategically rich as any other QGD variation.

By putting his knight on f3, White gives up the plan of f3 and e4 for the time being. But the knight controls e5 and can go there at the right moment, and then there can follow either f3 or the ambitious f4. Apart from that there are an array of other choices including playing e4, by which White takes on an isolated pawn in order to attack (usually after placing rooks on d1 and e1). The most famous strategy of all is the minority attack by b4-b5. When one includes other variations in which it occurs, thousands of games have been played using the minority

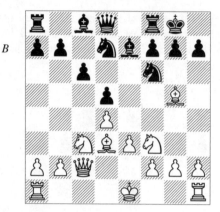

attack and thousands of pages written about it. As indicated before, the ideas behind the attack are relatively simple and easy to understand. Not surprisingly, actually putting them into practice is an art that depends upon profound understanding of the timing and therefore feasibility of each plan.

The interesting thing about the Carlsbad Variation is that White can mix and match these plans, switching from one to another in midstream! That factor makes it one of the most strategically complicated lines in chess and, I think, a much more difficult variation than the Modern Exchange with ♗d3 and ♘ge2.

Black needs to react to all this and can do so by knowing the major themes. As is the situation with White's ideas, the relevant manoeuvres have to be timed according to circumstance. Black's most rudimentary freeing plan is ...♘e4, which White avoids in certain lines and allows in others. Another favourite idea is to try to get some sort of kingside attack. This includes the move ...♗d6 in a majority of such cases. For example, White will often play ♗xf6 in order to divert Black's bishop to f6 and speed up his minority attack by b4. Then, even at the cost of two tempi, Black will use the time for ...♗e7-d6. Another standard idea is to challenge White on his own turf on the queenside. That can involve an early ...a5, or ...a6 with ...b5 (perhaps with ...♘b6-c4 to follow).

9...♖e8

This is almost always played. Black takes over the e-file in preparation for an eventual ...♘e4 and clears the way for ...♘f8 in order to protect h7. It's also very useful to play ...♘g6 or ...♘e6 in many variations.

10 0-0 ♘f8 *(D)*

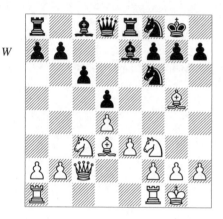

At this point White has many reasonable moves. Let's see some games.

Karpov – Ljubojević
Linares 1989

11 ♖ab1

We'll start with one of the oldest moves, preparing the direct b4-b5. Karpov plays White, which is interesting because he was the most prominent player to begin using 11 h3 (as played in the next few games). After you see this game you'll wonder why he switched!

11...♘e4 *(D)*

This is the traditional anti-Carlsbad procedure. Essentially, Black wants clarification and a strong central presence to counteract White's on the queenside. A good alternative is the queenside restraint plan by 11...a5, usually followed up by some sort of kingside attack (...♘g6, ...♗d6).

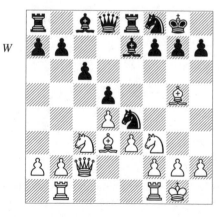

12 ♗xe7 ♕xe7 13 b4 a6 14 a4

Not only to prepare b5 but to play a5 and ♘a4 under some circumstances.

14...♗f5 15 ♘e5!?

Typically creative of Karpov, if a little odd-looking. In his notes, he analyses the obvious approach as follows: 15 b5 axb5 16 axb5 ♘xc3 (or 16...♖a3) 17 ♕xc3 ♖a3 18 ♖b3 ♖xb3 19 ♕xb3 ♗xd3 20 ♕xd3 c5 with equality. Hence he tries another strategy.

15...♖ad8

Henrichs suggests that 15...f6 is better, when Karpov's continuation 16 ♗xe4 ♗xe4 17 ♘xe4 fxe5 18 ♘g3'!?' is unconvincing after 18...exd4 (18...♘d7 is equal) 19 ♘f5 ♕f6 20 ♘xd4 ♘e6. Instead, Henrichs thinks that 16 ♘f3 produces only an "academic advantage".

16 ♖fc1 ♘g6 17 ♗xe4 ♗xe4 18 ♘xe4 dxe4 19 ♘xg6 hxg6 20 b5 *(D)*

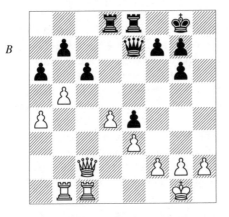

The ultimate minority-attack position. It looks like one of those skeleton pictures that they give in the textbooks, not something that was actually played! Henrichs mentions that it helps White to have the minor pieces off, although I'm not so sure. A knight might actually help to make direct threats against Black's weaknesses. With some exceptions, simplification makes White's task more pleasant in the minority attack if only because he can't be attacked on the kingside.

20...cxb5

20...axb5 21 axb5 ♖d6 22 ♕a4 ♖c8 23 ♕a7 ♖c7 24 ♖c5! would leave Black in a mess. A position like that may be salvageable with perfect defence (or it may not be), but in any event White has a clear advantage.

21 axb5 ♖d6 22 bxa6 bxa6 *(D)*

Henrichs gives 22...♖xa6 23 ♖b5! ♖c6 24 ♕b2 ♖xc1+ 25 ♕xc1 ♖a8 26 ♕b1 with a large advantage. It's funny how such a simple position can be so good. I should note, however, that Black's pawn on e4 is the deciding factor in this position. Without this extra weakness it's unclear whether White could win.

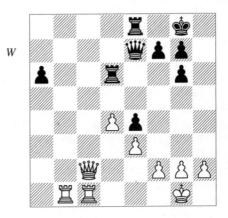

23 ♕a4 ♕d7 24 ♕xd7! ♖xd7

Now we get a little Rubinstein-like instruction from one of the all-time greats.

25 ♖c5 ♖a7 26 ♖a5 ♔f8 27 ♖b6 ♖ea8 28 h4!

In this book I keep emphasizing the second front. One would think that White's king might head to the centre, but it's on the kingside that he'll make inroads. Black's exposed pawn on e4 makes his situation worse, but at this point a central advance supported by White's king would do the trick anyway.

28...♔e7 29 ♔h2 ♔d7 30 ♔g3 ♔c7 31 ♖b2! *(D)*

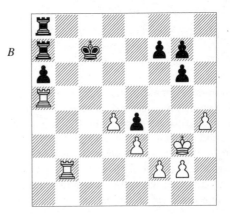

White protects his second rank against invasion. The rest is pretty clear, although not necessarily easy.

31...Rb7 32 Rc5+! Kb8 33 Ra2 Re7 34 Kf4 Kb7 35 Rb2+ Ka7 36 Rc6 Rh8 37 Ra2 a5 38 Rxa5+ Kb7 39 Rca6 Rxh4+ 40 Kg3 Rh5 41 Ra7+ Kc6 42 R5a6+ Kb5 43 Rxe7 Rg5+ 44 Kh2 Kxa6 45 Rxf7 1-0

Superb.

Djurić – Pfleger
Yugoslavia 1984

11 h3

This unassuming move has become White's most popular continuation. Yermolinsky describes it as a "useful waiting" move, noting that the 'useful' designation applies to covering g4, providing a retreat on h2 for White's bishop (following its common redeployment to f4), and "[underlining] how Black's 'liberated' c8-bishop suddenly finds itself deprived of activity".

11...Ne4

Again Black plays the classical freeing move. We'll see other schemes below.

12 Bf4 Ng5 13 Bxg5 Bxg5 14 b4 Be7 15 b5 *(D)*

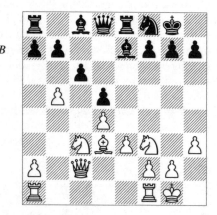

Another example of the pure minority attack unmixed with central or kingside action. Leaving the pawn on c6 gives Black a weak backward c-pawn after bxc6, but ...cxb5 instead leaves him with a weak d-pawn. Oddly enough, the first option is usually preferable for Black, following the notion that pawns on the third rank are easier to defend than ones on the

fourth rank. In this case the trade-off is the backward pawn on an open file (one on c6) versus the isolated pawn on a closed file (one on d5). Normally an isolated pawn on a closed file isn't hard to defend, but this is an exception.

15...Bd6 16 bxc6 bxc6 17 Bf5! *(D)*

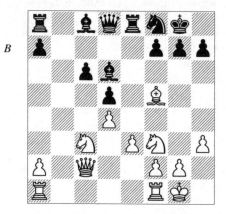

Both defensive and offensive. Obviously the bishop on c8 is aiming at White's king, and the idea of ...Bxh3 at some point is scary. But Black's 'bad' bishop (on the light squares, after all) is also an extremely valuable defensive piece when it stays on d7, so trading White's good bishop for it is not really a concession.

17...Qa5 18 Bxc8 Raxc8 19 Rab1 Ne6 *(D)*

It's always essential for White to make sure that 19...c5 doesn't work. Here it won't succeed because of 20 Rb5 Qa6 21 dxc5 Bxc5 22 Qb3.

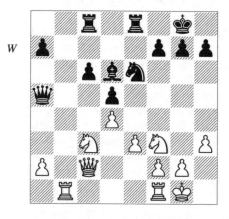

20 Rb7 Rb8

Bartashnikov shows the pretty line 20...c5 21 Nxd5 cxd4 22 Qf5 Bc7 23 Rxc7 Rxc7 24 Nf6+.

21 ♖fb1 ♖xb7 22 ♖xb7 ♖b8 23 ♖xb8+ ♗xb8 *(D)*

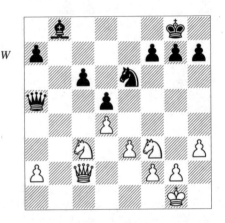

The presence of minor pieces for the defender isn't necessarily an improvement over what we saw in the last game, when there were only rooks left; what counts is their relative activity (the rooks were passively tied down). I think that practice shows how difficult it is to make some kind of general principle about piece combinations with this pawn-structure. Furthermore, Black's pieces are more actively placed here than we are used to, with the knight, bishop and queen all potentially covering c5. Presumably both of White's knights should be better than Black's bishop in this semi-closed position, but I suspect that it's defensible.

24 ♘a4 *(D)*

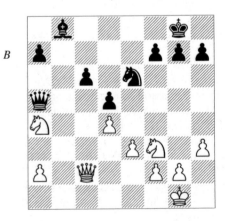

24...♕b5?

An unfortunate placement for the queen. Black should play 24...♕a6! 25 ♘c5 ♘xc5 26 dxc5 h6 with good defensive chances; e.g., 27 ♕b3 (27 ♘d4 ♗e5) 27...♗c7 28 ♘d4 g6. Perhaps we shouldn't make too much of White's success with his minority attack here.

25 ♘c5 g6?

After 25...♘xc5 26 dxc5 Bartashnikov says that 26...g6 27 ♘d4 gives a large advantage; that could certainly be argued after 27...♕a6 with the idea of ...♗e5. Still, the basic idea is right, because 27 ♕b3! is strong. Note that it's Black's lack of a back-rank escape-square that makes things difficult here, in a sequence such as 26...♕a6 27 ♕b1! ♕c8. And is 26...♕b4 27 ♕b3 a5 tenable? For example, 28 g3 ♗a7 29 ♘d4 ♗xc5 30 ♘xc6 ♕xb3 (again, only the lack of an escape-square even makes this necessary!) 31 axb3 ♗b4. See also 24...♕a6 instead of the unfortunate 24...♕b5. The point is that Black's sole weakness on c6 probably isn't fatal in this pawn-structure, and that relative piece placement is almost always the deciding factor.

26 a4!

This, however, does the trick since Black has to destroy his pawn-structure to avoid loss of material.

26...♕c4 27 ♕xc4 dxc4 28 ♘xe6 fxe6 29 ♔f1 ♗d6 30 ♘e5 c3 31 ♔e2 c5 32 ♔d3 cxd4 33 exd4 ♔g7 34 ♔xc3

White went on to win. A thought-provoking game.

Portisch – Larsen
Rotterdam Ct (4) 1977

10 h3 *(D)*

White makes this useful little advance a move earlier than in the previous game, which brings in the possibility of him not castling kingside. Black responds in traditional fashion.

10...♘f8 11 ♗f4!? ♘g6

Queenside castling for White usually only works if Black retreats his pieces and fails to strike back reasonably quickly against White's queenside. We get to see 0-0-0 in the main game as well as in the attractive example Khenkin-Bischoff, Bundesliga 2002/3, given without notes: 11...♘d7?! 12 0-0-0 ♘b6 13 ♔b1 ♗e6 14 h4 f6 15 ♖dg1 h5?! 16 g4!! hxg4 17 ♘h2 ♕d7 18 f3 f5 19 fxg4 fxg4 20 h5 ♘c4 21 h6 g5 22 ♗xc4 gxf4 23 ♘xg4! ♗xg4 24 ♗e2 ♔h8 25 ♖xg4 ♗f6 26 ♖hg1 ♘e6 27 ♕f5 ♕e7

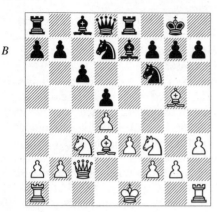

28 ♗d3 ♗g5 29 exf4 ♖f8 30 ♕e5+ ♗f6 31 ♖g7! ♖f7 32 ♕f5 1-0. Quite a picture at the finish!

12 ♗h2 ♗d6 13 ♗xd6 ♕xd6 14 0-0-0 *(D)*

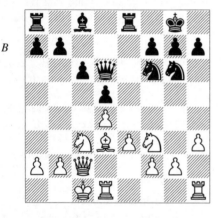

OK, White took three extra moves just to exchange his dark-squared bishop, but that got rid of Black's good bishop. And it's actually better for White to have 'lost' the tempo to ...♘g6 because g4 and h4-h5 can follow.

14...♕e7 15 g4 ♗e6 16 g5 ♘e4!

An excellent anti-queenside-castling pawn sacrifice, but here White still has an attack and extra space for Black to deal with. So perhaps we can call this 'dynamically balanced'.

17 ♗xe4 dxe4 18 ♕xe4 b5 19 h4 b4 20 ♘a4 ♕d6!?

Larsen foregoes 20...♗d5! 21 ♕xe7 ♘xe7 22 ♖h3 ♗e6! 23 ♖g3 (23 ♖h2 ♗g4) 23...♘f5 24 ♖gg1 ♗d5, when White's h-pawn falls, leaving an equal position.

21 h5 ♗d5 22 ♕g4 ♘f8 23 b3 ♕e6!? *(D)*
24 ♕f4

Not 24 ♕xe6? ♘xe6 25 ♖h3 ♗xf3 26 ♖xf3 ♘xg5. Black tries to show what he's gained by this unexpected trick in the next two moves.

24...♘d7

Versus ♘c5.

25 ♖he1 ♗xb3!? 26 axb3 ♕xb3

I don't know how sound this sacrifice is, but we've covered the opening, so let's just look at some more moves:

27 ♘b2 ♕a2!? 28 ♕f5 c5!? 29 ♕xd7 cxd4 30 ♖xd4 ♖ac8+ 31 ♖c4 ♖xc4+ 32 ♘xc4 ♕xc4+ 33 ♔d2 ♕a2+ 34 ♔d1 ♖f8 35 ♕d2 ♕a5 36 ♔e2 ♖d8 37 ♘d4 ♕xg5 38 ♕xb4 ♕xh5+ 39 ♘f3

White has obvious technical difficulties in this position, but he did win in the end.

M. Gurevich – Akopian
Barcelona 1992

11 h3 ♗e6 12 ♘e5 ♘6d7 13 ♗xe7 ♕xe7 14 f4

Yermolinsky calls this the 'post-up'.

14...f6 15 ♘f3 ♗f7 16 ♖ae1 c5! *(D)*

This is the natural counterattack against any such d4/e3/f4 structure; it should equalize.

17 ♕f2 ♘b6 18 ♘h4

Or 18 dxc5 ♕xc5 19 ♘d4 ♘c4 with equality.

18...cxd4 19 exd4 ♕c7 20 ♖c1 ♕d8 21 ♘b5!?

Dautov offers up 21 f5 ♖c8 22 g3 with the idea of ♘g2-f4; by then ...♘c4-d6-e4 will be fine for Black.

21...♘c4! 22 b3 a6! 23 bxc4 dxc4 24 ♗xc4 ♗xc4 25 ♖xc4 axb5 26 ♖c5

White can't be passive or Black will play ...♖e4 and ...♘e6.

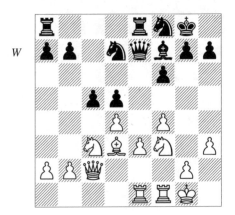

26...♘e6 27 ♖xb5 ♕xd4 28 ♕xd4 ♘xd4 29 ♖xb7 ♖xa2

Neither side made any obvious mistakes and a draw was the natural result.

Timman – Kasparov
London (USSR-RoW) (2) 1984

11 ♗xf6 ♗xf6 *(D)*

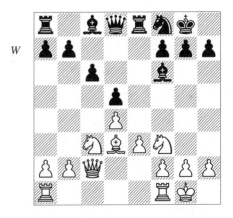

12 b4

White exchanges on f6 because he wants to speed up his minority attack. This is a standard idea which has been very popular, in part because the ideas are so clear and White has eliminated various moves such as ...♘e4 and ...♘g4. This raises the question of which minor pieces are best in the Carlsbad structure; as always, it depends upon time and activity. Black can't wait around for ♖ab1 and b5, so he has to pick a plan. Since ...♘e4 isn't possible, he can choose to play a restraint game on the queenside or organize an attack on the king. In

the event, Kasparov does both, but naturally looks towards the enemy king first.

12...♗g4

One of the standard anti-Minority Attack plans was first brought to notice in the game Timman-Spassky, Tilburg 1979: 12...a6 13 a4 g6 14 b5 a5! *(D)*.

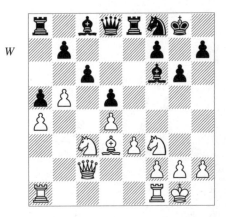

The idea is to prevent White's knight from getting to a4 and attacking c5 and b6 as it customarily does. Black had no troubles at all after 15 bxc6 bxc6 16 ♘b1! (the right solution, to reroute White's knight, which is currently doing nothing, to a useful post on b3) 16...♕d6 (16...♗d7 17 ♘bd2 ♗e7 18 ♘b3 ♗d6) 17 ♘bd2 ♘e6 18 ♖fc1?! (18 ♘b3) 18...c5! with equality.

13 ♘d2 ♗e7 14 ♖ab1 ♗d6 *(D)*

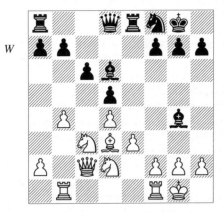

You'll see this regrouping idea in many Exchange Variation games. Black's dream (and sometimes it even comes true) is to play moves such as ...♖e6-h6, ...♕g5, ...♘g6-h4 and mate.

White tries to neutralize this with his following move:

15 ♗f5 ♗h5!

Black avoids simplification and retains the bishop for attack. This option wasn't available when his bishop was on c8.

16 ♖fc1 g6 17 ♗d3

17 ♗h3?! ♘e6 threatens ...♘g5.

17...♕g5 18 ♘e2 ♘d7 19 h3 *(D)*

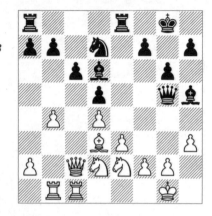

19...a6

Kasparov gives 19...♖xe3!? 20 fxe3 ♕xe3+ 21 ♔h1 (21 ♔f1? ♗xe2+ 22 ♗xe2 ♗g3 23 ♘e4 dxe4 and wins) 21...♗xe2 22 ♗xe2 ♕xe2 as unclear. It's still a little strange that he didn't play into this promising position; he may have thought that there was more to gain by waiting. That doesn't prove to be the case.

20 a4 ♖ac8 21 ♘f1 ♗xe2 22 ♗xe2 ♕e7 23 ♕b3 ♘f6 ½-½

Hjartarson – Short
Dubai OL 1986

11 ♖ae1 *(D)*

Thomas Henrichs, a leading expert on the Exchange Variation, recommends 11 a3. Much like 11 h3, this is a useful waiting move. Depending upon Black's reply, White will play a minority attack, a central attack, or both.

The text is an old move that prepares e4 and tries to lure Black into playing ...♘e4. It was seen in the games of Marshall and others and was revived about 20 years ago. However, this game and still another by Nigel Short sent Carlsbad players looking for new ideas.

11...♘e4!

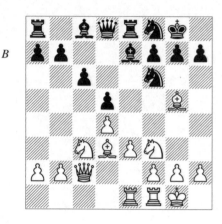

White had hoped that protecting his e-pawn had prevented this move but it turns out to be justified.

12 ♗xe7 ♕xe7 13 ♗xe4

White should consider 13 ♘d2 here.

13...dxe4 14 ♘d2 f5 15 f3

An old recommendation was 15 d5. Then 15...♗d7 with the idea 16 ♕b3 cxd5! solves Black's problems, as in L.Spassov-Van der Sterren, Albena 1983.

15...exf3 16 ♘xf3 ♗e6 17 e4 fxe4 18 ♖xe4 *(D)*

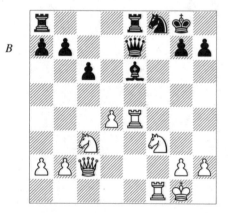

White has a lot of nice squares in this position, with pressure down the e-file and potential moves such as ♘e5 and d5. The question is whether that makes up for the weakness of his isolated pawn.

18...h6

Short preemptively stops ♘g5 and prepares to move his queen to, e.g., c7.

19 ♖fe1 ♖ad8 *(D)*

20 ♖e5

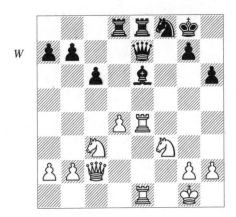

White would like to centralize with ♕e4. Short had success in another game following 20 ♖1e3 ♕f7! 21 ♘e5 (21 ♕e2 ♗c4 22 ♕e1 ♖xe4 23 ♖xe4 ♗e6!? 24 h4 ♖e8 25 ♘e5 ♕f6 26 ♕g3 ♕d8 with an eye on d4, Semkov-Dokhoian, Erevan 1988) 21...♕f5 22 ♕g3? ♖xd4! 23 ♘g4 ♔h8 24 ♘xh6? gxh6 25 ♕c1 ♕f6 26 ♖ee3 ♖f4 and the attack was over in Timman-Short, Amsterdam 1988. It's not clear what White overlooked.

20...♕f7 (D)

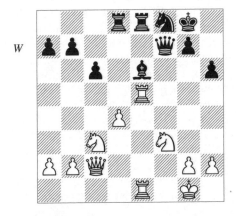

21 b4?!

Loosening. White may have been worried about his a-pawn, but ...♗xa2 isn't a threat yet. Better seems 21 ♕e2 with the idea 21...♗d7 22 ♖f1.

21...♘d7 22 ♖a5?

Losing the thread.

22...♗g4! 23 ♘e5 ♘xe5 24 dxe5 b6 25 ♖a3 ♖d4 26 ♕f2? ♖f4 27 ♕g3 ♖xe5 28 h3 ♖xe1+ 29 ♕xe1 ♗e6 30 ♕e5 ♗xh3! 31 ♘e4 ♖f1+ 32 ♔h2 ♖h1+! 0-1

Modern Exchange

9 ♘ge2 (D)

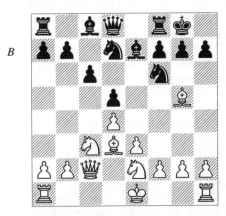

The Modern Exchange Variation is distinguished by the knight's development to e2, which strongly indicates White's desire to expand in the centre via f3 and e4. In this position most players pursue some combination of central expansion and queenside minority attack. The many versions of this strategy give us a deeper understanding of what both sides' ideas are and how they should be applied.

9...♖e8 10 0-0 ♘f8 (D)

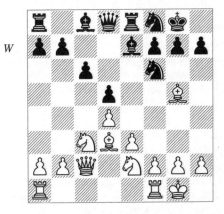

White has played various moves at this juncture. They all share the same goals, but initially go in different directions. In contrast to the Carlsbad Variation, White doesn't have ♘e5; furthermore, the move e4 without f3 will lead to an isolated pawn position in which having a knight on f3 would be much better than one on e2.

That leaves a series of ways to prepare for e4 by playing f3 and, for example, ♖ad1 and/or ♖fe1. Alternatively, White can play a3 and/or ♖ab1 to enforce b4 before turning his attention to the centre. We'll get a feel for the nature of the play by seeing the following games. This time the imbedded notes and games are particularly important because they show alternate set-ups for both sides.

Avrukh – Lugovoi
Beersheba-Peterburg 1999

11 f3 (D)

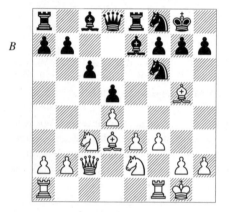

This has probably been played more than any other move. White makes no bones about playing for e4. But that's not necessarily as committal as it looks because by playing f3 instead of moving a rook or knight, White doesn't reveal which piece distribution Black will have to face.

11...g6

11...♘g6 is seen in the next game. With 11...g6 Black prepares ...♘e6, which if played at once loses a pawn to ♗xf6 and ♗xh7+.

The alternative 11...♗e6 was seen in Van Wely-Piket, Antwerp 1996, a well-played game that includes several themes that recur in this line: 12 ♗h4!? ♖c8 (in almost every line with f3, ...c5 is Black's way to try to equalize or take the initiative; however, if White is careful, he can either prevent the advance of the c-pawn or render it harmless) 13 ♖ad1 (a move with a double purpose: to prepare e4, and to discourage ...c5, which would expose Black's d-pawn after dxc5) 13...a6 14 ♔h1 ♘g6 15 ♗f2 (D).

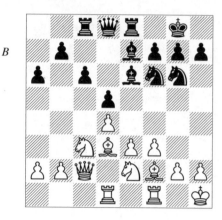

We can see this characteristic manoeuvre throughout the Modern Exchange Variation. It turns out that 12 ♗h4 is multifaceted. One motivation is escape: with the bishop on g5, the moves ...♘g6 and h6 might force its exchange. The other idea is to protect the two central pawns. The game continued 15...c5 16 dxc5!? ♗xc5 17 ♘d4 (White grabs the outpost, and his knight is so influential that Black trades it off, and then exchanges White's bishop on d3 as well; the only problem is that it's harder for Black to attack the resulting pawn-structure) 17...♗xd4 18 exd4 ♘f4! 19 ♖fe1 ♘xd3 20 ♕xd3 ♕b6 21 ♖d2 ♕c6 22 ♖de2 (taking stock, we see that White's bishop has more prospects than Black's, for example along the h2-b8 diagonal, and his rooks are more active; therefore Piket launches a queenside attack) 22...b5 23 a3 h6 24 g4! ♕c4! 25 ♕d2 ♘d7! 26 ♔g2 ♘b6 27 ♘d1 ♕c6 28 b3 (White really can't allow Black's knight into c4, so he has to create a minor weakness) 28...♗d7 (to exchange some pieces) 29 ♕a5! ♖xe2 30 ♖xe2 f5! (just as White was ready for ♗g3-e5, he has to deal with a counterattack) 31 h3 fxg4 32 hxg4 ♖f8 33 ♖e3 ♕g6 34 ♗g3 ♕c6 35 ♘f2 ♘c8. From this point White managed to generate a little pressure because of his active bishop, but the game was eventually drawn.

12 ♖ad1

This is a very common move: White wants to play e4 and therefore gives the pawn on d4 more support so that it will be less vulnerable when that advance is played.

12...♘e6 13 ♗h4 ♘h5

Black tries to swap bishops. He may want to attack the dark squares, notably White's weak

pawn on e3. Instead, 13...♘g7?! would intend
...♘f5, so White should expand in the centre to
prevent that by 14 e4. If he can get the move e5
in without an immediate undermining of his
centre he will usually stand very well. The advance f4-f5 may follow, perhaps supported by a
knight on g3.

14 ♗f2! *(D)*

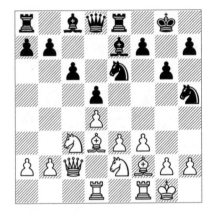

Much as ♖ad1 does, this prepares e4 by for-
tifying d4. So Black takes radical steps to hold
back the key advance:

14...f5! 15 ♔h1

The vital test is 15 e4. Baburin offers the
variation 15...♘ef4 16 e5!? (16 ♘xf4 ♘xf4 17
exd5 ♘xd5! 18 ♖fe1 is a strange kind of isolated queen's pawn position in which White's
pressure down the e-file gives him the edge)
16...♘xd3 17 ♕xd3 ♘g7!. Black wants to bring
a knight to the perfect blockading square on e6
and appears to stand well enough.

15...♖f8 16 a3

The centre is more or less in balance so
White begins a minority attack. Combining central and queenside advances is common in these
lines, just as in the Carlsbad Variation.

16...♘eg7 17 b4 a6 18 ♘a4 ♗d6

We know this move by now! Black wants to
organize a kingside attack, even though the c8-
bishop isn't taking part.

19 ♕c3 ♗c7 20 ♘c5 ♕d6 21 ♗g1 *(D)*

21...♕e7

Now he's contemplating ...f4. The only other
way to get developed is to kick out White's
knight even if that would create weaknesses;
e.g., 21...b6 22 ♘b3 ♗b7 23 a4!? (23 ♖c1 ♕e7)
23...♕e7!? (threatening ...♗d6) 24 a5 ♗d6 25

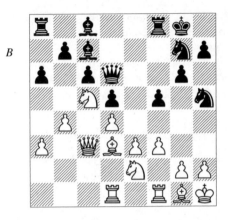

axb6 ♗xb4 26 ♕c2. This is hard to assess.
White still has the idea of e4, but has to make
sure that ...c5 doesn't break up his centre.

22 ♗c2 f4!? 23 ♘xf4

23 e4 ♘g3+! 24 ♘xg3 fxg3 is awfully risky
for White.

**23...♘xf4 24 exf4 ♗xf4 25 ♘d3! ♗d6 26
♘e5**

White is winning the important dark squares.
The opening has been over for a few moves so
we'll take the rest of the game more lightly.

**26...♗f5 27 ♗b3!? ♗e6 28 ♖de1 a5 29
bxa5 ♕c7**

29...♗xa3 30 ♘d3!? and ♘c5.

**30 a4 ♕xa5 31 ♕c1 ♗f5?! 32 g4! ♗e6 33
♗c2**

Back to the correct diagonal!

**33...♕c3 34 ♖e3 ♕a5 35 h3 c5 36 ♖b3 ♕c7
*(D)***

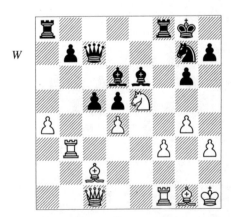

**37 ♕b2 ♖ab8 38 ♖b6 cxd4 39 ♗xd4 ♗c5?
40 ♗xc5 ♕xc5 41 ♘c6! ♖be8 42 ♖xb7 ♖f7 43
♖b6?**

He should exchange rooks and keep the pawn. Now it gets tactical, with Black calling the shots.

43...♕c4 44 ♖f2 ♕f4 45 ♔g2 ♘h5!! 46 ♕e5 ♕h6 47 h4 ♘f4+ 48 ♔g3 ♕f8 49 ♘d4? ♗xg4! 50 ♕d6 ♕g7 51 ♖b8 *(D)*

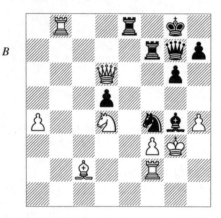

51...♖xb8??

Now the game should be drawn. Baburin pointed out 51...♘h5+ 52 ♔g2 ♖xb8 53 ♕xb8+ ♖f8 54 ♕b4 ♕f6, winning.

52 ♕xb8+ ♖f8 53 ♕xf8+ ♕xf8 54 fxg4 ♕a3+ 55 ♔xf4? ♕b4??

55...♕d6+! is correct, with winning chances.

56 ♔e3 ♕c3+ 57 ♗d3

White escapes all the checks. He won easily.

Neverov – Gelfand
Uzhgorod 1987

11 f3 ♘g6 *(D)*

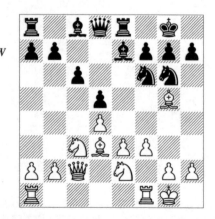

12 e4!?

White has to be careful not to play this too early. More sensible is the patient 12 ♖ad1 ♗e6 13 ♔h1 (he gets off the dangerous g1-a7 diagonal) 13...♖c8 14 ♘g3! ♘h5!? 15 ♗xe7 ♘xg3+ 16 hxg3 ♕xe7 17 ♔g1 (another waiting move; he can play for either the minority attack via b4 or slowly prepare e4) 17...c5? *(D)* (a positional mistake, as is soon evident).

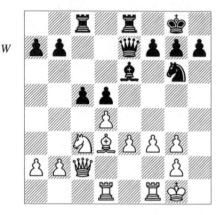

18 ♗xg6! hxg6 19 dxc5! ♕xc5 20 ♖d4 b5 21 a3 ♕b6 22 ♖fd1 ♖c4 23 ♔f2 a6 24 ♕e2 ♖xd4 25 ♖xd4, Tukmakov-Miladinović, Burgas 1995. We have a good knight versus a bad bishop in an IQP position, although Tukmakov failed to win after encountering tough defence. White certainly won the opening, but without the mistake 17...c5 things weren't so clear; probably he had a small advantage in any case.

12...dxe4 13 fxe4 ♗e6 14 ♖ad1 ♘g4!

This is the problem. White can hardly afford to let Black control e3, so he has to retreat, which gives Black just enough time to counter-attack in the centre with the key move ...c5.

15 ♗c1

15 ♗xe7 ♕xe7 16 ♖f3 c5! with the idea 17 d5 ♗d7 and a knight will settle in on e5.

15...c5 16 ♗b5!?

White tries to stir things up rather than concede the centre by 16 h3 cxd4. But Black has a little trick.

16...♕c7! *(D)*

17 g3 ♖ed8

It turns out that he wins the e5-square anyway, because now 18 h3? cxd4 19 hxg4 dxc3 contains the extra threat of ...♕c5+, picking up the bishop on b5.

18 d5 ♗c8

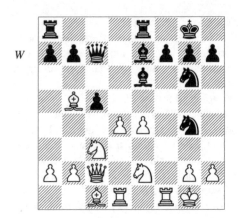

Now Black is simply better.

19 ♘f4 c4 20 ♔g2 ♘4e5 21 d6!

White attempts to activate his pieces with this pawn sacrifice; otherwise he's in terrible positional shape due to his bad bishop and inactive knights, whereas Black retains his outpost on e5.

21...♗xd6 22 ♘cd5?

A blunder. 22 ♘fd5! would have given White his own beautiful outpost and some if not sufficient play for the pawn.

22...♕c5 23 a4 ♗g4! 24 ♖de1 *(D)*

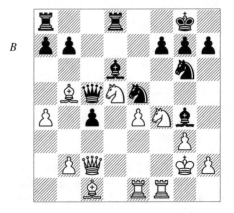

24...♕c8!

Black now has the double threat of 25...a6, winning the bishop, and 25...♘xf4+ followed by ....♗h3+. The alternative 24...a6 25 ♗e3 ♕c8 26 ♘b6 is superficially more complicated but it also wins after 26...♘xf4+ 27 gxf4 ♗f3+! 28 ♖xf3 ♘xf3 29 ♘xc8 ♘xe1+.

25 b3 ♘xf4+ 26 gxf4 ♗h3+ 27 ♔h1 ♘d3

The game is effectively over: Black is winning more material.

Kasparov – Beliavsky
Moscow (TV, rapidplay) 1987

11 a3 *(D)*

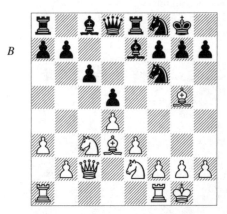

A flexible move. Black doesn't know on which side of the board White will operate.

11...g6!?

Here's an entertaining snippet from a brilliantly-played blindfold game: 11...♘g6 (probably one of the best moves) 12 b4 a6 13 ♘g3 ♗d6 14 ♖ae1 h6 15 ♗xh6!? gxh6 16 ♗xg6 fxg6 17 ♕xg6+ ♔h8 *(D)*.

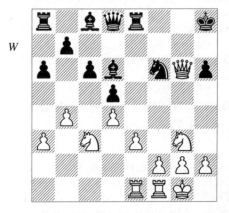

18 e4! ♗f4 19 e5 ♘g4 20 ♘ce2 ♗d2 21 ♖d1 ♖g8 22 ♕h5 ♕g5 23 ♕xg5 ♗xg5 24 h3 ♘xf2 25 ♔xf2 ♗h4, Zsu.Polgar-Ivanchuk, Monte Carlo (Amber blindfold) 1993, reaching a nutty position that White ultimately won.

12 b4 ♘e6 13 ♗h4 a6 14 f3

By an odd route, we have transposed to Kasparov-Short (page 51), which featured 14...♘h5.

14...♘g7 15 ♗f2! h5 16 h3 ♘h7 17 e4

Again, Black hasn't assessed any penalty for this move, so White must stand better.

17...♗h4 18 ♕d2 ♗xf2+ 19 ♖xf2 h4 20 ♗c2 ♘h5 21 ♘f4! ♘xf4 22 ♕xf4 ♕f6 23 ♕d2

Exchanging queens isn't bad either.

23...♗e6 24 e5 ♕g7 25 ♘a4 ♘f8 26 ♕g5 ♕h8 27 f4 f6 28 exf6 ♗f7 *(D)*

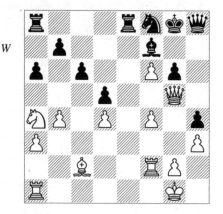

Now the pretty stuff begins. Since this was for TV, the time allotment was short.

29 ♗xg6 ♗xg6 30 f5 ♔f7 31 ♘c5!? ♗h5 32 ♘xb7 ♘d7 33 ♘d6+ ♔f8 34 ♕xh4 ♘xf6 35 g4 ♖e7 36 g5! ♖d7 37 gxf6 ♖xd6 38 ♖e1 ♖e8 39 ♖xe8+ ♔xe8 40 ♖e2+ ♔f8 41 ♖e6! ♕h6

The key calculation is 41...♖xe6 42 fxe6 ♕g8+ 43 ♔f2 ♕xe6 44 ♕xh5 ♕xf6+ 45 ♕f3 and White wins the pawn endgame.

42 ♖xd6 ♕e3+ 43 ♕f2 ♕xh3 44 ♕f4 1-0

Move-Orders in the Queen's Gambit Declined

Move-order issues are rife in the Queen's Gambit Declined. That's true in other openings that I deal with, but not to this extent or with this significance. Your choice of early moves directly bears upon your mastery of the opening and what positions you'd like to head for. Depending upon what sort of thinker you are, this situation can be either fascinating or appalling.

However, you don't need to know about all these move-order details (or for that matter, about any of them) to go out and start playing the QGD with either colour. If you want to do so, by all means skip this section. As you grow

curious about the subject, however, you may want to return here to supplement your practical knowledge. Even what is presented below is not complete, but most of what's important is covered.

I'm going to follow the same path of moves that I did at the beginning of this chapter, but I'll add details and expand the material. In what follows I won't assume that you've read the other sections of this chapter, although sometimes I'll refer you to one or another.

1 d4 d5 2 c4 e6 3 ♘c3

Before getting to more complicated material, let me repeat what I said about the immediate exchange of pawns, 3 cxd5 exd5 *(D)*, in the introduction to this chapter, adding some details.

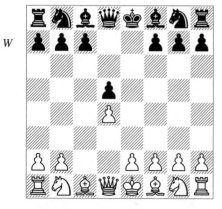

The sequence actually called the Exchange Variation goes 1 d4 d5 2 c4 e6 3 ♘c3 ♘f6 4 cxd5 exd5, generally with 5 ♗g5. But if White tries to get to that position by 3 cxd5 exd5 4 ♘c3, Black doesn't have to reply 4...♘f6. He can play 4...c6. Then 5 ♗f4 is outside the realm of a true Exchange Variation and anyway, Black can equalize easily by 5...♗d6, or go for more by 5...♗f5.

Notice that this differs from the important Alatortsev Variation, which goes 1 d4 d5 2 c4 e6 3 ♘c3 ♗e7 (which has its own section above). In that case, after 4 cxd5 exd5 5 ♗f4, Black would have to use up an extra tempo to play 5...♗d6, and the move 5...♗f5? is simply bad after 6 ♕b3. Conclusion: even though the Alatortsev order doesn't permit White to play an Exchange Variation, there is no automatic equalizer for Black after the moves 4 cxd5 exd5 5 ♗f4.

The remaining natural move after 3 cxd5 exd5 4 ♘c3 c6 is 5 ♘f3. After this Black can still avoid the Exchange Variation by 5...♗f5, which is incidentally considered a good move that equalizes. Then it's important to see that 6 ♕b3 can be safely answered by 6...♕b6 or 6...♕c8.

The position after 3 ♘f3 (D) is critical. It can arise from other move-orders, so sometimes White may be stuck with it. For example, one way in which this can happen us via 1 ♘f3; e.g., 1...d5 2 c4 e6 3 d4. Another route is 1 d4 d5 2 ♘f3 e6 3 c4.

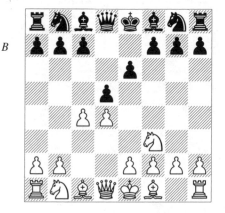

At this point there are quite a few issues:

a) I'm not too concerned here about transpositions to completely different openings, but here 3...c6 will usually transpose to a Semi-Slav; e.g., if White plays 4 ♘c3 or 4 e3.

b) Black also has 3...c5 4 cxd5 exd5, when 5 ♘c3 is the Tarrasch Defence to the Queen's Gambit. In this exact position, White can deviate from the 'pure' Tarrasch Variation by skipping ♘c3 for the moment and playing 5 ♗g5!?, which gives him some extra opportunities. That may be confusing if you're just starting out with this opening, but if you're curious you can find details in the books.

c) Usually Black will play 3...♘f6 here. Let me repeat what I said in the text and expand upon why this is an important position. The most common way to get to it is not by 1 d4 d5 2 c4 e6 3 ♘f3 ♘f6. It comes up more often via the move-order 1 d4 ♘f6 2 c4 e6 (D).

In this position a lot of players would like to avoid the Nimzo-Indian Defence (3 ♘c3 ♗b4), so they play 3 ♘f3 instead of 3 ♘c3. Then if

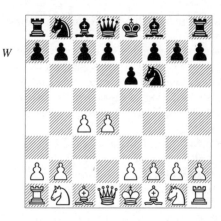

Black plays 3...d5, we're back to the basic position.

But Black doesn't have to play a Queen's Gambit. He can choose to play the Queen's Indian Defence by 3...b6, or the Modern Benoni by 3...c5 4 d5 exd5 5 cxd5 d6 6 ♘c3 g6, intending ...♗g7. There's more to be said about the Modern Benoni. Its standard order is 1 d4 ♘f6 2 c4 c5 3 d5 e6 4 ♘c3 exd5 5 cxd5 d6 and in most cases 6 e4 g6. However, by having included the move ♘f3, White has forfeited the chance to play popular Benoni variations such as 7 f4 ♗g7 8 ♗b5+. Thus ♘f3 limits White's options.

Now we return to 1 d4 d5 2 c4 e6 3 ♘f3 ♘f6 (D):

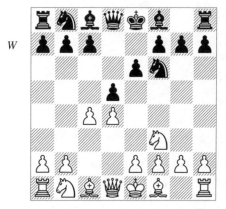

There are probably more serious negatives than positives for White with ♘f3 already having been played, but let's look at a few benefits for him first. Please remember that this is the complex and confusing version of the move-order presentation in the beginning of the

chapter – I'm trying to fit in as much information as I can!

Those who are experienced in the Queen's Gambit (or who have read this chapter) will see that this move-order avoids the main-line positions in which Black delays ...♘f6 in favour of 3...♗e7, that is, 1 d4 d5 2 c4 e6 3 ♘c3 (instead of 3 ♘f3) 3...♗e7, the Alatortsev Variation mentioned above. Notice also that if 1 d4 ♘f6 2 c4 e6 is Black's move-order, then 3 ♘f3 ♗e7?! is no longer logical as a substitute for 3...d5; apart from the answer 4 ♘c3, White could play 4 d5!?.

If White gets to this basic position (1 d4 d5 2 c4 e6 3 ♘f3 ♘f6), he has the choice of playing 4 g3, which is called the 'Catalan Opening'. It is absolutely sound, although rarely used on the lower and average levels of play. The Catalan is not optimally entered by 3 ♘c3 ♘f6 4 g3, because 4...dxc4 (or 4...♗b4 followed by ...dxc4) makes it awkward for White to recover his pawn.

White will usually answer 3...♘f6 with 4 ♘c3 (D).

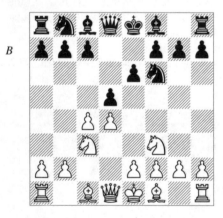

Now consider this further move-order information:

1) White has yet another benefit from having included ♘f3. If Black now plays 4...♘bd7, then 5 ♗g5 c6 6 e3 ♕a5!? is the Cambridge Springs Defence, which is considered quite playable. This can be forced by Black if White plays the main line 3 ♘c3 ♘f6 4 ♗g5 ♘bd7 5 e3 c6 6 ♘f3, and now 6...♕a5 is the Cambridge Springs.

However, if White has played 4 ♘f3 (instead of 4 ♗g5), then after 4...♘bd7, 5 cxd5 exd5 6

♗f4 is a promising order (this is analysed at the beginning of the Orthodox/Capablanca section). So having ♘f3 in discourages the Cambridge Springs!

2) What about the negative effects for White of 4 ♘f3 instead of 4 ♗g5? A couple of them are particularly significant:

2a) Black can choose to play 4...dxc4. Then what is considered the most challenging line goes 5 e4 ♗b4 6 ♗g5 c5 (6...h6 is also played). This introduces the Vienna Variation, which in contemporary chess will often lead to 7 ♗xc4 cxd4 8 ♘xd4 ♗xc3+ 9 bxc3 ♕a5 10 ♗b5+ (or 10 ♗xf6 ♕xc3+ 11 ♔f1 gxf6) 10...♘bd7 (or 10...♗d7) 11 ♗xf6 ♕xc3+ 12 ♔f1 gxf6 (D) with a real mess that is still unresolved in theory and practice.

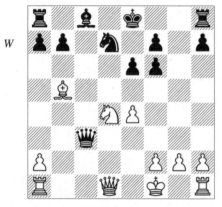

It's all about specifics at that point so I'll leave it to the reader to look up the theory. However, both players should know about the Vienna Variation. For Black, it's an opportunity to play something different, and for White, it's a potential problem to deal with. You can see that the Vienna Variation isn't an issue if White plays 3 ♘c3 and 4 ♗g5.

2b) After 4 ♘f3, Black can also continue 4...♗b4, leading to other complex variations such as 5 ♗g5 ♘bd7 6 cxd5 exd5 7 e3 c5 8 ♗d3 ♕a5 and 5 ♕a4+ ♘c6 6 a3 ♗xc3+ 7 bxc3 ♘e4 8 ♕c2. Again, it's the sort of thing that Black might consider playing (perhaps for surprise value) and that White should be prepared for.

2c) As explained in the beginning of the chapter, 4...♗e7 5 cxd5 exd5 6 ♗g5 0-0 7 e3 c6 gives us an Exchange Variation, but with

White's knight committed to f3. This is the Carlsbad Variation, given its own section. The only problem for White is that he's lost the option of placing the king's knight on e2, which is the favourite development for a majority of players.

2d) Black can still try to avoid the Carlsbad Exchange variation altogether by means of 4 ♘f3 ♗e7, and if 5 cxd5 cxd5 6 ♗g5, then 6...c6 *(D)*.

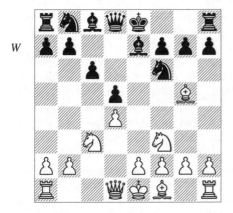

W

This has the idea 7 e3 ♗f5 with the easy play that usually comes from ...♗f5. To avoid this White can play 7 ♕c2 (to prevent ...♗f5) 7...g6!? (to enforce it, but creating a weakness) 8 e3 ♗f5 9 ♗d3 ♗xd3 10 ♕xd3 0-0 (10...♘bd7 is a good alternative) 11 ♗xf6 ♗xf6 12 b4 ♕d6 13 ♖b1 ♘d7 14 0-0 ♖fd8, Andersson-Kasparov, Belgrade 1988, and now 15 a4 seems like a good idea, countering ...b5 and considering a5 and ♘a4 at the right moment. Nevertheless, Black should know about these details because he can gain equality or very close to equality in these positions, and they provide a way to avoid the Exchange Variation.

2e) For the sake of completeness, I should add that White can also skip 5 cxd5 and go back to a traditional line by 5 ♗g5 0-0 and now play 6 e3, or he can try to get into another version of the Exchange Variation by 6 cxd5 exd5, but even then it's not easy because the books say that 6...♘xd5 is satisfactory.

2f) Finally, after 4 ♘f3, 4...♗e7 can be answered by the independent move 5 ♗f4 *(D)*.

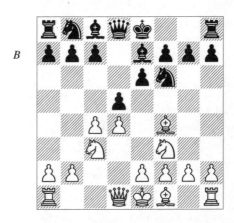

B

This important option has a long history, but I've had to forego an examination of it. One interesting aspect of 5 ♗f4 is that in the main lines Black will soon play ...c5, following the notion that an early move by the bishop on c1 will be met by queenside action. For example, 5...0-0 6 e3 c5 7 dxc5 ♗xc5 8 a3 ♘c6 9 ♕c2 (or the popular 9 cxd5 ♘xd5 10 ♘xd5 exd5 11 ♗d3 ♗b6 12 0-0 d4 13 e4, with a standard kingside majority structure that we see elsewhere in this book) 9...♕a5 10 ♘d2 or 10 0-0-0.

It goes on and on. All this makes quite a case for 3 ♘c3 and its predictability.

Such a barrage of move-order details can be disheartening, but they are important if you really want to master the Queen's Gambit and not merely play around with it. There are three redeeming features in this situation. First, you don't have to learn these details all at once. By playing the Queen's Gambit, you'll soon realize the importance of move-order subtleties, and either hearken back to this book or learn more by other means. The second piece of good news is that you can pick and choose what you want to do and avoid having to deal with most of these issues. That is especially true if you're Black. Finally, there is every chance that your opponent will know less about move-order issues than you do!

3 Slav and Semi-Slav

1 d4 d5 2 c4 c6 *(D)*

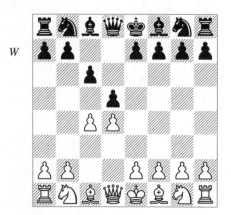

W

In this chapter we'll be investigating the Slav complex, embracing all variations of the Queen's Gambit that begin with 1 d4 d5 2 c4 c6. The Slav Defence is long-established as one of Black's most solid and effective answers to 1 d4. Max Euwe famously used the opening in his world championship matches versus Alekhine in the 1930s, and in the last two decades various forms of it (including the Semi-Slav, discussed in this chapter) have grown tremendously in popularity. Chess professionals in particular have found that the Slav's solidity is complemented by the dynamic counterattacks which can arise if White plays aggressively for an advantage

The Slav move 2...c6 reinforces Black's d5-pawn and it therefore begs comparison with the Queen's Gambit Declined (a.k.a. 'QGD': 1 d4 d5 2 c4 e6). In the QGD, Black's second move 2...e6 blocks off his own bishop on c8, making development of that piece difficult. That is not true of the Slav Defence, although 2...c6 uses up the c6-square, which in most openings is the best square for Black's queen's knight. This elimination of a possible ...♘c6, Black's 'ideal' development, is considered to be a prime drawback of 2...c6. A comparison of these two openings' respective disadvantages, however, would

seem to favour the Slav over the Queen's Gambit Declined, since after 1 d4 d5 the move ...♘c6 tends to be fairly ineffective anyway. A much more important consideration is that in the Slav, Black has wasted a tempo if he wants to play the important move ...c5, so often a key move (or positional threat) in the QGD.

It's also revealing to compare the respective Exchange Variations of these two openings. In the Queen's Gambit Declined, 1 d4 d5 2 c4 e6 3 ♘c3 ♘f6 4 cxd5 exd5 gives White a 2-1 central pawn-majority (a desirable feature for him); whereas in the Slav, 1 d4 d5 2 c4 c6 3 cxd5 cxd5 leaves the central pawn count the same. Superficially that would seem to favour the Slav version over the QGD. Again, things are not so easy. First, there are many players who prefer such imbalanced structures, and in the QGD Exchange, some would argue that Black's open e-file is more useful than White's open c-file. In addition, the QGD move 2...e6 affords Black the opportunity to develop his king's bishop quickly and thus enables the desirable move ...0-0 in short order. In the Slav Defence, by contrast, Black will take some time to play ...0-0 because he has to find a place for the f8-bishop, and trying to do so by a speedy ...e6 would seem to contradict the main advantage of 2...c6, i.e., to be able to develop the c8-bishop quickly.

I shall use the name 'Slav' for lines in which Black *doesn't* play ...e6 before bringing his queen's bishop out, or at least doesn't eliminate that option within the first few moves. By contrast, 'Semi-Slav' denotes a variation that begins with both ...e6 and ...c6 on the first few moves; for example, 1 d4 d5 2 c4 c6 3 ♘c3 e6, or here 3...♘f6 4 ♘f3 e6, or 1 d4 d5 2 c4 e6 3 ♘c3 c6, etc. This will include the Meran Variation, described in its own section. Although the most common lines in the Slav and Semi-Slav include ...dxc4, Black can also play moves such as ...a6 and ...g6. The latter moves hold the d5 point and emphasize the fundamental solidity of this defence.

Solidity tends to indicate lack of ambition, but that's not necessarily so in the Slav, since most of the main lines are unbalanced. It is true, however, that Black will seldom be playing for an early initiative or tactical chances unless White provokes him. A reason for this can be seen by the picture after the second move. Black is certainly not ready to waste a move on the pawn-break ...c5, but the only other way to challenge the centre would involve ...e5, a move unlikely to happen soon in view of the fact that White will almost always play ♘f3 on this or the next couple of moves.

Nevertheless, Black's second move has a potential dynamism that will express itself in specific situations. For example, in most variations of both the Slav and Semi-Slav, Black will play ...dxc4 at a fairly early stage. Then, although it may seem trivial, White needs to pay serious attention to recovering his pawn, because Black may play simply ...b5 and hang on to it (compare the Queen's Gambit Declined or Accepted, where this is a rare occurrence). Should this possibility require the move a4 on White's part, he has used up a tempo and weakened his b4-square. Already on his third move, then, White has a limited choice of continuations that avoid the forced loss of a pawn and yet still contain some punch. His candidates for the job are 3 cxd5 (the Exchange Variation), 3 ♘c3, and the main move 3 ♘f3. In the right situation White might prefer to gambit his c-pawn for compensation elsewhere, leading of course to unbalanced play.

You have seen or will see that all major openings have move-order issues. The Slav is no different but the majority of important decisions come on very early moves and mostly comprise independent set-ups rather than transpositions. The description that follows is a resource to which you can return after you gain some experience.

3 ♘f3

Although 3 ♘f3 is the main move, White sometimes uses 3 ♘c3 (D) in order either to bypass certain lines or to play independently.

Two of the most frequent continuations are 3...♘f6 4 cxd5 cxd5 5 ♗f4, which is considered in the Exchange Variation section, and 3...e6 4 e4, the Marshall Gambit, discussed in the Semi-Slav section.

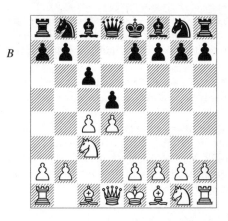

B

A couple of unique move-orders to watch out for as White, or to use as Black, are:

a) 3...dxc4, which is quite complex after 4 e3 b5 5 a4 b4 6 ♘b1 (6 ♘a2 e6 protects the pawn on b4; there usually follows 7 ♗xc4 ♘f6 8 ♘f3, again considered equal) 6...♗a6 7 ♕c2 ♘f6 8 ♗xc4 ♗xc4 9 ♕xc4 ♕d5. All this is theory that I won't pursue; it's simply good to know it exists. Or White can play 4 e4 (D).

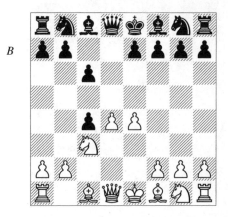

B

This is somewhat more ambitious: 4...b5 (or 4...e5 5 ♘f3 exd4 6 ♕xd4 ♕xd4 7 ♘xd4 with prospects of a small edge for White) 5 a4 b4 6 ♘a2 (6 ♘ce2!?) 6...♘f6 7 e5 ♘d5 8 ♗xc4, after which Black has various set-ups involving ...♗f5, ...♗a6, or simply ...e6. White would like to get in the moves ♗d2, ♘c1-b3 and ♖c1.

b) 3...e5!? is the Winawer Counter-Gambit, about which a lot has been written. Obviously if Black can get away with this move unpunished he will have freed his game entirely. I'll just give a skeletal structure of the main lines and refer you to theory to get the details: 4 cxd5 (4 dxe5 d4 5 ♘e4 ♕a5+ 6 ♗d2 ♕xe5 7 ♘g3; 4 e3 e4!? or 4...exd4) 4...cxd5 5 dxe5 (5 ♘f3 e4 6 ♘e5) 5...d4 6 ♘e4 ♕a5+ and now 7 ♗d2 ♕xe5 or 7 ♘d2 ♘d7!? or 7...♘h6!?.

c) After 3...♘f6, White can play 4 e3, often his main reason for using the 3 ♘c3 move-order. That's because 4...♗f5?! is now a mistake due to 5 cxd5 cxd5?! (5...♘xd5 6 ♕b3) 6 ♕b3 with the idea 6...♕b6 7 ♘xd5. Compare this with 3 ♘f3 ♘f6 4 e3 below, when 4...♗f5 is perfectly playable. After 3 ♘c3 ♘f6 4 e3, Black can instead play 4...g6, 4...a6 or 4...♗g4!?, the latter of particular interest to players who want to keep the game dynamic in character.

Chess is as flexible as you want it to be, although main lines usually give White the best chance to gain a lasting advantage.

3...♘f6 4 ♘c3

Conceding that the more aggressive variations involving ♗g5 against the Semi-Slav aren't to their taste, players are turning relatively often to the modest 4 e3 (D).

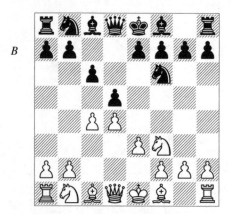

If White plays ♘c3 next he is likely to achieve a standard formation, but 4 e3 opens up some other possibilities for both sides. Without going into detail here, this move-order compares to 4 ♘c3 e6 5 e3 in the following ways:

1) It sidesteps 4 ♘c3 dxc4 5 a4 ♗f5 (the main line of the Slav proper), because 4 e3 dxc4 5 ♗xc4 is as favourable a development as White could wish for.

2) It gives White more leeway in replying to the Semi-Slav. That is, after 4...e6, White can revert to the main line by 5 ♘c3 (see the Semi-Slav section of this chapter), but he can also use some combination of the moves ♘bd2, ♗d3,

0-0 and b3. Those last formations are not pursued in this book but can hopefully be understood on general grounds, i.e. by omitting ♘c3, White avoids having to suffer the tempo-gaining moves ...dxc4 and ...b5-b4. This last sequence occurs in the Meran Variation of the Semi-Slav, and will be seen in that section.

3) After 4 e3, Black may decide not to cooperate in returning to Semi-Slav territory. He can instead play 4...♗f5 or 4...♗g4, placing his 'bad' bishop outside the pawn-chain and leaving White's bishop on c1 looking rather sad. In that case we return to the point made often in this book: in d-pawn openings, White should remember to look at ♕b3 or ♕a4, when responding to the early development of the c8-bishop. It's unlikely that any other course will yield an advantage versus Black's natural development.

To demonstrate that trade-off, let's take a look at the common Black deviations after 4 e3:

a) 4...♗g4 5 ♕b3 hits b7 and prepares ♘e5. Then 5...♕b6 (D) is a good way to continue.

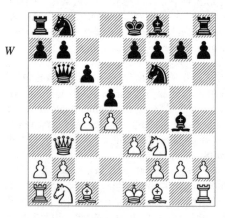

The game Korchnoi-Acs, Budapest 2003 saw 6 ♘e5 ♗f5 (Black wants to play ...e6 and ...♘bd7 with the freer development) 7 cxd5 ♕xb3 8 axb3 ♘xd5, when White's weak b4-square is a bother that at least compensates Black for his opponent's central majority: 9 ♘a3 (9 ♘d2?! ♘b4 is awkward; e.g., 10 ♖a4 e6 11 e4 ♗g6 12 ♔d1 {12 f3? b5} 12...♘d7, etc.) 9...f6 10 ♘d3 ♘a6 11 ♗d2 e6 12 f3 ♗g6 13 ♘c2 ♗xd3 14 ♗xd3 ♘ab4 15 ♔e2 ♘xd3 16 ♔xd3 ♗d6, and if anything Black has an edge.

Why can't White play the same game and get the advantage by 6 ♕xb6 axb6? Because he can't exploit the b5 outpost; for instance, 7 ♘c3 (7 cxd5 ♘xd5 and White still needs to take notice of ...♘b4; e.g., 8 ♘e5? ♘b4!; also ineffective is 7 ♘e5 ♗f5 8 ♘c3 e6 with equality) 7...e6 8 cxd5 exd5 9 ♗e2 ♗d6 10 0-0 b5!; note that White's bishop on c1 is bad in these lines.

b) 4...♗f5 and now:

b1) After 5 ♘c3 e6 6 ♘h4, both 6...♗g6 7 ♘xg6 hxg6 and 6...♗e4! 7 f3 ♗g6 8 ♘xg6 hxg6 have been tested in high-level grandmaster play, with and without the insertion of ♕b3 and ...♕b6. This has generally resulted in balanced play, especially after 6...♗e4. White has two bishops, but neither one is as good Black's bishop, and Black's open h-file can come in handy, often in conjunction with ...♗d6 and the aggressive move ...g5 to disturb things early on and force a change of structure that accommodates the knights.

b2) 5 cxd5 cxd5 6 ♕b3 (D).

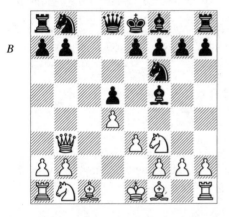

In this position Black must choose how he wants to defend the b-pawn. 6...♕b6 is possible but the more ambitious set-up is 6...♕c7, intending 7 ♗d2 ♘c6 8 ♗b5 e6. White's plan is to weaken Black's pawn-structure by ♗xc6 (when ...bxc6 is normally best), trade dark-squared bishops by ♗b4, and then mount pressure down the c-file. He might, for example, play a rook to c1 and occupy c5 with a knight after the preliminary ♘a4. From Black's perspective (after ♗xc6 and ...bxc6), he will have two bishops and pressure down an open b-file, with prospects of ...c5 after, say, the moves ...♕b6 and ...♘d7. At the moment White seems to be getting very slight advantages in this type of position, but even those may well prove to be

illusory. The whole line is quite playable for Black in any case.

c) 4...g6 5 ♘c3 ♗g7 is a hybrid Grünfeld/Slav variation that is known as the Schlechter Slav. This position can also arise via 1 d4 ♘f6 2 c4 g6 3 ♘c3 d5 4 ♘f3 ♗g7 5 e3 c6. After, for example, 6 ♗d3 0-0 7 0-0 ♗g4 8 h3 ♗xf3 9 ♕xf3 e6 10 ♖d1 ♘bd7 (D) White wants to use his two bishops and space advantage and slowly make progress on the queenside, whereas Black is happy that White's dark-squared bishop is restricted and will strive for ...e5.

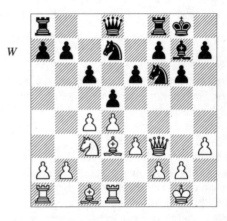

An ultra-solid position has arisen. Sometimes Black can consider ...dxc4 followed by ...e5 but that brings White's light-squared bishop to an aggressive diagonal. At the moment the desirable move ...e5 is difficult to implement because Black's d-pawn requires defence. As a general rule, the player with two bishops will have some advantage unless the opponent's knights already have an available outpost or he can create one by means of a forcing attack. Here, since Black cannot do so, White probably retains a small edge. Still, these positions are very resilient and one could also argue Black's bishop on g7 is so much superior to White's on c1 that he can claim full equality. Note that it doesn't help White to open the game immediately because that would activate his opponent's knights: 11 e4!? e5! 12 dxe5 (12 exd5 exd4 13 dxc6 ♘e5 14 ♕e2 ♘xd3 15 ♖xd3 bxc6 with an equal position; 12 ♗e3 dxe4 13 ♘xe4 ♘xe4 14 ♗xe4 ♕h4 15 d5 f5 16 dxc6? fxe4 17 ♕g4 ♕xg4 18 hxg4 ♘f6 and Black has the advantage) 12...♘xe5 13 ♕e2 ♘xd3 14 ♖xd3 ♖e8 with dynamic play that appears evenly balanced.

Slav Main Line

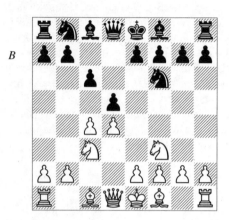

Now we move into the realm of the Slav proper, leaving the Semi-Slav (4...e6) for later. Black begins with:

4...dxc4

This is a rather strange-looking move, at least to the inexperienced player. With his first three moves, Black has carefully maintained his pawn on d5 and prevented e4. Now he surrenders his control of that square and grants White a central majority to boot! Perhaps that might make sense if 4...dxc4 won a pawn, but White can regain the pawn on c4 fairly easily.

As is often the case, Black's motivation follows from a combination of the goals and the specifics of the position. He would like to develop his pieces, and since 4...e6 cuts off the queen's bishop, it would be nice to place that piece on f5 to be followed by ...e6 and kingside development. However, the immediate 4...♗f5?! is one of those cases in which the bishop comes out a bit too early, because White has played ♘c3 instead of e3 (that is, as opposed to 3 ♘f3 ♘f6 4 e3 ♗f5 above). Play can continue 5 cxd5! and now:

a) 5...cxd5?! 6 ♕b3! *(D)*.

6...♕b6!? (6...♗c8 is an admission of failure but perhaps best; 6...b6 is always weakening in such positions – White can take advantage of Black's vulnerable light squares by 7 ♗f4 ♘c6 8 e4! dxe4 9 ♗b5 ♗d7 10 ♘e5 ♘xe5 11 dxe5 with the idea ♖d1) 7 ♕xb6!? (White can also grab a pawn by 7 ♘xd5 ♘xd5 8 ♕xd5 e6, and return it advantageously by 9 ♕b3 ♕xb3 10 axb3 ♗c2 11 ♗d2 ♘c6 12 ♖c1 ♗xb3 13 e4)

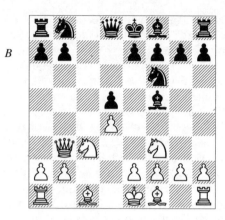

7...axb6 8 ♗f4 e6 9 e3 ♗b4 10 ♗b5+ and White stands better because Black's pawns are vulnerable.

b) 5...♘xd5 also seems to fall short of equality; e.g., 6 ♕b3 (6 ♘d2!? is strange-looking, but e4 can't be stopped so it probably produces some advantage; the benefit of the central majority outweighs White's loss of time) 6...♕b6! 7 ♘xd5 (or 7 ♕xb6 axb6 8 ♘xd5 cxd5 9 e3 ♘c6 10 ♗b5 ♗d7 11 ♗d2) 7...♕xb3 (7...cxd5 8 ♕xd5!? e6 9 ♕b3 ♕xb3 10 axb3 ♗c2 11 e3 ♗xb3 12 ♗b5+ ♘c6 13 ♘e5) 8 ♘c7+ ♔d7 9 axb3 ♔xc7 10 ♗f4+ ♔c8 11 ♘d2! e6 12 e4 ♗g6 13 ♗d3 ♗b4 14 ♔e2 ♖d8 15 ♘c4! with the twin ideas of ♘b6+ and ♘e5.

Instead of 4...dxc4 or 4...♗f5?!, 4...a6!? *(D)* is an ultra-sophisticated attempt that asks White what his plan is while preparing to develop his queen's bishop to f5 or g4.

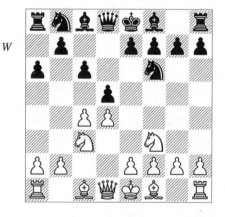

I won't go into theory, but a few features of this position are easily explained. In variations without ...a6, the usual response to ...♗f5 or

...♗g4 involves the move ♕b3, attacking the b-pawn. But after 4...a6, Black can play ...♗g4 or ...♗f5 and answer White's ♕b3 by either ...b5, which forces a resolution of the centre, or the remarkable ...♖a7!?. One point of the latter move is that Black needn't devote his queen to defence of b7 and thus it is less exposed to attack. To clarify that a bit you might want to compare the lines after 4 ♘c3 ♗f5?! 5 ♕b3 ♕c7 or 5...♕c8, which expose Black's queen to potential attack down the c-file. It's also worth noting that the move 4...a6 is a very useful one in the Exchange Variation after 5 cxd5 cxd5, since it prevents ♘b5 as well as White's standard move ♗b5. In fact, we shall look at a line that comes from 4...a6 in the Exchange Variation section below.

5 a4

The Geller Gambit 5 e4 b5 6 e5 attempts to use White's broad centre for attacking purposes and mix in some tactical opportunism. In the process there arise positional features involving the struggle for light and dark squares by both players. To give a taste of this complex gambit, let's take a brief look at the old main line, which goes 6...♘d5 7 a4 *(D)*.

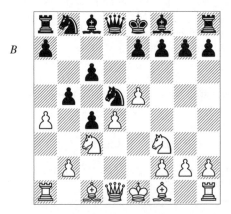

7...e6! (securing d5; other moves are risky – for instance, 7...♗b7 8 e6! shatters Black's pawn-structure) 8 axb5 ♘xc3 9 bxc3 cxb5 10 ♘g5 (threatening both 11 ♕f3 and 11 ♘xf7) 10...♗b7 11 ♕h5 (White creates dark-square weaknesses in Black's position) 11...g6 12 ♕g4 ♗e7 13 ♗e2 ♗d5! (13...♘d7 14 ♗f3 ♕c8! similarly protects the light squares and according to theory also favours Black) 14 ♗f3 h5 15 ♕g3 (most of White's moves have been forced)

15...♘c6 16 0-0 b4! and White's pawn-chain is collapsing before he can exploit Black's dark-square weaknesses. Needless to say, there is more theory on this complex line, but the conclusion is that Black stands well, in large part because White's attack has to depend upon pieces alone, and he can't wait around too long while Black prepares ...a5 and ...b4.

5...♗f5

Just in time, Black gets his bishop out and stops White from forming an ideal centre with e4. This is the choice of most players. There are a number of valid alternatives, including 5...c5 and 5...♗g4. Having to choose one, I'll look briefly at a third, highly interesting, alternative: 5...♘a6 *(D)*.

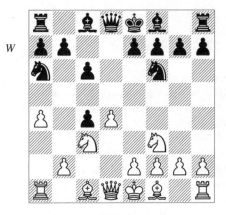

What on earth is Black doing, after first giving up the centre, by wasting time and putting his knight on the edge of the board? As Graham Burgess points out, this is to some degree a waiting move. Black wants White to move his e-pawn so that he can play ...♗g4. But if you think about it there are few if any other useful moves by which Black can temporize! Although 5...♘a6 doesn't exactly set the house on fire, it *is* a developing move, and sometimes the knight can occupy the b4 outpost. Otherwise it might recentralize by ...♘c7 or even give support to a ...c5 counterthrust.

White's most natural move is 6 e3, which can be met by 6...♗g4! (a trick is 6...♗f5 7 ♗xc4 ♘b4 8 0-0 ♘c2?? 9 e4 ♘xa1 10 exf5, etc.) 7 ♗xc4 e6 (7...♘b4? 8 ♘e5!) 8 h3 ♗h5 9 g4 (9 0-0 ♘b4 10 ♕e2 ♗e7 11 ♖d1 0-0 12 g4!? ♗g6 13 e4 is the kind of restraint centre explored in the chapter on structures in Volume 1;

here Black's bishop is outside the pawn-chain, but in real danger of being cut off, whereas Black's knight on b4 is a definite plus) 9...♗g6. At this point let's break off in order to explore an idea that many of you must have been wondering about: 10 ♗xa6!? bxa6 *(D)*.

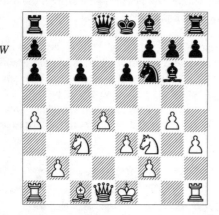

White captures the knight on a6 to double and isolate Black's pawns on a7, a6 and c6 (the latter on an open file). He also has two central pawns and a nice support point on e5 for his knight, so that moves like ♘e5 and ♕f3, perhaps followed by h4-h5, are potential threats. What are the downsides? First, he has given his opponent the two bishops, which happen to have attractive open lines available. Second, he has weakened his light squares, a serious issue with this particular pawn-structure. Black has also gained the b-file along which his rook can attack the backward pawn on b2. Finally, White has lost a move capturing the knight and will have a difficult time organizing an attack down the c-file before Black plays ...c5 and puts pressure on White's centre. Thus we have a typical trade-off between static and dynamic factors. White needs to respond firmly; for example, 11 ♘e5 ♗d6 (11...c5!? 12 a5! ♗d6?! 13 ♕a4+ ♔f8 14 ♕c6!) 12 ♘xg6 (12 ♕f3 ♖c8! 13 e4 ♗b4! 14 ♘xg6 hxg6 15 ♗e3 c5 16 ♖d1 ♕a5 and the dynamic side is getting the better of it) 12...hxg6 13 g5 with some kind of dynamic equilibrium after 13...♘h5 14 ♘e4 or 13...♘d5 14 e4 ♘xc3 15 bxc3 c5 16 dxc5 ♗xc5 17 ♕xd8+ ♖xd8.

In fact, this trade of bishop for doubled a-pawns arises repeatedly in chess openings. For example, there are several variations of the King's Indian Defence in which Black plays ...♘a6 and White bites with ♗xa6. One such is 1 d4 ♘f6 2 c4 g6 3 ♘c3 ♗g7 4 e4 d6 5 ♗e2 0-0 6 ♗g5 ♘a6 7 ♕d2 e5 8 d5 c6 9 f3 cxd5 10 cxd5 ♗d7 11 ♗xa6!? bxa6 12 ♘ge2 ♕b6 13 ♗e3 ♕b7 14 0-0 ♘e8, pitting Black's static weaknesses against two bishops and a potentially dynamic ...f5 thrust. Or the Glek Variation with 1 d4 ♘f6 2 c4 g6 3 ♘c3 ♗g7 4 e4 d6 5 ♘f3 0-0 6 ♗e2 e5 7 0-0 ♘a6, when an early c5 and ♗xa6 occurs in at least one of the main lines.

Some other examples: the Pirc Defence with 1 e4 d6 2 d4 ♘f6 3 ♘c3 g6 4 f4 ♗g7 5 ♘f3 0-0 6 ♗d3 ♘a6, inviting ♗xa6. Or a similar idea in the French following 1 e4 e6 2 d4 d5 3 ♘d2 ♗e7 4 ♗d3 c5 5 dxc5 ♘f6 6 ♕e2 0-0 7 ♘gf3 ♘fd7 8 ♘b3 ♘a6 9 ♗xa6 bxa6 10 c6 ♘b8 11 0-0 ♘xc6.

Of course White can also offer the trade-off. For example, a variation of the Réti Opening goes 1 ♘f3 d5 2 c4 e6 3 g3 ♘f6 4 ♗g2 c6 (or 4...dxc4 5 ♘a3 ♗xa3 6 bxa3!?) 5 0-0 dxc4 6 ♘a3 ♗xa3 7 bxa3 with the bishop-pair, dark squares, and b-file for the pawn. And so forth. You will find other examples as you move through the chess world. This is an example of cross-pollination: the point is that when you have a position in which your knight is about to be captured on a6 or a3, you will come to recognize the pros and cons of allowing that capture.

Returning to the main move 5...♗f5, we have a major split between 6 e3 and 6 ♘e5, with each now getting its own section.

Dutch Variation: 6 e3

1 d4 d5 2 c4 c6 3 ♘f3 ♘f6 4 ♘c3 dxc4 5 a4 ♗f5 6 e3 e6 7 ♗xc4

The lines are drawn. Both sides are reasonably well developed and White has the central majority. Black's task, then, is to make sure that it can't advance (i.e., e4 cannot be played) until he is ready to snipe at the centre and force White into some undesired change of structure. From White's point of view, Black's pawn-structure is super-solid and will only be completely broken down by e4 and d5. Alternatively, White has the option of e4-e5, seeking attacking chances.

7...♗b4

Black indirectly increases his control over e4.

8 0-0 *(D)*

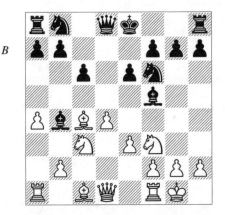

A basic position. We can see some general features of the game developing. White has a central majority (2:1), and Black has a restraint formation with the light-squared bishop in front of the pawn-chain (see Chapter 3 in Volume 1 on pawn-structures for an explanation of the various types of restraint centres). In the situation before us, Black is not waiting for e4 but preventing the advance of the e-pawn by piece-play. He has two pieces attacking e4 and a third ready to exchange off a piece defending that square. Whether or not that situation persists, he will try to gain time for the characteristic pawn-breaks ...c5 and ...e5.

Note that Black's bishop is on an outpost on b4 and cannot be expelled by pawns; therefore White may need to retreat his knight or divert resources to drive the bishop away. As a first plan, White would like to play f3 in order to get e4 in, but that would require either a knight retreat or advance to e5, and both moves will allow an early ...c5. This leaves White with two basic approaches:

a) He can support a central advance with his pieces, the classical approach. In that case, White wants to pose Black the challenge of confronting an ideal centre;

b) He can chase down Black's bishop on f5 by a variety of methods, including the direct 6 ♘h4. In that case, should White decide to capture the bishop on f5 he will have to forego e4 for some time, but that may not be a bad trade-off.

These goals can operate in tandem. The more specific decision about whether and when to try to expel Black's bishop on b4 will vary according to circumstance.

The 6 e3 variation is probably the most instructive one in traditional Slav practice. It produces games permeated by strategic and positional themes that will be usable in many contexts.

8...♘bd7

Black will normally choose between this move and 8...0-0. The decision comes down to one's goals and some tactical assessments. Depending upon your goals and who you're playing, a practical drawback of 8...♘bd7 is that it opens up some possibilities for an immediate draw. White can play 9 ♕b3, when Black has to choose between the following:

a) 9...a5, allowing a draw by 10 ♘a2 *(D)*.

10...♗e7 (10...♕e7? 11 ♘xb4 ♕xb4 12 ♕xb4 axb4 13 ♗d2 really isn't acceptable for Black) 11 ♕xb7 ♖b8 12 ♕a6 ♖a8 13 ♕xc6 ♖c8 with a draw by perpetual attack.

After 9...a5, Black can't really avoid this draw, but White can, and often does, playing either 10 ♘a2 ♗e7 11 ♘h4 or 10 ♘h4. The last move can lead to, for example, 10...♗g6 (10...♗g4 11 f3 ♗h5 is a good alternative) 11 g3!?, not just protecting the knight but also intending the exotic idea ♘xg6, ♖d1 and ♗f1-g2.

b) 9...♕b6 is an extremely risky variation that most players would like to avoid even though it may be survivable for Black: 10 e4 (10 ♘h4 is still possible) 10...♗g6 11 ♗xe6!? fxe6 12 a5! ♗xa5 13 ♕xe6+ ♔d8 14 e5 and as I customarily say about such random positions, please consult the books! Black may stand satisfactorily, but you should commit the tactics to memory if you want to live long against a strong player.

Instead of 8...♘bd7, 8...0-0 solves that problem, because now 9 ♕b3 ♕e7! (protecting b7 as well as b4) is considered fine. On the other hand, Black loses some flexibility and time in some variations (compare the ...♗g4 lines below, in which Black delays castling). Furthermore, he may not want to allow ♘e5; e.g., 8...0-0 9 ♕e2 ♗g6 10 ♘e5 ♘bd7 11 ♘xg6 hxg6, and here 12 ♘a2 is interesting. What is the solution to this quandary? Just come prepared!

9 ♕e2 *(D)*

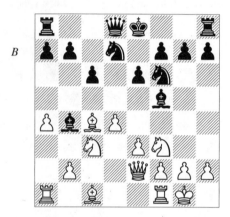

This is White's traditional and most popular plan, simply trying to enforce e4 while clearing d1 for a rook. We'll examine it in some detail via games beginning with:

A: 9...♗g4; and
B: 9...0-0.

A)

9...♗g4

Black has a simple idea: to eliminate White's f3-knight and then temporarily restrain White's pawns with his own on c6 and e6. I talked about this structure in Chapter 3 of Volume 1. As usual, ...c5 and/or ...e5 are Black's long-term goals.

Lugovoi – Kovalevskaya
St Petersburg 2000

10 ♖d1 ♕a5

Black wants to gain a tempo to implement his plans. Sensing no immediate attack, he doesn't feel that ...0-0 is necessary for the moment, and may even play ...0-0-0 later.

11 e4 ♕h5 *(D)*

You will see this idea in several lines: Black wishes to cripple White's kingside pawns. But in doing so he gives White the bishop-pair and an even stronger centre. Instead 11...0-0 transposes to a normal position, and 11...♗xc3!? 12 bxc3 ♕xc3 13 ♖a3!? or here 13 ♗b2 ♗xf3 14 gxf3 ♕a5 15 d5!? gives White a lot of compensation for a pawn. Regardless of the exact assessment, taking on that kind of position seems impractical for Black.

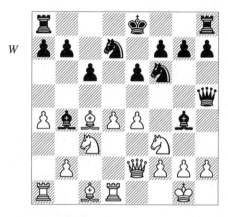

12 ♖d3!?

This interesting move avoids having doubled pawns on f3. One alternative is to force Black to carry out his plan by 12 h3!? ♗xf3 13 ♕xf3 ♕xf3 14 gxf3; e.g., 14...0-0 15 a5 (gaining space) 15...a6 16 ♗e2 (16 ♗f4!?) 16...♖fd8 17 ♖a4 ♗e7 (the position should be equal; White's structural immobility detracts from his two-bishop advantage) 18 f4 ♘e8 19 ♗e3 ♖ac8 20 ♗f3?! (20 ♗d3 looks better) 20...♘d6 (20...f5! and one prefers Black) 21 ♗e2 g6 22 ♖aa1 ½-½ Khalifman-Ki.Georgiev, Burgas 1994. The characteristic interaction of bishop-pair and doubled pawns leads to unpredictable play, as in many openings in which Black plays ...♗xf3.

12...e5 13 h3!?

White expends a whole tempo on this move but he wants to attack. 13 d5!? would be normal, when 13...♘c5 14 ♖e3 0-0! needs to be met, probably by 15 dxc6 bxc6 16 ♘a2. It's refreshing that so much unexplored territory remains in these older lines. That tends to be true when a variation is less tactical and/or forcing.

13...♗xf3 (D)

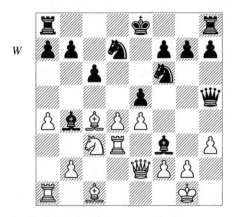

14 ♖xf3

White's attempt to drum up chances by sacrificing are typical but unless followed up precisely he can easily fail against Black's good development and solid structure. Instead, 14 ♕xf3 ♕xf3 15 gxf3 keeps the pawn with a balanced position. Here's a well-played example: 15...0-0 16 f4 exd4 17 ♖xd4 c5 18 ♖d1 ♖fd8 19 e5 ♘b6 20 ♖xd8+ ♖xd8 21 ♗b3 ♗xc3 22 bxc3 ♘e4 23 ♗e3 ♘xc3 24 ♗xc5 ♘e2+ 25 ♔f1 ♘xf4 26 a5 ♘c8 27 ♗e3 ♘e6 28 ♖c1 and the bishops provide at least enough counterplay for a pawn, Hillarp Persson-Hector, Malmö 2003. Having faith in the bishop-pair comes as you gain more experience.

14...exd4 15 g4 ♕c5 16 ♖f5!? ♕e7 (D)

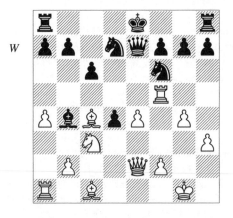

17 g5?

This kind of overextension is often how Black wins in the Slav. Such an attack is unlikely to succeed without the cooperation of White's dark-squared bishop and centre pawn. It's much better to count upon the two bishops for compensation by 17 ♘a2! 0-0!? (17...h6! is a helpful preventative move) 18 e5 ♘d5 19 ♗g5.

17...dxc3 18 gxf6 gxf6!?

Or 18...♘xf6 with the idea 19 bxc3?! ♗xc3 20 ♗a3 ♗b4!.

19 bxc3 ♗d6

There seems to be nothing wrong with playing 19...♗xc3; Black does have two extra pawns and good squares!

20 ♖b1 ♘c5 (D)

Perhaps 20...0-0-0 was even better. Black has a nice advantage in any case.

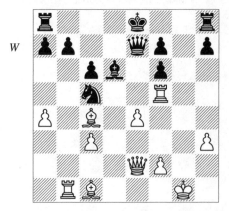

21 ♗a3 ♖g8+ 22 ♔h1 ♕xe4+ 23 ♕xe4+ ♘xe4 24 ♖xb7! 0-0-0! 25 ♗a6 ♗xa3 26 ♖e7+ ♔b8 27 ♖xe4 ♖d1+ 28 ♔h2 ♖dg1?

28...♗d6+ 29 f4 ♖c1 is simple and strong, with the idea 30 ♖xf6? ♗c5.

29 ♖e8+! ½-½

Black won the opening, but White had his chances to influence that situation between moves 13 and 17, so the verdict is unclear.

Khalifman – Anand
Linares 2000

10 ♖d1 ♕a5 11 e4 ♘b6!? (D)

As above, Anand delays castling in order to get all of his other desired moves in.

12 ♗b3!?

12 ♗d3 makes it more difficult to grab the pawn: 12...♗xc3 (not 12...0-0? 13 e5! ♘fd5 14

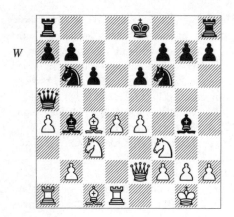

♗xh7+) 13 bxc3 ♕xc3 14 ♗b2 ♗xf3 15 gxf3 ♕b4 16 d5! with a very dangerous attack. Again and again we shall see the bishop-pair used in the most dramatic fashion against a solid Slav structure.

12...♗xc3 13 bxc3 ♕xc3 14 ♖b1 0-0

Getting castled is half the battle in these variations! Does White have compensation?

15 h3! ♗xf3 16 ♕xf3! ♕xf3 17 gxf3 *(D)*

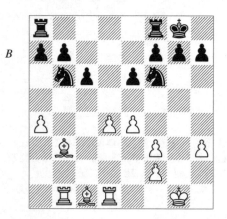

It's amazing that White can waste another tempo (h3) to enter a simplified position a pawn down with such a kingside structure! This is a lesson in the bishops and central majority. As the game goes on, the majority tends to get stronger and stronger. White also has some concrete ideas involving a5 and putting pressure on the queenside down his two open files on that side of the board.

17...♘bd7 18 ♗a3 ♖fc8! 19 ♗c4 ♘b6!

This knight will alternate between restraining White's centre and harassing him. Scherbakov analyses 19...c5?! 20 ♖xb7 cxd4 21 ♖xd4

e5 22 ♖dxd7! ♘xd7 23 ♗d5! *(D)*, when White is practically winning.

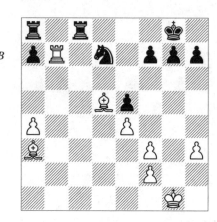

White will win the f-pawn, and when a player gets a pawn and the advantage of the bishop-pair in return for the exchange, the odds are that he's doing very well! A sample line: 23...♘b6 24 ♗xf7+ ♔h8 25 a5 ♘a4 (25...♘c4 26 ♗xc4! ♖xc4 27 ♗d6! ♖a4 28 ♗xe5 ♖xa5 29 ♗xg7+ ♔g8 30 ♗f6 with the idea e5 and e6, with f4-f5 and/or a king march up the board if White is denied e6) 26 ♗d6 ♘c5 27 ♖b1! and the e5-pawn will soon fall.

20 ♗b3

Or 20 ♗f1!? ♖c7! 21 a5 ♘c8 22 ♖dc1 ♘e7!, avoiding weaknesses.

20...♘bd7!

Black can hardly gain any activity, but it is not easy for White to find a plan either.

21 ♗c4

This works against ...b6 because the bishop would slide into a6.

21...♘b6 22 ♗b3 ½-½

The knights have reasserted themselves just in time. White can probably win another pawn, but at the cost of any winning chances. The result fairly reflects the opening.

Illescas – L. Dominguez
Dos Hermanas 2005

10 h3 ♗xf3 11 ♕xf3 *(D)*
11...0-0 12 ♖d1 ♖c8 13 ♘e4!?

One would think that simplifying would make Black's life easier, and in fact it's rare for White to forego central expansion and attack. But when you think about it, many if not most

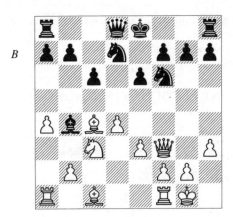

endings in which one side possesses the bishop-pair are won for their owner, as long as there are pawns on both sides of the board.

13...♘xe4

Or 13...♕a5 14 ♘xf6+ ♘xf6 15 e4 with advantage.

14 ♕xe4 ♕a5 15 ♕c2 ♘b6 16 ♗d3 g6 17 e4

As Illescas indicates, this restricts Black's knight.

17...c5?! *(D)*

17...♖fd8 18 ♗e2 h5!? had been played before, when Illescas likes 19 ♗f3 c5 20 d5 exd5 21 exd5 c4 22 ♗g5.

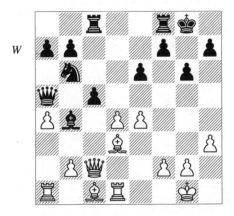

18 dxc5! ♗xc5

White is also better after 18...♖xc5 19 ♕b3 ♖fc8 20 ♗e3: centre and bishops!

19 ♕b3

Threatening to win with 20 ♗d2.

19...♕b4?

Black doesn't sense how bad the ending will become. Better was 19...♗b4.

20 ♕xb4 ♗xb4 21 a5! ♘a8

21...♘c4 22 ♖a4 ♘e5 23 ♗h6 doesn't help Black.

22 ♗h6 ♖fd8 23 a6! *(D)*

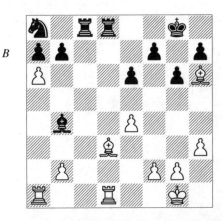

The opening ideas have expressed themselves and you can see that Black has gone wrong. It's not easy to say where, but an earlier ...c5 or ...e5 was needed in order to neutralize the bishops.

23...bxa6

Illescas gives the charming line 23...b6 24 ♗g5! ♖d7 25 ♗b5 ♖xd1+ 26 ♖xd1 ♘c7 27 ♗c6 and White is winning.

24 ♗xa6 ♖xd1+ 25 ♖xd1 ♖b8 26 ♗f4 ♖e8 27 ♖d7 ♗c5 28 ♗e5 ♗b6 29 g4 *(D)*

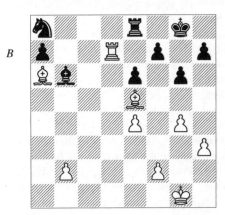

When your pieces are ideally placed then the pawns frequently have to be brought into action, either to break down the enemy structure or simply to help in the attack.

29...♖d8 30 ♖b7 ♔f8 31 ♗f6 ♖e8 32 ♗b5 ♖c8 33 ♗d7 ♖c1+ 34 ♔g2 ♗c7 35 ♖xa7 ♘b6 36 ♗b5 e5 37 b3 ♖c5 38 ♗c4! h6 39 h4 g5 40

hxg5 hxg5 41 ♗d5 ♔e8 42 b4 ♖c3 43 ♗xf7+!
♔xf7 44 ♗xe5 1-0

B)
9...0-0 10 e4 ♗g6 *(D)*

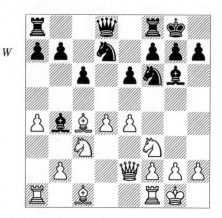

From g6 Black's bishop keeps pressure upon
White's centre and protects his king. Now Black
is threatening ...♗xc3 followed by ...♘xe4.
We'll look at several games from this position.

Bacrot – J. Gustafsson
Bundesliga 2003/4

11 ♗d3 ♗h5
This funny move is quite popular and makes
the game more like the lines with 9...♗g4
above. Black would like to play ...e5, since the
knight on f3 is pinned. Black feels that White's
bishop on d3 is to his advantage because it no
longer controls d5.

12 e5
The only logical plan left.

12...♘d5 13 ♘xd5 cxd5 14 ♕e3!? h6
Black doesn't want to give up the two bishops by capturing the knight on c3; instead, he
goes after White's good bishop. But first he has
to protect against ideas of ♘g5. White on the
other hand will prepare the advance of his f-
pawn.

15 ♘e1 ♗g6!?
A doubled-edged move, trading weak pawns
for freedom of activity. In the face of f4, an alternative is 15...f5 (seizing space) 16 exf6 (16 ♘c2
♗e7 looks satisfactory for Black) 16...♕xf6 17
♗b5 ♖f7! 18 ♘d3 ♗d6 with equality, Lutsko-
Lybov, Bydgoszcz 2001; Black can follow with

...♗g6; his lone weakness on e6 is compensated
by activity.

16 ♗xg6 fxg6 17 ♘c2! *(D)*
Now the knight can go to e3 where it covers
key squares. Compare the older line 17 ♘d3
♗e7 18 ♕h3 ♖f5! 19 ♘f4 ♘f8, when Black is
fairly solid.

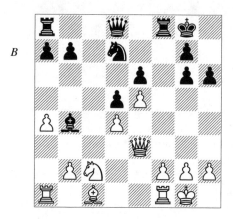

17...♗a5
The natural 17...♗e7 now runs into 18 ♕h3
♕b6 (this time 18...♖f5? fails to 19 ♘e3) 19
♗d2 and Black's position is awkward.

18 ♕d3 ♔h7 19 f4
Now the character of the game is set: Bacrot
has more space and can advance pawns on both
wings. Black's king is also vulnerable.

19...a6 20 b4 ♗b6 21 g4!? *(D)*

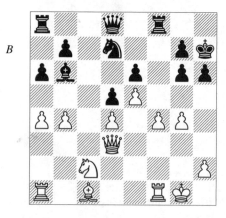

A little loosening. This could have been prepared.

21...♕h4 22 ♘e3
We see that the move 17 ♘c2 has come in
handy. In what follows Black fails to react well.

22...♖ac8?! 23 ♗d2 h5 24 ♖ae1! hxg4 25 ♖e2 ♖f7 26 ♖g2 ♘f8 27 ♖xg4 ♕e7 28 a5 ♗a7 29 ♖f3 ♔g8 30 ♖h3 ♕e8 31 ♖gh4 ♖fc7 32 f5! (D)

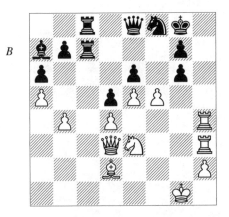

32...♔f7 33 ♖h8 ♕b5 34 fxg6+ ♔e7 35 ♖f3 ♖c1+ 36 ♔g2 1-0

Van Wely – Shirov
Wijk aan Zee 2004

11 ♗d3 h6 (D)

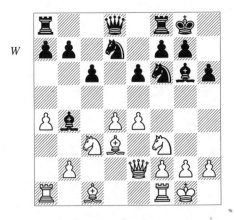

For a while this was the main line, eliminating ♘g5 and ♗g5 ideas.

12 ♖d1

The wonderful attacking game Christiansen-Sher, Wiesbaden 1994 illustrates how deceptive this quiet position can be: 12 ♗f4 ♖e8 13 h3 a6?! 14 ♖fd1 ♕b6? (after two passive moves Black already has to submit to a terrific attack) 15 e5 ♘d5 16 ♘xd5 cxd5 17 ♘h4! ♕xd4 (Christiansen offers the line 17...♗xd3 18 ♖xd3

g5 19 ♕h5 gxf4 20 ♕xh6, winning) 18 ♘xg6 fxg6 19 ♗g3! ♕b6 20 ♗xg6 ♖ec8 21 ♔h2 ♘f8 22 ♗d3 ♖c7 23 f4! g6 24 a5! ♕c6 (24...♗xa5?! 25 ♗f2 ♕b4? is disastrous: 26 ♗e1 ♕xf4+ 27 g3) 25 ♗f2 ♕e8 26 g4 ♖c6 27 ♖f1 ♗c5 28 ♗xc5 (or 28 ♗g3; White has too many forces on the kingside) 28...♖xc5 29 f5 exf5 30 gxf5 d4 31 fxg6 (or 31 ♗c4+ ♔h8 32 ♖ae1) 31...♖xe5? (Black would last longer after 31...♕xe5+ 32 ♕xe5 ♖xe5 33 ♖f7 ♖c8 34 ♖xb7) 32 ♗c4+ ♔g7 33 ♖f7+ ♕xf7 34 ♕xe5+ ♕f6 35 ♕c7+ ♔h8 36 ♖f1 ♕g7 37 ♖f7 1-0.

12...♕e7

12...♖e8 is also played here, to enforce ...e5 if possible.

13 h3 e5?!

This may be premature, at least in practical terms. The overall impression is that Black should have no serious difficulties in this variation, but soon after this move he's scrambling.

14 dxe5 ♘xe5 15 ♘xe5 ♕xe5 16 f4

White's exchanges were based upon preparing the advance of his kingside majority. In many openings this requires immediate action by Black before the pawns run him over.

16...♕a5!? 17 f5 ♗h7 (D)

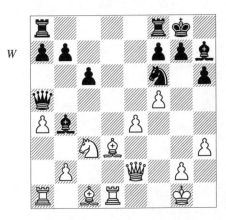

Now White has weaknesses (see his backward e-pawn, for one), but he's counting upon the miserable status of the bishop on h7. We're at the end of the opening and it looks like Black has more difficulties than his opponent.

18 ♗f4 ♖fe8 19 ♕f3!?

White sacrifices a pawn to get the attack rolling.

19...♗xc3 20 bxc3 ♕xc3 21 ♖ac1 ♕d4+

This is the picture that White is hoping for when he expands on the kingside. As Sherbakov points out, even though there's nominal material equality, the position of the bishop on h7 in some variations means that Black will effectively be playing a rook down.

22 ♔h2 ♕xa4 23 e5 ♘d5 24 ♖c4 ♕b3 25 ♖b1 ♕a3! (D)

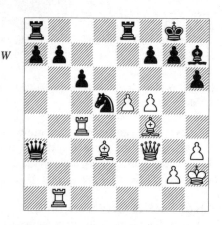

Otherwise f6 will be terribly strong. Shirov's legendary resourcefulness begins to show itself.

26 ♖xb7 ♘xf4 27 ♖xf4 ♖xe5

Scherbakov gives the line 27...♕c3? 28 e6! ♖f8 (28...fxe6 29 f6!) 29 ♖xf7 ♖xf7 30 exf7+ ♔f8 31 ♕e3! ♖d8 32 ♖e4! ♕f6 33 ♖e8+ ♔xf7 34 ♗c4+.

28 ♕g3 ♕d6 29 ♗c4 ♖xf5! 30 ♖xf5 ♕xg3+ 31 ♔xg3 ♗xf5 32 ♖xf7 (D)

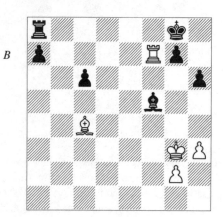

32...♗d3! 33 ♖xa7+ ♗xc4 34 ♖xa8+ ♔f7 35 ♔f4 ♔f6

and the players went on to draw. White cannot break through.

The same position sometimes arises if Black defers ...0-0, but he gains one major option.

1 d4 d5 2 c4 c6 3 ♘f3 ♘f6 4 ♘c3 dxc4 5 a4 ♗f5 6 e3 e6 7 ♗xc4 ♗b4 8 0-0 ♘bd7 9 ♕e2 ♗g6 10 e4 (D)

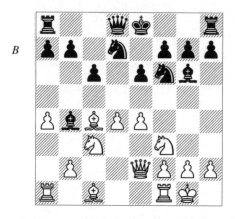

White leaves the e-pawn *en prise*, a sacrifice that has been played in a number of famous games. Accepting the gambit hasn't been popular for some time; however, that may be due more to the practical defensive difficulties than any actual advantage for White. In the following game Black holds his own and then outplays White in a back-and-forth contest.

Gligorić – Beliavsky
Belgrade 1987

10...♗xc3 11 bxc3 ♘xe4 12 ♗a3 (D)

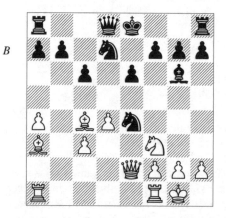

By now it should be easy to see what White is up to: the bishop-pair will serve as compensation for the centre pawn. Preventing Black from castling is important; if he had played an order with ...0-0 earlier, this sacrifice would be unsound.

12...♕c7 *(D)*

Black intends to castle queenside. At first, 12...♘xc3?! 13 ♕b2 ♘xa4 14 ♕xb7 ♘ab6 looks good. However, 15 ♘d2 ♕c8 16 ♗a6 ♖b8 17 ♕xc8+ ♘xc8 18 ♖fc1 leaves Black in a fix; e.g., 18...♘e7 19 ♘c4 ♖b3 20 ♘a5!? ♖b6 21 ♗f1! ♔d8 22 f3! (versus ...♗e4) 22...a6 23 ♗d6, etc.

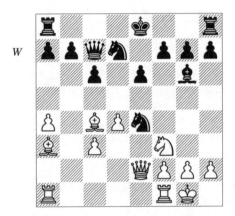

13 ♖fc1

Another try is 13 ♘d2!? ♘xd2 (these positions are extremely difficult to handle when the attacker has two bishops; 13...♘d6? would be a mistake due to 14 ♗xe6 and after 13...♘xc3? 14 ♕e3! ♘d5 15 ♗xd5 cxd5 16 ♖fc1, Black is two pawns ahead, but totally tied up) 14 ♕xd2 0-0-0 15 ♗e7! ♖de8 16 ♗h4 f6 17 a5! ♖hf8 18 ♗g3 e5 19 f4! with a strong attack, Razuvaev-Levitt, Reykjavik 1990.

13...0-0-0 14 a5 ♖he8 15 ♕b2! ♔b8 16 ♖cb1 ♔a8 17 ♗f1! *(D)*

White stays calm, confident in his bishops. He intends g3 and ♗g2 followed by a6, so Black moves quickly to disturb the central balance.

17...e5 18 ♖e1 ♘ef6 19 ♘d2 exd4 20 ♖xe8 ♖xe8 21 cxd4 ♘d5 22 ♘c4 ♗e6 23 g3 ♗e4!

Preventing ♗g2; otherwise things are falling apart. Black plays well throughout this game.

24 ♕d2 f5 25 ♖e1 ♘5f6 26 ♖a1

26 ♕g5! g6 27 ♕h6 intending ♕g7 was suggested.

26...♗d5 27 ♗c1 ♗xc4 28 ♗xc4 ♘d5!? 29 ♕c2 ♖e1+ 30 ♔g2 ♘7f6 31 ♕xf5 ♕d8 32 ♕g5

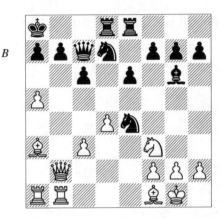

♕e7 33 ♗d3 ♘b4 34 ♕f5 ♕e8 35 ♗f1 ♘bd5 36 ♗b2 ♖xa1 37 ♗xa1 g6

At this stage the bishops don't look so great, especially the one on a1. Black's grip on d5 may be enough, although g4-g5 is a theme.

38 ♕e5 ♕d8 39 a6 b5?! *(D)*

39...bxa6! is probably better. The king will sit safely on b7, and I see no problems for Black.

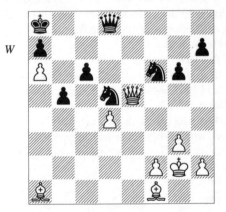

40 ♗e2?

The turning point of the game. 40 ♗b2! intends 40...♕a5?! 41 ♗c1 ♕xa6 42 ♗g5 ♘d7 43 ♕h8+ ♘b8 44 ♕xh7, etc.

40...♕c8! 41 ♗b2 ♕xa6 42 ♗c1

Too late.

42...♕b7 43 ♗g5 ♕f7

Everything is secured and there's no reason why the two passed pawns on the queenside shouldn't win.

44 ♗f3 ♔b7 45 ♔f1 a5 46 ♗d2 a4 47 ♗f4 ♕c7 48 ♕e2 ♕e7 49 ♗e5 a3 50 ♔g2 ♕e6 51 ♔g1 ♘c3 52 ♕d3 ♕c4 53 ♕d2 a2 54 ♕b2 ♘fd5 55 ♔g2 ♕b4 0-1

Modern Line with 6 ♘e5

1 d4 d5 2 c4 c6 3 ♘f3 ♘f6 4 ♘c3 dxc4 5 a4 ♗f5 6 ♘e5 *(D)*

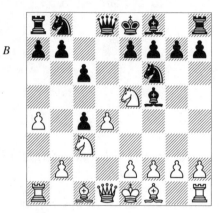

This main move is a strange one in many ways, since White is taking two extra moves to capture the pawn on c4. But he also opens up the possibility of f3 followed by e4, when Black's bishop would be blocked off after ...♗g6 but has nowhere else to go. Needless to say, this calls for action.

6...♘bd7

These days this is the most popular move. Black is loath to go into the complications that follow 6...e6 7 f3 ♗b4 8 e4 ♗xe4! (8...♗g6 9 ♗xc4 is everything that White wants) 9 fxe4 ♘xe4, when White's normal winning try is 10 ♗d2. 10 ♖a3!?? *(D)* is amazing but hard to believe.

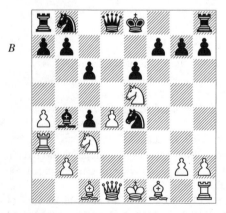

Then the highly entertaining game R.Janssen-E.Oostarom, Bussum 2001 went 10...♕h4+

11 g3 ♘xg3 12 hxg3 ♕xh1 13 ♕g4 ♘a6 14 ♖a1 0-0 15 ♔f2 f5 16 ♕e2 f4 17 ♗xf4 c5 18 ♕g4 cxd4?, and instead of 19 ♗xc4? he had the beautiful combination 19 ♕xe6+ ♔h8 *(D)*.

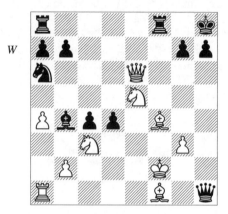

20 ♕g8+!! ♔xg8 21 ♗xc4+ ♔h8 22 ♘g6+ hxg6 23 ♖xh1#. I couldn't resist showing this although, sadly, the odds of 10 ♖a3 working are poor.

Returning to the (relatively) sane 10 ♗d2, the main line continues 10...♕xd4 11 ♘xe4 ♕xe4+ 12 ♕e2 ♗xd2+ 13 ♔xd2 ♕d5+ 14 ♔c2 *(D)*.

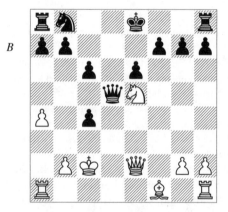

This is the starting point for truckloads of theory. White will usually recover the c-pawn and the game will move into an endgame with a piece versus three pawns. The resulting variations are engrossing and will repay study. Nevertheless, their theory is worked out to an exceptional depth; reluctantly, I'll refer those who are interested to specialized books and databases.

7 ♘xc4 *(D)*

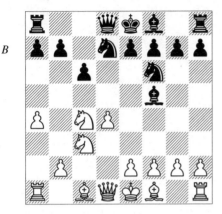

7...♕c7

This is really the most logical move, preparing ...e5. Otherwise f3 and e4 will again pose difficulties. A lesser option is 7...♘b6, intending 8 ♘e5 e6 (8...♘bd7 9 ♕b3!) 9 f3 ♘fd7. We won't go into that one, for which recent games are the best resource. Even Morozevich's 7...♘d5!? can be played, when 8 f3 is most interesting, or 8 ♗g5 (8...h6?? 9 ♘d6+!).

8 g3!

8 f3 now gives Black time for 8...e5 9 e4 exd4 10 ♕xd4 ♗e6 with a game that's easy to play.

8...e5 9 dxe5 ♘xe5 10 ♗f4 ♘fd7

10...♖d8 11 ♕c1 has been considered favourable for White going back to the earliest days of this variation. The point is that White has ♕e3 as an idea, so Black has to play 11...♗d6 12 ♘xd6+ ♕xd6, when White gets the two bishops, and after 13 ♗g2 he stands somewhat better.

11 ♗g2 *(D)*

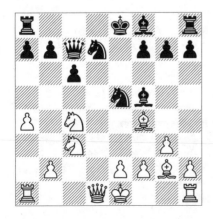

This position has been a fruitful source of strategic chess ideas, with the opponents competing for superiority in terms of activity, outposts, bishop-pairs, weaknesses, space, and king safety. Tactics are as always critical, but you will find that, even more than is usual in openings, the tactical and combinative elements flow from superior play in the positional and strategic realms. The play now divides into two paths.

The Established Move

11...f6 *(D)*

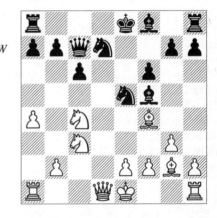

This is the obvious and traditional line. Black simply defends everything. The only problem is that White can get a space advantage on the queenside and along with other projects he may attempt to break down Black's structure on that wing.

Anand – Morozevich
Wijk aan Zee 2000

12 0-0 ♘c5

This is the contemporary favourite, introduced by Morozevich, who won 4½ of 5 points with it!

Going way back to the 1937 World Championship, Alekhine was dissuaded from 12...♖d8 after 13 ♕c1 ♗e6 14 ♘e4! ♗b4 15 a5 0-0 16 a6! *(D)*.

Here we have a common theme in any opening where a bishop is stationed on g2: White is concerned with weakening the base of the pawns on the long h1-a8 diagonal. The game continued

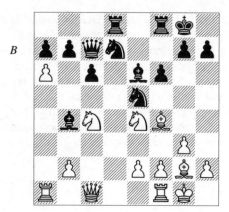

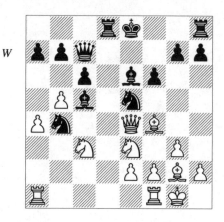

16...bxa6? (16...b6 17 ♕c2! "would hold Black under constant pressure" according to Kasparov) 17 ♘xe5 ♘xe5 18 ♘c5 ♗xc5 19 ♕xc5 g5? (Kasparov suggests 19...♕b6) 20 ♗e3 ♗d5 21 ♖xa6 ♗xg2 22 ♔xg2 ♖f7 23 ♖fa1 ♕d6 24 ♕xd6 ♖xd6 25 ♖xa7 ♖xa7 26 ♖xa7 ♘c4 27 ♗c5 ♖e6 28 ♗d4 ♖xe2 29 ♗xf6, Euwe-Alekhine, The Hague Wch (1) 1937. With an extra pawn and bishop versus knight, Euwe was able to win fairly easily.

We now return to 12...♘c5 (D):

13 ♘e3!

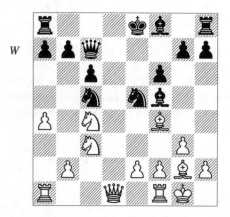

Certainly logical, since White aims at the weakened f5. In any event, Morozevich won games (as Black) that continued 13 ♘xe5 fxe5 14 ♗g5 a5!, and 13 e4 ♗g6 14 ♗xe5? fxe5 15 f4 ♖d8!.

13...♗e6

The idea behind 13 ♘e3 is 13...♖d8 14 ♘cd5!.

14 b4 ♖d8 15 ♕c2 ♘a6 16 b5 ♘b4! 17 ♕e4 ♗c5 (D)

18 ♖ad1

18 bxc6!? bxc6 19 ♖ac1 (this combination of moves logically targets Black's c-pawn, although Black's pieces are quite active; later Rogozenko came up with 19 ♘c4, but then 19...♗d4! is equal – you can see what a benefit all Black's centralized pieces are!) 19...0-0 20 ♘c4 ♖d4! (20...♗xc4 21 ♕xc4+ ♘xc4 22 ♗xc7 ♖d7 23 ♗f4 with the usual two-bishop advantage and Black's c-file pieces are problematic) 21 ♗xe5 ♖xe4 22 ♗xc7 ♖xc4 23 ♘e4 ♗e7 with equality, Gershon-Postny, Tel Aviv 2000.

18...0-0 19 ♘c4! (D)

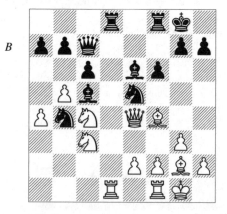

Without pressure on the c-pawn, White has to seek play elsewhere. This exchange sacrifice for a pawn at least mixes things up and gives enough compensation.

19...♖xd1 20 ♖xd1 ♗d5 21 ♘xd5 cxd5 22 ♖xd5 ♘xd5 23 ♕xd5+ ♔h8

After 23...♖f7 White plays 24 e3! and captures on e5 follow.

24 e3

Black threatened 24...♗xf2+ and ...♕xc4.

24...♖d8 25 ♗xe5 fxe5 26 ♕e4 ♖d1+!?

The rook gets exposed here. 26...♗d6! holds on to Black's material until he reorganizes; for example, 27 a5 b6 28 axb6 axb6 29 ♕d5 ♗c5! with equality.

27 ♗f1 ♗e7 28 ♔g2 (D)

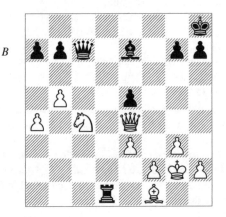

28...♕d7!?

28...♗f6 allows 29 ♗d3 g6 30 ♕f3! ♖xd3 31 ♕xf6+ ♔g8 32 ♘xe5, although 32...♖d6 isn't so bad.

29 ♘a5

29 ♘xe5! ♕d5 30 ♕xd5 ♖xd5 31 ♘f7+ ♔g8 32 ♗c4 ♖c5 33 ♘e5+ ♔h8 34 f4 g5 35 ♔f3 seems to favour White, again not by much.

29...♕d5!?

Or 29...♕c7 30 ♕xb7 ♕xb7+ 31 ♘xb7 ♖a1 32 a5 ♖b1.

30 ♕xd5 ♖xd5 31 ♘xb7 ♖d7 32 ♘a5 e4!

This pawn ties White's pawns and king down. The rest proceeds logically.

33 ♘b3 g6 34 a5 ♗b4 35 ♗c4 ♔g7 36 b6 axb6 37 ♗b5 ½-½

Morozevich's Variation

11...g5!? (D)

This was a shocking move when Morozevich offered it up for refutation, but we are still waiting for its demise. Although 11...f6 seems to equalize (or very close to it), it is rather passive. Instead, 11...g5 diverts the dangerous bishop from f4 and tries to force a clarification in the centre. In most variations this speeds up Black's development. From an outsider's point of view, the games in this line have been particularly

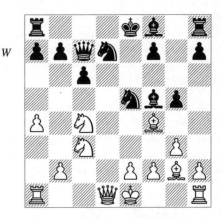

engaging because of White's ever-changing attempts to punish such a reckless advance. The resulting contest tends to revolve around White's attempt to exploit Black's kingside weaknesses and Black's active play in the centre and on the kingside. We'll look at some lines and games with 12 ♘e3, 12 ♘xe5 and 12 ♗xe5.

12 ♘e3 gxf4 13 ♘xf5

This knight is a superb piece, whose influence will be felt in all aspects of the game.

13...0-0-0 14 ♕c2 (D)

14 gxf4 ♘c5! 15 ♕c2 and now 15...♘c4! grants Black active play. Instead, 15...♘g6 16 e3 ♘d3+ 17 ♔f1 is messy.

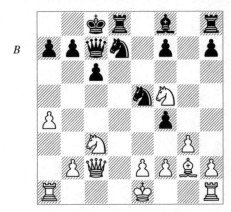

Here is a key position that began the whole ...g5 rage and is still unresolved.

Kasparov – Morozevich
Wijk aan Zee 2000

This seminal game illustrates many of the key ideas.

14...♘g4

A logical move which went out of favour once it appeared that Black's kingside pressure wasn't quite enough. Hübner's suggestion 14...♗b4 hasn't caught on.

15 a5!? fxg3

15...♗c5 16 0-0 fxg3 17 hxg3 threatens ♘e4, and 17...♗xf2+ 18 ♖xf2 ♘xf2 19 ♔xf2 ♘e5 20 ♔e1! or 20 a6 fails for Black because the knight on f5 covers everything.

16 hxg3 a6 17 ♖a4! ♘df6 18 ♘e4 (D)

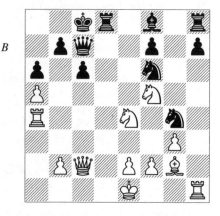

18...♘xe4?!

Kasparov suggested 18...♘d5 19 ♘c5 with some advantage. Even then White's knights are superbly placed and Black's f- and h-pawns are weak.

19 ♗xe4 h5 20 ♔f1! ♔b8 21 ♔g2 ♗e7 (D)

Perhaps 21...♘e5 improves.

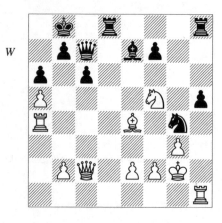

22 ♘xe7!

You have to know when to give up a good piece for a bad one! Normally it's done so as to assist the win of material or the last stages of an attack. Here Kasparov does it for purely practical reasons: without exchanging Black's bishop it might participate actively (opposite-coloured bishops help the attack, remember). White has plenty of other good pieces with which to work.

22...♕xe7 23 ♗f3 ♘e5

23...♕e6 24 ♕c5 hits the weak pawn on h5, and 24...f5 25 ♖b4 ♘e5 26 ♕b6 ♕e7 27 ♗xh5 wins it.

24 ♗xh5 ♕e6 25 ♕c3 f6 26 ♖ah4 ♕f5 27 ♗f3 ♖xh4 28 ♖xh4 ♕b1 29 ♖h1 ♖d1 30 ♖xd1 ♕xd1 31 b4

We're getting familiar with bishop versus knight and an extra pawn, and so I'll take my leave.

31...♔c7 32 ♕c5 ♕d6 33 ♕xd6+ ♔xd6 34 ♗e4 ♘c4 35 ♗d3 ♘b2 36 f4 ♘d1 37 g4 ♘e3+ 38 ♔f3 ♘d5 39 ♔e4 ♘xb4 40 ♗c4 c5 41 g5 fxg5 42 fxg5 ♔e7 43 ♔f5 ♘c2 44 ♔e5 ♘e3 45 ♗e6 c4 1-0

White wins the race after 46 g6 c3 47 g7 c2 48 g8♕ c1♕ 49 ♕f7+ ♔d8 50 ♕d7#.

L. Johannessen – Shirov
Bundesliga 2004/5

14...♘c5 (D)

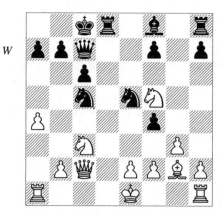

The contemporary move. Black turns his attention to the centre before dreaming about the kingside. One immediate idea is ...f3.

15 0-0 ♘e6!?

Later on Black took another and probably better course by keeping the knight active on c5: 15...fxg3! 16 hxg3 a5 17 ♖fd1 h5! 18 ♖xd8+

♕xd8 19 ♖d1 ♕f6 20 e4 h4 (20...♘g6 21 f4 h4 is easier, transposing) 21 f4 (21 ♘xh4 ♖xh4! is very complicated) 21...♘g6 22 e5 ♕e6 with a good game, Ivanchuk-Gelfand, Russian Cht (Sochi) 2005; 23 ♘d6+? ♗xd6 24 ♖xd6 ♕c4 followed, when Black had much the better game. Gelfand's treatment is consistent with the idea that active play is necessary to compensate for Black's kingside weaknesses.

16 ♕e4!?

A good move, but not the only one; on the downside, it uses up the e4-square. White has also played 16 a5 and 16 ♖ad1, with the same basic idea: White's knights are superior to Black's, and therefore Black's bishop has no square to go to without being vulnerable. On top of that, Black's h- and f-pawns are isolated. These factors only provide White with a moderate advantage, to be sure, but the position isn't easy for Black to play.

16...fxg3 17 hxg3 *(D)*

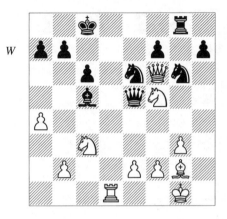

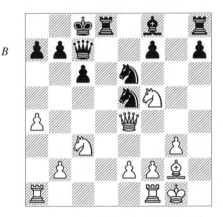

17...a5

Black holds up two of White's good moves, a5 and b4. But it turns out to be slow, and even weakening. Ftačnik-Sundararajan, Pardubice 2004 continued with the better 17...♖g8 (more active than 17...a5; still, Black has nagging positional problems) 18 ♖ad1 ♖xd1 19 ♖xd1 ♗c5 20 ♕h4 ♘g6 (Black goes tactical – what else?) 21 ♕f6 (not 21 ♕xh7?? ♖h8, but 21 ♕h5! would prepare e3 and ♘e4, and after 21...♘ef4 22 ♕h6 ♘xg2 23 ♔xg2, the knights are very strong) 21...♕e5!? *(D)*.

22 ♕xf7? (White shouldn't be afraid of simplification; after the superior 22 ♘e4! ♕xf6 23 ♘xf6 ♖d8 24 ♖xd8+ ♔xd8 25 ♘xh7 Black

will find it hard to recover his pawn without losing another) 22...♖f8! 23 ♕d7+ ♔b8 (all at once White has to defend) 24 e4 ♘e7! 25 ♕d3!? ♘xf5 26 exf5 ♖xf5 27 ♘e4 ♕xb2 28 ♖d2 ♕a1+ 29 ♖d1 ♕b2 30 ♖d2 ♕a1+ 31 ♖d1 ½-½.

18 ♘b5! *(D)*

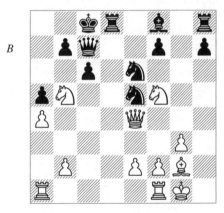

This time it's Black's queenside that comes under attack (a consequence of playing 17...a5). Whether or not the earlier play actually established an advantage for White, one can't be happy with Black's position.

18...cxb5 19 axb5 ♘c5!?

19...♘d7? 20 ♖xa5! and ♖fa1 is too much for Black's position to bear, but Scherbakov's 19...b6! is a brilliant defensive try. Black realizes that the attack via ♖xa5 is even worse than that along the diagonal. Still, one feels that he will have a difficult time gaining full equality against 20 f4 ♗c5+ 21 e3.

20 ♕e3 ♘g4 21 ♕c3 ♕e5

White was attacking a5 and h8.

22 ♕f3! *(D)*

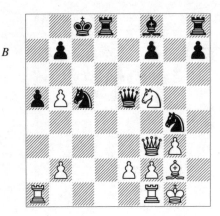

Always hold on to f5! Faced with many threats, Black returns the piece.

22...♕e4 23 ♕xe4 ♘xe4 24 ♗xe4

So the whole game came back to the weakness created by ...g5. Now Johannessen has a substantial advantage but fails to bring home the point, perhaps because he is playing against one of the world's top defenders. We'll just look at the moves. Needless to say, White had improvements:

24...♗b4 25 ♖fd1 ♔c7 26 ♔g2 ♔b6 27 ♖ac1 h5 28 e3 ♘e5 29 ♗d5 ♖d7 30 f4 ♖hd8 31 e4 ♘g4 32 ♔f3 ♗xb5 33 ♘e3 ♘xe3 34 ♔xe3 ½-½

Here 34...f5! would just about equalize.

Kramnik – Morozevich
Monaco (Amber rapid) 2002

12 ♘xe5!? (D)

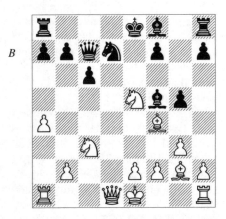

Since Black's resources may be sufficient after 12 ♘e3 (see especially the note about

15...fxg3! in the previous game), White has also tried this simple move.

12...gxf4 13 ♘xd7 0-0-0!?

It's going to be two bishops for a pawn again! 13...♗xd7 has been played in several games and seems to equalize. Also of interest would be 13...♕xd7, which in principle is the same idea as 13...0-0-0. However, the queen recapture is less risky since Black's bishops benefit from simplification and White's knight is restricted.

14 ♕d4 (D)

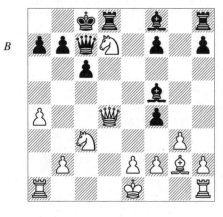

14...♕xd7!

Now this sacrifice is forced because of the threat to a7.

15 ♕xf4

15 ♕xh8?! ♕d2+ 16 ♔f1 ♕xb2 17 ♖e1 ♗b4 isn't worth playing around with.

15...♗d6 (D)

Black sacrificed a pawn but has obtained reasonable compensation thanks to the strong bishops and the lead in development.

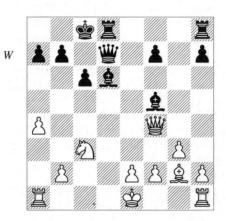

16 ♕c1

I'm sure that Kramnik is happy with his extra pawn, but Morozevich has some dynamic chances. Jobava-Khalifman, Bled OL 2002 seems to have a philosophy similar to that expressed in my description of 13...♕d7. It continued 16 ♕h6 ♔b8 17 0-0 ♕e6! 18 ♕xe6 ♗xe6 and the exchange of queens had helped Black. Khalifman had no problems equalizing and went on to win.

16...a5

Perhaps 16...h5!? 17 a5 a6 was worth trying.

17 0-0 ♗e5? *(D)*

Scherbakov prefers 17...♔b8!. The idea is to challenge White to find a way to his king while pursuing an attack against White's.

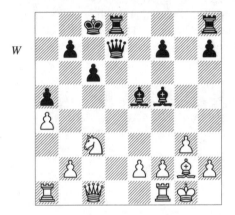

18 ♘b5!

White threatens ♕c5 and ♘a7+ followed by ♘xc6. It's already impossible to defend without conceding something else.

18...♕e7?

Not 18...♔b8? 19 ♕c5! cxb5 20 ♕xe5+ ♔a8 21 axb5; but 18...♗b8 would hold on for a while.

19 ♘a7+ ♔b8 20 ♘xc6+! bxc6 21 ♕xc6

Here White's attack is too strong, especially with more pawns to add to the three already captured. He won shortly.

Jobava – Carlsen
Warsaw Ech 2005

12 ♗xe5

In a manner typical of chess theory, we find White returning recently to a move originally condemned as harmless at best.

12...♘xe5 13 ♕d4 f6 14 0-0-0 *(D)*

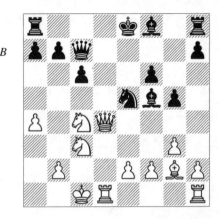

The starting position for many recent battles, in part because 11...g5 has successfully met other challenges.

14...♗e6

a) Jobava beat the 2700+ star Grishchuk (Calvia OL 2004) following 14...♗e7?! 15 ♘e3! ♗e6 16 ♕e4! (again, f5 is the square to remember! If you command that, you're halfway home) 16...♗b3 17 ♖d2 0-0 18 h4 gxh4 19 ♕xh4 ♖f7 20 ♘f5! *(D)*.

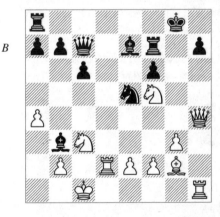

There you have it. The game concluded rapidly: 20...♔h8 21 ♗e4 ♖af8 22 f4 ♘c4 23 ♘g7! ♖xg7 24 ♗xh7 f5 25 ♕h5 ♗h4 26 ♗xf5+ 1-0.

b) 14...♘xc4 15 ♕xc4 ♗d6 is quite reasonable for Black. Then 16 h4 followed by e4 may be very slightly better for White; that remains to be demonstrated over the board.

15 f4 gxf4 16 gxf4 ♘xc4 17 ♕xf6

This time White snatches the material. We'll skip over the next few theoretical moves.

17...♗f7 18 ♕xh8 ♕xf4+ 19 ♔b1 ♗g6+ 20 ♔a1! ♘e3

This is virtually forced in view of a rook coming to f1.

21 ♖d2!? (D)

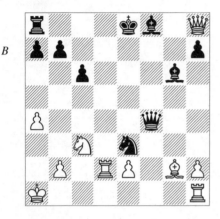

21...♘c2+?

White was greedy and now Black should be: 21...♘xg2! was analysed by Scherbakov in great detail, concluding that after 22 ♖d4! ♕f5! 23 ♘e4 ♔e7! 24 ♖hd1 ♘e3 25 ♖d7+ ♔e6! 26 ♕g8+ ♔e5 27 ♕h8+, the game could be drawn by repetition, but Black could also get ambitious and try 27...♔f4!?. As he points out, there's a good chance that White (or Black?) can improve!

22 ♖xc2 ♗xc2 23 ♖f1 ♕d6 24 ♗e4! ♗b3 (D)

24...♗xe4? is clearly hopeless after 25 ♘xe4.

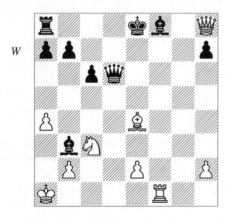

25 ♘b5!

It's typical of these high-theory battles that once the players are truly past their analysis there are wonderful moves still to come.

25...cxb5 26 ♗xb7 ♖b8 27 ♗c6+! ♔d8 28 ♕xf8+ ♔c7 29 ♕g7+! ♔xc6 30 ♕c3+ ♔b6

30...♗c4? 31 ♖f6.

31 ♕xb3

All that White got out of his spectacular play was a pawn! But he still has threats. The game concluded:

31...♔a5 32 ♕c3+ ♔b4 33 ♕c7+! ♖b6 34 ♕xa7+ ♖a6 35 ♕c7+ ♖b6 36 ♖f4! ♕b3 37 ♕a7+ ♖a6 38 ♕c5 ♖g6 39 axb5 1-0

Exchange Slav

1 d4 d5 2 c4 c6 3 cxd5

3 ♘c3 ♘f6 4 cxd5 cxd5 is another way to reach an Exchange Slav (see 3 ♘c3 in the general introduction to this chapter, which allows options like 3...dxc4). Then 5 ♗f4 has conventional answers such as 5...♘c6, but an unusual one is 5...♕b6!? (D).

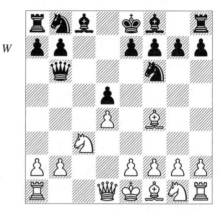

Black's idea is 6 e3!? (6 ♖c1 ♗d7 threatens ...♕xb2 and ends in some sort of equality – check theory, or you can wing this one) 6...♕xb2 7 ♖c1 e5! 8 ♘xd5!? (8 dxe5 ♗b4 9 ♘e2 ♘e4) 8...♗d7!. It all seems to work out.

3...cxd5 (D)

The Exchange Variation has traditionally been a slight disincentive to the Slav Defence and over the years some big names used it effectively as White. One basic idea is that White no longer has to worry about ...dxc4. These days Black has enough ways to defuse the resulting positions that it's not as much of a problem. Since the heavy pieces may be exchanged on the open c-file there can be drawish tendencies,

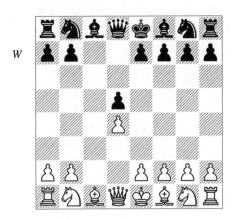

which might be upsetting to either party, or it might be their intended result. However, you'll find that if they want to, one or both players can muddy the waters enough to get to a legitimate middlegame without undue risk. I include a brief description of the Exchange Variation in this volume because we have few representatives of symmetrical opening play and because some typical Slav ideas arise.

4 ♘c3

Unfortunately, there are any number of move-orders, so in the interests of brevity I'll just show a couple of the common resulting positions. Obviously 4 ♘f3 might have distinctive effects, possibly leading to something such as 4...♘f6 5 ♗f4 a6!?, but generally we get transpositions.

4...♘c6 *(D)*

4...♘f6 transposes to 3 ♘c3 ♘f6 4 cxd5 cxd5 above.

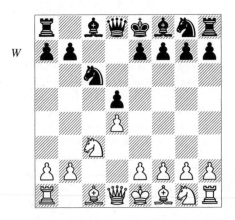

The position after 4...♘c6 is the takeoff point for our games.

Yusupov – Beliavsky
USSR Ch (Minsk) 1979

5 ♗f4 ♗f5

5...♘f6 6 e3 a6!? looks like a good version of the ...a6 move, because Black keeps options open for his c8-bishop; e.g., 7 ♗e2 (a clever move designed to prevent ...♗g4; instead 7 ♗d3 ♗g4! 8 f3 ♗h5 9 ♘ge2 e6 10 ♘g3 ♗g6 is equal) 7...♘e4 (or 7...♗f5) 8 ♘xe4 dxe4 9 f3 e5! *(D)*.

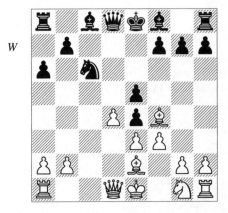

10 dxe5 ♕a5+ 11 ♔f2 ♗e6! 12 ♕c2! (12 fxe4 ♖d8 13 ♕c1 h6!; forget those horrid pawns, Black will gain e5; e.g., 14 ♘f3 g5 15 ♗g3 ♗g7 16 ♖d1 ♖xd1 17 ♕xd1 0-0 18 ♔g1 ♖d8 19 ♕c2 g4!) 12...♖d8! 13 ♕xe4 ♖d2 with equality, Azmaiparashvili-Anand, Las Palmas 1993. Black's handling of the opening was exemplary.

6 ♘f3

6 e3 ♘f6 7 ♗b5 e6 8 ♕a4 can be met surprisingly by 8...♕b6! 9 ♘f3 ♗e7! 10 ♘e5 0-0 11 ♗xc6 ♖fc8! (11...♕xb2 12 0-0!) 12 ♗b5 a6 13 0-0 axb5 14 ♕xb5 ♕xb5 15 ♘xb5 ♖c2 and Black is already ahead, Vera-Hector, Istanbul OL 2000.

6...e6 7 e3 ♘f6 8 ♗b5 ♘d7 *(D)*

This is Black's favourite place to break the symmetry, and the most important move to remember. He unpins the c6-knight and is thus in a better position to answer the typical moves ♘e5 and ♕a4.

9 ♕a4 ♕b6

Another idea is 9...♖c8 10 0-0 (10 ♗xc6! ♖xc6 11 ♕xa7! is the only chance for advantage: 11...♖b6?! 12 0-0 ♖xb2 13 ♖fc1! and

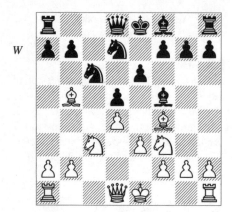

W

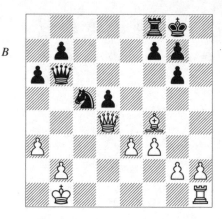

B

♘a4 and ♘d1 are threats) 10...a6 11 ♗xc6 ♖xc6 12 ♖fc1, Ki.Georgiev-Khalifman, Plovdiv 1986; now 12...♕b6! equalizes.

10 ♘h4 ♗e4 11 0-0-0! (D)

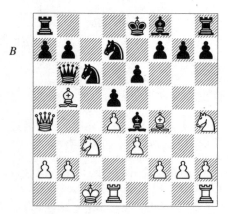

B

An unusual move in the Slav, indicative of how the play can heat up. Now that d4 is protected, f3 and e4 ideas will work better.

11...♖c8

11...♗e7 12 f3 ♗g6 13 ♘xg6 hxg6 14 e4 gave White an obvious advantage in Naumkin-Tan, Formia 1994.

12 f3 ♗g6 13 ♘xg6 hxg6 14 ♔b1 a6 15 ♗d3 ♗b4! 16 ♖c1 0-0 17 a3 ♗xc3 18 ♖xc3 e5! 19 dxe5 ♘cxe5 20 ♕c2 ♖xc3 21 ♕xc3 ♘xd3 22 ♕xd3 ♘c5 23 ♕d4 (D)

At first sight White has a theoretical edge because of the IQP and threats like ♖c1. On the other hand White's bishop is of the wrong colour.

23...g5!

This clears g6 for a check by Black's queen and thus gets out of the pin.

24 ♗e5 ♖d8 25 ♖c1 ♕g6+ 26 ♔a2 ♘e6 27 ♕b6 ♖d7 28 ♖c8+ ♔h7 29 g4 ♕d3 30 f4 ♕e4 31 ♕b3 ♖d8 ½-½

The alternative was 31...gxf4 32 exf4 ♘xf4 33 ♗xf4 ♕xf4 34 ♕d3+! ♕e4 35 ♕h3+ ♔g6 36 ♕h5+ ♔f6 37 ♕h4+ ♔g6 38 ♕h5+ with a draw.

1 d4 d5 2 c4 c6 3 cxd5 cxd5 4 ♘c3 ♘c6 5 ♘f3 ♘f6 6 ♗f4 a6!? (D)

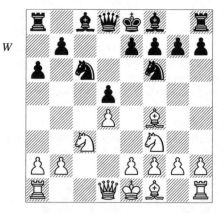

W

The move ...a6 is customary in contemporary Slav play; it can arise by means of 1 d4 d5 2 c4 c6 3 ♘f3 ♘f6 4 ♘c3 a6, for example. Black avoids all the many lines in which White plays ♗b5. An important benefit of the ...a6 systems is that if Black now moves his c8-bishop to f5 or g4, he can more easily answer White's ♕b3 by either ...b5 or even ...♖a7 (...♘a5 can also be more effective under some circumstances). Of course ...a6 also uses up an important tempo for development, a fact which White will try to exploit. We'll look at two games after 6...a6.

Kamsky – Short
Linares 1994

7 ♘e5 e6

Here the unconventional 7...♕b6! 8 ♘xc6 bxc6 9 ♕d2 ♘h5! looks equal.

8 e3 ♗d6!? *(D)*

8...♘xe5 9 ♗xe5 ♗e7 10 ♗d3! 0-0 11 0-0 ♗d7 12 ♕c2! h6 13 f3 gives White an edge; a future e4 can cause trouble.

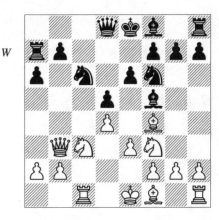

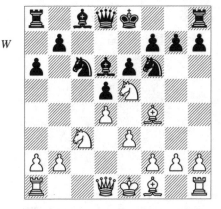

9 ♗g3

9 ♘xc6 bxc6 10 ♗xd6 ♕xd6 looks great at first (open file versus a backward pawn with the dark-square defender missing), but Black has the moves ...♖b8 and ...e5 at the ready, and even a well-timed ...c5 might rid him of weaknesses.

9...♗xe5 10 dxe5 ♘d7 11 f4 0-0 12 ♗e2 b5 13 ♖c1 ♗b7 14 0-0 ♖c8 15 ♗d3 ♕e7 16 ♗b1 ♖fe8 17 ♕c2 g6 18 ♕f2 f5 19 exf6 ♘xf6 20 ♗h4 ♕g7

With mutual weaknesses the game is probably about equal; it was eventually drawn.

Illescas – Topalov
Dos Hermanas 1999

7 ♖c1 ♗f5 8 e3 e6 9 ♕b3 ♖a7!? *(D)*

This strange-looking rook move has become a standard idea in the ...a6 lines! Black condemns his rook to temporary passivity to avoid making other concessions and to develop quickly.

10 ♘e5 ♗e7 11 ♘xc6 bxc6 12 ♗e2 ♘d7!

Now ...c5 is unstoppable.

13 0-0 c5 14 ♕a4 ♕b6?

Failing to see the tactics or to assess them correctly. 14...0-0 15 dxc5 ♘xc5 16 ♕d4 ♖b7! was equal.

15 dxc5 ♗xc5 16 b4! ♕xb4

Or 16...♗e7? 17 e4!, threatening both 18 exf5 and 18 ♗e3.

17 ♕xb4 ♗xb4 18 ♘xd5 ♗c5 19 ♘c7+ ♔e7 20 ♘xa6 ♗a3 21 ♖c3 ♗b2 22 ♖b3 ♗e5 *(D)*

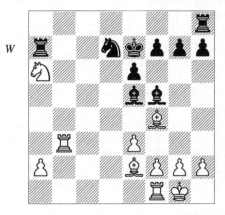

23 ♘b4!?

23 ♖c1! ♗xf4 24 exf4 with ♘b4 next seems even better, stopping ...♘e5. But White stands much better anyway, a pawn up for nothing.

Semi-Slav

1 d4 d5 2 c4 c6

We're going to be looking at the position that arises after 1 d4 d5 2 c4 c6 3 ♘f3 ♘f6 4 ♘c3 e6 (the Semi-Slav) 5 e3 ♘bd7. Both sides should be familiar with the various options that arise along the way, including move-orders that lead to the same endpoint. First, the move-order 2...e6 *(D)* is often used to get to the Semi-Slav, *if* Black wants to delay ...♘f6 on the third move.

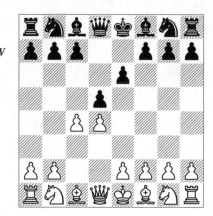

W

That is, Black can get to the desired Semi-Slav position by playing 2 c4 e6 3 ♘c3 c6 4 ♘f3 ♘f6 5 e3 ♘bd7. Why would he want to play 2...e6 first, and then 3...c6? Because once White is committed to 3 ♘c3, Black has gained in several ways:

a) He has eliminated any line in which White plays ♘d2;

b) He has helped himself in certain variations with ...dxc4 and ...b5, because ...b4 will then attack the knight on c3 with tempo.

c) Finally, Black may be happier playing the unbalanced pawn-structure that results from 2 c4 e6 3 cxd5 exd5 than the symmetrical one after 2 c4 c6 3 cxd5 cxd5.

All that sounds good, but there's always a trade-off. One drawback to this order is that it allows the Marshall Gambit, 4 e4. See the note on that below. A further move-order that avoids both the Exchange Slav and the Marshall Gambit is 1 d4 ♘f6 2 c4 e6 3 ♘f3 d5 4 ♘c3 c6. The trade-off then is that Black needs to be willing to play a Nimzo-Indian.

3 ♘c3

3 ♘f3 might discourage the idea of delaying ...♘f6 because White can try 3...e6 4 ♗g5!?, a rather obscure but interesting option. This would also not be possible with the 2 c4 e6 3 ♘c3 order. I'm not going to give you the details about all these choices, but want to make you aware of what's out there so that you can reflect upon what suits you best.

3...e6

3...♘f6 4 ♘f3 e6 transposes to the main position of the Semi-Slav. Other options are considered in the introductory notes to 3 ♘c3 at the beginning of this chapter.

4 ♘f3

An alternative is the Marshall Gambit, 4 e4!? *(D)*.

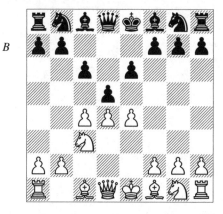

B

This usually leads to the gambit 4...dxe4 5 ♘xe4 ♗b4+ 6 ♗d2 ♕xd4 7 ♗xb4 ♕xe4+, when Black is a pawn up but has lost the dark squares. This is a sharp variation to which a very large amount of concrete theory has been devoted; it should probably be learned by heart. I won't go into the details here, but so far it has not deterred top players from using this move-order as Black. On the other hand it seems that White is always coming up with new ideas, and the gambit may suit players who enjoy speculative attacks.

There is also a positional way to answer the Marshall Gambit, namely, 4...♗b4 *(D)*.

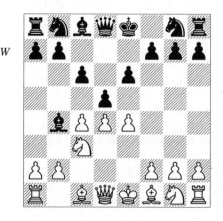

W

The resulting play is very instructive and will often bear a resemblance to variations of the French Defence. A few of many possibilities:

a) 5 e5 ♘e7 (5...c5 is more open but also a sound move) 6 a3 ♗xc3+ 7 bxc3 b6!? (7...c5!?) 8 ♘f3 ♗a6 with a complex game.

b) 5 cxd5 exd5 6 e5 is another pawn-chain approach, when play can go 6...♘e7 (or 6...c5 7 a3 ♗a5; or 6...♗f5) 7 ♘f3 c5 (or 7...♗f5 8 ♗e2 0-0) 8 a3 ♗xc3+ 9 bxc3 ♘bc6 10 ♗e2 ♗g4. It's fair to call this position dynamically equal. White has space, dark squares, and the bishop-pair. Black can either put pressure on the d-pawn (by ...cxd4, ...♘f5 and ...♗xf3) or play for the queenside light squares (by, for example, ...♘a5 and ...♖c8).

c) 5 ♕g4 ♘f6 6 ♕xg7 ♖g8 7 ♕h6 is very similar to a French Defence; here 7...dxe4, 7...♖g6 and 7...c5 are all equal or better for Black.

d) 5 ♗d2 can become sharp after 5...dxc4 6 ♗xc4 ♘f6 7 ♕e2 ♕xd4 8 ♘f3 ♕d8 9 0-0 with modest compensation for the pawn.

Quite a few top players have used 4...♗b4. It avoids extensive theory, and the result depends upon the strategic understanding of each player.

4...♘f6 *(D)*

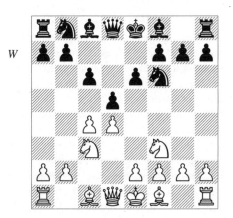

The combined moves ...e6 and ...c6 give us what is called the Semi-Slav Variation. It has become one of the most fertile areas for investigation in modern chess play. But what is going on here? First Black denies c6 to his knight and then blocks the open diagonal for his bishop on c8! Why? Obviously the answer cannot be rapid development, because he's making pawn moves. And although Black has a strong point at d5 (every one of his moves, including 1...d5, has increased control of that square), White has more space and better control of the centre as a whole. In general Black's position has to strike one as passive. And yet the Semi-Slav is associated with extraordinarily exciting play. Let's see why. In the first place, Black has a threat: 5...dxc4, after which his pawn on c4 can be defended by ...b5. To see that this is actually a threat, take a look at the move 5 g3 below, which turns into a gambit (not a terrible one, but still not to most people's taste). So White needs to do something that prevents, neutralizes, or compensates for the capture on c4. The obvious move for that purpose is:

5 e3

This is the main line that we shall explore.

I'll get to 5 ♗g5 in a short note below. Other moves have their disadvantages which are enlightening to look through, especially to understand why the main lines *are* main lines. Here are a few that may be of value in that respect:

a) 5 a4 (to prevent ...b5 should Black decide upon ...dxc4), when Black can simply develop by, e.g., 5...♘bd7, or exploit the new hole on b4 by 5...♗b4 (with ...♘e4 and perhaps ...♕a5 in mind) 6 ♗d2 0-0 (or 6...c5) 7 e3 c5. This exploits White's passively-placed bishop on d2, which is disconnected from the defence of d4. Black intends to play ...♘c6 and capture on d4, whereas 8 dxc5 ♘c6 takes over the centre; e.g., 9 cxd5 exd5 10 ♗e2 ♗xc5 11 0-0 ♖e8 with ideal activity for an isolated queen's pawn position.

b) 5 ♕b3 defends the c-pawn with the hope of developing via ♗f4 or ♗g5. It can be met by simple development such as ...♘bd7, but the forcing sequence 5...dxc4 6 ♕xc4 b5! is surprisingly effective and has more or less eliminated 5 ♕b3 as an attempt to gain the advantage (the same applies to 5 ♕d3 dxc4; in that case Black has another good option in 5 ♕d3 b6!). The play can proceed 7 ♕d3 b4!? 8 ♘e4 ♘xe4 9 ♕xe4 ♗b7 10 e3 ♘d7 11 ♗c4 ♗e7 12 0-0 0-0 with equality, Korchnoi-Tischbierek, Zurich 1999.

c) 5 g3 dxc4 6 ♗g2 *(D)* can turn into a real gambit.

6...♘bd7 (Black stops ♘e5 before he plays ...b5; the immediate 6...b5 7 ♘e5 ♘d5 is a good

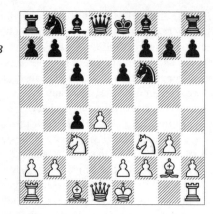

alternative; e.g., 8 e4 ♘b4 9 a3!? ♕xd4 10 axb4 ♕xe5 11 ♗f4 ♕f6 12 ♘xb5 ♗xb4+ 13 ♔f1 cxb5 14 e5 ♕e7 15 ♗xa8 ♗b7 with good compensation for Black according to Korchnoi, in view of 16 ♖xa7 ♗g2+ 17 ♔xg2 ♕xa7) 7 a4 (White should save the pawn; 7 0-0?! b5 8 e4 ♗b7 9 e5 ♘d5 10 ♘g5 h6! 11 ♘xe6 fxe6 12 ♕h5+ ♔e7 13 ♗g5+ hxg5 14 ♕xh8 ♘xc3 15 bxc3 ♘b6 16 ♕h5 ♔d7 and White lacks compensation) 7...♗b4 8 0-0 0-0 9 ♘a2 ♗d6 10 ♘d2 e5 11 ♘xc4 ♗c7 with equality, Dausch-S.Pedersen, Copenhagen 1995.

d) Now, what about 5 ♗g5 *(D)*?

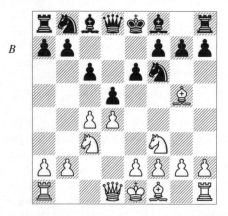

Then Black can play 5...♘bd7, intending 6 e3 ♕a5, which is the old Cambridge Springs Variation of the Queen's Gambit Declined (not too popular among defenders of the QGD, although it is certainly playable). He has two other moves within the Semi-Slav complex. One is 5...h6, which can in turn lead to 6 ♗xf6 ♕xf6, the Moscow Variation, or 6 ♗h4 dxc4 7 e4 g5 8 ♗g3 b5, known as the 'Anti-Moscow'

Variation (see the next paragraph). The Moscow is strategically interesting, but I think less so than the Meran and Anti-Meran, to which I'll be devoting my attention. I have given one example of the Moscow Variation in Chapter 3 in the first volume.

The other and most popular move after 5 ♗g5 is 5...dxc4, usually leading to 6 e4 b5 (Black holds on to his extra pawn; else White plays ♗xc4 with the ideal centre and better development). We enter the main line of the infamous 'Botvinnik Variation' once White plays 7 e5 h6 8 ♗h4 g5 9 ♘xg5! hxg5 10 ♗xg5 ♘bd7 *(D)*.

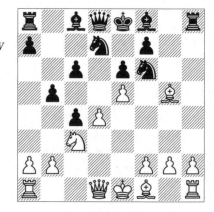

This is one of the most thoroughly played and analysed variations in modern chess. It is characterized by lengthy tactical and sacrificial sequences, with play in which half a tempo changes the entire nature of the game. Many fans and specialists devote their time to studying and extending Botvinnik Variation theory, and it would do you no good for me to rehash a selected fraction of it, since to master these lines on either side of the board requires a great deal of playing experience and very specific study of tactical sequences. The Anti-Moscow above (5...h6 6 ♗h4 g5 7 ♗g3 dxc4 8 e4 b5) is of the same nature, being extremely theoretical. It's not yet worked out to the outrageous extent that various Botvinnik lines are (30+ moves), but it's still dependent upon hoards of position-specific tactics. Neither variation is within the scope or intent of this book, but that should not discourage a lover of fascinating chess theory.

5...♘bd7 *(D)*

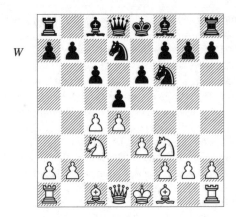

The natural 5...♘bd7 introduces the standard Semi-Slav lines that we'll examine. It is very flexible, allowing for Black's bishop on f8 to go to e7, d6 or b4. In the meantime, Black develops a piece and supports either ...c5 or ...e5 should the opportunity arise.

Before moving to what White plays next, let's examine the Semi-Slav from another perspective. Take the moves 1 d4 d5 2 ♘f3 ♘f6 3 e3 e6 4 c3 c5 5 ♘bd2 ♘c6 6 ♗d3 (D).

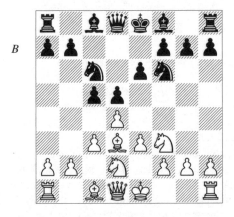

Do you recognize this position? It's the Classical Colle System, considered one of White's dullest variations in d-pawn chess! The Classical Colle is sound enough, but grandmasters rarely play it, and indeed I'm not sure that a top-ten player has tried to play this form of the Colle in decades. Ironically, the Colle System with the move b3 (omitting c3) has attracted a number of strong grandmasters over the last 15 years or so. But when one looks at the reversed Semi-Slav position, Black has forgone this possibility ...b6. So how can a notoriously dull opening be so popular with colours reversed, played a full tempo down? We'll discover some concrete reasons shortly, but more general issues apply. The nature of reversed openings is such that Black's goals can differ from White's in the same position. Obviously Black is usually satisfied with equality in a system where a dynamic imbalance cannot be achieved by force. Then, too, White has to commit himself to a specific 6th move versus the Semi-Slav set-up, giving Black some extra information with which to respond flexibly by choosing the appropriate counter.

Let's continue with our Colle example (from the diagram after 6 ♗d3): sometimes Black plays 6...♗d6 (6...♕c7 7 dxc5 ♗xc5 8 b4 ♗d6 is a better version for Black, but we're continuing with the analogy) 7 dxc5 ♗xc5 8 b4 ♗d6 (D).

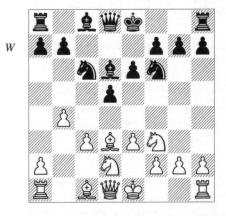

Here it might be useful to jump ahead and glance at the first few moves of the Meran Variation main lines below. In this position (after 8...♗d6), Black, who is a tempo down on the Semi-Slav lines, will not play ambitiously with ...e5 as White does in the Meran Variation. Rather, he will play something like ...♘e5, or ...a5, answering b5 with ...♘e5. Such a strategy is certainly dull, but it should equalize. That's the difference between a counterattack whose basis is the opponent's aggression (in the Meran, White usually plays for advantage with e4-e5 and exposes himself to attack), and Black's willingness to play more solidly in order to equalize in the reversed position.

Now we return to the subject of this section, 5 e3 ♘bd7. At this point White has two moves that we'll look at: 6 ♗d3 (with 6...dxc4), the Meran System; and 6 ♕c2, the Anti-Meran System.

The Meran

6 ♗d3 dxc4 7 ♗xc4 b5 (D)

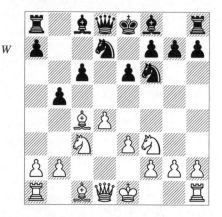

This sequence of moves defines the Meran System.

8 ♗d3

What is going on here? Briefly, White has a central majority, and given the chance, will play e4 followed by moves such as ♗g5, ♕e2 and the like. Or perhaps he will go for e5, ♘e4 and ♗g5. Thus White's play will be fairly transparent unless he is challenged in the centre. Sometimes the time-consuming move a3 might be mixed in, to counter ...b4. The somewhat better idea of a4 is positionally desirable, but has the particular drawback of taking away the a4-square for the knight after ...b4.

With 7...b5, Black has advanced a pawn that can be used to drive White's knight away from c3, from which position it controls e4 and influences the centre. The pawn on b4 might prove weak and the squares c5 and c6 may be vulnerable if Black doesn't quickly assert himself on the queenside. Ideally, Black would like to counter White's plan of e4 by a combination of bothersome moves like ...b4, ...♗b7 and ...c5, focusing his counterattack upon d4 and e4. In some lines he can afford the time for ...a6 and ...c5, and if White doesn't try for much, then ...♗d6 followed by ...e5 can be effective. In the position after 7...b5, we'll be looking mainly at the move 8 ♗d3. 8 ♗b3 isn't played much,

primarily due to 8...b4 and 9 ♘a4?! (a move which is normally desirable in order to control c5) 9...♗a6! (preventing 10 0-0), or 9 ♘e2 ♗b7 followed by ...♗d6, ...0-0 and ...c5.

However, 8 ♗e2 *(D)* is an important option, keeping the bishop out of the way of various attacks by ...c4 and ...e4 while keeping the d-pawn in sight of the queen. Its drawback is a lack of central protection, i.e., after White plays e4 his pawn has limited support. Nevertheless, White will have to play e4 soon or he'll have no chance for advantage because Black will implement a plan with ...c5 or ...e5.

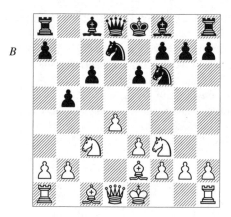

Here are two relevant games:

Hübner – K. Müller
Bundesliga 1998/9

8...♗b7

8...a6?! invites 9 e4, with greater effect than in what follows. With 8...♗b7, Black places his bishop on b7 with the faith that he will be able to achieve the move ...c5 and employ the bishop upon the long diagonal. White's next move seems overly optimistic.

9 e4!?

9 0-0 is seen in the next game.

9...b4 10 e5 bxc3 11 exf6 ♘xf6

Safe and sound, unlike the crazy alternative 11...cxb2 12 fxg7 bxa1♕ 13 gxh8♕ *(D)*.

This is the 'Four Queens Variation', which not surprisingly is theoretically unresolved! A critical line goes 13...♕a5+ 14 ♘d2!? ♕f5!? 15 0-0 0-0-0 (Vidoniak analyses 15...♕xa2! 16 ♘c4 0-0-0 17 ♗d3 ♕f6 18 ♕xh7 and now Pedersen suggests 18...♕xd4) 16 ♕b3 ♘c5

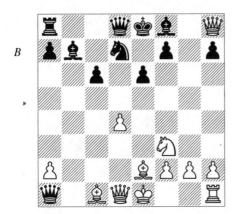

(16...♗e7! is equal) 17 ♕b4 ♕c2? (17...♘d7 with equality) 18 ♕f6! ♕cc3 19 ♕xc3 ♕xc3 20 ♘f3 ♘e4 21 ♕xf7 c5 22 ♗f4 ♗d6 23 ♕xe6+ ♔b8 24 ♗xd6+ ♘xd6 25 ♕e7 ♕a5 26 dxc5 ♘c8 27 ♕e5+ ♕c7 (27...♔a8 28 c6!) 28 ♕xc7+ ♔xc7 29 ♖d1 ♖e8 30 ♗b5 ♖g8 31 ♖d7+ ♔b8 32 c6 ♗a8 33 ♘e5 a5 34 ♖xh7 1-0 Sadler-Kaidanov, Andorra 1991. Crazy stuff that I just had to mention, regardless of its marginal instructional value.

12 bxc3 ♗d6 13 0-0 0-0 *(D)*

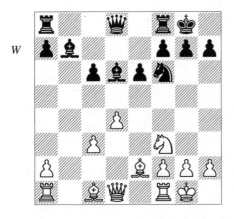

Black stands quite well here, because ...c5 is coming and his bishops will be especially active.

14 c4?!

14 ♗g5?! ♕c7! (now ...♘e4 is an issue, but doubling pawns by ♗xf6 only helps Black's kingside ambitions because White gives up the bishop-pair and opens himself to attack along the g-file) 15 ♗d3!? c5 gives Black a small edge, Potapov-Galkin, St Petersburg 1998. Perhaps a modest continuation such as 14 h3 (to protect against ...♘g4) 14...c5 15 ♗e3 is called for.

14...c5 15 ♗a3 ♘e4 16 dxc5 ♗xc5 17 ♗xc5 ♘xc5 18 ♕xd8 ♖fxd8 *(D)*

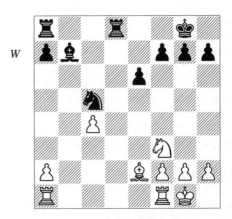

With White's isolated pawn, and Black's better knight and bishop, Black has a substantial advantage. Notice how the ideal blockade on c5 keeps White's bishop out of play.

Now for our second game with 8 ♗e2:

Lputian – Anand
New Delhi FIDE KO 2000

8...♗b7 9 0-0 ♗e7

A solid move, and perfectly adequate. 9...a6 is more popular; in that case Black plays directly for ...c5. Compare the 8 ♗d3 lines.

10 e4 b4 11 e5 *(D)*

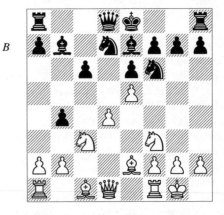

Already we see the shortcomings of ♗e2: if the knight on c3 moves, the pawn on e4 falls. Of course White could have played more slowly, but he's hoping that forcing the pace will favour him.

11...bxc3 12 exf6 &xf6 13 bxc3 0-0 14 &b1 Wc7 15 &f4!

Otherwise ...c5 will follow.

15...Wxf4 16 &xb7 &b6 17 g3 Wf5 18 &d3 Wa5 19 Wc2 ½-½

Returning to the main move 8 &d3, there are three principal continuations, often transposing. I'll examine 8...a6 and 8...&b7. 8...Wc7 is a good transpositional tool, but it's easier to present the material via the other two moves.

Classical Meran

8...a6 *(D)*

This is the traditional move, preparing ...c5. White can try to take advantage of Black's lack of development by attacking with his central majority.

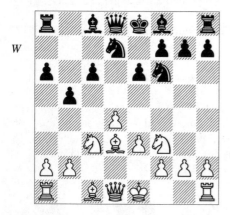

9 e4

Pedersen gives a 'rule of thumb' that ...a6 in the Semi-Slav should be met by e4. Oddly enough, White already gives up all chances for advantage after 9 0-0 c5, when 10 We2 is a sort of Queen's Gambit Accepted with a harmless reputation and 10 a4 b4 at best transposes to the next note but also gives Black options of ...&d6 instead of ...&e7.

9...c5 *(D)*

9...b4?! 10 &a4 transposes to a Modern Meran (which we'll be looking at below) except that Black has spent a move on ...a6, which is less than optimal for that variation.

You'll have to bear with me on these comparisons and transpositions. It isn't necessary to know them, but you might want to return here after you have played some games and want to make sense of them.

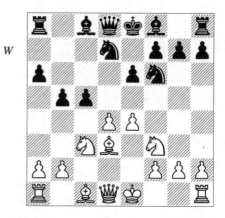

We come to a crossroads. White can play 10 d5 or 10 e5.

Reynolds Attack

10 d5

This introduces the wild Reynolds Variation, ideal for specialists or for anyone who thinks that his opponent won't be prepared for it! The move d5 is always critical in such positions because it opens lines for White's pieces to work with. The positional basis for d5 also stems from the fact that if White waits for ...cxd4, both Black's bishop on f8 and knight on d7 will have active posts, whereas now they are limited by their c-pawn. Variations stemming from 10 d5 constantly interact with those beginning with the moves 8...&b7 and 8...Wc7, so I'll mix the material.

10...Wc7

The most 'flexible' move. Unfortunately, it's hard to decide upon which move should be played first. For example, White can toss in the exchange of pawns dxe6 and ...fxe6 just about anywhere. Fortunately we're more concerned with the resulting positions than the details of how to get there. Of course there are alternatives, such as 10...c4, which very often transposes to 10...Wc7. But 10...e5 is independent. Then 11 b3! prevents ...c4 and prepares a4. Black usually disturbs things by 11...c4!? 12

bxc4 &b4 13 &d2 ♛c7 14 0-0 bxc4; e.g., 15
&c2 0-0 16 ♘h4! ♘b6 17 ♛f3 with some advantage to White, Krasenkov-Moroz, Lubnie-
wice 1994.

11 0-0 &b7 12 dxe6 fxe6 *(D)*

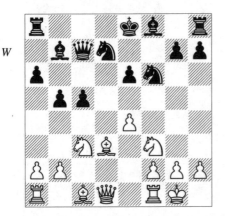

Black's pieces are active and his majority on
the queenside is threatening. Given a few moves,
the combination of ...c4, ...0-0-0 and ...♘c5
will give Black a terrific game. But in the meantime White can organize for e5, play against
Black's e-pawn, and/or attack via a4. A high-
profile game follows.

Kasimdzhanov – Kasparov
Linares 2005

13 &c2

After 13 ♘g5?! ♛c6 14 &f4 c4 15 &c2 &c5
16 b3 ♘b6!, as in Al.Panchenko-Dreev, Kazan
ECC 1997, Black will gain even more activity
down the f- and d-files. He stands better. In fact,
White now retreated with 17 ♘f3, not a good
sign!

13...c4 14 ♘d4 ♘c5 15 &e3 e5

Black must take care not to get too greedy.
Capturing the e-pawn by any means exposes
him down the e-file and lets White have time to
pile up on e6.

16 ♘f3 &e7 17 ♘g5 *(D)*

17...0-0!

Typical Kasparov. He gets two bishops and
an attack in return for sacrificing the exchange
– not such a surprising decision, in fact.

18 &xc5 &xc5 19 ♘e6 ♛b6 20 ♘xf8 ♖xf8

Apart from Black's superior development
(see the rook on a1, for example) and attack on

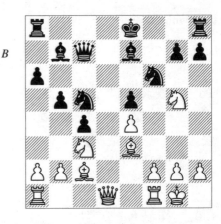

f2 (by ...♛e6 and ...♘g4, for example) he has
moves such as ...&d4 and ...b4 to look forward
to. All this is hardly decisive, but very difficult
to defend against in practice.

21 ♘d5

Kasparov gives analysis to suggest that 21
♔h1 and 21 a4 lead to roughly equal and/or unclear play.

21...&xd5 22 exd5 *(D)*

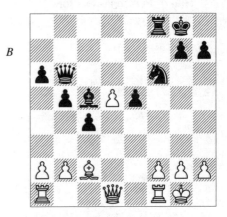

22...&xf2+! 23 ♔h1

Not 23 ♖xf2? ♘g4! with the idea 24 ♛xg4??
♛xf2+ 25 ♔h1 ♛f1+ and mates.

23...e4! 24 ♛e2?

A real mistake. Kasparov suggests that both
24 a4 and 24 d6 were playable.

24...e3 25 ♖fd1 ♛d6 26 a4 g6!

Now the idea is ...♘h5-f4. These notes are
hardly comprehensive, of course.

**27 axb5 axb5 28 g3 ♘h5! 29 ♛g4 &xg3! 30
hxg3 ♘xg3+ 31 ♔g2 ♖f2+ 32 ♔h3 ♘f5! 33
♖h1 h5! 34 ♛xg6+ ♛xg6 35 ♖hg1 ♛xg1 36
♖xg1+ ♔f7 0-1**

Classical with 10 e5

10 e5 *(D)*

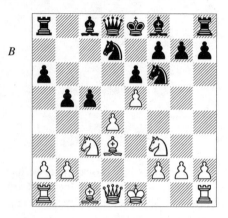

This older move, clearing the way for ♘e4 or ♗e4, also has a lengthy history of theory and practice. It can be avoided by 8...♕c7, however, so we'll just cover one game.

Hillarp Persson – Hector
Malmö/Copenhagen 2004

10...cxd4 11 ♘xb5 *(D)*

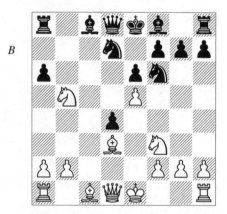

11...axb5
Recently this has been Black's most popular move. 11...♘g4 has been analysed for years, with the main line being 12 ♕a4 ♗b7 13 ♘bxd4 ♕b6 14 0-0 ♗c5 15 ♗e3 ♘xe3 16 fxe3 h6. Instead, 11...♘xe5!? 12 ♘xe5 axb5 used to be considered Black's safest line, although there have been quite a few challenges to that view.

12 exf6 gxf6 13 0-0 ♕b6 14 ♕e2 b4

At first sight Black's king looks completely secure; then again, it has to find a home somewhere.

15 ♖d1 ♗c5 16 a4!? *(D)*

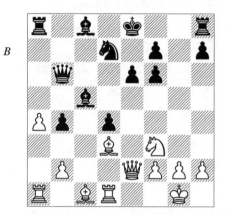

An odd idea, but with some good points. Positionally, White gains a passed pawn which can be a tactical diversion at the right moment. Furthermore a2 won't be a target any more. Depending upon what Black does, White can also consider anchoring a bishop on b5.

16...bxa3!?
A tactical point of 16 a4, such as it is, is 16...♗a6 17 a5!? (17 ♗xa6 looks as good or better, however), after which Black must avoid 17...♗xd3?? 18 axb6.

17 bxa3 ♗b7 18 ♗e4! *(D)*

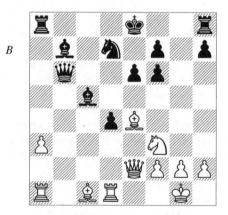

A simple solution: get rid of the powerful bishop on b7.

18...♗a6
Black refuses the offer. 18...♗xe4 19 ♕xe4 ♖a4 is a little wobbly following 20 ♖b1.

19 ♕e1 ♖d8 20 ♗d2 ♕d6 21 ♗b4! d3 22 ♕c3 ♕b6?! 23 ♕d2!

White threatens ♗a5 and ♗xd3 and clearly has the upper hand.

The Modern Meran

8...♗b7 (D)

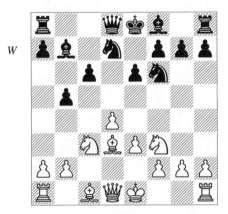

By these means Black saves the move ...a6 in some lines and gets more active play. 8...♗b7 also signals that Black's main freeing move will be ...c5 rather than ...e5. Play may easily transpose into the previous section; however, it does so in lines that Black is clearly satisfied with. Therefore it's the positional continuations that take the centre stage and White will turn his attention there. With Black's pawn still on a7, ...c5 will not be available until ...b4 is played. Then White still has the advantage that after ...c5, ♗b5+ will be worrisome. Playing ...♗e7 and ...0-0 before counterattacking is generally too slow. Finally, an early ...b4 allows White to play ♘a4 and fight for the c5-square. Remember that if White provokes ...b4 by playing a4, that square will be occupied and his knight will have to retreat.

9 e4

In other lines Black will just shoot for ...c5; for example, 9 0-0 a6 10 e4 c5 11 e5 cxd4 12 ♘xb5 looks like one of our previous Classical lines, but in this case Black has the extra option 12...♗xf3 13 ♕xf3 ♘d5 (13...♘xe5?! 14 ♕xa8! ♕xa8 15 ♘c7+) 14 ♘xd4 ♘xe5 15 ♕e2 ♘xd3 16 ♕xd3 ♗c5 with equality, Piket-Kramnik, Monaco (Amber blindfold) 1996.

9...b4 (D)

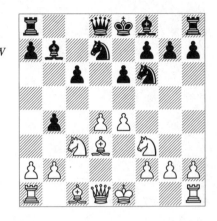

This is the idea of 8...♗b7: Black will play ...c5 next and save the move ...a6.

10 ♘a4

The knight is well enough placed here because when Black plays ...c5 it will be traded for an active piece. The most entertaining alternative goes 10 e5?! bxc3 11 exf6 cxb2 12 fxg7 bxa1♕! 13 gxh8♕. We've reached another 'four queens' position, but this one's clearly in Black's favour. A cute game went 13...♕a5+ 14 ♘d2 ♕5c3! 15 ♔e2 ♘c5 16 ♕xh7 ♘xd3 17 ♕xd3 ♕xd3+ 18 ♔xd3 ♗a6+ 19 ♔c2 ♕xa2+ 20 ♗b2 ♖b8 21 ♕a1 ♖xb2+! 22 ♕xb2 ♗d3+! 23 ♔c3 ♗b4+! 0-1 I.Johannsson-Z.Nilsson, Amsterdam OL 1954.

10...c5 (D)

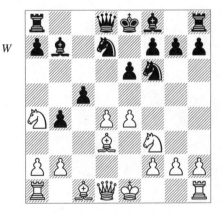

11 e5

This is the only serious try for advantage. White's pawn on e4 is attacked and he needs to keep the initiative. In the meantime he sets his eye on the dark squares.

11...♘d5 (D)

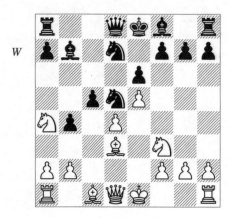

You can see how powerful this knight is on the d5 outpost. The question is whether White can use his central space advantage and squares such as e4, c4 and g5 to launch an attack on Black's king or otherwise compromise Black's position.

12 0-0

White would like to attack by ♗g5, or even ♘g5!?. He has the choice between this calm development or taking immediate action. Doing so by 12 ♘xc5 ♗xc5?! (12...♘xc5 will transpose to the 12 dxc5 line) 13 dxc5 ♘xc5 14 ♗b5+ hasn't worked out well, as the two bishops eventually prove their worth. For many years, White has tried to make something of 12 dxc5 ♘xc5 (D), and now:

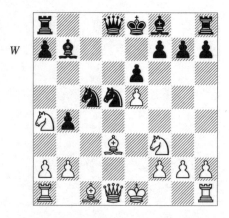

a) 13 ♘xc5 ♗xc5 14 0-0 (14 ♗b5+ ♔e7 15 0-0 ♕b6 16 ♗d3 h6! 17 ♕e2 ♖hd8 18 ♗d2 ♔f8, castling by hand, illustrates Black's general strategy, Uhlmann-Larsen, Las Palmas Ct (6) 1971) 14...h6 15 ♘d2 ♕c7! 16 ♖e1 ♖d8 17 ♘e4 ♗e7 18 ♘g3 g6! 19 ♗d2 ♔f8 20 ♕e2

♔g7 21 ♖ac1 ♕b6 22 ♗c4 ♕d4 23 ♗b3 h5 24 ♖ed1 ♕b6 with equality, Epishin-Dreev, Tilburg 1994.

b) 13 ♗b5+ ♘d7 14 ♗g5 ♕a5! 15 ♗xd7+ ♔xd7 16 0-0 (D).

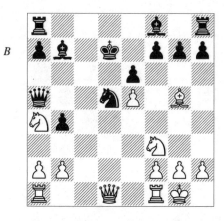

This is an archetypal position for the Meran. Black's king is stuck in the centre and, given time, White could attack it by, for example, some combination of moves such as ♘d4, ♕h5, ♖c1 and f4-f5. This basic advantage is significant, and such attacks do sometimes succeed, but they are rendered difficult by Black's outpost on d5 and lack of weaknesses. Furthermore, Black's position is superior in almost every other respect. Compare the knight on d5 to the ones on f3 and a4, or Black's powerful bishop on b7 to White's bad bishop on g5 (about to be driven away should Black want to). Black's queen is also very active, whereas White's is tied to a4. All in all, it's not surprising that variations with this kind of position have grown increasingly attractive to Black. Yusupov-Kramnik, Horgen 1995 continued 16...♗e7!? (Dreev suggests 16...h6!, and indeed, there's no reason why Black shouldn't stand better with his bishop-pair and clearly superior pieces) 17 b3 h6 18 ♗xe7 ♔xe7 19 ♘d2! (heading for the weakness on d6) 19...♘f4 20 ♘c4 ♘d5 21 ♕xd5 ♗xd5 22 ♘e3. This is almost equal, since White can re-route by ♘b2-c4. Nevertheless, Black has the better pawn-structure and can bring his rooks to the centre. Yusupov suggests 22...♖hd8 23 ♘b2 ♘e2+ 24 ♔h1 ♘c3 with a small advantage.

We return to 12 0-0 (D):

We'll now follow a characteristic game.

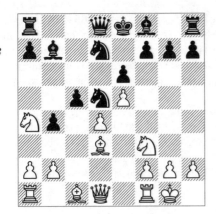

B

Alterman – L. Spassov
Munich 1991/2

12...cxd4

A natural and good move, weakening White's grip on the centre. On the other hand, it does give White's knight a good post on d4. Another satisfactory move is 12...h6; for example, 13 dxc5 ♗xc5 14 ♘xc5 ♘xc5 15 ♗b5+ ♔f8 16 ♕d4 ♖c8! 17 ♗d2 ♕b6 18 ♗e2 g6 19 ♕h4 ♔g7 20 ♖ac1 ♗a6!, Gelfand-Oll, Vilnius 1988. By seizing the d3-square and eliminating half of the bishop-pair, Black secures approximate equality.

13 ♖e1

The pawn sacrifice 13 ♘xd4!? leads to a dynamic imbalance; for example, 13...♘xe5 14 ♗b5+ ♘d7 15 ♖e1 ♖c8 16 ♕h5 (threatening ♘xe6) 16...g6 17 ♕e5 ♕f6 18 ♘f3!? ♗g7 19 ♗xd7+ ♔xd7 20 ♕e2 ♕d8!? 21 a3! b3 22 ♗d2 ♔e7 23 ♕b5 ♗c6 24 ♕xb3 ♔f8 with a complex position in which Black's problems finding a place for his king are balanced by his central majority and bishop-pair, Obukhov-Doroshkevich, RSFSR Ch (Kuibyshev) 1990.

13...g6 14 ♗d2 *(D)*
14...♗e7?!

This lets up the pressure on e5. Better was 14...♗g7 15 ♗b5 (15 ♖c1!?) 15...♖c8 16 ♗g5 ♕a5 17 ♘xd4 ♖c7 (Stohl suggests 17...a6!? 18 ♗xd7+ ♔xd7, which again shows the relative safety of Black's king when it is shielded by the knight on d5; then 19 ♘b3 ♕b5 20 ♘d4 ♕a5 21 ♘b3 ♕b5 repeats) 18 ♖c1 (18 a3!? a6 19 ♗xd7+ ♖xd7 20 ♗d2 ♗f8 21 ♕b3 ♘f4! 22 ♗xb4 ♕d5 23 ♕xd5 ♖xd5 leaves weaknesses in White's camp) 18...0-0 19 ♗xd7 ♖xd7 20

♖c5 ♕a6 21 ♖c1 ♕a5 22 ♖c5 ♕a6 ½-½ Alterman-Pinter, Beersheba 1991.
15 ♘xd4 0-0 16 ♗h6! ♖e8 17 ♕g4 ♗f8 18 ♗xf8 ♖xf8 19 h4! *(D)*

An attacking move that takes advantage of the fact that Black doesn't have a lot of useful moves.

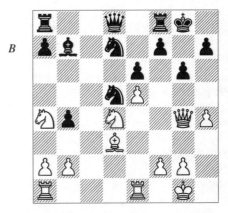

B

19...♕e7

The critical tactical line is 19...♕a5 20 h5! ♕xa4 21 hxg6 hxg6 22 ♗xg6! fxg6 23 ♕xg6+ ♔h8 24 ♘xe6 with mate next.

20 h5 ♖fe8 21 ♖ad1 a6?! 22 ♗b1 ♕f8!? 23 hxg6 hxg6 24 ♕g5! ♖ac8 25 f4! ♕g7?!

25...♖c7! was a better defensive try.

26 ♗e4 ♖c7?! 27 ♖c1 ♖xc1 28 ♖xc1 ♘f8 29 ♗xd5 ♗xd5 30 ♘b6 ♘h7 31 ♕g4 ♖d8 32 ♘xd5 ♖xd5 33 ♖c8+ ♘f8 34 ♘c6 f5 35 ♕g5 ♖d7 36 ♕f6! ♕f7

36...♕xf6 37 exf6 ♖f7 38 ♘e7+ ♔h8 39 ♘xg6+ ♔g8 40 ♖a8 ♖xf6 41 ♘e5 and Black's queenside pawns fall. The rest of the game is routine:

37 ♕xf7+ ♔xf7 38 ♘xb4 ♖d1+ 39 ♔h2
♖d4 40 ♖c7+ ♔g8 41 ♘xa6 ♖xf4 42 b4 g5 43
b5 ♖h4+ 44 ♔g1 ♖a4 45 b6! ♖xa6 46 b7 ♖b6
47 a4 ♖b1+ 48 ♔h2 g4 49 a5 f4 50 a6 ♖b2 51
a7 1-0

Anti-Meran (6 ♕c2)

1 d4 d5 2 c4 c6 3 ♘f3 ♘f6 4 ♘c3 e6 5 e3 ♘bd7
6 ♕c2 (D)

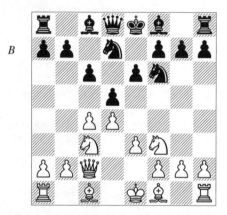

With this move White covers the critical e4-
square, begins to clear the back rank, and discourages Black's plan of ...dxc4 and ...b5.

6...♗d6

Black's idea is to enforce ...e5, either directly
or after ...dxc4. White's job is to render that
move ineffective or worse.

7 ♗e2

White simply prepares castling. There's a
subtle point here: White is now allowing the
same move ...dxc4 (with the loss of tempo that
entails), precisely what he avoided when he
played 6 ♕c2. It turns out that Black's bishop
on d6 doesn't go well with ...dxc4 and ...b5. For
one thing, White's advance e4 will threaten e5,
forking the bishop and knight.

Before investigating that, here are some alternatives:

a) 7 ♗d3 is another common order for
White, when 7...0-0 8 0-0 dxc4 9 ♗xc4 transposes to the main line. But 7 ♗d3 has the serious drawback that Black seems to equalize if he
knows his stuff after 8...e5, answering 9 cxd5
with 9...cxd5.

b) 7 e4 is pretty well worked-out, the most
entertaining line going 7...dxe4 8 ♘xe4 ♘xe4 9

♕xe4 e5 10 dxe5 0-0! 11 exd6 ♖e8 12 ♕xe8+
♕xe8+ 13 ♗e3 with a kind of material equality
after which Black can easily go wrong but may
even stand slightly better if he plays accurately.
Not surprisingly, there are other ways to equalize.

c) 7 ♗d2, intending to castle queenside followed by an attack, comes across the most
problems in the line 7...0-0 8 0-0-0 b5!, intending 9 cxb5 c5! with a strong queenside attack.
This line could use more attention, however.

d) 7 b3 is solid and interesting but fairly
easy to meet. One well-established line goes
7...0-0 8 ♗e2! (8 ♗b2 e5! 9 cxd5 cxd5 10 dxe5
♘xe5 11 ♗e2 ♘xf3+! 12 ♗xf3 d4! 13 exd4
♖e8+ 14 ♔f1 ♕a5 with excellent compensation, Korchnoi-Beliavsky, Leon 1994) 8...dxc4
9 bxc4 e5 10 0-0 ♕e7; for example, 11 ♗b2
♖e8 12 ♖fe1 e4 13 ♘d2 ♘f8 14 f3 exf3 15
♗xf3 ♘g4 16 ♘f1 ♕g5 17 e4 ♘e6! 18 ♖ad1
(18 e5? ♘xd4! 19 exd6 ♘e5 20 ♖xe5 ♘xf3+
21 ♔h1 ♘xe5 and Black is winning, as given
by Scherbakov) 18...♘xd4! 19 ♖xd4 ♘xh2 20
♘xh2 ♗xh2+ 21 ♔f1 ♗e5 22 ♖d3 ♗e6 (D).

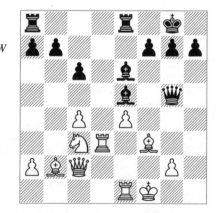

With two pawns, far superior pieces, and
White's four isolated pawns, Black clearly has
enough if not more than enough compensation
for the knight, Gelfand-Anand, Monaco 2000 –
a rapid blindfold game!

e) 7 g4!? (D).

This radical move was discovered by Sha-
balov in the early 1990s, and leading grandmasters such as Gelfand and Shirov have helped to
popularize the idea. I have reluctantly decided
not to delve into its extensive bank of ideas and
theory, but should emphasize that it is the most

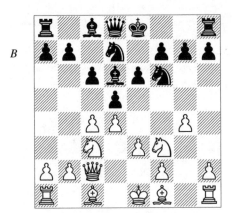

aggressive and exciting way to attack the Semi-Slav once you've played 6 ♕c2. Naturally this comes with considerable risk, since 7 g4 sacrifices the g-pawn temporarily (or permanently in some lines), and weakens the kingside. The initial idea is to meet 7...♘xg4 with 8 ♖g1 and, after the knight moves, play ♖xg7. Barring Black's acceptance of the pawn by ...♘xg4, White has gained space and hopes either to drive away the knight on f6 or, if Black defends by ...h6, to enforce g5 and open lines. His over-all strategy is to play for 0-0-0 and (usually) e4. Black has a large choice of counter-strategies, including variations in which he plays for an early ...e5, which is in line with the old saying about flank attacks being best answered by central attacks. Alternatively, Black has had mixed success with an attempt to control e4 by 7...♗b4, and he can also develop slowly by ...b6 and ...♗b7. Sadly the initially anarchic 7 g4 has turned into a highly theoretical line with a heavy dose of tactics and forcing lines, so those who are tempted to play it should be sure to devote a lot of study time to its intricacies. As Black, you should master at least one defensive solution.

In contemporary chess we find a strong disposition towards playing g4 in many openings, even in situations where it would previously have been thought to be an amateurish error. The Sicilian Defence stands out in this respect, but the move has cropped up all over the theoretical spectrum. It was undoubtedly the success of 7 g4 in the anti-Meran that gave impetus to this surge of similar ideas. Such sharing of ideas constitutes one of the most striking instances of the 'cross-pollination', a subject that I discuss in the first volume.

We turn to a game with 7 ♗e2 (D):

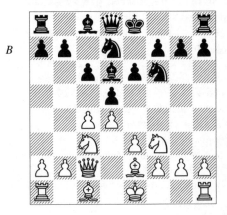

Karpov – Anand
Brussels Ct (8) 1991

For this positionally-oriented variation, I am not presenting current theoretical lines but games that show the most important ideas, or at least a clear contrast of strategies. This game in particular has been eclipsed by various refinements, yet the players' overall handling of the position holds up perfectly well.

7...0-0 8 0-0 dxc4

A logical and straightforward approach. Black wants to get ...e5 in without allowing White to play cxd5 and isolate his d-pawn. Nevertheless, 8...e5 has proven satisfactory after 9 cxd5 cxd5 10 ♘b5 ♗b8 11 dxe5 ♘xe5 (D), and now:

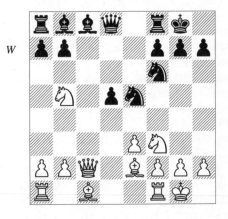

a) 12 ♗d2 ♗g4 13 ♘bd4 ♘e4 with equality, Karpov-Korchnoi, Amsterdam 1991 and later games. The same old story: Black's active pieces around the isolated pawn make up for the potential weakness.

b) 12 ♖d1 a6 13 ♘c3 ♕c7 14 g3 ♘eg4 15 ♗d2 ♗e6 16 ♖ac1 ♕e7 17 ♘d4 h5! 18 ♘a4 ♗d6 19 ♘f5 ♗xf5 20 ♕xf5 g6 21 ♕f3 ♕e6 22 ♗e1 ♖ac8 23 ♖xc8 ♖xc8 24 ♘c3 ♗b4! 25 ♗d3 ♘e5 26 ♕e2 ♕h3 27 f3 ♗c5 28 ♗c2 ♖e8 with a winning attack, Granda-Illescas, Pamplona 1991/2. An entertaining game.

Finally, 8...♕e7 and 8...♖e8 are the other common options, intending to play ...dxc4 and ...e5, but at a time of Black's choosing. If White tries to play e4 against either move he gets little; e.g., 8...♖e8 9 e4 dxe4 10 ♘xe4 ♘xe4 11 ♕xe4 e5.

9 ♗xc4 ♕e7 (D)

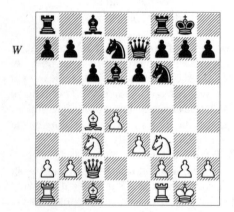

10 a3

White's is a prophylactic strategy, specifically aimed at thwarting Black's intentions. First, he secures a place for the bishop on a2, both to avoid a tempo loss after ...♘b6 and to neutralize ...b5-b4. 10 ♗b3 is another way to pursue this strategy, and over time it has become favoured over 10 a3. White also has tactical motivations, in that Black's ...e4 and ...♗xh2+ is not to be feared in that order.

10...e5 11 h3!

A good idea anyway, directed against the move ...♘g4. Here it also prevents the tactical idea of ...e4 followed by ...♗xh2+, and allows White to maintain the central tension. In turn, Black is challenged to find a useful move. Incidentally, this is precisely what is considered one of Black's best ways of playing against the main-line Colle System that runs 1 d4 d5 2 ♘f3

♘f6 3 e3 c5 4 c3 e6 5 ♘bd2 ♘c6 6 ♗d3 ♗d6 7 dxc5 ♗xc5 8 0-0 0-0 9 e4 ♕c7 10 ♕e2 h6.

11...♗c7

11...exd4?! 12 exd4 (D) gives White an isolated queen's pawn:

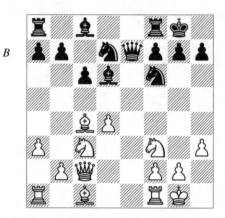

But as always he gets great piece activity, especially with his lead in development and rooks connected on the first rank. For example, 12...♘b6 13 ♗a2 ♗e6 14 ♖e1 ♘bd5 15 ♗g5 with very good attacking chances.

12 ♗a2 h6 13 ♘h4!

Periodically throughout this entire book we see how important and effective a knight on f5 can be. Of course before that it threatens to go to g6.

13...♖e8! 14 ♘f5 ♕f8 (D)

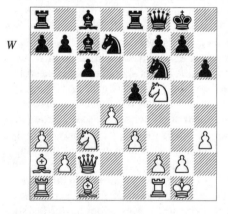

15 ♘b5!?

Tricky, although simply 15 ♗d2 might have been better, maintaining the positive points in his position and threatening ♘b5 for real.

15...♗b8 16 ♗d2!

Now 16...cxb5? loses after 17 ♗b4. Still, Black's next move stops these ideas and leads to a reasonable game.

16...a5 17 dxe5 ♗xe5?! *(D)*

Anand gives 17...♖xe5 18 ♘c3 ♘c5, which looks OK for Black.

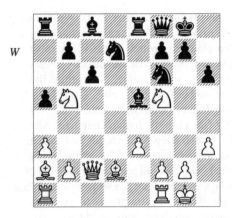

18 f4!

Trying to mobilize his 4:3 majority. Imagine the effect of e4-e5. We are entering the middle-game. White's opening has been fairly success-ful, but nothing that would forever dissuade Black from playing the variation.

18...♗b8

Not 18...cxb5? 19 fxe5 ♘xe5? 20 ♘xh6+.

19 ♘c3 ♖d8!?

19...b5 and 19...♗a7 are probably better moves. Then White might throw caution to the

wind and play g4 with the idea g5-g6. 19...g6!? is another thought.

20 ♗e1! ♘h7 21 ♗h4 ♘df6 *(D)*

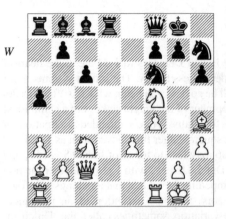

22 ♖ad1 ♖xd1 23 ♖xd1 ♗e6??

A huge mistake. 23...♗xf5 24 ♕xf5 ♗a7 is reasonable, although 25 ♗f2 ♖e8 allows 26 ♕xa5 or 26 e4, which will favour White gener-ally, especially in a bishop vs knight ending, should one be reached. The rest is easy:

24 ♗xe6 fxe6 25 ♕b3 ♕e8 26 ♘xg7! ♕f7 27 ♘xe6 ♗a7 28 ♗f2 ♖e8 29 ♘d4 ♕xb3 30 ♘xb3 ♗xe3 31 ♗xe3 ♖xe3 32 ♘xa5 1-0

A sort of model game for the 8 ♗e2 varia-tion. However, it also shows how solid Black's defence is, in that he could still reach or come very close to equality at several points well into the game.

4 Introduction to the Indian Defences

The Indian Defences to 1 d4 are at the heart of modern chess theory. The Indian systems that I shall be covering all begin with 1...♘f6. This development of the knight stakes out a claim to e4 and forestalls White's intended occupation of that square. Other first moves such as 1...c5 and 1...d6 may lead to forms of Indian Systems, and the Dutch Defence with 1...f5 is another method of impeding 2 e4. I feel that it belongs in its own category, with the exception of an infrequent side-variation, sometimes called the 'Dutch Indian', which involves 1...e6 and ...♝b4+ at an early stage.

After 1...♘f6 we see the move 2 c4 *(D)* in the clear majority games by masters. By this move White inhibits 2...d5 and prepares 3 ♘c3 without blocking his c-pawn. The second most popular move 2 ♘f3 will often be followed by c4 on one of the next few moves, sharing the same basic idea. Experience has shown that 2 ♘c3 lacks the punch to threaten Black's position, mainly because it isn't possible to enforce e4 after 2...d5. However, I should say that this is a result of specifics and not of inviolable principles. The idea that one shouldn't block the c-pawn in 1 d4 openings has its exceptions; a couple occur as early as the second move, as in the Dutch Defence variation that goes 1 d4 f5 2 ♘c3 and the Chigorin Defence, 1 d4 d5 2 c4 ♘c6.

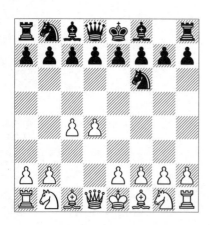

At this point (following 2 c4), White would like to play e4, establishing a broad centre and laying claim to central space. Black must decide upon a strategy. He can directly thwart that advance by, for example, controlling the e4- and d5-squares; e.g., 2...e6 3 ♘c3 ♝b4 (the Nimzo-Indian Defence) or here 3 ♘f3 b6 and ...♝b7 (the Queen's Indian Defence). Alternatively, he can allow White to play e4, setting up his strong pawn-centre. The establishment of an ideal centre would seem to be the goal of all openings and therefore advantageous for White. But for White's centre pawns to give him the advantage two things must hold true:

a) The pawns must actually control the central squares, which is usually the case against the Indian Defences.

b) They must be secure against dissolution, which may or may not be the case in the Indian Defences.

Thus Black plans to attack White's centre and/or to arrange things such that any advance by White backfires. Even in the latter case he must eventually attack and compromise White's centre or suffer under a cramped and probably untenable situation. The strategy just described is usually introduced by ...g6 in conjunction with either ...d6 (the King's Indian Defence), ...d5 (the Grünfeld Defence) or ...c5 (the Benoni). The latter is a sort of hybrid solution, since 2...c5 (threatening to impair White's centre by ...cxd4) already allows the incursion of White's pawn to d5, and e4 will follow if White wishes. Whether White's centre has been strengthened or weakened thereby is open to dispute.

Let's take a quick look at how the major Indian defences unfold in the first few moves. The King's Indian Defence (1 d4 ♘f6 2 c4 g6 3 ♘c3 ♝g7; e.g., 4 e4 d6 5 ♘f3 0-0) is in one sense the most radical one: it doesn't put a piece or pawn on the fourth rank for the first five moves! That phenomenon doesn't usually continue further, although we have some funny lines in the KID like the Panno System with 4

♘f3 d6 5 g3 0-0 6 ♗g2 ♘c6 7 0-0 a6 followed by 8...♖b8 and often 9...♗d7, in which case Black has gone 9 moves without placing anything beyond his third rank. When Black instead plays his usual ...e5 at an early stage, he blocks off his own bishop, but creates a dilemma for White about how to react. At first sight the Grünfeld Defence (1 d4 ♘f6 2 c4 g6 3 ♘c3 d5) is superior to the King's Indian in vital respects: the move ...d5 directly challenges White's centre, so that Black gains some space to work with. His bishop on g7 will be unblocked and remain so indefinitely, sometimes well into the endgame. In conjunction with the moves ...c5 and ...♘c6, for example, the queen on d8 and the bishop on g7 exert strong pressure upon the key d4-square (the move ...♗g4 can also come in handy in that respect if White has a knight on f3). In reality, White is compensated due to some specific features of play. If White plays 4 cxd5 ♘xd5 and then makes the principled move e4, then either Black's knight must retreat, giving White time to bolster his ideal centre, or the knight has to exchange on c3, when of a sudden White has shored up d4 with a pawn and is able to fight for control of that square. The outcome of that engagement, combined with some other factors, produces a competitive balance which attract players on both sides of the Indian Systems.

The Nimzo-Indian was the first of the Indian openings that really caught on among the world's top players, and it's easy to see why, The Nimzo-Indian combines rapid development with central control, to the extent that Black may even be said to be on equal footing with White in the centre proper (depending upon the variation, of course). Furthermore, he faces only rare situations like those in the King's Indian and Grünfeld in which White has a formidable set of pawns on e4 and d4. One might complain that Black therefore has no particular target, but the main action results from the exchange ...♗xc3, which cedes the bishop-pair to White but often saddles him with doubled c-pawns.

The Queen's Indian Defence also deploys Black's forces so as to control e4 and d5. Black receives a bit of a break in that regard because White's 3 ♘f3 not only fails to control e4 and d5, but interferes with potential central occupation that might follow from White's moves f3 and e4. Thus the Queen's Indian has been considered a safe and solid defence. You should keep in mind, however, that White controls more space, and surprisingly dynamic play can result from the natural imbalance that entails.

The Modern Benoni involves a different set of issues. On the positive side, Black has the quasi-permanent advantages of a powerful, unobstructed bishop on g7 and an open and very useful e-file. But unlike practitioners of the other Indian Defences, he faces a powerful and almost irremovable pawn on d5 that restricts his mobility and development.

Of course there is much more to say about the Indian Defences in general, but the real differences and similarities are best shown in their individual contexts.

5 Nimzo-Indian Defence

1 d4 ♘f6 2 c4 e6

2...e6 is a quintessentially flexible move that leaves Black's options open while increasing his control over d5. Now he has several ways to prevent White's key move e4. He can:

a) play ...d5 (usually transposing to the Queen's Gambit Declined);

b) develop by ...b6 and ...♗b7, to strengthen control of d5 and e4; or

c) bring the f8-bishop to b4, either giving check or pinning a knight on c3. All of these moves focus on the central light squares, with the intention of precluding e4 by White. Even ...♘e4 followed by ...f5 can contribute to this purpose.

Note that the immediate 2...b6?! fails in this respect because White can play 3 ♘c3 (or 3 f3) 3...♗b7 (3...d5 4 cxd5 ♘xd5 5 e4 ♘xc3 6 bxc3 isn't disastrous, but compares poorly with the Grünfeld Defence of Chapter 8) 4 f3 (or 4 ♕c2 followed by e4) 4...d5 5 cxd5 (D).

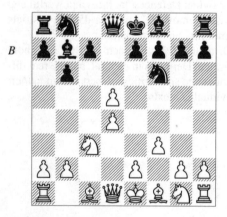

After Black recaptures, there follows 6 e4. When White establishes the ideal e4/d4 centre and it isn't subject to an effective attack, you can be pretty sure that he'll have the advantage. For this reason one hardly ever sees an experienced player make the move 2...b6.

We return to 2...e6 (D):

3 ♘c3

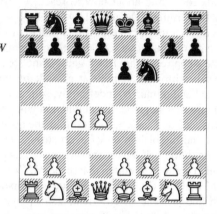

This is the obvious move (to prepare the advance e4), but in fact White makes a major decision thereby. 3 ♘c3 allows Black to play 3...♗b4, pinning the knight. Whether White wants to allow this determines his choice of moves. The main alternative, very often played, is 3 ♘f3; this also develops a piece and controls the important central squares d4 and e5. As we shall see in Chapter 6, 3 ♘f3 has its own pluses and minuses. Refer to Chapter 2 for the implications of 3 ♘f3 if Black chooses to play the Queen's Gambit Declined by 3...d5.

Other third moves are either dubious or generally less ambitious. Sometimes it helps to look at weaker moves to understand the good ones. Here are some relatively logical continuations for White:

a) After 3 f3?! d5!, White cannot manage to play e4 and thus has used up a move and taken away the best spot for White's knight on f3. An example of how the play might go is 4 ♘c3 (this amounts to a poor version of the Queen's Gambit Declined) 4...c5 (Black strikes back in the centre, but he can also play 4...♗e7) 5 cxd5 cxd4! (D).

6 ♕a4+ (6 ♕xd4 ♘c6! takes advantage of White's pinned d-pawn to gain more time by attacking White's queen) 6...♘bd7 (not the only move, but it shows up how weak White's dark squares are). Then White can choose between:

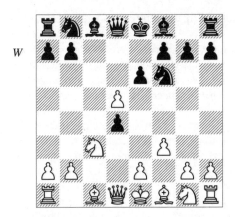

W

a1) 7 dxe6 dxc3 8 exd7+ ♗xd7 9 ♕b3 ♗c5! 10 bxc3 0-0 11 e4? ♘xe4! 12 fxe4 ♕h4+ 13 ♔d1 ♕xe4 results in devastating threats like ...♗a4, ...♗g4+ and ...♖fd8.

a2) 7 ♕xd4 ♗c5! again targets the weakened dark squares in White's camp. White would be temporarily a pawn ahead after 8 ♕d1 exd5 9 ♘xd5 ♘xd5 10 ♕xd5 but things would turn sour after 10...♕a5+!: 11 ♔d1 (11 ♗d2?? fails to 11...♗f2+ 12 ♔xf2 ♕xd5) 11...♘f6 12 ♕e5+ ♗e6 13 e4 ♖d8+ and there are too many pieces attacking White's king. This line serves as a warning about weakening pawn moves, the importance of piece activity and the risks of early queen development.

b) 3 a3 prevents ...♗b4 but doesn't control a central square or develop a piece. Black can equalize immediately by playing 3...d5 (3...c5 is another aggressive move) 4 ♘c3 c5 (or, of course, 4...♗e7, since White wouldn't play a3 in the first few moves of the Queen's Gambit Declined!) 5 e3 with equality, and not 5 ♘f3?! cxd4 6 ♘xd4 dxc4 7 ♕a4+ ♗d7 8 ♕xc4 ♘c6, when Black has good development whereas White's queen is out there a bit early; for example, ...♖c8 might soon follow. Compare this with 1 d4 ♘f6 2 c4 e6 3 ♘f3 b6 4 a3. The difference in that case is that 4...d5, while playable, doesn't go well with the move ...b6.

c) A much better move is 3 g3 preparing ♗g2, which contests both e4 and d5. It's a little too slow to give White an advantage, but it can easily transpose to another opening; for example, 3...d5 4 ♘f3 is a Catalan, comfortable enough for Black, and 3...c5 4 d5 exd5 5 cxd5 d6 6 ♗g2 g6 is a Modern Benoni, analysed in the chapter on that opening. For those wanting

an independent line, 3...♗b4+ is a good alternative, when Black is already prepared to castle.

3...♗b4 *(D)*

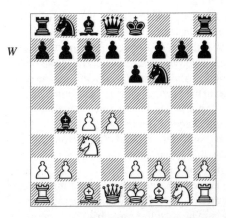

W

This move defines what is called the Nimzo-Indian Defence. It is named after the brilliant and creative thinker Aron Nimzowitsch, who both played and had the most to do with promoting 3...♗b4 in the early part of the 20th century. The Nimzo-Indian has been played by just about every World Champion and nearly every challenger going back to the 1920s. It is arguably the most difficult opening to play against after 1 d4.

Why 3...♗b4? The most obvious and important answer is that it prevents White from playing 4 e4. Let's make sure. The sequence 4 e4 ♘xe4 5 ♕g4 isn't in books on chess theory, although perhaps it should be in the opening primers, since White attacks both the e4-knight and the g7-pawn. The best reply is 5...♘xc3 *(D)*.

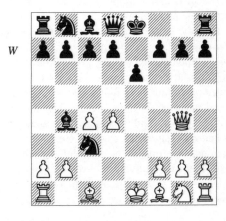

Black threatens discovered check and the knight can't be captured. Still, White can try 6 a3 (6 ♕xg7? ♘e4+ 7 ♔e2 ♕f6 and Black remains a piece ahead), when the trap that Black has to avoid is 6...♗a5? 7 ♕xg7 ♘e4+ 8 b4 and after Black defends his rook, his bishop will be captured. Instead, 6...♗e7! 7 bxc3 0-0 leaves Black with an extra pawn and a great position. Thus 4 e4 deserves a '?' after all. These moves are good to play through if you are inexperienced in the opening phase of the game. Similar ideas can arise in other openings including the Sicilian Defence and French Defence.

Let's return to 3...♗b4. Apart from preventing e4, this move fights for control of the central light squares. All three of Black's moves have directly or indirectly helped him control d5, and two of them have done the same for e4. This emphasis on light squares is characteristic of most Nimzo-Indian variations, at least for the first five or six moves. For example, Black will frequently play ...b6 and ...♗b7 next, also watching over the d5- and e4-squares.

That's not all. Whether or not Black chooses to play ...b6, he has other light-square themes. The move ...d5 is a part of many variations, staking further claim to e4 and adding the queen to the mob of pieces defending d5. In addition, occupation of the light squares by ...♘e4 is common, followed by ...f5 to cement control of e4.

Chess being what it is, of course, this delightfully simple picture proves deceptively complex as Black may later turn to moves such as ...c5, ...♘c6, ...d6 and ...e5 in order to challenge or defend *dark* squares! Still, the abundance of light-square themes lends a distinctive character to Nimzo-Indian play that often extends well into the middlegame.

One of the most obvious features of 3...♗b4 is that it introduces the possibility of ...♗xc3+, giving White doubled pawns. As we discussed in the introductory chapters of Volume 1, those doubled pawns are particularly bad because the forward pawn on c4 is incapable of being defended by pawns, and it can easily be attacked (see below). The better part of Nimzo-Indian variations have one or more points at which ...♗xc3 is the best move. However, that capture usually comes at the cost of giving White the bishop-pair. In some cases White also takes

command of the centre, although if embarked upon too early, the occupation of the centre may have drawbacks, such as queenside weaknesses, overextension, or simply the inability to exploit extra space. Another advantage that Black has is speedy development in the first few moves. After his third move he is already ready to castle, whereas White has quite a few moves to go, perhaps e3 followed by ♗d3, ♘f3 and 0-0. In the meantime, he may throw in moves such as a3 and ♕c2, which don't contribute much to getting White's pieces out.

Thus White's policy in most variations is a cautious consolidation of his position involving protection of his centre and development. Black would like to disturb the position's balance in his favour, usually combining piece-play with one or more pawn-breaks. White almost inevitably has to make pawn-structure concessions, either the aforementioned doubled c-pawns, an isolated pawn, weak light squares on the queenside, or loss of space in the centre as Black advances. The issue becomes whether the situation stabilizes enough for White's bishop-pair to exert itself, in which case Black can be in real trouble. The bishops' merits vary from position to position; we'll see both how ineffectual they can be in some of the variations that follow, and how devastating in others.

Sämisch and Related Lines

Under this heading we shall be covering lines where White plays an early a3, and Black captures on c3, doubling White's pawns. There are several forms that this can take, depending on whether White plays a3 immediately, or after 4 f3 or 4 e3, often waiting until Black has played ...d5 before playing a3. The traditional form of the Sämisch is as follows:

1 d4 ♘f6 2 c4 e6 3 ♘c3 ♗b4 4 a3!? ♗xc3+ 5 bxc3 *(D)*

The Sämisch Variation is in many ways the most instructive of all Nimzo-Indian lines. It seems odd to force Black into ...♗xc3+, a move that he is likely to play anyway, and thus to accept the weak doubled c-pawns while losing time. For some rather subtle reasons, however, it turns out that there are advantages to forcing Black to commit to a strategy before he can

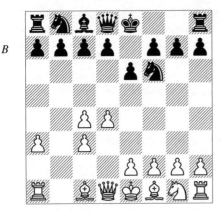

react to White's. Indeed, 4 a3 was one of the earliest methods of play versus the Nimzo-Indian and many of the best players of the time, including the long-time World Champion Botvinnik, were infatuated with possession of the bishop-pair. Remember that having two bishops versus a bishop and a knight, or two bishops versus two knights, is generally advantageous, although you have to assess each case individually (especially in this opening). White's idea is to compel Black to part with his bishop before he changes his mind and retreats, something that occurs in other lines. In contemporary chess, both 4 a3 and its cousin 4 f3 have once again become quite popular. Similarly, White can follow up the move 4 e3 with 5 a3, or even 5 ♗d3 and 6 a3, often producing the same basic structure. As mentioned above, the motivation for this is often to wait for Black to commit himself to playing ...d5. The reason for this is that some of the most challenging lines at Black's disposal against the 4 a3 move-order involve him avoiding ...d5 and attacking White's c4-pawn with his pieces.

The Sämisch Variation is the ideal starting point for discussing the Nimzo-Indian because it contains a majority of the fundamental themes that arise from the opening. On a simple level, we may say that the strategies resulting from 4 a3 can usually be characterized as one of the following:

a) White undertakes to gain ground with his central and kingside pawns, creating threats or forming a basis for a direct attack by pieces. Typically this involves ideas such as f3 and e4 (or g4, which also grabs space), e4-e5 and/or f4-f5-f6. For his part, Black attempts to block

those pawns with his own, usually with moves like ...e5 and/or ...f5.

b) White tries to activate his bishop-pair, which requires line-opening pawn advances or exchanges. Black endeavours to restrict White's bishops to passive roles behind their own pawns.

c) Black wants to win White's weak forward c-pawn or expose his weaknesses on the key queenside light squares. He tends to exchange pieces in order to neutralize White's kingside efforts. White can either strain to protect his weak c4-pawn with pieces, or sacrifice it for activity.

d) Alternatively, Black will play moves to contest the centre: either ...d5, or some combination of ...d6, ...e5 and ...c5. Then he can even think about initiating play on the kingside.

I shall devote an exceptional amount of space to exploring these schemes. They will play out in the following variations:

A: Systems with ...d6 and ...e5;
B: Systems with ...d5;
C: Systems with ...c5 and/or ...b6.

As this is a book of ideas, the latest theory will not always be covered (the last section is exceptional in that respect), and I'll be using some classic games that throw the strategies and set-ups into relief. Before moving ahead I shall very briefly mention a curious move:

5...♘e4 (D)

This received several tests in the 1961 World Championship match between Tal and Botvinnik, the latter playing White.

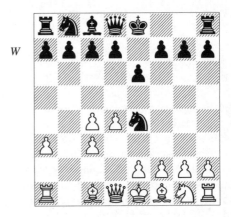

Black attacks White's c3-pawn but this advanced knight is subject to being driven back with gain of time by f3. Tal is trying to make way for the move ...f5 (emphasizing light-square control). The immediate 6 f3? fails to 6...♕h4+, when Black wins major material, and the attempt to prepare f3 by 6 ♘h3 allows 6...c5! in order to answer 7 e3 or 7 ♕c2 with 7...♕a5. After trying a variety of moves, Botvinnik found a fairly effective one:

Botvinnik – Tal
Moscow Wch (20) 1961

6 e3 f5

6...♘xc3?? 7 ♕c2 traps the knight. 6...0-0 may be more accurate. Nevertheless, White can play 7 ♗d3 f5 8 ♘e2, when White will soon play f3 and chase Black's knight away with a central advance in store.

7 ♕h5+! g6 8 ♕h6

Now Black's kingside squares are a tad weak by virtue of his 3rd and 5th moves.

8...d6

8...♕f6 was played in later games, but note that 8...♘xc3? 9 f3! threatens e4. The most interesting choice is 8...♕g5 9 ♕xg5 ♘xg5 10 f3 *(D)*, when the move e4 is coming.

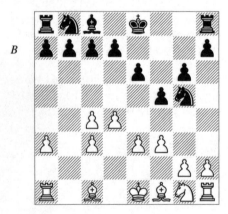

This is an instructive queenless middlegame (not ending!) because Black is far away from mounting an attack on White's c4-pawn (in fact, c5 may become an option for White at some point) and his dark squares are weak. White's two bishops and centre wield considerable influence and guarantee some advantage.

9 f3 ♘f6 10 e4! e5 11 ♗g5

White has achieved his main goals of expanding in the centre and getting his bishops out.

11...♕e7 12 ♗d3 ♖f8 13 ♘e2 ♕f7

and Botvinnik was doing well. He should now have played 14 0-0, when he gives the instructive line 14...♘g8 15 ♕h4 f4 16 c5! ♕g7 17 cxd6 cxd6 18 ♕e1 h6 19 ♗h4 g5 20 ♗f2 with a clear advantage. See how the two bishops cooperate with the centre and queenside.

Lines with ...d6 and ...e5

When the Nimzo-Indian Defence and Sämisch Variation became respectable in the 1920s and 1930s, one of the first ideas that Black employed involved the moves ...d6 and ...e5. This made eminent sense: why not prevent White from expanding in the centre before one turns one's attention to the queenside and its more-or-less permanent weaknesses?

White's response to that question is to use his space in the centre to support an attack on Black's kingside. This is a difficult task. However, since Black is playing in the centre instead of attacking on the queenside, White's pieces will be relieved of their duty to protect his queenside (in particular, Black is not attacking White's pawn on c4 by means of ...b6 and ...♗a6; later on you will see that this is a major strategy). Notice too that the ...d6/...e5 defence already shifts the focus of the game from the central light squares to central dark squares. Although the combination of ...d6 and ...e5 is seen less frequently than in earlier times, it still constitutes a legitimate answer to White's ideas. What's more, the same structure arises in other variations of the Nimzo-Indian.

Let's start with two older games, because they contain mistakes that illustrate important themes.

Gligorić – Plater
Warsaw 1947

1 d4 ♘f6 2 c4 e6 3 ♘c3 ♗b4 4 a3 ♗xc3+ 5 bxc3 d6!? 6 f3

White intends e4. Capablanca once played 6 ♕c2?!, with the same goal, versus Ragozin in Moscow 1935. It turns out that this is inaccurate, because Black could have grabbed the opportunity to generate counterplay against the centre by 6...e5 7 e4 ♘c6!. The point is that White's 6th move has taken protection away from his d-pawn. Now he hasn't time for ♗d3, and 8 d5 ♘b8! 9 ♗d3 ♘a6 *(D)* (or 9...♘bd7) lets Black take over the inviting c5-square for his knight. Indeed, the c5-square is a 'true' outpost, in that it can't be attacked by enemy pawns:

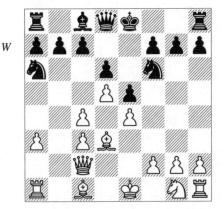

W

In this position it will prove difficult for White to organize any pawn-breaks, since f4 will be met by ...exf4 with additional Black firepower along the e-file aimed at the backward pawn on e4. Furthermore, the a4-square is an inviting target for Black, who can play ...♗d7 and ...♕e8 at some point, complementing a knight on c5. Another theme that we shall see throughout this chapter concerns the possible move ...c6. Here Black may play ...c6 and ...cxd5 to open the c-file for his rook (...♖c8), which puts considerable pressure on White's pawns on that file. This all stems from the inaccuracy 6 ♕c2. Of course White's position isn't hopeless. He can still play for ♘e2 and ♘g3 or f4 at some point.

But the timing of all this is delicate. After 6 ♕c2, Ragozin actually played 6...0-0?! 7 e4 e5 8 ♗d3! c5!? (now 8...♘c6 9 ♘e2! holds the centre together nicely) 9 ♘e2 ♘c6 10 d5 ♘e7 11 f3 ♘d7 12 h4 (here's the problem: left to his own devices White will launch his pawns forward to take over as much space as he can; then he can mount an attack) 12...♘b6 13 g4! *(D)*.

Compare this with the last diagram: Black has lost his outpost on c5 and can't play ...c6 to create pressure on the queenside. Staking out as much space as possible is a key element of White's strategy in the Sämisch. The game continued 13...f6 14 ♘g3 ♔f7! 15 g5 ♘g8 16 f4

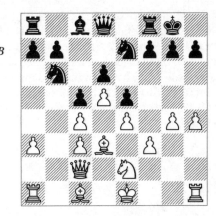

B

♔e8 17 f5. Black's king has escaped but his pieces are confined to the first few ranks and he stands poorly.

6...0-0 7 e4 e5 8 ♗d3 c5!?

Black's choice is important. He tries to force things in the centre and on the queenside but it's nice to have ...c6 in reserve; for example, 8...♘c6 9 ♘e2 h6 (versus ♗g5) 10 d5?! ♘a5 11 ♗e3 b6 12 ♘g3 ♗a6 13 ♕e2 c6! 14 0-0 ♖c8 *(D)*.

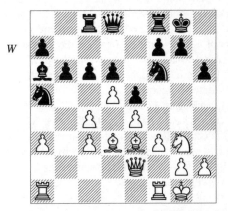

W

In that case Black can attack along the c-file by exchanging pawns to control the c4-square. Had he played ...c5, he would have run out of pieces able to attack White's pawn on c4. Of course, 10 d5 wasn't forced.

9 ♘e2 ♘c6 10 0-0!?

An intentional pawn sacrifice.

10...b6

The question is whether Black should stand pat or win a pawn and liquidate White's centre. If you play either side of the Sämisch or another Nimzo-Indian variation involving e3 and ...c5, you will run into this issue. Accepting the sacrifice might lead to a line such as 10...cxd4 11 cxd4 exd4 (11...♘xd4 12 ♘xd4 exd4 13 ♗b2 ♕b6 14 ♕d2!, and in most cases ♕f2 recovers the pawn, with White having mobile bishops on open lines) 12 ♖b1 (or 12 ♗g5 h6 13 ♗h4 g5 14 ♗f2) 12...♘d7 13 ♗b2 ♘c5 14 ♘xd4 ♘xd3 15 ♕xd3 (D).

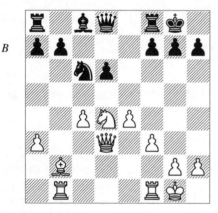

What's going on in such positions? You'll notice that White has a weak pawn on c4 but Black has problems with his vulnerable d-pawn. White has the more powerful bishop and prospects of advancing his pawns on the kingside. In general, Black should only win the pawn on d4 if he can hang on to it or otherwise achieve immediate counterplay.

11 ♗g5! ♗a6 12 f4!

Here we have a basic idea that applies to this kind of centre: Black should not normally 'mix systems' when he has played ...e5 by trying to attack White's c-pawns at the same time. Since Black's centre and kingside need to be continually monitored, it's risky to park a bishop on a6 and/or a knight on a5, away from the kingside action. Below we shall see a more sophisticated defence involving the same queenside moves but without ...d6 and ...e5.

12...cxd4 13 cxd4 exd4

After 13...h6, White decimates Black's kingside by 14 fxe5! hxg5 15 exf6 gxf6 16 ♘g3! ♘xd4 (what else?) 17 ♕h5 with too many threats, such as ♕h6 in combination with ♘h5 or e5.

14 ♘g3 (D)

White threatens both ♘h5 and ♘f5. Suddenly Black is lost, and it's only move 14!

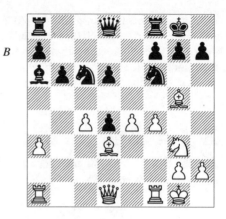

14...♔h8 15 ♘h5

Once White captures on f6 and doubles White's pawns, Black's kingside will be horribly exposed.

15...♕e7 16 ♕e1

There's no hurry, although White can also win with 16 ♘xf6 gxf6 17 ♗h4. Then what's to be done about ♕h5 and e5?

16...♕e6 17 f5! ♕e5 18 ♗xf6 gxf6 19 ♕h4 ♖g8

At this point Gligorić won relatively slowly following 20 ♖f3 ♖g5 21 ♖h3 ♔g8, but there was an immediate win to be had by 20 ♘xf6! ♖g7 21 ♖f3. White has the standard tactical idea of 22 ♖h3 and 23 ♕xh7+ and there's nothing that Black can do about it except to give up his queen on f6.

Lines with ...d5 and the Botvinnik Approach

1 d4 ♘f6 2 c4 e6 3 ♘c3 ♗b4 4 a3 ♗xc3+ 5 bxc3 d5 (D)

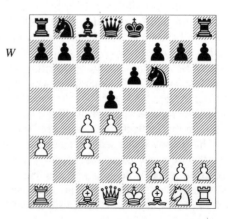

Black plays what may seem the most natural move on the board (though is not so common via this precise move-order), staking out territory in the centre to neutralize White's usual advantage in space. True, White can and usually will 'undouble' his pawns by cxd5, but that has some drawbacks after the simple reply ...exd5:

a) it frees Black's bad bishop on c8; and

b) gives his king's rook good scope along an open central file.

6 e3 *(D)*

This move reaches a position that is more often seen via the move-order 4 e3 d5 5 a3 &xc3+ 6 bxc3. In that sequence, White doesn't play a3 until Black is committed to ...d5.

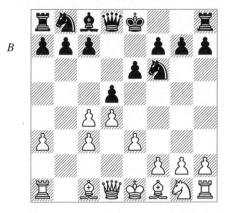

Instead of 6 e3, it's tempting to bring the queen's bishop out before shutting it in by e3. That brings us to our first example of ...d5 in the Sämisch, an illustration of how White can go fundamentally wrong.

Botvinnik – Kotov
Groningen 1946

1 d4 &f6 2 c4 e6 3 &c3 &b4 4 a3 &xc3+ 5 bxc3 d5 6 cxd5!?

Now White could have achieved the normal position by 6 e3. See the next game.

6...exd5 7 &g5?! *(D)*

The strongest player in the world at that time shows us what *not* to do when playing his own system! White's logic is to place his dark-squared 'bad' bishop outside the central pawn-chain that will be formed by e3 and d4. However, this slows down the important development

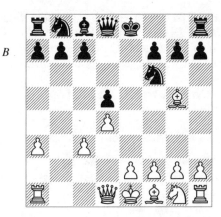

of his kingside and weakens White's queenside dark squares.

7...c5!

A dynamic response. Black has ...&a5 in mind, hitting the c3-pawn and unpinning the knight on f6. 7...h6 is also not a bad move, because if White plays 8 &xf6 &xf6, he loses his most important asset, the bishop-pair. Nevertheless, Black would have used the extra tempo ...h6 to achieve this and the position would be objectively equal, with a technical battle in store. By the way, the obvious alternative after 7...h6 is 8 &h4, but that is even worse for White because it allows the direct attack 8...g5 9 &g3 &e4, when Black is attacking the c3-pawn and would like to threaten the g3-bishop by ...h5 or play ...c5 followed by ...&a5. The point to remember here is that the rapid exertion of queenside pressure definitely outweighs the weaknesses created by ...h6 and ...g5. A useful old saying is "Weaknesses aren't weaknesses unless they can be attacked". This may not be 100% accurate, but is a good rule of thumb.

8 f3!?

White tries to stop ...&e4 and may have ideas of playing e4 later. The move f3 is always dangerous (great reward but great risk). The problem is that after the natural 8 e3, 8...&a5 forces some awkward defence like 9 &c2 &e4 10 &f4 cxd4 11 exd4 &c6. Then Black is threatening ...&xd4!, and 12 &f3 &g4! can be followed by ...&xf3 and/or ...&c8, putting pressure on White's backward c-pawn. 12 &e2 &f5 is a perfect picture of light-square domination.

8...h6 9 &xf6

But now the *dark* squares are in trouble (look at that weakness on e3!)! Retreat isn't attractive either: 9 ♗h4 0-0 10 e3 ♖e8 11 ♗f2 (11 ♕d2 ♕e7 12 ♔f2 ♘e4+! 13 fxe4 ♕xh4+) 11...cxd4 (11...♕a5 12 ♕d2 ♗f5) 12 cxd4 ♘c6 and White is having a hard time getting his pieces to active squares.

9...♕xf6 10 e3 0-0 11 ♘e2 ♖e8 *(D)*

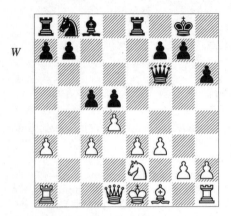

12 ♔f2

A sad move to make but it will be forced soon anyway. One example is 12 ♕d2 ♘c6 13 dxc5 (ruining his pawn-structure, but what else?) 13...♕h4+ 14 ♘g3 ♕e7 15 ♔f2 ♕xc5 with a dominating position.

12...♕e7 13 ♕d2 ♘d7 14 ♘f4 ♘f6 15 ♗d3

White has managed to get his pieces out, but e3 is still weak.

15...♗d7 16 h3 ♕d6 17 ♖hb1 b6 18 ♗f1 ♖e7! *(D)*

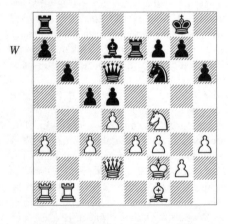

19 a4 ♖ae8 20 ♖e1 c4!

One of those paradoxical moves that grandmasters are good at finding. Releasing the pressure on d4 in this way is generally bad but here

it stops ♗d3 and ♘d3 while containing the terrible threat of ...g5. The rest of the game is short and sweet:

21 g4 g5 22 ♘e2 ♖xe3! 23 ♘g3 ♕xg3+! 24 ♔xg3 ♘e4+ 0-1

White's problems stemmed from the over-ambitious 7 ♗g5.

Let's return to the position after 1 d4 ♘f6 2 c4 e6 3 ♘c3 ♗b4 4 a3 ♗xc3+ 5 bxc3 d5:

6 e3 *(D)*

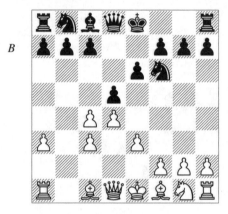

6...c5

Now for an important move-order issue. The position after 6...c5 could also have occurred via the common move-order 4 e3 d5 5 a3 ♗xc3+ 6 bxc3 c5 or 4 e3 c5 5 a3 ♗xc3+ 6 bxc3 d5. In the move-order here, however, Black isn't already committed to ...c5 and he doesn't have to play it yet (the trade-off, of course, is that in the 4 a3 move-order, Black is not committed to playing ...d5). For example, he can insert 6...0-0, when 7 cxd5 exd5 8 ♗d3 b6 9 ♘e2 ♗a6 tries to get the light-squared bishops off the board immediately. The obvious continuation for White is 10 0-0 ♗xd3 11 ♕xd3. Then Black might play 11...♕c8!? 12 f3 ♕a6, winning light squares like c4. But that simplification doesn't solve the problem of the centre after 13 ♕xa6 ♘xa6 14 ♘g3 *(D)*. Then the advance e4 will follow, emphasizing the superiority of the white bishop over the poorly-placed knight on a6.

For example, 14...♖fe8 15 ♖e1 c5 16 e4 dxe4 17 fxe4 cxd4 18 cxd4 ♖ad8 19 ♗b2 ♘b8 20 ♖ac1 ♘bd7 21 ♖c7 and White clearly has the upper hand. In general, space and mobility are

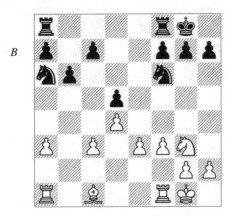

just as much advantages in queenless middle-games as they are with queens still on the board.

7 cxd5 exd5 8 ♗d3 0-0 9 ♘e2! *(D)*

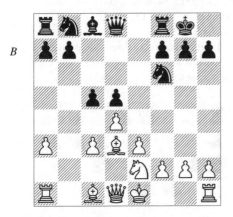

This move defines White's strategy. By developing the knight to e2 he gives his centre pawns the freedom to advance, namely, by f3 and e4, often supported by a knight on g3. In spite of White's lagging development, this set-up tends to bring out the best in White's centre and bishop-pair. Placing a knight on f3 would allow Black to prevent e4 indefinitely.

The arrangement of pieces and pawns after ♗d3, ♘e2, 0-0 and f3 was developed and popularized by Botvinnik, and was used by him in one of his most famous victories, over Capablanca in the AVRO 1938 tournament. Since then many great players have employed it, including Kasparov.

9...b6 10 0-0 ♗a6 11 ♗xa6

Many players prefer 11 f3 immediately. Then after 11...♗xd3 12 ♕xd3, Black can develop his knight to a square other than a6, but White

has prevented the useful manoeuvre ...♘a6-c7. This trade-off of advantages is hard to assess.

11...♘xa6 12 f3!

The beginning of a dynamic strategy to over-run Black's position with pawns by e4-e5, f4-f5, etc. Right now it's time to see some general strategy by examining White's alternatives to the move 12 f3:

a) The above-mentioned Botvinnik-Capablanca, Rotterdam (AVRO) 1938 was a seminal game, so we'll skip over the technical inaccuracies in the next few moves: 12 ♗b2?! ♕d7! 13 a4 (13 ♕d3 ♕a4! with the kind of queenside light-square control that White needs to avoid for as long as he can) 13...♖fe8 14 ♕d3 c4? *(D)*.

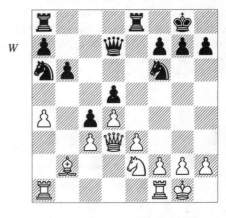

With the benefit of hindsight just about every commentator agreed that this is a positional mistake because it gives up the option of ...cxd4 and releases the pressure on White's centre. Years of master games have confirmed that general view. Let's see how this works: 15 ♕c2 ♘b8 16 ♖ae1 ♘c6 17 ♘g3 ♘a5 18 f3 ♘b3 *(D)*.

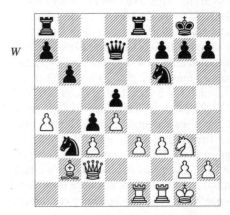

19 e4! (this is the whole point of the system. White will try to blow Black away in the centre and kingside before too much damage occurs on the queenside) 19...♕xa4 20 e5 ♘d7 21 ♕f2! (otherwise Black might employ the trick 21...♘bc5!) 21...g6! 22 f4 f5 (White threatened f5 with too much attack for Black to handle, but Capablanca prepared this defensive resource; it's not easy to defeat an immortal!) 23 exf6 ♘xf6 24 f5 (normally this would be decisive, but Black can reduce the attacking material) 24...♖xe1 25 ♖xe1 ♖e8 (the key point of the game; isn't the attack at a standstill?) 26 ♖e6!. This frustrates Black's plan and turns the tide, because now simplification comes at the cost of a powerful passed pawn. The 'opening' phase is past and I'll stick with the bare moves now. The wonderful thing is that White succeeds here in spite of minimal material and an apparently awful bishop on b2. 26...♖xe6 27 fxe6 ♔g7 28 ♕f4 ♕e8 29 ♕e5 ♕e7 (D).

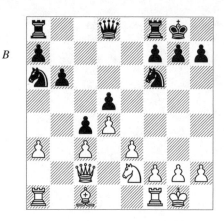

B

24 ♘f1! b5 25 ♘e3 ♘b6 26 g4 fxg4 27 ♘xg4 ♖f8 28 ♘f6+ ♔h8 29 ♕g2 ♘c6 30 ♕h3! (White stops ...♘e7) 30...♘d8 31 ♗c1! ♘c8 32 ♔h1 ♖a6 33 f5 gxf5 34 ♗h6 1-0.

Let's return to 12 f3!.

12...♖e8 (D)

Without counterplay down the e- and c-files, Black would have nothing to do but wait for White's attack.

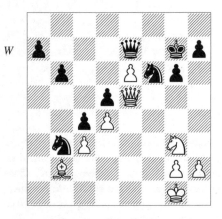

W

30 ♗a3!! ♕xa3 31 ♘h5+! gxh5 32 ♕g5+ ♔f8 33 ♕xf6+ ♔g8 34 e7 ♕c1+ 35 ♔f2 ♕c2+ 36 ♔g3 ♕d3+ 37 ♔h4 ♕e4+ 38 ♔xh5 ♕e2+ 39 ♔h4 ♕e4+ 40 g4 ♕e1+ 41 ♔h5 1-0.

b) Gligorić-Benko, Budapest 1948 solidified the idea that after ...c4, the e4 advance couldn't be stopped forever: 12 ♕d3 c4?! 13 ♕c2 (D).

13...♘b8 14 f3 ♖e8 15 ♘g3 ♘c6 16 ♕f2 ♕d7 17 ♗b2 ♖e6 18 ♖ae1 ♖ae8 19 ♖e2! g6 20 ♖fe1 (here we see application of brute force! White finally gets e4 in and from there on things go well) 20...♘a5 21 e4 ♕b7 22 e5 ♘d7 23 f4 f5 (this appears to block White's attack yet it turns out that Black has little positive to do while White organizes another pawn-break)

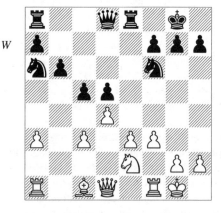

W

This position has occurred scores of times in master play, normally via 4 f3 or 4 e3. We'll follow a game that is instructional because we get to see White's plans in pure form, and also a straightforward strategy for Black.

Tisdall – Bjarnason
Reykjavik 1989

13 ♘g3 ♕d7!

As in Botvinnik-Capablanca, Black takes aim at the light squares, in this case a4 and b5. Even ...♕b7 might operate against the e4 push.

14 ♖a2! *(D)*

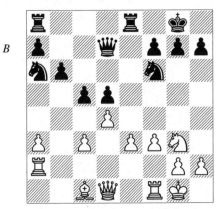

Strange to say, this manoeuvre of the queen's rook to the centre may be the only way to play for advantage. Not only does White swing over to support the e4 push, he does so while still preventing ...♕a4 and keeping his queen's bishop free to go in either direction. The idea of ♖a2-e2 (or ♖e2-f2) followed by e4 in this type of position goes back to the 1940s and early 1950s (at least in terms of consistent usage) and has become a standard part of White's weaponry in this and even a couple of other openings, notably Queen's Gambits. Sometimes ♖a2 is played with the knight still on e2, in which case White has the new idea of g4 and ♘g3 with g5 and e4 to follow. Naturally Black has his own resources, and in spite of most writers' and players' mistrust of his position he hasn't scored that much worse than in other variations.

14...♖ac8! *(D)*

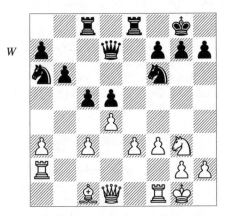

15 ♕d3!?

Perhaps more accurate is 15 ♖e2, which has indeed played in a few games. Then Black's most successful idea has been 15...cxd4 16 cxd4 ♖c4! *(D)* with double-edged play.

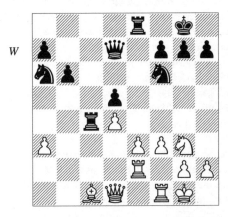

White will have to place his bishop passively on b2 to enforce e4. Lutsko-Kveinys, Tallinn 2001 continued 17 ♕d3 b5 18 ♗b2 ♘c7! 19 e4 ♘e6 (this standard defensive move hits f4 and d4) 20 ♖d2 ♘f4 21 ♕e3 ♘6h5 22 ♘xh5 ♘xh5 23 g4?! ♘f6 24 e5 ♕c6 25 ♖g2 ♘d7 with advantage to Black. 26 f4 would be met by 26...♘f6 and ...♘e4, and 26 ♕d3 by 26...♘b6! 27 f4 ♘a4. In lines like these White's bishop on b2 really *is* a bad bishop! But his play is fairly easy to improve upon.

15...♕a4 16 ♖e2 ♘c7!?

The logical follow-up to Black's play is 16...cxd4 17 cxd4 ♕c4! 18 ♕xc4! ♖xc4. After 19 ♗b2, White has a mobile centre. Still, Black can play 19...♘c7 intending 20 e4 dxe4 21 fxe4 ♘b5! and gain counterplay.

17 e4 *(D)*

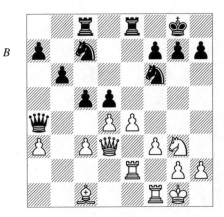

17...♘b5

Black's plan is logical and appropriate to the position, but a tad slow. Of course, his defence is extremely difficult. Notice that if 17...cxd4 18 cxd4 ♘e6, White's bishop can now settle in on e3, whereas if it were already committed to b2, he would have to deal with ...♘f4. From here on things proceed thematically, and typically easily, for White after e5 is achieved:

18 e5 ♘d7 19 ♗b2 cxd4 20 cxd4 ♘f8 21 f4 ♕c4 22 ♕e3 ♕c6 23 f5 ♔h8 24 ♘h5 ♘d7 25 ♕g5 ♖g8 26 e6! fxe6 27 fxe6 ♘f8 28 ♘f4 ♘c7 29 ♕e5 ♕e8 30 ♖c1! 1-0

To balance out that one, here's a near-perfect strategy employed by Black against Milov, a leading advocate of the Sämisch Variation (via the 4 e3 and 4 f3 move-orders):

V. Milov – Campora
Andorra 2001

1 d4 ♘f6 2 c4 e6 3 ♘c3 ♗b4 4 e3 0-0 5 ♗d3 d5 6 a3 ♗xc3+ 7 bxc3 c5 8 cxd5 exd5 9 ♘e2 b6 10 0-0 ♗a6 11 f3 ♖e8 12 ♘g3

Allowing Black to capture on d3, a subtle difference as compared to ♗xa6.

12...♗xd3 13 ♕xd3 ♘c6 14 ♖a2 ♕d7 15 ♖e2 ♖ad8! 16 ♗b2

We've seen this kind of thing before, but not with the knight on c6. The move ♗b2 helps to prepare e4, although right now the d-pawn would fall to ...dxe4 and multiple captures on d4. Thus White needs one more preparatory move, probably ♖d1. It seems as though Black can do little but wait.

16...h5! *(D)*

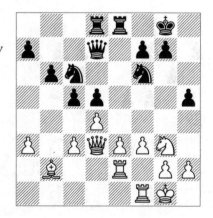

This advance is beautifully timed and works out nicely. Normally such a pawn turns into a weakness.

17 ♖d1

17 ♘h1 h4 18 ♘f2 is the standard idea versus ...h5 in such positions in order to enforce e4, but here 18...♘a5 19 e4 ♘h5! creates problems for White. When White's bishop goes to b2, f4 is a potential home for Black's knight.

17...h4 18 ♘f5 c4

Or 18...h3! intending 19 g3 g6, when White's knight will sit very awkwardly on h4.

19 ♕c2 ♘e7 20 ♘xe7+ ♖xe7?!

20...♕xe7! holds down e4 and keeps the advantage – the move ...h3 is still in the air.

21 e4 dxe4 22 fxe4 ♖de8 23 ♖de1 *(D)*

White in turn misses the best time for 23 e5!.

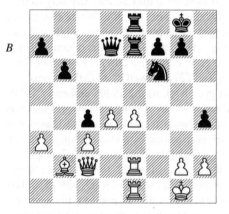

23...h3 24 e5 ♘d5

This knight guarantees at least equality. Black went on to win after some ups and downs:

25 ♗c1 ♕g4 26 ♖f2 b5 27 ♖ee2 f6 28 ♖f3 fxe5 29 ♖g3 ♕xe2 30 ♕xe2 exd4 31 ♕h5 ♘f6 32 ♕g6 ♖e1+ 33 ♔f2 ♖8e2+ 34 ♔f3 ♖e7 35 gxh3 ♖xc1 36 cxd4 ♘d5 37 ♕c6 ♖f1+ 38 ♔g2 ♖f5 39 ♖f3 ♘f4+ 40 ♔g3 ♖ef7 41 ♔g4 ♖5f6 42 ♕a8+ ♖f8 43 ♕xa7 ♖g6+ 44 ♔h4 ♔h7 45 ♖g3 ♘g2+ 46 ♖xg2 ♖xg2 47 ♕e7 ♖f4+ 48 ♔h5 ♖f5+ 49 ♔h4 ♔h6 0-1

Central Strategies against the Botvinnik

What about variations with ...d5 in which Black foregoes the ...♗a6 bishop exchange and concentrates instead upon the centre? These lead to a difficult fight in which e4 for White is not always possible. Instead we see White expanding on the kingside, both for the sake of attack there and to drive Black's pieces away so that he can play e4 after all. In the meantime Black has a greater emphasis on preventative measures against attack by White.

Many such variations arise via the move 4 f3; for example, 4 f3 d5 5 a3 ♗xc3+ 6 bxc3 0-0 7 cxd5 exd5 8 e3. Then the position may reach a standard Botvinnik variation if White plays ♗d3, ♘e2 and 0-0 while Black is playing ...0-0, ...b6 and ...♗a6. But Black has a lot of alternatives. For one thing, he can choose 6...c5! instead of 6...0-0, and if White plays 7 cxd5, respond with 7...♘xd5!. Currently, at least, White's extensive and varied efforts to gain an advantage in that position have proven fruitless, although a robust middlegame may ensue. There are also independent moves for Black within the basic Botvinnik structure, as in this game:

Gheorghiu – Fischer
Havana OL 1966

1 d4 ♘f6 2 c4 e6 3 ♘c3 ♗b4 4 f3 d5 5 a3 ♗xc3+ 6 bxc3 0-0 7 cxd5 exd5 8 e3 *(D)*

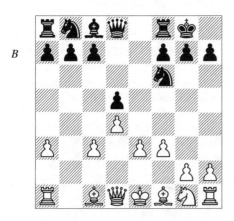

8...♘h5!?

Black threatens ...♕h4+ and prepares ...f5-f4 under the right circumstances.

The alternative 8...♗f5!? militates against 9 ♗d3?!, because after the exchange 9...♗xd3 10 ♕xd3 c5 (or 10...♖e8), Black has dispensed with the weakening move ...b6 and gained time in comparison to the plan of ...b6, ...♗a6 and ...♗xd3. So instead of 9 ♗d3, White will try instead to exploit the bishop's presence by playing the advance g4. Play might go 9 ♘e2 c5 10

g4!? (not the only idea, of course) 10...♗g6 11 ♘f4!? ♘c6 (although Black's development and centralization are visually impressive, it's difficult to find anything to attack in the white camp; while White has to deal with his own awkwardly-placed pieces, he is counting upon his space advantage, two bishops, and potential central expansion) 12 ♗g2 ♖c8 13 0-0 ♘a5! 14 ♖a2! h6 15 ♘xg6 fxg6, Malaniuk-Ivanchuk, Lvov 1988. White now played 16 ♖e1, and 16...♖c6! was fine for Black, who is ready to play ...cxd4 and ...♕c7 with effect (the game was drawn).

9 ♕c2

This is a flexible move directed against ...♕h4+; it also supports ♗d3.

9...♖e8

As usual in this line, the queenless middlegame after 9...♕h4+ 10 ♕f2 ♕xf2+ 11 ♔xf2 favours White's space and his two bishops: 11...♘f6 12 g4!? (or 12 c4 or 12 ♗d3 ♖e8 13 g4!? b6 14 g5 ♘h5 15 e4) 12...h6 13 ♘e2 b6 14 ♘g3 ♗a6 15 ♗xa6 ♘xa6 16 h4 with good prospects.

10 g4

White plays on the flank in order to drive Black's pieces off before he attacks in the centre. The drawback in such positions is his development, so Black will try to act quickly with his pieces.

10...♘f4! *(D)*

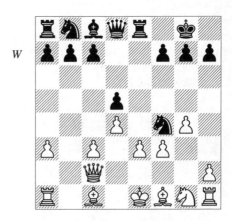

11 h4!

White still only has one piece out and it's his queen! 11 h4 accrues more territory while preventing counterplay by ...♕h4+.

11...c5 12 ♔f2

'Developing' the king with tempo.

12...♘g6 13 ♗d3 ♘c6

13...♘xh4?! allows 14 ♗xh7+ ♔f8 15 ♔g3 g5 16 ♘h3 f6 17 ♘f4!? with the idea 17...gxf4+ 18 exf4!.

14 ♘e2 ♗e6 15 g5 ♖c8 *(D)*

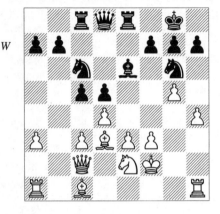

W

16 h5!

Although it's logical and safe to retreat White's queen from the indirect attack along the c-file, Gheorghiu bravely ignores the pressure in order to get his attack going.

16...♘f8 17 g6! fxg6?! 18 hxg6 h6 19 ♕b1 ♘a5 20 ♘f4

The opening is over and White has pretty much what he wants: two bishops, a cramping space advantage, and prospects to play e4.

20...c4

Trying to use b3 for his pieces. The problem is that there's not much else for Black to do that doesn't help White; for example, 20...cxd4 21 cxd4 b6 22 ♕b5 ♘c4 23 ♖h5!.

21 ♗c2 ♖c6 22 ♖a2! *(D)*

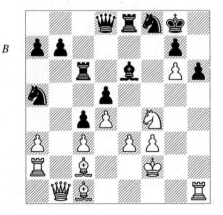

B

Moving to a second front. The player who commands more space can often do this.

22...♘d7 23 a4! ♘f6 24 ♗a3 ♕d7 25 ♖b2 b6 26 ♖b5 ♘b7 27 e4

Finally this push, and it's decisive!

27...dxe4 28 ♗xe4 ♖cc8 29 ♖e5 ♗g4

White was threatening ♗xb7, d5, ♖he1 and more. The alternatives were 29...♘d8 30 ♕b5 ♘xe4+ 31 ♖xe4 ♕xb5 32 axb5 and everything hangs; and 29...♘d6 30 ♗xd6 ♕xd6 31 ♘xe6 ♖xe6 32 ♖xe6 ♕xe6 33 ♗f5, which is a pretty piece of geometry. The rest is easy.

30 ♘d5! ♖xe5 31 ♘xf6+ gxf6 32 dxe5 ♘c5 33 ♗xc5 ♕d2+ 34 ♔g3 ♗xf3 35 ♗xf3 ♖xc5 36 ♕c1 ♕xc1 37 ♖xc1 ♖xe5 38 ♔f4 ♔g7 39 ♗e4 h5 40 ♖d1 ♖e7 41 ♖d5 ♔h6 42 ♖d6 ♔g7 43 ♖c6 h4 44 ♖xc4 h3 45 ♔g3 ♔h6 46 ♗b1 ♖e3+ 47 ♔h2 ♖e1 48 ♗d3 ♖e3 49 ♖h4+ ♔g5 50 g7 1-0

Finally, there's the case where Black sets up 'normally' by ...c5, ...♘c6 and ...♖e8. One problem that arises is where to put the c8-bishop.

Kacheishvili – Jenni
Linares 2001

1 d4 ♘f6 2 c4 e6 3 ♘c3 ♗b4 4 e3 0-0 5 ♗d3 c5 6 ♘e2 ♘c6 7 0-0 d5 8 cxd5 exd5 9 a3 ♗xc3 10 bxc3 ♖e8

A roundabout way to the Sämisch structure.

11 f3 b6 12 ♖a2 ♗b7 13 g4! *(D)*

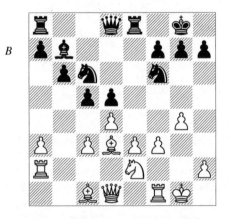

B

13...c4

Black is at a loss for an effective plan.

14 ♗b1 ♘a5 15 ♘g3 ♘b3 16 g5 ♘d7 17 e4 ♘xc1 18 ♕xc1

In spite of losing his dark-squared bishop, White enjoys control of the centre and king-side. It turns out that his attack almost plays it-self.

18...b5 19 e5 a5 20 ♘h5 ♕b6 21 ♘f6+ gxf6 22 gxf6 ♚h8 23 ♕h6 ♖g8+ 24 ♚h1 ♘f8 25 ♖g1 ♘g6 26 ♖g5 1-0

An interesting relationship exists between the same ♗d3, ♘ge2, f3, ♘g3 set-up that oc-curs in the Nimzo-Indian and in the Exchange Queen's Gambit. In both cases White wants to use his central majority and enforce e4 fol-lowed by e5. Of course, the bishop on g5 in the Queen's Gambit is outside the central pawn-chain and seems to play a completely different part from that on b2 or c1 in the Nimzo-Indian, especially when ♗xf6 is played with ...♗xf6 as a reply. In both cases, however, White's main idea is e4-e5 (driving a piece away from f6 with tempo), followed by f4-f5. And there is another connection, as illustrated by this po-sition:

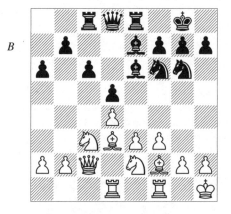

This comes from our section on the Ex-change Queen's Gambit. The bishop has re-treated from g5 to f2 via h4, in part to avoid a forced exchange that can occur if the bishop re-mains on g5 too long (by ...♘h5 or ...♘g6 and ...h6, for example), but also in order to defend the e3/d4 centre and allow for e4. Isn't this pretty much the function of the 'bad' bishop on b2 in the Nimzo lines that we have just seen? In simi-lar fashion, Black will play ...c5 to increase pres-sure on d4 and discourage the key advance e4. In both openings White may well switch to an attack via g4. Obviously meaningful differences

exist. In the QGD, Black hasn't exchanged his dark-squared bishop for a knight. But we see how White in the Nimzo-Indian can achieve an effective attack with surprisingly reduced ma-terial, a prime example being the Botvinnik-Capablanca game above.

Sämisch Main Line with ...c5 and ...♗a6

After the 4 a3 move-order, Black frequently adopts a set-up in which he doesn't move the d-pawn or e-pawn, but plays to blockade White's potential advances on both sides of the board. This strategy has been strengthened by specific move-orders in recent years. First let's see how the issues evolved with practice.

1 d4 ♘f6 2 c4 e6 3 ♘c3 ♗b4 4 a3 ♗xc3+ 5 bxc3 0-0

For a few comments on this move-order, see the next section.

6 e3 c5

This fixes the forward doubled pawn on c4 as an easy target of attack and eliminates any idea of White freeing his pieces by pushing his pawn to c5.

Amongst the large set of options in the Sämisch (and Nimzo-Indian), Black has 6...b6 7 ♗d3 ♗b7, when 8 f3 is the normal move and has had mixed results. Much more interesting is Vaganian's recent move 8 ♘e2!?, offering a promising gambit: 8...♗xg2 9 ♖g1 ♗f3 (if 9...♗e4, then 10 ♘g3!) 10 ♖g3 ♗e4 11 f3 ♗xd3 12 ♕xd3 with compensation for the pawn. Nevertheless, both sides have chances for ad-vantage.

7 ♗d3 ♘c6 8 ♘e2 b6 9 e4 ♘e8! *(D)*

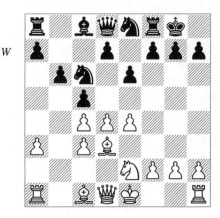

At first sight this gives a strange impression: Black doesn't develop a piece and moves the knight backwards. The retreat is justified by three considerations: Black avoids the annoying pin ♗g5, he prepares to answer f4 with ...f5, and he manoeuvres the knight towards the d6-square from which point it will attack c4 again.

An early game Bronstein-Najdorf, Budapest Ct 1950 illustrates what *not* to do as Black: 1 d4 ♘f6 2 c4 e6 3 ♘c3 ♗b4 4 a3 ♗xc3+ 5 bxc3 c5 6 e3 ♘c6 7 ♗d3 0-0 8 ♘e2 d6 9 e4 ♘e8 (the procedure with ...♘e8 and ...f5 works best with the pawn on d7 supporting the pawn-chain, but this is still a sensible way to play) 10 0-0 b6 11 f4 (11 ♗e3!?) 11...♗a6? (there was still time for 11...f5!) 12 f5! e5? (an innocent-looking move which loses the game!) 13 f6! *(D)*.

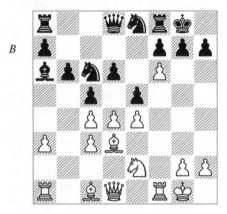

There is no good answer; for example, 13...♘xf6 14 ♗g5! and Black will not survive ♘g3-h5 and/or ♗xf6 with ♘g3 and ♕h5; and 13...gxf6 14 d5 ♘e7 15 ♗h6 ♘g7 16 ♘g3 is almost as bad. This is why f5 is seldom allowed and f6 almost never. You can see the rationale behind the blocking manoeuvre ...f5. The game concluded 13...♔h8 14 d5 ♘a5 15 ♘g3 gxf6 16 ♘f5 ♗c8 17 ♕h5 ♗xf5 18 exf5 ♖g8 19 ♖f3 ♖g7 20 ♗h6 ♖g8 21 ♖h3 1-0.

10 0-0 ♗a6

Getting to work on that c-pawn. Black's plan is simple and White needs to create something in the centre or kingside to counter it.

11 f4 f5

There's the blockading move that we mentioned. Notice how, by preventing f5, Black has prevented White's queen's bishop from moving to the kingside and perhaps joining in an attack.

This same idea occurs in the Closed Sicilian line 1 e4 e5 2 ♘c3 ♘c6 3 g3 g6 4 ♗g2 ♗g7, where White plays f4 soon thereafter and Black replies ...f5. Similarly, in the King's Indian Attack, White will often arrange the move f4 and run into ...f5.

Black has alternative approach: he can allow White to go one step further and then blockade by 11...f6!? (11...♘a5 12 f5 f6 is a similar idea) 12 f5 *(D)*.

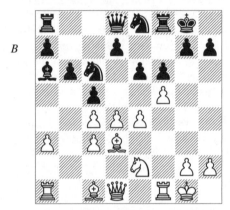

The board is full of tension. A game Tisdall-Arnason, Husavik 1985 went 12...cxd4 13 cxd4 ♖c8 14 ♗d2! exf5! 15 ♕a4 fxe4 16 ♗xe4 ♗b7; here 17 ♕c2! looks good, when 17...g6 18 ♗d5+ ♔g7 19 ♕c1 g5 20 ♘g3 ♘d6 21 ♕d1 is a sample line. Black has all kinds of options, however (12...♖c8 is an obvious one). I wouldn't bet on either side after 11...f6.

We now return to 11...f5 *(D)*:

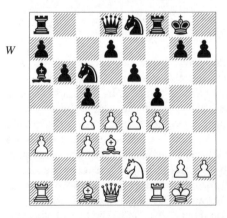

From the position after 11...f5, we look at two games:

Yusupov – Karpov
Linares 1993

12 ♘g3 *(D)*

At almost every juncture White has tried to exchange pawns, sometimes gaining a small advantage. In this position the exchange seems to help Black's structure as much as White's; e.g., 12 exf5 exf5 13 dxc5 bxc5 14 ♗e3 d6 15 ♗f2 ♕d7 is a simple example. But the assessment of these and similar plans can and will change as players refine their move-orders.

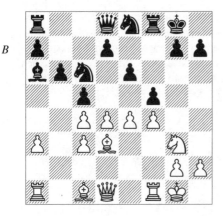

12...g6

This move took over theory and practice for a while after Karpov won two games versus Yusupov. But 12...♘d6 is logical, attacking the c4-pawn and defending f5. One possible problem for Black is 13 exf5 exf5 (13...♘xf5 14 ♘xf5 exf5 15 dxc5 bxc5 16 ♕f3; 13...cxd4!?) 14 dxc5 bxc5 15 ♗e3, when his loose pieces make the defence difficult.

13 ♗e3 *(D)*

Keeping the tension in the centre. Again White can open the position with 13 exf5 exf5 14 dxc5 bxc5. Then 15 ♕a4 is very interesting, and a tactical line that has occurred several times is 15 ♗e3 d6 (15...♕a5 16 ♗e2 ♖f7 or 16...♘f6 is unclear) 16 ♗xf5!? gxf5 17 ♕d5+ ♖f7 18 ♕xc6 ♗xc4 (the riskier pawn sacrifice 18...♗b7 has also been tried, with mixed results). Black can follow up with moves like ...♕c8 and ...♖b8 with a complex position that like so much else may be worked out by the time you read this book! What's important here are not the specific moves and ever-changing theory, but the overall situation: the burden is

on White to alter the pawn-structure and/or dynamics of the position before Black consolidates and wins positionally. This applies to a great number of Nimzo-Indian positions that involve ...♗xc3+ and bxc3, and is worth keeping in mind over-the-board.

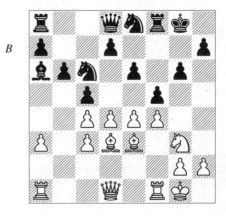

13...cxd4!?

Karpov's idea, designed to improve upon (or merely pose other problems than) his earlier game with Yusupov, which went 13...♘d6 14 exf5!? (initiating a bold sacrifice, although possibly something simple along the lines of 14 dxc5 ♘xc4 15 ♗xc4 ♗xc4 16 ♖e1 is the reason why Karpov didn't repeat 13...♘d6) 14...♘xc4 15 ♗xc4 ♗xc4 16 fxg6 (16 ♖f2) 16...♗xf1 17 ♕h5 ♕e7 18 ♖xf1 hxg6!? (18...cxd4! is probably better) 19 ♕xg6+ ♕g7, and in Yusupov-Karpov, London Ct (3) 1989 White eventually lost in the unclear complications after 20 ♕d3. The endgame after 20 ♕xg7+ ♔xg7 21 dxc5! was a promising option. These lines should definitely help you to understand the opposing strategies.

14 cxd4 d5!

The fascinating thing here is that Black, who has the knight-pair, forces open the position, as opposed to the strategies of previous players who tried to keep everything closed.

15 cxd5 ♗xd3 16 ♕xd3 fxe4 17 ♕xe4

A fair alternative is 17 ♘xe4, when 17...♕xd5 leads to complex play that I'd assess as equal. This whole line may be superseded in the future so I'll spare the details.

17...♕xd5 18 ♕xd5 exd5 *(D)*

The basic concept remains: Black works on the light-square complex, as he has done since

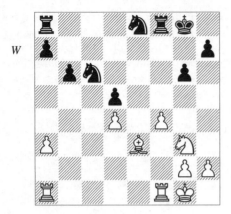

the very first move. Looking at this structure for a moment we see that c4 and e4 are weak whereas the bishop on e3 is passive. If Black could now play ...♘d6, preventing f5 and keeping White's bishop entombed on e3, his advantage would be very significant. But it's White's move:

19 ♖ac1 ♖c8 20 f5! ♘d6 21 fxg6

This isn't a theory book but 21 ♗h6!? ♖f7 22 fxg6 hxg6 23 ♘e2 is also interesting and again the chances seem about equal. Something similar applies for the next two moves, but soon after that Karpov's well-posted knights and White's weak pawns turn the game in Black's favour.

21...hxg6 22 ♖xf8+ ♔xf8 23 h4 ♘c4 24 ♗g5 ♘xd4 25 h5 gxh5 26 ♖f1+ ♔e8 27 ♘xh5 ♘xa3 28 ♘g7+ ♔d7 29 ♖f7+ ♔c6 30 ♖xa7 ♘ac2! 31 ♗f6 b5! 32 g4 b4 33 ♖a2 b3 34 ♖b2 ♔c5 35 ♘f5 ♖g8! 36 ♘xd4 ♖xg4+ 37 ♔f2 ♘xd4 38 ♗xd4+ ♔xd4 39 ♖xb3 e4 40 ♖a3 ♖e8 0-1

Here's another example of how White, not wanting to wait around for Black's queenside attack, takes drastic action:

V. Milov – J. Polgar
Moscow FIDE KO 2001

1 d4 ♘f6 2 c4 e6 3 ♘c3 ♗b4 4 e3 0-0 5 a3 ♗xc3+ 6 bxc3 c5 7 ♗d3 ♘c6 8 ♘e2 b6 9 e4 ♘e8 10 0-0 ♗a6 11 f4 f5

This is the same main line that we have just seen. After many years of following the same themes, a new idea appeared:

12 d5!? ♘a5 13 e5! ♗xc4!?

Especially in view of what happens, it's logical to try to prove that White's centre is overextended. Thus 13...d6!, and if 14 dxe6, 14...♕e7!. Then it's natural to play 15 g4!? (blasting away; White tries to force the position open...) 15...g6!? (...and Black to keep it closed! A real mess occurs after 15...fxg4 16 ♘g3) 16 gxf5 gxf5 17 ♘g3, but then 17...♕xe6! has the idea 18 ♗xf5 ♖xf5 19 ♘xf5 ♕xf5 20 ♕d5+ ♔f8! 21 ♕xa8 ♗b7 and Black has too much attack. Instead of all this, 14 ♘g3 g6 emphasizes the essential solidity of Black's position; for example, 15 ♕e2 ♘c7. In the spirit of the position, then, White might try 14 g4!?, which is not at all clear. At any rate, 13...d6 would be a consistent way for Black to proceed. One can see why White might choose the more straightforward lines with exf5 and dxc5 mentioned above.

14 ♗xc4 ♘xc4 15 d6 *(D)*

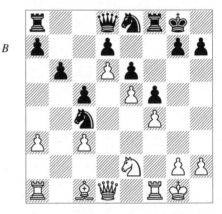

Quite a position! Black is a pawn ahead with a solid pawn-structure, but the knight on e8 and rook on f8 are hemmed in, and White has ambitions to attack on the queenside. The main point is that it's hard to break down White's cramping central pawn-structure. On the other hand Black still has good control over the light squares.

15...b5

Again there have been several games that were played after this one. Since the opening issues have been defined, I'll merely point out that Black's options include 15...g6 and 15...♕c8, the latter from the stem game for this line, Ziatdinov-T.Georgadze, USSR 1985.

16 a4 a6 17 ♕d3 g6 18 axb5 axb5 19 ♗e3!

This attacks c5 once, and ♘c1-b3 will do so once more.

19...♖xa1 20 ♖xa1 ♕b6 21 ♘c1 ♘g7 22 ♘b3 ♖c8 23 ♗f2 *(D)*

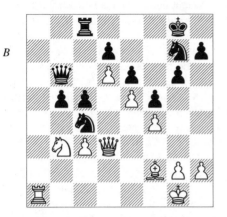

The game continued and White recovered his pawn with a superior position. Some wild tactics ensued but eventually he won:

23...♘b2 24 ♕c2 ♘a4 25 c4 ♕b8 26 ♘d2 ♘b6 27 cxb5 c4 28 ♘f3 ♘h5 29 g3 ♕b7 30 ♖a3 ♔g7 31 ♘d4 ♔f7 32 ♕a2 ♘e4 33 ♖a7 g5 34 ♕e2 ♕b1+ 35 ♕f1 ♕e4 36 ♕e2 ♕b1+ 37 ♔g2 ♔g6 38 fxg5 c3 39 ♕c2 ♕b4 40 ♖b7 ♖c4 41 ♘xe6 dxe6 42 ♖xb6 ♕b2 43 ♕d3! ♖f4 44 ♕e3 c2 45 d7 c1♕ 46 d8♕ ♖xf2+ 47 ♕xf2 ♕xe5 48 ♕e8+ ♔xg5 49 ♕xe6 ♕xe6 50 ♖xe6 f4 51 ♖e5+ ♔g6 52 ♖c5 f3+ 53 ♔xf3 ♕h1+ 54 ♔e3 1-0

4 e3 and the Hübner Variation

1 d4 ♘f6 2 c4 e6 3 ♘c3 ♗b4 4 e3

For most of the modern history of the Nimzo-Indian Defence, this modest advance has been played more often than any other move. Over the last decade or so 4 ♕c2 has become a top-level favourite and has recently surpassed 4 e3 on most levels of tournament play, but not by much. Between them these moves dominate Nimzo-Indian practice. In general one can say that 4 e3 is more flexible for both sides, leading to a remarkable number of formations, sometimes only barely related! I'll stick with a few popular variations whose lessons extend into other lines. We'll look at 4...0-0 and 4...c5, each in their own section.

Another important move is 4...b6. I'm not devoting space to it, but compare the Queen's Indian Defence of the next chapter.

At this point we have some move-order issues that are seldom addressed although obviously known to most masters. It says something about the technical nature of the Nimzo-Indian that tiny differences in move-order have such important positional effects. Because this is all rather confusing, I'm going to make a comparison of the consequences of playing 4...0-0 and 4...c5 in terms of reaching desired positions. Otherwise, whether you're White or Black, it will be easy to get off on the wrong foot.

Early Castling

4...0-0 *(D)*

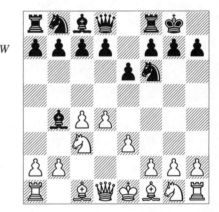

Castling is the most popular move at the top levels versus 4 e3. It is nevertheless a committal decision and it's interesting to see which of White's standard set-ups will achieve more or less against a castled king. White has four primary options (which are the same ones he plays versus 4...c5): 5 a3, 5 ♗d3, 5 ♘e2 and 5 ♘f3.

I'll look at the knight moves as main lines. 5 a3 enters into Sämisch territory, which we've been over. And 5 ♗d3 is a transpositional beehive, as follows:

a) Should Black play 5...d5, then 6 a3!? ♗xc3+ 7 bxc3 followed by ♘e2 should be compared with the Botvinnik Sämisch.

b) Alternatively, 5...c5 leads to a number of positions depending upon what White chooses. I should mention that 6 ♘f3 d5 7 0-0 is one of the classic positions of the Nimzo-Indian. It can lead to positions that are familiar to us; for example:

b1) 7...dxc4 8 ♗xc4 cxd4 9 exd4 b6 10 ♗g5 ♗b7.

b2) 7...♘c6 8 a3 dxc4 (8...♗xc3 9 bxc3 dxc4 {or 9...♕c7} 10 ♗xc4 ♕c7 is one of the oldest Nimzo-Indian variations) 9 ♗xc4 cxd4 10 exd4 ♗e7 (after 10...♗xc3 11 bxc3, Black has committed his knight to c6 rather than d7, which some players don't like; however, that's another story) 11 ♗g5 b6 12 ♖e1 ♗b7 (D).

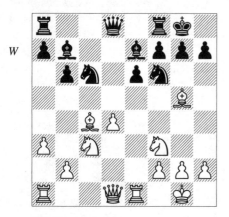

Both 'b1' and 'b2' are the type of IQP positions which we discussed and of which I gave numerous examples in Chapter 3 of Volume 1.

Torre – Unzicker
Wijk aan Zee 1981

5 ♘e2 (D)

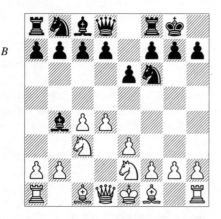

White plays conservatively, hoping to avoid the doubled pawns that would otherwise arise

after ...♗xc3+. He wants to drive away the bishop and then expand in the centre. The drawbacks to this knight move include hemming in the bishop on f1 and developing rather passively.

5...d5!

Because this counter is available, 4...0-0 is arguably the best order versus the ♘e2 systems, or at least the easiest to play. Another strategy to exploit White's slow development and knight placement is 5...♖e8 6 a3 ♗f8!?, when a recent game continued 7 d5 d6 8 g3 ♘bd7 9 ♗g2 ♘e5! 10 b3 exd5 11 cxd5 ♗g4 12 f4 ♘ed7 13 ♕c2 ♗xe2 14 ♔xe2!? c6 15 dxc6 bxc6 16 e4 ♘c5 17 ♗e3 d5! 18 e5 ♘g4 19 ♗d4 f6 20 ♗xc5 fxe5! 21 ♔f3 e4+ 22 ♔e2 ♗xc5 23 ♘d1 ♗b6 with enormous centre pawns, Avrukh-P.Carlsson, Turin OL 2006.

6 a3 ♗e7 7 cxd5 exd5!?

7...♘xd5 is the safer move, equal if unambitious: 8 g3 c5! 9 dxc5 (9 ♗g2 ♘xc3 10 ♘xc3 ♘c6) 9...♘xc3 10 ♕xd8 ♖xd8 11 ♘xc3 ♗xc5 12 ♗g2 ♘c6 13 0-0 (13 ♔e2 is an option) 13...♗e7 14 ♖b1? (14 ♖d1 ♖xd1+ 15 ♘xd1 e5 16 ♗d2 ♗e6 17 ♗c3 f6 with equality) 14...♗d7 15 b4 ♖ab8 16 ♗b2 ♘e5 17 ♘e4 ♘c4, Ki.Georgiev-Sax, Warsaw Z 1987. Black has far better piece placement and a significant advantage.

8 g3 ♘bd7 9 ♗g2 c6 10 0-0 ♖e8 11 h3 ♘f8

In traditional Queen's Gambit fashion, Black shifts his eyes to the kingside and e4; moves such as ...♗d6, ...♗f5 and ...♘e6-g5 are on the cards.

12 b4 (D)

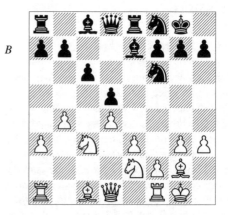

Here we see a conventional minority attack by White designed to weaken Back's queenside by b5. That takes a long time, however, so

White also tries to undercut Black's kingside advance by establishing the Exchange Variation pawn-structure g4/f3/h3 and prevent ...♗f5 or ...♘e4. All this is obviously double-edged because of White's own weaknesses.

12...a6 13 ♘f4 ♘g6 14 ♘xg6 hxg6 15 g4 ♗d6 16 f3 a5 17 ♖b1 axb4 18 axb4 ♗c7 19 ♕c2 ♕d6

A primitive yet effective attack.

20 ♘e2 ♗xg4!

The move that White missed. 20...♕h2+ 21 ♔f2 is harmless.

21 ♕c5

White also loses after 21 fxg4 ♕h2+ 22 ♔f2 ♘e4+ 23 ♔f3 ♖e6 or 21 hxg4 ♕h2+ 22 ♔f2 ♕h4+ 23 ♔g1 ♕h2+ 24 ♔h1 ♗g3+.

21...♕h2+ 22 ♔f2 ♗xh3 23 ♖g1 ♖a2! 24 ♖b2 ♖xb2 25 ♗xb2 ♗xg2 26 ♖xg2 ♕h4+ 0-1

The e-pawn falls, and then the game.

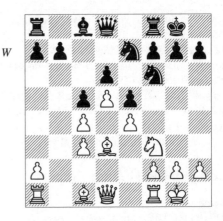

W

Pliester – Rosten
Isle of Man 1995

5 ♘f3 *(D)*

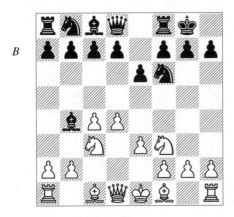

B

5...c5 6 ♗d3 ♗xc3+

Black wants to fix White's c-pawns before setting up a ...d6/...e5 pawn-structure. He can also play 6...♘c6, when 7 d5 ♘e7! is considered equal, and 7 0-0 d5 will transpose to the main line above (which arose from 5 ♗d3). In this respect, then, 5 ♗d3 is more flexible than 5 ♘f3. As always, you might want to play a few games before you try to absorb these subtleties.

7 bxc3 ♘c6 8 0-0 d6 9 e4 e5 10 d5 ♘e7 *(D)*

This is a Hübner Variation pawn-structure, but with Black having castled early. Castling

has cost Black a move in terms of his central reaction to White's strategy and, ironically, it can make his king more exposed by eliminating the option of ...0-0-0. Compare the 'Hübner Proper' below, which goes 4...c5 5 ♗d3 ♘c6 6 ♘f3 ♗xc3+ 7 bxc3 d6. In our position White has more options, which is not to say that he stands better.

11 ♘h4 h6 12 ♖b1

This is an interesting move that again would count for little if Black could still castle queenside. Alternatively, 12 g3!? ♗h3 13 ♘g2 intending f4 has also caused Black some trouble; and the fairly conservative 12 f3!? was seen in Gelfand-Short, Dos Hermanas 1997, which continued 12...g5 13 ♘f5 ♘xf5 14 exf5. White has a small edge because Black lacks counterplay, although that's hardly fatal and with accurate play Black could have equalized later.

12...♖b8 13 ♕f3! *(D)*

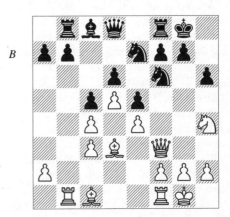

B

Here's the point. Upon the normal move ...♘g6 White will have the reply ♘f5, but Black has to find another constructive plan in the meantime.

13...♚h7 14 h3 ♘g6 15 ♘f5 ♘g8

Black's play deteriorates a bit but he definitely has the worse of it.

16 g4 ♘h4 17 ♕g3 ♘xf5 18 exf5 f6?! 19 f4! ♕e8? 20 fxe5 dxe5 21 ♗e3 ♕e7 22 ♖b5 a6 23 ♗xc5 ♕c7 24 ♗b6 1-0

White's strategy deserves attention.

4...c5 and the Hübner Proper

4...c5 *(D)*

This is the best path to take if you want to end up in the Hübner Variation, which is the subject of this section.

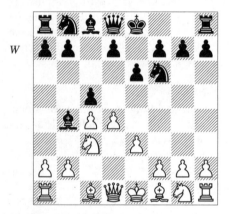

5 ♗d3

Now 5 ♘e2 gives White some aggressive options and causes much more trouble for Black than does the position after 4...0-0 5 ♘e2 d5. The extra complications that come with 4...c5 could be a disincentive for Black in practice, but that depends upon specific variations. Here's an overview of 5 ♘e2 lines: 5...cxd4 (5...d5 6 a3 ♗xc3+ 7 ♘xc3 cxd4 8 exd4 dxc4 9 ♗xc4 is satisfactory for Black but not to everyone's taste; Black can also play 5...b6!? 6 a3 ♗a5, which has traditionally been a sideline but is considered fully playable) 6 exd4 d5 (6...0-0 7 a3 ♗e7 8 d5 exd5 9 cxd5 ♖e8 10 d6 ♗f8 has a lot of theory attached to it, with difficulties for both sides, but perhaps a little more for Black if White really knows what he's doing) 7 c5 ♘e4 8 ♗d2 ♘xd2 9 ♕xd2 *(D)*.

9...a5 (9...0-0 10 a3 ♗a5!? is also possible) 10 a3 ♗xc3 11 ♘xc3 a4 12 ♗d3 ♗d7 13 0-0

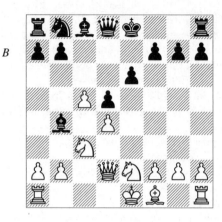

♘c6 14 ♗c2 and White gets genuine attacking chances. It just takes some study to catch up with this, especially by White.

5...♘c6

5...♗xc3+ 6 bxc3 ♘c6, trying to get to a Hübner Variation, is a big positional error because White can play 7 ♘e2! instead of 7 ♘f3. Then he is a full tempo ahead of a normal Sämisch position because he skipped a3.

6 ♘f3 ♗xc3+

Only now does Black play this way, when White's knight on f3 obstructs its own pawns.

7 bxc3 d6 *(D)*

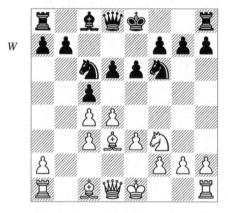

This is the 'real' Hübner Variation, made famous by Hübner himself, but also by Fischer with his positionally devastating win over Spassky in their world championship match. Black has intentionally 'wasted' a move by exchanging on c3 without waiting for White to play a3. The point is that he plans ...e5, a move that wouldn't be particularly attractive if the c-pawns hadn't been doubled; e.g., if White had ♕c2 in before ...♝xc3. The irony here is that in the Sämisch Variation White is happy to 'waste' the tempo a3 in order to make his ideas work; whereas in the Hübner Variation, Black does the opposite (wastes a move by *not* waiting for a3) for much the same reason!

What are the general characteristics of the variation? Black is about to play ...e5, so as to partially close the position, and if White plays e4 and d5 (a common set-up) then the position is blocked on at least the queenside and in the centre. Therefore we expect more action on the king's wing. That explains why Black may not rush to castle, as he did above; he may well play ...0-0-0. White may also choose not to castle, according to taste. On the one hand castling gives White an extra move to see what Black is doing. On the other hand, since the closed centre renders White's king safe enough, foregoing 0-0 can give him an extra tempo to carry out other manoeuvres.

At this point the play therefore splits into 8 0-0 and lines in which White plays without (or delays) 0-0.

Lukacs – Stohl
Austrian Cht 1994

8 0-0 e5 9 ♘d2

A typical reorganization, going for f4 without blocking off the d3-bishop, but it's hard to achieve that.

9...0-0 *(D)*

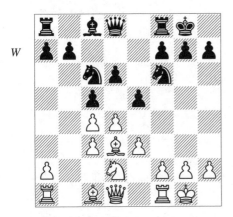

10 d5 ♘e7 11 f3!

This is better and more realistic than trying to get f4 in: 11 ♕c2?! ♘g6! 12 f4? (White's

position is too loose for this move, and he exposes his internal weaknesses on e3 and d3; 12 f3 was still the better choice) 12...exf4 13 exf4 ♖e8 14 h3 (versus ...♘g4) 14...♘h5! 15 ♘e4 ♝f5 16 ♔h2 ♕h4 (Black's pieces are swarming all over the place) 17 ♘f6+ (what else?) 17...gxf6 18 ♝xf5 ♕g3+ 19 ♔g1 ♖e1! 20 ♕f2? (but 20 ♖xe1 is met by 20...♕xe1+ 21 ♔h2 ♖e8!) 20...♕xf2+ 21 ♔xf2 ♖xf1+ 22 ♔xf1 ♘g3+ 0-1 Spiegel-Mednis, Wattens 1994.

11...♘e8

Jakab-K.Szabo, Budapest 2003 went 11...h6 12 ♖f2 ♘e8 13 e4 ♘g6 14 g3 with a sound, flexible set-up for both sides.

12 e4 ♘g6 13 g3 f5! *(D)*

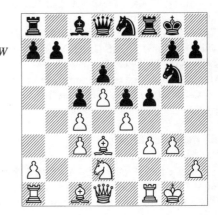

A standard counterattack. White wins e4 but Black activates his pieces against White's slightly weakened kingside. He also has another idea.

14 exf5 ♝xf5 15 ♘e4! ♕d7 16 ♕c2 ♘f6! 17 ♘xc5!?

White intentionally falls for it. Otherwise pieces are coming off and he'll have to suffer a long defence.

17...♝xd3 18 ♘xd3 ♖ac8 19 ♘b2

Black has a good game for a pawn and especially after his next move:

19...b5! *(D)*

20 ♝g5

20 cxb5 ♕xb5 21 c4 ♕xd5! with good pressure on White's weak queenside.

20...bxc4 21 ♝xf6 ♖xf6 22 ♕e4 ♕b5 23 ♘d1 ♘e7?!

23...♕a5! would completely tie White down.

24 ♘e3 ♕a5 25 f4!

The only shot: diverting the marauder.

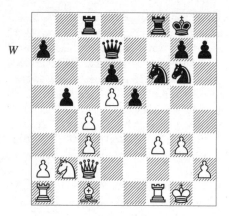

W

25...♕xc3 26 fxe5 ♕xe5!?

26...♖xf1+ 27 ♖xf1 ♕xe5 28 ♕xe5 dxe5 29 d6 ♘g6 is also advantageous but difficult.

**27 ♕xe5 dxe5 28 ♖xf6 gxf6 29 ♖c1!? ♖d8!
30 ♖xc4 ♘xd5 31 ♘xd5 ♖xd5 32 ♖c8+ ♔g7
33 ♖c7+ ♔g6 34 ♖xa7**

Although Black failed to convert his advantage into victory, his opening play is a model treatment.

White Avoids or Delays 0-0

**1 d4 ♘f6 2 c4 e6 3 ♘c3 ♗b4 4 e3 c5 5 ♗d3
♘c6 6 ♘f3 ♗xc3+ 7 bxc3 d6 8 e4 e5 9 d5**

This is the most direct way: White closes up the centre and proceeds to reorganize his pieces as quickly as possible.

9...♘e7 10 ♘d2 (D)

The knight on f3 is blocking White's position (compare the Sämisch, where the knight is on e2), so White gets it out of the way.

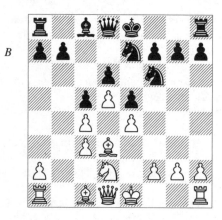

B

We look at two games.

Petrosian – Ivkov
Nice OL 1974

10...0-0 11 ♘f1! ♕a5 12 ♗d2 ♘e8

A plausible sequence is 12...♘g6 13 ♘e3 (13 g3) 13...♘f4 14 ♗c2 ♗d7 15 h4! ♔h8 16 g3.

**13 ♘g3 f5?! 14 exf5 ♘xf5 15 ♕c2 g6 16 0-0
♗d7 17 ♘e4 (D)**

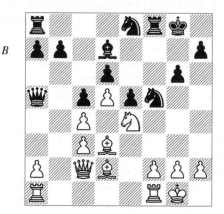

B

This looks like a King's Indian Defence where White has obtained his usual e4 outpost but Black has been denied his on d4. We've talked about the usefulness of doubled c-pawns in covering key central squares.

17...♘f6 18 ♘g5!?

Perhaps 18 f4!? could be tried.

18...♖ae8 19 f3 ♘g7 20 g4! (D)

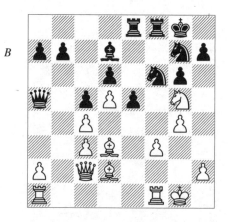

B

Petrosian typically wants to take the very last squares away from both the g7- and f6-knights.

20...♕a4!?

The right idea, but Black apparently missed White's next move, which was probably too simple to see.

21 Wb3! Rb8! 22 Ac2!? Wa5

Or 22...Wxb3 23 axb3, when White is potentially better on both sides of the board. White also has an edge after 22...b5!? 23 cxb5 Wxb5 24 c4. Don't forget that he still owns the kingside!

23 a4 Wc7 24 h3

Now f4 is always a possibility.

24...a6?! *(D)*

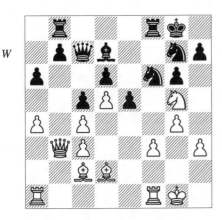

He's got to play ...h6 soon.

25 a5?!

After 25 f4! b5 26 axb5 axb5 27 fxe5 dxe5 28 Ra6!, White has decisively infiltrated Black's position.

25...b5 26 axb6 Rxb6 27 Wa3 Wd8 28 Wc1! We7 29 We1 Rb2 30 Ad3 Ac8 31 Ac1 Rb3 32 Ac2 Rb6 33 f4!

The rest is easy. This game illustrates Petrosian's customary way of playing the slowest possible attack while preventing counterplay.

33...h6 34 fxe5 Wxe5 35 Wxe5 dxe5 36 De4 h5

36...Dxe4 37 Rxf8+ Kxf8 38 Axe4 and Black can't protect the h- and c-pawns.

37 Aa3 Dxe4 38 Rxf8+ Kxf8 39 Axe4 Rb3 40 Axc5+ Ke8 41 Rf1 1-0

Knaak – Vaganian
Sochi 1980

1 d4 e6 2 c4 Df6 3 Dc3 Ab4 4 e3 c5 5 Ad3 Dc6 6 Df3 Axc3+ 7 bxc3 d6 8 e4 e5 9 d5 De7 10 Dd2

A similar case of running the other way was Hübner-Timman, Tilburg 1981. When Black gets such a great game against the leading proponent of a defence he must be doing something right: 10 Dh4 h6 11 g3 g5 12 Dg2 Ah3 13 De3 Wd7 14 f3 0-0-0! 15 Rb1 Kb8 16 Rb2 h5! 17 Rf2 Rdf8 18 Rg1 Dh7 19 g4?! Dg6 20 Rg3 Df4 with a big advantage. What did Hübner have in mind?

10...h6 11 h4!? Ad7 12 Df1 Wa5 13 Ad2 0-0-0! *(D)*

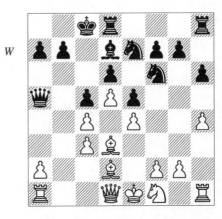

Now Black will be safe and doesn't have to worry as much about White's plans to expand on the kingside.

14 De3 h5 15 g3?

15 f3! has to be played, to retain the knight.

15...Dg4! 16 Dxg4 Axg4 17 f3 Ad7 *(D)*

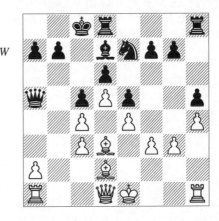

Now that the smoke has cleared, White has weaknesses and Black has none. So it's not hard to see who has the advantage!

18 Wc2 Rdf8 19 Rb1 Wc7

This is a typically solid position for Black's king when White's c-pawns are doubled and can't advance to create threats.

20 ♖b2 ♔b8 21 ♔d1 f6 22 ♔c1 ♗c8 23 ♕d1 ♖fg8

This was a good time for 23...f5! with the idea 24 ♗g5 f4!.

24 ♗e3 ♕a5?!

He really should have played 24...f5!.

25 ♕b3 ♕d8 26 f4!? ♘g6! 27 ♗e2? *(D)*

The play isn't too accurate hereabouts. White can hold tight by 27 f5! ♘e7 28 ♖f1 g6 29 fxg6 ♖xg6 30 ♗f2.

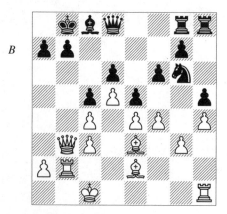

27...♕e7 28 ♗f3 f5!

Now White can't hold his centre together and his king is exposed.

29 ♕c2 ♖e8 30 exf5? exf4! 31 ♗d2 ♘e5 32 ♗e2 fxg3 33 ♗g5 ♕f7 34 ♖g1 ♗xf5 35 ♕d1 ♗g4! 36 ♖xg3 ♘xc4 37 ♗xg4 ♘xb2 38 ♗e6 ♕f2 39 ♕f3 ♖ef8 40 ♕xf2 ♖xf2 0-1

Finally, we look at another, more flexible move for White. It leads to typically slow manoeuvring, then White comes up with an ingenious plan.

Yusupov – Lalić
Erevan OL 1996

1 d4 ♘f6 2 c4 e6 3 ♘c3 ♗b4 4 e3 c5 5 ♗d3 ♘c6 6 ♘f3 ♗xc3+ 7 bxc3 d6 8 e4 e5 9 h3!? *(D)*

White prepares ♗e3 by protecting against ...♘g4.

9...h6 10 ♗e3 b6 11 d5 ♘e7 12 ♘d2 g5!? 13 ♘f1 ♘g6 14 g3 ♗d7 15 ♗d2 ♕e7! 16 ♘e3 0-0-0 17 ♕f3 ♘e8

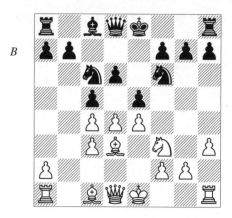

Lalić offers 17...♘f4!? as a possibility.

18 0-0-0 ♔c7 19 ♖h2! *(D)*

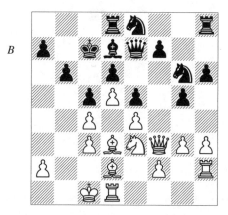

There it is! This may not get an advantage by force, but White comes up with a definite plan.

19...♘g7 20 ♖dh1 ♖de8 21 ♗c2!

The idea is ♕d1 and ♗a4. So next you'll see White trying to close the kingside (temporarily).

21...h5 22 h4 gxh4!

22...g4 is well met by 23 ♕d1!, because after White plays ♗a4 he can return to play f3 with f-file control. These are typically extended strategies when you play with or against the Hübner.

23 gxh4 ♘f4 24 ♘g2! f5 25 ♘xf4 exf4

Instead, 25...fxe4 26 ♕xe4 ♗f5? loses to the simple 27 ♘xe6+.

26 ♖e1!

White has much the better game. His bishops are simply too strong on the open board and he went on to win. This is an example of how the player with the bishop-pair can afford to be patient.

Classical Nimzo-Indian: 4 ♕c2

1 d4 ♘f6 2 c4 e6 3 ♘c3 ♗b4 4 ♕c2 *(D)*

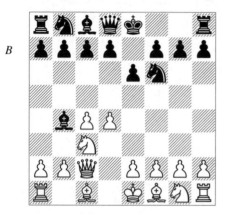

This is called the Classical Variation of the Nimzo-Indian. One advantage of 4 ♕c2 is obvious right away: it prevents doubled pawns! That is indeed its most important function. But the queen move also threatens the advance e4, which is of course the dream of every 1 d4 player. Another possibility is that White will develop his dark-squared bishop and clear the back rank for ♖d1 or 0-0-0. After 4 ♕c2 White's pieces and pawns can end up on a variety of squares, as needed. He can play pawns to f3 and/or e3, a knight to f3, h3 or e2, and a bishop to f4 or g5.

From Black's standpoint there are some encouraging factors that put him on an equal footing. The most important one may well be that 4 ♕c2 abandons White's protection of the d-pawn. This shows up in quite a few continuations; for example, 4...c5 attacks the d-pawn directly, as does the relatively rare 4...♘c6. More importantly, when Black plays 4...d5, he indirectly threatens the d4-pawn, and even should White capture on d5, a queen recapture will still attack that pawn. Since most lines include the move ...c5 and/or ...♘c6 at some point, those moves will gain in effect. Black can also look forward to his usual lead in development that accompanies the Nimzo-Indian, especially if you consider the queen on c2 (or c3) as only 'half-developed', since it is subject to attack by Black's pieces. Generally Black will get castled

quickly (in fact 4...0-0 is one of his main replies), and variations with an early ...d5 are particularly likely to give him extra pieces out. Naturally, White will argue he has control of the centre and two bishops (in many lines), major factors that compensate for Black's development. He'd be right. But whether this leads to more than equality is still an open question. Let's turn to a few of the many possible continuations that can stem from 4...d5 and 4...0-0.

As always I'm being selective. A great deal of theory surrounds the move 4...c5, for example, and 4...♘c6 has a long history behind it. I should note, however, that 4...b6?! lets White occupy the centre by 5 e4! in a way that is more favourable than 4 ♕c2 0-0 5 e4 below. It can't be recommended.

Central Counter-Attack: 4...d5

1 d4 ♘f6 2 c4 e6 3 ♘c3 ♗b4 4 ♕c2 d5 *(D)*

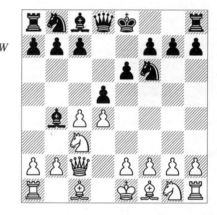

This is the most direct and one of the two most important replies to 4 ♕c2. In many ways it is the most logical. As indicated above, White's queen has abandoned defence of d4, so the threat of ...dxc4 is a serious one. If you think in terms of the Queen's Gambit Declined, it seems awfully early for White to have his queen on c2. In fact, the first thing that we'll look at can turn into the equivalent of the QGD Exchange Variation, 5 cxd5. That can lead to a quiet game or a complex tactical game depending upon what the players want. We'll get an overview of the material by looking at instructive games, which as usual are mainly aimed at strategy and less at bringing you up to date with theory.

5 cxd5

I shall just give an outline of the alternative 5 a3 ♗xc3+ 6 ♕xc3. Much of its theory has become a matter pure analysis, heavy on tactics. Black has a wide choice over the next few moves; for example, recently 6...c5 has gained a lot of attention, intending 7 dxc5 d4, and if 8 ♕g3, either the double gambit 8...♘c6!? with the idea 9 ♕xg7 ♖g8 or simply 8...0-0 9 ♗h6 ♘e8. Modern chess is full of all these dynamic counterattacks.

Instead 6...♘e4 7 ♕c2 (D) has produced the most analysed position of the 4 ♕c2 Nimzo-Indian:

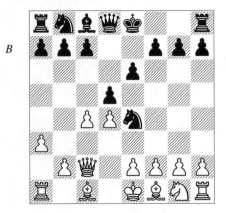

Here are mere snippets that give an idea of the complexities that await you if White chooses to go that route:

a) 7...c5 8 dxc5 ♘c6 9 cxd5 exd5 10 ♘f3 ♗f5 11 b4 0-0 (11...d4!? has been played in some big-name games) 12 ♗b2 ♖e8 (the main alternatives are 12...d4 and 12...b6!?, when 13 b5 bxc5 14 bxc6 ♕a5+ 15 ♘d2 ♖ab8! is a wild sacrifice; Cox draws attention to 13 ♕a4! instead; then 13...♗d7 14 cxb6 ♕xb6 15 e3 ♖fc8 and ...a5 might follow, but for now White seems to stand better) 13 ♕b3 (13 ♖d1 b6! throws everything into turmoil) 13...♘a5!? 14 ♕d1 ♘c4 15 ♕d4, Bareev-Zhang Zhong, Beersheba 2005, and it seems that White has the advantage. Now all you have to do is memorize all the side-variations and check the latest improvements!

b) Kasparov-Adams, Izmir ECC 2004 tested umpteen moves of theory in the infamous line 7...♘c6 8 e3 e5 9 cxd5 (Cox has recently brought Sokolov's suggestion of 9 f3 to the fore; it might well lead to a positional advantage for White, but has barely been tested) 9...♕xd5 10 ♗c4 ♕a5+ 11 b4 ♘xb4 12 ♕xe4 ♘c2++ 13 ♔e2 ♕e1+ 14 ♔f3 ♘xa1 15 ♗b2 0-0 (D).

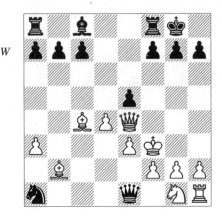

16 ♔g3 (a position that has arisen with amazing frequency over the years; I'll skip the outrageously deep analysis and follow the game) 16...h6 17 h4 ♖e8 18 ♔h2 ♕xf2 19 ♗xa1 ♗f5 20 ♕xb7 exd4 21 ♘f3 ♗e4 22 ♕xc7 ♗xf3 23 ♕xf7+ ♔h8 24 ♕xf3 ♕xh4+ 25 ♔g1 ♕e1+ 26 ♗f1 ♕xa1 27 ♖xh6+ gxh6 28 ♕f6+ ½-½. Great stuff, but involving 50 years in development and countless alternative paths that you may or may not want to master.

There are many fascinating opening variations whose existence is tactically based in the extreme and require many very specific moves to stay viable at all. It seems to me that when such variations survive a few decades of practice and fend off attempts at refutation, they will continue to defy other threats that come up later. That is, at some point we can almost guarantee that the latest 'refutation' will lead to a satisfactory counter, however improbable, that preserves the line from extinction or even disadvantage. Some primary examples are the Dragon and Poisoned Pawn variations of the Sicilian Defence (as well as perhaps the Sveshnikov), and the Marshall Attack of the Ruy Lopez. Others might include the black side of various main lines of the Exchange Grünfeld, the 7 ♕g4 Winawer French, the Four Pawns Attack main lines versus the Alekhine Defence, and this last Nimzo-Indian line above (beginning with 10...♕a5+ or thereabouts). In some of these cases (and I'm sure there are more), White may be able to avoid the variation in question and gain some advantage before the fireworks begin, but he can't do so in the main lines. This is merely a proposition, and there may prove to be exceptions, but to me it indicates that a fundamental dynamic balance exists in some opening variations that cannot be overcome even by the most ingenious ideas.

We now return to the position after 5 cxd5 (D):

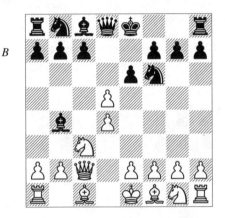

This is an odd place to put a diagram as you'd think that it would go after the recapture 5...exd5. But there are two absolutely legitimate moves here:

A: 5...♕xd5;
B: 5...exd5.

A)

5...♕xd5 *(D)*

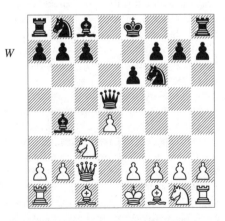

Popularized by Romanishin, this has been a major line for at least 15 years.

6 ♘f3

Feeling dissatisfied with this simple knight development, White sometimes turns to 6 e3, preparing 7 ♗d2. Black replies 6...c5! *(D)*.

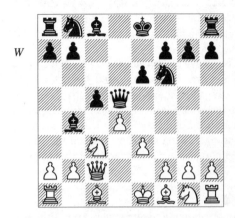

Black has to break up the centre immediately. This resembles the Chigorin Queen's Gambit line 1 d4 d5 2 c4 ♘c6 3 cxd5 ♕xd5 4 e3 e5 5 ♘c3 ♗b4 6 ♗d2 ♗xc3 7 ♗xc3.

After 6...c5!, the play can continue 7 ♗d2 ♗xc3 8 ♗xc3 cxd4 9 ♗xd4 ♘c6 10 ♗c3 (or 10 ♗xf6 gxf6 11 ♘e2 ♗d7 12 a3 ♕e5 with equality, Kasparov-Anand, New York PCA Wch (2) 1995) 10...♗d7 11 ♘f3 ♖c8 *(D)*.

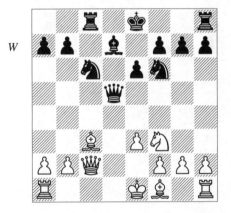

Again, we have the bishop-pair versus rapid development. In these situations Black has to play actively, because given time the bishop-pair will be a decisive force. Here's a model treatment about how to maintain the initiative in a lifeless-looking position: 12 a3 ♘e7! (among other things Black would like to play ...♗b5) 13 ♖d1 ♕c5 14 ♕b3!? ♘ed5 15 ♗d2 (Gavrilov analyses 15 ♗d4 ♕a5+ 16 ♘d2 ♗c6 17 ♗e2

0-0 18 ♕d3 a6!) 15...♕b6! 16 ♕xb6 ♘xb6 17 ♘e5 (17 b3!? tries to stop ...♗a4 or ...♘a4, but Black is quicker: 17...♘e4 18 ♗a5 ♘d5 19 ♘e5 ♖c5!) 17...♗a4 18 ♖b1 ♘e4 19 ♗a5 ♖c5 20 ♗xb6 axb6 21 ♘d3 ♖c8 22 ♘b4 ♗e7 with equality, Zakhartsov-Gavrilov, Vladimir 2004.

6...♕f5

This move broke onto the scene in the early 1990s when Romanishin used it successfully. Initially, opinion was largely negative, because it seemed that Black was weakening his pawn-structure by allowing 7 ♕xf5, while actually losing time doing so! The nature of the subsequent play has had influence upon chess theory as a whole, in that the resulting pawn-structure now appears in several new opening variations.

7 ♕xf5

a) For a while, players were trying the unlikely-looking retreat 7 ♕d1!?. It doesn't help White's development, but he would like to gain his time back by e3 and ♗d3. Black can strike first by 7...e5! intending 8 ♘xe5 ♘e4 or 8 dxe5 ♘e4 9 ♗d2 ♘c6 10 e3 ♘xd2 11 ♕xd2 ♘xe5 with roughly equal play. Black's idea is alive and well at the time of writing.

b) 7 ♕b3!? *(D)* is also slow but keeps the central structure intact and hits b4.

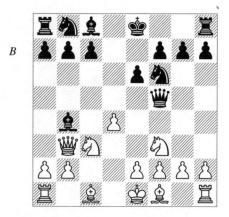

We'll follow the game Dreev-Bareev, Elista 1998: 7...♘c6!? 8 g3 (White continues his tactic of controlling key central squares, but again at the loss of time a fianchetto involves; he could also play moves such as 8 ♗d2, 8 e3 and 8 a3) 8...0-0 9 ♗g2 e5! (still attempting to disturb the equilibrium in quick-hitting style; although it looks silly, even 9...♕d5!? is possible) 10 d5!? (after 10 dxe5 ♗e6! Black gains time

too quickly) 10...♗xc3+ 11 bxc3 ♘a5! (for the next few moves, Black's control of the light squares takes centre stage) 12 ♕a4 b6 13 ♘d2 ♕h5! (preventing castling) 14 h3 ♗d7 15 ♕b4?! e4! 16 c4 e3! 17 fxe3 ♖fe8! 18 e4? (18 ♕c3 was the best chance to avoid what follows) 18...♕e5! 19 ♔f2! ♘h5 20 ♕a3 ♕d4+! 21 e3 ♕e5! 22 g4 ♕f6+ 23 ♗f3 ♕h4+ 24 ♔g1 ♘xc4! 25 ♕d3 ♕g3+ 26 ♗g2 ♘f4! (a cute finishing touch) 27 ♕f1 ♕xe3+ 28 ♔h2 ♘xd2 29 ♕d1 ♘xg2 (or 29...♘e2! 30 ♕e1 ♕f4+ 31 ♕g3 ♕xg3#) 30 ♗xd2 ♕xe4 31 ♔g3 ♘e3 32 ♔f2 0-1. Black's sustained initiative kept the bishops in check.

7...exf5 *(D)*

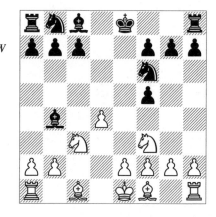

At first this may make a strange impression, but when you get used to the many openings in which Black is playing with doubled f-pawns these days it won't surprise you. Black's basic idea is that White's 2:0 central majority is restrained by the c- and f-pawns, so it simply won't be able to expand. In particular a rook on e8 renders the advance e4 on White's part extremely unlikely.

We aren't looking at many queenless middlegames in this book, partly because the opening features can disappear so quickly. In this case it's different: the central pawn-structure often remains the same well into the middlegame, and we get to see the minor pieces' relative worth. Black's strategy is to present a compact centre with reasonably active pieces. White's is to use his space advantage (and, sometimes, the bishop-pair).

8 a3

Now Black has a choice of retreats.

Gagunashvili – N. Pedersen
Vlissingen 2004

8...♗e7 9 ♗f4

Another try is 9 b4 c6 10 e3 0-0 11 ♗d3 g6 12 ♗b2 ♘bd7 13 ♘a4 ♘d5 14 ♖c1 ♗f6 15 0-0 ♘5b6 16 ♘c5 ♘xc5 17 bxc5 ♘d5, Arlandi-Romanishin, Turin 1998. Black's strongpoint, supported by the doubled pawn and (potentially) a bishop on e6, gives him close to equality, but White has space and a small advantage.

9...c6 10 e3 ♘bd7 11 ♗d3 ♘b6 12 0-0

White must be a little better with his space advantage.

12...0-0 13 ♖fc1 ♗e6 14 ♘d2 ♖fc8 15 ♗g3 ♘h5 16 b4 ♘xg3 17 hxg3 *(D)*

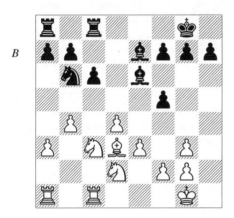

When one side is conducting a classical minority attack like this, knights can be at least as useful as bishops. Nevertheless, Black should wait to see how White will make progress. In most cases b5 can be answered by ...c5, or even ...cxb5. So White needs to use piece-play instead; e.g., ♖ab1 and ♘b3. In the game, Black tries to compromise White's pawn-structure:

17...a5!?

White can be satisfied after 17...g6 18 ♖ab1 ♔g7 19 ♘e2 intending ♘b3-c5/a5.

18 bxa5 ♖xa5 19 ♖cb1 ♘a4?

This lands Black in trouble. Accurate play is needed: 19...♗d8! 20 ♘b3! ♖a7 (20...♗xb3 21 ♖xb3 with the idea ♖ab1) 21 ♘c5 ♖b8 22 a4 and Black is under slight pressure. The good news for him is that White's ♘xe6 will achieve little by itself.

20 ♖xb7 ♘xc3 21 ♖xe7 ♘b5 22 ♗c4 ♖xa3 23 ♖xa3 ♘xa3 24 ♗xe6 fxe6 25 ♘b3

and White won material and the game. But as for the variation in general, it's likely that with good defence Black can keep his disadvantage to a minimum.

Dreev – Short
Reykjavik (rapid) 2004

8...♗d6 *(D)*

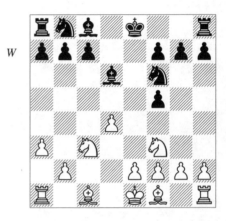

9 ♗g5

White can also play the natural and obvious 9 ♘b5!?, gaining the bishop-pair; e.g., 9...♗e6 10 e3 ♘c6 11 ♗d2 a6 12 ♘xd6+ cxd6 13 ♗d3 ♘e7 *(D)*.

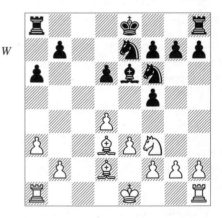

This is Timman-Yusupov, Frankfurt (rapid) 1998. We have a picture of what's at the heart of ...♕f5: Black has an isolated d-pawn and doubled f-pawns whereas White has the bishop-pair. But both the d-pawn and f5-pawn prevent incursions, and Black will undoubtedly be able to exchange off a bishop. White has seldom won such a position at the high levels of play, and indeed Timman-Yusupov was drawn.

9...♘e4!? 10 ♘xe4 fxe4 11 ♘d2 f5 12 e3 ♗e6 13 g4 h6 14 gxf5 ♗xf5 15 ♗h4 ♔d7

Here White should have simply developed, rather than play 16 f3?! exf3 17 e4? ♖e8, when Black was distinctly better.

B)

5...exd5 *(D)*

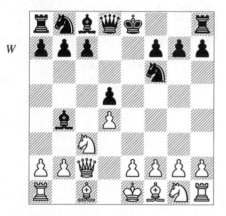

Although 5...♕xd5 comes close to equality, the positions are a bit difficult to handle. It's also hard to imagine Black winning many games versus relatively strong opposition. That being the case, many players on all levels have used the older recapture with the pawn. This introduces an Exchange Queen's Gambit structure wherein Black's bishop on b4 can be either an advantage or a disadvantage. Indeed, the Queen's Gambit analogy continues after White's next move.

6 ♗g5 h6

This poses White a stark decision between a purely positional effort (which Black may nevertheless counter actively) and a variation that has produced spectacular tactical struggles on a regular basis. We'll look at both approaches:

The Positional Line

7 ♗xf6 ♕xf6 8 a3 ♗xc3+ 9 ♕xc3 *(D)*

We have a standard Nimzo-Indian trade-off: Black is going to castle way before White (maybe next move), but White has pressure down the c-file and the better bishop (his pawns will be on e3 and d4). As usual, White's

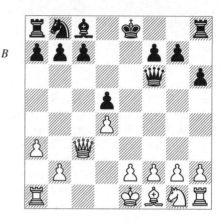

long-term advantages, which include a minority attack, must be countered by Black's activity, customarily on the kingside and in the centre. To help with that, Black has a lead in development, at least in terms of being ready to castle and bring pieces out rapidly. On the other hand, he lacks a dark-squared bishop to place on d6 as part of his attack. These factors make the variation instructive and attractive to both sides. It has numerous themes, including those dealing with the minority attack in a pure form.

Petrosian – Botvinnik
Moscow Wch (1) 1963

9...c6 10 e3 *(D)*

This is the Carlsbad pawn-formation, which pops up in a number of d-pawn openings but especially the Queen's Gambit Declined, where it is discussed in detail. By playing ...c6, Black has acceded to the pure form of White's minority attack by b4-b5 in order to solidify d5. The solid-looking 10 ♘f3!? allows Black to place his bishop on f5 where he wants it, without being challenged by White (see the next game). On the plus side, ♘e5 might follow.

10...0-0 11 ♘e2 ♖e8!?

Since White wants to play ♘g3, Black decides not to commit his bishop to f5 yet.

12 ♘g3

Not 12 ♘f4?? ♕xf4. But 12 b4 would initiate the queenside attack and ask Black where he's putting his pieces. Finally, 12 ♘c1!? with the idea of ♘d3 (probably prefaced by ♗e2) has been suggested. It would place the knight optimally at the cost of time and development.

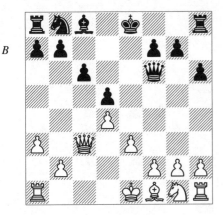

12...g6!

With the idea of ...h5-h4, a plan that arises whenever the knight is on g3. Still, for once Black has no lead in development and if White consolidates, his queenside attack will take over.

13 f3?!

This move, exposing the light squares, is too loosening. Ironically, Botvinnik once lost by making a similar move in the Sämisch Variation with an early ♗g5xf6, as you can see by looking back to that section.

13 ♗d3! h5 14 ♕c2! *(D)* is a much better idea.

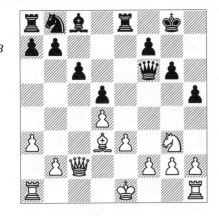

14...♘d7 (14...h4 15 ♘e2 h3?! 16 ♖g1! has the idea of gxh3 and 0-0-0 with a terrific attack) 15 h3 ♘f8! (a nice reorganization that leaves Black in fair shape) 16 0-0 h4 17 ♘e2 ♘e6 18 b4 a6 19 a4 ♗d7 20 ♖ab1! (White doesn't consolidate by 20 b5 due to 20...axb5 21 axb5 ♖xa1 22 ♖xa1 c5 with equality) 20...♖ac8 21 ♕d1 ♘g5. Beliavsky-Balashov, Minsk 1983, and now 22 ♘f4 is very probably best, to protect White's

kingside and prepare the minority attack with b5. White should have some advantage in that case, although it's not much.

13...h5 14 ♗e2 ♘d7 15 ♔f2

15 0-0 h4 16 ♘h1 ♕g5! forces a response to the attack on e3; for example, 17 e4 ♘f6! 18 e5 ♘h5 and White has difficulties untangling his pieces.

15...h4 16 ♘f1 ♘f8 17 ♘d2 ♖e7 18 ♖he1 ♗f5 *(D)*

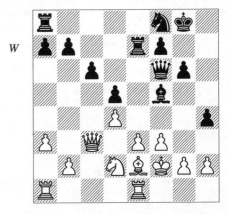

What is White's plan? The opening is past and we can only assess it as a smashing success for Black.

19 h3!? ♖ae8 20 ♘f1 ♘e6 21 ♕d2 ♘g7?!

This backwards move intends ...♘h5, and it does give Black a distinct advantage. Nevertheless, Ripperger gives analysis to show that 21...♘g5! 22 ♔g1 ♗xh3! 23 gxh3 ♘xh3+ leads to a winning game. That might be difficult to play in the very first game of a world championship match!

22 ♖ad1 ♘h5 23 ♖c1 ♕d6 24 ♖c3! *(D)*

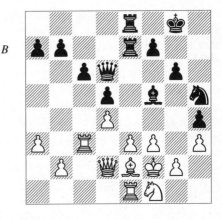

24...♘g3?!

24...♖e6! is better.

25 ♔g1!

25 ♘xg3? ♕xg3+ and 26 ♔f1 ♕h2 or 26 ♔g1 ♖xe3 27 ♖xe3 ♖xe3, etc.

25...♘h5!? 26 ♗d1!? ♖e6 27 ♕f2

Petrosian's defence is effective as usual, and White has put things together nicely in the face of severe pressure. Only his mistake on move 30 negates this hard work.

27...♕e7 28 ♗b3 g5 29 ♗d1 ♗g6 30 g4? hxg3 31 ♘xg3 ♘f4! 32 ♕h2 c5 33 ♕d2 c4 34 ♗a4 b5! 35 ♗c2 ♘xh3+ 36 ♔f1 ♕f6 37 ♔g2 ♘f4+ 38 exf4 ♖xe1 39 fxg5 ♕e6 40 f4 ♖e2+! 0-1

Seirawan – Portisch
Rotterdam 1989

9...0-0! *(D)*

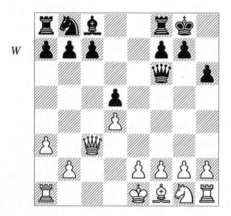

As we shall see, spending a tempo on ...c6 may not always be the best idea.

10 e3

10 ♘f3 gives Black the chance to develop ideally: 10...♗f5 11 e3 (not 11 ♕xc7? ♘c6! 12 e3 ♖fc8 and Black has way too much attack) 11...♘d7 12 ♗e2 c5! 13 0-0 c4, Boleslavsky-Borisenko, USSR Ch (Moscow) 1950. This is an idea to remember: White can't effectively expand on the queenside in the face of Black's activity; for example, 14 b3 b5 15 a4 b4! 16 ♕xb4 ♖fb8.

10...♗f5!

Skipping ...c6 is very useful unless White can capture on c7 or attack the f5-bishop.

11 ♘e2 ♖c8

11...♘d7! *(D)* is the most active approach which (as the game demonstrates) is what Black needs:

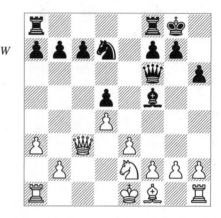

12 ♘g3 (12 ♕xc7 ♖fc8 13 ♕xb7 ♖ab8 14 ♕xd5 ♖xb2 is very risky for White; these active lines are exactly what he's trying to avoid) 12...c5! (12...♗g6 13 ♕xc7) 13 ♘xf5 ♕xf5 14 dxc5?! (14 ♗d3 ♕g4 15 0-0 c4!) 14...d4! 15 ♕xd4 (15 exd4 ♖fe8+) 15...♘xc5 16 ♖d1 ♖ad8! 17 ♕xd8 ♖xd8 18 ♖xd8+ ♔h7, Vera-Delanoy, Pau 1988. Black's advantage would be within limits after 19 ♗c4!; e.g., 19...♕b1+ 20 ♖d1 ♕c2 21 b3 ♕c3+ 22 ♔e2 ♘xb3 23 ♗xb3 ♕xb3 24 ♖d3 ♕b2+ 25 ♔f3!, etc., but who would want to play White?

12 ♘g3!?

Or:

a) 12 ♘f4?! c5! *(D)*.

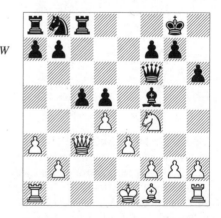

White can't ever allow this move without getting something valuable in return, especially when he is undeveloped. 13 dxc5 (13 ♘xd5

♕d6) 13...♕xc3+ 14 bxc3 ♖xc5 15 ♖d1, Korchnoi-Beliavsky, USSR Ch (Moscow) 1973; and here 15...♗e6! makes White's weak queenside the issue.

b) A better plan for White is 12 ♖d1 ♘d7 13 ♘f4! c6!? (Black should also think about opening things up by 13...c5 14 ♘xd5 ♕d6 15 dxc5 ♘xc5) 14 ♗e2 ♕e7 15 0-0 ♘f6 16 b4 with at best a small edge, Shabalov-Dzhandzhgava, Riga 1988.

12...♗e6?!

A passive retreat. Every long-term element favours White, as Seirawan so brilliantly demonstrates. Therefore Black needs to disturb the equilibrium and look towards immediate counterplay:

a) 12...c5?! falls a bit short after 13 ♘xf5 ♕xf5 14 dxc5!, when 14...b6?! 15 ♗d3 ♕g5?? allows White the startling trick 16 cxb6! ♖xc3 17 b7. Instead, 14...a5 15 ♗d3 ♕e6 is preferable, but this is positionally suspect after 16 0-0 b6 17 ♗c2! ♖xc5 18 ♕d3 g6 19 b4.

b) 12...♗g6! is best because Black keeps his bishop on its most influential diagonal and will achieve either ...c5 or ...h5. For example, 13 b4 (13 ♗e2 c5; 13 ♕b3 c5) 13...h5 14 ♗e2 h4 with the initiative.

13 b4!

White's ideal set-up: he doesn't have to worry much about the kingside and Black has few options on his queenside.

13...a5 14 ♗e2! axb4 15 axb4 ♖xa1+ 16 ♕xa1 ♕e7 17 ♕c3 *(D)*

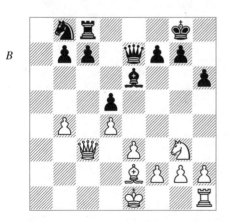

17...♕d6

Seirawan got a similar advantage against Tal in Nikšić 1983: 17...♘c6 18 b5 ♘d8 19 0-0 c5

20 bxc6 bxc6 21 ♖c1 ♗d7 22 ♕a5; Black is in terrible shape positionally.

18 0-0 ♘c6 19 b5 ♘e7 20 ♖a1! g6 21 ♕c5 *(D)*

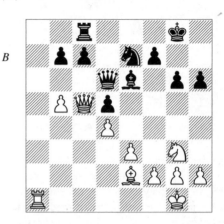

21...b6?!

21...♕d7 22 ♖a7 ♖b8 23 ♗d3. Black will have to defend for ages, and a well-timed e4 could pose big problems.

22 ♕xd6 cxd6

From now on White is in charge. Notice the opening of a second front that is almost always necessary to win a game if the defender passively protects his weaknesses on his vulnerable side of the board.

23 ♔f1 ♔f8 24 ♔e1 ♔e8 25 ♗d3 ♔d8 26 ♔d2 ♖b8 27 ♘e2 ♔c8 28 ♘c3 ♗b7 29 ♘a4 ♗c8 30 ♖c1 ♗e6 31 ♖c2 ♖b7 32 ♖a2 ♖a7 33 ♔c3 ♔c7 34 ♔b4 ♔b7 35 ♖c2 ♖a8 36 ♖c1 ♖c8 37 ♘c3 ♖a8 38 ♗c2! f5 39 ♗b3 ♗g8 40 h4 ♖f8 41 ♘e2! ♖f6 42 ♖h1 ♗f7 43 ♘f4 ♔c7 44 ♗d1! ♗g8 45 g4! fxg4 46 ♗xg4 ♔b8 47 ♖c1 ♖f8 48 h5 gxh5 49 ♗xh5 ♗h7 50 ♖h1 ♗e4 51 f3 ♗f5 52 ♗g4 ♗xg4 53 fxg4 ♖f6 54 ♔c3 ♔c7 55 ♔d3 ♔c8 56 ♔e2 ♔c7 57 ♔f3 ♔c8 58 ♔g3 ♔c7 59 ♖c1+ ♔b7 60 ♖c2 ♔b8 61 ♖f2 ♔c7 62 ♖h2 1-0

Uncompromising Attack

After all that technical material, we turn to 7 ♗h4, which signals a disinclination to simplify. White generally gets his wish in that respect.

7 ♗h4 c5 *(D)*

This must be considered one of the most important variations stemming from 4 ♕c2 d5,

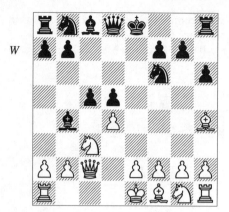

particularly in the main line 7 ♗h4 c5 8 dxc5 g5, etc. Like its counterpart 5 a3 ♗xc3+ 6 ♕xc3, correct play is usually dependent upon lengthy analysis in positions of mad disarray, and should only be used by those who are either very well-prepared or know full well that their opponents, by virtue of their playing strength or habits, couldn't know as much as they do! I have to say that this is a wonderfully entertaining variation whose tactics are of an original nature. Since it is of such a forcing and heavily-analysed nature, however, I'll only provide two revealing examples.

Keres – Botvinnik
Leningrad/Moscow 1941

We'll start with this famous game in order to show that from the very beginning White had to face dynamic counterattacks in this variation. That continues right up to the present.

8 0-0-0?

We'll see the modern 8 dxc5 next.

8...♗xc3! 9 ♕xc3

Perhaps this move is wrong already! 9 ♗xf6 ♗xb2+! gives Black some advantage, but less than in the game.

9...g5 10 ♗g3 cxd4 11 ♕xd4

Now White loses a tempo and is exposed to a vicious attack down the c-file. The result isn't much better after 11 ♕a3 ♗f5 12 ♘f3 ♘e4! 13 ♖xd4 ♘c6 14 e3 (14 ♖d1 ♖c8!) 14...g4! and Black is winning, Lukin-Estrin, USSR corr. Ch 1960-3.

11...♘c6 12 ♕a4 ♗f5! 13 e3 ♖c8 14 ♗d3?

A better chance was offered by Botvinnik's suggestion 14 ♘e2! a6 (but 14...0-0! 15 ♘c3

♘e4 looks very strong) 15 ♘c3 b5 16 ♕xa6 (16 ♕b3!?) 16...b4 17 e4! ♗xe4 18 ♗b5.

14...♕d7! *(D)*

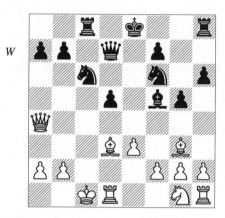

One move and it's over! The knight is unpinned and threatens ...♘b4+.

15 ♔b1 ♗xd3+ 16 ♖xd3 ♕f5 17 e4 ♘xe4 18 ♔a1 0-0 19 ♖d1 b5! 20 ♕xb5 ♘d4 21 ♕d3 ♘c2+ 22 ♔b1 ♘b4 0-1

As Botvinnik says, "White's kingside pieces took no part in the game". This is a comprehensible and analytically limited contest, which one cannot say about the variation that follows.

The Modern Line

8 dxc5 *(D)*

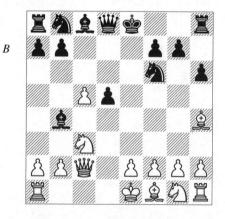

As indicated before, this position can and usually does lead to outlandishly complicated positions that are mostly the result of massive home analysis. There's nothing wrong with that – think of the Poisoned Pawn Najdorf Sicilian or Botvinnik Variation of the Semi-Slav – but there's really very little for me to explain or suggest except that you hit the books, computers, or whatever scheme you might have for studying/learning. To give you a flavour of the action, I'll squeeze some positions into a sample game that follow the most popular and critical variations.

R. Ibrahimov – Mamedyarov
Baku 2006

8...g5 9 ♗g3 ♘e4 10 e3

A recent game went 10 ♗xb8 ♕f6! 11 ♗g3 ♘xc3 12 a3 ♗f5 13 ♕d2 ♗a5 14 b4?? (White goes wrong in the complications; instead, 14 e3 is a risky winning try, while White can also try to bail out with the forcing line 14 ♘f3!? ♕b1! 15 ♕xa5 ♕xb2 16 ♕a4+ ♗d7 17 ♗e5 ♘c3 18 ♕d1! ♘xd1 19 ♗xb2 ♘xb2, when ...♘a4 follows with a small edge) 14...♘e4 15 ♕c1 ♖c8! 16 ♖a2 ♖xc5 17 ♕a1 ♕c6 18 ♕e5+ ♔d8 19 ♕xh8+ ♔d7 0-1 I.Sokolov-Aronian, Turin OL 2006. A treacherous line, as we can see by the fact that a game between such powerful players lasted less than 20 moves.

10...♕a5 11 ♘e2 ♗f5 *(D)*

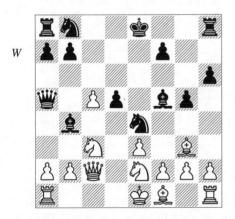

The basic position. What follows is representative of some recurring tactical ideas.

12 ♗e5

Who knows what's happening in lines like 12 ♗xb8!? ♖xb8 13 ♘d4? Only the experts... maybe. You may get a feel for the nature of the tactics by 13...♗d7!? (not a very intuitive move, but 13...♗g6 14 ♗b5+ ♔f8 15 ♗d3! gave Black problems in Dreev-Zhang Zhong, Moscow

(Russia vs China) 2004; best play is then 15...♕xc5 {15...♘xc3 16 0-0!} 16 0-0 with some advantage to White) 14 ♘b3! ♗xc3+ 15 bxc3 ♕xc3+ 16 ♕xc3 ♘xc3 17 f3 ♔e7 18 ♔d2 ♘a4, I.Sokolov-Van Wely, Wijk aan Zee 2005. A difficult position to assess, but in any case close to equality.

12...0-0 13 ♘d4 ♖e8!?

This may be the most important move of all. Maybe ten years from now we'll know something definitive.

13...♘xc3 has been the most explored alternative; here are a few samples:

a) 14 ♕xf5 ♘e4+ 15 ♔d1!? (Emms suggests 15 ♔e2 ♗xc5!? 16 ♘b3 ♕a6+ 17 ♔f3 ♕e6!) 15...♘c6 16 ♘b3 ♕a4 17 h4?! ♘xe5 18 hxg5 ♘g4 19 ♖xh6, Bu Xiangzhi-Sargisian, Moscow 2006, and here 19...♖fc8! is strong.

b) 14 ♘xf5 ♘e4+ 15 ♔d1 ♘c6! *(D)*.

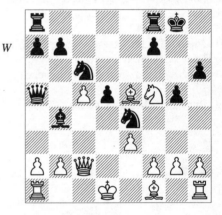

16 ♗d4 (16 ♗g3? ♗xc5 17 f3 ♖fd8!! with a mega-attack, Law-Ward, London 1994; 16 ♗d6!?) 16...♘xd4 17 exd4! ♗e1! 18 ♘xh6+? (18 ♔c1! ♘xf2 19 ♖g1 is not clear – Emms) 18...♔h8! 19 ♔c1 ♖ac8! 20 ♔b1 ♗xf2! 21 ♗d3 ♗xd4 22 ♗xe4 dxe4 23 h4 ♖xc5 24 ♕xe4 ♕d2 25 ♘xf7+ ♔g7 0-1 Devereaux-Emms, British League (4NCL) 2004/5. Very nice.

We now return to 13...♖e8 *(D)*:

14 ♗xb8

Emms offers 14 ♘xf5 ♖xe5 15 ♘xh6+ ♔g7 16 ♘g4 ♖e6, when 17 ♗d3 may be one of those fortunate moves that is effective for no logical reason.

14...♘xc3!?

Giving up a piece. Some simplification took place in Atalik-Short, Sarajevo 2004: 14...♗g6

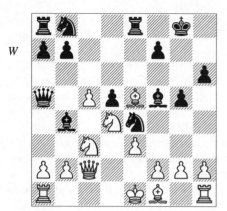

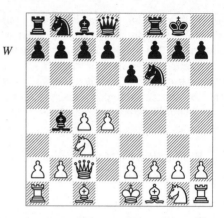

15 ♗d3 ♖axb8 16 0-0 ♕xc5 17 ♖ac1 ♖ec8 18 f3 (18 ♕e2 ♗xc3!?) 18...♘xc3 19 ♗xg6 ♘e2+ 20 ♕xe2 ♕xc1 21 ♗f5! with equality.

15 ♘xf5 ♘e4+ 16 ♔e2 ♕a6+ 17 ♔d1 ♕f6 18 f3

18 g4! looks clever, cementing the super-knight. Maybe 13...♘xc3 is best after all?

18...♕xf5 19 fxe4

19 a3 looks like the best try. The great thing about Black's combination is that it develops so slowly and without a great deal of material remaining.

19...dxe4 20 ♗d6 ♖ed8 21 ♔e2 (D)

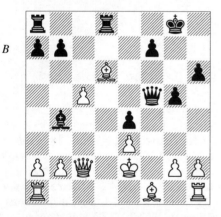

21...♖ac8 22 ♕a4 ♖xc5! 23 ♕xb4 ♖xd6 24 ♔e1 a5 25 ♕xb7 ♖f6 26 ♕b8+ ♔g7 27 ♕g3 ♖c2 28 ♗e2 a4 29 b4 axb3 30 axb3 ♕d5 0-1

That's what 'real chess' looks like in the sharp theoretical lines!

Classical with 4...0-0

4...0-0 (D)

By choosing this move, Black refuses to commit to a plan and waits to decide upon his choice of ...d5, ...c5, or ...b6. Rather than cover the tens of subvariations that can follow, I'll give a few examples of a fairly recent and thematic continuation, followed by a brief look at the 'main line'.

Central Occupation

5 e4 (D)

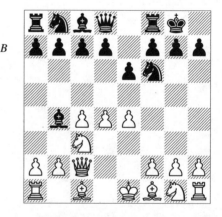

Talk about a fundamental challenge to 4...0-0! White simply takes over the centre. This had been condemned for years and designated an error by some sources; then someone decided that it might be OK to suffer a little as long as he could win the battle of control over vitally important central turf. As of this writing 5 e4 has been doing about as well as any other variation in the Nimzo-Indian. It is so committal, however, that I wouldn't be shocked if it were 'solved' in the sense of giving Black a clear path to equality or even better. Whatever happens, however, an examination of 5 e4 must be worth it, if only for the average player to understand why such a natural move hasn't always been one of White's main choices and why it has become one. We'll first look at 5...d6, a response that Black has used to avoid the most critical lines, and then 5...d5, directly challenging the centre. For the curious, other moves such as 5...c5 seem playable.

The Slow Line

5...d6 *(D)*

Apparently unchallenging, Black's simple move has its strengths. Much as in other variations of the Nimzo-Indian, he wants to blockade the big centre in order to attack it later.

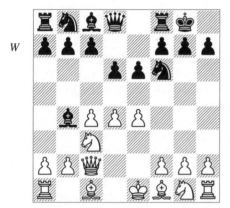

6 a3

a) The logical alternative 6 ♗d3 avoids doubled pawns, but anything that doesn't support d4 allows Black to transform the pawn-structure to his liking: 6...e5! 7 ♘e2!? (7 a3! ♗xc3+ 8 bxc3 transposes to our main game; 7 d5 allows for a variety of choices, since the c5-square has opened up for Black's bishop on b4 or his knight on b8; e.g., 7...♘a6 8 a3 ♗xc3+ 9 ♕xc3 ♘c5 10 f3 ♘h5 intending ...♕h4+ and/or ...f5) 7...exd4 8 ♘xd4. This position was contested as far back as the 1930s. Black can continue 8...♗xc3+ 9 ♕xc3 ♖e8 10 f3 d5 11 cxd5 ♘xd5 12 ♕b3 ♘b6 with complications. Or he can choose 8...♖e8 9 0-0!? ♗xc3 10 ♕xc3 ♘xe4 11 ♕c2 ♘f6 12 ♗g5 h6 13 ♗h4 with some compensation. Even 8...♘c6 9 ♘xc6 bxc6 has been tried with reasonable prospects. One other thing

to note is that Black can retreat to c5 with his bishop in all these lines, especially after a3, and have satisfactory play.

b) I should mention that 6 e5!? is also played, when White's centre isn't as vulnerable as it looks. 6...dxe5 7 dxe5 ♘g4 8 ♘f3 ♘c6 9 ♗f4 or 9 a3 can follow, with complex play that I won't pursue here.

6...♗xc3+ 7 bxc3 e5

We have a Sämisch Variation in which Black has played ...e5, with the important difference that White has played e4 in one jump. On the other hand the move ♕c2 isn't necessarily that useful, and the advanced centre is potentially exposed. The resulting strategies can vary wildly. To begin with, Black threatens ...exd4 followed by ...♘xe4, so White's next move is natural:

8 ♗d3 *(D)*

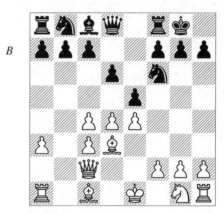

Here the main moves are 8...♘c6 and 8...c5, for which I shall give game examples.

Black's other continuation is 8...b6 9 ♘e2 ♗b7 10 0-0 ♖e8, which attempts to force White into playing d5. This is a traditional way for Black to proceed in the Nimzo-Indian, but White doesn't have to oblige (perhaps having the queen on c2 is worthwhile after all!): 11 ♘g3 ♘c6 12 ♗b2 ♘e7!? 13 f4 ♘g6 14 ♗c1! ♘d7!? 15 f5 ♘gf8 16 f6! (a trick that keeps coming up!) 16...♘xf6 17 ♗g5 ♘8d7 18 ♘h5 ♔h8 19 ♖f3 ♖g8 20 ♖af1. White had a terrific attack in Leitão-Urday, Americana 1997.

Short – Karpov
Dortmund 1997

8...♘c6 9 ♘e2 b6 10 0-0 ♗a6

Standard stuff. Black lines up to attack c4.

11 f4! ♘d7 12 ♗e3 ♘a5 *(D)*

W

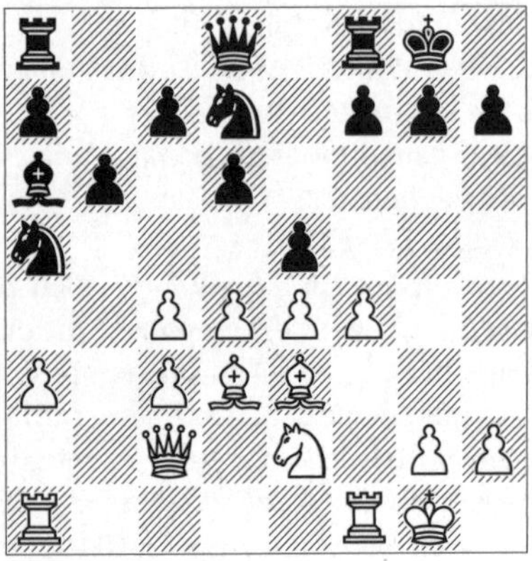

13 c5!?

Although highly praised, this advance does have the problem that it will inevitably open the c-file and expose White's weaknesses. On the positive side, White staves off material loss and weakens Black's centre. 13 ♕a2 with the idea ♖ad1 and/or ♖f3 is another approach.

13...♗c4?!

Black might do better with 13...♗xd3! 14 ♕xd3 dxc5! (14...exd4? 15 cxd4 bxc5 16 dxc5 ♘xc5 17 ♗xc5 dxc5 18 ♕c3 and White has a big advantage). Then 15 dxe5 looks good at first for White due to his kingside pawn-mass. But Black can move his knight and count upon long-term advantages: 15...♘b8! 16 ♖ad1!? (16 ♕c2 ♘c4 17 ♖f3) 16...♕xd3 17 ♖xd3 ♘c4. This is hard to assess but should be OK for Black.

14 cxd6 cxd6 15 ♘g3 ♕c7 16 ♘f5 *(D)*

B

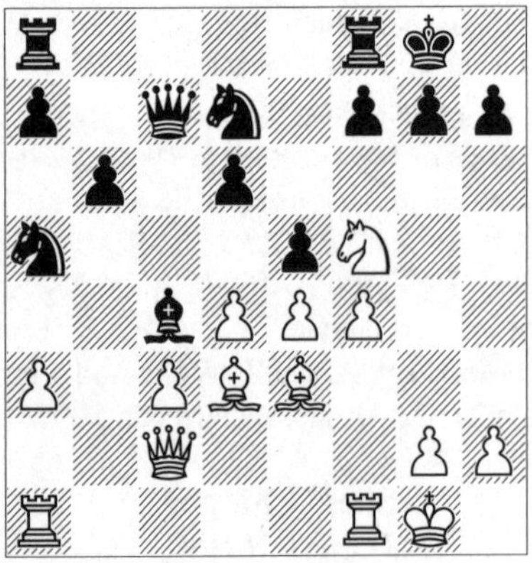

16...♔h8

16...♗xd3 17 ♕xd3 ♘c4 wins c4 but is too slow: 18 fxe5 dxe5 (18...♘xe3 19 exd6) 19 ♗h6!.

17 ♖f3 ♖ac8 18 ♖af1! *(D)*

B

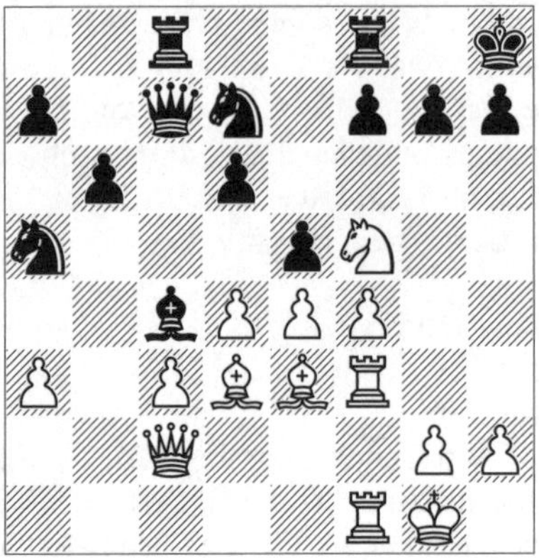

18...f6

Regardless of what follows, we can say that White has won the opening. Short anticipated 18...♗xd3 19 ♕xd3 ♕xc3 20 ♕xc3 ♖xc3 21 fxe5 dxe5 22 ♗h6! ♖xf3 23 ♗xg7+ ♔g8 24 ♖xf3, winning. At this point we're seeing one of those positions in which the knight on a5, the strongest minor piece on the board if Black breaks through on the queenside, is the weakest when attention turns kingside. The game remains complicated. I'll present it with a minimum of notes.

19 ♗f2 b5 20 ♗g3 a6 21 h4!? ♗f7?! 22 ♗e1 ♘b6 23 ♕f2 ♘ac4 24 ♖g3 g6 25 ♘h6 ♗e6 26 f5 gxf5 27 ♘xf5 ♖g8!?

27...♘xa3 28 ♘g7 ♗g8 29 ♗d2! threatens ♗h6.

28 ♘xd6!

Now White is winning, although it still takes accuracy.

28...♖cf8 29 ♖xg8+ ♔xg8 30 ♘f5 ♕d7 31 ♕g3+ ♔h8 32 d5 ♗xf5 33 ♖xf5 ♘d6 34 ♖f1 ♘bc4 35 h5 ♕g7 36 ♕h4 ♖g8 37 ♕xf6 ♘e3 38 ♕xg7+ ♔xg7 39 ♖f3 ♘ec4 40 ♗h4 ♔h6 41 ♗e7 ♔xh5 42 ♖f6 ♖g6 43 ♖f5+!

A nice finishing touch. There's nothing like two bishops and a passed pawn.

43...♘xf5 44 exf5 ♖g4 1-0

Ivanisević – Nisipeanu
Istanbul Ech 2003

8...c5!? 9 ♘e2 ♘c6 10 d5 ♘e7 *(D)*

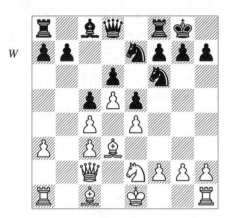

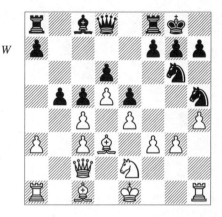

11 f3!?

This has become a typical Hübner Variation structure (see that section), but with a knight on e2. White's most pointed strategy is to counter Black's typical development by playing 11 ♘g3; for example, 11...♘g6! 12 ♘f5 ♘f4 13 0-0 ♗xf5!? 14 exf5 ♖e8 15 f3 ♘xd3!? 16 ♕xd3 e4 17 fxe4 ♘xe4 18 f6!, again with the idea 18...♘xf6 19 ♗g5. Of course this is just a sample out of scores of continuations; the flexibility of strategies by both sides is an attractive feature of such positions.

11...♘g6 12 h4 ♘h5!? (D)

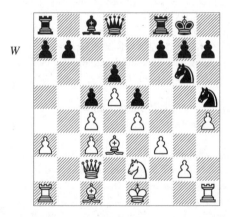

13 g3?

The idea is to stop either knight from coming to f4, but Black finds an ingenious rejoinder. Much better would be 13 g4 ♘hf4 14 h5 ♘g2+ 15 ♔f2 ♘6f4 16 ♖h2! ♘xe2 17 ♕xe2 ♘f4 18 ♗xf4 exf4 19 e5!, when White has ideas of ♕e4 and e6.

13...b5!! (D)
14 cxb5 c4! 15 ♗xc4 f5

Black has a promising kingside attack, his amazing moves ...b5 and ...c4 serving to clear the way to White's weakened kingside pawns.

16 ♗g5 ♕b6 17 exf5 ♗xf5 18 ♕d2

Emms gives the line 18 ♗d3 ♗xd3 19 ♕xd3 e4! 20 fxe4 ♘e5, when White is three pawns up but he'll be lucky to survive.

18...e4! 19 f4 ♖ac8

Black has taken over. White's next move is a bit desperate, but it's hard to find a good one:

20 ♕d4 ♕xd4 21 ♘xd4 ♖xc4 22 ♘xf5 ♖xf5 23 g4 (D)

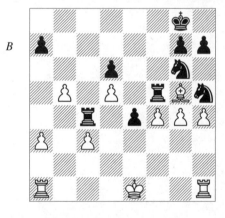

23...♖xg5! 24 fxg5 ♘hf4 25 a4 ♖xc3 26 a5 ♖c2 27 b6 ♘g2+ 0-1

There follows 28 ♔d1 ♘e3+ 29 ♔e1 ♘e5 and checkmate.

Challenging the Centre

5...d5 (D)

This starts a direct assault on White's broad centre, leading to a set of critical variations that

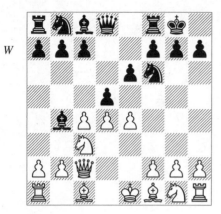

W

have to be assessed on an individual basis. It's surprising that White can allow Black to develop so quickly with threats; after all, he only has two pieces out and is far from castling. White's contention is that his central advantage will overcome temporary tactical and developmental difficulties. There are many paths to consider here; I won't begin to try to cover all the complexities of 5...d5, but will follow what currently seems to be the main line:

6 e5 ᐁe4 7 a3

7 ᐃd3 c5 8 a3 ᐃxc3+ 9 bxc3 transposes but is less forcing.

7...ᐃxc3+ 8 bxc3 c5 9 ᐃd3 *(D)*

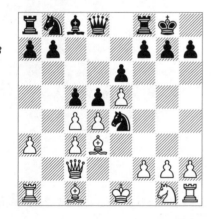

B

A key position. We look at two games. Theory is exploding in this line, so they are merely examples.

Vallejo Pons – Schandorff
St Vincent ECC 2005

9...cxd4 10 cxd4 ᐎa5+ 11 ᐕf1 ᐃd7!?

Another course is 11...ᐁc6; for example, 12 ᐁe2 ᐁb4 13 axb4 ᐎxa1 14 f3 f5 15 ᐎb1! ᐎa4 16 ᐃc2, Pogorelov-An.Rodriguez, Calvia open 2004; now 16...ᐎa6! is extremely complicated.

12 ᐁe2 f6 13 ᐃxe4! dxe4 14 exf6 ᐉxf6 15 ᐃe3 ᐃc6 16 ᐁg3

Shariyazdanov-Pikula, Biel 2002 had gone 16 h4!? ᐁd7 17 ᐉh3, and here 17...ᐉaf8! 18 ᐁg3 ᐉ6f7! is strong, with the idea 19 ᐁxe4?? ᐎf5.

16...ᐉf8 17 ᐕg1 ᐁd7 *(D)*

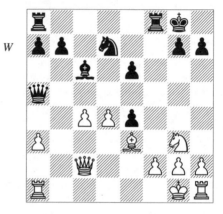

W

18 h3

Vallejo Pons analyses 18 ᐁxe4 ᐎf5 19 f3 ᐎg6 20 h4 ᐉxf3! 21 h5 ᐎg4 22 ᐁf2 ᐎf5 23 ᐎxf5 ᐉxf5 with approximate equality.

18...ᐁf6 19 ᐕh2 ᐉac8 20 ᐉhc1 ᐎc7

This position is called unclear by Vallejo Pons. The game was ultimately drawn.

Vallejo Pons – Leko
Morelia/Linares 2006

9...ᐎa5 10 ᐁe2

Euwe tried 10 ᐃxe4 versus Muhring in Johannesburg 1955. Alas, 10...dxe4 11 ᐃd2 ᐎa6 12 ᐎxe4 ᐎxc4 13 ᐁe2 ᐁc6 14 0-0 ᐉd8 was pleasant for Black. This is the sort of evidence that got 5 e4 discarded in the first place.

10...cxd4 11 cxd5

11 0-0 dxc3 12 ᐃe3 ᐁc6 13 cxd5 exd5 14 f3 ᐁd2 15 ᐃxh7+ ᐕh8 16 ᐃxd2 cxd2 was good for Black in Kelečević-Abramović, Yugoslavia 1984. Again, this was well before contemporary players began to look into 5 e4 in earnest.

11...exd5 12 f3 ᐁxc3 13 ᐁxd4 ᐁe4+ 14 ᐕe2 *(D)*

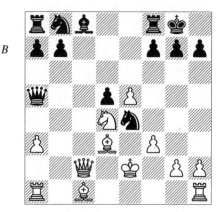

14...f5! 15 ♗e3

Kasparov suggests another crazy line: 15 e6! ♘c6! 16 ♘xc6 bxc6 17 e7 ♖e8 18 ♕xc6 ♖xe7! 19 ♕xa8 ♘g3++! 20 ♔d1 ♕c3 21 ♗d2! ♕xa1+ 22 ♗c1 ♕c3! 23 ♗d2 ♕a1+ with a repetition. Whether any or all of this is correct, it shows what fantastic play is hidden in this variation.

15...♘c6!? (D)

15...♘d7!? both threatens the pawn on e5 and has ...♘dc5 in mind. One line would be 16 ♖hf1!? (16 fxe4 fxe4 17 ♗b5 ♘xe5) 16...♘xe5 17 fxe4 fxe4 18 ♖xf8+ ♔xf8 19 ♗b5 ♗g4+ with compensation. Who knows what's happening in such a position? It's refreshing to have so much unknown territory.

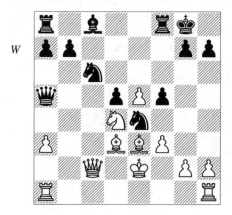

16 ♘xc6 bxc6 17 ♖hc1?!

The best idea seems to be 17 ♖ac1! ♖b8 18 ♖hd1, bringing every piece to the defence.

17...♖b8 18 ♔d1 ♖d8 19 ♗d4 ♗e6

Or 19...c5!? 20 ♗xc5 ♗e6.

20 ♖ab1? ♖xb1 21 ♖xb1 c5 22 ♖b5 ♕xa3
(D)

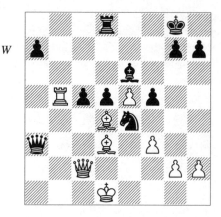

With two extra pawns and an attack, Black is winning. Only capturing the knight on e4 gives White any hope, but then he opens lines against his own king.

23 ♗b2 ♕a2 24 ♗e2 ♗d7 25 fxe4 ♗xb5 26 ♗xb5 ♖b8 27 ♗c6 ♕xb2 28 ♗xd5+ ♔h8 29 ♕xb2 ♖xb2 30 exf5 ♖b4 31 ♔c2 ♖d4 32 ♗f7 ♖e4 33 e6 h5 34 ♗xh5 ♔g8 35 g4 ♔f8 36 g5 ♔e7 37 h3 a5 38 ♗g4 a4 39 f6+ gxf6 40 g6 ♔f8 0-1

Modern Line: Going for the Two Bishops

4 ♕c2 0-0 5 a3 ♗xc3+ 6 ♕xc3 b6 *(D)*

Needless to say, there are alternatives; e.g., the gambit 6...b5!? 7 cxb5 c6! tries to dominate the light squares by ...♗b7 in conjunction with opening lines and accelerated development.

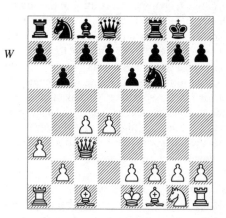

7 ♗g5

White plays his most ambitious move, putting his bishop outside a potential pawn-centre with e3 and fighting directly for e4.

7...♗b7 *(D)*

There is a considerable body of theory and practice behind the move 7...♗a6, although it is still not considered as important as the simple fianchetto.

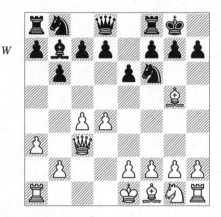

In grandmaster games in which 4 ♕c2 is played, this position is reached more often than any other. For the most part the variations turn technical, however, which dampens the interest of many lower-level players. I'll give a couple of games to indicate what both sides may be after.

Kasparov – Timman
Linares 1993

8 f3

There's a logic to this move that goes beyond enforcing e4, namely, that control of the square itself lies behind most of White's strategies in this variation. For example, apart from 8 f3, White sometimes plays 8 ♘f3 and then 9 ♘d2, as in the next game. Or, in other lines, a knight will come to c3 via e2. White does have one other idea that is specifically connected with 8 f3: his knight can develop to h3 and then perhaps f2. But this highlights a negative aspect to White's whole approach: he is still a long way from developing his kingside.

8...d5!? *(D)*

Black employs the easiest idea, which is to challenge White's centre before it becomes mobile. But 8...h6! is helpful in several lines, since after 9 ♗h4 it takes the bishop away from the queenside and centre, in particular e3. There's also a tactical point to forcing the bishop back, as seen in the note to move 10.

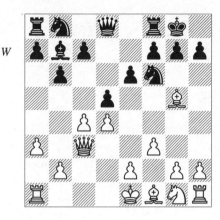

9 e3 ♘bd7

These last two moves have become so customary that (ignoring the omission of ...h6 for the moment) the majority of games with a ...d5 defence begin here.

10 cxd5! exd5

A tactic that often applies in these positions is 10...♘xd5?! 11 ♗xd8 ♘xc3 12 ♗xc7 ♘d5 13 ♗f4 ♘xf4 14 exf4. White's pawns are crippled, but he's still a pawn ahead and this position has lacked takers from Black's side. ♗d3 and ♘e2 will follow in most lines, with ♔f2 a good centralizing move.

However, it's important to note that if the moves 8...h6 9 ♗h4 were inserted, as they usually are, then in this line Black could answer ♗f4 with ...g5! and win the e3-pawn. That position is known to be equal. In fact, White hasn't been able to prove any advantage in the lines after 8...h6 9 ♗h4 d5, although the debate continues.

11 ♗d3 *(D)*

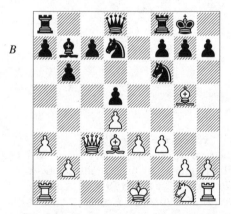

11...♖e8

Targeting the e-pawn right away. Now it looks as though ...h6 is a threat.

12 ♘e2! h6 13 ♗h4!

In fact, we've transposed to a normal position except that Black didn't have the opportunity for an effective ...♘xd5.

13...c5

The point is that 13...♖xe3? loses to 14 ♗xf6! ♘xf6 15 ♗h7+.

14 0-0 ♖c8 15 ♕d2 ♕e7 16 ♗f2 ♗c6

An important positional idea is that 16...cxd4 is well answered by 17 exd4! (D), even though 17 ♘xd4 places a knight in front of the isolani opposing the bad bishop. That latter position isn't bad, but it does give Black nice posts on e5 and c5 for his d7-knight.

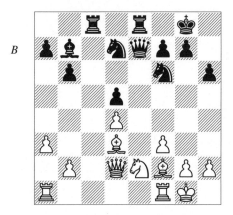

After the recapture by the pawn, we have a position that could come from the Queen's Gambit. Every key central square is covered and White, whose position looks innocuous at the moment, can slowly activate his pieces, in particular a rook to the e-file and his bishop to g3. Again, stability favours the bishop-pair.

17 ♘c3! ♘f8 18 ♖fe1 ♘e6 19 ♗h4 ♘g5

19...g5 weakens Black's kingside and especially his f5-square.

20 ♗f5 ♗d7 21 ♗c2 ♗c6 22 ♖ad1 ♕e6 23 ♕f2

When you have the bishop-pair you can take your time and play for the long run. Most endgames will be winning for you. White has won the opening.

23...♖cd8 24 h3

24 ♗xg5 hxg5 25 ♕g3 g4 is nothing special, but after 24 h3, the same idea will win a pawn. So Black retreats.

24...♘gh7 25 dxc5

Kasparov mentions 25 ♗b3!?, when 25...c4 (to stop 26 e4) 26 ♗c2 again prepares the advance e4. But he has a different version in mind.

25...bxc5 26 e4! (D)

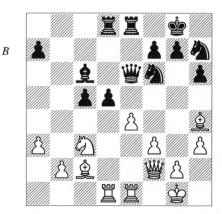

26...dxe4

26...d4 27 e5! results in a very large advantage for White.

27 ♖xd8 ♖xd8 28 ♕xc5 ♘g5 29 ♗xg5 hxg5 30 ♕xg5 ♕c4 31 fxe4 ♕d4+ 32 ♕e3 ♕xe3+ 33 ♖xe3 ♖d2 34 ♖e2 ♖xe2 35 ♘xe2 ♘xe4 36 ♗xe4 ♗xe4 37 ♔f2

and White eventually won the ending.

In general, however, it is difficult for White to counter Black's rapid development and central counterattack after 8 f3, whether Black plays 8...h6 9 ♗h4 d5 or 8...d6. So White has looked for other approaches, as in the next game.

Krush – Shirov
Edmonton 2005

1 d4 ♘f6 2 c4 e6 3 ♘c3 ♗b4 4 ♕c2 0-0 5 a3 ♗xc3+ 6 ♕xc3 b6 7 ♘f3 ♗b7 8 ♗g5

Obviously, White can employ the order 7 ♗g5 ♗b7 8 ♘f3 as well.

8...d6 9 ♘d2!? (D)

White wants to control e4 by another means, the advantage of which is that his knight on d2 contributes significantly to central play, especially in contrast to ♘h3.

9...♘bd7 10 e3

10 f3 is another matter. Then one possibility is 10...c5, to contest d4. A fascinating game

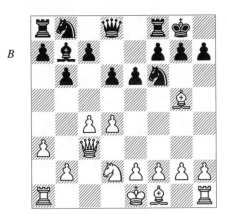

Van Wely-Timman, Breda (7) 1998 continued 10...d5 11 e3 ♖e8!? (anticipating 12 cxd5 exd5, opening the e-file) 12 ♗d3 h6 13 ♗h4 e5!. Here's an example of the fundamental conflict: Black's central advances force White to alter the pawn-structure before he can consolidate his bishop-pair advantage. Whether or not this succeeds, both sides are pursuing their philosophic goals: White to prevent the weakening of his pawns in order to win in the long run, and Black to rip into the position as best he can.

10...♖c8!? (D)

An odd-looking move whose point becomes clear in a moment. Instead, 10...c5 11 dxc5! is a way to gain time for development.

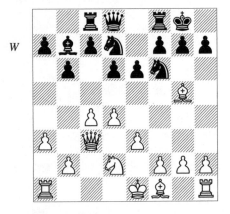

11 f3 c5 12 dxc5!?

Played to release the pressure on White's centre and get castled quickly. One drawback is that White cedes a central majority to Black; the other is tactical:

12...♖xc5!

This attacks the bishop on g5 with tempo.

13 ♗h4 b5!

13...♘d5? fails to 14 ♗xd8 ♘xc3 15 ♗e7 ♖e8 16 ♗xd6 ♖c6 17 ♗g3.

14 b4 ♖c6 15 ♘b3 bxc4 16 ♘a5 ♖c7 17 ♘xb7 ♖xb7 18 ♗xc4 ♖c7! 19 ♕d4

Now things are looking up for White. In addition to the advantage conferred by his two bishops, Black's pawns are a bit weak.

19...e5! 20 ♕d3 e4! (D)

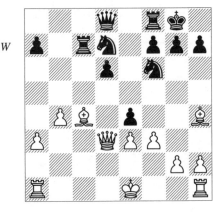

As the owner of the knight-pair, Shirov must continue the policy of disturbing White's pawn-structure to open lines and create outposts for his knights.

21 ♕e2

21 fxe4? loses a piece to 21...♘e5.

21...♘e5 22 ♗b5?

It turns out that the c8-square needs to be covered, so 22 ♗a6! is better, with a double-edged game still in store. But that's certainly not easy to see at this point.

22...exf3 23 gxf3 (D)

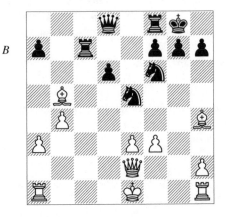

Now White's kingside is weakened, but how does Black follow up?

23...♕c8! *(D)*

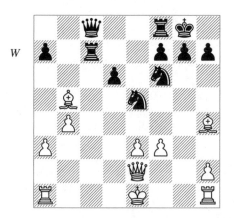

As so often, Shirov finds a creative way to seize the initiative.

24 0-0

After 24 ♗xf6? ♖c2 25 ♕d1 gxf6 26 0-0 ♔h8 27 ♔h1 ♖g8 28 ♗e2 d5! Black has decisive threats.

24...♖c2 25 ♕d1 ♘d5! *(D)*

26 ♕e1

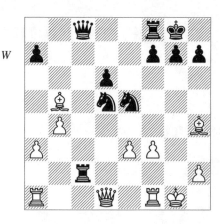

26 ♕xd5 ♕h3 27 ♖f2 ♖xf2 28 ♔xf2 (or 28 ♗xf2 ♘xf3+ 29 ♔h1 ♕xh2#) 28...♕xh2+ 29 ♔f1 ♕h1+ 30 ♔e2 ♕xa1 might be a reasonable exchange sacrifice for White but his king is too exposed. The rest is easy.

26...♘c3 27 a4 a6! 28 ♗e7 axb5 29 ♗xf8 ♕h3 0-1

There follows 30 ♖f2 ♘xf3+ 31 ♔h1 ♕xh2+! 32 ♖xh2 ♖xh2#. The system with ♗g5 and ♘f3-d2 is hard to assess, even after the ...♖xc5 idea. My overall impression is that the play is dynamically equal.

6 Queen's Indian Defence

Introduction to 3 ♘f3

1 d4 ♘f6 2 c4 e6 3 ♘f3 *(D)*

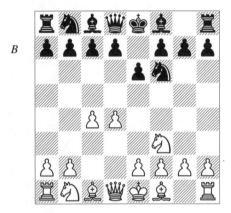

B

By playing 3 ♘f3 White enters into a contest about move-order choices. By omitting or putting off ♘c3 he avoids the highly-respected Nimzo-Indian Defence (1 d4 ♘f6 2 c4 e6 3 ♘c3 ♗b4) and indeed, this is generally considered the main motivation behind 3 ♘f3. Otherwise, with a few exceptions mentioned below, White gains little by delaying 3 ♘c3 versus the main defences to 1 d4, and he can sacrifice some popular options. Let me clarify that by examples. After 3 ♘c3, White might want to enter into a variation not accessible after 3 ♘f3, such as the Exchange Queen's Gambit 3...d5 4 cxd5 exd5 5 ♗g5 c6 6 e3 ♗e7 7 ♗d3 0-0 8 ♘ge2. White's commitment to ♘f3 precludes a number of popular options. In fact, even the Classical Queen's Gambit Declined that arises from 1 d4 ♘f6 2 c4 e6 3 ♘f3 d5 4 ♘c3 differs in several ways from 1 d4 d5 2 c4 e6 3 ♘c3, although they will often transpose. In the latter order, for example, Black might play 3...♗e7. These positions are dealt with at some length in Chapter 2 on the Queen's Gambit.

Another restriction imposed by 3 ♘f3 comes up in the Modern Benoni. White has eliminated certain options that arise after 3 ♘c3 c5 4 d5 exd5 5 cxd5 d6 6 e4 g6; for example, 7 ♗d3 ♗g7 8 ♘ge2 0-0 9 0-0, 7 f4 ♗g7 8 ♗b5+ (or here 8 ♘f3) or 7 f3 ♗g7 8 ♗g5. Obviously, none of those variations can be played after 3 ♘f3.

Thus, when playing 3 ♘f3, it's necessary to build a repertoire around these limitations. In actual practice, most players are not deterred by that task.

3...b6 *(D)*

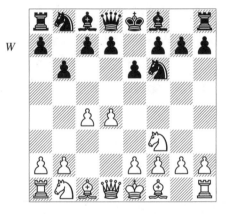

W

The Queen's Indian Defence (a.k.a. 'QID') is defined by this move. Notice that after 3 ♘c3, 3...b6?! allows 4 e4 with superior central control, something Black really doesn't want to let happen. After 3 ♘f3 b6, however, Black intends to keep a determined hold on the central light squares and permit neither a successful e4 nor d5. This can involve the moves ...d5 or ...f5, if necessary, and often includes occupation of e4 by either a knight or a bishop.

White for his part may strive directly to enforce e4 by moves such as ♘c3 (perhaps prefaced by a3 to prevent ...♗b4) and ♕c2. Or he can do the same, but slowly, by means of g3, ♗g2 and ♘c3 or ♘bd2 depending upon the situation. His ultimate set-up and strategy will depend upon what Black specifically undertakes in the centre. The resulting tension can produce both strategically and tactically interesting chess. This is a lesson to players everywhere, because for many years the Queen's Indian Defence had the reputation of being a dull opening that normally led to a drawish position. In fact, that reputation still holds among some lower-rated players, although it shouldn't.

I'm going present an overview of the variations and ideas of the Queen's Indian, with a mix of older and newer games. The emphasis will be on a few of the typically dynamic ideas that are being played in modern chess. To this end the material divides into two sections: the Fianchetto Variation (4 g3), and the Petrosian System (4 a3).

Fianchetto Variation

1 d4 ♘f6 2 c4 e6 3 ♘f3 b6 4 g3

Historically this has been White's main choice and it remains so in spite of the emergence of new strategies. Straight away, White's fianchettoed bishop anticipates opposing its counterpart on b7 and indirectly looks at the same key e4- and d5-squares as his opponent does. White also clears the way for early castling. A quick look at obvious alternatives might clarify White's choice:

a) White can play 4 ♘c3 but then after 4...♗b4 we're back in a kind of Nimzo-Indian, which may not be the type of position most players are looking for when they play 3 ♘f3 instead of 3 ♘c3.

b) 4 ♘bd2 takes the sting out 4...♗b4, a move which would no longer threaten to double White's pawns as it would after 3 ♘c3. But this comes at the cost of blocking the c1-bishop and reducing the white queen's influence over d4. Most importantly, White chance of ever playing d5 is greatly reduced. Black can continue simply by 4...♗b7 with ...d5 or ...♗e7 and ...0-0 next.

c) 4 ♗f4 is a perfectly good move, in order to get the bishop out before hemming it in by e3. A typical sequence would be 4...♗b7 5 e3 (5 ♘c3 ♗b4 is a type of Nimzo-Indian, easy to play for Black because White's f4-bishop neither hampers Black's knight on f6 nor defends the queenside; thus, for example, 6 e3 ♘e4 7 ♕c2 f5 8 ♗d3 0-0 9 0-0 ♗xc3 10 bxc3 d6 11 d5

♘c5 12 dxe6 ♗xf3 13 gxf3 ♘xd3 14 ♕xd3 ♘c6 with good play) 5...♗e7 (5...♗b4+ is a well-known option) 6 h3 (versus ...♘h5, which would track down and exchange the bishop on f4 and leave Black with the two bishops) 6...0-0 7 ♘c3 d5 (D).

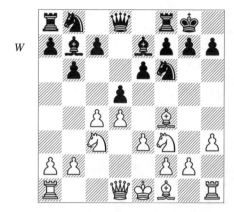

Here White's move h3 (as opposed to developing) leads to a balanced version of a Queen's Gambit. An intriguing gambit goes 8 cxd5 (8 ♗e2 c5) 8...♘xd5 (8...exd5 is also reasonable, with ideas of ...c5 and ...♘e4) 9 ♘xd5 ♕xd5! 10 ♗xc7?!, and now 10...♕a5+! (10...♗b4+ is the normal move) 11 ♘d2 ♘d7 intending ...♖ac8 and ...e5 with more than enough play for a pawn.

d) 4 e3 is a solid, risk-free move that prepares ♗d3 and 0-0. I won't be covering the details here. White might want to look into this modest line to avoid main-line theory, and Black should be ready to respond to it. Probably 4...♗b7 5 ♗d3 d5 6 0-0 ♗e7 or 6...♗d6 is the easiest way to approach the position.

We now return to 4 g3 (D):

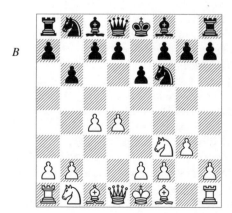

After 4 g3, Black makes a decision as to how he wants to counter White's space advantage: 4...♗b7 or 4...♗a6.

The Classical 4...♗b7

4...♗b7

This is the older move, which generally leads to a quieter game but not always so.

5 ♗g2

White's plan is 0-0, ♘c3, and then d5 or ♕c2 and e4.

5...♗e7 *(D)*

Where do the pieces belong? Basically Black has to develop his kingside, get castled, and make sure that White doesn't play d5. His other natural choice is 5...♗b4+, when 6 ♗d2 ♗xd2+ (6...♗e7!?) 7 ♕xd2 ♘e4 8 ♕c2 0-0 9 ♘c3 sets up an old trap: 9...♘xc3? 10 ♘g5! and Black is losing material! This is a typical tactic that is worth knowing, although Black had to make some weak moves to allow it.

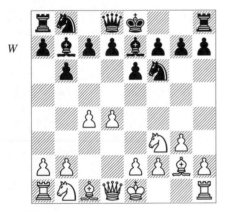

W

6 0-0

6 ♘c3 will transpose to our main line after 6...♘e4 7 ♗d2 ♗f6 8 0-0 0-0. A famous game Korchnoi-Karpov, Moscow Ct (21) 1974 went 6...0-0 7 ♕c2 c5 8 d5!? *(D)*.

This is a standard break that both sides always have to be aware of. White's idea is to shut the b7-bishop out of play. He will play e4 next, so Black has to capture, when tactics erupt: 8...exd5 9 ♘g5 (now the d-pawn is pinned) 9...♘c6 (best was 9...h6! 10 ♘xd5 ♗xd5 11 ♗xd5 ♘c6) 10 ♘xd5 g6 11 ♕d2! ♘xd5 12 ♗xd5 ♖b8? 13 ♘xh7! ♖e8 (the main line goes 13...♔xh7 14 ♕h6+ ♔g8 15 ♕xg6+ ♔h8 16 ♕h5+ ♔g8 17

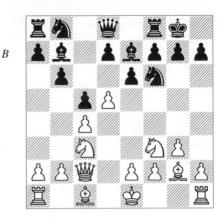

B

♗e4 f5 18 ♗d5+, etc.) 14 ♕h6 ♘e5 15 ♘g5 ♗xg5 16 ♗xg5 ♕xg5 (16...♕c7 17 ♗f6) 17 ♕xg5 ♗xd5 18 0-0 ♗xc4 19 f4 1-0.

6...0-0 7 ♘c3 ♘e4

Otherwise White will prevent this by ♕c2.

8 ♗d2!

A very instructive move. If White plays 8 d5 instead, then 8...♘xc3 cripples his pawns. So 8 ♗d2 is logical, preparing 9 d5. But the interesting part is that if Black captures White's bishop on d2, White counts upon having a big centre and better development that will outweigh the bishop-pair. That is a bit unusual when there are no weaknesses in Black's camp, but it has been shown to be true in this particular position. Thus you will very seldom see 8...♘xd2.

8...♗f6

The other well-known move is 8...f5, when 9 ♕c2 ♗f6 10 ♖ad1! has won some nice games.

9 ♖c1 *(D)*

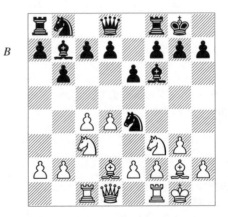

B

This is the basic position of the main line. Let's see how a World Champion handles it:

Kasparov – Ponomariov
Linares 2003

9...d5

White wants to play d5, so Ponomariov blocks it. 9...c5 is more frequently played, leading to a Benoni-like position after 10 d5 exd5 11 cxd5 and, for example, 11...♘xd2 12 ♘xd2 d6.

10 cxd5 exd5 11 ♗f4 ♘xc3

Korchnoi-Salov, Belgrade 1987 may have helped to inspire Kasparov. That game continued 11...♘a6 12 ♗e5 ♖e8 13 ♗xf6 ♕xf6 14 e3 c5 15 ♘e5 ♕e7 16 ♖e1 ♘c7 17 ♘d3 ♘xc3 18 bxc3 c4 19 ♘f4 ♕d6 *(D)*.

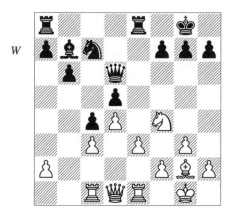

W

20 f3! (shades of the Exchange Queen's Gambit and Nimzo-Indian Sämisch Variation! White intends to play e4; this came out of nowhere) 20...♖e7 21 e4 f6 22 ♖c2 ♖ae8 23 ♖ce2 b5 24 h4! (a sort of second front; watch how terrifically White's pieces coordinate over the next few moves) 24...a5 25 ♔h2 ♗c6 26 ♕c2 g6 27 ♗h3 ♔g7 28 h5! g5 29 ♘g6! *(D)*.

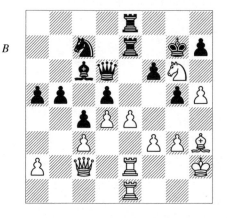

B

A terrific combination follows: 29...hxg6 30 e5 fxe5 31 dxe5 ♕c5 32 ♕xg6+ ♔h8 33 ♕f6+ ♔g8 34 h6! ♖f8 35 ♕xg5+ ♔h8 36 f4 (the attack is so slow!) 36...♖h7 (it's surprising how little Black can do; maybe 36...b4 37 f5 bxc3 38 f6 ♖g8, but White has a huge attack in any event) 37 f5 ♗e8 38 e6! ♕e7 39 ♕xe7 ♖xe7 40 g4! b4 41 cxb4 c3 42 g5 (White will win the race) 42...d4 43 g6 d3 44 g7+ ♖xg7 45 hxg7+ ♔xg7 46 ♖g1+ ♔f6 47 ♖e3 ♗b5 48 ♖g6+ ♔e7 49 ♖g7+ ♔d6 50 a4! ♘d5 51 e7 ♖e8 52 ♖e6+ ♔c7 53 axb5 c2 54 ♖c6+ ♔b7 55 f6 d2 56 f7 d1♕ 57 fxe8♕ ♕d2+ 58 ♖g2 ♕f4+ 59 ♖g3 1-0. A great game.

12 bxc3!

12 ♖xc3 is the move most players would make, but 12...c5 gives enough counter-pressure; for example, 13 ♖c1 (to get out of the pin) 13...♘a6! (a typical move in such positions; the knight doesn't get in the way and it may continue on to c5 in some lines) 14 ♖e1 ♖e8 with equality.

12...♘a6 *(D)*

Allowing a tactic that secures White the better centre. Black's problem after 12...♘d7 13 c4! dxc4 14 ♖xc4 is that he can't get 14...c5 in due to 15 d5! ♖e8 16 ♖e1 b5 17 ♖c1. Perhaps 12...c5 immediately was correct.

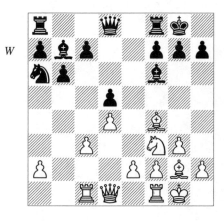

W

13 e4!

A nice pawn sacrifice to break down the centre. Black has to accept, but then weakens his position trying to hang on to the pawn.

13...dxe4 14 ♘d2 g5!?

14...c5 15 ♘xe4 threatens ♘xf6+; 14...♖e8 15 ♖e1 also favours White.

15 ♗e3 ♖e8 16 f4!

Somehow Kasparov always manages to get open lines!

16...exf3 17 ♗xf3 ♗d5!?

17...♗xf3? allows a winning attack after 18 ♕xf3 ♕e7 19 ♖ce1.

18 ♗xd5 ♕xd5 19 ♖xf6 ♖xe3 20 ♕g4! *(D)*

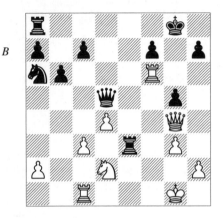

Now both ♖cf1 and ♘f3 are threats.

20...♖e6 21 ♖f5 ♕c6 22 ♕xg5+ ♖g6 23 ♕h5 ♖f8 24 ♘f3

What's that knight doing on a6?

24...f6 25 ♘h4 ♖g7 26 ♕h6 ♘b8 27 ♖h5 f5 28 ♕f4 ♕e4 29 ♖f1 ♕xf4 30 ♖xf4 ♖g4 31 ♖fxf5

White is a clear pawn up.

31...♘d7 32 ♖xf8+ ♘xf8 33 ♔f2 ♘d7 34 ♘f5 *(D)*

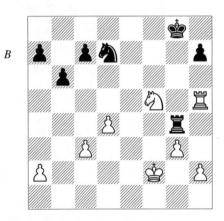

If there is ever a Kasparov decal, it should have a picture of the board with a knight on f5.

34...♔h8 35 ♔f3 ♖g8 36 ♖h6 ♖f8 37 g4 ♘f6 38 c4 ♔g8 39 ♔f4 ♖f7 40 g5 ♘e8 41 ♔e5 ♖d7 42 ♔e6 ♖f7 43 ♖f6! ♘xf6

43...♘xf6 44 gxf6 ♖f8 45 f7+ ♔h8 46 ♔e7 and White's pawn promotes.

44 gxf6 ♖f8 45 f7+ ♔h8 46 ♔e7 1-0

Here's a well-known older game in which Black demonstrated what to do when White overextends:

Euwe – Keres
Rotterdam (9) 1939/40

1 d4 ♘f6 2 c4 e6 3 ♘f3 b6 4 g3 ♗b7 5 ♗g2 ♗e7 6 0-0 0-0 7 ♘c3 ♘e4 8 ♕c2

This move is logical.

8...♘xc3 9 ♕xc3 d6 10 ♕c2 f5

Black's philosophy: don't allow e4 for free!

11 ♘e1

11 d5! is more promising, based on the idea 11...exd5? 12 ♘d4!.

11...♕c8! 12 e4 ♘d7 13 d5!? fxe4 14 ♕xe4 ♘c5 15 ♕e2 ♗f6! *(D)*

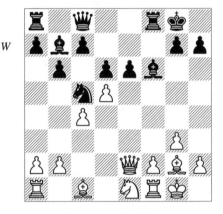

Look how active Black's pieces are. Now White embarks upon unjustified tactics:

16 ♗h3 ♖e8 17 ♗e3 ♕d8! 18 ♗xc5 exd5! 19 ♗e6+ ♔h8 20 ♖d1

No better is 20 ♗a3 ♕e7 21 cxd5 ♗xd5 with an extra pawn and much better pieces.

20...dxc5 21 ♘g2 d4 22 f4 d3!

Initiating a winning combination.

23 ♖xd3 ♕xd3! 24 ♕xd3 ♗d4+ 25 ♖f2 ♖xe6 26 ♔f1 ♖ae8!?

But here he slips up a bit. 26...♗xf2! 27 ♔xf2 ♖ae8 was winning.

27 f5?

27 ♖d2! would have been a more stubborn defence.

27...♖e5 28 f6 gxf6 29 ♖d2 ♗c8! 30 ♘f4 ♖e3 31 ♕b1 ♖f3+ 32 ♔g2 ♖xf4 33 gxf4 ♖g8+ 34 ♔f3 ♗g4+ 0-1

The Modern 4...♗a6

4...♗a6

Black plays an 'extended fianchetto', the modern favourite. although it dates all the way back to Nimzowitsch himself. I'll mainly give illustrative examples without many detailed analytical notes.

5 b3

The attack on the c-pawn proves annoying, and 5 ♕a4 has generally been ineffective (one good line is 5...♗b7 6 ♗g2 c5), as has 5 ♕b3, so 'everybody' plays 5 b3.

5...♗b4+

This check is designed to disrupt the coordination of White's pieces.

5...♗b7 is rarer but playable. Adams, who is arguably the best Queen's Indian player around, shows us a beautiful example of how to equalize and then get a counterattack in Morović-Adams, Istanbul OL 2000: 6 ♗g2 ♗b4+ 7 ♗d2 a5 8 0-0 0-0 9 ♕c2 d6 10 ♘c3 ♘bd7 11 ♖ad1 ♗xc3 12 ♗xc3 ♗e4 13 ♕c1 a4 14 ♗h3 b5! *(D)*.

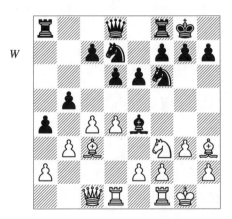

The QID is ideally about light-square control. This is true and then some in what follows: 15 ♘d2 axb3 16 axb3 bxc4 17 bxc4 ♖a2 18 f3 ♗c2 19 ♖de1 c5 20 d5 exd5 21 ♗xd7 ♘xd7 22 cxd5 ♕a8! 23 ♗b2 ♕a4 (every piece ends up transferring from one light square to another) 24 ♗c3 ♘b6 25 e4 ♗d3! 26 ♖f2 ♖c2 27 ♕a1 ♕xa1 28 ♗xa1 ♖a8 29 ♘b3 ♘c4 (now White's

knight on b3 is trapped) 30 e5 ♖xf2 31 ♔xf2 ♗c2 32 ♘d2 ♘xd2 33 exd6 ♘c4 34 d7 ♗a4 35 ♖c1 ♗b5 0-1.

6 ♗d2 ♗e7 *(D)*

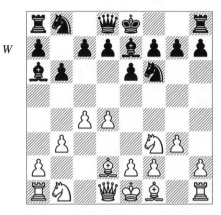

The starting point for the majority of the Queen's Indian battles between top grandmasters for the last 10 years. With the extra move 5...♗b4+ Black has lured White's bishop to d2, from where it has less effect than on b2. His next plan is to enforce ...d5, which will both give him space and attack c4.

Wojtaszek – Macieja
Krakow 2006

7 ♗g2 c6

This move may look strange, but Black wants to be able to play ...d5 and have the option of recapturing with the c-pawn should White play cxd5. He might also play ...b5 to increase pressure on c4. By contrast, 7...d5 8 cxd5 exd5 9 0-0 0-0 10 ♘c3 with the ideas ♗f4 and ♖c1 gives White free development and pressure along the c-file.

8 ♗c3

White's simple idea is to defend the d-pawn and then play ♘bd2, often prefaced by ♘e5.

8...d5 *(D)*

9 ♘e5

Karpov-Anand, Warsaw 2000 was a model of Black's strategy: 9 ♘bd2 ♘bd7 10 0-0 0-0 11 ♖e1 ♗b7 12 ♖c1 (after 12 e4, multiple exchanges followed by ...c5 will equalize) 12...c5 13 ♗b2 ♖c8 14 cxd5 exd5 15 ♖c2 ♖e8 16 ♗h3 ♖c7 (typical and equal; now maybe 17 dxc5 was best) 17 ♘f1? c4! 18 ♘e3 b5 19 bxc4

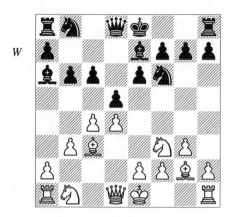

W

dxc4! (this time the flank outweighs the centre, if only because the centre pawns will take too long to mobilize) 20 &g2 &e4 21 &c1 &b6 (the whole situation has changed in a few moves: Black's pieces are swarming all over the queenside and ...b4 is coming) 22 &e5 &xg2 23 &xg2 b4 24 &c2 c3 25 &c1 &d6 26 f4 &a8+ 27 &g1 &bd5 28 &xd5 &xd5 29 &d3 &e4 (compare each sides' pieces) 30 &d1 f6 31 &g4 &f8 32 &e3 &c6 33 d5 &c5 34 &g2 &d6 35 &f5 &xf5 36 &xf5 a5 37 e4 a4 38 &e2 b3 39 axb3 axb3 (White's centre pawns are finally rolling, but Black's are already there) 40 &f1 &b7 41 &ff2 &c8 42 &xc8 &xc8 43 e5 &c5 0-1.

9...&fd7 10 &xd7 &xd7 11 &d2 0-0 12 0-0 &c8 13 e4 *(D)*

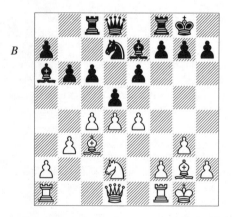

B

13...b5

This is one of Black's standard plans. In the next game we see 13...c5.

14 &e1 dxe4

Both sides have tried all sorts of moves here. I'm ignoring most of the theory.

15 &xe4 bxc4 16 &e2 &f6

Intending 17 bxc4 &d5!.

17 &c5! *(D)*

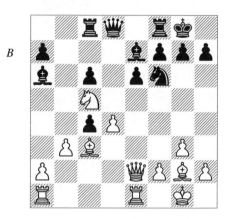

B

It's worth putting up with some trouble to get the bishop-pair and dark-square control, even if the latter is limited.

17...&xc5

17...&d5? fails for tactical reasons: 18 &xd5! &xc5 19 &xe6!.

18 dxc5 &e7

18...&d5 19 &e5!? &b4 20 &ed1! favours White.

19 b4!

Now it's a pawn sacrifice. Neither side has a great advantage, but White has the more attractive deployment of forces.

19...&fd8 20 &b2 &e8 21 a4 h6 22 &e2 &d3 23 &e4 &d7 24 &ee1 *(D)*

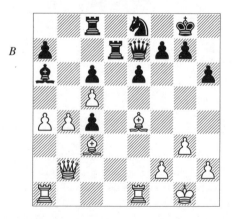

B

24...&b7?!

24...&f6 looks right. The bishop returns anyway.

25 ♕a2 ♗a6 26 ♖ab1 ♘f6 27 ♗g2 ♘d5 28 ♗e5 ♕f8

28...f6! may be better; e.g., 29 ♗d6 (29 ♗a1) 29...♖xd6 30 cxd6 ♕xd6 31 ♖bd1. Unclear? In any case, White's exchange sacrifice would be risk-free.

29 ♖ec1 ♖b7 30 ♕a3 ♕d8 31 h4 f6 32 ♗d6 c3?! 33 ♖xc3! *(D)*

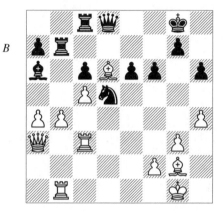

Minor pieces actually have more effect than rooks in such a position. White has better practical chances and he managed to break down Black's defences:

33...♘xc3 34 ♕xc3 ♕d7!? 35 ♖b2 ♕f7? 36 b5! cxb5 37 ♕a5! bxa4 38 ♕xa6 ♖xb2 39 ♕xc8+ ♔h7 40 ♕a6 ♖b1+ 41 ♔h2 ♕g6 42 ♕xa4 ♖b2 43 ♕d4 ♖e2 44 c6 e5 45 ♕xa7 ♖c2 46 c7 1-0

Topalov – Anand
San Luis Wch 2005

7 ♗g2 c6 8 ♗c3 d5 9 ♘e5 ♘fd7 10 ♘xd7 ♘xd7 11 ♘d2 0-0 12 0-0 ♖c8

This variation had been a main line for some time, but now the following 8-10 moves have been torn apart by games and analysis. No wonder that some players keep switching to new lines in the QID. Fortunately there are a lot of ideas out there.

13 e4 c5 14 exd5 exd5 15 dxc5 dxc4 *(D)*

16 c6! cxb3! 17 ♖e1! b2! 18 ♗xb2 ♘c5 19 ♘c4

There have been several other moves played at this point and unsurprisingly, given the high publicity accorded this game, over the next several moves as well.

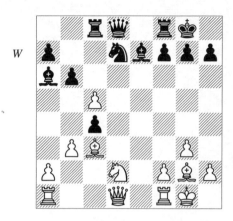

19...♗xc4 20 ♕g4 ♗g5 21 ♕xc4 ♘d3 22 ♗a3!? ♘xe1 23 ♖xe1 ♖e8 24 ♖xe8+! ♕xe8 25 ♗d5! *(D)*

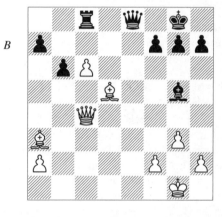

This is arguably the end of the opening! White is a full exchange down, counting upon his passed pawn and two bishops. Normally that would be a pretty good situation, but there isn't a great deal of material left, and Black would love to give back the exchange for a pawn by ...♖xc6. As it turns out, White can prevent that and tie Black down enough to prevent active counterplay. As a result, White seems to have a draw in hand, and can try for more.

25...h5 26 ♔g2 ♗e7 27 ♗b2 ♗f6 28 ♗c1! ♕e7 29 ♗e3 ♖c7 30 h4 ♗e5 31 ♕d3 ♗d6 32 ♗g5 ♕e8 33 ♕f3 b5 34 ♗e3

34 ♕xh5 ♖xc6 should be equal.

34...♕e5 35 ♕d1 ♕e8 36 ♕xh5!

Allowing the simplifying sacrifice on c6 only in order to reject it! White will now have a pawn for the exchange with very limited material, yet he's definitely the one playing for a win.

36...♖xc6 37 ♗xa7 ♖a6 38 ♗d4 ♗f8 39 ♗e5 b4 40 ♕f5 g6 41 ♕f4 ♕e7 42 ♗d4 ♖a5 43 ♕f3 ♗g7 44 ♗b6 ♖b5 45 ♗e3 ♗c3 46 ♗g5! *(D)*

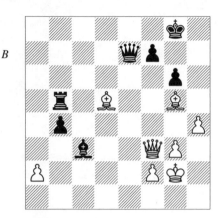

46...♕a7?

46...♕f8! is correct; obviously defending is a tremendous burden in such a situation.

47 ♕d3! ♖b6? 48 ♗e3! ♕a6 49 ♗xf7+! ♔xf7 50 ♕d7+ ♔f8 51 ♕d8+ ♔f7 52 ♕c7+ ♔g8 53 ♕xb6

At this point Topalov was objectively winning, but Anand kept finding clever ways to confuse things. After a late-night exchange of errors the players eventually drew. But this was a brilliant performance by Topalov and some indication of how much room for creativity exists in the QID. Let's try another game between the same two players in the same time period:

Topalov – Anand
Sofia 2005

1 d4 ♘f6 2 c4 e6 3 ♘f3 b6 4 g3 ♗a6 5 b3 ♗b4+ 6 ♗d2 ♗e7 7 ♘c3

Instead of 7 ♗g2, White plays directly for e4, a natural and logical plan. The main problem is that the knight can no longer defend c4 against attacks by ...d5 and ...b5.

7...c6 8 e4 d5

Here we are again with the basic idea. The combination of ...c6 and ...d5 (with perhaps ...b5 to come) militates against White's bishop straying from f1, from where it defends c4, even though it 'belongs' on g2.

9 ♕c2!? dxe4 10 ♘xe4 ♗b7 11 ♘eg5!?

A novelty at the time.

11...c5 12 d5! exd5 13 cxd5 h6 14 ♘xf7! *(D)*

This is truly incredible, as is what follows. Notice White's slow development and his serious weakness along the h1-a8 diagonal. It's inspiring that such ideas are possible!

14...♔xf7 15 0-0-0! ♗d6

Safest, under the circumstances.

16 ♘h4 ♗c8 17 ♖e1 ♘a6 18 ♖e6!

Is the opening over yet? A lot has changed when the Queen's Indian Defence starts looking like the Najdorf Sicilian. Ironically, Topalov's whole conception from start to finish depends upon the bishop on f1. This is the 'problem piece' that wasn't able to get developed!

18...♘b4

After 18...♔xe6? 19 dxe6+ ♔g8 20 ♗xa6, Black would still be under a ferocious attack.

19 ♗xb4 cxb4 20 ♗c4 b5! 21 ♗xb5 ♗e7? 22 ♘g6! ♘xd5 *(D)*

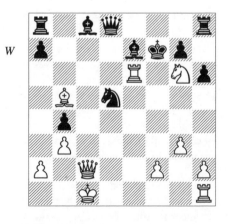

23 ♖xe7+?

This turns out to be a serious mistake. Topalov undoubtedly saw that 23 ♖e5! ♗b7 24 ♕f5+ ♔g8 25 ♗c4 was winning, but decided to keep it simple and safe. He must have missed Anand's 25th move.

23...♘xe7 24 ♗c4+ ♔f6 25 ♘xh8 ♕d4!

After the expected capture 25...♕xh8?, 26 ♖d1! wins.

26 ♖d1 ♕a1+ 27 ♔d2 ♕d4+ 28 ♔e1 ♕e5+ 29 ♕e2 ♕xe2+ 30 ♔xe2 ♘f5 31 ♘f7

After all that, Topalov eventually won this pawn-up endgame.

The theory of the variation with 4 g3 ♗a6 5 b3 ♗b4+ is ever-expanding. We may soon find out if Black can effectively neutralize White's play in this manner or will have to suffer under a long-term disadvantage. Whether the Queen's Indian supplies a satisfactory defence to 3 ♘f3 depends in part upon his solution to 4 g3.

Petrosian System (4 a3)

1 d4 ♘f6 2 c4 e6 3 ♘f3 b6 4 a3 *(D)*

B

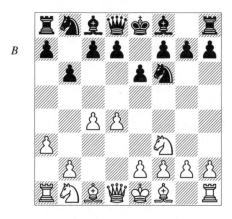

At first you may think that this move is a terrible waste of time. Obviously, White is trying to prevent ...♗b4, but is it worth a tempo? And what else does 4 a3 do? To begin with, preventing ...♗b4 is worth a lot more than it may seem. It's not just that the Nimzo-Indian (3 ♘c3 ♗b4) is such a bother to play against, but that Black has already committed himself to ...b6 (and thus ...♗b7 or ...♗a6). That is a set-up in which a knight on c3 is particularly useful. Specifically, a knight there not only supports e4 (as does a knight on d2 or queen on c2), but also the pawn

advance d5 (a move that *loses* its support after ♘d2 or ♕c2). This is important because once Black has fianchettoed his queen's bishop, a white pawn on d5 can become particularly irritating. In response to this potential threat, Black can of course play ...d5, but that accedes to a type of pawn-structure that Black may not prefer once committed to ...b6. To understand this, let's compare that formation with the Queen's Gambit Declined. The only major variation in which Black plays ...b6 is the Tartakower. Indeed, if play from the diagram proceeded 4...d5 5 ♘c3 ♗e7 6 ♗g5 0-0 7 e3 ♗b7 (7...h6 is a potential waste of tempo: 8 ♗xf6!), Black would have a standard position of the Tartakower Variation in which the move a3 can justifiably be regarded as useless, or nearly so. But once Black has weakened his queenside squares, White has other options; e.g., 6 cxd5! exd5 (6...♘xd5 7 e4) 7 ♗f4 0-0 8 e3 *(D)*.

B

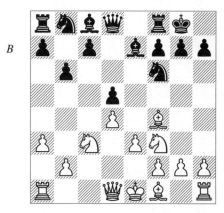

White has serious queenside pressure because of Black's weaknesses there (♖c1 and either ♕b3 or ♕a4 might prove useful). In fact, the move ♘b5 becomes an immediate theme (e.g., 8...♗f5 9 ♘b5 ♘a6 10 ♕a4), because White's profligate 4 a3 actually prevents ...♗b4+ in response!

4...♗b7

We'll follow this as the main line but it's quite possible that other moves are as good or better:

a) 4...♗a6 is very popular. Black has done well in this line, and he retains a degree of flexibility in his choice of piece placements. The main line goes 5 ♕c2 ♗b7! (this is a hypermodern idea: first Black diverts the queen and then wastes a move to cover e4; but what's the point?) 6 ♘c3 c5! (the queen no longer supports the move d5, so Black can break up the centre in this way) 7 e4! (taking over the largest share of the centre; 7 dxc5 would concede d4) 7...cxd4 8 ♘xd4 *(D)*.

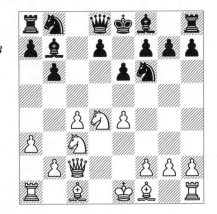

B

As in the Sicilian Defence, Black has a central majority and would love to achieve ...d5. For the moment, that move fails to cxd5 and ♗b5+, so White has some time to strengthen his centre. The queen on c2 can either be a drawback (it sits on the open c-file) or an advantage (it allows White's rooks to connect more quickly). Here Black has played 8...♘c6 and 8...d6 with reasonable success. A complicated alternative is 8...♗c5 9 ♘b3 ♘c6! (not only does Black develop quickly but he also targets the only weakness in White's position: the hole on d4) 10 ♗g5 h6 11 ♗h4 ♘d4! 12 ♘xd4 ♗xd4 13 ♗d3 (the white e-pawn needs protection) 13...♕b8!? (or 13...♗e5; the dark squares are key) 14 ♗g3 ♗e5 15 0-0-0 0-0 16 ♔b1 d6 17 ♗xe5 dxe5 *(D)*.

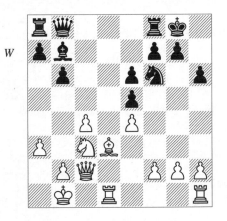

W

There's that doubled e-pawn structure that we talk about periodically through the book. Whether the pawns are ultimately useful or a problem is as yet unclear, but notice that both d5 and d4 are covered so that White can't put a piece on either square, and of course d4 will serve as an outpost for Black's pieces. On the other hand, White has no targets for Black to attack and he has a potentially important queenside pawn-majority. Khenkin-Adams, Bundesliga 2002/3 continued 18 ♕e2 ♖d8 19 ♕e3 (White could consider some kingside attack with, say, 19 g4 or 19 f3 and g4 next) 19...♖d4! 20 f3 ♗a6!? 21 b3 ♕c7 22 ♔b2 ♖ad8 23 ♘e2 ♖4d7 24 ♗c2! b5!? (Black's pieces are well-placed for this, but he invites active counterplay) 25 c5! b4! 26 axb4 ♖b8. This complicated position is dynamically equal.

b) 4...c5 *(D)*.

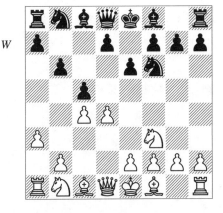

W

Now White's most ambitious move is 5 d5. Then:

b1) It's instructive to see why 5...exd5 6 cxd5 d6 (6...g6!?) 7 ♘c3 g6?! isn't supposed to be good: 8 e4 ♗g7 9 ♗b5+! ♗d7 10 ♗e2 (or 10 ♗d3) 10...0-0 11 0-0 *(D)*.

Note that we've arrived at a Benoni in which Black has two extra moves ...b6 and ...♗d7 for White's one. Nevertheless, this trade-off favours White, who can handily play moves such as ♗f4 with tempo. Conversely, Black's plans are disrupted because he would like to play either ...♘a6-c7 (not possible here) or ...♖e8 and ...♘bd7, in which case he needs to move the d7-bishop. That points to the move 11...♗g4, when 12 ♗f4 ♗xf3 13 ♗xf3 ♕e7?! prepares ...♘bd7, a familiar plan from the Modern Benoni of

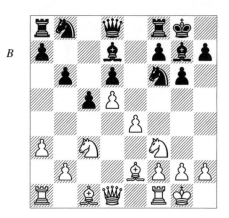

B

Chapter 9. Unfortunately, White can then play 14 e5! and, because of the insertion of ...b6, the 'normal' 14...dxe5 loses to 15 d6. The situation is more complicated than this (as always) but those are basic indications of why Black will probably want to avoid this version of a Benoni set-up.

b2) 5...♗a6! *(D)* and now:

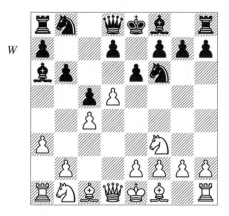

W

This leads to a better Benoni-type position. Play generally proceeds along the lines of 6 ♕c2 exd5 7 cxd5 g6 (7...♘xd5?? 8 ♕e4+) 8 ♘c3 ♗g7 9 g3 0-0 10 ♗g2 d6 11 0-0 ♖e8 12 ♖e1 ♘bd7 (12...b5!?) 13 ♗f4 ♕e7. We've arrived at a Fianchetto Benoni in which Black has achieved a theoretically ideal set-up, in that e5 is under control and his pieces are well-placed for action; e.g., ...♘g4-e5 is a good reorganization. However, there's still a question of the specific effects of Black's extra moves ...b6 and ...♗a6. White can try to exploit the queenside vulnerability immediately by 14 ♕a4 ♗b7 15 ♘b5, when we see how

positional factors in chess suddenly devolve into tactics. Pelletier-Gelfand, Biel 2001 continued 15...♘e5!? 16 ♘xe5 dxe5 17 d6! ♕d7 18 ♗xb7 ♕xb7 19 ♗g5 with some advantage. Instead, Black might have gone for decimation of the centre by 15...♘xd5!? with the idea 16 ♗xd6?! ♕d8 17 e4 ♗xb2! 18 exd5 ♗xa1 19 ♖xa1 ♕f6 and ...a6.

Let's return to the main move, 4...♗b7 *(D)*:

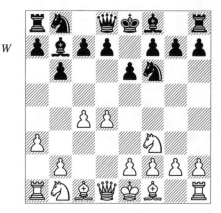

W

5 ♘c3 d5

Of Black's other moves, only 5...g6!? merits a look. The underlying idea is that if White presses forward with his plan of 6 d5, in order to block out Black's bishop on b7, Black has another strong bishop on g7 along the open a1-h8 diagonal. In turn, White has other answers to 5...g6; for example, developing quickly by means of 6 ♗g5 ♗g7 7 ♕c2 (intending moves such as ♖d1 and e4), or 6 ♕c2 (intending e4). In both cases, the critical reply is ...♗xf3. White's bishop-pair should more than make up for his pawn-structure. This is especially so since Black has made no fewer than three moves with his bishop to remove the f3-knight (...b6, ...♗b7 and ...♗xf3) and that leaves him behind in development. After 6 ♕c2 ♗xf3, White has recaptured the bishop in both ways, the safe course being 7 gxf3 (doubled f-pawns have advantages that we discuss from time to time in this book) 7...♘c6 (7...♗g7 8 ♗g5 gets White's bishop in front of his central pawns once e3 is played) 8 e3 ♗g7 9 f4 followed by ♗g2 and 0-0. White's f-pawn helps to restrain ...e5.

6 cxd5

White has several other moves here, but I'll only mention 6 ♗g5, when the most popular line is 6...♗e7 7 ♕a4+!? c6 (7...♕d7 challenges White to enter an apparently equal endgame; for example, 8 ♕xd7+ ♘bxd7!? 9 ♘b5 ♗d8 10 cxd5 ♘xd5 11 e4 ♘5f6; so 8 ♕c2!? is often played) 8 ♗xf6 ♗xf6 9 cxd5 exd5 10 e3 0-0 11 ♗e2 *(D)*.

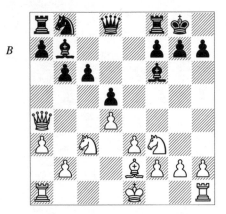

Recognize this? In both structure and piece placement we have a QGD Tartakower Defence! Play might develop along the same lines; for example, 11...♖e8 12 0-0 ♘d7 13 ♖fd1 ♘f8 14 ♖ac1 ♘e6 15 ♕c2 or something similar, with equality. At least 4 a3 comes in handy here in order to prepare b4. More challenging is 10 g3 0-0 11 ♗g2, putting pressure on d5; compare the next note.

6...♘xd5

An instructive decision. 6...♘xd5 is easily Black's most popular choice, leaving the bishop's path unobstructed on the long diagonal. But 6...exd5 has also been played a fair amount. In that case we again have a typical Queen's Gambit. White has the mediocre move a3 in, but Black has played ...b6 and ...♗b7 rather early on. Instead of transposing to a kind of Tartakower, which is perfectly playable, White will sometimes put his bishop on g2, as in the last note. Then out of many possibilities a classic trade-off may occur: 7 g3 ♗e7 8 ♕a4+ c6 (8...♕d7 9 ♕xd7+ can be followed by moves like ♘b5, ♗f4 and ♗h3) 9 ♗g2 0-0 10 0-0 ♘bd7 11 ♗f4 ♘h5 12 ♖ad1! ♘xf4 13 gxf4 *(D)*.

What are the characteristics of this position? Black has the bishop-pair and White's f-pawns are doubled. Nevertheless, White light-squared bishop is better than its counterpart on b7, he

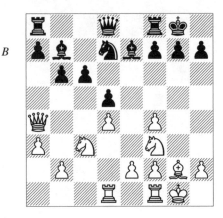

has the g-file, and a well-timed knight jump to e5 can be useful. Black can try to gain space on the queenside (...b5 and ...a5 or ...♘b6, for example) or use piece-play on the kingside (...♖e8, ...♘f8-g6). In the meantime, White might shift his pieces to the kingside (♔h1, ♖g1, ♕c2, e3, ♘e2-g3), especially since any attempt to play b4 can be weakening.

But 6...♘xd5 *(D)* is the most important continuation:

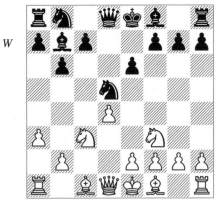

Apart from the main lines with 4 g3, this is probably the most heavily analysed position from the Queen's Indian Defence. By 'surrendering the centre' but keeping the long diagonal open for his bishop, Black announces his policy of allowing White to form a strong centre and then sniping at it from the wings. The resulting positions resemble the Grünfeld Defence in spirit. Black's bishop will usually be on e7 instead of g7, but Black's quest for the queenside light squares gives the two openings a similar flavour.

At this juncture White normally plays:

A: 7 e3 or

B: 7 ♕c2.

We'll look at games that express typical ideas behind both moves, by no means attempting to recreate the current theoretical standing of the variation. A complex alternative is 7 ♗d2, which intends a recapture with the bishop after ...♘xc3; this idea normally appears after 7 ♕c2. There are also a number of variations with 7 ♕a4+ and/or ♗g5 that haven't produced spectacular results, probably because the move a3 isn't so useful in that case.

A)

7 e3 *(D)*

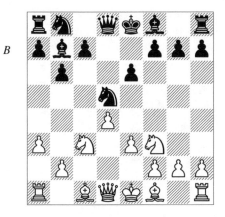

This is a somewhat older line that can transpose to the more modern 7 ♕c2 with small but significant differences. What is 'old' and 'modern' may be changing, however, and 7 e3 is getting some renewed attention. The variations are also deserving of study because certain ideas correspond with those in other openings such as the Grünfeld and Queen's Gambit.

Kasparov – Korchnoi
London Ct (1) 1983

7...g6 *(D)*

Ever since this high-profile game, 7...g6 has been considered the toughest move for White to meet.

8 ♗b5+

For 8 ♘xd5, see the next game.

8...c6 9 ♗d3 ♗g7 10 e4 ♘xc3 11 bxc3 c5 12 ♗g5 ♕d6! 13 e5 ♕d7 14 dxc5?

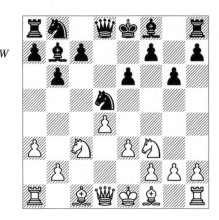

Van der Wiel suggested 14 0-0 0-0 15 ♕d2! cxd4 16 cxd4 ♘c6 17 ♕f4.

14...0-0! 15 cxb6 axb6 *(D)*

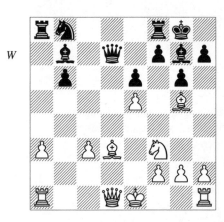

Black borrows a pawn sacrifice from the Grünfeld Defence. His basic idea is that White has weak pawns on the open a- and c-files, while even the e-pawn requires defence in the face of ...♕c7 and ...♘d7. In the meantime, that knight on b8 could easily end up on c5 or c4 to great effect. As in the Grünfeld, Black has more than enough for a pawn and great winning chances.

16 0-0 ♕c7

Black keeps the advantage with this move, but 16...♖a5!? may actually be better because Kasparov manages to get some counterplay here.

17 ♗b5! ♗xe5

Again, 17...♖a5 is an idea; on the other hand, 17...♘c6 18 ♗f6! isn't so easy.

18 ♗h6 ♗g7 19 ♗xg7 ♔xg7 20 ♕d4+ ♔g8 21 ♘g5 h6 22 ♘e4 ♗xe4 23 ♕xe4 ♘a6 24

♕e3? ♕c5! 25 ♕xc5 ♘xc5 26 ♖fb1 ♖fd8 27 ♗f1 ♖d6

White's weaknesses are quite serious and Kasparov went on to lose.

Portisch – Palo
Kallithea ECC 2002

8 ♘xd5 *(D)*

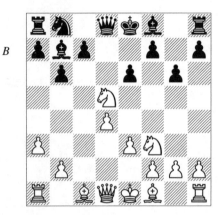

This exchange has been used quite a bit recently. It leads to strategic/positional play that may not appeal to the attacking players who have used 4 a3 to emulate Kasparov's aggressive style.

8...exd5 *(D)*

8...♕xd5 doesn't look very good after simply 9 ♗d3 intending to castle quickly and play e4. A tactical melee came about after 9 ♗d2 ♗g7?! 10 ♖c1 0-0!? 11 ♖xc7!? (very risky) 11...♗c6 12 ♗b4 ♖e8 13 ♘e5 a5 (13...♗xe5 14 dxe5 ♕xe5 15 ♕d6!?) 14 ♗e7 ♘a6?? (14...♗xe5! 15 dxe5 ♕xe5 16 ♕d6 ♕xb2) 15 ♖xc6 ♗xe5 16 ♖xb6 ♗c7 17 ♖b5 and White was two clear pawns up in Rowson-Brunello, Verona 2006.

8...exd5 produces an interesting position. White can choose between a variety of ideas. If Black's bishop goes to g7, then White will play for a classic minority attack following b4. Notice that the pawn-structure is the same formation that we've seen in so many openings, famously the Exchange Variation of the Queen's Gambit Declined. The exchange of a pair of pieces may favour White under those circumstances. In fact, Black's best idea may consist of foregoing ...♗g7 to point his dark-squared bishop towards the kingside, perhaps from d6.

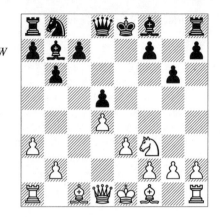

From there it also covers Black's queenside dark squares.

9 ♗d2!?

Apart from clearing the c-file, this move has an intriguing idea. A derivative game went 9 ♗e2 ♗d6 10 ♗d2!? ♘d7 11 ♗b4! *(D)*.

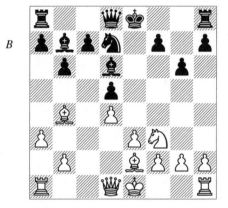

White tries to exploit the absence of Black's bishop from the long diagonal. 11...c5 (by no means forced) 12 dxc5 bxc5 13 ♗c3 0-0 14 b4! (breaking up Black's pawn-structure) 14...♖c8 15 0-0 cxb4 (15...♕e7 16 bxc5 ♘xc5 17 ♕d4 f6 18 ♖ab1) 16 ♗xb4 ♘c5 17 ♖b1 ♗a6!? 18 ♗xa6 ♘xa6 19 ♕d4?! (19 ♗xd6! ♕xd6 20 ♕d4 with a pleasant advantage) 19...♘xb4 20 axb4 ♕e7 21 b5!? ♖c5 ½-½ Elianov-Bologan, Sarajevo 2005.

9...♘d7 10 ♗b4! ♗g7

10...c5 11 dxc5 bxc5 12 ♗c3 is awkward for Black. In that case, White not only forces weaknesses but will play b4 early on.

11 a4!? c5 12 ♗a3 0-0 13 ♗b5 ♖e8 14 a5 a6 15 ♗xd7 ♕xd7 16 0-0 cxd4 17 ♘xd4 bxa5 18

♗c5 ♗c6 19 ♖xa5 ♗b5 20 ♖e1 ♖ac8 21 b4 ♗c4

Black has equalized. It's hard to believe that he can stand too badly in these lines, but the ♗d2-b4 idea is intriguing.

Let's return to Black's 7th move and see his alternative to a fianchetto. The ...♗e7 lines are especially important as similar positions may also arise from other move-orders.

7...♗e7 8 ♗b5+ c6 9 ♗d3 *(D)*

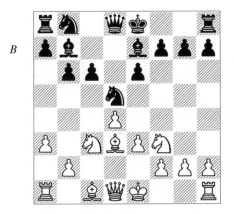

We have reached a position that has occurred frequently over the years. The basics are easy to understand: White wants to protect his centre and then shift towards the kingside or, sometimes, simply push the d-pawn down the board. Black tries to counterattack on the queenside, usually via the c-file. Eliminating the light-squared bishops goes a long way towards protecting his king. We'll look at two games from this position.

Epishin – Beliavsky
USSR Ch (Leningrad) 1990

9...0-0 10 ♕c2 h6 11 e4 ♘xc3 12 bxc3 c5 13 0-0 *(D)*

13...♕c8!?

This odd-looking move has the most immediate goals, threatening ...cxd4 and preparing to rid the board of White's dangerous bishop on d3. That would leave him with one less attacking piece and weak light squares on the queenside.

After 13...♘c6, a seemingly more logical move, 14 ♗b2 ♖c8 15 ♕e2 cxd4 16 cxd4 gives

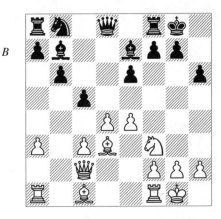

White the better of it with his central advantage.

14 ♕e2

Perhaps 14 ♕a2!? could be tried in order to get a passed pawn after 14...♗a6!? 15 ♗xa6 ♕xa6 16 d5. These are more or less typical ideas of the line 4 a3 ♗b7 5 ♘c3 d5 6 cxd5 ♘xd5. Interestingly, this conflict between White's good centre and Black's restraint of it in combination with counterplay on the queenside light squares is extremely similar to both the Semi-Tarrasch (see page 46) and the Grünfeld Defence (see page 46).

14...♗a6 15 ♖d1 ♗xd3 16 ♖xd3 ♘d7! 17 ♗f4 ♖d8 18 ♖e3

Or 18 ♖ad1 cxd4 19 cxd4 ♕c4 with equality.

18...cxd4 19 cxd4 ♕c6 20 ♖d1 ♖ac8 *(D)*

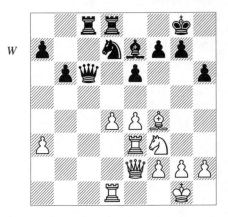

21 d5 exd5

Maybe 21...♕a4!? is a better try.

22 exd5 ♕c4 23 ♖xe7 ♕xf4 24 d6 ♖c1 25 g3 ♖xd1+ 26 ♕xd1 ♕f6 27 ♕d5 ♘f8 28 ♖xa7 ♖xd6 29 ♕e5 ♖d1+ 30 ♔g2 ♕d8 31 ♕f5 ♕d5 32 ♕xd5 ♖xd5 33 ♖a8! g5 34 ♖b8 b5 35 a4

bxa4 36 ♖a8 g4 37 ♘h4 h5 38 ♖xa4 ♘e6 39 h3 ♘d4 ½-½

Kožul – Naiditsch
Kusadasi Ech 2006

9...♘xc3 10 bxc3 c5 11 0-0 ♘c6
Black chooses a more active square for his knight.

12 ♗b2 ♖c8 13 ♕e2 0-0 14 ♖ad1 cxd4 15 exd4!? ♗f6 16 c4! ♘a5 17 ♘e5 ♗xe5 18 ♕xe5 ♕c7 19 ♕h5! g6 20 ♕h6 ♘xc4 *(D)*

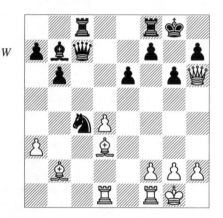

As so often, Black puts most of his pieces on light squares. As a consequence, White's daring attack on the dark squares is unobstructed.

21 ♗xc4 ♕xc4 22 d5 f6 23 ♖d4 ♕b3 24 dxe6 ♕xe6
Not 24...♕xb2?? 25 ♖d7.
25 ♖fd1 ♖fe8 26 h3 ♕c6 27 f3
Because of the opposite-coloured bishops the defence is difficult. But Naiditsch, probably in time-trouble, blunders.
27...♖e2?? 28 ♖d8+ ♖xd8 29 ♖xd8+ ♖e8 30 ♗xf6 ♔f7 31 ♕g7+ ♔e6 32 ♖d1 1-0

B)
7 ♕c2 *(D)*

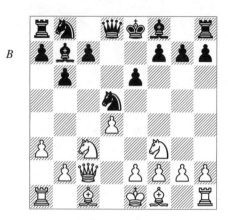

A popular move, trying to get e4 in without further ado. The queen will also exert pressure down the c-file in cases where Black doesn't exchange on c3.
7...♘xc3
An illustrative excerpt is 7...♗e7!? 8 ♗d2!? (8 e4 ♘xc3 9 bxc3 transposes to the main line) 8...0-0 9 e4 ♘xc3 10 ♗xc3 (this time White's bishop assumes an active role and Black must

be ready for the move d5, creating a passed pawn) 10...♘d7 11 ♖d1 ♕c8! (aiming for ...c5 and in some cases ....♗a6, to eliminate White's best bishop) 12 ♗d3 ♖d8 13 0-0 c5 *(D)*.

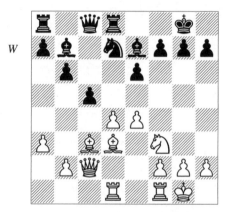

14 d5! (a Grünfeld-like passed pawn) 14...c4! 15 ♗e2 exd5 16 exd5 ♗f6 and the play was almost equal in the game Miles-Polugaevsky, Biel 1990, since the d-pawn won't get any further even if White advances it to d6.

8 bxc3
Naturally 8 ♕xc3 is sometimes played, when apart from 8...h6, Black has the sequence 8...♘d7, and if 9 ♗g5, 9...♗e7! 10 ♗xe7 ♔xe7. In spite of the black king's odd placement, White isn't able to make any progress, and moves like ...♖c8 and ...c5 will follow, or in some circumstances ...♘f6, ...♕d6 and ...c5. Such a line reflects a master's pragmatism: instead of worrying about the principle of king safety in the abstract, he makes a real-world assessment of White's actual attacking chances.
8...♗e7 9 e4 0-0 10 ♗d3 c5 *(D)*

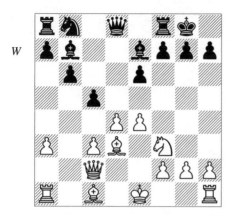

11 0-0

You may recognize that this is the main line after 7 e3, with the sole exception of the pawn on h6. This illustrates the consistency of ideas that follows logically from a given pawn-structure.

11...♛c8!

11...cxd4 12 cxd4 ♘c6 isn't necessarily bad, but doesn't actually infiltrate on the queenside and thus risks White building up his attack relatively unperturbed. Here's a nice example: 13 ♗b2 ♖c8 14 ♕e2 (D).

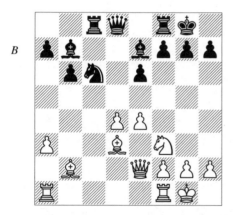

14...♘a5?! (since Black isn't getting through on the queenside yet, maybe it's better to keep the pieces centralized; 14...♕d6 looks like a good alternative) 15 ♖ad1 ♖e8 16 ♘e5! ♗f8 17 f4 f6 18 ♘g4 ♖e7?! 19 f5! ♕e8 20 e5! exf5 21 ♗xf5 fxe5 (21...♖d8 22 ♕c2 and White's attack is already winning) 22 ♗xc8 ♕xc8 23 ♖c1 (from here on out it's really just a matter of time) 23...♕e8 24 ♗c3 ♖e6 25 ♘xe5 ♗xa3 26 ♖a1 ♗d6 27 ♕a2 ♗xe5 28 dxe5 h6 29 ♗xa5 bxa5 30 ♖ab1 ♗c8 31 ♖b8 ♕c6 32 ♕a3 ♖e8 33

♖c1 ♕d7 34 ♕d6 1-0 Gelfand-Naiditsch, Pamplona 2004.

12 ♕e2 ♗a6 13 ♖d1 ♖d8 (D)

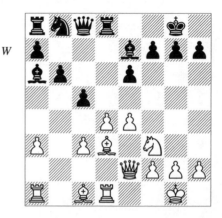

We'll look at two games from this position.

I. Sokolov – J. Polgar
Hoogeveen 2003

14 h4!

Grabbing space on the kingside and preparing an advance that ultimately pays dividends.

14...cxd4 15 cxd4 ♗xd3 16 ♖xd3 ♘d7 17 ♗g5 f6 18 ♗f4 (D)

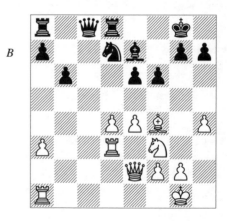

18...♕b7?!

A waste of precious time. 18...♕a6! is much better.

19 h5 ♖ac8 20 ♖ad1 ♕a6 21 e5 f5 22 d5! exd5

Emms gives 22...♘c5 23 d6! ♘xd3 24 ♕xd3 ♕xd3 25 ♖xd3 with advantage.

23 ♘d4

Here White had the nice option 23 ♕a2! ♕c4 24 ♕xc4 ♖xc4 25 ♖xd5 ♖xf4 26 ♖xd7.

23...♖f8 24 ♕f3 ♘c5 25 h6! *(D)*

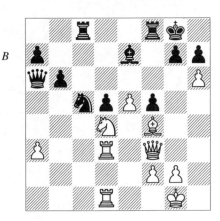

25...g5!?

25...♘xd3 26 hxg7 ♔xg7 27 ♖xd3 is dangerous for Black but not completely clear. The rest of the game flows smoothly.

26 ♗xg5! ♗xg5 27 ♕h5 ♗f4 28 ♖f3 ♗xe5 29 ♘xf5 ♕b7 30 ♖xd5 ♖ce8 31 ♕g5+ ♔h8 32 ♖xe5! ♖xe5 33 ♘e7! ♖e1+ 34 ♔h2 ♕b8+ 35 ♖g3 ♖xe7 36 ♕xe7 ♘e6 37 ♕xe6 ♕f4 38 a4 a6?!

Black's problem is that she's tied to defensive squares; e.g., 38...♕xf2? 39 ♖g8+! ♖xg8 40 ♕e5+; best but hopeless in the long run is 38...♖f7.

39 ♕xb6 ♖b8 40 ♕e3 ♕h4+ 41 ♖h3 ♕f6 42 ♕c3 1-0

Krasenkow – Navara
Antalya Ech 2004

14 e5!? ♗xd3 15 ♖xd3 cxd4 16 cxd4 ♘c6

Black stands somewhat worse after 16...♕c4 17 ♗g5 ♘c6 (17...♗xg5 18 ♘xg5 ♘c6 {18...h6? 19 ♘xf7!} 19 ♕e4) 18 ♖c1 ♕d5 19 ♖xc6 ♗xg5 20 ♖c7.

17 ♕e4 ♖d5!?

Navara suggests 17...♕d7! 18 ♘g5 ♗xg5 19 ♗xg5 ♕d5 20 ♕h4 ♘xe5 21 ♖h3 h6 22 ♗xd8 ♖xd8 23 ♖d1 ♘c6 with compensation. A good illustration of how, because of White's compromised centre, Black gets to have some fun instead of always defending.

18 ♗e3 ♕e8!?

Clearing d8. Black has emerged from the opening with an inferior but defensible position.

19 ♖c3 ♖ad8 20 ♖ac1 ♘a5 *(D)*

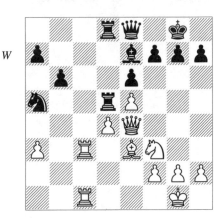

This is the real beginning of Black's light-square strategy (beyond his concentration upon d5, that is). He wants to play ...b5 and ...♘c4, and of course a4 is open to the queen. These are all Grünfeld and Semi-Tarrasch themes.

21 h4!

White too abandons all pretence of profound strategy and launches the kingside attack that typifies such variations.

21...b5!? 22 ♘g5 g6

Not 22...♗xg5 23 ♗xg5 ♖xd4? 24 ♕xd4! ♖xd4 25 ♖c8. This theme persists for many moves.

23 h5 h6!

Krasenkow gives the pretty line 23...♘c4? 24 hxg6 hxg6 25 ♕h4 ♗xg5 26 ♗xg5 ♖xd4 27 ♕h8+!! ♔xh8 28 ♖h3+ ♔g8 29 ♗f6 and mate follows.

24 ♘h3 g5

Another aesthetic attacking sequence is Krasenkow's 24...♘c4 25 hxg6 fxg6 26 ♘f4 ♗xa3 27 ♖xa3! ♘xa3 28 ♖c6!! ♕xc6 29 ♕xg6+ ♔f8 30 ♕f6+ ♔e8 (30...♔g8 31 ♘g6) 31 ♘g6 ♔d7 32 ♕f7+ ♔c8 33 ♘e7+.

25 f4 ♘c4

Everything on light squares.

26 ♗f2?

26 fxg5 ♘xe3 27 ♕xe3 ♖xd4 28 gxh6 favours White because of Black's king position.

26...f5! 27 exf6 ♗xf6 28 fxg5 hxg5

The game is approximately equal. It was eventually drawn.

7 King's Indian Defence

Before we even begin, I should explain that the King's Indian Defence (a.k.a. 'KID') is actually a set of moves that has no specific starting point. That is to say, Black plays 1...♘f6, 2...g6, 3...♗g7, ...d6 and almost always ...0-0 (normally in that order), versus almost any first move by White other than 1 e4. But we shall concern ourselves with the King's Indian Defence in its original meaning, that is, versus d4.

The best way to introduce ourselves to the KID is to take a stroll through the first few moves.

1 d4

1 c4 ♘f6 can transpose into a 1 d4 version of the King's Indian Defence should White play d4 on any of the next several moves. The same applies to 1 ♘f3; for example, 1...♘f6 2 d4 g6, etc.

1...♘f6 *(D)*

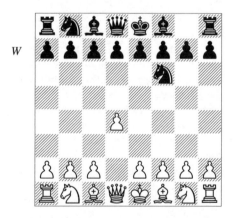

2 c4

2 ♘f3 g6 is another route that often transposes to c4 lines. Of course that order might lead to independent systems; for example, 3 ♗g5, 3 ♗f4, and a number of lesser options that are not covered in this book. A very brief word on the first two, since I'll have a bishop-development theme over the next few moves.

a) 3 ♗g5 is an offshoot of the Torre Attack. Black can play any number of systems and any

number of move-orders, but in deference to my lectures about ...c5 in these contexts, I'll point out that after 3...♗g7 4 ♘bd2 (versus ...♘e4) 4...c5 is a legitimate choice, with one important line proceeding 5 ♗xf6 ♗xf6 6 ♘e4 ♗xd4 (or 6...♕b6 7 ♘xf6+ ♕xf6) 7 ♘xd4 cxd4 8 ♕xd4 0-0 9 0-0-0 ♘c6 (9...♕a5 10 ♘c3 ♘c6 is also possible) 10 ♕d2, and now 10...d5! 11 ♕xd5 ♕c7 is an effective sacrifice, intending ...♗e6 and play along the c- and d-files.

b) 3 ♗f4 is the London System, a good choice to avoid theory but perhaps not a good one to learn from. Again ...c5 is to be considered at most points; e.g., 3...c5 is theoretically equal and 3...♗g7 4 e3 d6 5 h3 (to have a place to hide after ...♘h5) 5...0-0 6 ♗e2 c5 can be played, among others. In both cases Black has an eye on the move ...♕b6. This is relevant to points that I make below.

2...g6 3 ♘c3

This time 3 ♘f3 ♗g7 4 g3 can be of independent significance and will generally transpose to the Fianchetto System, which I shall not be covering in this book.

3...♗g7 *(D)*

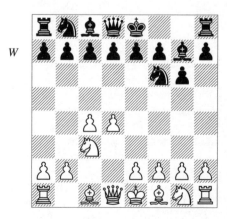

This position may be considered the beginning point for the King's Indian Defence, a storied opening associated with dynamic slugfests of the highest order. It was championed by

Fischer and Kasparov, who helped to keep the King's Indian popular in spite of its reputation as a risky proposition for the defender. Kasparov in particular revolutionized the strategic and even philosophical elements of the opening. The theory of the King's Indian has undergone constant changes for 60 years including wild shifts of strategy and assessment. Flexible play and the possibility of both players working on either or both wings makes this an opening for those with an inclination towards complex strategic thinking. At the same time, attacking players can get addicted to it! Today the King's Indian is enjoying a comeback among leading masters after a temporary decline in usage; at the club and open tournament level it has never stopped being popular.

To speak briefly about some general characteristics of the King's Indian, let me take the main-line position following 1 d4 ♘f6 2 c4 g6 3 ♘c3 ♗g7 4 e4 d6 5 ♘f3 0-0 (D).

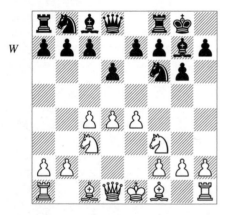

It's no wonder that players of the 19th century and first half of the 20th century took relatively little interest in this opening. After all, Black has failed to move a pawn to the fourth rank within the first five moves! No respectable opening at the time had such consistent disregard for classical principles, particularly when Black doesn't even have a grip on any of the four central squares. It wasn't until the late 1940s and 1950s that creative minds from the Soviet Union, including Bronstein, Boleslavsky, Geller, and a host of other strong players and analysts, began to find merit in Black's setup. The virtues of White's position are fairly obvious and have served him well up to the

present day: space, central control, a broad and mobile centre, and convenient squares for his pieces. But what sustains Black's game? His development has been faster than White's, which is a start. More significant than any other factor, however, is the relative weakness of White's d4, a consideration neglected in much of the literature. The d4-square will never be protected by a pawn and is always a potential point of attack or outpost for Black's pieces. In some variations we see ...c5 and ...♘c6 targeting that point, but most of the variations in the position above involve the move ...e5. Even then, only a minority of systems combine ...e5 with the direct assault by ...♘c6 and ...♗g4 in combination with the bishop on g7. Instead, the move ...e5 sets up a simple dynamic. Three things can happen:

a) White can capture on e5 by dxe5, but this reduces the vitality of White's centre and exposes d4 to occupation in conjunction with the d-file. See the Exchange Variation below and similar positions in the main lines.

b) Black can capture on d4 by ...exd4 with unpredictable effects. But what attracts King's Indian adherents about that trade is the extension of the range of the powerful bishop on g7 and the opening of the e-file for a rook. Moreover, Black often gains the handy squares c5 and e5 for his knights. In return, White has an ideal restriction of Black's 'surrendered' centre (the pawn on d6 can't advance), which means that Black has to operate within a limited region. Furthermore, White's pieces can take up active squares in a harmonious manner; for example, a knight on d4 and bishop on e3.

c) White can advance his pawn to d5. This generally eliminates any designs that Black has on the d4-square and extends White's space advantage. But now we can begin to see why the King's Indian is viable. With d5 relieving pressure on Black's centre and rendering any direct attacks unlikely, both sides can expand along the pawn-chains on opposite wings. For White, the move c5 leads to the opening of lines and pressure on Black's pawns on c7 and d6. For Black the move ...f5, and in the main lines ...f4 and ...g5-g4, leads to the opening of lines and pressure on White's kingside. That is at least a reasonable bargain for Black, whose bishop on g7 is a threat to become free should White try to stop his ...f5-f4 advance by exf5 or by f4.

That's quite a superficial account of play in the King's Indian, and such positions don't even arise in many variations. But the 'threat' of their occurrence underlies a lot of what both sides actually do in terms of strategy. The other positional factors that interact with this opening are too numerous to mention, so I'll leave that to analysis and examples in specific variations.

My emphasis will be on the major systems that begin 1 d4 ♘f6 2 c4 g6 3 ♘c3 ♗g7 4 e4 d6. They constitute the large bulk of master practice, and along with g3 systems they account for well over 90% of grandmaster games. Because the main lines are so instructive, I'll only briefly examine some instructive alternatives in what follows.

Selected Alternatives to 4 e4

1 d4 ♘f6 2 c4 g6 3 ♘c3 ♗g7 (D)

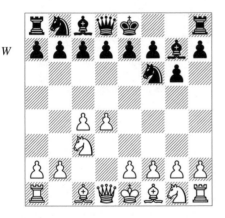

There are of course many alternatives to 4 e4, but none of them except the g3 variations are very popular. Therefore I'll point out only a few options with ideas that you might want to be aware of. I'll try to tie this section together a bit by emphasizing the move ♗g5 in many contexts.

4 ♘f3

This flexible development of the king's knight introduces most serious deviation from main lines. Almost any set-up following from 4 e3 can be met by ...d6, ...0-0 and ...e5 (supported by a piece if necessary). 4 ♗f4 is a legitimate move and will usually transpose into some other variation after 4...d6. Both sides should be aware that Black's attempts to exchange

such a bishop by means of ...♘h5 (for example) are an important consideration. Compare lines below.

Our main theme is the development of the queen's bishop to g5 at various stages. Here 4 ♗g5 can be met by 4...c5 (4...h6 5 ♗h4 d6 is normal and fine, of course; ...c5 may follow soon anyway), and if 5 d5, 5...h6 6 ♗h4 ♕a5 7 ♕d2 g5 8 ♗g3 ♘h5 (D) followed ...♘xg3 with equality.

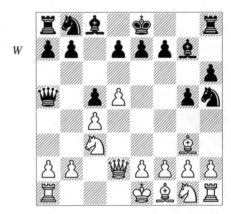

What should be noted is that, unsupported by a knight on f3, the move 9 ♗e5 cannot be played. That is the move that White should look for if Black has not yet played ...d6 (see the next note).

In this kind of position, which is ubiquitous in the King's Indian and Benoni, hundreds of top-level games have confirmed that Black's two bishops at least compensate for his slightly weakened pawn-structure. Regarding the latter, we can apply the old saying: weaknesses aren't weak unless you can exploit them.

4...d6

Once White is committed to 4 ♘f3, castling by Black seems to have lost the disadvantages that it has in the order 4 e4 0-0. That doesn't mean that it's a better move than 4...d6, but it allows Black a few new options; for example, 4...0-0 5 ♗g5 c5 (the move ...c5 is thematic if the c1-bishop strays to the kingside; see below) 6 d5!? h6 7 ♗h4 d6 (watch out for 7...g5 8 ♗g3 ♘h5 9 ♗e5!, and if 9...f6?, 10 ♗xb8! ♖xb8 11 d6!, when things are getting awkward for Black) 8 e4!? (not the only move) 8...g5 9 ♗g3 ♘h5 with equality.

5 ♗g5

This is known as the Smyslov System, which is very solid and a good choice for White if he doesn't fancy too complicated a position. He opts for quick development and well-placed pieces without trying to capture too much of the centre. For his part, Black doesn't feel very threatened and can play to gain some space on either wing. He also hopes to chase down White's dark-squared bishop as above.

As for 5 ♗f4, Farago-Bilek, Budapest 1965 saw a creative solution to 5...0-0 6 h3, a rather irritating move which is frequently played to preserve the f4-bishop and avoid having it chased down as in the examples that we keep seeing. The game went 6...c5 (6...♘h5 7 ♗h2 is the point) 7 e3 ♛a5! 8 ♛d2 cxd4 9 exd4 e5! *(D)*.

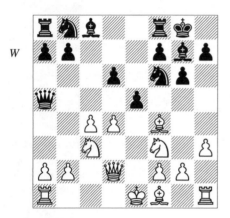

W

10 ♗e3 (not 10 dxe5? dxe5 11 ♗xe5, when 11...♖e8 wins material, and 11...♘c6 is also very strong) 10...♘c6 11 d5 ♘e7 12 ♗d3 ♘e8 (12...♘f5 13 ♗g5 h6) 13 0-0 f5 with equality. This even *looks* like a King's Indian!

We now return to 5 ♗g5 *(D)*:

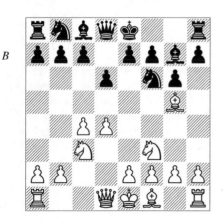

B

5...h6

Black prepares yet another combination of chasing the knight and ...c5. After 5...0-0 6 e3, the obvious 6...♘bd7, to prepare ...e5, can be met by the sophisticated and well-tested move 7 ♛c2!; e.g., 7...e5?! (7...c6 8 ♗e2 e5 9 0-0 ♛e7 10 b4! is White's idea) 8 ♖d1!, threatening dxe5, when 8...h6 9 ♗h4 ♖e8 10 ♗e2 leaves Black cramped. Instead of this, 6...c5 7 ♗e2 ♗f5 intending ...♘e4 is often recommended, as Smyslov himself played when Black versus Pachman. That is hardly the most incisive line, however, and shouldn't put anyone off playing 5 ♗g5.

6 ♗h4 g5 7 ♗g3 ♘h5

Once again both sides have to decide where to put their pieces. The following is a logical way to continue:

8 e3 c5 9 d5 *(D)*

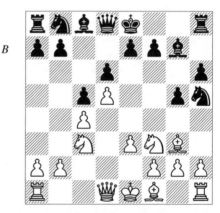

B

Not the only move, but an instructive one.

9...♛a5 10 ♛d2 ♘d7 11 ♗e2 ♘xg3 12 hxg3 ♘f6

With equality.

The nice thing about this position for Black is that he still has the option to castle queenside if he wants to. Of course, this is hardly all that there is to the Smyslov System.

The Orthodox 4 e4

1 d4 ♘f6 2 c4 g6 3 ♘c3 ♗g7 4 e4

As mentioned above, this move accounts for the bulk of games in the King's Indian Defence. White's intentions are not subtle: he wants to play with a central space advantage so as to limit Black's development and make more room for his own pieces. The conflict between this wish and the vulnerability of his centre to Black's attacks underlies the players' strategies for most of the opening phase and sometimes well beyond.

4...d6 *(D)*

This is almost universally played after 4 e4. Black's intent is to restrain e5 and stake out some claim to the centre. I shall only remark upon 4...0-0 in the introductory note to the Four Pawns Attack below, in the context of that variation.

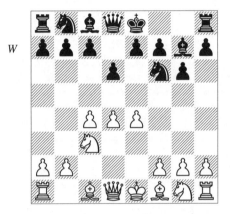

Although I won't entirely neglect other variations, I shall devote most of this chapter to the Four Pawns Attack (5 f4), and the Classical Variation (5 ♘f3), with an emphasis on the latter. The King's Indian is so vast that one could devote this book to its many fascinating variations, but in line with the philosophy that understanding can only be gained by attending to details, I have decided to specialize in those two variations. The examination of the Four Pawns continues my policy of taking the most obvious attempt at refutation of an opening in order to gain some insight into its character. To do this we might ask which moves would probably be proposed by the average player if he were seeing an opening for the first time, especially if he'd heard that the opening wasn't supposed to be any good. That is, which variation would he instinctively use to demonstrate that the opening was disadvantageous? For the King's Indian Defence, the Four Pawns Variation seems the obvious choice in that respect, because it attempts to punish Black immediately for not occupying the centre.

The Classical Variation of the King's Indian Defence is one of the most subtle and complex variations in chess, but at the same time it has some broadly applicable ideas that are quite straightforward, especially about pawn-structures and their treatment. Thus the inexperienced player can gain insights that will help him begin to play the KID, and there will be material that should help players of any level to refine their understanding.

In addition to these two systems, I have included sections on the Averbakh Variation (5 ♗e2 0-0 6 ♗g5) and the Sämisch Variation (5 f3). They feature a few unique pawn-structures and in particular emphasize the formations with the move ...c5 that don't appear in the Classical Variation.

First, to complete the discussion that we've had about ♗g5 lines, I'll focus on the move 5 ♗g5 and tie it in with the earlier examples we looked at, both practically and philosophically. After 5 ♗g5, Black can castle, but one might argue that 5...0-0 isn't optimal because it justifies White's play after 6 ♕d2, preventing ...h6 and preparing attack in many lines. Of course that's hardly disastrous, but 5...h6 is the more ambitious choice: 6 ♗h4 (if instead 6 ♗e3, 6...♘g4 is a good response, and 6 ♗f4 can be met efficiently by 6...♘c6 7 d5 e5!); and now 6...c5! *(D)*.

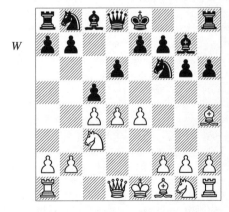

We've now seen this move several times; in the King's Indian and most 1 d4 openings, an early move of White's queen's bishop to f4 or g5 indicates that Black should strongly consider ...c5 as his reply (immediately or within the next few moves), rather than ...e5, which is the normal KID move. You'll find the ...c5 strategy all the more effective if Black can nudge White's bishop to h4 (via ...h6) or g3 (via ...h6 and ...g5). Why? Because moving that bishop removes a defender from White's queenside, so the moves ...♕b6 and ...♕a5 become more attractive. Of course, the reverse is also true: from White's side of the board, we can say that if Black's bishop goes to f5 or g4, he should strongly consider playing c4. This comes up many times in the Queen's Gambit and Slav chapters.

A primitive example is the Trompowsky Attack 1 d4 ♘f6 2 ♗g5, when of course Black can play 2...e6, 2...d5, or even head for a King's Indian Defence by 2...g6 (allowing 3 ♗xf6 exf6, which may or may not be to his taste). But there are two major lines involving a ...c5 counter-attack: the immediate 2...c5 (when ...♕b6 will generally follow if possible), and 2...♘e4, when play can go 3 ♗h4 c5! or 3 ♗f4 c5! followed by ...♕b6 or ...♕a5+, depending upon the circumstances. Another case in point is the Grünfeld Defence, in which the ♗f4 variations for White tend to be answered by ...c5.

The associated warning is simply that, before developing your queen's bishop early on in a 1 d4 opening, take care to anticipate and prepare for any queenside attack by your opponent. Naturally there are plenty of instances in which it is completely safe and even best to do so (e.g., variations involving ...♕b6 tend to be inferior versus 4 ♗g5 in the Queen's Gambit Declined), so don't be intimidated, just proceed with caution.

At any rate, let's take a look at the line 5 ♗g5 h6 6 ♗h4 c5 (as seen in our last diagram) 7 d5 (7 dxc5 ♕a5 8 ♗d3 ♕xc5 with equality; again the bishop on h4 is not available to bother Black's queen) 7...g5 8 ♗g3 ♕a5! (D).

9 ♗d3 (to parry the threat of 9...♘xe4; 9 ♕d2 is natural, but on d1 White's queen was watching over h5, whereas with the queen on d2, 9...♘h5! followed by ...♘xg3 would be both playable and good; the two bishops and beautiful long diagonal are particularly strong in this case) 9...♘xe4! (a known trick, which is again successful due to the absence of White's dark-squared bishop from the queenside) 10 ♗xe4 ♗xc3+ 11 bxc3 ♕xc3+ 12 ♔f1 f5! (either

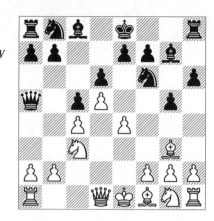

winning the bishop on e4 or trapping the other one by ...f4). Then:

a) 13 ♖c1 ♕f6 (or 13...♕b2! 14 ♖c2 ♕f6, in order to have the last rank available, a nice refinement) 14 h4 (14 ♕h5+ ♔d8 15 h4 g4 16 ♗d3 f4) 14...g4 15 ♗d3 f4 16 ♘e2 fxg3 17 ♘xg3 ♖f8 18 ♖c2 ♘d7 19 ♕xg4 ♘e5 with a large advantage for Black, Spassky-Fischer, Sveti Stefan/Belgrade (16) 1992.

b) 13 ♘e2 ♕f6 14 ♗c2 f4 15 h4 ♖f8! 16 hxg5 hxg5 17 ♘xf4?! gxf4 18 ♗h2 (Black's point is 18 ♗h4 ♖h8!) 18...♘d7 19 g3 ♘e5 20 ♕h5+ ♔d8 21 gxf4 ♘g4 22 ♖e1 ♖h8 23 ♗h7 ♕g7 0-1 Stein-Geller, USSR Cht (Moscow) 1966. White's resignation is due to 24 ♗g3 ♘f6. A classic victory by Geller, one of the great King's Indian players.

Four Pawns Attack

To discuss this variation, let's return to the fourth move:

1 d4 ♘f6 2 c4 g6 3 ♘c3 ♗g7 4 e4 d6

4...0-0 (D) has advantages in some lines, especially if Black wants to play ...c5 without a preliminary ...d6; Fischer played it at least once. In doing so, we run into a couple of thought-provoking issues.

Surprisingly, Black needn't be too afraid of 5 e5 ♘e8 6 f4 d6 because White will have difficulty maintaining his centre in the face of ...c5; for example, 7 ♘f3 c5 8 d5 (8 dxc5 ♘c6 with tremendous compensation if White tries to hang onto his pawn by multiple exchanges on d6; see how the bishop on g7 comes to life) 8...♗g4 9 ♗e2 (9 ♕e2 ♗xf3) 9...♗xf3 10 ♗xf3 dxe5 11

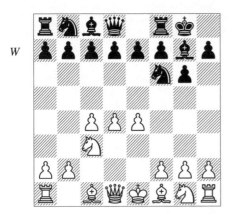

fxe5 ♘d7!. These lines are well worth playing over if you're fairly new to this opening or the concept of how to undermine a large centre.

On the other hand, a conventional move such as 5 ♗g5, which we just saw is not dangerous if ...d6 has already been played, can be trickier after 5...d6 6 ♕d2 (now there's no ...h6/...g5 sequence); or 5...h6 6 ♗e3! and Black lacks the normal harassing move ...♘g4 while he has weakened his kingside. After 5...c5, 6 d5 ♕a5 7 ♕d2 h6 8 ♗xh6! ♗xh6 9 ♕xh6 ♘xe4 10 ♖c1 leaves Black's kingside vulnerable to h4-h5, ♘f3-g5, etc. White could also play 6 dxc5 ♕a5 7 ♕d2 to greater effect, because an early ♘d5 can be effective.

This incomplete discussion of 4...0-0 isn't directly important (after all, hardly anyone plays the move!), but we can begin to get a feel for typical King's Indian considerations.

5 f4 *(D)*

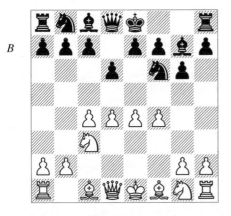

The Four Pawns Attack, White's most ambitious approach and probably the first one that would occur to a player who has never seen the King's Indian, but knows the importance of central control and occupation by pawns. In the 1920s when the King's Indian became more than a curiosity, the Four Pawns was indeed used by the likes of Alekhine, Bogoljubow, among other leading players. The dynamic possibilities and chances for a quick knockout were surely considerations in their reaction.

Most textbooks (and this one) will show some examples of the triumph of the centre in other openings; e.g., something along the lines of 1 e4 e5 2 ♘f3 ♘c6 3 ♗c4 ♗c5 4 c3 ♘f6 5 d4 exd4 6 cxd4 ♗b6? 7 d5 ♘e7 8 e5 and Black's pieces are driven into passivity as a result of the unopposed onslaught by White's centre pawns. How much better it should be to play moves like e5 and d5, when they are protected by pawns on either side! Furthermore, Black is supposed to stake a claim in the centre before he is overrun, right? Of course, it's not so easy for White; advantages of this nature always have their accompanying disadvantages. In the case of the Four Pawns KID, we see that the pawns on c4 and f4 are also restricting the scope of White's bishops on f1 and c1. Perhaps this isn't a dominant concern because once the pawns advance, at least one is normally exchanged. For example, in the main lines Black will trade off his e-pawn for White's c-pawn or e-pawn. Still, the cost in time to erect such a centre has to be considered.

Furthermore, the advance of pawns in any chess opening leaves open the risk that they might become weak. In the Four Pawns KID, we see that the squares e4 and d4 are no longer able to receive the support of the pawn moves c3 and f3, so they are more exposed to attack; this is particularly true of d4, since it is indirectly attacked by Black's bishop on g7 and can be disturbed by the pawn moves ...c5 and ...e5. Furthermore, the squares e3 and d3 may be considered 'interior weaknesses', since they are also without support. In most situations, interior weaknesses on the third rank are difficult to exploit, being within the defensive range of so many pieces. But that can be a different matter if the centre in front of them is compromised. If and when White's pawns advance further to d5 and/or e5 (which is the plan, after all), e4 and d4 become interior weaknesses as well. Then those front pawns are within range of Black's forces, which are waiting on the second and third ranks for just such an opportunity to tear into the ill-protected foot soldiers. That worst-case scenario for White would result from his over-enthusiasm. It turns out that White should usually marshal his pieces to support the centre pawns and wait for the right opportunity to press forward. Or in some cases he will count upon them as cramping influences and forego a general advance indefinitely. These methods provide the rationale for White's entire enterprise.

5...0-0 6 ♘f3 (D)

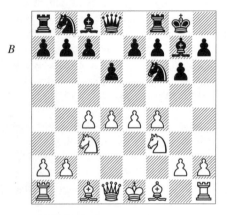

These first six moves are normally played (6 ♗e2 will follow in this note). How does Black react to this powerful front, and how does he get his pieces out to any but passive squares? There are three basic ideas. One is to grab one's share of the centre directly by ...e5, which is not immediately feasible, and unfortunately the preparatory 6...♘bd7 is met by either 7 e5 or 7 ♗d3 without giving Black sufficient counterplay. So Black needs to snipe at the centre from a distance, preferably using his bishop on g7. He can therefore consider 6...c5, which tries to extend the scope of Black's bishop on g7 and attack the centre at the same time. Something similar can occur after 6...♘a6, but in that case ...e5 becomes a major idea and piece placement is a key for both sides. The resulting battle will demonstrate many themes universal to the KID. Taken as a whole, the Four Pawns Attack gives us a thorough course in the handling of broad centres by both sides.

Before moving on, the often-played 6 ♗e2 (presumably to avoid 6 ♘f3 ♗g4) restricts White's options in a number of lines, notably 6...♘a6. White might want to try the move-order 7 ♗e3, to control c5 after 7...e5 8 fxe5 dxe5 9 d5. But Black can also get ambitious after 6 ♗e2 by the underrated 6...e5!; for example, 7 dxe5 (7 fxe5 dxe5 8 d5 ♘a6 with equality; compare the 6...♘a6 main line, where White has been limited to the move ♗e2 instead of the important options that he enjoys there, in particular ♗d3) 7...dxe5 8 ♕xd8 ♖xd8 9 fxe5 ♘fd7 (D).

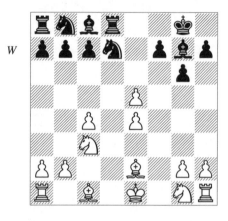

This is the first of a lot of King's Indian positions in which White tries to make something of his extra pawn and direct threats. Given an extra move, Black will have the advantage because of White's inferior pawn-structure, so White must strike first: 10 ♘d5 (10 e6 fxe6 covers d5; then Black can turn his attention to occupying the weak squares e5 and d4) 10...♘a6 11 ♗g5 ♖e8 12 ♘e7+ ♔f8 13 ♘xc8 ♖axc8 14 ♗g4 (otherwise Black captures on e5 exposing the isolated pawn behind it) 14...♘xe5! (a positionally-motivated exchange sacrifice; instead, 14...f5 15 exf5 ♘xe5 is equal) 15 ♗xc8 ♖xc8 (D).

Black controls every important square and has ideas like ...♘d3+, ...♘c5, ...♖e8 and ...♘xc4. A sequence such as 16 ♖d1 ♘xc4 17 b3 ♘d6 18 ♘f3 ♗c3+ 19 ♔e2 ♘xe4 may be the best that White can do, but he then stands worse because Black has two pawns and superior piece placement. This is worth checking for yourself.

After 6 ♘f3, we turn to the variations beginning with 6...c5 and 6...♘a6.

Incidentally, why don't masters play 6...♗g4? After all, that move puts pressure directly on White's vulnerable d4-square by pinning the

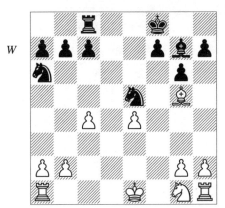

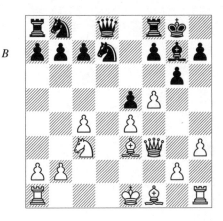

knight and sometimes threatening to exchange it. In conjunction with a combination of moves like ...c5, ...♘c6 and/or ...e5 this is certainly attractive. For no obvious or even logical reasons, the specifics of the position interfere. A good line for White is 7 ♗e3 (often the bishop on this square is vulnerable to ...♘g4, but not this time) 7...♘fd7!? (the thematic move in such positions, supporting ...e5 or ...c5 and unmasking the bishop; instead, 7...♗xf3 8 ♕xf3 e5 9 fxe5 dxe5 10 d5 favours White, who will play 0-0-0; in this type of position, check to see if White has a bishop on e3 fighting for c5) 8 h3!? (White loses a tempo in order to set up the idea that follows; 8 ♗e2 is also advantageous since d4 is well covered) 8...♗xf3 9 ♕xf3 e5 (9...c5!? 10 d5 ♗xc3+! 11 bxc3 ♕a5 has positional points in its favour, but White still has his advantage on both wings with his space and bishop-pair after simply 12 ♗d2, ♗e2 and 0-0; also, 9...♘c6 falls short due to 10 e5!) 10 dxe5! (10 fxe5? runs into the surprise 10...c5! – a tactic to remember, since it applies to other positions) 10...dxe5 11 f5 *(D)*.

In spite of his command of d4, Black lacks sufficient compensation for White's bishop-pair and the eventual attack by playing g4. This is not at all obvious, so let's go a few moves further and look at two moves:

a) 11...♘c6 12 0-0-0 ♘d4 13 ♕f2 c6 (13...c5 14 g4 ♕a5 15 ♔b1 and White simply marches forward with moves such as g5 and h4-h5 in some order, with ♘d5 another potential factor) 14 g4 ♕a5 15 g5. The opening is basically over, with White well on top with the ideas h4-h5 and/or f6, Glek-Damljanović, Belgrade (GMA) 1988.

b) 11...♗h6!? 12 0-0-0! (12 ♗xh6 ♕h4+) 12...♗xe3+ 13 ♕xe3 *(D)*.

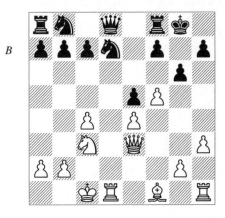

We have reached one of those fairly common cases in which exchanging a 'bad' fianchettoed bishop (in this case on g7) for the opponent's very good one (on e3) can be disadvantageous due to the weaknesses left unprotected; for example, 13...♘c6 14 g4 ♘d4 and Black has a superb knight versus a very bad bishop and yet after 15 h4 he is in serious trouble in the face of g5 and h5; for example, 15...c6 16 ♘e2 (a simple move to get rid of Black's best piece; also good is 16 ♗d3 ♕e7 17 g5) 16...♘xe2+ (16...c5 17 ♘c3!) 17 ♗xe2 ♕e7 (17...♕b6 18 ♕h6; Black could use a bishop on g7!) 18 h5 ♖ad8 (18...g5 19 ♖xd7!) 19 hxg6 fxg6 20 ♖h6! ♕g7 21 c5! ♘xc5 22 ♗c4+ ♔h8 23 ♖dh1 ♖d4 24 ♕e2 ♖xe4 25 fxg6! and wins.

Central Break

6...c5 *(D)*

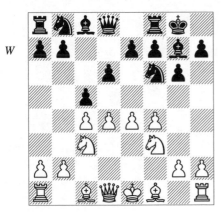

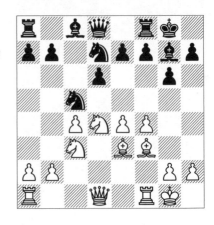

This is Black's traditional main line. He attacks the centre at its weakest point on d4; but at the same time wants to unleash the power of the bishop on g7.

7 d5

There are two frequently-used ways to deviate from this natural move:

a) White might want to take the King's Indian player out of his normal channels by 7 ♗e2 cxd4 8 ♘xd4 (D).

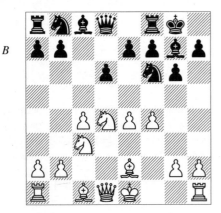

White aims for a Maroczy Bind structure (characterized by c4 and e4). This is a safe choice, but compared to the Sicilian Defence version in Volume 1, the move f4 instead of f3 weakens e4 and makes it easier for Black to find counterplay; for example, 8...♘a6! (an ambitious move that refuses to simplify; Black has a few cards up his sleeve – the immediate ideas are ...♘c5 and ...♛b6) 9 ♗e3 ♘c5 10 ♗f3 ♘fd7 (10...♗h6 is also considered equal) 11 0-0 (D).

11...e5! 12 ♘db5 exf4! 13 ♗xf4 ♘e5 14 ♗e2 (14 ♘xd6 ♘ed3 15 ♘xc8 ♛d4+ 16 ♔h1

♖axc8; 14 ♛xd6 ♘cd3) 14...♗e6 15 b3 a6 16 ♘d4 ♘c6! 17 ♘xc6 (17 ♗e3 ♗e5!; again e5 comes in handy) 17...bxc6 18 ♖c1 ♛a5 19 ♗d2 ♛b6 20 ♗e3 ♖ad8!? 21 ♔h1 ♛b8 22 ♗f3 ♗e5, Bisguier-J.Watson, Minneapolis 1982. White's knight is restricted on c3 and because of e5 and the e-file Black had some advantage. These dark-square themes are ubiquitous in the KID.

The alternative 8...♘c6 (D) is of course playable but gives few positive prospects for Black.

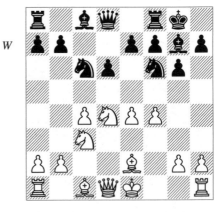

9 ♗e3 ♘xd4 10 ♗xd4 e5 11 fxe5 dxe5 12 ♗c5 ♖e8 13 ♛xd8 ♖xd8 14 0-0 ♖d2 15 ♖ad1 ♖xd1 16 ♖xd1 ♗e6 17 h3 ♗f8 with equality, Tarasov-Geller, USSR Ch (Moscow) 1961.

b) 7 dxc5 got a short burst of attention from some top players but doesn't have much punch: 7...♛a5! 8 ♗d3 (to protect the e-pawn; instead, 8 cxd6 ♘xe4 9 dxe7 ♗xc3+ 10 bxc3 ♖e8 is terrible for White: it's not just the doubled pawns but his weaknesses on d3, e3 and e4) 8...♛xc5 9 ♛e2 (to kick the queen out by ♗e3 and be able to castle; this is a little like the Austrian Attack in the Pirc Defence from Volume 1) 9...♗g4 10 ♗e3 ♕a5 11 0-0 ♘c6 *(D)*.

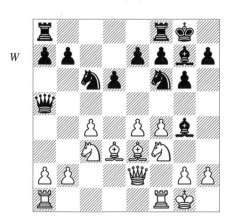

Both sides are fighting for d4:

a) 12 a3 ♘d7 13 b4 ♕d8 (13...♕h5 makes sense because now that White's c-pawn is a target and the g7-bishop is unleashed, Black needn't fear any simplification) 14 ♖ac1 a5! 15 b5?! (15 ♕b2) 15...♘d4; here Black owns c5 and the c-file versus White's weak c4-pawn, Dlugy-Schmaltz, Internet 1999.

b) 12 ♖ac1 ♘d7! 13 ♕f2 *(D)*.

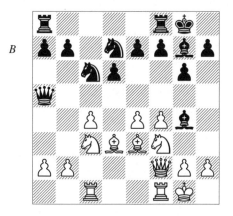

13...♗xf3 14 gxf3 ♘c5 15 ♗b1 ♘a4! (a move that's been emulated more than once; it eliminates White's most annoying idea, i.e. ♘d5; Black's position is without weaknesses, so even if White has a nominal advantage because of his space advantage, the practical chances are equal) 16 ♘xa4 ♕xa4 17 b3 ♕a3 18 c5 dxc5 19 ♗xc5 ♕xc5! 20 ♖xc5 ♗d4 21 ♖d1 ♗xf2+ 22 ♔xf2 ♖fd8 23 ♖cd5 e6 with equality, Topalov-Kasparov, Linares 1994.

7...e6 *(D)*

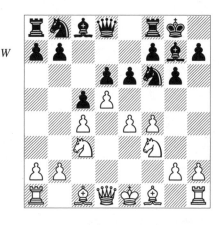

Black has to strike back at White's centre.
8 ♗e2
Periodically someone tries to open up the d-file by 8 dxe6, but 8...fxe6 covers d5, preventing White from landing a knight on that square. In the meantime Black has an outpost on d4, one that masks his potentially weak pawn on d6. A famous example went 9 ♗d3 ♘c6 10 0-0 a6 (or 10...♘d4, as Kasparov once played) 11 a4 (...b5 would greatly benefit Black's pieces, so White stops it) 11...b6 12 ♘g5 *(D)*.

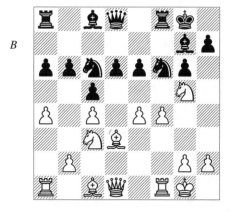

12...♖a7! (an example of second-rank defence, and preparation for a counterattack) 13 ♖a3 ♖e7! 14 ♗b1 ♘d4 15 ♗e3 ♗b7 16 ♕e1 e5 17 f5 (White doesn't want to allow ...exf4, but 17 fxe5 ♖xe5! also establishes an outpost on an open file) 17...h6 18 ♘h3 (18 fxg6 hxg5 19 ♗xg5 ♕e8! recovers the pawn with dividends) 18...gxf5 19 exf5 ♕e8 20 ♕h4 e4! 21 ♕g3 (Black's opening has been a total success and his second-rank strategy comes in handy after 21 ♗xh6 ♗xh6 22 ♕xh6 ♖g7, threatening ...e3 and starting a huge attack) 21...♘h5 22 ♕g4 ♔h8 23 ♘f4 ♘xf4 24 ♖xf4 ♗e5 25 ♖f2 ♘f3+! 26 ♔h1 ♘xh2 27 ♕h4 h5! (threatening ...♘g4; the rest is easy to understand) 28 f6 ♖h7 29 ♗xe4 ♗xe4 30 ♘xe4 ♘g4 31 ♖f5 ♗xb2 32 ♘xd6 ♕g6 33 ♖b3 ♗xf6 34 ♗g5 ♗g7 35 ♖xf8+ ♗xf8 36 ♗f4 ♖d7 37 ♖xb6 ♗xd6 38 ♗xd6 ♖xd6 39 ♖b8+ (or 39 ♖xd6 ♕b1+) 39...♔g7 40 ♖b7+ ♔h6 41 ♕e1 ♖e6 42 ♕d2+ ♕g5. Black won quickly in Hjartarson-Larsen, Reykjavik 1986.

8...exd5 *(D)*

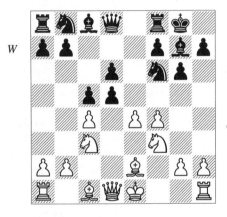

9 cxd5

a) 9 e5?! is still being played and has been analysed for many years. In most examples it is a classic case of overextended pawns. The easiest road to some advantage is 9...♘e4 10 cxd5 (10 ♘xd5 might be the best way to bail out, although 10...♘c6 11 ♗d3 f5 12 exf6 ♘xf6 favours Black) 10...♘xc3 11 bxc3 ♘d7! *(D)*.

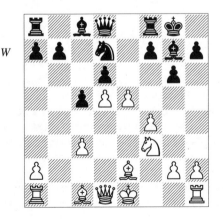

Remarkably, White is already much worse. For example, 12 0-0 (12 e6 is weak after either 12...♗xc3+ 13 ♗d2 ♗xd2+ 14 ♕xd2 fxe6 15 dxe6 ♘b6 or 12...fxe6 13 dxe6 ♘b6 and Black corrals the d-pawn; for example, 14 0-0 ♗xe6 15 ♘g5 ♗d5 16 ♖b1 ♗xc3 17 ♔h1 ♗d4, Fyllingen-Djurhuus, Norwegian Ch (Rorøs) 2002) 12...dxe5 *(D)* and now:

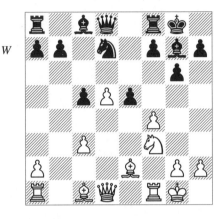

a1) 13 ♔h1 e4! (this is a key move even when the pawn can be taken! Here Black opens up the h8-a1 diagonal without losing a pawn) 14 ♘g5 ♘f6 15 ♗c4 h6 16 ♘h3 ♗f5, Ruhrberg-Kopp, Hessen 1992.

a2) 13 fxe5 ♘xe5 14 ♗e3 ♘xf3+ 15 ♗xf3 ♕d6 16 ♕d2 ♗e5 17 h3 b6 18 ♗h6 ♖e8 19 ♖ae1 ♗a6 20 ♗e2 ♗xe2 21 ♖xe2 c4! (isolating White's d-pawn) 22 ♖ef2 ♖e7 23 ♔h1 ♖ae8 24 ♗g5 ♖d7 25 ♖e2 ♕xd5! 26 ♕e3 ♖e6 and Black is clearly better, Li Zunian-Gheorghiu, Dubai OL 1986.

b) 9 exd5 is also instructive. One good response is 9...♗f5! (this stops White's only real threat: activation of his c1-bishop and f1-rook by the advance f5) 10 0-0 ♖e8 (10...♘a6 11 ♗d3 ♕d7 is the same strategy) 11 ♗d3 *(D)*.

This is White's idea. He wants to exchange bishops on d3, then advance his pawn to f5, bring his dark-squared bishop onto an active square, and attack. Now:

b1) 11...♘a6 12 ♗xf5 gxf5 gives us a position of a type that arises in other openings. Basically a knight on e4 will block off serious threats to the f-pawn, and meanwhile Black gets the g-file.

b2) 11...♕d7 (Black takes a stand on f5; until White breaks down that square, his pieces

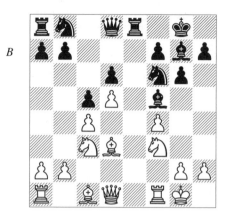

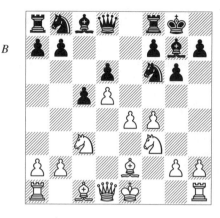

will be cramped and his interior weaknesses on e3 and d3 will come into play) 12 h3 ♘a6 (now the idea is ...♘c7 and ...b5; notice how ...♕d7 helps in that respect as well) 13 a3 (13 g4 ♗xd3 14 ♕xd3 ♘b4 15 ♕d1 h5! 16 g5 ♘e4! 17 ♘xe4 ♖xe4 and White's king is exposed; 13 ♗xf5 gxf5! prepares ...♘e4 with total control along the e-file) 13...♘c7 14 ♕c2 (14 g4 allows a promising piece sacrifice by 14...♗xg4, which will generally give Black a perpetual check at worst; and Black can also play for queenside files by 14...♗xd3 15 ♕xd3 b5! 16 cxb5 ♖eb8 17 a4 a6 18 bxa6 ♘xa6; Black has excellent play on both wings) 14...b5! 15 cxb5 ♘fxd5 16 ♘xd5 ♘xd5 (D).

From the position after 9 cxd5, I'll present a short overview of the daring 9...♘bd7 and then look at two main moves, 9...♖e8 and 9...♗g4, citing games with a selection of the most essential treatments and tactical motifs of the Four Pawns. Several of these also apply to other openings. The main alternative 9...b5!? expresses a different philosophy, trying to divert White from protection of his centre. The first threat is ...b4, which limits White's options. If White plays the obvious move 10 ♗xb5?!, Black has a tactic that you simply have to know if you're playing the King's Indian or Benoni with either colour: 10...♘xe4! (D).

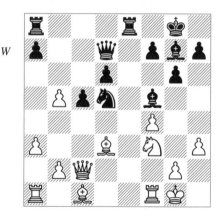

17 ♗xf5 gxf5! (that e4 outpost again! Also, compare the remaining bishops) 18 ♖b1 ♖e4 19 ♖d1 ♘b6 20 b4 ♕xb5 21 ♖xd6 c4 22 ♕f2 c3 23 ♕g3 ♕e2 24 ♘e5 c2 0-1 Peng Zhaoqin-J.Polgar, Novi Sad (women) OL 1990.

We now return to the position after 9 cxd5 (D):

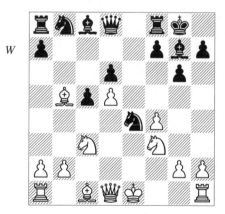

11 ♘xe4 ♕a5+ with the idea 12 ♘c3 (12 ♔f2 ♕xb5 13 ♘xd6 wins a pawn but misplaces White's king and weakens his light squares) 12...♗xc3+ 13 bxc3 ♕xb5. White has trouble on the light squares, his c1-bishop is restricted, and he can't even castle.

Having said all that, the drawback to 9...b5 is 10 e5! dxe5 11 fxe5 ♘g4 12 ♗g5 (or 12 ♗xb5

♘xe5 13 0-0 and White has a passed d-pawn and attacking pieces); for example, 12...♕b6 13 0-0 c4+ 14 ♔h1, when after 14...♘f2+? 15 ♖xf2 ♕xf2, 16 ♘e4 or (even better) 16 ♘xb5 gives White a great game.

Central Provocation

9...♘bd7

Here Black attempts to restrain White's centre before attacking it. This is an underrated system that was held to be inferior due to 10 e5, but then Black can launch a dynamic counterattack. Here's one example:

Kopionkin – Ulko
Russian Cht (Smolensk) 2000

10 e5 dxe5

Even 10...♘e8!? is an instructive position to play around with: is White's centre weak or strong? I think you'll find that Black is doing well.

11 fxe5 ♘g4 12 e6! ♘de5 13 ♘g5!? fxe6!?
A bold sacrifice.

14 ♗xg4 ♘xg4 15 ♕xg4 exd5 *(D)*

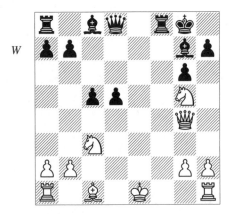

Black has two mobile pawns for a piece, two bishops, and open lines against White's exposed king.

16 ♕h4
After 16 ♕g3, 16...♖e8+ 17 ♔d1 ♗f5 looks extremely strong.

16...h6 17 ♘f3 g5 18 ♕a4?! *(D)*
But it would be surrender to play 18 ♗xg5 hxg5 19 ♕xg5 ♕xg5 20 ♘xg5 ♗g4! and Black has the piece back with a much superior game.

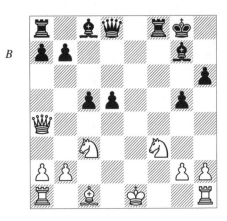

18...g4! 19 ♘d2 ♗d7 20 ♕b3 c4! 21 ♕xb7 ♕e7+ 22 ♘e2
Even worse is 22 ♔d1?? ♗a4+.

22...♖ae8 23 ♕xd5+ ♔h8 24 ♕xc4 ♖f4!
Black wins the queen in one way or another; e.g., 25 ♕a6 ♖a4 26 ♕d3 ♗f5 27 ♕b5 ♖b4.

Attack on the Centre

9...♖e8 *(D)*

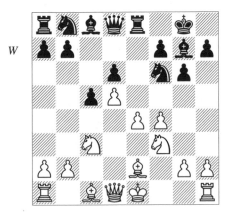

Black makes a direct, provocative move that attacks the pawn on e4. This brings to the fore the conflict between White's direct e5 and Black's attempts to destroy the central pawns before they strangle him. I'll use two exemplary games to investigate the nature of the resulting play:

Blokh – A. Feldman
USSR 1982

10 e5 dxe5 11 fxe5 ♘g4 12 ♗g5

The slower-looking 12 0-0 doesn't force Black's queen to move, but retains some attack. Here's a tricky example: 12...♘xe5 13 ♗f4 ♘bd7 14 d6! (this is the move that opens up White's pieces: his important moves are ♘d5 and ♗c4 or ♗b5) 14...♘xf3+ 15 ♗xf3 ♘f8! (heading for the important d4-square) 16 ♕d2 (16 ♕b3) 16...♘e6 17 ♗g3 ♕g5?? (17...♘d4! looks solid enough, when 18 ♗d5 keeps some initiative for the pawn) 18 d7! ♗xd7 (18...♕xd2 19 dxe8♕+) 19 ♕xd7 ♖ed8 20 ♕xb7 (Black is just a piece down) 20...h5 21 ♗d5 ♗xc3 22 ♕xf7+ ♔h8 23 bxc3 1-0 Vaïsser-Wohlers Armas, Cannes 2000.

12...♕b6 *(D)*

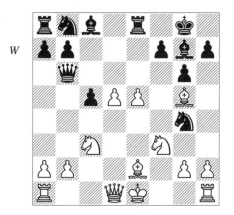

13 ♕d2!?

An exciting move invented by the Four Pawns theoretician Blokh. Instead, one of the main lines of theory goes 13 0-0 ♘xe5 14 ♘xe5 ♗xe5 15 ♗c4 ♗f5! 16 ♘b5 a6! 17 d6! axb5 18 ♗xf7+! ♔xf7 19 ♖xf5+! gxf5 20 ♕h5+ ♔f8 21 ♗h6+ ♗g7 22 ♗xg7+ ♔xg7 23 ♕xe8 c4+ 24 ♔h1 ♖xd6 25 ♖e1 ♕f8! 26 ♕e5+ ♔g8 27 ♕d5+ with a draw, Vaïsser-Bauer, France 1992. OK, this is all theory (and was at the time), but it shows the near-perfect balance between attack and defence that typifies this main line of the 9...♖e8 Four Pawns Attack.

13...♘d7

It's always a critical decision for Black whether to capture the important e-pawn. The danger is that it will take too much time from Black's development. For example, Blokh analyses 13...♘xe5 14 0-0-0 c4 15 ♘xe5 ♗xe5 16 ♗xc4 ♕c5 17 ♗b3 ♘a6 18 ♖hf1 ♗g4 19 d6! *(D)*.

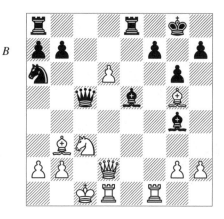

That essential move again! This time it's based upon the line 19...♖f8 20 ♖de1! ♗xd6 21 ♗f6 and ♕h6.

14 e6!

A typically strong thrust when Black plays too passively.

14...fxe6 15 dxe6 ♗xc3?

The best line may be 15...♕xe6 16 ♘d5 ♗e5 17 ♘xe5 ♕xe5 18 ♗f4 ♕d4 19 ♕xd4 cxd4 20 ♔d2! with some advantage, or here 20 ♘c7 ♖e4 21 0-0!?.

16 bxc3 ♕xe6 17 0-0! ♘df6

Or 17...♕xe2 18 ♖ae1! ♕xd2 19 ♖xe8+ ♔f7 20 ♖e7+ ♔g8 21 ♘xd2.

18 ♖ae1 ♕c6 19 h3! ♘e4 20 ♕f4 h6 21 hxg4 hxg5 22 ♘xg5 ♘xg5 23 ♕xg5 ♔g7 24 ♗c4 ♖xe1 25 ♖xe1 ♕f6 26 ♖e7+ 1-0

Not surprisingly, Black could have defended better but this is a good illustration of what damage White's centre can do.

Piskov – Parmentier
Budapest 1989

10 ♘d2 *(D)*

At first this move looks passive, merely protecting e4, but it has a very dynamic plan behind it: White wants to get his knight to c4 and force e5 through. Why not just leave the knight on f3 and do the same? For one thing, advancing to e5 immediately gambits a pawn, as in the previous game. It also happens that a knight on c4 is ideally placed to attack the d-pawn (and the d6-square itself) if, for example, Black plays ...♘fd7 at some point. Another very important advantage to ♘d2-c4 is that a bishop can go to f3 to strengthen White's centre. Then if White

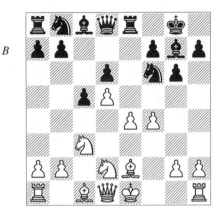

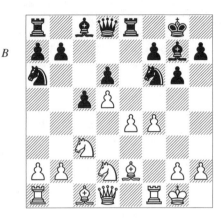

plays e5, this piece will defend the d-pawn against attack and can grow greatly in range. The formation with a bishop on f3 and knight on c4 also allows a rook on e1 to provide direct support for a central thrust. Finally, it turns out that there is a dangerous sacrifice initiated by e5 and then playing ♘c4 with tempo.

What should Black do? It's all a matter of timing. First of all, ♘c4 isn't a threat yet because the pawn on e4 hangs. Queenside activity is called for to activate his pieces before White can implement his plan. Specifically Black would like to play ...b5 and/or ...c4 to try to get a knight to squares like d3.

10...♘a6

A good defensive example was 10...a6 11 a4 ♘bd7 12 0-0 c4!? 13 ♔h1 (13 ♘xc4 ♘xe4 14 ♘xe4 ♖xe4 is equal, and has the point 15 ♘xd6?? ♕b6+) 13...♘c5 14 e5 dxe5 15 fxe5 ♖xe5 16 ♘xc4 ♖xe2! (Black must not fear sacrificing the exchange in this line to maintain the initiative; otherwise White has moves like a5, d6, ♗g5, etc.) 17 ♘xe2 ♗g4 18 ♘e5 ♘ce4, Glek-Tseshkovsky, Budapest 1989. Black has activity for the pawn and the d-pawn is weak but the position is still hard to assess.

11 0-0 (D)

11...c4!?

A characteristic idea. The other strategy is to play for ...b5; e.g., 11...♖b8 12 ♔h1 ♘c7 13 a4 a6 14 a5 ♗d7! (this is a customary Benoni manoeuvre) 15 ♗f3 ♘b5 16 e5 dxe5 17 fxe5 ♖xe5 18 ♘c4 ♖f5!? (ingenious; Tal introduces an elaborate exchange sacrifice) 19 ♘e3 ♖f4! 20 ♘e2 ♖h4! 21 g3 ♖e4 22 ♗xe4 ♘xe4 23 ♘f4 ♘d4 24 ♔g2 ♕e7 25 ♖e1 h5 26 ♖a3 ♖e8 27 ♘e2? ♗h3+! 28 ♔xh3 ♘g5+ 0-1 Ufimtsev-Tal,

USSR Spartakiad (Moscow) 1967. The finish would be 29 ♔g2 ♕e4+ 30 ♔f2 ♕f3+ 31 ♔g1 ♘h3#.

12 ♔h1! ♘c5 13 e5!

Again White sacrifices a pawn so that ♘c4 can come with tempo.

13...dxe5 14 fxe5!

14 ♘xc4 e4! 15 ♗e3 ♘d3 16 ♗xd3 exd3 17 ♕xd3 ♗f5 18 ♕d2 ♖c8 19 ♘e5 ♘e4 20 ♕d4 ♘d6 gives Black wonderful compensation for a mere pawn, Meduna-Vokač, Olomouc 1995. Every black piece is on the right square.

14...♘fd7?

14...♖xe5! could lead to consecutive exchange sacrifices: 15 ♘xc4 ♖xe2!? 16 ♕xe2 ♗f5 17 ♖xf5!? gxf5 18 ♗g5 with complications.

15 e6 fxe6 16 ♘xc4 ♘e5 17 d6 (D)

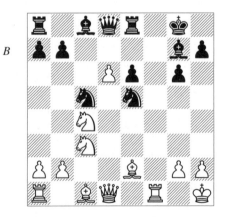

This pawn is going to cause a lot of trouble, pinning down Black's pieces.

17...♗d7 18 ♗f4 ♘c6 19 ♕d2 ♕h4 20 g3 ♕h3 21 ♗f3 ♘d4 22 ♗g2 ♕h5 23 b4! ♘a4 24 g4! ♕xg4 25 ♘e5!?

Or 25 ♘xa4 ♗xa4 26 ♘e5.

25...♗xe5 26 ♗xe5 ♘xc3 27 ♗xd4 ♘e2??
28 ♗e5 ♕h5 29 ♕e3 1-0

The knight is trapped.

Restraint of the Centre

9...♗g4 *(D)*

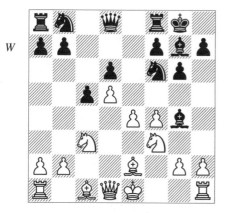

Black attempts to prevent White's centre from advancing by exchanging the piece that most supports e5: White's knight on f3. This results in a position in which Black's play is almost exclusively of the queenside, involving expansion and routing his pieces in that direction. White either plays in the centre by marshalling his forces to break through on the restricted square e5, or uses pawn advances on the kingside to launch a direct attack on that lightly-populated area of the board.

10 0-0 ♘bd7 11 ♖e1

11 h3 ♗xf3 12 ♗xf3 wastes a bit of time to force the exchange. There may follow moves like 12...♖e8, 12...♖b8, or even 12...♘e8 intending ...♘c7 and ...b5.

11...♖e8 12 h3 ♗xf3 13 ♗xf3 ♕a5! 14 ♗e3
(D)

White is still trying to blast through in the centre. He needs ♗e3 so as to answer ...c4 with ♗d4. Both sides have to keep an eye on the plan ...c4, ...♘c5-d3, exploiting White's interior weaknesses. As usual, it's all a matter of timing, not only tactically but also for the achievement of positional goals such as winning key squares. Here are two older games from this position, both played in the same year and still relevant.

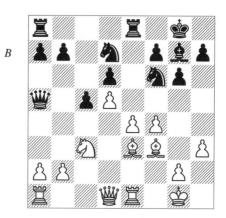

Vaïsser – Kindermann
Biel 1991

14...♖ac8!?

Intending ...c4 and ...♘c5; this has been criticized but may not be bad.

15 g4!?

This aggressive advance is one of White's main attacking ideas in this variation, although the kingside weakening can cause it to backfire. White really does need to react to the idea of ...c4 and imitating the next game by 15 ♗f2 doesn't seem to do enough.

15...h6 16 h4 *(D)*

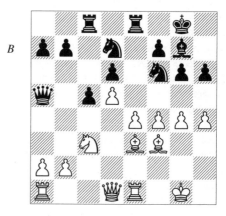

16...b5?!

Here's a trick that players of both colours should know: 16...h5!. Now if 17 g5, 17...♘g4! 18 ♗xg4 hxg4 19 ♕xg4 ♘b6! intends ...♘c4 or in some cases ...♗xc3; White's attack has disappeared. And after 17 gxh5 ♘xh5 18 ♗xh5 gxh5 19 ♕xh5 ♕b4!, White has to watch out for ...♘f6 and ...♘xe4. These positions are unclear but at least as dangerous for White as Black. The ...h5 idea is useful if it looks as though other measures will be inadequate.

17 g5 hxg5 18 hxg5 ♘h7 19 ♗g4!

One of the major points behind g4-g5 is to activate this often-passive bishop.

19...♖cd8

Now we see White explode in the centre just in time:

20 e5! *(D)*

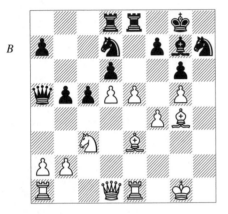

B

20...dxe5 21 f5! e4!

Freeing Black's bishop and preparing to bring pieces to e5 and d4. This is normally the best way to respond to an e5 sacrifice in the Four Pawns.

22 fxg6!

Kindermann's clever trick was 22 f6? ♘hxf6 23 gxf6 ♘xf6 and White's extra piece means nothing because his kingside is too exposed and Black, already with three extra pawns, threatens to win the d-pawn by ...b4.

22...fxg6 23 ♗e6+ ♖xe6?

Correctly trying to keep the initiative, but it doesn't work; 23...♔h8 is best, and difficult to crack.

24 dxe6 ♘e5 25 e7! ♖e8 26 ♕d5+ ♔h8 27 ♔g2! ♖xe7 28 ♖h1 ♖f7 29 ♖af1 ♖xf1 30 ♔xf1 1-0

Kožul – Nunn
Wijk aan Zee 1991

14...b5 15 a3 ♘b6!

Heading for c4, to target the weakness on e3 and supplement the pressure exerted by Black's bishop along the a1-h8 diagonal. But White

still has the bishops and centre, so this isn't a one-way street; 15...b4 16 axb4 ♕xb4 is also played.

16 ♗f2!? *(D)*

16 e5 is the consistent move *if* it works! Then a controversial line is 16...♘c4 17 exf6 ♘xe3 18 ♖xe3 ♗xe3 19 fxg7 ♖ae8 and only the real experts know what's happening, or maybe they don't!

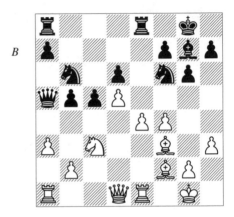

B

16...♘c4 17 ♕c2 ♘d7

Black discourages e5, that square now being controlled five times! 17...♘xb2? fails to 18 e5!.

18 ♗e2 ♖ab8!

A perfectly-timed move, avoiding the tempting 18...♘xb2 19 ♘xb5.

19 a4 b4! 20 ♗xc4

Later 20 ♘b5!? was played.

20...bxc3 21 b3 a6 22 ♖ec1 ♘b6 23 ♗f1 c4! *(D)*

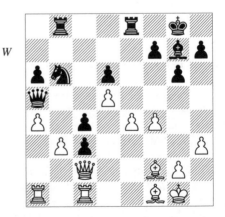

W

24 ♗xc4!?

The prettiest of winning ideas is 24 b4 ♕xb4 25 a5 ♘d7 26 ♖cb1 ♕b3!! 27 ♖xb3 cxb3 28 ♕d3 c2 29 ♖e1 ♖ec8.

24...♘xc4 25 bxc4 ♖b2 26 ♕d3 ♖d2 27 ♕f3 f5 28 e5 dxe5 29 fxe5 ♖xe5 30 ♔h1 ♖e4 31 ♗e1 ♕c7 32 ♖ab1 ♖de2! 33 ♗xc3 ♖2e3 34 d6 ♕xd6 35 ♗b4 ♕c6! 36 ♕f1 ♖xh3+! 37 gxh3 ♖e2+ 0-1

A classic game. Black's queenside attack beat White's central one.

6...♘a6 vs the Four Pawns

1 d4 ♘f6 2 c4 g6 3 ♘c3 ♗g7 4 e4 d6 5 f4 0-0 6 ♘f3 ♘a6 (D)

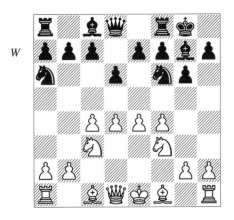

W

At first this may seem to be a strange way to counter a formation so imposing as the Four Pawns. As it happens, moving a knight to the rim is routine in the King's Indian Defence and relates directly to the centre. For one thing, the usual choices of a square for this piece are:

a) c6, where it can be attacked by d5, and

b) d7, where it gets in the way of Black's light-squared bishop.

In this particular situation neither of those options is realistic. The strategy behind ...♘a6 is to play ...e5 and then have the c5-square available for the knight in case White grabs the e5-pawn and tries to hold it. That will yield active play. On a secondary level, 6...♘a6 is a waiting move to see what White is up to. Black can still change his mind about ...e5 and play something like ...♗g4 or ...c5 instead.

7 ♗d3

This is probably the most logical continuation if White is planning to answer ...e5 with

d5 at some point. Then his e-pawn is covered, a nice thing in view of a coming ...♘c5. Some of the alternatives are just as important, however.

a) 7 e5 might be the Four Pawns player's instant reaction, since it stops ...e5 and at first the knight on a6 doesn't look relevant with regard to central play. But the latter part isn't true. 7...♘d7 (D) follows, when Black is about to play ...c5.

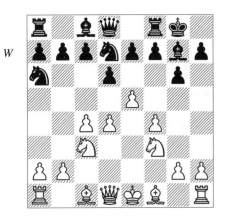

W

Then one of several ideas is 8 ♗e2 (White would like to be able to play d5 in response to ...c5 without losing his e-pawn; the only move that keeps the pawns intact on d5 and e5 is 8 ♕e2, but then 8...c5 9 d5 ♘b6! prepares ...e6 to crack open the e-file *vis-a-vis* White's queen, so 10 ♗e3 ♗g4! could follow, with good play for Black) 8...c5 9 exd6 exd6 (9...cxd4 10 ♘xd4 ♘b6 11 0-0 ♕xd6 12 ♗e3 leaves White's pieces nicely centralized, and 12...♘c5? fails to 13 ♘db5) and now:

a1) 10 0-0 is reasonable. Then Black should probably attack the loose e-file squares by 10...♘f6 (or maybe 10...cxd4 11 ♘xd4 ♕b6 12 ♘cb5 ♘ac5 13 ♔h1 ♘f6 with the same notion) 11 d5 (11 ♗e3 ♘g4) 11...♖e8, intending 12 ♗d3 ♗f5! with a position from 9 exd5 in our last section!

a2) 10 d5 (D).

Here Black has two moves of note:

a21) 10...♘c7 11 0-0 and we should note that 11...b5? is premature (but 11...♘f6! should be fine, and 11...♗xc3 is also possible): 12 f5! bxc4 13 fxg6 (or 13 ♗g5! f6 14 ♗f4) 13...fxg6 14 ♗g5 with an initiative for White, Vaïsser-Golubev, Biel 1995.

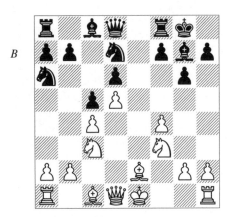

a22) 10...♗xc3+ 11 bxc3 f5 is better and intriguing – it will take White a long time to get his bishops out! Then 12 ♘g5 ♘f6 13 0-0 ♘c7 (13...h6? 14 ♘e6) 14 ♗f3 ♖e8 seems to cover White's ♘e6 plan, so White might have to start an arduous preparation for g4. Black could focus on achieving the advance ...b5 (he potentially has four pieces and a pawn to support that) and use his e-file control to discourage White's forces from straying. Of course ...b5 might well activate White's pieces (imagine a bishop on b2), so that has to be well-timed. It may be that this is simply equal.

b) 7 ♗e2 is the main alternative (to 7 ♗d3), and more frequently played. 7...e5 and now play comes down to a struggle over the dark squares:

b1) 8 fxe5 dxe5 *(D)* and now:

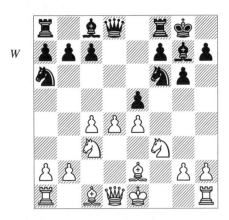

b11) 9 ♘xe5 c5!. This undermining attack is the consistent theme and justification for the ...♘a6 lines. Then 10 d5? allows 10...♘xe4!, so 10 ♗e3 appears to be best, after which

10...♘g4?! 11 ♗xg4! ♗xg4 12 ♘xg4 cxd4 13 ♘d5 dxe3 14 0-0 is the kind of thing White wants: while Black is scrambling to recover his pawn, White switches to the attack. But Black also has 10...♘b4!?; for example, 11 d5!? ♘xe4! 12 ♘xe4 ♗f5 with equality, Huerta-Arizmendi, Madrid 2000.

b12) 9 d5 ♘c5 10 ♗g5 (White's problems defending his e-pawn indicate why 7 ♗d3 might be preferable; a mistake is 10 ♕c2?! ♘fxe4! 11 ♘xe4 ♗f5 12 ♗d3 ♗xe4 13 ♗xe4 f5 recovering the piece with the better game) 10...h6 11 ♗xf6 ♕xf6 12 b4 ♘a6 13 a3 c5! (I'm not sure that until this game, players in general realized how strong this move is when White's dark-squared bishop is gone; White's queenside progress is completely stifled) 14 ♖b1 ♗d7 (or 14...♕d6) 15 b5!? ♘c7 16 d6 ♘e6 17 ♘d5 ♕d8 18 ♕d2, Lautier-Kasparov, Amsterdam 1995. This is unclear, and the game was drawn.

b2) 8 dxe5 dxe5 *(D)* is a key type of gambit position.

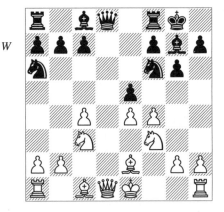

Then:

b21) 9 ♘xe5 ♘c5 10 ♗f3 ♕xd1+ 11 ♔xd1 ♖d8+ 12 ♔c2 ♘fxe4! 13 ♘xe4 ♗f5 14 ♖e1 ♗xe5 15 fxe5 ♖d4, and 16 b3 is the only idea White can try if he is to search for an advantage, but Black's activity always seems good enough to hold the balance: 16...♘xe4 17 ♔b2 ♘c5 18 ♔a3 ♘d3 19 ♖d1 ♖e8 20 ♗xb7 ♖xe5 with equality, Peng Zhaoqin-M.Socko, Groningen (women) 1998.

b22) 9 ♕xd8 ♖xd8 10 ♘xe5 ♘c5 11 ♗f3 ♗e6! is similar: 12 0-0 (12 ♘d5 ♘fd7! 13 ♘xd7 ♖xd7 with straightforward ideas such as

...♖e8 and ...c6; White's e-pawn is a problem, he has lost control of d4, and is vulnerable on d3) 12...♘fd7! 13 ♘xd7 ♗d4+! 14 ♔h1 ♖xd7 15 ♘d5 c6, A.Geller-Belov, USSR 1988; White is poorly coordinated, and ...♘d3 or ...♗xc4 is coming.

After all that, let's return to the position after 7 ♗d3 *(D)*:

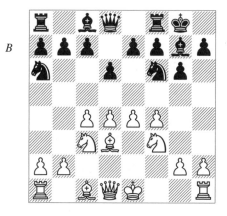

7...♗g4

Developing quickly is usually recommended. The engaging thing about 6...♘a6 is that the play stays alive regardless of what either side does. Instead of 7...♗g4, for example, 7...e5 8 fxe5 dxe5 9 d5 *(D)* illustrates a different set of themes.

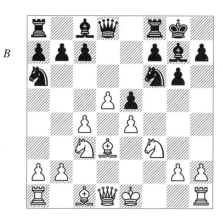

Now 9...♘c5 10 ♗c2 a5 11 0-0 is attractive for White, who has easy build-ups with ♗g5 or ♗e3 and ♕d2 available, or can pursue the traditional expansion with b3, a3 and b4. So Black usually prefers 9...c6 10 0-0 cxd5 11 cxd5 ♘e8 (11...♕b6+ 12 ♔h1 ♘e8 13 ♕e2 protects the

b-pawn and prepares ♗e3; White's position makes a good impression) 12 ♕e2 ♘ac7 13 ♗g5 f6 14 ♗h4!. The bishop is well placed here, stopping ...f5 and ready to go to f2 when that's desirable. You should consider the idea ♗h4-f2 in other branches of the 9...c6 line. Vaïsser gives 14...♕e7 15 ♘d2!, when White is better.

8 0-0

8 ♗e3 is promising, trying not to waste a tempo by castling: 8...♘d7 9 h3! ♗xf3 10 ♕xf3 (White wants to go throw everything at Black and go queenside when appropriate) 10...e5 (what else?) 11 dxe5 dxe5 (11...♘ac5 12 ♗c2 dxe5 13 0-0-0! ♘e6 14 f5 ♘d4 15 ♕f2 with an edge) 12 f5! ♘dc5 (12...♗h6!? 13 0-0-0! ♗xe3+ 14 ♕xe3 is very similar to the position that we saw above in the line with 6...♗g4; play might continue 14...c6 and now 15 ♖hf1 or 15 h4!? ♕b6 16 ♕h6, etc.) 13 ♗e2 ♘d3+ (13...♗h6? 14 ♖d1; 13...gxf5 14 exf5 e4 15 ♕g3!) 14 ♗xd3 ♕xd3 15 ♖d1 ♕xc4 16 f6 ♗h8 17 ♘d5 ♖fd8 18 b3! ♕c2 19 0-0 ♕xa2 20 ♗h6 ♖xd5 21 ♖xd5 ♘b4 22 ♖xe5, winning, J.Watson-Becerra Rivera, Linares 1999.

8...♘d7 9 ♗e3 e5 10 fxe5 c5! *(D)*

This is a major theme of the 6...♘a6 lines. White can't hold his centre together, whereas 10...dxe5 11 d5 will favour White due to his ready-made queenside play.

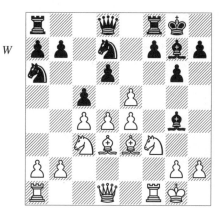

11 d5

11 dxc5 accedes to breaking up the centre, which usually indicates that Black will have few problems; e.g., 11...dxc5 12 ♗e2 ♘c7 13 h3 ♗xf3 14 gxf3!? ♗xe5, Peev-Spasov, Tsarnovo 2001. A better option for White is 11 ♘d5, with

the possible reply 11...cxd4 (11...♗xf3 12 ♖xf3 cxd4 13 ♗xd4 ♘xe5) 12 ♗xd4 ♘ac5!? 13 ♕d2. Then Black needs to take some care; for example, 13...dxe5 14 ♗e3 f5!? 15 ♗g5 and his position is under pressure.

11...♘xe5

Now White has to press on quickly or Black will remain with a powerful central outpost at e5:

12 ♗e2! *(D)*

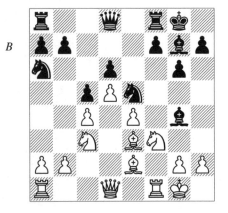

12...♗d7!?

This still maintains the e5 outpost but also preserves Black's good bishop. The accepted continuation has been 12...♘xf3+ 13 ♗xf3 ♗xf3 14 ♕xf3 ♕e7, when White followed older theory in Beim-Kindermann, Bundesliga 1999/00: 15 ♗f4 (White has to think about winning the dark squares if he's to makes any progress) 15...♘c7 16 ♕g3 ♖ad8 17 ♔h1! (getting out of the way of inconvenient checks but also preparing the knight manoeuvre that follows) 17...♗d4 18 ♖ae1 f6 *(D)*.

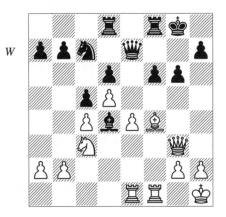

19 ♘e2!? (19 h4 might be worth playing in order to have h5 in reserve, especially if White has ♘e2-f4 in mind) 19...♗e5 20 ♘g1 (or 20 h4) 20...♗xf4 21 ♕xf4 ♘a6! (odd-looking, but the knight wants to cover or occupy e5, and the way to get there is via b8! In the meantime Black has the irritating plan of ...♘b4-c2-d4) 22 ♖f3!? (22 ♕d2 ♖de8 23 ♘f3 ♘b8 24 b3 ♘d7 25 ♕c3 ♘e5 26 ♘d2 ½-½ Parker-Gallagher, British League (4NCL) 2001/2) 22...♘b8 23 ♖a3 a6 24 ♖b3 ♕c7 25 ♕f1 ♘d7 26 ♘e2!? ♖fe8! 27 ♘f4 ♘f8 28 ♖g3 ♕f7 29 ♖f3 ♕g7 30 ♖g3 ♕f7 31 ♖f3 ½-½.

13 ♕d2 ♘c7

13...♕e7 also appears satisfactory: 14 ♗g5 ♘xf3+ 15 ♗xf3 ♗d4+ 16 ♔h1 f6 17 ♗h6 ♖fe8 18 ♘e2 ♗e5 19 ♘f4 ♘c7 and White isn't making progress. Black can contemplate ...b5 at some point.

14 ♗g5 ♕e8 15 ♖ae1 ♘xf3+!? 16 ♖xf3 ♗d4+ 17 ♗e3!? *(D)*

Probably White should keep the bishops on. 17 ♔h1 f6 18 ♗h6 ♖f7 19 ♖ef1 ♕e5 20 ♗f4 ♕e7 resembles the last note.

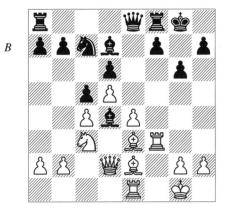

17...♗xe3+ 18 ♕xe3 ♕e5 19 ♖ef1 f6 20 ♕f2 ♔g7 21 ♔h1 a6 22 a4 ♖ab8

Black has some queenside play and the chances are roughly equal, Mercadal-Buraschi, corr. 2001.

Classical King's Indian

1 d4 ♘f6 2 c4 g6 3 ♘c3 ♗g7 4 e4 d6 5 ♘f3 *(D)*

This may be considered the start of the Classical Variation of the King's Indian Defence.

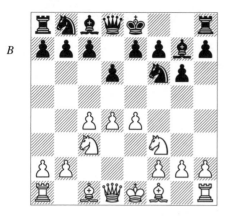

B

5...0-0 6 ♗e2

White's overwhelming favourite. As always, there are many options; for example, 6 h3 and 6 ♗g5.

6...e5 *(D)*

Also almost automatic, although 6...♘bd7 can safely introduce ...e5, as explained in the 6...e5 7 0-0 ♘bd7 line of this chapter. 6...c5 is outside the scope of the discussion, sometimes transposing to a Maroczy Bind Sicilian (7 0-0 cxd4 8 ♘xd4) or to some kind of Benoni (7 d5).

For a discussion of why exactly Black takes two moves to fianchetto his bishop and then promptly turns it into a bad bishop, see the discussion of this very subject in Volume 1, Chapter 2.

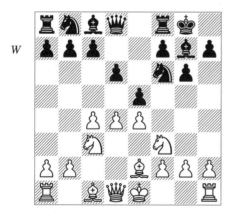

W

From the position after 6...e5, it's difficult to select some variations to talk about while ignoring others. As always, I shall try to discuss variations that are important for practical play, but even more so ones whose characteristic positions will apply to other variations in the King's Indian and openings in general. The following section is fitting that regard.

Exchange Variation

7 dxe5 dxe5

White exchanges pawns and then queens. He either hopes that his quick development will allow him to get the better game, or that the simplified position will suit his playing style. Some players use the Exchange Variation to obtain a draw, but that is a tricky business, to say the least. I repeatedly point out in this book that queenless middlegames are not endgames. That is all the more the case with so many pieces left on the board.

8 ♕xd8

Although 8 0-0 is sometimes tried, this exchange is really the point of 7 dxe5. Upon slower moves, Black can develop freely and gain time to cover the d5-square against invasion.

8...♖xd8 *(D)*

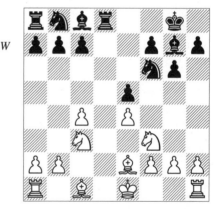

W

The Exchange Variation may appear rather dull, and even a reason to avoid playing the King's Indian Defence. But the variation embraces positional ideas that are basic to KID play. First of all, you should always keep in mind that in most chess openings, the early exchange of queens will not eliminate winning chances for either side, and in some cases may even increase them. With that in mind let's try to understand what's going on in general terms. Initially White counts upon his central space and relatively fast development (e.g., by ♗g5, ♘d5 and 0-0-0). These represent short-term advantages that might be transformed into something more permanent. But White also cedes his opponent a true outpost on d4; a knight occupying that square will generally have great influence, so much so that White will usually not be able to gain concrete advantages by 'working around' it. If Black successfully implements the move ...c6, it leaves White's knights and rooks without the d5 pivot point, whereas the d6 point isn't easily accessible to knight nor to more than temporary occupation by a rook (Black responds by ...♘e8, ...♗f8, etc.). The situation with respect to each side's bishop is also significant. White's dark-squared and Black's light-squared bishops have excellent scope – they are 'good'. But White has to deal with a very bad bishop on f1 (cut off by both the c- and e-pawns), whereas Black has blocked off his own bishop by ...e5. The second situation is not so grave in that Black strengthens his control of d4 thereby, and later the g7-bishop can be activated by a couple of different methods. A typical way to enliven things is ...♗f8 and ...♗c5 or ...♗b4 as appropriate. Even ...♗f6-d8-b6 puts the bishop on an effective diagonal. How these trade-offs play out will determine the course of the game.

As indicated, Black will attempt to post a piece on d4. Sometimes the move ...f5 can be useful but that is generally not played until the pieces are reorganized. The c5-square is also crucial: a knight occupying it hits several important points in the enemy position, and the potential for ...♘e6-d4 can cause White headaches. If Black gets a knight to c5 he will generally try to support it by ...a5. Finally, ...♖e8 (protecting the e-pawn) and ...♘d7-f8-e6 may prove feasible.

For his part White would love to achieve the moves b4 and c5 (or ♘a4 and c5), opening up the f1-a6 diagonal for the previously passive bishop and clearing c4 for pieces (a knight, for example, might travel to it by ♘d2-c4). Another set-up is with a3, b4, ♗e3 and ♘d2-b3. Once Black plays ...c6 and ...a5, his b6-square can be inviting to White's pieces. Finally, as mentioned before, White's lead in development may help him to force changes in the initial pawn-structure which, if it persists, will favour Black in the long run.

Let's start out with a game in which White succeeds in achieving his goals.

Born – Tonneman
corr. 1978

9 ♗g5

9 ♘d5 ♘xd5 10 cxd5 c6 11 ♗c4 cxd5!? 12 ♗xd5 ♘d7 13 ♗g5 ♖e8 transposes to the next game.

9...♖e8 10 0-0-0

Again, 10 ♘d5 ♘xd5 11 cxd5 c6 12 ♗c4 cxd5 can transpose, but 12...b5 13 ♗b3 c5!? is also played.

10...♘a6

10...♘c6 is an option, aiming directly for d4, with approximate equality following 11 ♘d5 (11 ♗e3 ♘d4 12 ♘xd4 exd4 13 ♗xd4 ♘xe4 with equality) 11...♘xd5 12 cxd5 ♘d4 13 ♘xd4 exd4 14 ♗d3 c6.

11 ♘e1 (D)

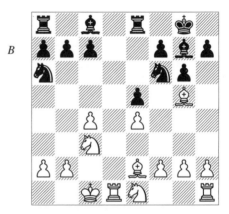

This has several points. White wants to play f3 to solidify his centre, and by playing ♘e1 he avoids ...♗g4 (when ...♗xf3 would strengthen Black's control of d4). Most importantly, he wants to bring his knight to the queenside to support expansion on that wing.

11...♘c5

11...♗e6 is another good move, simply developing.

12 f3 c6

12...♘e6 is also sensible. You can see that Black hasn't had trouble with the opening yet, but neither has White, who is slowly solidifying his position.

13 ♘c2 ♘e6!?

Reorganization by 13...a5 14 ♗e3 ♗f8 is also possible.

14 ♗e3 ♗f8 15 b4!?

The right idea: White grabs space and the c5 idea looms. It does allow an unclear tactic, so 15 ♖d2 first might have been better.

15...a5 16 a3 axb4 17 axb4 ♖d8?!

Black's first mistake. A better if messy idea was 17...♘d4!? 18 ♘xd4 ♗xb4; for example, 19 ♔c2! exd4 20 ♗xd4 ♘d7 21 ♖a1 ♖xa1 22 ♖xa1 f5!? with complications.

18 ♔b2! ♖xd1 19 ♖xd1 ♗e7 20 ♔b3

White has a small advantage because Black lacks a plan.

20...♔f8 21 ♘a4 ♘d7 22 c5 (D)

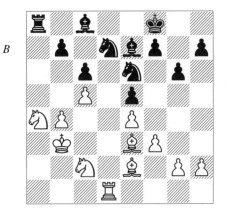

There it is. White has finally made the desired move.

22...♗d8 23 ♘a3! ♔e7 24 ♖d2 ♗c7 25 ♘c4

The opening is over and White controls the board. He went on to win the game.

Danailov – Kasparov
Dortmund jr Wch 1980

1 c4 g6 2 ♘f3 ♗g7 3 ♘c3 d6 4 d4 ♘f6 5 e4 0-0 6 ♗e2

Before continuing, let's look at a different game. It's a model for Black, with the inclusion of 6 h3 instead of 6 ♗e2. White could have played much better, but we see Black's systematic exploitation of the dark squares in ultraclear fashion. Note particularly that the rook ends up on d4; that square is not exclusively reserved for knights: 6 h3 e5 7 dxe5 dxe5 8 ♕xd8 ♖xd8 9 ♗g5 c6 10 ♗e2 ♘a6 11 0-0 ♖e8 12 ♗e3 ♗f8 13 ♘d2 ♘c5 14 ♖fd1 ♘e6 15 ♘b3 a5 16 a4 ♗b4 17 f3 ♘d7 18 ♖ac1 ♘dc5 (D).

19 ♘xc5 ♘xc5 20 ♖a1 ♗e6 21 ♗f1 ♖ed8 22 ♔f2 ♔f8 23 g3 ♘b3 24 ♖ab1 ♗c5 (still working

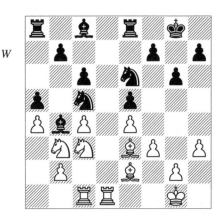

on the dark squares) 25 ♗xc5+ ♘xc5 26 h4 ♔e7 27 ♔e3 ♘b3 28 g4 ♖d4 29 ♗d3 ♗xc4 30 ♗c2 ♖ad8 0-1 Borsuk-Kaminski, Warsaw 1992.

6...e5 7 dxe5 dxe5 8 ♕xd8 ♖xd8 9 ♗g5 ♘bd7 10 ♘d5 c6 11 ♘e7+ ♔f8 12 ♘xc8 ♖dxc8 13 0-0-0 ♘c5 14 ♗xf6 ♗xf6

One of the main lessons of this game is that simplification will not solve White's underlying positional problems.

15 ♗d3 a5 16 ♖he1 (D)

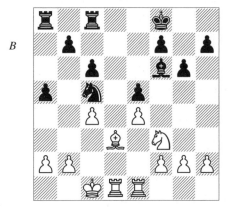

16...♖e8!

Protecting e5 and freeing the bishop on f6 to move. The future World Champion activates his last piece and makes it look easy.

17 ♗f1 ♗d8 18 g3 a4 19 ♔c2 ♗a5 20 ♖e3 ♖ad8 21 ♖xd8 ♖xd8 22 ♗h3 f6 23 ♖e2 ♔e7 24 ♗g2 ♘d3

Threatening ...♘b4+.

25 a3

On top of everything else, there goes the b3-square. But 25 b3 ♘b4+ 26 ♔b1 (26 ♔b2? a3+!

27 ♔xa3?? ♘d3 28 b4 ♗xb4+ 29 ♔b3 ♘c1+)
26...a3 27 ♔c1 ♗b6 28 ♘e1 ♗d4 wins for
Black. This time it's the bishop that uses d4!
25...♘c5 *(D)*

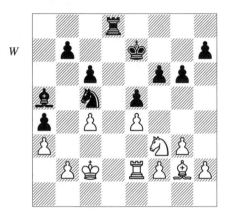

W

White's bad bishop haunts him to the very
end. We see why either ♘d5 or b4 and c5 is so
desirable for White in this variation.

**26 h4 h5 27 ♖e3 g5 28 hxg5 fxg5 29 ♖e2
♘b3 30 ♔b1 ♔f6 0-1**

Zugzwang. For example, 31 ♖e3 ♖d1+ 32
♔c2 ♖c1+ 33 ♔d3 ♘c5+ 34 ♔e2 g4 and the
knight can't move because of mate on e1.

The Main-Line King's Indian

**1 d4 ♘f6 2 c4 g6 3 ♘c3 ♗g7 4 e4 d6 5 ♘f3 0-0
6 ♗e2 e5 7 0-0**

White normally chooses not to enter into the
Exchange Variation, which can be understood
from the examples in the last section. 7 0-0 is
the most flexible move, not committing to any
central pawn-structure.

Strongpoint Variation

7...♘bd7 *(D)*

This solid knight development was the primary way of playing for several decades after
the King's Indian Defence first gained attention
in the 1920s. During that time 7...♘bd7 naturally generated many new ideas and wonderful
games, but now has been overtaken by 7...♘c6
and 7...♘a6. Nevertheless, specialists still find
ways to benefit from it, sometimes moving beyond minor improvements to new methods of
play. One appealing feature of 7...♘bd7 is that

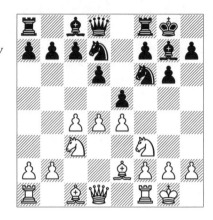

W

it is a central move and thus stays in contact with
c5, e5 and f6, all key King's Indian squares.
Compare 7...♘a6, which only controls c5; or
7...♘c6 8 d5 ♘e7, a two-move continuation
based largely upon transfer to the kingside. Situ-
ated on d7, Black's knight can be used to support
e5 as a strongpoint, or to play ...♘e5 or ...♘c5
if Black chooses to play ...exd4 at some point.

The disadvantages of 7...♘bd7 relate primarily to its failure to challenge White's space
advantage and the fact that it blocks off Black's
bishop on c8. This latter circumstance (which
you'll note does not apply to 7...♘a6 or 7...♘c6)
means that achieving the move ...f5 may be
problematic, and that White can keep the centre
fluid without worrying as much about immediate attacks on the kingside. Thus Black is unlikely to dominate one side of the board or the
other, although he has access to and plays on
both wings. Another drawback has to do with a
concrete feature of the King's Indian, that c7 is
left unprotected, so that Black hasn't as much
leeway to move his queen as he does after
7...♘a6.

I haven't mentioned the greatest virtue of
7...♘bd7 from our point of view: the play
stemming from this move includes a majority
of themes and concepts that characterize the
entire Classical King's Indian! After 7...♘bd7
we see properties of the KID that don't appear
after 7...♘c6 8 d5 ♘e7 (the main line of most
of this chapter). For example, lines in which
Black plays ...♘c5 or ...exd4, and situations in
which White plays dxe5 in a more effective
way than in the Exchange Variation. For those
reasons we'll delve into some details of three
variations:

A: 8 ♗e3;
B: 8 ♖e1;
C: 8 d5.

A)

8 ♗e3 *(D)*

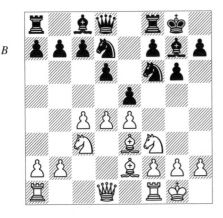

This is the most common and highly-regarded move, of which I'll give two examples:

Donaldson – Browne
Reno 1992

8...♘g4

a) 8...a5?! was played for some time with considerable success. In fact, a great blow to 7...♘bd7 adherents was delivered when White found the right plan: 9 dxe5! dxe5 10 ♕c2 (10 c5! is another way to implement White's strategy; the tactical point is that Black can't win White's c-pawn after 10...♘g4 11 ♗g5 f6 due to 12 ♕d5+ ♔h8 13 ♗d2!? c6 14 ♕d6) 10...♘g4 11 ♗d2! c6 (11...f5? 12 h3 ♘h6 13 ♗g5!) 12 ♘a4! *(D)*.

Here is a great example of what can happen in any King's Indian if the centre is fluid, as opposed to the 7...♘c6 8 d5 lines when a locked structure arises. If White can play dxe5 followed by a pawn advance to c5, it can outweigh Black's potential occupation of d4 and f4. The combination of ♘a4 and ♘d2-c4 with an open d-file can be deadly, because knights can end up on d6 and/or b6, whereas even the nominally 'bad' bishop on e2 can get into the action on c4. It should be said that with a slightly different placement of Black's pieces the position would be unclear; for example, if Black's knight were

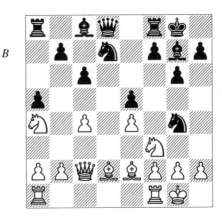

on h5 or f4 instead of g4, or if ...♖e8 had already made room for ...♘f8-e6-d4 – you might want to compare the Exchange Variation above. Which positions to allow or reject is a matter of judgement and specifics. In the example we follow White goes about a similar reorganization, whereas Black simply doesn't have the piece disposition to counter White's plans: 12...h6 (12...f5? is even worse: 13 ♘g5! ♘df6 14 h3 ♘h6 15 c5) 13 h3 ♘gf6 14 ♗e3 ♘h5 15 ♖fd1 ♕e7 16 g3! (keeping Black's knight out of f4) 16...♖e8 17 ♔h2 ♕e6?! 18 ♘g1! ♘hf6 19 ♖d2 ♗f8 20 c5! ♕e7 21 ♖ad1 ♖b8 22 ♘f3 ♗g7 23 ♗c4 ♘f8 24 ♘b6 ♘8d7 25 ♗b3! ♘xb6 26 cxb6, Uhlmann-Knaak, Leipzig 1980. With control of c5 and the d-file, White has things well in hand.

b) 8...c6 used to be considered the main line; however, 9 d5 forces a decision about how to defend the d-pawn. Then the natural move 9...♘g4 fails tactically to 10 ♗g5 f6 11 dxc6! ♘c5 (11...fxg5 12 cxd7) 12 cxb7 ♗xb7 13 ♗c1, winning a pawn because 13...♘xe4?? 14 ♘xe4 ♗xe4 15 ♘d2 costs Black a piece. And 9...c5 *(D)* establishes the kind of structure that generally favours White, particularly since Black took two moves to get his pawn there.

This is a pawn-chain situation, and the two breaks are b4 and f4. The latter is less appealing because after ...exf4 it opens up the long diagonal for Black's bishop. Play can proceed 10 ♘e1 (the standard idea to put the knight on d3 and play for b4 to break down Black's pawn-structure) 10...♘e8 (there's no plan except ...f5) and now White can flout the older rules by playing 11 g4!? in order to discourage ...f5; e.g., 11...f5 12 exf5 gxf5 13 gxf5 ♖xf5 14

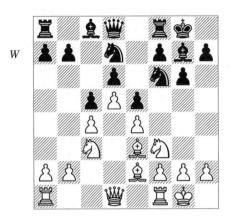

W

♗g4 ♖f8 15 ♗e6+ ♔h8 16 ♘f3 and ♘g5. Then Black comes under attack and suffers because of White's outposts. He also stands worse positionally because White has penetrated to Black's interior weakness on e6.

9 ♗g5 f6 10 ♗d2 c6 11 d5

Normally White should play this after Black plays ...c6. It forces Black to commit and eliminates any dynamism that might result from ...exd4 followed ...d5. After d5, White is ready to expand upon the queenside.

11...♕e7 12 b4! ♔h8

12...♘h6 13 dxc6 bxc6 14 b5 ♗b7 15 bxc6 ♗xc6 16 ♘d5 is similar.

13 dxc6! bxc6 14 b5 *(D)*

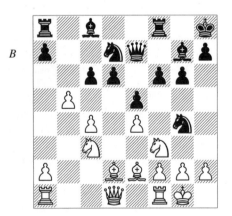

B

This is almost a refutation of Black's play, and applies both here and in some other ...c6 lines. White gains the d5 outpost by force. The moral is that once White plays d5, Black should be ready to play either ...c5 or ...cxd5.

14...♗b7 15 bxc6 ♗xc6 16 ♘d5 ♗xd5 17 cxd5 ♘c5 18 ♘e1 ♘h6 19 f3

White has the bishop-pair, space and open lines on the queenside. The game flows surprisingly smoothly hereafter.

19...♘f7 20 ♘d3 ♘xd3 21 ♗xd3 ♗h6

As good as anything. At least Black gets rid of a problem piece. But for one thing his knight won't be able to get back in time to defend the queenside.

22 ♗xh6 ♘xh6 23 ♕d2 g5 24 ♖ac1 f5 25 ♖c6! f4 26 h3

See how difficult it is for Black to play the standard kingside assault ...g5-g4 when he has no light-squared bishop?

26...♘g8 27 ♖fc1 ♖fd8 28 ♗a6! *(D)*

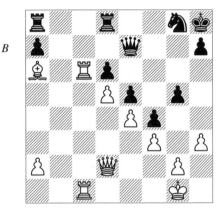

B

Placing the bishop here not only stops any ...♖c8 forever but threatens ♗c8-e6, which can't be stopped for long.

28...♕f8 29 ♖c7 ♘f6 30 ♕c2 ♘h5

Even worse is 30...♘d7 31 ♗c8 ♘c5 32 ♗f5.

31 ♗c8 ♘g3 32 ♗e6 ♖db8 33 ♖f7 ♕h6 34 ♔h2 ♖f8 35 ♖d7 g4!? 36 ♗xg4 ♕g6 37 ♕c6?

Easier was 37 ♕c7 with the idea 37...h5 38 ♖xd6 ♕g5 39 ♖cc6.

37...♖ad8 38 ♖e7 ♖g8 39 ♖e6 ♕g5 40 ♖xd6 ♖xd6 41 ♕xd6 h5 42 h4! ♕xh4+ 43 ♗h3 ♕g5 44 ♖c6

Donaldson avoids the last trick: 44 ♖c7? ♘xe4 45 fxe4 ♕g3+.

44...♔h7 45 ♕e6 ♘f1+ 46 ♔g1 ♘e3 47 ♖c7+ ♔h8 48 ♕e7 ♕xe7 49 ♖xe7 ♖b8 50 d6 ♖b1+ 51 ♔f2 ♖b2+ 52 ♔e1 ♖b1+ 53 ♔e2 ♖b2+ 54 ♔d3 1-0

A graceful and well-executed win. It shows what the possession of space and creation of enemy weaknesses can do for you.

Krush – Bologan
Edmonton 2005

8...♖e8!?

As explained above, this rook move (threatening ...exd4) has been considered inferior because after 9 d5, Black's rook will have to return to f8 to support the thematic ...f5. But Black is working with other ideas:

9 d5

9...exd4 was threatened with an attack on the e4-pawn. Instead, 9 ♕c2 ♘g4 10 ♗g5 f6 11 ♗d2?! exd4 12 ♘xd4 ♘c5 13 h3?! f5! (a tactical theme to remember) 14 hxg4 ♗xd4 15 gxf5 gxf5 16 exf5 ♕h4 is good for Black.

9...♘h5!?

This is a relatively recent idea (at least in its present form). It's worth noting that ...♘h5 is normally an inferior move if White can prevent ...♘f4 by the move g3, as he does here:

10 g3 ♗f8! *(D)*

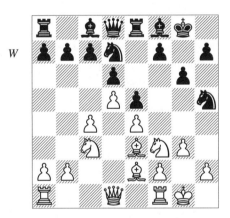

This is the beginning of Black's reorganization: he directs another piece to prevent White's c5 advance, and he makes room on g7 for a knight.

11 ♘e1 ♘g7

Normally one would not expect to fianchetto a knight, but it supports the attacking move ...f5 and makes it possible to play ...h5-h4. Black's pieces are achieving a weird sort of coordination!

12 ♘d3

12 b4 is a reasonably good move, although it didn't turn out well in Kutsin-Komliakov, Nikolaev 1995: 12...♗e7 13 ♘d3 f5 14 ♕d2 ♘f6 15 f3 h5 16 ♖ac1?! h4! 17 c5 ♘gh5 18 ♔g2 ♖f8 19 cxd6 cxd6 20 exf5 gxf5 21 gxh4 f4 22 ♗g1 ♖f7 23 ♘f2 ♖g7+ 24 ♔h1 ♗f8 25 ♕e1 ♘g3+! with a winning attack.

12...f5 13 f3 *(D)*

13 b4 fxe4 14 ♘xe4 ♘f5 is fine for Black, whose knight will probably end up on d4 once the bishop on e3 moves.

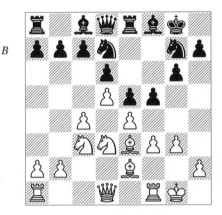

13...a5!?

A recent arrangement of pieces, not necessarily superior to the old one. But it's intriguing because it boldly fights for the queenside, where Black is assumed to be inferior. That is in fact a common theme in the modern King's Indian. The old move was 13...♗e7, when a wonderful example was 14 b4 (14 ♕d2 ♘f6 15 c5 fxe4 16 fxe4 ♘g4 with equality) 14...♖f8 15 c5 ♘f6 (another idea is 15...♗g5!? 16 ♗f2 h5 17 ♕b3 ♘f6 18 cxd6 cxd6 with the idea ...h4) 16 ♖c1! h5 17 ♘f2! (an extremely original manoeuvre that depends upon material sacrifice) 17...h4!? (17...a5) 18 g4!! (Black's attack via ...hxg3, ...♘h5, etc., is permanently stopped, at a cost of two pawns) 18...f4 19 ♗d2 dxc5 20 ♘d3! cxb4 21 ♘b5, Onishchuk-Florean, USA Ch (San Diego) 2006. White will recover the b-pawn with a powerful queenside attack; he went on to win.

14 a3 *(D)*

14...♘c5!?

This is a surprising scheme for Black, to say the least. Now it will take some time for White to organize a successful queenside attack.

15 ♕c2 ♘h5 16 ♘xc5 f4!?

Bologan is simply going for it in this game, without regard to safety or positional niceties. Perhaps this move isn't objectively best.

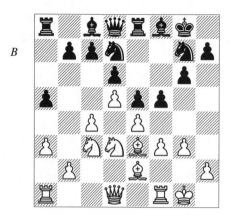

17 ♘e6!

Not 17 ♘xb7 because of 17...♕g5.

17...♗xe6 18 dxe6 fxe3 19 ♕d3?

After this Krush has a few problems. At this point 19 f4! was the right move because f5 is threatened and 19...exf4 20 gxf4 ♖xe6 21 ♗g4 prevents any surprise attacks.

19...♘g7 20 ♕xe3 ♘xe6

As so often in the King's Indian, Black has an outpost on d4 to play with; next he denies d5 to White's pieces:

21 ♔h1 c6! 22 ♖ad1 ♕c7 23 ♖d3 ♗e7 *(D)*

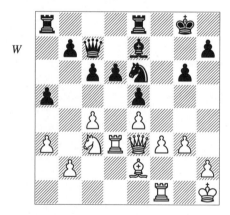

24 h4?

Again 24 f4 was best. From here on out it proves difficult for White to find good moves.

24...♖f8 25 ♖fd1 ♖f7 26 ♗f1 ♖af8 27 ♘e2?

White covers d4, but the cure is worse than the disease:

27...♘c5 28 ♖c3 ♕b6 29 b3 ♖xf3 30 ♕xf3 ♖xf3 31 ♖xf3 ♘xe4 32 ♔g2 ♘f6 33 ♘c1 e4 34 ♖f4 ♕e3 35 ♗e2 d5 36 cxd5 cxd5 37 ♖ff1 ♗d6 38 ♖xf6 ♕xg3+ 39 ♔f1 ♕h3+ 0-1

B)

8 ♖e1 *(D)*

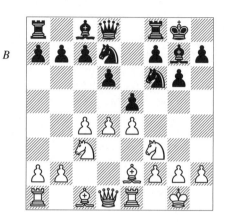

By this move White develops and prepares to defend the e-pawn so that ...exd4 won't be effective. This is very solid and maintains the tension; on the slightly negative side, White hasn't a positive plan yet and he does weaken f2 in some lines.

8...c6

Black has some alternatives, but this is a flexible move that covers d5 and allows Black's queen to move if needed.

Sakaev – Svidler
St Petersburg Ch 1997

9 ♗f1 *(D)*

9 ♖b1 is also popular: 9...a5 10 ♗f1 ♖e8 (Black tries to gain a tempo for ...exd4 by strengthening its effect down the e-file) 11 d5 (this is the standard remedy to ...♖e8 in almost any setting). Lerner-Kovalevskaya, Moscow 2002 continued 11...♘c5 12 b3 ♗d7 13 ♘d2. Then 13...♗h6 worked out reasonably well, but trading the dark-squared bishop can be dicey. A good alternative would be 13...♘h5!; for example, 14 dxc6 (14 g3 cxd5 15 cxd5 f5) 14...♗xc6 (or 14...bxc6 with equality) 15 ♘f3 ♘f4 16 g3 ♘fe6! 17 ♘d5 ♘d4 18 ♗b2 ♘ce6 19 ♗g2 ♘xf3+ 20 ♕xf3 ♘d4 21 ♕d3 a4 22 b4 ♗xd5 23 cxd5 ♕b6 is equal.

9...exd4

Opening the board to activate Black's pieces. This is one of Black's approaches in many KID variations. A 'strongpoint' approach is 9...♕e7 10 d5 a5 11 a3 ♘c5 12 b3 ♘e8 13 ♗b2 f5,

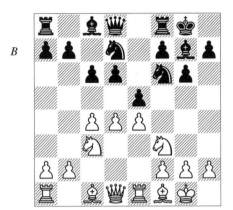

B

Mikhalevski-Sutovsky, Tel Aviv 1994. The tactical 9...♘g4!? 10 h3 exd4 11 ♘xd4 ♕b6! 12 hxg4! ♕xd4 is another main line whose assessment swings between equal and slightly better for White. Black has some initiative but his d-pawn is weak. In this line 12...♗xd4 can be answered by 13 ♗e3! ♗xe3 14 ♖xe3 with the advantage, because 14...♕xb2?? 15 ♖b1 ♕a3 16 ♘a4 ♕xa2 17 ♖b2 traps the queen.

10 ♘xd4 ♘g4 11 ♕xg4 ♗xd4 12 ♕d1 ♕f6 13 ♗e3 ♗xe3 14 ♖xe3 ♘e5 *(D)*

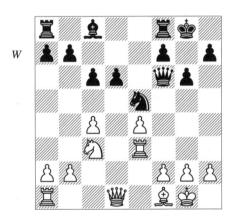

W

These last moves are well-known and logical. Now Black has to make up for his weak d-pawn by posting his pieces more actively than his opponent's.

15 ♕d2 h5!?

Possibly Black should just get his bishop out by 15...♗e6 to connect rooks.

16 ♖d1 ♖d8 17 b3 h4

Black is grabbing space, which is eminently logical. As it turns out, the march of the h-pawn also creates weaknesses.

18 ♗e2!

The 'bad' piece peeks out!

18...♗e6 19 g3! *(D)*

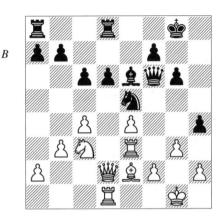

B

Since 19...hxg3 is answered by 20 ♖xg3!, the move f4 looms. Svidler tries to become active:

19...♘g4 20 ♗xg4! ♗xg4 21 f3 ♗e6 22 g4!

A safe space advantage on the kingside for White is not something Black wants in the KID!

22...♖d7 23 ♖d3 ♖ad8 24 ♕h6 a6 25 g5 *(D)*

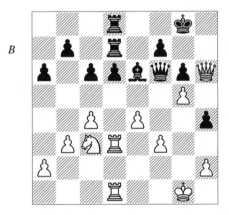

B

25...♕f4

This cedes a pawn; Sakaev analyses 25...♕h8 26 ♕xh8+ ♔xh8 27 a4 a5 28 ♘e2 ♔g7 29 ♘f4 ♔f8 30 ♘g2, when the h-pawn will fall.

26 ♘e2 ♕e5 27 ♕xh4 d5 28 ♕f4 ♕xf4 29 ♘xf4 dxe4 30 ♖xd7 ♗xd7 31 fxe4 ♔f8 32 e5 ♔e7 33 e6! 1-0

The forced continuation would be 33...♗xe6 34 ♖xd8 ♔xd8 35 ♘xe6+ fxe6 36 c5 and White wins the ending. Along with his better pawn-structure, White can create an outside passed pawn by h4-h5 if he needs to. This game provides an example of the fight between central control and piece activity.

C)

8 d5 *(D)*

The important position that this leads to can arise from two other variations:

a) The Petrosian System: 1 d4 ♘f6 2 c4 g6 3 ♘c3 ♗g7 4 e4 d6 5 ♘f3 0-0 6 ♗e2 e5 7 d5 ♘bd7 8 0-0.

b) The Glek Variation of the Main Line: 1 d4 ♘f6 2 c4 g6 3 ♘c3 ♗g7 4 e4 d6 5 ♘f3 0-0 6 ♗e2 e5 7 0-0 ♘a6 8 d5 (assuming Black plays ...♘c5 next).

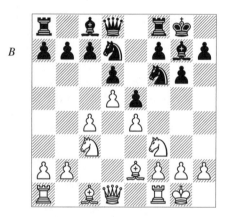

Why is this obvious move relatively rare? The first-level answer is that it's somewhat awkward for White to answer the following direct attack on the e4-pawn:

8...♘c5 9 ♕c2

White only has two reasonable ways to protect his pawn, neither without drawbacks. 9 ♘d2 blocks the development of the queen's bishop. It is generally answered by 9...a5 (securing Black's knight from being kicked out by b4), when for the moment neither of White's knights can move, whereas Black can develop and begin to organize for his standard move ...f5. That's enough to get a feel for what's going on, but let's take this a step further. If White tries 10 ♖b1 ♗d7 11 a3?! (ready to play b4), Black answers with 11...a4! *(D)*. This is a familiar positional trick described by the phrase 'one pawn holding up two' (referring to the pawns on a4, a3 and b2).

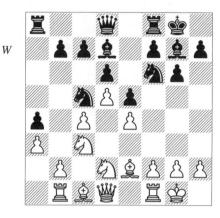

The idea of 'one pawn holding up two' is that White cannot play b3 or b4 without giving himself an isolated a-pawn on an open file, and in particular one that can be easily blockaded because the rook, knight, and a bishop on d7 all control a4 (for the moment, b3 or b4 would be especially awkwardly met by ...axb3, but barring that peculiarity the situation in general is still very good for Black). This stratagem is obvious to the advanced player, but it may not be so to the inexperienced player, who should add it to his stock of standard patterns.

Moving back, what if (after 9 ♘d2 a5), White plays 10 ♕c2? Then play can follow along the lines of our main move; e.g., 10...♘e8, and we'll see that Black is doing fine. He also has the positionally double-edged move 10...♗h6!? *(D)*, to get rid of his 'bad' bishop.

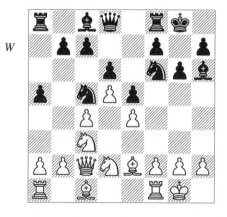

As is often the case when exchanging off a g7-bishop, Black must take care that the squares around his king don't become too weakened. On the other hand the c1-bishop is quite a valuable piece and nice to get rid of. A couple of games have continued 11 ♘b3 ♗xc1 12 ♖axc1 ♘fd7 13 ♘xc5 ♘xc5, and now White should play something like 14 ♕d2, ready to answer 14...f5?! (not the best) with 15 exf5 gxf5 16 f4. Then the disadvantage of ...♗h6 is shown: it can no longer command the long diagonal by playing ...e4 or ...exf4. The above is a rather stylized explanation, but true in essence.

9...a5

Securing the knight on c5. Now White plays the most logical continuation.

10 ♗e3 *(D)*

Watch out for another typical trick that comes up in more than one variation: 10 ♖b1? ♘fxe4! 11 ♘xe4 ♘xe4 12 ♕xe4 ♗f5 and ....♗xb1.

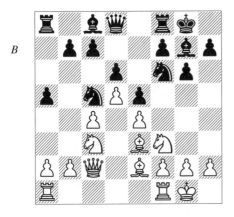

10...♘g4

This stock King's Indian manoeuvre has been the most popular choice here. 10...♘e8!? (preparing ...f5) also leads to particularly informative lines. 11 ♘d2 f5 12 f3 gives White a near-ideal minor-piece configuration. His pieces retain maximum flexibility and the knights both cover the critical e4-square. In spite of those advantages, Black has scored well in practice after the usual pawn-storm attack 12...f4 13 ♗f2 g5; e.g., 14 b3 (or 14 a3!, to speed up the attack even further, when 14...a4!? 15 ♗xc5 dxc5 16 ♘xa4 ♕e7 provides some compensation for the pawn), and now:

a) 14...♗d7 15 a3 ♖f7 16 ♖ab1 ♗f8 17 b4 axb4 18 axb4 ♘a6 19 c5?! (this looks right, but ends up bringing one more black piece to the attack; regardless of the objective assessment, defending against a kingside attack over the board can be a thankless task) 19...dxc5 20

♗xa6 ♖xa6 21 bxc5 g4!? 22 ♖xb7 ♖g6 23 fxg4 (23 c6 gxf3 24 cxd7? ♖xg2+ 25 ♔h1 ♕xd7 and wins) 23...♗xg4 24 ♔h1 ♕g5 25 ♖g1 ♖fg7 26 ♖bb1? ♕h5 27 ♘f1 ♗f3 0-1 Tillmann-Karl, Berne 1998.

b) A good illustration of White's strategy would be 14...♘f6 15 a3 h5 16 b4 axb4 17 axb4 ♖xa1 18 ♖xa1 ♘a6 19 c5! *(D)*.

The idea is 19...♘xb4 20 ♕b1 dxc5 (20...♘a6 21 c6!) 21 ♗xc5. Otherwise, White's twin ideas are c6 and ♘c4.

Compare this piece configuration with that in the lines that follow. There White gets either a knight on d2 or a bishop on e3, but not both.

11 ♗g5

Better than 11 ♗d2 f5 12 exf5? ♗xf5 13 ♕d1 e4!. White mustn't let the g7-bishop get loose.

11...f6 *(D)*

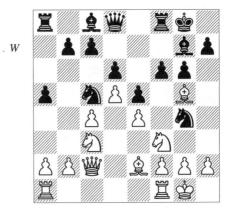

Now we get an instructive split into moves that you'll see in the many KID variations with this sequence (that is, ...♘g4 followed by ♗g5 and ...f6):

Nor – Peter
Budapest 1997

12 ♗h4 g5 13 ♗g3 f5 *(D)*

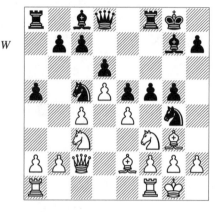

W

14 ♘d2!?

14 exf5 ♗xf5 15 ♕d2 h6 16 h3 ♘f6 is equal. Black's pawn-structure isn't optimal but he controls the important e4-square.

14...f4 15 ♗xg4 ♗xg4 16 f3 ♗d7!? 17 ♗f2 h5 18 a3 g4 19 b4 ♘a6

The position is dynamically balanced. White has to be careful not to grab meaningless material on the queenside while he's getting mated on the other wing.

Costas Varela – J. Ivanov
Marin 2001

12 ♗c1 f5 13 ♗g5 ♗f6! 14 ♗xf6 ♘xf6 *(D)*

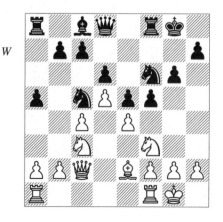

W

Breaking up White's centre. The next six or seven moves are almost forced from a positional point of view.

15 ♘d2 fxe4 16 ♘dxe4 ♘fxe4 17 ♘xe4 ♗f5 18 ♗d3 ♗xe4 19 ♗xe4 ♕g5 20 ♖ae1 ♖f4 21 ♖e3 ♖af8 22 ♖g3 ♖g4 23 ♖xg4 ♕xg4 24 f3 ♕g5 25 ♕e2

White stands a little passively but should be OK.

Most of what is shown in this last section applies in one form or another to other systems in which White plays d5. The specifics of how both players implement their ideas determine who stands better. Nevertheless, you can see why 8 d5 is not a terribly popular move.

The Classical Main Line with 7...♘c6

1 d4 ♘f6 2 c4 g6 3 ♘c3 ♗g7 4 e4 d6 5 ♘f3 0-0 6 ♗e2 e5 7 0-0 ♘c6 *(D)*

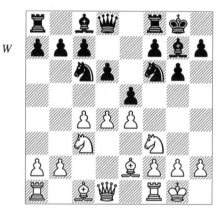

W

With this move, by contrast with 7...♘bd7, Black forces the pace. He threatens 8...exd4 9 ♘xd4 ♘xe4!, so White has to respond directly.

8 d5

White usually makes this choice without much thought. He has other moves such as 8 dxe5 and 8 ♗e3, when a standard sequence is 8...♘g4 9 ♗g5 f6 10 ♗c1 f5!? normally leading to a number of central exchanges in the midst of unclear complications. Nevertheless, moves other than 8 d5 constitute a very small percentage of all master games played.

8...♘e7 *(D)*

The knight moves to support a kingside attack. 8...♘b8 loses too many tempi.

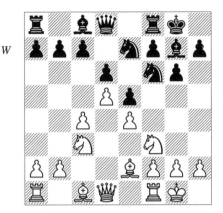

W

This position, introducing what is often called the Mar del Plata Variation, is the most popular one in the King's Indian Defence, and indeed one of the best-known in chess practice. I shall examine this variation in greater depth than it would normally merit because only a close investigation can give us an insight into how delicately balanced the game of chess can be. The persistence of dynamic equality in variations with frenetic activity on both wings borders on the miraculous. Indeed, variations stemming from 8...♘e7 have survived more than 50 years of intense scrutiny by the world's strongest professionals (and computers), only to remain mysteriously resistant to solution. Players of all ages are taught this variation because it exemplifies the pawn-chain as well as the flank attacks that are designed to break it up.

From the diagram, the lines that best illustrate the traditional strategies arise from 9 ♘e1 and 9 ♘d2. In both cases White is not only initiating a reorganization of forces but anticipating Black's plan of moving his knight and playing ...f5 in order to claim some territory. By moving his knight from f3, White does two things. First, by unmasking the e2-bishop, he prevents what is in general the most irritating knight move by Black, namely ...♘h5; once that is played, the knight often goes to f4 and hovers uncomfortably close to White's king. After 9 ♘e1 or 9 ♘d2, Black has to shelve ...♘h5 ideas for the time being. Black will have to be content with the move ...♘d7 or ...♘e8 if he wishes to make way for ...f5. Once Black's knight retreats,

White is able to meet ...f5 by bolstering his centre with f3, though he often avoids this until ...fxe4 is a real threat. The reason is that f3 can clarify Black's plans, and encourage ...f5, ...g4, etc.

In a majority of games White will get a pawn to c5. Then he will:

a) pile up pressure on the d6-pawn, perhaps by ♘c4, ♗a3 and ♘b5;

b) infiltrate down the c-file by means of some combination of doubling or tripling on it with his rooks and queen;

c) if necessary, advance his a-pawn to further enhance his queenside assault and in particular his threat to occupy the a7-square.

Black on the other hand will get his pawns to f4 and g4 (sometimes supported by ...h5), in order to:

a) play ...g3 and dare White to find an answer that avoids his sacrificial onslaught;

b) play ...gxf3 and open the g-file for a direct assault.

Notice that in most Mar del Plata games, Black runs right past the base of the pawn-chain with the move ...g3, putting no pressure whatsoever on it! So much for traditional pawn-chain theory, which would suggest ...h4-h3 instead.

It is often said that Black gets the better of this deal because his object of attack is the king, which no one can afford to lose, whereas if White captures a few queenside pawns and queenside squares, that's not immediately fatal. Indeed, Black's attack can succeed precisely because of the extra few tempi that he can use to punish White's king while his queenside and centre are collapsing. But the compensating factor for White is that his attack tends to proceed just a bit faster than Black's while his defensive walls are harder to breach. This not-so-delicate balance creates beautiful games on a regular basis.

After 8...♘e7, White can also forego 9 ♘e1 or 9 ♘d2 and permit Black to play ...♘h5 and ...f5. In those lines White will often end up playing on the queenside *and* kingside. The most important case of this arises when White plays 9 b4, the so-called 'Bayonet Variation'. It is very popular and also has a massive body of theory related to it. I have given it a brief treatment at the end of the chapter. The themes associated with 9 b4 are so variegated and tempo-dependent that only a thorough examination would impart to the reader genuine understanding and competence. Therefore I have concentrated upon two systems that feature pawn-chain themes in a wide variety of contexts. Such lengthy pawn-chains don't consistently appear in most chess openings, and certainly not with such clarity of purpose.

9 ♘e1

9 ♘e1 *(D)*

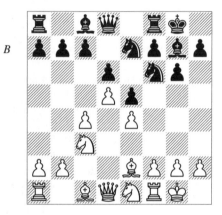

9 ♘e1 is a multipurpose move that has traditionally been White's most popular choice. On a fundamental level, it frees the f-pawn to go to f3 for defence (or to f4, but that move has become rare). Apart from the functions described above that apply to both 9 ♘e1 and 9 ♘d2, the retreat to e1 has its own virtues. It keeps a diagonal clear for White's bishop on c1. This turns out to be no small matter, since the move ♗e3 is the key to the favourite modern variation that 9 ♘e1 leads into. In addition, after the knight moves to d3 it supports the key pawn-break c5, attacking Black's pawn-chain. A major difference between this and 9 ♘d2 is that White's knight on d3 can swing back to f2 for defensive purposes, i.e., to discourage Black's advance ...g5-g4. In combination with the move h3 (not always desirable because of the hole left on g3), White could actually have five defenders of g4 (queen, bishop, knight, and two pawns), with the knight being particularly important because capturing and leaving a piece on g4 is normally much better defensively than having to leave a

pawn on that square. Finally, the knight will sometimes go to g2, in cases where White tries to stake out territory by g4; that plan is useful to be aware of but is not one that White implements much these days.

There's always a drawback to any such move, and this time it has to do with the forward reach of White's knight in the two situations. Even if it has successfully supported the c5 pawn advance from its post on d3, White's knight is too far away Black's queenside and centre to put pressure on the d6-pawn, much less give weight to a further advance of White's queenside pawns. And of course from f2 it will do nothing in those respects.

9...♘d7

There used to be more discussion about the merits of this retreat. Some books (and conventional wisdom?) dismiss the alternative 9...♘e8 *(D)* on the grounds that it does nothing versus White's advance c5; others that by not covering the e5-square it encourages White's f4 advance.

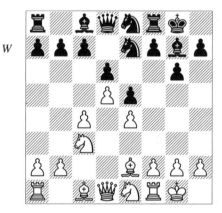

But in theory there isn't anything wrong with 10 f4 exf4 11 ♗xf4 h6! with ideas of ...g5. Then 12 ♘c2 f5 13 exf5 g5 followed by ...♘xf5 is a standard idea, with approximate equality. Black may want more, of course, but presumably White won't be thrilled with such a result. The similar 10 ♘d3 f5 11 f4 exf4 12 ♗xf4 (12 ♘xf4 c6!?) 12...fxe4 and ...♘f5 is not considered bad for Black either.

When assessing 9...♘e8, issues connected to White's move c5 are much more interesting. In several other lines of the Mar del Plata we see the knight go from d7 to f6 (to provoke White to play f3) and then backwards to e8(!) to defend Black's d6- and c7-squares, the latter being a common intrusion square for a rook, knight or queen. This is particularly the case when Black is defending against the ♘d2-c4 strategy examined in the next section, but also at a later stage of the main lines with ♘e1. Moreover, while there are some subtleties to consider in this massively complicated situation, it turns out that Black's defence in the older lines featuring ♘d3 (with c5) and ♘d2 (with c5 and ♘c4) don't suffer with a knight on e8.

So what's the point of foregoing the immediate 9...♘e8 in favour of 9...♘d7? In my opinion, it's the fact that White's 'newer' strategy with an early a4 and attack on the a-pawn seems to gain in strength, since both the move ...b6 and the c6-square are more important in those lines. You can understand this by examining, for example, 9...♘e8 10 ♗e3 f5 11 f3 f4 12 ♗f2 g5 13 a4, when 13...a5 (13...♘g6 14 ♘b5) 14 c5 ♘g6 15 ♘b5 would improve for White upon the main ...♘d7 lines that follow below. All this may sound picky, but anyone who is going to go into these heavily theoretical pawn-storm variations should know something about such details. Whether the above is true is another matter! I'm not sure that the distinction between knight retreats has ever been truly investigated in depth, and wouldn't be surprising if 9...♘e8 were revived once the details were worked out. At any rate, here's an entertaining game with various pawn-storm themes in which it was effective for a unique reason:

Gelfand – Kantsler
Israel 2001

9 ♘e1 ♘e8 10 ♗e3 f5 11 f3 f4 12 ♗f2

You will also see this ♗e3-f2 manoeuvre in the next section, but with Black's knight on d7 rather than e8.

12...h5 13 c5

13 a4!? would be the test that corresponds to my speculation above, because Black wouldn't have the handy defensive idea 13...a5 14 c5 ♘xc5 which is available if the knight is on d7, but illegal here. OK, we can skip over that thought and have fun with the game.

13...g5 14 a4 ♘g6 15 a5 ♖f7 16 cxd6 ♘xd6! *(D)*

W
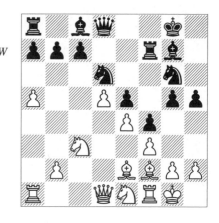

17 ♘d3 ♗f6 18 ♘c5 ♘f8

Covering e6.

19 ♘b5 ♖g7 20 a6 bxa6! 21 ♘xa6 g4!

The attack always takes priority over material in this variation.

22 ♘xa7 *(D)*

B
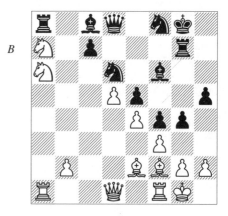

22...g3

This idea will become familiar to you if it isn't already. Unless White plays h3 and allows some kind of ...♗xh3 sacrifice, Black's knights will gain squares close to White's king.

23 ♗c5

Upon 23 hxg3 fxg3 24 ♗c5 ♗g5! 25 ♘xc8 ♗f4! 26 ♖e1 ♕h4!, Black's attack will at the very least give him the better game.

23...♗h3!! *(D)*

This is yet another attacking theme to remember. Since White wants to capture on c8 and play h3 to thwart the attack, Black simply occupies that square. The less glamorous 23...♗d7 and 23...gxh2+ 24 ♔h1 ♗h4!? are also options, both unclear.

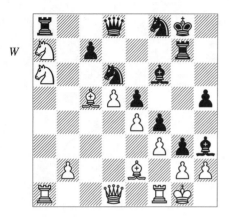

24 gxh3?

Underestimating the attack. Best was 24 hxg3 ♖xg3 (24...♗xg2 25 ♘c6!? ♕d7 26 ♔xg2 ♖xg3+ 27 ♔f2 ♗h4 28 ♗d3! and unbelievably White escapes; a little hard to see, that one!) 25 ♖f2 and it's still unclear.

24...♕d7 25 ♗d3 ♕xh3 26 ♕e2 ♘g6

Unfortunately for White, this knight always seems to get to f4 or h4.

27 ♕g2

27 ♘b5 ♘h4 28 ♘bxc7 ♘g2!! 29 hxg3 ♖xg3 30 ♔f2 ♗h4 and this time there's no escape.

27...♕d7! 28 ♘xc7 ♘h4 29 ♕e2 ♕h3! *(D)*

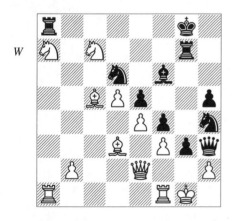

Black has the same idea two moves later! But what can White do?

30 ♘e6 ♘g2!! 31 ♖fc1 ♕xh2+ 32 ♔f1 ♕h1+ 33 ♗g1 ♘h4

Now the threat is 34...♘xf3 35 ♕g2 ♘h2+.

34 ♘xg7

34 ♖c2 ♖gxa7! 35 ♖xa7 ♖xa7 opens that second front we always look for!

34...♘xf3 0-1

Having learned something, we'll return to the main line 9...♘d7 *(D)*.

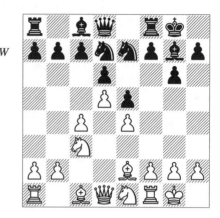

At this point our focus will be on the old main line 10 ♘d3, after which we'll return to the 'newer' one 10 ♗e3. Because 10 a4!? belongs with the a4 themes in the next section, we'll talk about it there.

Old Main Line

10 ♘d3 f5 11 ♗d2

This very old variation still has some life in it.

11...♘f6 12 f3 f4 13 c5 g5 *(D)*

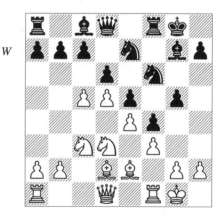

The strategies thus far should be self-evident. White is trying to infiltrate Black's queenside and Black is set upon an all-out assault on White's king.

14 cxd6 cxd6 15 ♘f2 h5 16 ♖c1 ♘g6 17 ♘b5 ♖f7 18 ♕c2 ♘e8 19 a4 *(D)*

These games are in an old and only recently revived variation. Theory only went 19 moves

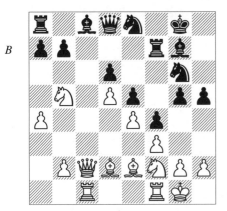

deep back then before someone deviated! Today, frightening though it may be, we can get mutual preparation beyond move 30. That's OK: there are also new ideas at around move 10 for you to dip into. And ultimately, if you play one of those, you'll still be able to build your game around the same ideas and themes that you're seeing here.

We'll look at two games. To be fair, they arose from very different move-orders and only merged at this point.

Ftačnik – Sznapik
Baile Herculane Z 1982

19...♗f8 *(D)*

Black wants to reorganize, as in thousands of Mar del Plata games, with the moves ...♖f7, ...♗f8, ...♖g7 and at the right moment, ...♘f6. It sometimes seems as though ...g4 can be played at any time along the way.

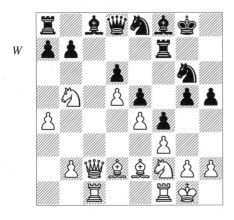

20 ♘xa7!?

20...♗d7!

Normally (but not always), trading off the light-squared bishop on c8 makes a kingside breakthrough impossible.

21 ♘b5 ♖g7 22 h3

A known defensive trick is to wait until Black has everything ready for ...g4, and then play g4 yourself! Thus White has 22 g4 *(D)*.

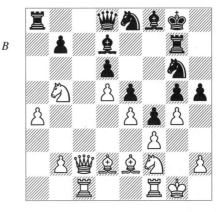

This advance is worth remembering, whether or not it works in the exact situation before us. Something like 22...fxg3 (22...hxg4 can be answered with 23 ♘xg4!? or 23 fxg4 ♘h4 24 ♕b3) 23 hxg3 h4 24 g4 might free White to pursue his queenside attack.

22...♘h4 23 ♕b3 g4! 24 fxg4 hxg4 25 hxg4

A pretty mate follows 25 ♗xg4 ♘f6! 26 ♘c7 ♘xg4 27 ♘e6? ♘xf2! 28 ♘xd8 ♖xg2#.

25...♘f6 26 ♗e1 *(D)*

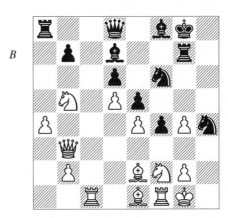

26...♘h5!!

This is not only visually pleasing but also necessary. For example, 26...♘xg4 27 ♘xg4

♗xg4 28 ♗xg4 ♖xg4 29 ♕h3 ♕g5 30 ♗xh4!
♖xh4 31 ♕e6+ ♔h8 and now 32 ♖f3! (32...♕h5
33 ♘xd6!) or 32 ♖c8. It's typical of these positions that after simplification, White has significant positional advantages; here the big one is
Black's awful bishop.

27 ♖c3!

27 gxh5? ♖xg2+ 28 ♔h1 ♕g5! threatens
...♖h2+.

27...♘g3

Otherwise White's move ♖h3 will stop things
cold.

28 ♖xg3

Forced. The knight was wreaking havoc.

**28...fxg3 29 ♕xg3 ♖xa4 30 ♘c3!? ♖a1 31
♘fd1 ♗e7** *(D)*

Improve the position of your worst-placed
piece!

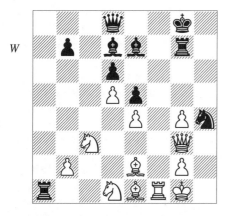

**32 ♘e3 ♘g6! 33 ♕f2! ♗h4 34 g3 ♘f4! 35
♔h2! ♘xe2 36 gxh4!? ♘f4 37 g5 ♖h7! 38
♘f5?**

Finally a serious mistake, doubtless in time-
trouble. Better is 38 ♕g3, thinking about 39 g6.

**38...♗xf5 39 exf5 ♘d3! 40 ♕g3 ♖xe1 41
♖xe1**

After 41 ♕xd3 ♖xf1 42 ♕xf1 ♕xg5 Black
wins the queen.

41...♘xe1 42 ♔h3

White's got some passed pawns but his king
is too loose. The game is over, as shown by 42
♘e4? ♖xh4+! and 42 ♕xe1 ♕xg5.

**42...♕c8! 43 ♕g4 ♘d3 44 ♘e4 ♕c1! 45
♕f3 ♘f4+ 46 ♔g4 ♕g1+ 0-1**

There follows 47 ♘g3 (47 ♕g3 ♕d1+ 48
♕f3 ♖xh4+ 49 ♔g3 ♖h3+) 47...♖xh4+! 48
♔xh4 ♕h2+ 49 ♔g4 ♕h3#.

Kožul – Radjabov
Sarajevo 2003

19...♗d7 20 ♕b3 ♗f8 *(D)*

20...♗f6 was tried in one game. Generally
this is played in order to move the queen somewhere and then the bishop to d8, finishing its
trip on a more active square, such as b6 or a5.
Notice that the central structure hasn't changed
fundamentally for a long time, nor will it soon.
In such positions, long journeys by single
pieces are not uncommon.

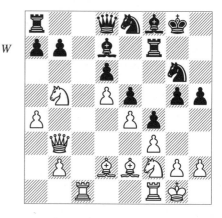

21 ♖c4!?

This is slightly strange; normal is ♖c2 (or
maybe ♖c3). Perhaps White envisioned a tripling of heavy pieces with either ♕c3 and ♖c1,
or ♖fc1, ♖1c3 and ♕c2.

21...a6 22 ♘a3 ♖g7 *(D)*

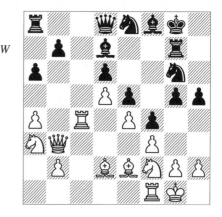

Not a subtle plan, but then play in this variation usually isn't. Black aims for ...g4.

23 a5

White on the other hand has a wide range of choices for his pieces. The only sure thing is that he has to move fast!

23...♘f6 24 ♕b6 ♕e8

An exchange of queens would cripple Black's kingside attack.

25 h3

The defensive effort begins. Not 25 ♕xb7?? ♗b5 (discovery on the queen) 26 ♕b6 ♖b8.

25...g4! 26 fxg4 hxg4 27 hxg4 ♘h4 *(D)*

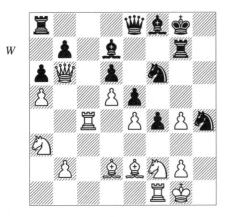

28 ♖c7 ♕g6 29 ♗e1! ♖h7!

29...♘xg4 30 ♘xg4 ♗xg4 would be deadly were it not for the defensive bishop on e1: 31 ♖xg7+ ♕xg7 32 ♗xg4 ♕xg4 33 ♗xh4 ♕xh4 34 ♕xb7, etc.

30 ♕b3

White's retreat is a moderately bad sign, because he would like to carry out a breakthrough on the queenside. Unfortunately, ...♕h6 was threatened. Now White's queen maintains contact with h3. It's hard for Black actually to get through to the king in such positions – you'll see both sides achieve their share of points if it gets this far.

30...♘xe4!

Centre pawns tend to be worth more than flank pawns. 30...♕h6 31 ♘h3 ♘xe4 32 ♗d3! ruins everything.

31 ♕d3?

This fails miserably (or ought to). White should get some pieces off the board by 31 ♘xe4! ♕xe4 32 ♖f2. Although 32...f3!? is scary, White has good control of the light squares: 33 ♖c4! ♕xd5 34 ♗d3! and ♗e4. Black could play simply 32...♖b8, however, with perhaps a very small advantage.

31...♘g3! *(D)*

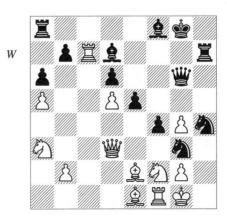

32 ♖xb7

This time a queen exchange is welcome, because after 32 ♕xg6+ ♘xg6 33 ♗d3 ♗e8! Black wins material.

32...e4?

Black returns the favour. 32...♗f5! is terribly strong, because 33 gxf5 ♘xe2+ is mate in two.

33 ♘xe4! ♘xe4 34 ♖xd7

Eliminating pieces is life-or-death in this variation. White usually has long-term advantages that are worth a little material.

34...♖xd7 35 ♗xh4 ♕h7 36 ♖xf4 ♕xh4 37 ♖xe4 ♗g7 38 ♗f3? *(D)*

Better was 38 g3. From now on almost every move can be either questioned or praised, so I'll leave them alone:

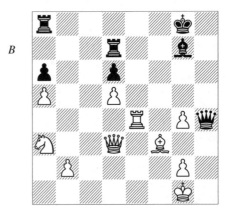

38...♖f8 39 ♘c4 ♖df7 40 ♖e3 ♖f4 41 ♖e4 ♖xf3 42 gxf3 ♕g3+ 43 ♔h1 ♔f7 44 ♘xd6+ ♕xd6 45 ♔g2 ♖h8 46 ♕b3 ♕h2+ 47 ♔f1 ♕h1+ 0-1

Modern Main Line with 10 ♗e3

1 d4 ♘f6 2 c4 g6 3 ♘c3 ♗g7 4 e4 d6 5 ♘f3 0-0 6 ♗e2 e5 7 0-0 ♘c6 8 d5 ♘e7 9 ♘e1

Let's return to this move and look at one more idea. There's a lot to learn by examining games with loads of theoretical content, even if you don't want to play anything of the sort. But for those of you who are either tired of or frightened by the theoretical wilderness, 9 a4!? *(D)* might be of interest:

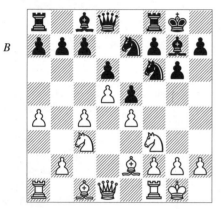

I place it in this section because it goes with the contemporary a4 ideas that are associated with 10 ♗e3, and in fact Korchnoi tried 9 a4 versus Kasparov during a period when he was experimenting with several other schemes involving that move at a later stage. The main idea is simply a5, gaining important space and extra control over b6. White's knight or rook may also use the a3-square. There's little theory attached to this line, but a small selection of games. Here are some ideas: 9...a5 (after 9...♘h5, White can go ahead with 10 a5, when 10...♘f4 11 ♗xf4 exf4 12 ♕d2 favours White, and 10...f5 11 c5!? is also promising) and now:

a) 10 ♘e1 ♘d7 11 ♗e3 f5 12 f3 ♘c5!? 13 ♘d3 b6 14 b4 ♘xd3 15 ♕xd3 axb4 16 ♘b5 ♔h8 and then:

a1) 17 ♕b3!? ♘g8 18 ♕xb4 ♘f6 with a very unclear position, Korchnoi-Kasparov, Barcelona 1989. When Kasparov won this game, it unjustly dampened interest in 9 a4 for years.

a2) 17 ♗d2! is probably best, intending simply ♗xb4 and then a5; White seems well ahead of the normal 10 ♗e3 lines with 13 a4 a5. In two games with this move White stood clearly better.

Even when deviating from the main lines, it still helps to study them!

b) Garcia Palermo-Flores, Pinamar 2002 saw 10 ♖a3 ♘d7 11 ♘h4!? f5 12 exf5 gxf5 13 f4 *(D)*.

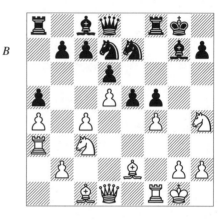

Very interesting! You'd think that more people would be investigating this sort of thing, if only to duck theory. The game continued 13...♘g6?! 14 ♘xg6 hxg6 15 ♘b5 ♖f7 16 ♖g3! with a clear advantage. There were few if any typical Mar del Plata themes in that one! It shows that one needn't be prisoner of the latest innovation on move 25.

9...♘d7 10 ♗e3

Similarly, 10 a4 is playable and has even enjoyed a modest popularity in the past few years. I would rather not commit my knight to e1, so I feel that 9 a4 is more promising.

10...f5 11 f3 f4 12 ♗f2 *(D)*

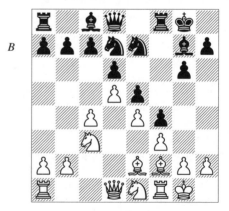

It's ironic that of all the many systems played by White after 9...♘d7, the line that most grandmasters and strong players had strongly rejected from the early days on was 10 ♗e3 and 12 ♗f2, now the most popular Mar del Plata set-up. The problem, gleaned from some horrible experiences, was that White was taking two moves to put the bishop in a position where it would lose more tempi to Black's onrushing pawns or at least provide a target and thereby help Black to open kingside lines. One of the initial and most famous Mar del Plata games, Taimanov-Najdorf, Zurich Ct 1953, was a disaster for White, the game proceeding 12...g5 13 ♘d3 ♘f6 14 c5 ♘g6 15 ♖c1 ♖f7! 16 ♖c2? ♗f8! 17 cxd6 cxd6 18 ♕d2? g4 19 ♖fc1? g3! 20 hxg3 fxg3 21 ♗xg3 ♘h5 22 ♗h2 ♗e7! *(D)* (with the bishop headed for g5, it's hard to believe that White can hold the position).

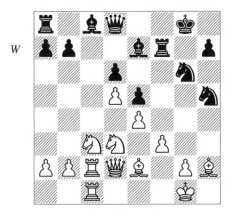

23 ♘b1 ♗d7 24 ♕e1 ♗g5 25 ♘d2 ♗e3+ 26 ♔h1 ♕g5 27 ♗f1 ♖af8 with a winning attack.

There were similar experiences in high-profile games until players started looking in another direction for White. Many years later, someone decided that they were tired of having their bishop on the passive square d2, which makes it so hard to get c5 in, so he took the time to look at 10 ♗e3 again. Fairly quickly it became evident that the earlier conceptions of how to attack the queenside and defend the kingside had evolved greatly due to the experiences with ♘d3, such that Taimanov's play seemed primitive indeed. Basically, White needs to play c5, open up the c-file and occupy it with heavy pieces, play ♘b5, etc. True, an all-out pawn assault with b5-b6 is still rather slow but much more likely than after 10 ♘d3. Remember that in the 9 ♘d2 variation that procedure

was a realistic one. The big difference is that after 12 ♗f2, White has an attractive new target on a7, to be attacked in conjunction with ♘b5. Upon ...a6 or ...a5, the idea of c5 and cxd6 creates a hole on b6. The other major difference, and the reason for the fully-fledged revival of 10 ♗e3, came with ideas involving a4, most of them the inventions of Korchnoi, who has spent many years trying to refute the King's Indian (as yet, unsuccessfully). We shall talk about them next move.

What should Black be doing? Obviously it depends upon what plan White pursues (for example, sometimes the straightforward c5 and ♖c1 are played, omitting a4). If there is anything approaching a general philosophy of defence here, it would be to leave the queenside completely alone and pursue the kingside attack as fast as possible, sacrificing pawns if necessary but not being diverted by White's queenside activity. Timing is everything in this line, and the faster runner generally wins, so Black should be wary of queenside moves such as ...a6 and ...b6. A major exception to this is the move 13...a5 versus 13 a4, currently considered Black's best course. The preservation of the light-squared bishop is a priority that outweighs the loss of a tempo, so ...♗d7 may be necessary in some cases. On the other hand, Black may not want to move his knight from d7 too quickly, because it is important to force White to use an extra move to get the advance c5 in. That is, the knight on d7 will help to stop c5 and White may need to play b4 (or the clumsy ♘d3) to enforce it. That seems trivial, but b4 is not the move that White would ideally spend time on if he could avoid doing so.

On the kingside itself, Black's normal plan is to play the conventional moves ...f4, ...g5, ...♖f7-g7, ...♗f8, ...♘f6, ...h5 (if necessary), and usually throwing his g-pawn forward without regard to doing anything but opening lines. If White captures a few times on g4 Black may lose the g-pawn but gain both the g- and h-files. If White ignores Black's pawn on g4, the move ...g3 can be a precursor to combinative play against the white king. The other main idea on the kingside is to omit ...h5 and play ...♖f6-h6 with an eye towards ...♕e8-h5 and direct attack. This seems more effective against ♖c1 ideas than those with a4.

Unfortunately, both sides should probably know quite a lot of theory to play these lines. To some extent studying examples and playing as many games as possible will make up for straight memorization. Ideally one would do a little of both.

12...g5 *(D)*

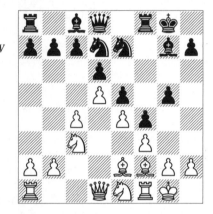

Black begins the usual assault. He can also play ...h5 first, probably because he isn't happy to confront White's defensive idea g4 and wants to be able to capture the pawn if that occurs. Of course ...h5 preempts any idea of ...♖f6-h6, but that only works in a minority of cases and may not appeal to everyone. After 12...g5, we have the straightforward move 13 ♖c1 and the more sophisticated 13 a4.

The Unpretentious Rook Move

13 ♖c1 *(D)*

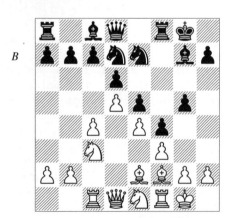

I'll offer two games from this position:

del Rio – Illescas
Dos Hermanas 2004

13...♘g6 14 c5!? *(D)*

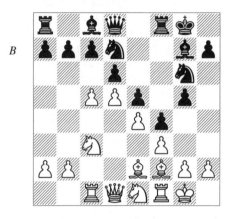

This is a standard but adventurous sacrifice that succeeds or fails under circumstances that vary only slightly from one position to another. The idea is that White gets the c-file and the initiative while Black's knight is stuck offside. At the very least White generates considerable pressure on the queenside.

14...♘xc5 15 b4 ♘a6 16 ♘b5 ♗d7

Another recent game continued 16...♖f7 17 ♘d3 ♗d7 18 a4 with mutual and dynamic chances, Pavlović-Fedorov, Warsaw Ech 2005.

17 a4 *(D)*

There have actually been a lot of games from this position, including some with 17 ♘xa7. Rather than dig into very technical theory we'll follow the main game.

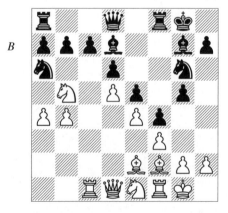

17...♕b8!?

Presumably the idea of ♘xa7 was getting too annoying for Black's taste. 17...♖f7 has been seen in many games, with White doing pretty well. After the obvious 17...♘xb4?!, Mikhalevski offers the continuation 18 ♘xc7 ♖c8 19 ♘b5 a5 20 ♖xc8! ♗xc8 21 ♘c2! with advantage.

18 ♘d3! ♖f7 19 ♘a3 (D)

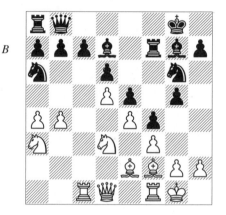

Threatening b5 because Black's knight has nowhere to go.

19...♕d8 20 b5 ♘b8 21 a5 a6

This looks awful but Black *is* a pawn ahead, so White has to prove something. The opening has come to an end and we'll follow the middlegame because of its astonishing character.

22 b6 c5 23 dxc6 ♘xc6 24 ♕d2!

A very subtle move. Instead of the direct threat of ♗c4, which might have followed 24 ♘b2 (with 24...♗e6 25 ♗c4 ♕d7 as a probable continuation), White keeps his knight on an active square and plans a surprise.

24...♗e6 25 ♖xc6!! bxc6 (D)

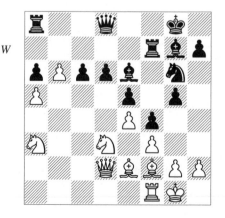

Amazing. Now we can see the point of 24 ♕d2.

26 ♘b4 g4!?

Probably a good idea, so that White has something to think about too. Naturally ...g3 can't be allowed. Instead, 26...♕d7 27 ♘xa6 gives White two passed pawns and guess what? His queen protects a5 so that the knight can get out via c7!

27 fxg4 f3! 28 ♗xf3 ♕d7! (D)

Black protects c6 and hits g4.

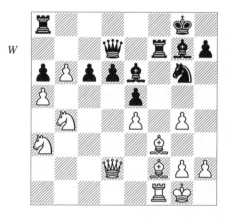

29 h3?!

29 ♖b1 with the idea ♘xa6! was better.

29...♘f4 30 ♗e3 c5 31 ♘bc2 ♗h6? 32 ♔h2

Black's 31st move loses the initiative since now White threatens g3.

32...♗g7 33 g3 ♘g6 34 ♗g2 ♘e7 35 ♖d1 ♖d8 36 ♕e2! ♕c8 37 ♗g5

This frees the c2-knight to get to f5 or d5.

37...♗f6 38 ♗xf6 ♖xf6 39 ♘e3 ♘c6 (D)

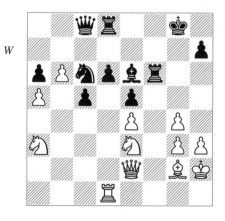

40 ♘f5 ♗xf5

Mikhalevski analyses 40...♘d4? 41 ♖xd4! ♗xf5 42 b7!! ♕b8 43 ♖d2! (43 exf5!?) 43...♗e6 44 ♕xa6 ♖f7 45 ♖b2 "and when the a-pawn reaches the a6-square the game will be over".

41 exf5 ♔h8 42 ♘c4

From here on out it's pretty easy. White owns the light squares and has the powerful passed pawn.

42...♘d4 43 ♕e4 h5 44 b7 ♕c7 45 ♘e3 ♕h7 46 g5 ♖ff8 47 f6 ♕xe4 48 ♗xe4 ♖b8 49 ♖b1 ♘b5 50 ♖xb5 axb5 51 a6 b4 1-0

Speelman – Uhlmann
Leningrad 1984

13...♖f6 14 b4

It seems generally agreed that if any attack with ...♖f6-h6 works it's going to be in this position. Another way for White to continue is 14 c5 a6 15 c6 bxc6 16 dxc6 ♘f8 17 ♘d5.

14...♖h6 15 c5 a6 16 cxd6 cxd6 17 g4

If this had to be played, it may have been smarter to do so a move or two ago.

17...fxg3 18 hxg3 ♘g6! 19 ♘g2 ♘f4!

Easy to spot but still daring for one to actually play it!

20 gxf4 gxf4 21 ♗h4 ♗f6! *(D)*

Perhaps this is what Speelman missed, expecting 21...♕b6+ 22 ♗f2, etc.

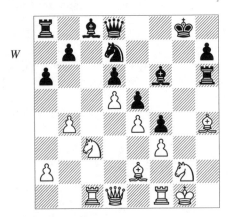

22 ♗xf6 ♘xf6

Black is a full piece down but it's hard to know what to do for White. The first problem is ...♕b6+, and ...♗h3 looms as well, so Speelman tries to escape with the king.

23 ♔f2 ♖h2 24 ♔g1 ♖h3 25 ♔f2 ♖g3 26 ♘xf4

Or 26 ♘a4 b5 27 ♘c5 dxc5 28 bxc5 ♗h3.

26...exf4 27 ♕d4 ♘g4+!? 28 ♔e1

A last chance might be 28 fxg4 ♕h4 29 ♔e1 ♖xc3+ 30 ♔d2, however unlikely.

28...♘e5 *(D)*

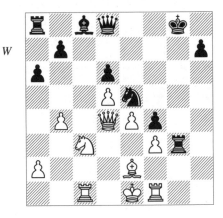

A monster knight!

29 ♔d2 ♗h3 30 ♖g1 ♗g2 31 ♘a4 ♗xf3 32 ♘b6 ♖xe2 33 ♔xe2 ♕g5 34 ♘xa8 f3+ 35 ♔f2 ♖g2+ 36 ♖xg2 ♕xg2+ 37 ♔e3 ♕g5+ 0-1

Sophisticated Assault

13 a4 *(D)*

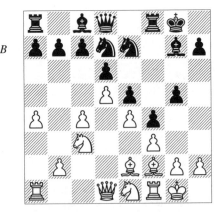

What is this move all about? With a4 on the board, White can more productively attack the a7-pawn (or square) with his knight on b5 and bishop on f2. This is so because ...b6 is met by a5, whereas if Black plays ...a6, ♘a7 has the important goal of eliminating Black's bishop on c8. As we have seen, that bishop is almost essential to Black's kingside attack. Barring that possibility, White has direct ideas such as a5 and even a6. In other cases a4 allows for a rook to come to a3 both in order to defend the kingside (e.g., Black plays ...g4 and White answers fxg4, unmasking the rook on a3 horizontally), and to double or triple major pieces along the c-file.

Right now 13...a5 seems to be Black's best solution to 13 a4, which is paradoxical because it 'weakens' the queenside with tempo. But it also stops b4, which in turn makes c5 more difficult to achieve. A few examples out of many demonstrate what 13 a4 is about:

a) 13...a6 14 a5 ♖f6 and now:

a1) 15 ♘a4 ♖h6 16 c5 ♕e8 17 ♔h1 ♕h5 18 ♗g1 ♘f6 19 cxd6! cxd6 20 ♘b6 ♕h4 21 ♘xc8!. This is a good example of getting rid of the key attacking piece. Now, although Black gave it an inspired try, he wasn't able to get through to the king in Summerscale-Snape, Coulsdon 2002.

a2) 15 g4!?. We've talked about this idea, which Shirov has used before. Here Shirov-Tkachev, Biel 1995 continued 15...fxg3 16 hxg3 h5! 17 ♘g2 ♖h6 18 ♘e3 ♘f6 19 ♔g2 ♗d7 20 b4 ♕e8 21 c5 ♕g6 22 cxd6 cxd6 23 ♘c4 g4?! (23...h4!?) 24 ♘b6 gxf3+ 25 ♗xf3 ♖f8 (White looks better to me, but this is too complex to say for sure) 26 ♘xd7 ♘xd7 27 ♖h1 ♘f6 28 ♕e2 h4 29 ♖h3 ♖c8 30 ♕d2 hxg3 ½-½.

b) 13...♖f6?! 14 ♘b5 a6?! 15 ♘a7 (D).

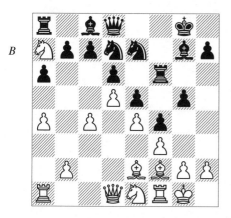

15...♖xa7 16 ♗xa7 ♖h6 (a remarkable piece of optimism; 16...b6 never seems to trap the bishop in such positions, in this case because of 17 a5! ♗b7 18 axb6 cxb6 19 c5! ♘xc5 20 b4 ♘d7 21 ♗xa6, etc.) 17 ♘d3 ♘f6 18 c5 (18 ♘f2

has also won some games) 18...g4 19 fxg4 ♘xe4 20 ♗f3 ♘g3!? 21 cxd6 cxd6 22 hxg3 fxg3 23 ♖e1 ♘g6 24 ♖e4!, and White's king was able to get to the safe haven on e2, Krivoshei-Cherkasov, Koszalin 1999.

c) 13...♘g6 is under a cloud because after 14 a5 ♖f7 (or 14...h5 15 ♘b5) 15 c5, Black's counterplay is too slow. The knight gets in the way of ...♖f6-h6.

We now turn to an example with 13...a5.

P.H. Nielsen – Kotronias
Hastings 2003/4

13...a5

As mentioned earlier, this move weakens Black's queenside and even spends a tempo doing so, but these drawbacks appear to be outweighed by the fact that it also frustrates White's active plans.

14 ♘d3 b6 *(D)*

Black tries to undercut both c5 and a5. This is the structure that he's been aiming for, with the benefit that ...♘c5 can be a valuable defensive resource at some point.

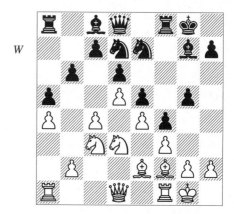

15 ♗e1!?

In many ways retreating the bishop is White's most logical move. The reasoning is as follows:

a) White needs to get b4 in.

b) Once he's made that move and Black has captured with the move ...axb4, White will set his eyes upon his next queenside break, which is a5.

c) Capturing on b4 with the bishop (or even aiming it that way) is the best way to achieve a5 and continue his queenside attack. Then, whether Black captures White's pawn on a5 or not, White will gain targets on the queenside, such as c7, b6 or d6.

d) Finally, by capturing on b4 with the bishop, White preserves his knight on d3 to go to f2 and protect against ...g4 in the traditional fashion.

Of course there are difficulties with this procedure in terms of time; the whole thing's rather slow. White's bishop has to travel to e3, f2, e1 and b4, conceivably hurting his kingside defences thereby (for example, there won't be a ♗g1 defence). White's knight on c3 will have to get out of the way, although ♘b5 may be a tempo well spent. And the move c5 will still be a long way from realization even after White completes the a5 plan. Nevertheless, Black's knight on d7 will have to move to f6 (or perhaps c5) at some point in order to continue with his kingside attack, at which point White's queenside chances will inevitably improve.

For all that, 15 b4 immediately makes sense too, mainly because White must play b4 if he is going to open the queenside and he may be able to make use of the knight on b4 by, for example, going to c6 and supporting a5. However, it should be noted that a knight on c6 in the King's Indian will often be stranded there as Black moves to the kingside to pursue his attack. Let's see a couple of the main ideas in practice: 15...axb4 16 ♘b5 (after 16 ♘xb4 ♘c5 17 a5? bxa5 18 ♗xc5 dxc5 19 ♘d3 ♘c6! 20 dxc6 ♕d4+ Black wins back the piece with an extra pawn and pressure) 16...♘f6 (D).

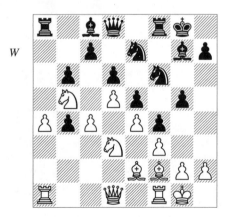

17 ♗e1 (17 ♘xb4 h5; 17 ♕b3!? might plot ♕xb4 and a5; I don't know if that's been tried)

17...g4 (17...h5 18 ♘f2!?) 18 fxg4 (White gives up a centre pawn, usually a bad idea if you can avoid it, but 18 ♗xb4 g3! 19 h3 ♗xh3! 20 gxh3 ♕d7 would be a dangerous standard attack; note how useful the light-squared bishop can be) 18...♘xe4 19 ♗xb4 ♗d7 20 ♕c2 ♘g5 21 h4!? ♘e4 22 ♗e1 ♘g6 23 h5 ♘g3! 24 hxg6 ♕h4 with a powerful attack, Chabanon-Degraeve, French Cht 1999.

15...♘f6 16 ♘f2 h5 17 h3 ♔h8 (D)

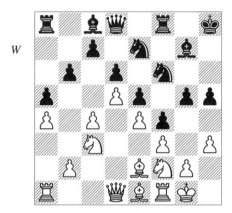

18 ♘b5 ♘eg8 19 b4 ♖f7

Some recent games from this critical position have favoured White; for example, 19...♘h6 20 c5 bxc5 21 bxc5 ♖f7 22 ♘a3! ♗f8 23 ♘c4 g4 24 fxg4 hxg4 25 hxg4 ♖g7 (D).

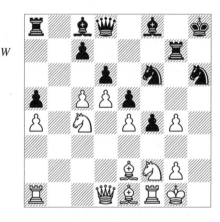

26 ♖a3! ♘hxg4 27 ♘xg4 ♘xg4 28 ♖h3+ ♔g8 29 ♖h4!? ♘f6?! 30 ♕c2! and Black's attack looks dead, Zakhartsov-Voicu, Alushta 2005.

20 bxa5 bxa5 21 c5 ♗f8 22 cxd6 cxd6 23 ♖c1 ♘h6 24 ♖c4 ♖g7 25 ♕c2 g4 26 ♗xa5!?

Perhaps the most critical line is the greedy 26 hxg4!? hxg4 27 ♘c7 g3 28 ♘xa8, N.Brunner-Helstroffer, Nancy 2006, agreed drawn at this point! We'll just enjoy the rest of our game, in spite of the fact that White could have played better.

26...♕e8! 27 h4 gxf3 28 ♗xf3 ♗g4! 29 ♗xg4 ♘fxg4 30 ♗b6 ♕e7 31 ♘xg4?! ♘xg4 32 ♗f2 f3! 33 g3 ♘e3! 34 ♗xe3 ♖xg3+ 35 ♔f2 ♖g2+ 36 ♔xf3 ♖xc2 37 ♖xc2 ♕xh4 38 ♖g1 ♖xa4 39 ♘c3 ♖c4 40 ♔e2 ♗h6! 41 ♗b6 ♖xe4+ 0-1

9 ♘d2

9 ♘d2 (D)

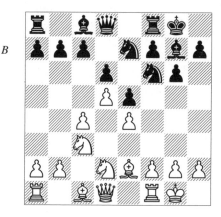

There's a legitimate question whether this move or 9 ♘e1 is better. As mentioned above, once White plays ♘d2 it is unlikely that he will return to defend against, say, the standard pawn attack via ...f5, ...f4 and ...g5-g4. On the other hand, 9 ♘d2 supports more aggressive intentions on the queenside. White's idea is to play c5 (ultimately this is difficult to stop) and then place the knight on c4, which exerts tremendous pressure on Black's queenside and centre, most obviously on the d6-pawn but also supporting b5-b6, and infiltrating by ♘a5-c6 in some lines. All the time, the knight keeps an eye on the e5-pawn, the foundation of Black's position. If Black lets the e-pawn go (say, by ...dxc5, when White also has a bishop on b2), then the collapse of his centre causes an immediate crisis (essentially, he has to get through to White's king immediately thereafter). A further consideration which affects the entire course of

the play is the slow pace at which White is able to mobilize his c1-bishop and a1-rook. This gives Black opportunities to play on the queenside as well. In fact, Black's play on that wing crops up in almost every major King's Indian system.

These ideas are best illustrated by example. We look at 9...♘e8 and 9...a5. There are of course numerous alternatives, with the most important being 9...c5. I'll forego that in favour of giving more detailed coverage of the other two moves.

Pawn Race

9...♘e8 (D)

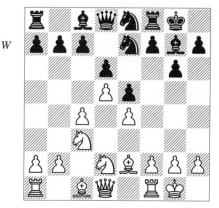

After both 9 ♘d2 and 9 ♘e1 there are disagreements over whether 9...♘e8 or 9...♘d7 is more accurate.

In this position I won't go into that except to say that:

a) 9...♘d7 protects against c5, with the caveat that after b4 White might play c5 as a pawn sacrifice;

b) 9...♘e8 supports d6 so that a 'traditional' plan with c5, cxd6, ♘c4 and ♘b5 doesn't threaten the d-pawn or the c7-square. That may be more important.

See the more detailed discussion of the same choice after 9 ♘e1.

10 b4 f5

So now it's a pawn-race, *à la* 9 ♘e1 ♘d7.

11 c5 ♘f6

Bringing the knight back to f6 negates the difference between 9...♘d7 and 9...♘e8.

12 f3 f4 13 ♘c4 g5

This is familiar territory. Here are two instructive and entertaining games:

Bogdanovski – Golubev
Skopje 1991

14 ♗a3 (D)

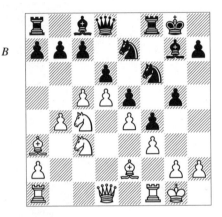

14...♘g6 15 b5 ♘e8!?

It's hard to believe that Black can get away with making this passive move twice! But he succeeds in this game, which says something about how dangerous ...f4, ...g5 and ...g4 can be even in an inferior line. More likely to be good is 15...dxc5, as seen in Bunzmann-Golubev.

16 b6 axb6 17 cxb6 cxb6 18 ♕b3 h5 19 ♖ab1 g4 20 ♘xb6 ♕g5! (D)

What material?

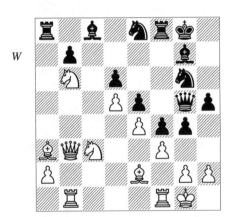

21 ♔h1?!

21 ♘xa8?! g3 22 h3 ♕h4! 23 ♖b2 ♗xh3 24 gxh3 ♕xh3 25 ♗b5 ♘h4 is utterly depressing for White, who might have thought he had the game in the bag. There can follow 26 ♗d7 ♕xd7 27 ♘b1 ♕h3, but it doesn't help much.

21...♘h4 22 ♘xc8?!

Normally, getting rid of this bishop is key to successful defence, but now White hasn't even won any material! Other moves are not much easier, however.

22...♖xc8 23 ♖g1 ♖f7 24 ♖bc1 ♗f8 25 ♘a4 ♖xc1 26 ♗xc1 ♖g7 27 ♕d1 ♘f6 28 ♘b6 ♕g6 (D)

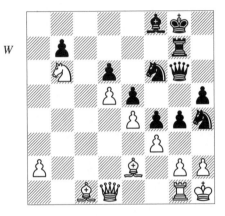

29 ♗d2

Golubev offers the charming analysis 29 ♕e1 g3 30 h3? ♘g4! 31 fxg4 hxg4 32 ♗xg4 ♕xg4!! 33 hxg4 ♖h7 and mates!

29...♘h7 30 ♕f1 g3 31 ♗e1 ♖c7 32 ♗c4 ♗e7!

Black begins a standard manoeuvre to free his bad bishop. In this case it serves a defensive function, but in many openings it will make the trip ...♗g7-f6-d8-b6/a5 for attacking purposes.

33 a4 ♗d8 34 a5 ♔h8 35 ♕e2 ♖g7 36 ♗b5 ♕f6! 37 ♗e8 gxh2 38 ♔xh2 ♕e7?!

In time-trouble Golubev backs off. He wasn't sure about what would follow 38...♖g3!.

39 ♗a4?!

This was the last chance for 39 ♗d7!.

39...♖g3!

Black finds a very pretty and original combination.

40 ♗xg3 (D)

40...♘f5!! 41 ♖c1

Everything loses: 41 exf5 fxg3+ 42 ♔xg3 ♕h4#; 41 ♗e1 ♘g3 42 ♗xg3 fxg3+ 43 ♔xg3 ♕h4#.

41...fxg3+ 42 ♔g1 ♕h4 43 ♕b5 ♕h2+ 44 ♔f1 ♕h1+ 45 ♔e2 ♕xg2+ 0-1

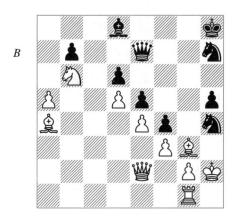

Somehow this great game just feels like another few hundred King's Indians. I guess that says something about the opening!

Instead of 14 ♗a3, White can also add fuel to his pawn advance by pushing the a-pawn first:

Bunzmann – Golubev
Bethune 2002

14 a4 ♘g6 15 ♗a3 ♖f7 16 b5 *(D)*

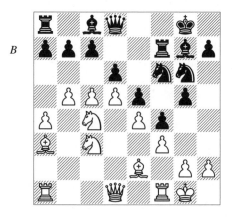

16...dxc5!?

This strange move is actually a plausible attempt to get Black's attack going; he prefers to face the move d6 rather than b6. The game R.Hernandez-J.Gunnarsson, Santa Clara 2002 is terribly instructive: 16...♗f8 17 a5!? (17 b6 is also promising, in view of the line 17...axb6?! {17...dxc5! is probably the best way to defend} 18 cxb6 cxb6 19 ♖b1 ♖a6 20 ♕b3!) 17...dxc5! (Martin offers 17...b6 18 cxb6 axb6 19 axb6 cxb6 20 ♘a2! g4 21 ♘b4 g3 22 ♘c6 and White

has made too much progress too fast) 18 b6 axb6?! (a possible improvement is 18...cxb6) 19 axb6 cxb6 20 ♕b3! ♖a6 21 ♗b2?! (21 ♖fb1! must be strong; the overall impression is that White is better after 16...♗f8) 21...♘d7? (Bogdanovski-Rosiak, Lodz 1989 actually favoured Black after 21...g4!) 22 d6! *(D)*.

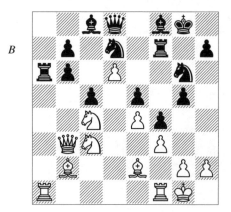

After this powerful breakthrough the situation is still complex, but we may consider the opening ideas complete. So we'll sit back and watch how Black can get slaughtered before his attack could take effect: 22...h5 23 ♘d5 ♔h7 24 ♖fd1 b5 25 ♕xb5 g4 26 fxg4 ♕g5? 27 ♖xa6 bxa6 28 ♕c6 hxg4 29 ♕xc8 f3 30 ♕e8! ♖g7 31 ♗f1! g3 32 h3 ♕h5 33 ♖d2 f2+ 34 ♔h1 ♕h4 35 ♖e2 ♕g5 36 ♕e6 1-0.

17 ♗xc5 h5!? *(D)*

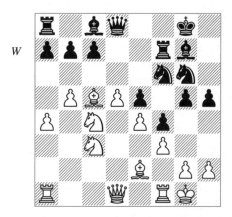

18 d6

The combination in Ftačnik-Cvitan, Bundesliga 1997/8 has been shown in umpteen books, but not everyone reads these things, so a quick run-through: 18 a5 g4 19 b6 g3 20 ♔h1! ♘h7 21 d6 ♕h4 22 ♗g1 ♗h3 23 bxc7?? ♗xg2+! 24 ♔xg2 ♕h3+!! 25 ♔xh3 ♘g5+ 26 ♔g2 ♘h4+ 27 ♔h1 g2#.

18...♗f8

Or 18...♗e6!?; this ...dxc5 idea isn't looking half bad!

19 ♗f2 cxd6 20 b6! a6 21 ♘d5 ♘xd5 22 ♕xd5 ♕f6 23 ♖ac1 g4 24 ♘xd6?! ♗e6 25 ♕xe6 ♕xe6 26 ♘xf7 g3! *(D)*

The typical Black KID counterattack! Not 26...♖c8?! 27 ♘g5!.

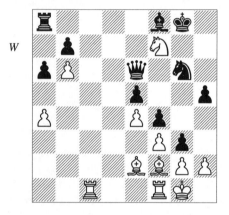

27 hxg3 fxg3 28 ♗xg3 ♖c8 29 ♘g5 ♕xb6+ 30 ♗f2 ♗c5 31 ♖xc5 ♖xc5 32 ♗c4+ ♔h8 33 ♖d1 ♕a5 34 ♗f7 ♘f4 35 g3 ♖c1 36 ♖xc1 ♘e2+ 37 ♔f1 ♘xc1 38 ♗e3 ♕xa4 39 ♔g2 ♕c2+ 40 ♔h3 ♕d3 0-1

I'm not confident that this line fully equalizes for Black if White plays extremely accurately. However, Black's disadvantage will very likely be within manageable bounds in any case. The view that after 9 ♘d2, Black can't compete against White in a pawn-race holds some truth, but only some.

Queenside Manoeuvres

9...a5 *(D)*

Black turns his attention to the queenside. At the very least, he wants White to spend extra time to get the move b4 in. After this minor victory, Black can rush off to pursue his kingside attack, or try other ideas on the queenside, which is the strategy that most players prefer. While White gets on with a3 and b4, Black can play ...♗d7 with the idea ...a4 and, more abstractly,

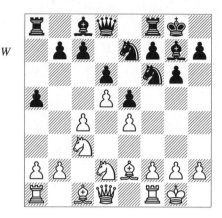

...c6. There is more than one point to the latter move, but a major one is to play ...cxd5, and after cxd5 to mobilize his own pieces on the queenside and neutralize White's attack there. For example, a queen move may follow, clearing the back rank for action, and ...♘c8-b6 covers the key square c4. On an elementary level, ...c6 and ...cxd5 also removes a pawn from potential attack should White eventually make queenside progress. In the meantime, Black can always make a few kingside motions to prepare a delayed attack on that side of the board. As you might expect, this is all stretching Black's forces rather thin and White is really more naturally placed to make progress on the queenside. He has a much simpler task than Black: to evict all those jumbled pieces that we just referred to, or open queenside lines and bypass them.

Ftačnik – Topalov
Polanica Zdroj 1995

10 a3 ♗d7 11 b3

White wants to prevent ...a4, with one pawn holding down two.

11...c6

As described above, Black needs to clear out some pawns and open files to gain active play on the queenside and spots for his pieces. Of course for every such exchange White will also gain squares.

12 ♗b2

Or:

a) Black's forces made a pretty picture in Nemet-Gallagher, Swiss Cht 1994: 12 ♖b1 ♕b8 13 b4 cxd5 14 cxd5 ♖c8 15 ♗b2 axb4 16 axb4 b5! *(D)*.

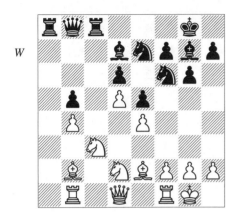

17 ♗d3 ♕b6 18 ♘b3 ♗h6 19 ♘a5 ♖c7 20 ♗e2? ♖xc3! 21 ♗xc3 ♘xe4 (an exchange sacrifice tends to be pretty safe when you get a centre pawn and mobile majority) 22 ♗e1 ♖c8 23 ♗f3 ♘f6 24 ♗d2 ♗xd2 25 ♕xd2 e4 26 ♗e2 ♘exd5. A second centre pawn has fallen, and Black is clearly better.

b) White played a better idea in Sharavdorj-Al Modiahki, Yangon 1999, but didn't get much after 12 ♖a2 ♕b8 13 ♖c2! ♖c8 14 ♘db1!? (perhaps 14 a4!? intending ♗a3 could be tried; then White could play on the kingside too) 14...b5 15 cxb5 (15 dxc6 ♗xc6 16 cxb5 ♗xe4 17 ♘xe4) 15...cxb5 16 b4 axb4 17 axb4 ♖a1 18 ♗d3 ♘h5 19 g3 (19 ♗b2 ♖a7 20 ♘a3) 19...♖a7 with equality.

12...♗h6!? (D)

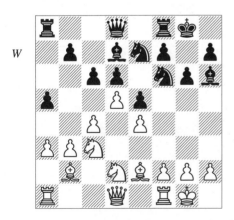

Black considers getting rid of this 'bad' bishop, but is also covering f4. Exchanging on d2 carries with it the risk that the dark squares near his king will become too weak.

13 ♖b1 ♘c8 14 dxc6 ♗xc6

14...bxc6 is met by 15 b4! with a small advantage.

15 ♗d3

15 b4! with the idea 15...♗xd2 16 ♕xd2 ♘xe4 17 ♘xe4 ♗xe4 18 ♖bd1 is a promising pawn sacrifice, intending f4. As so often, White is winning the theoretical battle but is faced with great practical difficulties in neutralizing Black's activity.

15...♘b6 16 b4 axb4 17 axb4

At this point White simply seems to have the better game: space and the d6 weakness are the first two reasons.

17...♘h5! (D)

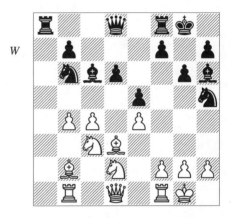

Watch out for this knight. Topalov already sees the contours of the game.

18 g3 ♗d7 19 ♕e2 ♖c8 20 ♘b3 ♘a4 21 ♘xa4 ♗xa4 22 ♗c1 (D)

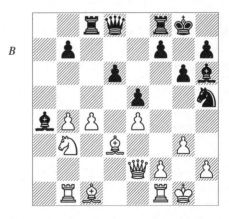

22...♗xc1!

Topalov's idea is simply to eliminate a potential defender. White has little left to attack with.

23 ⟂fxc1 ⟂xb3!

The same reasoning. But what are those pieces defending?

24 ⟂xb3 ⟂g7!

The main point of ...⟂h5: d4 is there for the taking with nothing to challenge it.

25 c5!

He shouldn't wait around for ...⟂e6-d4 without activating his bad bishop.

25...⟂e6 (D)

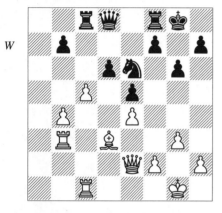

26 ⟂bc3?!

26 ⟂e3! was better, when 26...b5 (26...⟂c7 27 ⟂c4!) 27 cxb6 (27 ⟂xb5 ⟂d4) 27...⟂xc1+ 28 ⟂xc1 ⟂xb6 29 b5 is almost equal, but Black's knight still looks somewhat better than White's bishop; e.g., 29...⟂c5 30 ⟂e3! ⟂a5 31 ⟂b1 ⟂c3 32 ⟂d1 ⟂b8.

26...dxc5 27 bxc5 ⟂a5! 28 ⟂c2?!

But 28 ⟂e3 might run into 28...b6! 29 c6 ⟂c5, etc.

28...⟂g7 29 ⟂g2 ⟂c6! 30 ⟂b2 ⟂c7 31 ⟂c4 ⟂xc5 32 ⟂b5 ⟂b6 33 ⟂1c2? ⟂c7 34 ⟂c1 ⟂fc8! 35 ⟂f1 ⟂e6 36 ⟂xc7 ⟂xc7 37 ⟂xc7 ⟂xc7

Black is a pawn ahead and has a winning position.

The Bayonet Variation

9 b4 (D)

Here we have the popular Bayonet Variation, which I shall only briefly examine. The Bayonet is characterized by play on both wings. Because the move 9 b4 allows Black to claim specific squares on the queenside via ...a5 and attempt to block White's traditional advances there, we find Black concentrating upon that

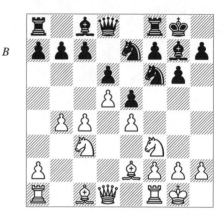

region of the board before he undertakes kingside action, if indeed the latter occurs at all. Ideally, some important ideas will come across in what follows, but it is essentially an very abbreviated outline of today's favourite variations. The following game and notes may shed a little light on the ensuing themes.

Black's principal choice, both originally and in current practice, is 9...⟂h5, which will be the subject of the illustrative games below. 9...a5 has been the primary alternative for years. Here's a recent example: 10 ⟂a3 (10 bxa5 has also been used extensively) 10...axb4 (Black also plays a variety of other moves such as 10...⟂d7, 10...⟂h5 and 10...b6; at the moment it seems that several are quite playable, but that none fully equalize) 11 ⟂xb4 b6 12 a4 ⟂e8 13 ⟂b5 (this stops ...c5, an important defensive idea for Black) 13...f5 14 ⟂d2! ⟂h8!? (D).

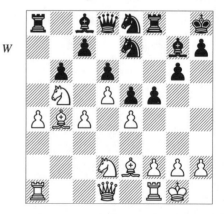

15 ⟂c3!. White's last two moves combine well; he can now play a5 without having to lose a critical tempo after the replies ...c5 and ...c6,

whereas the bishop on c3 makes f4 possible. A standard trick is 15 a5?! c6 16 dxc6 ♘xc6 and Black will capture on a5 with some advantage. After 15 ♗c3, Mikhalevski-Finegold, Schaumburg 2006 continued 15...c6 16 dxc6 ♘xc6 17 exf5 gxf5 18 f4! ♗b7 19 ♘f3!, and White's creative reorganization had secured him a definite advantage. A model game.

We now move on to Black's main continuation, 9...♘h5.

Bareev – Polzin
Rethymnon ECC 2003

9...♘h5 10 ♖e1

White has tried a number of moves here, particularly 10 g3 and 10 c5. But the move 10 ♖e1 is the overwhelming choice of masters today and indeed the reason why the Bayonet has come from relative obscurity to its current prominence. Now White can meet ...♘f4 with ♗f1.

10...f5

There have been very many games with 10...a5 11 bxa5 ♖xa5 12 ♘d2 ♘f4 13 ♗f1, a recent example going 13...♖a8 14 c5!? dxc5 15 ♘c4 ♗d7 (Mikhalevski offers up 15...b6 16 a4 ♗a6 for consideration) 16 ♖b1 b6 17 a4 ♘c8 18 a5 bxa5 19 ♗e3 ♘d6 20 ♗xc5 ♘xc4 21 ♗xc4! ♖e8 22 g3 ♘h3+ 23 ♔g2 h5 24 ♗b5! with advantage for White, Ponomariov-Bologan, Foros 2006.

11 ♘g5 ♘f6 *(D)*

This is currently the main line of the Bayonet, although that could always change.

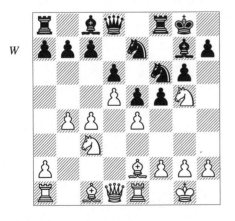

12 f3

12 ♗f3 is the other important move. A line that has been repeatedly tested over the years is 12...c6 13 ♗e3 h6 14 ♘e6 ♗xe6 15 dxe6 fxe4 16 ♘xe4 ♘xe4 17 ♗xe4 d5 18 cxd5 cxd5; e.g., 19 ♗c5 (19 ♗c2 is the older move, perhaps a better try) 19...dxe4 20 ♕xd8 ♖fxd8 21 ♗xe7 ♖e8 22 ♗c5 ♖xe6 23 ♖xe4 ♖d8 24 h4 a6 25 a4 ♖d5 with equality, Gyimesi-Baklan, Romanian Cht (Tusnad) 2005.

12...c6

12...♘h5!? and 12...♔h8 have also been played recently and should be researched by the serious student of this variation.

13 ♔h1 h6 14 ♘e6 ♗xe6 15 dxe6 ♘e8!

With the idea ...♘c7 and ...♘xe6. Essentially, Black counts upon gaining some material or a huge centre to offset White's bishop-pair.

16 ♕b3 ♘c7 17 c5 d5

So Black didn't get the e-pawn immediately but has the centre and can attack the pawn later. This requires a quick response by White.

18 exd5 cxd5 19 ♗b2! ♕c8!? *(D)*

A logical move that gets to the point: removal of White's pawn on e6. Both 19...♕e8 and 19...b6 have been tested without the final word having been said. 19...♕c8 has the advantage of avoiding certain problems along the e-file which are associated with 19...♕e8.

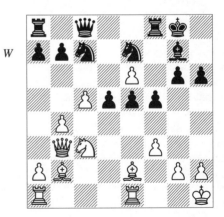

20 ♘b5!

The best way to counter Black's threat of ...♕xe6. White's play is very tactical in this line.

20...a6

A trick is 20...♘xb5?! 21 ♗xb5 ♕xe6 22 ♗xe5! ♗xe5 23 f4 with some advantage for White.

21 ♘d6 ♕xe6 22 ♘xb7 ♖ab8 23 ♘d6 ♘c6 24 a3 ♔h7 25 ♕a4 ♕d7 26 ♖ad1 ♖fd8

It has come down again to centre (and centralized pieces) versus the bishop-pair. Assuming that the tactics work, Black should be fine.

27 ♗xa6!?

Avrukh gives deep analysis on a variety of lines, the most thematic of which is 27 f4 (to define the central situation and exchange pieces before trying to win material) 27...e4 28 ♗xg7 ♔xg7 29 ♗xa6 ♘xb4! 30 ♕xd7+ ♖xd7 31 ♗c8 (31 axb4 ♘xa6 32 ♖xd5 ♖c7!) 31...♖xc8! 32 ♘xc8 ♘d3 and if anyone is better, it's Black. If he is allowed to capture a pawn on f4 or c5, his d- and e-pawns will become extremely strong.

27...♖a8 28 b5 ♘d4! 29 ♗xd4 exd4 30 ♕a5 ♘xa6 31 bxa6 ♕a7! 32 ♖b1 ♕xa6 *(D)*

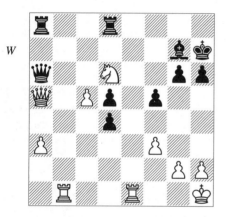

Black has achieved dynamic equality. The rest of the game is complex and full of alternatives, but the bottom line is that a draw is the fair result.

33 ♕c7 ♖g8 34 h4 ♖a7 35 ♕b6 d3 36 h5 gxh5 37 ♖ed1 ♕xb6! 38 cxb6 ♖xa3 39 ♘xf5 ♗f6 40 ♘e3 ♗d4! 41 ♘xd5 ♖a2 42 b7 ♗e5 43 ♘f6+ ♗xf6 44 b8♕ ♖xb8 45 ♖xb8 d2 46 ♔g1 ♗g5 47 ♖b4 ♔g6 48 ♔f1 ♔f5 49 ♔e2 h4 50 ♖c4 ♔e5 51 ♖e4+ ♔d5 52 ♖e8 ½-½

Averbakh Variation

1 d4 ♘f6 2 c4 g6 3 ♘c3 ♗g7 4 e4 d6 5 ♗e2 0-0 6 ♗g5 *(D)*

In the Averbakh, White tries to limit Black's options while keeping his own development flexible. I won't go into all the positional

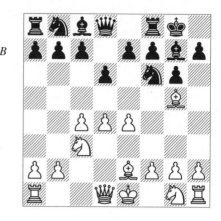

trade-offs between 5 ♘f3/6 ♗e2 and 5 ♗e2/6 ♗g5, but one of White's immediate ideas is to attack Black's king via ♕d2, ♗h6 and h4-h5. For this, the bishop on e2 is useful in that after 6...h6 7 ♗e3, 7...♘g4 is prevented. Another motivation for 5 ♗e2 and 6 ♗g5 is to prevent the natural 6...e5?? because of 7 dxe5 dxe5 8 ♕xd8 ♖xd8 9 ♘d5 ♘bd7 10 ♖d1! (or 10 ♘xc7) 10...♖f8 11 ♘xc7 with a winning game. Even the dynamic counter-attempt 11...♘xe4? falls on its face after 12 ♗e3 ♖b8 13 ♗xa7.

I shall use the Averbakh Variation mainly to discuss ...c5 structures in the King's Indian, something that we haven't seen much in other parts of this chapter. We shall also examine several Sämisch Variation games for that purpose.

6...c5

Naturally Black has alternatives. The popular 6...♘a6 is a typical modern move which can lead us back to the structures that we saw in the Classical KID lines with ...♘bd7. For example, 6...♘a6 7 ♕d2 e5 8 d5 c6 9 ♗d3 ♘c5 10 ♗c2 a5 11 ♘ge2 cxd5 12 cxd5 ♗d7 13 a4 *(D)*.

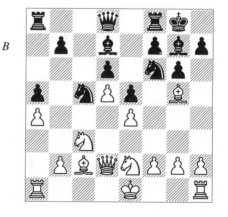

In this position, 13...♕b6 would be a natural move, but I like the idea 13...♖a6!?. Black intends ...♖b6 and in most cases ...♖b4. This is an example of Black abandoning ...f5 plans in favour of queenside action, as we saw in various lines with ...e5 earlier in this chapter. Of course, kingside expansion may follow later.

7 d5 h6 8 ♗f4

8 ♗e3 is another idea; it allows Black to play 8...e6 without immediately sacrificing his d-pawn.

8...e6!

A positional pawn sacrifice to activate all Black's pieces, with an emphasis on the dark squares. But White gets a free centre pawn.

9 dxe6 ♗xe6 10 ♗xd6 ♖e8 *(D)*

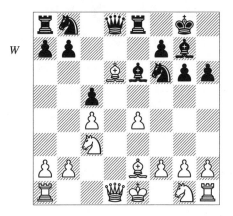

11 ♘f3 *(D)*

11 ♗xc5 is another can of worms. 11 e5!? is rare, but shows typically dynamic themes:

a) 11...♘fd7 12 f4 ♘c6 with the idea of an early ...f6 would be wild after 13 ♘d5 ♗xd5!? 14 cxd5 (14 ♕xd5 ♕b6 15 b3 ♖ad8) 14...♘d4 15 b4!? ♘xe5! 16 ♗xe5 ♗xe5 17 fxe5 ♖xe5 with a terrific attack for the piece.

b) 11...♘g4!? 12 ♗xg4 ♗xg4 13 ♕xg4 ♕xd6 14 f4 ♕d4! 15 ♘ge2 ♕xc4 with equality.

Now (after 11 ♘f3) Black must seek a way to use the power of the g7-bishop.

11...♕b6

11...♘c6 is an alternative that has been analysed out 25-30 moves to a drawish ending. I'll pass on that.

12 ♗xb8

12 e5 ♘fd7 13 ♘b5 ♘c6! is one of those typical exchange sacrifices for the dark squares: 14 ♘c7 (14 ♗c7 ♕a6 15 0-0 ♖ec8 and White's

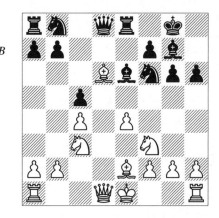

e5-pawn falls) 14...♘dxe5 15 ♘xe5 ♘xe5 16 ♘xa8 ♖xa8 and Black has compensation. Here 16...♕b4+ 17 ♔f1 ♘xc4! 18 ♘c7 ♖d8 is a good winning attempt.

12...♖axb8 13 ♕c2 ♘h5! 14 g3 ♗xc3+!?

Only one of several moves, including the logical and arguably superior 14...♗h3!?. That hasn't been tested as much, however.

15 ♕xc3

In the game Yermolinsky-Kindermann, Groningen FIDE KO 1997, White took a bold but risky decision after 15 bxc3 ♗g4 16 h3 ♗xf3 17 ♗xf3 ♕e6, and instead of 18 0-0 ♕xh3 (which was the theoretical continuation at the time) or 18 ♗xh5!? ♕xe4+! 19 ♕xe4 ♖xe4+ 20 ♔d2! gxh5, he played 18 0-0-0!?, to which Black responded with the dynamic 18...b5! *(D)*.

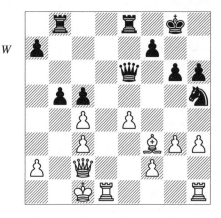

19 ♖he1 (White has options here such as 19 ♗xh5 and even 19 cxb5!?; the position is hard to assess, and harder still to play) 19...b4!? (later, 19...bxc4 20 e5 ♕a6 21 ♖d2 ♘g7 with the idea ...♘e6 was tried; that produced equal

chances) 20 e5 ♕a6! 21 ♖d7 ♘f6 with a messy, unclear position.

15...♗h3 16 e5 ♗g2 17 ♖g1 ♗xf3 18 ♗xf3 ♕d6 *(D)*

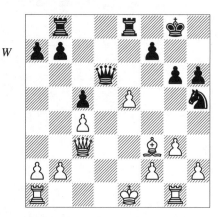

W

Preventing 0-0-0.

19 ♔f1

19 ♖d1 ♕xe5+ 20 ♕xe5 ♖xe5+ 21 ♔f1 ♘f6 22 ♔g2 b6 23 ♖d6 ♔g7 24 ♖gd1 ♖be8, Sorokin-Kaminski, Wisla 1992. Hazai makes the point that White has no squares to penetrate on. Still, with bishop for knight, there's no risk in playing on.

19...♕xe5 20 ♕a3

20 ♕xe5 ♖xe5 21 ♔g2 ♘g7!? is a better version of what follows.

20...♘g7!?

Black's ambitious idea is to bring this knight to the wonderful outpost on d4, by way of either e6 or f5. This runs into some problems, however, and Golubev feels that Black is only slightly worse after 20...b6 21 ♔g2 a5.

21 ♔g2 ♘e6 22 ♖ge1 ♕f6 23 ♗d5! *(D)*

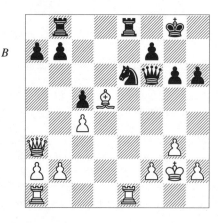

B

This is Bareev-Golubev, USSR jr-Wch qualifier (Klaipeda) 1985. Black came out worse in the enticing complications introduced by 23...♘d4? 24 ♕xc5 ♘c2 25 ♖xe8+ ♖xe8 26 ♖d1! ♖e2 27 ♔f1! ♖xf2+?! 28 ♔g1!. White eventually won. All in all, you can see how 6...c5 changes the King's Indian dynamic.

Sämisch Variation

1 d4 ♘f6 2 c4 g6 3 ♘c3 ♗g7 4 e4 d6 5 f3 *(D)*

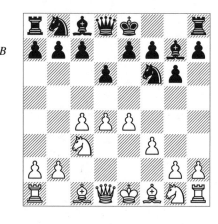

B

The Sämisch Variation is characterized by White's desire to protect his central squares e4 and d4, the first by a pawn and the second by pieces. This set-up is more difficult to attack by the means that we saw in the Classical Variation. If Black plays ...e5 and White replies d5 (by no means forced; see the first game), his favourite attack by ...f5-f4 and ...g5-g4 will achieve less for two reasons. First, White won't have to go through gyrations like ♘f3-e1 in order to attack on the queenside; that is, the moves f3 and ♗e3 come without hindrance. Moreover, White will often castle queenside and sidestep a direct attack on his king. He can then attack on either or both sides of the board, by means of h4-h5 or b4 and c5. I'll present examples below.

Black has many approaches to the Sämisch, but in general has benefited from remaining flexible. For some time now, 6...c5 has been the main weapon of top players. As in the Averbakh Variation, we'll see Black trying to pry open the long diagonal. Of course, there is a very wide variety of other strategies that both players can employ after 5 f3. My primary goal is to show a couple of typical structures that do not arise in the Classical lines.

Sämisch with ...e5

Shirov – Kasparov
Dortmund 1992

5...0-0 6 ♗e3 e5 7 ♘ge2 c6 8 ♕d2 ♘bd7 9 0-0-0 *(D)*

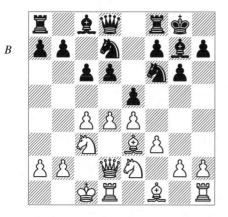

Here White is content to keep the centre fluid for the time being, much as he does in variations such as 1 d4 ♘f6 2 c4 g6 3 ♘c3 ♗g7 4 e4 d6 5 ♘f3 0-0 6 ♗e2 e5 7 0-0 ♘bd7. At any point he can play d5, which leads to another large set of variations and subvariations. Now the challenge is for Black to scare up play versus White's advantage in space. He does so by expanding on the queenside.

9...a6 10 ♔b1 b5 11 ♘c1

White needs to protect c4 and clear the way for his bishop on f1. The moves d5 and c5 are in the air, sometimes supported by a knight on b3. Black sidesteps them both.

11...exd4 12 ♗xd4 ♖e8!? *(D)*

Kasparov voluntarily gives up his grip on the centre by ...exd4 in order to open the long diagonal for his g7-bishop and the e-file for his rook. As in many variations of the King's Indian Defence (and for that matter in the Sicilian Defence), this creates a weak pawn on d6 that is a direct target down White's open d-file. With 12...♖e8, Black decides that it's not worth it to defend that pawn as yet. In fact, he also opens a square for the move ...♗f8, which in some variations provides solid support for that pawn.

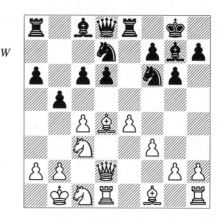

13 ♗xf6!?

Shirov accepts the sacrifice, but in doing so gives up the valuable dark-squared bishop that opposes its black counterpart. With hindsight, safer and more effective alternatives were found; for example, modern theory concentrates upon 13 ♗f2 and 13 ♘b3. But I'll stick to my main theme rather than get lost in those options.

13...♕xf6! 14 ♕xd6 ♕xd6 15 ♖xd6 ♘e5 *(D)*

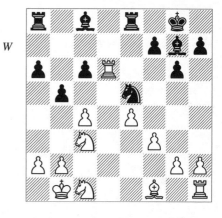

Remember that attacks can be just as deadly in queenless middlegames as when the queens are still on the board. For his pawn, Kasparov has two beautiful bishops as opposed to White's bad bishop, and his eye is on the king. Black's immediate intention is to play ...♗e6, sometimes in conjunction with ...♗f8, exploiting White's weak dark squares. Nevertheless, White is still a pawn ahead, which is no small matter.

16 f4!?

It's almost impossible to resist driving away the beautiful knight, especially as what follows isn't obvious. Perhaps better would be the seemingly suicidal 16 cxb5! axb5 17 f4 (17 ♘d3 b4! 18 ♘d1 ♗f8! 19 ♖d4 c5) 17...♘g4 18 ♖xc6! b4! (18...♘f2 19 ♖g1 b4 20 ♘d5 ♘xe4 21 ♗b5!) 19 ♘d5 ♗b7 20 ♗b5, although Black can get enough compensation for his material in several ways. To defend this general type of position is extremely difficult, all the more so against Kasparov!

16...♘g4! *(D)*

White was hoping for 16...♘xc4?! 17 ♗xc4 bxc4 18 e5.

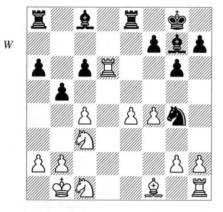

17 e5 ♘f2 18 ♖g1 ♗f5+ 19 ♔a1 b4! 20 ♘a4 f6! *(D)*

Cracking open the all-important long diagonal or winning a pawn.

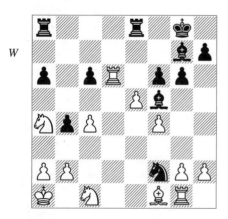

21 e6

The most spectacular line given by Kasparov is 21 g4!? ♘xg4! 22 ♗d3 fxe5!! 23 ♗xf5 gxf5 24 h3 exf4 25 hxg4 f3 26 ♘d3 (26 gxf5 f2 27 ♖f1 ♖e1 28 ♖d1 ♖xd1 29 ♖xd1 ♖e8 30 ♘d3

♖e2) 26...fxg4 27 ♖xg4 and after all those complications, the elegant 27...♖e1+! 28 ♘xe1 f2.

21...♖xe6 22 ♖xe6 ♗xe6 23 ♗e2 f5 24 ♘b3 ♗f7! 25 ♘a5 ♖d8! 26 ♖f1 ♘g4! 27 ♖d1 ♖xd1+ 28 ♗xd1 ♘e3! 29 ♗f3 ♘xc4 30 ♘xc6

Or 30 ♘xc4 ♗xc4 31 ♗xc6 ♗d4. The rest of the game is an application of technique. At the points where White is able to simplify, Black's two bishops will win the ending.

30...a5 31 ♘d8 ♘d2! 32 ♗c6 ♗h6! 33 g3 ♘f1 34 ♘b6 ♘xh2 35 ♘d7 ♗g7 36 ♘e5 ♗xe5 37 fxe5 ♔f8 38 e6 ♗e8 39 ♗xe8 ♔xe8 40 ♘c6 ♘f1 0-1

Let's see what happens when White closes the centre and Black tries his standard pawn-chain attack:

Platonov – Gulko
USSR Ch semi-final (Kiev) 1969

1 d4 ♘f6 2 c4 g6 3 ♘c3 ♗g7 4 e4 d6 5 f3 0-0 6 ♗e3 e5

There are funny move-order issues here. Black can play 6...♘bd7, intending to set up a system that avoids weakening d6; for example, 7 ♕d2 c6 8 0-0-0 a6. A popular option after 6...♘bd7 is 7 ♘h3!? (since ...♗xh3 isn't possible), with the basic idea of ♘f2 and perhaps ♘d3. Both sides' strategies are typically flexible and at that point Black sometimes reverts to 7...e5 8 d5 ♘h5, when White's knight may stay on h3 to help on the kingside. And so forth. It takes some study to master these nuances.

7 d5 ♘h5 8 ♕d2 *(D)*

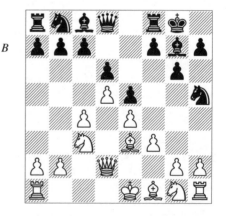

8...f5

A famous line is 8...♕h4+ 9 g3 (9 ♗f2 offers repetition by 9...♕f4 10 ♗e3, etc., or Black can try 9...♕e7) 9...♘xg3! 10 ♕f2 (10 ♗f2? ♘xf1) 10...♘xf1 11 ♕xh4 ♘xe3. This is Bronstein's idea. Black has only two pieces and a pawn for the queen, but threatens ...♘g2+ and will pick up the c-pawn with chances based largely upon queenside activity. With accurate play, this variation may favour White slightly, but that assessment is still being debated today.

9 0-0-0 *(D)*

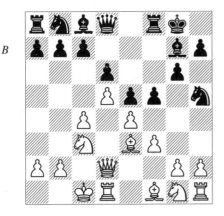

9...f4?!

This familiar advance is Black's most primitive approach, imitating the one that he uses against the Classical King's Indian. Perhaps my designation of '?!' is a bit harsh, but ...f4 is generally not a good idea for the reasons mentioned above. We shall examine it because the resulting positions illustrate White's core strategy versus ...e5/...f5 in clearest form. This situation can also arise in other variations in the Sämisch such as 5 f3 0-0 6 ♗e3 ♘c6 (with a later ...e5); it is also seen in the King's Indian Attack, and even in the Modern Defence (1...g6).

Over the years, Black has had more success with the flexible 9...♘d7, preparing ...♘df6 or ...♘c5. White can react in various ways; a classic and still popular possibility is 10 ♗d3 *(D)*.

Now:

a) 10...♘df6 11 ♘ge2 introduces another classic line. It affords White multiple choices such as exf5 followed by ♘g3, or simply h3, preparing g4. Ceding e4 by 11...fxe4 12 ♘xe4 ♘xe4 13 ♗xe4 ♗f5 14 ♘c3 gives White a small but certain advantage, in view of 14...♘f6

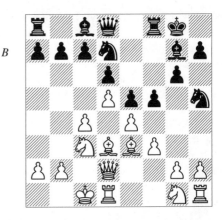

15 ♗g5 and White's e4 strongpoint cannot be broken down.

b) 10...♘c5!? 11 ♗c2 a6. Here Black prepares a counterattack by ...b5; for example, 12 ♘ge2 b5 13 b4 ♘d7 14 cxb5!? axb5 15 ♘xb5!? ♖xa2 16 ♘ec3 ♖a8, which has always been considered better for White, but Ward points out that this is not entirely clear.

10 ♗f2 ♗f6

Intending ...♗h4, to trade his bad bishop for White's good one on f2. Naturally White doesn't allow the exchange.

11 ♘ge2

In Gheorghiu-Angantysson, Reykjavik 1986, White got in every move of his ideal plan: 11 ♕e1 ♘d7 12 ♔b1 ♗e7 13 ♘ge2 b6 14 b4! a5 15 a3 ♗b7 16 ♘c1 ♘b8 17 ♘b3 axb4 18 axb4 ♘a6 19 ♘a2 ♕d7 20 ♔b2! ♔h8 21 ♖a1 h6 22 ♖ac1 *(D)* with the idea ♘d3 and c5.

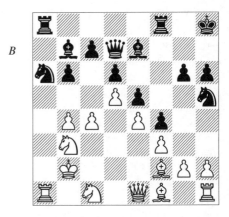

Although Black could have set up differently, we see what he is up against.

11...♗h4 12 ♗g1

By playing ...♗f6-h4, Black has imprisoned White's rook on h1. The problem is that he needs something positive to do.

12...♘a6

Black tries to slow down White's idea of a pawn-storm on the queenside. As before, if not disturbed, White has the simple plan of ♔b1, ♘c1-d3/b3, ♖c1 and launching his pawns forward with b4 and c5. In the early game Petrosian-Gligorić, Zurich Ct 1953, for example, Black let White have his way by 12...g5? 13 c5 g4 14 ♔b1, when Black was stuck for an idea. The game isn't that much better:

13 ♔b1 g5 14 ♘c1 g4 15 ♘d3 gxf3 16 gxf3 ♕e7 17 b4 ♔h8 18 ♖c1 ♖g8 19 c5 *(D)*

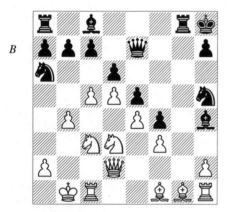

19...♘f6 20 ♘b5 ♗d7?

But White was getting through anyway. Now Black's pawn-chain collapses.

21 ♘xc7! ♘xc7

21...♖xg1 22 ♖xg1 ♘xc7 23 cxd6 ♕xd6 24 ♕c3! hits both c7 and e5.

22 cxd6 ♕xd6 23 ♗c5 ♘xe4

Forced, to save the queen; otherwise 23...♕a6 24 ♘xe5 followed by ♕xf4 is resignable.

24 fxe4 ♕g6

Even sadder is 24...♕f6 25 ♘xe5! and ♗d3.

25 ♘xf4! exf4 26 ♗d4+ ♖g7 27 ♖xc7 ♗f6 28 ♗xf6 ♕xf6 29 ♕b2! ♕xb2+ 30 ♔xb2 ♖e8 31 ♖xd7 ♖xd7 32 ♗b5 ♖dd8 33 ♗xe8 ♖xe8 34 ♖e1 f3 35 ♔c3 f2 36 ♖f1 ♖xe4 37 ♖xf2 ♔g7 38 d6 ♖e6 39 ♖d2 ♖e8 40 ♔d4 ♖c8 41 ♔d5 ♔f7 42 d7 1-0

Defence by means of ...e5 is still respectable, but these kinds of difficulties are one reason why Black has turned toward systems with ...c5.

Sämisch with ...c5

1 d4 ♘f6 2 c4 g6 3 ♘c3 ♗g7 4 e4 d6 5 f3 0-0 6 ♗e3 c5! *(D)*

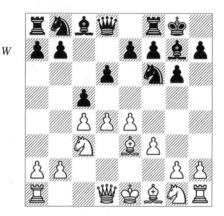

This variation begins with a pawn sacrifice in order to enhance the power of Black's bishop on g7 and to increase control of the dark squares in general. Remember that when White plays d4, c4 and e4, his most vulnerable square is d4, because it can't be supported by adjacent pawns.

7 dxc5

This variation is presented for instructional purposes; otherwise I would need to go into the alternatives 7 ♘ge2 and 7 d5. Their theory is extensive, but for once it's fair to say that mastery of the typical tactics and positional ideas will allow you to play either side with confidence.

7...dxc5 8 ♕xd8 ♖xd8 9 ♗xc5 ♘c6 *(D)*

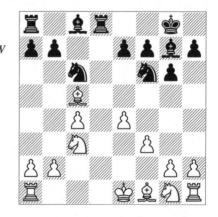

For his pawn, Black has both dark-square control and a lead in development. At this point we'll look at a few games:

Kramnik – Shirov
Bundesliga 1992/3

10 ♗a3 a5! 11 ♖d1 ♗e6 12 ♘d5 ♘b4! *(D)*

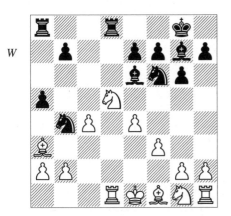

This move was Shirov's innovation, which changed both the assessment of this particular line and the reputation of the 6...c5 variation as a whole.

13 ♘xe7+!

13 ♗xb4?! axb4 14 ♘xb4 ♘d7! 15 ♖d2 ♘c5 *(D)* illustrates the power of the two bishops and open files:

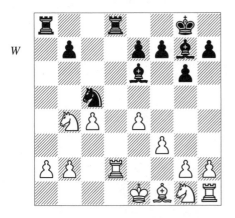

In spite of White's temporary two-pawn advantage, he is already in trouble and all three of his queenside pawns could easily fall. Otherwise we can get a position in which White's pieces won't be able to unravel; for example, 16 ♖xd8+ ♖xd8 17 ♘d5 ♗xb2 18 ♘xe7+ ♔f8 19 ♘d5 ♖a8! 20 ♗e2 ♖xa2 21 ♘h3 ♗xd5 22 exd5 ♗c3+ 23 ♔f2 ♗d4+ 24 ♔e1 ♘a4, etc.

13...♔h8 14 ♖xd8+ ♖xd8 15 ♘d5!

Gallagher gives the line 15 ♗xb4? axb4 16 ♘d5 ♖a8 17 ♘xb4 ♘d7! and Black stands better, although this time he's three pawns down! Compare the game.

15...♘c2+ 16 ♔d2 ♘xa3 17 bxa3 b5! *(D)*

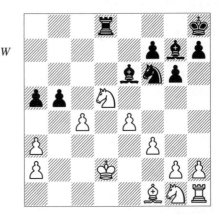

This key move takes the legs out from under the knight on d5 by liquidating the pawns that support it.

18 ♘h3 ½-½

Unfortunately, the game was agreed drawn at this point, but there's plenty more to say. Shirov gives the line 18...bxc4 19 ♗xc4 ♘xd5 20 exd5 ♗xd5 21 ♗xd5 ♖xd5+ 22 ♔e2. As Gallagher notes, Black could well play on, since he has the better minor piece.

He also draws attention to the alternative 16 ♔f2 *(D)*, first analysed by Shirov and then played in the game *Fritz6 – Har-Zvi*, Israeli Cht 2000.

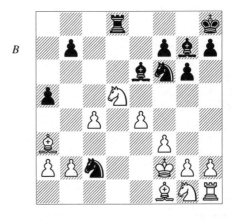

16...♘xa3 17 bxa3 b5! (Black is two pawns down but will again rid himself of White's strong knight and then either recover his material or sweep into White's position) 18 ♘h3 ♖c8!? (Shirov shows that 18...bxc4 19 ♗xc4 ♖c8! eventually leads to a drawn opposite-coloured bishop ending) 19 ♘xf6?! ♗xf6 20 cxb5 ♖c2+! 21 ♔e3 ♖xa2 22 f4 ♗d8! (the ...♗d8-b6 manoeuvre, standard in many KID positions, has decisive effect) 23 ♗d3 ♗b6+ 24 ♔f3 ♖xa3 (Black is a pawn down but the a-pawn and bishops are decisive) 25 ♖d1 a4 26 ♘f2 ♖b3 27 ♖b1 a3 28 ♖xb3 ♗xb3 29 ♗b1 a2 30 ♗xa2 ♗xa2 and Black won easily.

Razuvaev – Shirov
Bundesliga 1991/2

In this brief game we see Black's strategy at its most devastating. I won't give many notes because we've seen the basic ideas.

10 ♖d1!? ♖xd1+ 11 ♘xd1 ♘d7! 12 ♗a3 a5! 13 ♘e3

White can almost certainly do better in what follows, but it's no fun in any case.

13...♘b4 14 ♘h3 ♘c5 (D)

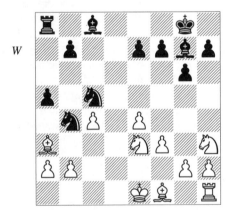

15 ♘f2 e6

Black takes away d5.

16 ♗e2 b6! 17 ♘fd1

17 0-0 ♗d4! (17...♘xa2 18 ♖d1 is unclear) 18 ♘ed1 ♘xa2 recovers the pawn, and White is even more tied up.

17...♘xa2 18 ♘c2 ♗a6

18...♗b7 with the idea ...f5 is another standard possibility, although it's unnecessary in this position.

19 ♗xc5 bxc5 20 ♘a3 ♘c1! 21 ♘b5 ♖b8 22 ♗f1 a4 23 ♔d2 ♘b3+ 24 ♔c2 ♖d8! 25

♘bc3 ♖d2+ 26 ♔b1 ♘a5 27 g3 a3 28 bxa3 ♗xc4 29 f4 ♗b3 0-1

Ro. Gunawan – Gelfand
Minsk 1986

10 ♘ge2 ♘d7 11 ♗e3

White tries something different, abandoning the placement of the bishop on a3. Now Black targets d3.

11...♘de5! 12 ♘f4 ♘b4 (D)

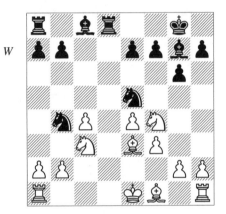

13 ♔f2!

Gallagher shows the lovely line 13 ♖d1 ♘xf3+! 14 gxf3 ♗xc3+ 15 bxc3 ♘c2+ 16 ♔e2 ♖xd1 17 ♔xd1 ♘xe3+ 18 ♔d2 ♘xf1+ 19 ♖xf1 b6 and White has multiple pawn weaknesses including those on the open c-file.

13...♗e6!? (D)

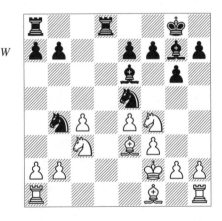

14 ♘cd5

14 ♘xe6 fxe6 leaves White without access to this important square.

14...♗xd5 15 ♘xd5 ♘c2 16 ♖c1 ♘xe3 17 ♔xe3 e6 18 ♘c3 ♗h6+! 19 f4 g5! *(D)*

Remarkably, Black is winning now because all the dark squares fall.

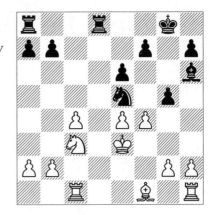

20 g3 ♘g6! 21 ♖c2

Or 21 ♘e2 gxf4+ 22 gxf4 e5.

21...gxf4+ 22 gxf4 ♗xf4+ 23 ♔f3 ♖d2!? 24 ♖xd2 ♗xd2 25 ♘b1 ♘e5+ 26 ♔f2 ♗f4 27 ♗e2 ♖d8 28 b3 ♖d4 29 h4

29 ♘c3 ♖d2 30 h4 ♖c2.

29...♖xe4 30 h5 ♗e3+ 31 ♔g2 ♗d4 32 ♗f3 ♘xf3 33 ♔xf3 ♖e3+ 34 ♔f4 ♖e2 35 ♖d1 e5+ 36 ♔f5 ♖h2 0-1

8 Grünfeld Defence

1 d4 ♘f6 2 c4 g6 3 ♘c3 d5 *(D)*

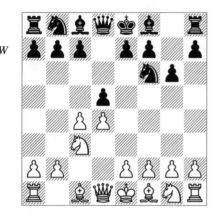

W

With 3...d5, Black sets White an entirely different set of problems from those he does with the King's Indian Defence (3...♗g7 followed by ...d6). Black challenges the centre immediately, and temporarily prevents White's advance e4. The combination of a dark-square strategy (...g6 and ...♗g7) with a light-square one (the move ...d5 will often lead to concentration upon the queenside light squares) is unusual in Indian systems where, at least initially, a particular colour complex is the focus of play (light squares in the Nimzo- and Queen's Indian, and dark squares in the King's Indian and Benoni). Similarly, the Queen's Gambit Declined and Slav Defences begin with concentration upon light squares.

This attention to both colour complexes lends a particular flavour to the Grünfeld. In the main lines, when White captures on d5 and Black recaptures with the knight followed by ...♘xc3, he immediately focuses on the dark squares (...♗g7, ...c5, ...♘c6 and ...♗g4), but soon turns his attention to light squares, either for purposes of restraint or occupation (...b6, ...♗b7, ...e6, ...f5 and ...♘c6-a5 or ...♘d7-f6/b6). White too has a flexible set of formations that typically encompass both colours in the vicinity of his exposed centre. The moves c4, ♘c3, e4, ♕b3 and ♗c4 attend to the light squares, whereas ♘f3/e2, ♗e3 and ♕d2 oversee the dark squares. In addition, White's central advances are divided between e5 and d5.

All this makes it difficult for those new to the Grünfeld to get a handle on what they should be doing. As is so often true, the central situation defines the optimal piece placement. If White creates a central majority by cxd5, he will generally concentrate upon establishing and then protecting an ideal e4/d4 structure. In a large majority of Grünfeld games by masters, White plays one of two systems that establish such a centre:

A: The Exchange Variation: 4 cxd5 ♘xd5 5 e4 ♘xc3 6 bxc3 (or 4 ♘f3 ♗g7 5 cxd5 ♘xd5 6 e4 ♘xc3 7 bxc3);

B: The Russian System: 4 ♘f3 ♗g7 5 ♕b3 dxc4 6 ♕xc4 0-0 7 e4.

These are the archetypical Grünfeld variations, which I shall call 'Main Lines'. Black will try to undermine White's structure, normally by pawn attacks early on, but sometimes by piece-play first and pawn moves later (especially so in the case of the Russian System). In both instances we have a classic situation where one side captures the centre with support from his pawns, and the other tries to control the centre from the outside of it. I shall concentrate upon precisely that situation.

Are there any elements common to all Grünfeld systems? Not quite, but in most significant variations, Black plays ...c5 in order to break up White's centre. This applies to most of the main lines above but also to primary alternatives such as 4 ♗f4 ♗g7 5 e3 c5 (or 5...0-0 and 6...c5); 4 ♘f3 ♗g7 5 ♗f4 0-0 6 e3 c5; 4 ♗g5 ♘e4 5 ♗f4 ♘xc3 6 bxc3 ♗g7 7 e3 c5; 4 ♘f3 ♗g7 5 e3 0-0 6 ♗e2 (or 6 ♗d2 or 6 ♗d3) 6...c5; 4 ♘f3 ♗g7 5 ♗g5 c5 (5...♘e4 6 ♗f4 ♘xc3 7 bxc3 c5), etc. In addition, we have 4 f3 c5, 4 h4 c5 and the like. As a practical matter, Black's instinctive reaction to less ambitious White play should be an early ...c5. Black's two other standard methods for resolving central issues are ...dxc4 (as in the Russian System) and ...c6. But ...c6 is infrequently played, and it can easily lead into variations that are properly Slav Defences. For example, 1 d4 ♘f6 2 c4 g6 3 ♘c3 d5 4 ♘f3 ♗g7 5 e3 c6 can come from the Slav move-order 1 d4 d5 2 c4 c6 3 ♘f3 ♘f6 4 e3 g6 5 ♘c3 ♗g7, etc.

The move ...c5 is therefore key to most Grünfeld lines, for reasons that are pretty obvious. First, it's easier for Black to attack d4 than e4. Then, you will notice that after the exchange ...cxd4 and cxd4, White's d-pawn is particularly vulnerable to the bishop on g7 and queen on d8, so that White can sometimes be pressured or even compelled to play either d5 or dxc5. The dxc5 option will often win a pawn, but it leaves White's pawn-structure shattered, with his c-pawn(s) exposed along an open c-file; we shall see more about this below. The advance of White's d-pawn to d5 is critical in a wide variety of middlegame situations, and it will be discussed in context.

Queenless middlegames appear more often in the Grünfeld than in other Indian systems. White's central majority may well be pitted against Black's queenside majority. In the Exchange Variation, without the c-pawns, Black is inclined to hold back his 2:1 majority throughout the opening and early middlegame. A fianchetto by ...b6 is safe, and by comparison with ...a6 and ...b5, it reduces the impact of a4 and protects c5 from occupation by a knight or bishop. The further advance of Black's a- and b-pawns is usually weakening. In the Russian System, White is more likely to play d5 before ...cxd4 occurs; in those cases, Black temporarily retains his 3:2 majority on the queenside, and we sometimes see a general advance by those pawns (for example, in the Hungarian Variation with ...a6 and ...b5 or the Prins Variation with ...♘a6 with ...c5 – see below). The moves ...c6 and ...e6 are often employed to isolate or eliminate White's pawn on d5.

With or without the c-pawns, White's d-pawn can also become a passed pawn, and indeed in the queenless middlegames or endgames arising from our main lines it is very often the centre of attention. In more cases than not, the d-pawn is a strength with which Black must

contend; even in the optimal cases in which he succeeds in securely blockading it, there may result only a stand-off, and White's space advantage can still be a factor. Frequently, both White's d- and e-pawns will survive long enough to be used to assist in space-gaining and attacking opportunities.

We'll look at these and more specific issues as we move to the main variations.

Exchange Variation

The most popular variation of the Grünfeld has always been the Exchange Variation:

1 d4 ♘f6 2 c4 g6 3 ♘c3 d5 4 cxd5 ♘xd5 5 e4 ♘xc3 6 bxc3 ♗g7 *(D)*

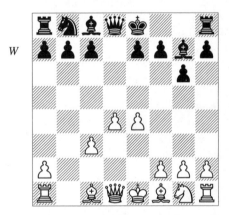

W

Note that 4 ♘f3 ♗g7 5 cxd5 ♘xd5 6 e4 ♘xc3 7 bxc3 is a common transposition to the contemporary 7 ♘f3 system.

First, we shall look at an extremely instructive sequence:

A: 7 ♗e3 c5 8 ♕d2.

Then we'll turn our attention to the two main-line systems:

B: 7 ♗c4;

C: 7 ♘f3.

These are examined in detail here because the positions are so fundamental to Grünfeld play:

7 ♗e3 with 8 ♕d2

7 ♗e3 c5 8 ♕d2 *(D)*

This system was made famous by Karpov's repeated use of it in his 1990 World Championship match versus Kasparov. The idea is not to

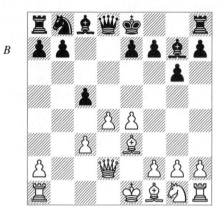

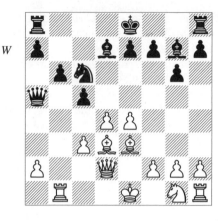

commit White's pieces (rooks, light-squared bishop, and knight) until Black does so. This is the best place in this chapter to look at the characteristics of queenless middlegames. I'll lay out two game excerpts with ideas that are typical of the Grünfeld in general:

H. Olafsson – Khuzman
Moscow 2004

8...♕a5 9 ♖b1

The tricky 9 ♘f3 transposes into 7 ♘f3 c5 8 ♗e3 ♕a5 9 ♕d2.

9...b6 *(D)*

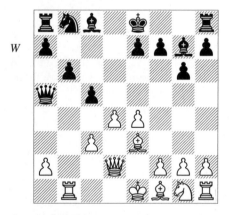

10 ♗b5+

This draws Black's bishop away from a spot on a6, from where it could exchange a pair of bishops and win light squares.

10...♗d7 11 ♗d3

11 ♗e2 ♗c6! and it's awkward to defend the e-pawn.

11...♘c6 *(D)*

The lines are drawn. White can take comfort from the fact that the bishop on d7 blocks the d-file and is poorly placed to put pressure on White's position. However, Black is well-developed and has the very useful threat of playing ...cxd4, exchanging queens, and winning the d4-pawn if White castles.

12 ♘f3

The (better?) alternative is 12 ♘e2 0-0 (after 12...cxd4 13 cxd4 ♕xd2+ 14 ♔xd2 White has an advantage because Black has no way to get at his centre) 13 dxc5 (often a poor choice in positional terms, but 13 f4 ♗g4! gets rid of a key defender) 13...♘e5 14 cxb6 axb6 *(D)*.

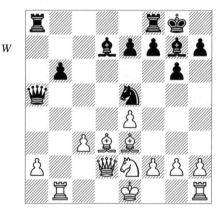

Here's a standard Grünfeld sacrifice of Black's c-pawn in return for pressure down the a- and c-files against weak pawns and possession of the c4 outpost. The situation is about equal: 15 0-0 ♕xa2 (threatening ...♕xd2 followed by ...♘xd3) 16 ♖b2 ♕a3 17 ♖xb6 ♖fd8 18 ♘d4 (18 ♗d4 ♗c8!) 18...♘xd3! 19 ♕xd3 ♖ac8 20 ♖b3 ♕a8!? (or 20...♕a5 with equality)

21 ♕b1 e5 ½-½ Hillarp Persson-Rõtšagov, Gothenburg 1999.

12...0-0 13 ♖c1?!

13 0-0? cxd4 wins a pawn. Perhaps White should already be willing to accede to a line like 13 ♖b5! ♕a4 14 ♖b2! in order to be able to castle. Then 14...♖fd8 (14...♗g4?? 15 ♗b5) 15 0-0 ♘a5 16 ♗h6 ♘c4 17 ♗xc4 ♕xc4 18 ♗xg7 ♔xg7 19 ♘e5 ♕e6 looks dynamically equal.

13...♗g4! 14 d5 ♖ad8! (D)

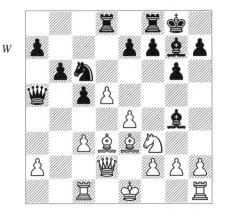

A manoeuvre to remember. Black prepares ...e6 and his knight will go to e5 or d4 depending on the situation.

15 ♕c2

White steps out of the pin. 15 0-0 ♗xf3 16 gxf3 e6! 17 c4 ♕a3! is slightly better for Black due to his control of d4 and White's weaknesses.

15...♗xf3 16 gxf3 ♘d4 17 ♕d1 ♘b5 18 ♗d2 ♘d6 (D)

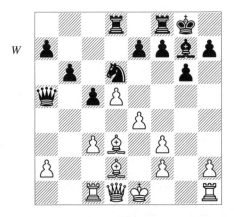

An ideal blockader. Black has won the opening. It's important to remember that the usual

counterplay for White in these positions comes from either f4 (and in this case e5) or a4-a5. But neither is available.

19 ♕b3

Not so much to protect the a-pawn as to discourage ...e6.

19...f5 20 exf5

20 c4 ♕a6 is awkward to meet, since 21 0-0 fxe4 22 fxe4 ♖f3! is extremely strong.

20...c4! 21 ♗xc4 ♖xf5 22 ♗e2 (D)

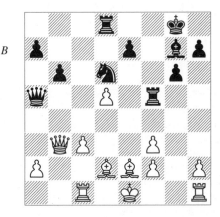

22...♖xd5

This leaves White with five isolated pawns! 22...♕xd5 would also be good, since 23 ♕xd5+ ♖xd5 24 ♗e3 (24 c4 ♖xd2) 24...♖c8 25 c4 ♖a5 dominates the queenside.

23 0-0 ♔h8 24 ♗f4 ♖f8 25 ♗g3 ♖d2 26 ♖c2 ♖xc2 27 ♕xc2 ♗xc3

Black is winning.

Yusupov – Khalifman
Ubeda 1997

8...cxd4 9 cxd4 ♘c6 10 ♖d1 ♕a5

10...♗g4!? is a tricky alternative. Then:

a) 11 f3 ♗d7 is considered equal. White can no longer bring his knight to f3, and must watch over the light squares as usual; e.g., 12 ♗b5 0-0 13 ♘e2 ♘a5! 14 ♗xd7 ♘c4! 15 ♕c3 ♘xe3 16 ♕xe3 ♕xd7 with an edge, Krush-Lalić, Hastings 2000. Black has bishop vs knight and will be able to use his queenside majority before White can use her central one.

b) 11 ♗e2! ♗xe2 12 ♘xe2 and now:

b1) 12...0-0 13 0-0 e6 14 d5!? exd5 15 exd5 ♘e5, as in Kožul-Avrukh, Belgrade 1999, is a typical d-pawn vs queenside fight. There could have followed 16 ♖c1 ♕d7 17 d6! ♖fc8 18 ♗f4 ♘c4 19 ♕d5.

b2) 12...♘a5!? (D).

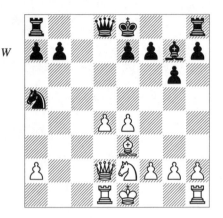

The fight begins for c4. Lputian-Kasparov, Wijk aan Zee 2000 went 13 ♕b4! 0-0 14 0-0 b6 15 d5 (White must be slightly better after 15 ♖c1 ♕d7 16 d6! ♖fc8 17 ♖fd1) 15...♕d6 16 ♕b5 ♕e5 17 ♖d4!? ♕b8!? 18 ♖a4?! ♖c8 19 ♘d4 ♖c5 20 ♕d7 ♖c7 21 ♕b5 ♕c8 22 h3 ♖c5 23 ♕b1? ♕d7 24 ♖b4, and here Black neglected to play the obvious 24...♘c4! with much the better game. Then Black's bishop is stronger than White's knight, because ♘c6 can be answered by ...e6. Instead of this Kasparov played 24...♖ac8 and ended up drawing a few moves later. But the overall lesson is that with accurate play, White's space and d-pawn seem to give him a small advantage.

11 ♕xa5 ♘xa5 12 ♗d3 0-0 13 ♘e2 ♗d7 14 ♖b1!

White intends ♗d2, so that a knight retreat would lose the b-pawn.

14...b6 15 ♔d2! ♖fc8 16 ♗a6!

Temporarily taking over the c-file in time to get his h1-rook out.

16...♖d8 17 ♖hc1 ♗c8 18 ♗d3! ♗b7 19 ♖c7 ♖ac8 20 ♖bc1 ♖xc7 21 ♖xc7 ♖c8!? 22 ♖xc8+

22 ♖xe7 ♗f8 23 ♖e5 ♗b4+ 24 ♔d1 ♗c6 intending ...f6 and ...♗a4+ or ...♘c4 is unclear.

22...♗xc8 23 ♘c3 (D)

Yusupov assesses this as clearly better for White. This is remarkable, since all he has is the big centre and centralized king. But that's the point: in the absence of other factors, it takes only a few small advantages for the 2:1

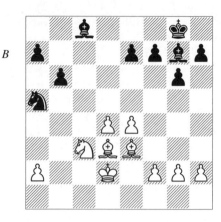

central majority to beat the 2:1 queenside majority.

23...♘c6 24 ♘b5 ♗a6 25 ♔c3!

25 ♘xa7 ♗xd3 26 ♘xc6 ♗xe4 27 ♘xe7+ ♔f8 28 ♘c8 ♗xg2 29 ♘xb6 is hardly clear due to Black's two bishops and White's four isolated pawns.

25...♔f8 26 a4!? ♗b7

26...h5 was widely recommended to stop White's next move but for one thing allows 27 e5! e6 (27...♗b7 28 ♗e4) 28 ♘xa7! ♗xd3 29 ♘xc6 ♗e4 30 ♘b8 ♗xg2 31 ♘d7+ ♔e8 32 ♘xb6.

27 g4! (D)

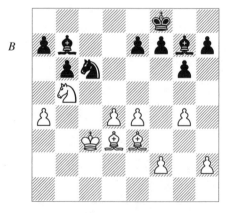

This move, pinning down Black's kingside and gaining more space, allows White to concentrate on the queenside.

27...♔e8 28 ♗c4 ♘b8 29 ♔d3 a6 30 ♘c7+ ♔d8 31 ♘d5 ♘d7 32 ♘b4!

Threatening a6 and f7.

32...a5 33 ♗d5! ♗xd5 34 ♘xd5 e6 35 ♘c3 ♔c7 36 ♘b5+ ♔c6 37 ♔c4

White's mobile centre is ultimately the decisive factor.

37...♗f8 38 ♗f4 ♗b4 39 f3 ♗f8 40 d5+

40 ♗d6! ♗xd6 41 d5+ is a clearer path to victory.

40...exd5+ 41 exd5+ ♔b7 42 ♘d6+! ♗xd6 43 ♗xd6

The rest is fairly simple: bishop versus knight with pawns on both sides of the board wins more often than not.

43...g5 44 ♗g3 ♘f6 45 ♗e5 ♘d7 46 ♗d4 ♔c7 47 ♔b5 f6 48 ♗f2 ♔d6 49 ♗xb6 ♘e5 50 ♗xa5 ♘xf3 51 ♗c3 1-0

7 ♗c4 and the Classical Exchange

7 ♗c4 (D)

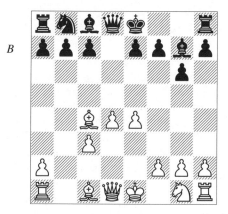

7...0-0

Over the next few moves there are many combinations of ...b6 and/or ...♘c6. We shall take time off for a couple of these because they show strategies unique to the Grünfeld which also contain themes and manoeuvres common to other chess openings. Theory from several sources approves of some of these lines to the extent that may worry players of 7 ♗c4. But Black must be careful; for example, 7...b6?! 8 ♕f3 (8 ♘e2 ♗b7) 8...0-0 9 e5 ♗a6!? 10 ♗d5 (10 ♕xa8? ♗xc4 with terrific compensation: the bishop-pair, light-square domination, etc.; White is undeveloped, and passive rooks in the middlegame are often worse than bishops) 10...c6 11 ♗b3 ♕d7 (D) (11...♕c7 led to a severe disadvantage after 12 h4!? c5 13 h5 cxd4 14 cxd4, with an ideal attack, in Yusupov-Timman, Tilburg Ct (7) 1986; the general rule is

that h4-h5 can work if Black has made no progress against the centre).

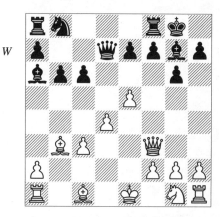

12 e6! (theory talks only about 12 ♘e2 and 12 h4, which are only equal, but not this simple move, nor the seemingly effective 12 ♘h3 e6 13 ♘g5!) 12...fxe6 13 ♕h3 ♔h8 14 ♗xe6 (or 14 ♘f3) 14...♕c7 15 ♘f3, etc. Maybe 7...b6 is just bad.

8 ♘e2

White played the variation with 7 ♗c4 and 8 ♘e2 almost exclusively for decades. It represents a kind of classical logic: develop the bishop actively to c4 (as opposed to e2), and put the knight on e2, a square from which it supports the centre but cannot be pinned (as opposed to ♘f3). White also castles as quickly as possible, something that is usually delayed in the variations with 7 ♘f3.

Now we briefly examine a variation without ...c5 (8...♘c6), and then turn to the main move 8...c5.

Playing without ...c5

Razuvaev – Stohl
Burgas 1992

8...♘c6 (D)

Another option is 8...b6. Although we won't look at it here, theory's overall verdict seems to be that the move is playable with precise defence. The attacking move 9 h4 is particularly dangerous and needs to be part of any preparation that one might make as Black.

The text-move blocks the c-pawn, but contains two other ideas to disturb White's game:

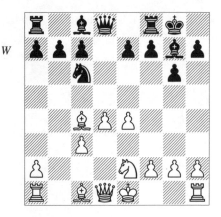

a) ...♘a5, driving away White's aggressively-placed bishop, often with ...c5 to follow;

b) the central advance ...e5, to block the position.

9 0-0 *(D)*

Natural. White has tried all kinds of things against 8...♘c6 without achieving a great deal. The advance h4 is sometimes White's reaction in the Grünfeld if Black hasn't challenged d4 with a pawn; but here it looks as though 9 h4 ♘a5 10 ♗b3 (10 ♗d3!?) 10...c5 11 h5 ♘xb3 12 axb3 cxd4 13 cxd4 isn't much of a problem; e.g., 13...♗d7!? (not the only move) 14 hxg6 hxg6 15 ♕d3 ♕b6, Spassky-Stein, USSR Ch playoff (1) 1964.

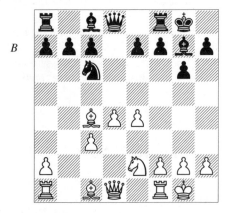

9...e5!?

An entirely different structure from in the main lines. Black's move restricts the scope of his g7-bishop but changes the pawn-structure so that a plan like ...b6, ...♘a5, and either ...♘b7-d6 or a well-timed ...c5 becomes possible. 9...♘a5 10 ♗d3 ♗e6 is also played, when

11 ♗g5 followed by f4 has caused Black problems. This sort of aggressive expansion by White becomes possible when his centre pawns aren't attacked by ...c5.

9...b6 *(D)* is another popular move-order now that h4-h5 doesn't activate White's rook.

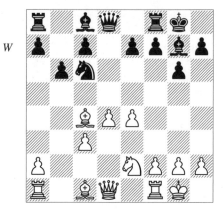

The ideas are simple: ...♗b7 and ...e5 or ...♘a5 with ...c5. Quick development by White can be dangerous, although with accurate play Black should be OK: 10 ♗g5 ♗b7 (10...♘a5 11 ♗d3 c5 is about equal; Black meets d5 with ...♕d7 and ...e6) 11 ♕d2 ♕d6?! 12 ♖ad1 ♘a5 13 ♗d3 c5 14 d5 e6 15 c4 (now Black has to watch out that White doesn't achieve f4 and e5) 15...♗a6 16 ♕c1 exd5 17 exd5 ♖ae8 18 ♘g3! ♕d7 19 ♖fe1 f5? (to stop ♘e4, but it creates an easily-accessible interior weakness on e6) 20 ♘e2! ♗b7 21 ♘f4 ♖xe1+ 22 ♖xe1 ♖e8 23 ♘e6 with a dominant position, Beliavsky-Gulko, Linares 1990.

We now return to the position after 9...e5 *(D)*:

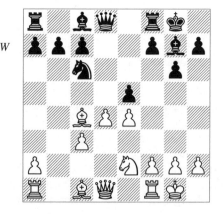

10 d5

This is the most instructive move, yielding a characteristic pawn-formation.

a) Suffice it to say that the controversial sequence 10 ♗a3 ♖e8 11 ♗xf7+!? ♔xf7 12 ♕b3+ ♔f6 13 f4! ♗h6! 14 fxe5++ ♔g7 15 ♕f7+ ♔h8 16 ♘f4 ♘e7 is quite a mess, and might even make this move-order undesirable for Black. You'll have to look at these particulars on your own time!

b) 10 ♗e3 ♕e7 (or 10...♘a5 11 ♗d3 b6) 11 d5 ♘a5 12 ♗d3 *(D)*.

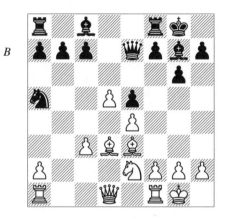

12...b6!? 13 ♕d2 ♗d7 14 ♖ac1 ♘b7 15 f4 ♗h6 16 ♖ce1 ♘c5 (we see the advantage of foregoing ...c5) 17 fxe5 ♗xe3+ 18 ♕xe3 ♕xe5 and Black is equal with a firm blockade and the e5 outpost, Tisdall-Stohl, Gausdal 1991.

10...♘a5 11 ♗d3 b6 12 c4 ♘b7 13 ♘c3 ♗d7 14 ♗c2 f5 15 ♗a4 ♖f7 16 ♗a3 ♘d6 17 ♗xd7 ♕xd7 18 c5 ♘xe4 19 ♘xe4 fxe4 20 ♕b3 ½-½

White has managed to keep the game open for his pieces, but he is also a pawn down and his centre isn't mobile. A possible continuation would be 20...♗f8 21 ♕c4 bxc5 22 ♗xc5 ♗xc5 23 ♕xc5 ♕a4 with equality.

Main Line with ...c5

1 d4 ♘f6 2 c4 g6 3 ♘c3 d5 4 cxd5 ♘xd5 5 e4 ♘xc3 6 bxc3 ♗g7 7 ♗c4 c5

Black's thematic move, targeting d4.

8 ♘e2 0-0

8...♘c6 9 ♗e3 will usually transpose after 9...0-0, but can also be used to get into early ...cxd4 lines. One such is 9...cxd4 10 cxd4

♕a5+!? 11 ♗d2 ♕d8!?, an implicit draw offer (or probing move) in that White can play 12 ♗e3 and repeat. Regardless of the theoretical details, the game Kramnik-Svidler, Dortmund 1998 is a superb example of Exchange Grünfeld themes, as well as the virtues of central pawn-masses: 12 d5! ♘e5 13 ♗c3 0-0 14 ♗b3 ♕b6 *(D)*.

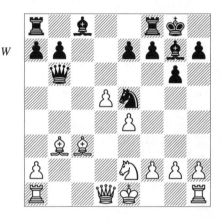

15 f4! ♘g4 16 ♗d4 ♕a5+ 17 ♕d2 ♕xd2+ 18 ♔xd2 e5 (it looks as though Black has solved his central problems) 19 h3! exd4 (19...♘f6 20 fxe5 ♘xe4+ 21 ♔e3 shows the power of a centralized king, yet another recurring theme in the Exchange Variation!) 20 hxg4 g5!? (20...♗xg4 21 e5 ♗xe2 22 ♔xe2; 20...d3 21 ♘c3 ♗xg4 22 ♔xd3 and in both cases the king supports the broad centre with a clear advantage) 21 g3! and now:

a) Analysis by Kramnik continues 21...d3 22 ♘c3 ♗xg4 23 ♔xd3 ♗f3 24 e5!? ♗xh1 25 ♖xh1 *(D)*, which he assesses as winning for White:

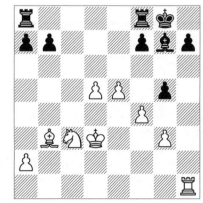

The diagram position is a demonstration of the power of White's central pawns. Although White is a full exchange down, all of his pieces are centralized and he has available an assortment of possible moves such as ♘e4, ♔e4, d6 and ♘d5, with Black's f7-pawn being particularly vulnerable and his bishop on g7 shut out. Most importantly of all, the opposite-coloured bishops ensure that White's bishop on b3 can't be exchanged off.

b) The game continued 21...♗xg4 22 e5! ♗xe2 23 ♔xe2. Again, White has the big centre, and the opposite-coloured bishops contribute to the winning scenario. As so often in the Grünfeld, we get a d-pawn marching down to deliver the final blow: 23...♖fc8 24 ♖ad1 ♖c3 25 ♖d3! ♖ac8 26 d6 b5 (26...♖xd3 27 ♔xd3 ♖c3+ 28 ♔xd4 ♖xg3 29 d7) 27 ♖xc3! dxc3 (27...♖xc3 28 d7) 28 e6! *(D)*.

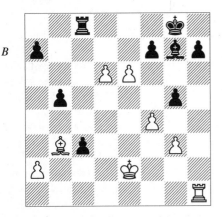

28...♔f8? (but 28...♗f8 29 e7 ♗xe7 30 dxe7 ♖e8 31 fxg5 ♖xe7+ 32 ♔d3 is convincing) 29 e7+ ♔e8 30 ♗xf7+! 1-0, in view of 30...♔xf7 31 d7. A wonderful game.

9 0-0 ♘c6 10 ♗e3 *(D)*

Just in time. Now White has defended the d4-pawn.

What are the characteristics of this main-line position? Both kings are safe, so it comes down to several factors. First of all, there's White's central majority, with pawns ideally placed on e4 and d4. That by itself isn't necessarily bad for Black, who may be able to restrain and then attack them. The question is whether the pawns can advance or cause other damage. With that in mind, let's consider what White would do if you gave him a move. The expansion via 11 f4

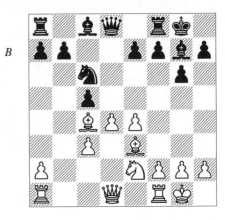

allows 11...♗g4. Playing h3 as a preparatory move can be considered, but at this point it looks slow. The advance 11 e5 is plausible, but creates central light-square weaknesses that Black is likely to be able to occupy. The move 11 d5 can be answered by 11...♘e5 12 ♗b3 b6 and ...♗a6 (or even 11...♘a5 12 ♗d3 e6); in both cases White has difficulty in playing c4 to protect the centre. That suggests some ideas: ♖c1, allowing d5 in many variations without the rook hanging, and/or a combination of ♕d2 and ♗h6. Some attack by f4 may follow later, all the more so if White can eliminate the powerful g7-bishop by means of ♗h6. If White achieves these things, his centre pawns and piece-play will control the board.

What advantages does Black have? First, as usual, the c4-square is loose and a potential outpost for a knight or bishop. The fact that ...♘a5 can be played with tempo is especially encouraging in that regard. Black also controls the open d-file and can play ...cxd4 to put pressure on the d-pawn and open his c-file. Since White is on the verge of consolidating as described above, that leads one towards two fundamental strategies. Black can get a rook to d8 and assault White's centre straight on. That is the classical approach, which often begins with ...♕c7, giving Black the subsequent choice of ...e5 to challenge d4, or ...e6 and ...b6 to restrain White's pawns. No immediate action is taken to attack White's side of the board. Alternatively, Black can try to exploit the enemy queenside light squares as quickly as possible, ideally by moves such as ...♘a5-c4 supported by the light-squared bishop, a rook on c8, pawn on b5, and so forth. One problem with this second plan is finding a good square for the bishop on c8. Thus if Black wants to follow the light-squares strategy, he will probably require an early series of forcing moves to carry it out. Let's look at both plans.

Classical System

10...♕c7 *(D)*

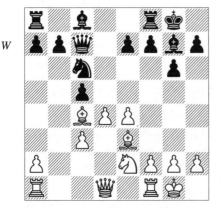

This is sometimes called the Smyslov Variation, and elsewhere the Shamkovich Variation. The traditional reason for this move is to follow up by ...♖d8. A disadvantage to that policy is that it weakens f7, not only directly but in the long term if White plays for f4-f5.

11 ♖c1

White is responding to an indirect threat of ...cxd4, although at the moment (were it Black's turn to move) 11...cxd4 12 cxd4 ♘xd4 13 ♗xf7+ and ♘xd4 would favour White. Nevertheless, ♖c1 gets off the long diagonal, protects c3, and most importantly serves as a strong disincentive for ...cxd4. The immediate 11 ♗f4 is also critical: 11...e5 12 ♗g3 (compare 11 ♖c1 ♖d8 12 ♗f4 e5 13 ♗g5!, hitting the rook) 12...♘a5!? (12...♕e7 13 d5 ♘a5 14 ♗d3 f5 is equal) 13 ♗d5 ♗e6! (grabbing light squares even if it means crippling one's pawns!) 14 ♗xe6 fxe6 15 ♖b1 a6, intending ...♘c4, is equal.

11...♖d8 *(D)*

This position is strategically very rich and after many years no clear verdict has been reached. I'll give two classic but genuinely illustrative game excerpts to demonstrate the main themes.

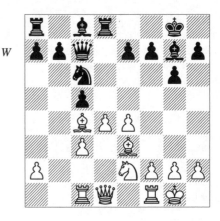

Gligorić – Smyslov
Yugoslavia-USSR 1959

This is one of the original, archetypal games that showed the latent strength of Black's position.

12 h3

White wants to play f4 without facing ...♗g4 with the idea of ...♗xe2. Since 12 h3 uses time, however, the immediate 12 f4 was nevertheless a main line for some years, with the idea 12...♗g4 13 f5!? gxf5 (or 13...♘a5) 14 h3 ♗xe2 15 ♕xe2. This attack eventually seemed to peter out after, for example, 15...cxd4 16 cxd4 ♕d6 (or 16...♕g3 17 ♖f3 ♕g6! 18 exf5 ♕f6, blocking the attack and targeting the centre, with equality) 17 exf5 (17 ♖xf5 ♘xd4 18 ♗xf7+ ♔h8) 17...♘a5 18 ♕g4 ♘xc4 19 ♖xc4 ♔h8 with equality. Generally the disappearance of White's powerful light-squared bishop means an end to Black's problems.

A logical alternative is 12 ♕d2, when Black can play the solid 12...♕a5 intending ...cxd4, or go for more with 12...a6!? 13 f4!? (White can also play 13 ♗h6 b5 14 ♗d3 ♕d7 15 ♗xg7 ♔xg7 16 d5; e.g., 16...♘e5 17 c4 or 16...c4 17 ♗c2 e6 18 ♘f4!?) 13...b5 14 ♗d3 f5! (compare the main game) 15 exf5 (15 ♘g3 e6) 15...c4 16 ♗b1?! (16 ♗e4! gxf5 17 ♗f3 with the idea ♘g3-h5) 16...gxf5! 17 ♘g3 e6 18 ♘h5 ♗h8 19 ♖f3 ♘e7 20 ♗f2 ♗b7 21 ♖e3 ♔f7!, Haïk-Kouatly, Cannes 1986. This is a superb demonstration of determined pursuit of the light squares by Black. Nevertheless, White could have played better and the whole line is unclear.

12...b6 13 f4 e6

First, Smyslov restrains the centre.

14 ♕e1 ♗b7

Later the direct attack 14...♘a5 15 ♗d3 f5, with the same basic idea, was played in Spassky-Fischer, Siegen OL 1970.

15 ♕f2!? ♘a5 16 ♗d3 f5! *(D)*

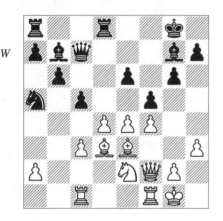

This is the key to Black's game. Without the move f5 at White's disposal, his bad bishop on e3 is reduced to defence and Black has greater pressure along the a8-h1 diagonal.

17 e5

A real concession, because White no longer has an effective pawn-break. However, he maintains a space advantage. What's more, the alternative 17 exf5 exf5 would leave d4 vulnerable to the bishop on g7.

17...c4 18 ♗c2 ♘c6!

Heading for d5 via e7.

19 g4 ♘e7 20 ♔h2 ♕c6 21 ♘g3 b5! 22 a4 a6

White has little to do, and Black's opening strategy has clearly won the day.

Spassky – Fischer
Santa Monica 1966

This game shows how White can sometimes use his centre to thwart Black's plans.

12 ♕e1!?

Getting out of the pin and planning something like f4-f5, ♕h4, etc.

12...e6!? *(D)*

As with other 12th moves in this line, White has not been able to get a forced advantage after 12 ♕e1 because Black can neutralize White's attacking plans by 12...♕a5! 13 ♖d1 (13 dxc5 ♘e5) 13...cxd4 14 cxd4 ♕xe1 15 ♖fxe1 b6 16 d5 (16 ♖c1!?) 16...♘a5 17 ♗b5 ♗d7 with equality.

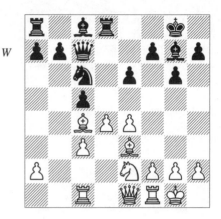

13 f4

Another promising idea is 13 ♗g5!? ♖d7 14 d5.

13...♘a5 14 ♗d3 f5 15 ♖d1 b6

Fischer has followed the Smyslov formula and hemmed in White's pieces. That's not the end of the story, however, because White's large centre is a potential force.

16 ♕f2!

Although it's not always the case in the Grünfeld, 17 dxc5 is a real threat in this position.

16...cxd4

16...fxe4 17 ♗xe4 ♗b7 18 ♘g3 gives White the edge.

17 ♗xd4 ♗xd4 18 cxd4 ♗b7 19 ♘g3 ♕f7

Every light square is guarded, but...

20 d5! *(D)*

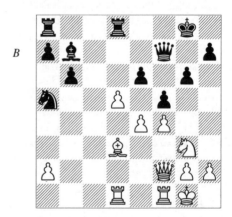

White's chances in these lines depend upon central activity, which in this case means breaking down Black's blockade.

20...fxe4 21 dxe6 ♕xe6 22 f5! ♕f7

Not 22...gxf5? 23 ②xf5 exd3 24 ♕g3+ ♕g6 25 ②e7+.

23 ♗xe4 ♖xd1 24 ♖xd1 ♖f8!

Another mistake would be 24...♗xe4? 25 ②xe4 gxf5 26 ♖d7! ♕g6 27 ♕d2! and White's attack is irresistible.

25 ♗b1 *(D)*

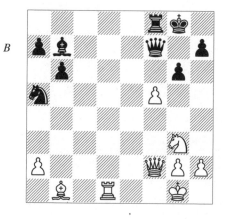

White has a small but definite edge. I'll continue the game without notes.

25...♕f6 26 ♕c2 ♔h8 27 fxg6 hxg6 28 ♕d2! ♔g7 29 ♖f1 ♕e7 30 ♕d4+ ♖f6 31 ②e4 ♗xe4 32 ♗xe4 ♕c5 33 ♕xc5 ♖xf1+ 34 ♔xf1 bxc5 35 h4!

Spassky went on to win this famous bishop vs knight ending. With pawns on both sides of the board, the bishop has a substantial advantage.

Kiselev – Epishin
Barnaul 1988

12 ♗f4 *(D)*

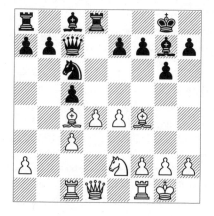

Here's the most difficult move for Black to meet. It turns out that the queen has trouble finding a good square.

12...♕d7

This awkward move is explained by a look at the alternatives:

a) 12...♕a5? strays too far from the second rank: 13 ♕b3!, when 13...e6 14 d5 exd5 15 ♗xd5 is awful.

b) 12...e5?! 13 ♗g5 puts the question to Black's rook and there's nothing satisfactory: 13...♖d7 (13...♖d6 14 ♕a4!; 13...♖e8 14 d5 ②a5 15 ♗b5 ♗d7 16 d6 ♕c8 17 ♖b1) 14 d5 ②a5 15 ♗b5 ♖d6 16 c4. Generally the achievement of c4 for White translates to some advantage, assuming that Black's pieces can't use d4 effectively.

c) 12...♗e5!? 13 ♗g3! ♗xg3 14 fxg3! e6 15 ♕d2 launches a nice attack. Black's bishop on c8 doesn't participate in the defence.

13 d5 *(D)*

This is purely a case of space and centre vs restraint and counterplay. As usual, 13 dxc5 allows compensation after 13...②e5! 14 ♗xe5 ♗xe5.

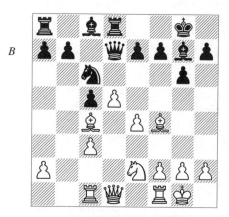

13...②a5

Or 13...②e5 14 ♗b3 b5.

14 ♗d3 b5!?

Black's most positive try. Otherwise he tends to acquiesce to more passive defence; for example, 14...e5 15 ♗e3 (or 15 ♗g5) 15...♕e7 (15...b6 16 f4! exf4 17 ♗xf4 is clearly better for White) 16 ♕d2 b6 17 f4 exf4 18 ♗xf4 ♗g4 19 ②g3 c4 20 ♗e2! ♗xe2 21 ♕xe2, Polugaevsky-Tukmakov, Moscow 1985.

15 ♖b1 a6 *(D)*

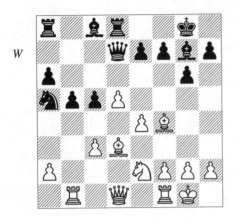

W

16 ♕c1!?

16 ♗e3 may grant White some advantage. Again, Black should stay active: 16...e6! 17 ♗xc5 ♕c7 18 ♗d4 exd5 19 exd5 ♗b7 20 a4! ♗xd5 21 axb5 axb5, when White keeps some edge by 22 ♖xb5 or 22 ♗xb5.

16...♘b7!?

Black would like to play ...e5 and at some point blockade by ...♘d6. A reasonable option is 16...e6.

17 ♕a3 e5! (D)

It's too early for 17...c4 due to 18 ♗c2 with the idea ♖ad1 and ♘d4.

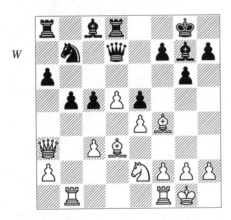

W

18 ♗g5 c4! 19 ♗c2 ♖e8 20 ♕c1 ♘d6 21 ♗h6 ♕e7!?

Easier is 21...f5! 22 exf5 gxf5 23 ♕g5 ♕e7 with no problems.

22 ♘g3 ♗xh6 23 ♕xh6 ♕f8 24 ♕e3 ♕e7 25 ♔h1 h5 26 h3 h4 27 ♘e2 f6 28 ♖g1 ♔g7

and the game is level.

Probably White has the edge in this variation by means of 12 ♗f4, but Black's position is certainly playable. Thus the Shamkovich Variation remains a viable option.

Modern Main 7 ♗c4 Line

1 d4 ♘f6 2 c4 g6 3 ♘c3 d5 4 cxd5 ♘xd5 5 e4 ♘xc3 6 bxc3 ♗g7 7 ♗c4 0-0 8 ♘e2 c5 9 0-0 ♘c6 10 ♗e3 (D)

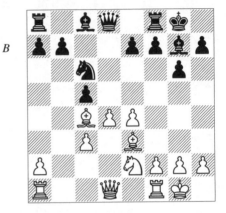

B

10...♗g4

This sortie has always been important, but has taken over modern theory for the last few decades. First let's mention the alternative 10...♘a5 11 ♗d3 cxd4 12 cxd4 at this point:

a) It's interesting that 12...♗e6 looks very much like the main line 10...♗g4 11 f3 ♘a5 12 ♗d3 cxd4 13 cxd4 ♗e6 below, except that White hasn't strengthened his centre by f3 (you may want to consider this again after you read the chapter). So how can it be that Black almost never plays this way? It turns out that by inserting 10...♗g4 11 f3, Black gains several advantages that arise in specific lines. The main difference is that he has the options of ...♕b6+, ...♕xd4+ and ...♗xd4+ (or ...♗xe3+) in some situations. Furthermore, the bishop on e3 can be attacked by moves such as ...♕a3 or in a few cases even ...♗h6.

b) Black's attempt to force a draw by means of 12...♘c6 (i.e. 13 ♗c4 ♘a5, etc.) fails to do so after 13 ♗b5 (13 ♗c2 b6 14 ♗a4 and ♖c1 is also advantageous) 13...♗g4 (13...♗d7 14 ♖b1 e6 15 ♕d2) 14 f3 ♗d7 15 ♖b1 e6 16 ♕d2 with an edge.

c) The most positionally interesting of deviations with this order is 12...b6!?, with the intention of ...e6 and ...♖e8. White has generally gained a small advantage here by normal means (♕d2, ♖ad1 and ♗h6, for example), but it's not much. The game Gligorić-Tukmakov, Odessa 1975 illustrates another plan in the Grünfeld that we haven't seen. It comes up when ...e6 has been played: 13 ♖c1 e6 14 e5!? ♗b7 15 ♘f4 ♕e7!? 16 ♕g4 ♘c6 17 h4! ♘b4 18 ♗c4 b5 19 ♗b3 *(D)*.

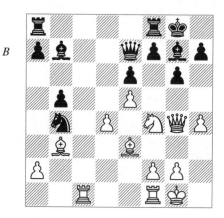

White has a kingside bind and the better prospects. The question is one of timing: if Black can plant and keep a piece on d5 right away, he should be OK. The problem is that White not only threatens to attack on the kingside but has the c5 outpost (♘d3-c5), which ensures his superiority.

11 f3 ♘a5

Issues of move-order are confusing here, but if you want to understand the position they are important. If Black now plays 11...cxd4 12 cxd4 ♘a5 *(D)* (this can also be arrived at by 10...cxd4 11 cxd4 ♗g4 12 f3 ♘a5), we reach this position:

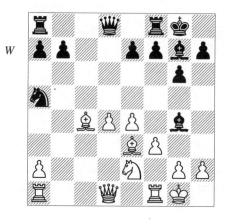

Then 13 ♗d3 ♗e6 will transpose to the main line in games below. There are, however, two differences. First, by capturing on d4, Black is allowing White the option of 13 ♗d5 *(D)*, which is theoretically equal but can be annoying in practice.

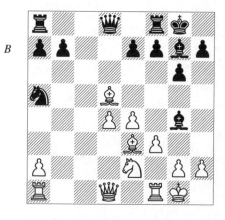

13...♗d7 14 ♖b1 a6 15 ♗xb7 (15 e5!? ♗b5 16 ♗e4 ♘c4 17 ♗f4) 15...♖a7! 16 ♗d5 ♗b5 17 a4 (17 ♖e1!? e6 18 ♗b3; these untested possibilities for White are a bit worrisome to Black, which argues for delaying ...cxd4) 17...♗xe2 18 ♕xe2 e6 19 ♗c4 ♗xd4 20 ♖fd1 ♗xe3+ 21 ♕xe3 ♖d7. Theory calls this equal, although Black still has to play accurately.

Then there's 13 ♖c1 ♘xc4 14 ♖xc4, to which a lot of theory is also attached. Again Black needs to be a little careful even if winning the bishop-pair can't be objectively worse for him. Neither of these options is a problem if the pawns on c5 and c3 are retained (see below).

A further significant difference between 11...♘a5 and 11...cxd4 12 cxd4 ♘a5 is that in the 'Seville Variation' below with 12 ♗xf7+, the pawns are still on c3 and c5, whereas with the 11...cxd4 order we have 13 ♗xf7+ ♖xf7 14 fxg4 and those pawns are traded. (You'll have to jump ahead to make sense of this description.) At this point the question becomes whether Black prefers the ♗xf7+ lines with the pawns still on the board. Unfortunately, one needs loads of specific study to answer that. But there's a possible saving grace. If Black believes that the best defence to the Seville (or a good one) is to play ...cxd4 and ...e5 later (see below), then you will see that the move-order is unimportant and that you don't need to exchange now, thus avoiding 13 &d5 and 13 Ec1. Hopefully some or all these nuances will become clearer as you go through the following material.

We now return to 11...♞a5 (D):

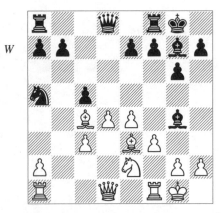

This is the main-line position of the ♗c4 Exchange Variation. We now have two basic variations that have thus far been taken seriously.

Seville Variation

12 ♗xf7+!?

It's pretty easy to see that 12 fxg4? ♞xc4 (with tempo!) is positionally bad. We look at 12 ♗d3 cxd4 13 cxd4 ♗e6 below.

12...♖xf7 13 fxg4

The 'Seville Variation' was so named because of several games that Karpov played with it against Kasparov in their 1987 match in Seville. The ideas behind it are intriguing, in part because they are superficially unprincipled.

13...♖xf1+ 14 ♔xf1 (D)

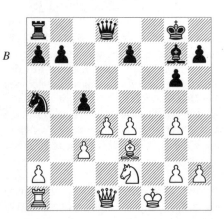

White has won a pawn, which is of some value even though it consists of a doubled g-pawn. His centre is superior to Black's and, given time, potentially mobile. Black has his own advantages; for example, a wonderful outpost on c4 for his knight and some play against White's rather draughty kingside.

In spite of a large body of theory and experience with 12 ♗xf7+, the ensuing play is not of such a critical nature that one needs to commit much to memory. I'll look at two games that should cover the main ideas and strategies.

Karpov – Kasparov
Belfort 1988

This game has been used in many books, deservedly so. It is representative of White's ideas and beautifully played. To get a more balanced view of the opening, see the game excerpts within the notes.

14...♕d6

14...♕d7 15 g5 (this is along the lines of Karpov's idea, to imprison the bishop on g7) 15...♖d8 (15...♞c4! and 15...cxd4 16 cxd4 e5 are good alternatives) 16 ♔g1 e5 17 d5 b6 18 h3 ♞c4 19 ♕d3 ♞d6 20 a4! (D).

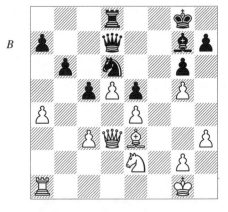

We'll see this more than once: the problems that Black has when he sets up this blockade with ...e5, ...c5, ...b6 and ...♞d6 tend to come from a4-a5. That can be surprisingly difficult to meet, as here: 20...c4 (else White plays c4 and a5) 21 ♕c2 ♗f8 22 ♔h1 ♞b7 23 ♞g1 ♗c5 24 ♕e2 ♗xe3 25 ♕xe3 ♕f7 26 ♞f3 with much the better game for White, Sakaev-Van Wely, Internet blitz 2004.

15 e5! ♕d5 *(D)*

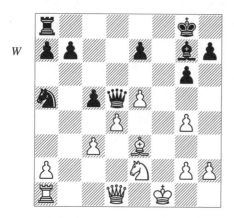

What's this? With 15 e5, White just ceded all those light squares Black loves so much! In addition, for a mere extra doubled pawn, White has exposed his king, given himself a bad bishop, and hardly attended to his development! For all that, there are some real dangers for Black. If, for example, White plays g5, his bishop's problem will be less important than that of Black's 'good' one, which is imprisoned indefinitely. Also, White has the easy-to-underestimate advantages of space and a central majority. Notice that if he gets moves like ♔g1 and ♘f4 in, Black will have serious weaknesses to cover.

For his part, Black's advantages are fairly obvious: a beautifully centralized queen on d5, an outpost for the knight on c4, and numerous possible open files for his rooks. One difficulty, however, is that he has to achieve any progress by use of his pieces alone, since he has no pawn-breaks.

16 ♗f2!

The immediate 16 g5 is worse for concrete reasons: 16...♕e4 17 ♗f2 ♖f8 with serious pressure.

16...♖d8 17 ♕a4! b6 *(D)*

18 ♕c2

Having provoked a weakness, Karpov returns to cover the central squares. A recent approach with the same ideas of pawn-structure versus piece-play went 18 ♘f4 ♕f7 19 ♘h3! ♕e6 20 g5 (now White has the ideal pawn-formation and needs to prepare for ♘f4 again) 20...♕f5!? (here I think 20...♕c6! is more thematic, with the idea 21 ♕a3? cxd4 22 cxd4 ♖xd4! 23 ♗xd4 ♕c4+, or 21 ♕xc6! ♘xc6 22

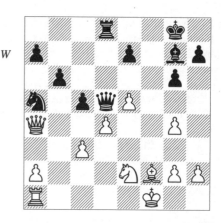

♘f4 ♔f7) 21 ♔g1 ♕d3 22 ♖d1 (or 22 dxc5 ♕xc3 23 ♖f1) 22...♕xc3 23 dxc5 ♖xd1+ 24 ♕xd1 ♗xe5 25 cxb6 axb6 26 ♗xb6 ♘c4 27 ♗f2 with a small advantage for White in the game P.H.Nielsen-Sutovsky, Dortmund 2005, which was eventually drawn.

18...♖f8

Later 18...♖c8! was discovered to be better and fully satisfactory. The trade-off of activity for structure is a very difficult one to handle.

19 ♔g1 ♕c4 20 ♕d2

White would like to continue with ♘g3-e4.

20...♕e6 21 h3 ♘c4 22 ♕g5! *(D)*

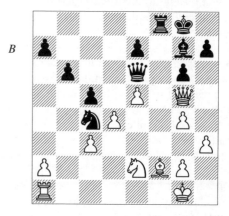

One of the best moves of the game and still part of the opening strategy! White wants to keep the bishop off h6 and at the same time get ready to mobilize by ♘f4 or ♘g3-e4. This provokes the next move which further restricts Black's bishop:

22...h6 23 ♕c1 ♕f7 24 ♗g3 g5

This move, trying to prevent ♘f4, has been criticized, although the suggested 24...♕d5!?

25 ♘f4 ♕e4 isn't really better after 26 ♘e6. Now the game is positionally won for White, so here are the moves alone:

25 ♕c2 ♕d5 26 ♗f2! b5 27 ♘g3 ♖f7 28 ♖e1 b4 29 ♕g6 ♔f8 30 ♘e4 ♖xf2 31 ♔xf2 bxc3 32 ♕f5+ ♔g8 33 ♕c8+ ♔h7 34 ♕xc5 ♕f7+ 35 ♔g1 c2 36 ♘g3 ♗f8 37 ♘f5 ♔g8 38 ♖c1 1-0

Van Tilbury – Zadrima
Moscow OL 1994

14...cxd4 15 cxd4 e5 *(D)*

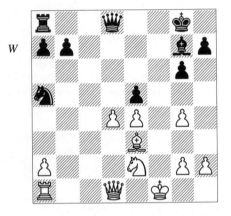

A completely different approach. In many cases Black will now play on the dark squares!

16 d5

Now the game once again takes on the character of superior pawn-structure (a dangerous protected passed pawn on d5) versus active piece-play. This time it will be difficult to prevent Black's bishop from coming quickly into play via h6 or f8. White has often tried 16 ♔g1 instead, when Black seems to have established equality by 16...♖c8; for example, 17 d5 ♘c4 (heading for a blockade on d6) 18 ♗f2 ♕d7 19 ♖c1 b5 20 g5 a5 21 ♘g3 ♘d6! is equal, Van Wely-Leko, Monaco (Amber rapid) 2001. You can still have fun playing this type of position in practice.

16...♘c4 17 ♕d3 *(D)*

For a while, 17 ♗f2 was considered a more dangerous try, retaining the good bishop, but this costs time after 17...♕f6 18 ♔g1 ♖f8 19 ♕e1 ♗h6!, leading to equality.

17...b5

This is a relatively safe move that secures the powerful knight's position. Kasparov played

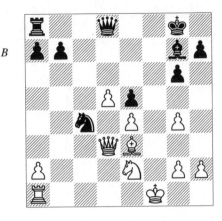

the paradoxical 17...♘xe3+!? 18 ♕xe3 ♕h4 versus Kramnik in Linares 1999, this time playing for dark squares and depending upon tactics in the face of White's extra and extremely dangerous d-pawn. The theory on this line extends past move 30 and is very specific, so I'll ignore it except to quote that game: 19 h3 ♗h6 20 ♕d3 ♖f8+ 21 ♔g1 ♕f2+ 22 ♔h1 ♕e3 23 ♕c4 b5 24 ♕xb5 ♖f2 25 ♕e8+ ♗f8 26 ♕e6+ (a very pretty line is 26 d6 ♕xe2 27 d7 ♕xe4 28 ♖g1 ♖f3! 29 ♕e6+ ♔h8 30 g5 ♗e7 31 gxf3 ♕xf3+ 32 ♖g2 ♕f1+ 33 ♔h2 ♕f4+ with a draw) 26...♔h8 27 d6 ♕xe2 28 ♕xe5+ ♗g7 29 ♕e8+ ♖f8 30 d7 ♕d3 31 e5 h6 32 e6 ♔h7 33 ♖g1 ♖f3 34 ♕b8 ♖xh3+ 35 gxh3 ♕e4+ ½-½.

18 g5 *(D)*

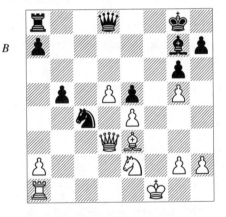

Cutting off the bishop, but Black activates it the other way.

18...♗f8 19 ♘g1 a6!

19...♘xe3+ 20 ♕xe3 ♕b6 has been played, but then 21 ♕xb6 axb6 22 ♘f3 ♗c5!? 23 ♖d1 might be a serious problem.

20 ♘f3 ♗d6

with a very solid position and equality. Neither side can undertake much.

The Gambit Lines

12 ♗d3 cxd4 13 cxd4 ♗e6 (D)

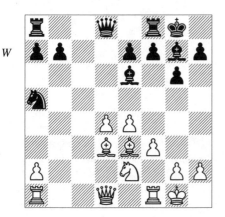

Now White really needs to do something about incursions on c4, because ...♗c4 threatens to win the light squares and ...♘c4 would create immediate tactical problems. Since 14 ♕a4 a6! threatens ...b5, White has only two serious moves that protect c4, both requiring material sacrifice. The first is the gambit 14 ♖c1 ♗xa2 15 ♕a4. White also has the exchange sacrifice 14 d5!? ♗xa1 15 ♕xa1, whose assessment at the moment is not fully resolved. In spite of over 45 years of investigation into 14 d5 by hundreds of grandmasters, a few new ideas are still being found at the top levels. Nevertheless, the play is dependent upon countless tactics which don't lend themselves to general understanding, so in this case there is only a limited amount to be gained through broad discussion of the opening as such. In fact, the specifics of the attack are really in the realm of the middlegame proper. Thus I shall limit my discussions of both 14 ♖c1 and 14 d5, providing some general contours of the play.

Geller's 14 ♖c1

14 ♖c1

With this move White covers c4 and offers a pawn. Black must accept or be driven back by the move 15 d5.

14...♗xa2 (D)

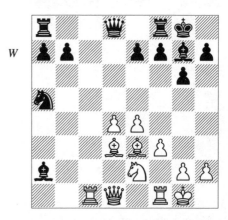

This position has fascinated players and theoreticians for many decades. After many years of intense scrutiny, Black seems to have solved his problems in the very main lines with the move 15...♗b3. Whether that will remain true is still an open question, and both sides can still experiment with little-played moves.

I'm only going to show one game, because White hasn't made much progress in the last few years.

Hillarp Persson – Rowson
Torshavn 2000

15 ♕a4 (D)

This is the most popular move by a huge margin: White forces Black's bishop to move and gets his pieces out as quickly as possible. Black's light-square strategy, with which we are so familiar, should work well after the straightforward attack 15 f4 a6! 16 f5 b5 17 e5, Nenashev-Notkin, St Petersburg 1995, when Notkin suggests 17...♘c4! 18 ♗g5 ♘b2 19 ♕d2 ♘xd3 20 ♕xd3 ♗c4 21 ♖xc4 (otherwise the d4-pawn falls) 21...bxc4 22 ♕xc4 ♕d7! 23 f6 exf6 24 exf6 ♖fc8 and ...♗f8 with a winning advantage. This is an instructive example of a queenside pawn expansion supporting Black's pieces.

15...♗b3

This move was discovered late in the development of theory. It has challenged White to find something new in order to justify 14 ♖c1 as a winning weapon. The time-honoured line

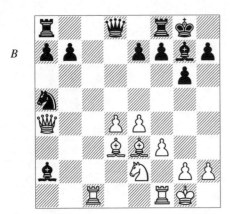

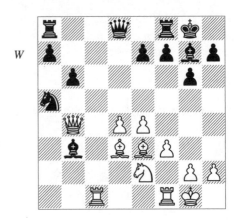

is 15...♗e6 16 d5 ♗d7, which may also be equal. Many years of theory and hundreds of high-level games have established the various ways to proceed in this position. Best play seems to be 17 ♕b4 e6 18 ♘c3 exd5 19 ♘xd5 ♗e6 20 ♖fd1 ♗xd5 21 exd5 ♖e8 (D).

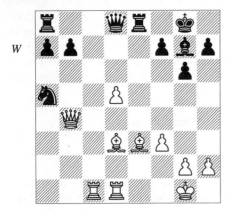

This position has arisen in many games and until recently was the main line of the 14 ♖c1 variation. Remarkably, my database gives a game with it that goes back to 1978! At first White's positional pluses – his bishop-pair, open lines, powerful passed d-pawn, and imprisonment of the knight on a5 – led to some nice wins in spite of his being a pawn behind. Over the past few years, however, Black has been drawing most games. In the diagram, Yusupov-Leko, Istanbul OL 2000 was drawn after the simple 22 ♗f2 ♗f8 23 ♕b2 (others have tried 23 ♕a4 here, with ongoing action) 23...♗g7 24 ♕b4 ½-½. It's fun to play around with the ideas here.

16 ♕b4 b6 (D)

White's whole idea is that Black's pieces are a little loose while his own centre is mobile. Although Black's queenside passed pawns are typically harmless for the time being, his pieces are protected here and it's been hard for even the world's best players to achieve anything; however, developments will probably continue for many years to come.

17 ♗g5

Or:

a) The revival of 15...♗b3 began with 17 d5 ♕d6! 18 ♗d2?! (18 ♕xd6 exd6 19 ♗a6 could be met by 19...f5! 20 ♖c7 fxe4 21 fxe4 ♖xf1+ 22 ♔xf1 ♗a4!, with the idea ...♘b3) 18...♖fd8! 19 ♕xd6 exd6 20 ♗g5 ♖dc8 21 ♗a6 ♖c5! with the superior game for Black, Yusupov-Anand, Wijk aan Zee Ct (2) 1994.

b) Another unclear line with a little more experimental leeway for both sides is 17 ♖c3 ♗e6 18 ♘f4 ♗d7 (D).

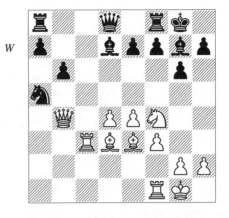

Now 19 ♖fc1 e6 20 e5, as in Barkhagen-Åkesson, Stockholm 1998, is hard to assess, but here 19 ♘d5! e6 20 ♘e7+ ♚h8 21 e5 looked promising for White in Zawadski-Quizielvu, ChessFriend.com 2004. Perhaps 17 ♖c3 is the direction in which to look.

17...f6

Not 17...♖e8? 18 ♗b5.

18 ♗h4 *(D)*

18 ♗f4 e5! breaks loose from the pressure. Arguably the most interesting move is 18 ♗d2: 18...♗f7 19 d5 e6 20 ♗f4!? e5!? (20...f5!) 21 ♗e3 ♘b7! heading for c5, with equality. There are plenty of possibilities in any position like this.

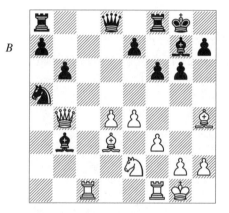

18...♕d6

A good alternative is 18...♗f7!? 19 d5 ♕d6. White's activity may compensate for a pawn, but certainly no more than that.

19 ♕xd6 exd6 20 d5 ♖fc8 21 ♘d4 ♗h6 22 ♖xc8+ ♖xc8 23 ♘xb3 ♗e3+ 24 ♚h1 ♘xb3 25 ♗xf6 ♚f7 26 ♗b2 ♗d4 27 ♗xd4 ♘xd4 28 ♗a6 ♖c3

with equality.

Sokolsky Exchange Sacrifice

14 d5!? ♗xa1 15 ♕xa1

Here's another sacrificial idea, again analysed in great depth but still affording new opportunities for both sides. Right now the attack on e6 isn't real (16 dxe6 ♕xd3), but it will be soon enough. 16 ♗h6 will come next, so Black nearly always defends g7:

15...f6 *(D)*

White has given up a rook for a bishop. What does he have? First of all, it was Black's dark-squared bishop that disappeared in the trade, so

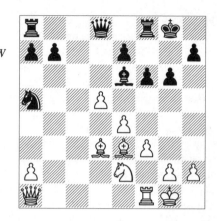

Black's kingside dark squares (and even his central dark squares) have become more vulnerable. The move ...f6 is weakening, this time of the squares e6 and g6. White also has an important lever with the move e5, in order to crack open the long diagonal or at least take over the centre. The g6-pawn can also become a target after e5 and ♘f4. Remember that pieces alone, however ideally placed, won't generally win the game until there is some kind of supporting pawn-break. Furthermore, it's generally true that possession of the bishop-pair can be enough to compensate for the loss of the exchange until the endgame approaches (and sometimes even thereafter). So there's no hurry to win back material or even to blast through to the king. With all that, is Black simply lost? Not really. It's up to White to find a way to break through, which is hard enough, but Black also has potential counterplay on the queenside (...♖c8, ...a6, ...b5, etc.) and the important defensive/offensive moves ...e6 and ...e5, which can sometimes neutralize the attack altogether.

Those are the basic ideas. Unhappily for the average player, this particular sacrifice requires considerable knowledge and specific memorization for which there is simply no substitute. Thus I'll give just a single game with one of the variations that seems topical and leave the reader to his own devices (= serious study).

Van Wely – Sutovsky
Dortmund 2005

16 ♕d4

16 ♖b1 and 16 ♕b1 are also played. But 16 ♗h6 was the most important move for years,

so thoroughly analysed that it could easily be the subject of a whole book. The main defence is 16...♖e8 17 ♔h1 ♖c8 18 ♘f4 ♗d7 19 e5! (otherwise ...♘c4-e5 would cut off the attack) 19...♘c4 20 e6 ♗a4 21 ♘xg6! hxg6 22 ♗xg6 ♘e5 (the computer says instantly that after 22...♕xd5? 23 ♕e1 and ♕h4 White wins without any complications) 23 ♗e4 ♗c2! (always light squares!) 24 ♗xc2 ♖xc2 25 ♕d1 ♔h7 26 f4 ♔xh6 27 fxe5 ♕c7 (I'm skipping loads of burdensome games and analysis here, such as 27...♖c4, 27...♖c5 and 27...♖c1) 28 exf6 ♕c4, with further messy analysis to follow.

16...♗f7 17 ♗h6 ♖e8 18 ♗b5 e5 19 ♕f2

These are all the best moves, according to theory. Maybe 19 ♕e3 would establish a new direction.

19...♖e7 20 f4! *(D)*

Way back in 1974, Gligorić played 20 ♗e3 versus Portisch, unsuccessfully. 20 f4 is now considered the only move.

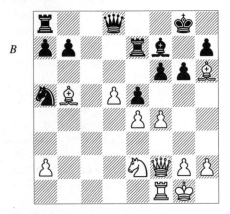

20...♖c8!?

An indication of the power of the bishops is that getting the queens off only enhances their effectiveness: 20...♕b6 21 ♕xb6 axb6 22 fxe5 ♖xe5 (22...fxe5 23 ♘c1! renders the a5-knight a prisoner) 23 ♘g3 f5 24 ♗f4 ♖xe4 25 ♘xe4 fxe4 26 d6 and the d-pawn is very strong, Degtiarev-Ernst, Hamburg 2005.

Nevertheless, Black can play 20...exf4 21 ♕xf4 ♕b6+ 22 ♔h1 ♗xd5! 23 exd5 ♕xb5 24 ♕xf6 ♕e8, Nayer-Krasenkow, Saint Vincent ECC 2005; then, oddly enough, Black might be doing well enough after the seemingly best line 25 ♗d2 (25 ♘f4 ♖f7) 25...♘c4 26 ♗c3 ♘e5 27 ♘g3 ♖d8.

21 fxe5 ♖xe5 22 ♘g3 ♘c4 23 ♕xf6 ♕xf6 24 ♖xf6

Here White has more than enough compensation for an exchange, and Black's practical difficulties make the situation worse for him. Van Wely went on to win.

Right now the 16 ♕d4 line of the exchange sacrifice seems to have more possibilities than others, although this is a situation that is subject to change with the next novelty. One point of the last two sections with 14 ♖c1 and 14 d5 is to show the sort of compensation required when one sacrifices material in a weakness-free position.

Modern 7 ♘f3 System

1 d4 ♘f6 2 c4 g6 3 ♘c3 d5 4 cxd5 ♘xd5 5 e4 ♘xc3 6 bxc3 ♗g7 7 ♘f3 *(D)*

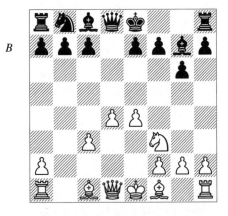

In spite of the continuing popularity of the traditional 7 ♗c4 among experts in the lines, 7 ♘f3 has taken over as the main line of the Exchange Variation at the grandmaster level. Its dynamic nature has led to many beautiful games and its appeal will be obvious when you see some games. Once again there's a tremendous amount of raw material in the main lines that defies unified description and can't really be expressed in terms of strategic principles. Recently a 208-page book has been written solely about specifically recommended lines for White in the line 7 ♘f3 c5 8 ♖b1. Whether playing White or Black, average and/or aspiring players needn't therefore avoid 7 ♘f3 variations, which are as rich as any in chess, but those who are less theoretically inclined may wish to specialize in less volatile lines. Once you've seen enough of the recurrent motifs in this variation you'll understand how to apply them to original positions.

In the early days of the Grünfeld Defence, 7 ♘f3 received little attention because it was supposed that Black could pin the knight with ...♗g4 at some point and nullify its role as protector of the centre. But it turns out that White's centre can stay intact in such situations and that ...♗g4 can have some serious drawbacks. Knowing that, White can settle back and enjoy the fact that his knight is more aggressively placed on f3 than e2. There's of course much more going on, as I'll try to indicate as we move along.

7...c5

7...0-0 8 ♗e2 only reduces Black's options if he plays 8...c5 next. Instead, it makes the most sense to combine 7...0-0 8 ♗e2 with 8...b6, because the bishop on e2 would have to move again to protect e4. Then 9 0-0 ♗b7 10 ♕c2 is a fairly comfortable position for White, who can play moves like ♗g5, ♖d1, d5, etc. But Lautier actually assigns 8...b6 a '?!' and I can't resist showing the game Lautier-Mirallès, Swiss Cht 1995, with a selection of his notes: 9 h4! *(D)*.

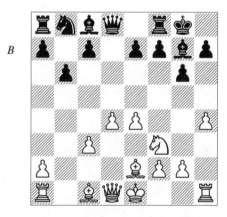

White's attack is seemingly innocuous, and yet Lautier shows that it's not so easy for Black:

a) 9...♗b7 10 h5! ♗xe4 11 ♘g5 ♗xg2 12 ♖h2 ♗d5 13 hxg6 hxg6 14 ♕d3 and White's attack is already on the verge of winning.

b) Lautier also mentions 9...♗g4!? without comment, after which I suspect that he had planned the surprising 10 h5!, and 10...gxh5 11

♘e5! or 10...♗xh5 11 e5!? with quite a good attack.

c) The game proceeded 9...c5 10 h5! ♗a6 11 hxg6 hxg6 12 ♗h6! ♗xh6 (12...♗xe2? 13 ♔xe2! allows White to connect rooks: 13...♗xh6 14 ♖xh6 cxd4 15 cxd4 ♕c8 16 ♕d3 ♕a6 17 ♖ah1 with a winning advantage) 13 ♖xh6 ♔g7 14 ♕d2 ♖h8 15 ♘e5! (just in time to keep the attack going, based upon 15...♖xh6 16 ♕xh6+! ♔xh6 17 ♘xf7+) 15...♕f8 16 ♘g4! cxd4 17 cxd4 ♗xe2 18 ♔xe2 ♕c8 19 ♖xh8! ♕xh8 (19...♕xg4+ 20 ♔d3 ♔xh8 21 ♕h6+ ♔g8 22 ♖h1) 20 ♖c1 ♕h5 21 f3 ♘d7 22 ♕b2! (with the idea ♖c7 and d5) 22...f5 (22...♘f6 23 d5) 23 exf5 gxf5 24 ♕b5! ♖d8 25 ♘e3 ♔g6 26 ♕d5 ♕g5 (26...f4 27 ♖c6+ ♘f6 28 ♕xd8 ♕b5+ 29 ♘c4!) 27 ♖c6+ ♔g7 28 ♖c7 1-0. Quite a pretty game.

After 7...c5, the variation that has dominated practice has been 8 ♖b1. But the flexible bishop development 8 ♗e3 is also fascinating.

♘f3 and ♗e3

8 ♗e3 *(D)*

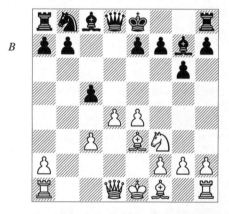

This keeps a lot of White's options open. Now the f1-bishop may still go to c4 or d3 instead of the conventional e2. White might also like to play a quick ♖c1. Finally, it would be great to get ♕d2 and ♗h6 in, eliminating White's greatest enemy. That isn't likely, but Black needs to react. He normally does so by entering some kind of endgame via ...♕a5 and ...cxd4, but can also play slowly to restrain and ultimately break down White's centre. We'll follow two games.

Lagowski – Shishkin
Kazimierz Dolny 2001

8...♕a5 9 ♕d2 ♘c6

The famous game Kramnik-Kasparov, London BGN Wch (2) 2000 went 9...♗g4 10 ♖b1 a6 11 ♖xb7 ♗xf3 12 gxf3 ♘c6 13 ♗c4 0-0 (the immediate 13...cxd4 14 cxd4 ♕xd2+ 15 ♔xd2 ♘xd4 16 f4 or 16 ♗xd4 ♗xd4 17 ♔e2 favours White because of his active pieces and centralized king) 14 0-0 cxd4 15 cxd4 ♗xd4 (15...♕xd2 16 ♗xd2 ♘xd4 17 ♔g2 gives White the two bishops) 16 ♗d5 *(D)*.

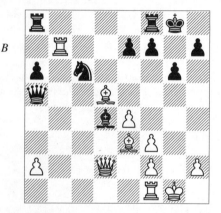

The bishop will remain a monster in the centre for a long time. 16...♗c3 17 ♕c1 ♘d4?! (Black wants an endgame with opposite-coloured bishops, but maybe 17...♖ac8 is better) 18 ♗xd4 ♗xd4 19 ♖xe7 ♖a7 20 ♖xa7 ♗xa7 21 f4! ♕d8 22 ♕c3 ♗b8 23 ♕f3 ♕h4 24 e5! (blocking the dark squares) 24...g5!? 25 ♖e1! ♕xf4 26 ♕xf4 gxf4 27 e6 fxe6 28 ♖xe6. Now White goes a pawn up. The opening is certainly over, so I'll just leave you with the moves: 28...♔g7 29 ♖xa6 ♖f5 30 ♗e4 ♖e5 31 f3 ♖e7 32 a4 ♖a7 33 ♖b6 ♗e5 34 ♖b4 ♖d7 35 ♔g2 ♖d2+ 36 ♔h3 h5 37 ♖b5 ♔f6 38 a5 ♖a2 39 ♖b6+ ♔e7 40 ♗d5 1-0. This was arguably the most important game in Kramnik's chess career.

10 ♖c1

10 ♖b1 has the drawback of allowing a tricky line stemming from Adorjan: 10...0-0 11 ♖b5 cxd4! 12 ♖xa5 dxe3 13 ♕xe3 ♘xa5 *(D)*.

Black has a rook and bishop for the queen, with the advantage of the bishop-pair and no weaknesses, while White's queenside pawns

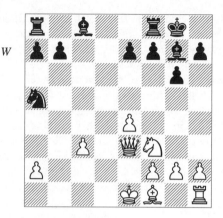

are weak. I'd be amazed if this weren't at least equal: 14 h4 (the only move that has had any success) 14...♗e6 (I can't see any problem after either 14...h5 or 14...h6) 15 h5 (or 15 ♘g5 ♗xa2 16 h5 ♖fc8 with equality) 15...♖fc8 16 e5 ♘c4 17 ♗xc4 ♖xc4! 18 hxg6 hxg6 19 ♘g5 ♖ac8 20 ♘xe6 ♖xc3 21 ♕g5 ♖c1+ ½-½ Dautov-Svidler, Istanbul OL 2000.

10...cxd4 11 cxd4 ♕xd2+ 12 ♔xd2 0-0 13 d5 ♖d8 14 ♔e1 ♘b4!

Black needs some tempi so that he can organize the destruction of White's centre.

a) Kramnik won an attractive and highly instructive game versus Leko in Budapest 2001 after 14...♘e5?! 15 ♘xe5 ♗xe5 16 f4 ♗d6 (16...♗g7 17 ♔f2!) 17 ♔f2 e5 18 ♗c5! *(D)* (breaking Black's hold on the centre).

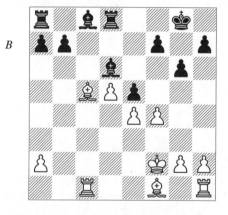

18...♗xc5+ (18...exf4!? 19 ♔f3! has some deceptively simple ideas, one of them being 19...g5 20 ♗xd6! ♖xd6 21 h4 h6 22 hxg5 hxg5 23 ♖h5 f6 24 ♗c4 ♔g7 25 ♖ch1, winning! And after 18...f6 19 ♗xd6 ♖xd6 20 fxe5 fxe5 21

♗e2, White's rook can't be stopped from coming to c7 – all this with White's bad bishop opposing Black's good one!) 19 ♖xc5 exf4 20 ♔f3 ♗d7 21 ♗d3 ♖ac8 22 ♖hc1 g5 23 ♖c7 ♖xc7 24 ♖xc7 ♗a4 25 ♔g4 h6 26 ♖xb7 ♖d7 27 ♖b4 ♗d1+ 28 ♔f5 (the king has done a lot of wandering, and now finds a dominant position) 28...♔g7 29 h4 f6 30 hxg5 hxg5 31 e5!! (D).

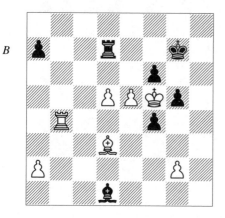

31...fxe5 (White's 31st depends upon the astonishing line 31...♖xd5 32 ♖b7+ ♔h6 33 ♗b1!!; for example, 33...fxe5 34 ♔e6) 32 ♔xe5 f3 33 gxf3 ♗xf3 34 d6 (as always, it's the d-pawn in the end!) 34...♖d8 35 ♗f5 ♗c6 36 d7 ♖f8 37 ♖d4 1-0.

b) 14...♘a5 (D) tests White's large centre against Black's attempts to undermine it.

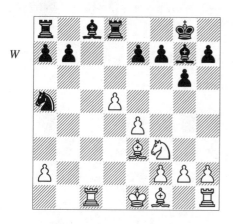

It seems to work out satisfactorily for Black. Kramnik-Kasparov, Astana 2001 continued 15 ♗g5 ♗d7 16 ♗d3 ♖dc8 17 ♔e2 e6 18 ♖xc8+ ♖xc8 19 ♖c1 ♖xc1 20 ♗xc1 exd5 21 exd5 b5! 22 ♗f4 ♘c4 23 ♗xc4 bxc4 24 ♗e5 ♗f8!

(Black's pieces are activated just in time) 25 ♘d2!? ♗b5 26 ♘e4 f5 27 ♘c3 ♗d7 28 ♔e3 ♗c5+ 29 ♗d4 ♗b4 30 ♗e5 ½-½.

We now return to 14...♘b4 (D):

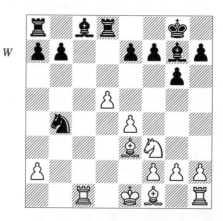

15 ♗c5?!

Underestimating Black's queenside pawns. Better was 15 ♗d2! ♘a6 (15...♘xa2?? 16 ♖c2), when 16 ♗xa6 bxa6 pits Black's poor structure versus the two bishops. Generally doubled a-pawns aren't so bad until a true ending arises, and the undermining move ...f5 will become a factor, so Black stands satisfactorily: 17 ♗b4 (17 ♗a5 ♖d7 18 ♘d2 f5! 19 f3 fxe4 20 fxe4 e6! 21 dxe6 ♖e7, Atalik-Karr, Cappelle la Grande 2000) 17...♖b8! 18 a3 f5! 19 ♗xe7 ♖e8 20 d6 fxe4 21 ♘d2 ♗f5 with equality, Zlochevsky-Egiazarian, Ohrid Ech 2001.

15...♘xa2 16 ♖c2 ♘c3 17 ♘d2 ♗d7 18 ♗xe7 ♖e8 19 d6 a5! (D)

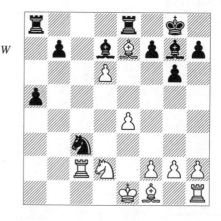

Starting the queenside pawn advance. What's to stop them?

20 f4 a4 21 ♗c4 b5 22 e5 b4 23 ♔f2 ♗f5 24 ♖b2 ♖eb8 25 d7 ♗f8 26 d8♕ ♖xd8 27 ♗xd8 ♖xd8 28 ♘f3 ♗c5+ 29 ♔g3 ♘e4+ 30 ♔h4 ♗e7+ 31 ♘g5 ♘xg5 0-1

Black has his share of fun in these endings.

Karpov – Kasparov
New York/Lyons Wch (17) 1990

8...0-0 9 ♕d2 ♗g4

Kasparov liked playing this move in various contexts.

10 ♘g5!? cxd4

The trick is 10...h6 11 h3 ♗h5 12 g4!.

11 cxd4 *(D)*

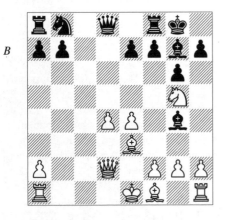

11...♘c6

Again, 11...h6 is answered by 12 h3.

12 h3 ♗d7 13 ♖b1 ♖c8 14 ♘f3 ♘a5

As so often, Black skirts around White's centre and eyes c4.

15 ♗d3 ♗e6 16 0-0 ♗c4 17 ♖fd1 b5?! 18 ♗g5 a6 *(D)*

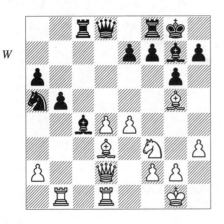

19 ♖bc1 ♗xd3

Black has systematically conquered the light squares but taken a lot of time.

20 ♖xc8 ♕xc8 21 ♕xd3 ♖e8 22 ♖c1 ♕b7 23 d5! *(D)*

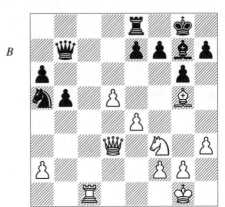

Here's Black's greatest enemy in the Grünfeld: White's d-pawn marching steadily up the board!

23...♘c4 24 ♘d2 ♘xd2 25 ♗xd2 ♖c8 26 ♖c6! ♗e5 27 ♗c3! ♗b8 28 ♕d4 f6 29 ♗a5! ♗d6 30 ♕c3 ♖e8 31 a3 ♔g7 32 g3 ♗e5 33 ♕c5 h5 34 ♗c7 ♗a1 35 ♗f4 ♕d7 36 ♖c7 ♕d8 37 d6 g5 38 d7

Through the breach!

38...♖f8 39 ♗d2 ♗e5 40 ♖b7 1-0

One nice continuation goes 40...h4 41 ♗a5! ♕xa5 42 ♕xe7+ ♔g6 43 ♕h7+! ♔xh7 44 d8♕+.

Modern Main Line with ♖b1

8 ♖b1 *(D)*

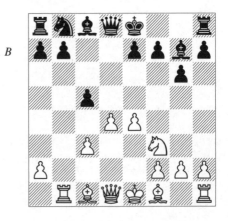

This move is played in the majority of contemporary games with 7 ♘f3. It's odd to move a rook instead of developing the kingside, especially when you've left your pawn on a2 undefended versus ...♕a5. But it's consistent with ♘f3 to discourage ...♗g4, which ♖b1 does by aiming at the b7-pawn. The other convenient advantage is that now the rook is off the long a1-h8 diagonal, so the important move d5 can occur without losing a rook!

8...0-0

There are countless minor lines along the way and we won't look at most of them. Here Black can lose in a few moves by 8...♕a5 9 ♖b5 ♕xc3+? (9...♕xa2 10 ♖xc5 ♘d7 11 ♖b5 leaves White with some advantage because the pressure has been released from his centre) 10 ♗d2 ♕a3 11 ♕c2! ♘c6?? (but 11...c4 12 ♗xc4 is pretty awful) 12 ♖b3 1-0 Polovodin-Maslov, USSR 1984.

9 ♗e2

At this juncture the material divides. I'll take a look at selected lines stemming from the two major moves: 9...♘c6 and 9...cxd4.

a) A solid variation that many strong players have used and avoids massive theory, is 9...b6 10 0-0 ♗b7 (D).

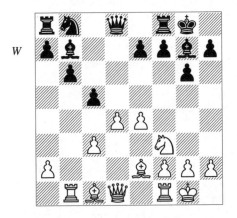

White's most common and logical response is to defend the d-pawn by 11 ♕d3 (although 11 ♕c2 deserves a closer look). Then:

a1) 11...e6 can be countered in several ways but the obvious one is 12 ♗g5. Then Black probably wants to avoid 12...♕d6 13 e5!?, and 12...♕c7 13 ♕e3 ♘d7 can be met by 14 e5!?, to restrict the knight on d7, or simply 14 ♖fc1 ♘f6 15 e5 ♘d5 16 ♕d2. Notice that the move e5

makes much more sense when ...e6 has been played.

a2) 11...♗a6 (Black wants to exchange the light-squared bishops as soon as possible) 12 ♕e3 e6!? (one of various moves designed to restrain the dangerous d-pawn; instead, 12...♕d7! would both prepare ...e6 and eye the a4-square) 13 ♗xa6 ♘xa6 14 ♕e2 ♕c8, Pelletier-Banas, Mitropa Cup (Bükfürdo) 1995, and either 15 ♗g5 or 15 ♖d1 might be played, probably with some advantage. But 9...b6 is a good practical choice.

b) 9...♕a5 is purely tactical, rather messy, and maybe better than its reputation. The game Shirov-Akopian, USSR U-26 Ch (Tbilisi) 1989 gives a brief indication of its risks: 10 0-0! ♕xa2 (10...♕xc3 11 d5 ♕a5 12 ♗g5 with compensation) 11 ♗g5 ♕e6 12 ♕d3 b6 13 d5 ♕d6 14 e5! (this is the essence of 8 ♖b1 Grünfeld play!) 14...♗xe5 15 ♘xe5 ♕xe5 16 ♕d2 (D).

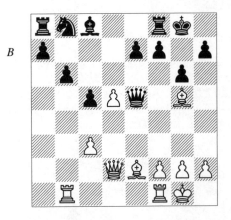

Shirov has sacrificed two pawns in exchange for some dark squares! The game continued 16...♕d6 17 ♕e3!? ♖e8 18 ♗f3 ♘d7 19 ♗f4!? ♕f6 20 d6 ♖b8 21 ♖bd1 e5? 22 ♗g5 ♕g7 23 ♗h6 ♕f6 24 ♗c6 ♖e6 25 ♗g5 ♕g7 26 f4! h6 27 ♗e7 exf4 28 ♕xf4 g5 29 ♕a4 ♘e5 30 ♗d5 ♗b7 31 ♕xa7 ♘d7 32 ♗xb7 1-0.

Direct Central Attack

9...♘c6 10 d5! ♘e5

Black can also accept the sacrifice. Here's one of the games that got the whole 8 ♖b1 rage started: 10...♗xc3+ 11 ♗d2 ♗xd2+ 12 ♕xd2 ♘d4 (later 12...♘a5 was played more often, White attacking by 13 h4 ♗g4 and now 14 h5!?

♗xf3 15 gxf3, or 14 ♘g5!? ♗xe2 15 ♔xe2, which isn't clear at all!) 13 ♘xd4 cxd4 14 ♕xd4 ♕a5+ 15 ♕d2! ♕xd2+ 16 ♔xd2 ♖d8 17 ♔e3 (the key to these endings is whether White's king can step out of the way of Black's central attack and at the same time connect rooks; here Kasparov achieves both) 17...b6 18 ♖bc1 e6 19 ♗c4 e5 20 ♗b3 ♗d7 21 ♖c7 a5 22 d6! (D) (invasion of the Grünfeld killer!).

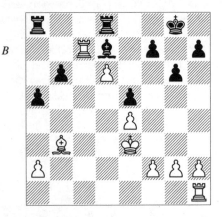

22...b5 23 f4 exf4+ 24 ♔xf4 ♖a6 25 e5 a4 26 ♗d5 a3 27 ♖f1 ♖a4+ 28 ♔e3 ♗e6 29 ♗xe6 fxe6 30 ♖ff7 ♖h4 31 ♖g7+ ♔h8 32 ♖ge7 1-0 Kasparov-Natsis, Malta OL 1980. A seminal game.

11 ♘xe5 ♗xe5 (D)

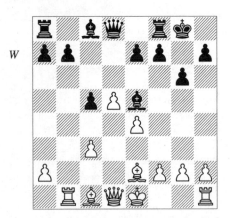

This used to be the main line before 9...cxd4 10 cxd4 ♕a5+ took over. Not everything is fully resolved here, but the top players don't seem to trust it any more. I'll give two games illustrating the main ideas. As always, the battle is between White's large centre and Black's attempts to immobilize and undermine it.

S. Ivanov – Mikhalevski
St Petersburg – Beer-Sheva 1999

12 ♖b3 (D)

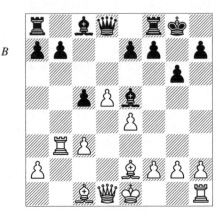

This is a fascinating alternative to the main move 12 ♕d2. It has the following features:

a) It protects the c-pawn;

b) It intends to play c4, after which the rook may swing over to the centre or kingside;

c) Unlike 12 ♕d2, it keeps the path of the c1-bishop free.

On the negative side:

a) The move ...c4 can force the rook to an awkward square with tempo. If it occurs, the rook will want to go to b4, when the move ♕d2 will be necessary to protect the c-pawn. But that blocks off the c1-bishop anyway!

b) Whereas 12 ♕d2 gives extra support to White's attack with f4, the rook on b3 does nothing in the centre.

12...e6

Natural, but this simple move allows White's centre to go on a rampage. Black can gain dynamic counterchances by 12...♕c7 with the idea of ...c4. White must either stop this or be able to play ♖b4 in response. For example, 13 ♕d2!? (the other move is 13 c4, when 13...e6 tries to open files before White gets castled and brings his pieces out) 13...e6 14 f4 c4! 15 ♖b4 ♗d6! 16 ♖xc4 ♕b6 (for the price of a pawn, Black has temporarily stopped White from castling and threatens ...exd5) 17 dxe6?! ♗xe6 18 ♖d4 ♖ad8! 19 f5 (19 0-0 ♗b4!! 20 ♕e3 ♗c5!) 19...♗c5! 20 ♖xd8 ♖xd8 21 ♕b2 ♗f2+! 22 ♔f1 gxf5 23 ♕xb6 ♗xb6 and White was hopelessly tied down in S.Ivanov-Greenfeld, Bugojno 1999.

13 f4 ♗g7 14 c4 ♖e8

14...exd5 15 cxd5 ♗d4 16 ♗e3 gets rid of the intrusive bishop.

15 e5!? f6 16 f5! *(D)*

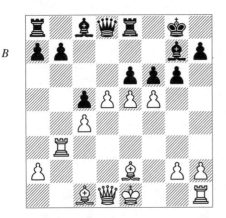

The ultimate centre vs undermining picture!

16...gxf5?!

The situation is not necessarily hopeless for Black, but he surely must have been intimidated! I won't even begin to go into the pages of notes that can accompany this game, but will just toss in a variation or two that shows how vital the initiative and two bishops are to White's attack. Here 16...exd5 can be met by 17 e6!? or 17 fxg6, neither leading to a clear assessment. From now on White's initiative is almost impossible to deal with.

17 ♗h5 ♖e7

17...♖f8 18 ♖g3 ♔h8 19 ♗b2 fxe5 20 ♖xg7! ♔xg7 21 ♗xe5+ ♔g8 22 0-0 gives White and his bishops a terrific attack.

18 d6 ♖d7 19 ♖g3 fxe5 20 ♗b2! *(D)*

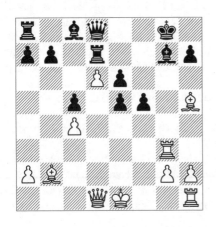

20...♔h8

Other moves like 20...♔f8 may be somewhat better, but here are two that are entertainingly worse: 20...♖xd6? 21 ♖xg7+! ♔h8 22 ♗xe5! ♖xd1+ 23 ♗xd1 and White wins; and 20...e4? 21 ♕a1! ♕f8 22 ♗e8! ♕xe8 23 ♗xg7 f4 24 ♖g5, etc.

21 0-0 ♖xd6

Not 21...b6? 22 ♕a1!.

22 ♕e2 ♖d4 23 ♖xg7 ♔xg7 24 ♕xe5+ ♔g8?

24...♕f6 is better but ultimately loses to 25 ♕xc5 e5 26 ♗xd4.

25 ♖f4! ♕g5 26 ♖xd4

Even prettier is 26 ♗xd4 cxd4 27 ♖g4!.

26...cxd4 27 ♕xd4 ♔f8 28 ♕h8+ ♔e7 29 ♗a3+ ♔d7 30 ♕d4+ 1-0

Kiriakov – Sowray
Hastings 1998/9

12 ♕d2 e6 13 f4 ♗c7

Retreating the bishop to help on the queenside is a more modern approach than the originally-played 13...♗g7. The latter move is just as important, but full of lines worked out to 25 moves and more (one famously extends to move 50 or so!). You really need to memorize this sort of thing to succeed, and there are books to help you do so. I'll just point out that it's the same story of White trying to blast through with his central pawns and Black trying to break them up. Wherever the bishop retreats, Black must beware of the white pawn if it reaches d6 and is still well-supported. Sometimes it takes 20 more moves, but it's a very good bet that you'll see it on d7!

14 0-0 exd5 15 exd5 *(D)*

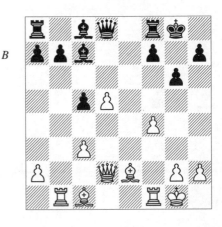

15...♗a5 *(D)*

It is strange to see a bishop so far away from the kingside and at such cost of time, but now that White's e-pawn is gone Black wants to combine forces on the c-pawn and White's queenside in general. Giving up a pawn by 15...♗f5?! 16 ♖xb7 ♗b6 hasn't panned out after 17 d6 (uh-oh) 17...♕f6 18 ♖d1!. The fatal move d7 won a piece for White on move 31 in Van Wely-Timman, Breda rapid playoff (1) 1998.

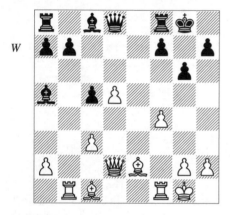

16 ♖b5

Not the most popular move but it brings home the point that the bishop-pair and some enemy weaknesses can be worth the exchange. Instead, White can get open lines at the cost of allowing Black rapid development by playing 16 f5!? ♗xf5 17 ♖xb7 ♕f6 18 ♖f3 (not so heavily tested for a change). Or you can do a little studying and plunge into the main line 16 d6 (I'm going to skip mountains of notes and alternatives) 16...b6 17 ♗f3 *(D)*.

17...♗f5! 18 ♗xa8 ♗xb1 19 ♗c6! ♕f6 (19...♗f5! leads to one of those long-winded lines, a bit better for White) 20 ♗b2 ♗xa2?! (20...♗f5) 21 c4! (now White is clearly better) 21...♗xd2 22 ♗xf6 ♗xc4 23 ♖f3! ♗e6 24 d7 (whoops) 24...♗xd7 25 ♗xd7 (Black has three pawns for the piece, but it's two bishops – no contest) 25...a6 26 ♔f1 b5 27 ♔e2 ♗a5 28 ♖a3 ♗d8 29 ♗e5 ♗e7 30 ♖xa6 and White won shortly in Van Wely-Van der Werf, Netherlands 1998/9.

16...b6 17 ♗b2

17 ♖xa5! bxa5 18 c4 is a better move-order, to avoid ...♗a6.

17...♕d6 18 ♖xa5! bxa5 19 c4 *(D)*

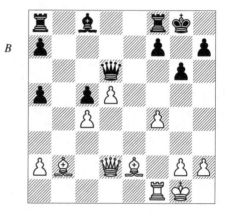

Again we have a situation in which White is an exchange down but has the two bishops and some attack on Black's weakened dark squares. The position isn't clear and Black can definitely improve upon what happens, but we'll just follow the moves:

19...f6 20 g4 ♖b8 21 ♗a1 ♖e8 22 ♗f3 ♖b4 23 ♖c1 ♗a6 24 g5 ♖xc4 25 ♖xc4 ♗xc4 26 ♗xf6 a4 27 ♔f2 ♕d7 28 ♔g3 a3 29 ♗a1 ♗f1 30 ♗g4 ♕b5 31 d6 ♕d3+ 32 ♕xd3 ♗xd3 33 d7 ♖b8 34 ♗e6+ ♔f8 35 ♗f6 c4 36 d8♕+ ♖xd8 37 ♗xd8 c3 38 ♗a5 c2 39 ♗b4+ 1-0

8 ♖b1 Exchange with 10...♕a5+

9...cxd4 10 cxd4 ♕a5+ 11 ♗d2 ♕xa2 12 0-0 *(D)*

This is the very main line of the Modern Exchange Grünfeld. Given the back-and-forth nature of chess fashion, that probably won't be the case in a few years; still, we have to work with

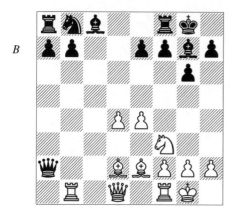

B

what we know. As with most main lines, theoretical analysis has developed over many years and is extremely dense. Therefore I'm going to cover only certain characteristic ideas, basic and otherwise, with little pretence to following the 'best' lines. My concentration is upon the variation that has been Black's favourite solution for some time.

I shall present more White wins, not only because they tend to be more thematic (advance the pawns, sacrifice, etc.), but because at the top levels White has such an overwhelming score after 11...♕xa2 (66%, with very few losses). Nevertheless, my notes indicate Black's possibilities of equalizing in key lines, so the reader shouldn't be overwhelmed by White's brilliant victories.

OK, what is going on in the diagram position? First of all, White has gambited a pawn and he has given Black two connected passed pawns on the queenside. Why? One reason for doing so is simply a practical one: years of experience have shown that 11 ♕d2 (in response to 10...♕a5+) results in a queenless middlegame (after 11...♕xd2+) in which there are no prospects for White to win if Black plays even moderately good moves. As might be expected, Black can even get the advantage in such an ending if White overextends his centre pawns. So with his pawn sacrifice by 11 ♗d2, White is trying to win. But upon what basis? First, he has more pieces out. Black's queen's knight and bishop have reasonably good squares to go to when they get out, but the presence of the rook on b1 means that at some point Black will have to use a tempo to defend b7. And although the b8-knight can be aggressively developed to

c6, it may well be kicked around by d5. A second advantage for White is our favourite one: the ideal Grünfeld centre. Not only does it remain a great threat to advance, but because of White's faster development it's less likely to be broken up. As indicated above, Black has to watch out for the d-pawn getting to d6. In addition, White can make use of the traditional advantage of having more space under control, i.e., he has the freedom to shift his pieces more easily from side to side and front to back than Black does. In our games you will see White's pieces occupying aggressive posts on the fourth and fifth ranks.

Other aspects of the position offer food for thought. Black's queen, for example, might seem to be exposed to attack, and in particular to time-gaining attacks that will help White's pieces to better posts. That is sometimes true, but in fact, the queen can also interfere with White's ability to place his pieces where he wants them. Right off you can see that White's passively-placed bishop would like to go to c4 but can't, and just as importantly, White's queen can't get to c2, b3 or a4. Sometimes those bishops on d2 and e2 will be targets that prevent White from straying too far. This issue varies from position to position, but it's worth noting how often the retreat of Black's queen (to e6, for example) is advantageous for White.

Another subtlety has to do with those passed a- and b-pawns. Often players assume that connected passed pawns are a cause to panic and that one needs to undertake immediate action against them. However, the pawns here can hardly advance without creating serious weaknesses, and would have to be well up the board before their aggressive potential would outweigh their vulnerability. Nevertheless, all this does point to some positive features of Black's position: he has no weaknesses at the moment and none of his pawns are past the third rank, nor are they likely to be so soon. It is notoriously difficult to break down such a structure; consider, for example, the many variations of the Sicilian Defence which share this characteristic. And in the long run the passed a- and b-pawns will become of decisive importance, especially in a simplified position.

A good way to think about White's strategy is in terms of piece placement. You will find that White's queen's bishop tends to go to e3, but sometimes to g5 or b4 to harass Black's e-pawn. The other bishop is an opportunist, heading to c4 if possible, but being quite content on the long diagonal if there is an exchange of Black's bishop on g4 for a knight on f3. White's rook on b1 likes to swim around on the fourth rank via b4, and his other rook on f1 will often go modestly to e1 to protect the e4-pawn, or to d1 to help advance the d-pawn.

For his part, Black simply needs to develop his pieces safely. His bishop on g7 is ideally placed, and his knight would usually like to attack White's centre from c6, although ...♘d7-b6 is also played. Obviously, Black's rooks belong on open files, but the one on a8 may stay there in order to support and advance the a-pawn. Finally, we have Black's light-squared bishop, which can go to d7 or b7, but in view of White's attack will usually go to g4 in order to exchange off a white piece.

The ideas above are only starting points, and you'll need to look at a lot of games in various books to get a deep understanding for how to play these lines.

12...♗g4

This is (or seems to be) the most important move because it gets a piece out and indirectly attacks d4. Let's see game excerpts from two other tries:

a) With 12...♘d7, Black is simply trying to get his pieces out. One instructive game continued 13 ♖e1 (13 ♗b4 is more common) 13...♘b6 (the rook on e1 protects the e-pawn so, for example, 13...♘f6 might be met by 14 ♖b4!? ♕e6 {14...♘xe4?? 15 ♗c4} 15 ♗c4 with a growing initiative) 14 ♖a1 (14 ♗b4!? puts the bishop on a promising diagonal) 14...♕b2 15 h3 (versus ...♗g4) 15...f5 16 ♗d3 fxe4 17 ♗xe4 ♕b5 18 ♖a5! ♕e8 19 ♗b4 (Black has managed to eliminate the e-pawn and thus reduce the danger of a passed d-pawn, but in return every one of White's pieces except the queen is very active) 19...♖f6 20 ♗c5 ♔h8 21 ♕b3 (one threat here is to play 22 ♗xb6 ♖xb6 23 ♕xb6! axb6 24 ♖xa8, etc.) 21...♕d8 22 ♘g5 ♘c4 *(D)* (Black is hoping that this trick saves him).

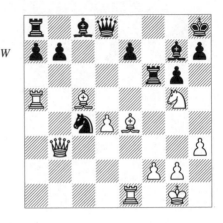

23 ♖a6!! (a lovely move) 23...♕g8 (23...bxa6 24 ♗xa8 ♗f5 25 ♗xe7 ♕xa8 26 ♗xf6 ♗xf6 27 ♕xc4 ♗xg5 28 ♕f7) 24 ♗xb7 ♖xa6 25 ♗xa8 h6 26 ♗b7 ♗xb7 27 ♕xb7 ♖f6 28 ♘f3 ♖e6 29 ♖b1 ♘d6 30 ♕xa7 ♔h7 31 d5 ♖f6 32 ♗xd6! ♖xd6 (32...exd6 33 ♖b7 ♔h8 34 ♘d4 and ♘e6 will follow) 33 ♕xe7 ♖xd5 34 ♖b7 (from now on it's a fairly easy win) 34...♖d1+ 35 ♔h2 ♖d8 36 ♘e5 ♕f8 37 ♘xg6! ♕xe7 (37...♔xg6 38 ♕e4+ ♔f6 39 g3!! h5 40 ♖b6+ ♖d6 41 ♕d4+ ♔e6 42 ♖xd6+ ♕xd6 {now this isn't with check!} 43 ♕xg7) 38 ♘xe7 ♖f8 39 ♔g1 ♖f7 40 ♖d7 ♗c3 (40...♖f8 41 ♘d5 ♖xd7 42 ♘f6+) 41 ♔f1 ♗e5 42 ♔e2 1-0 Noomen-Corti, corr. 2000.

b) 12...a5 used to be played quite a bit, but it doesn't develop a piece and the a-pawn is a long way from queening. Here's an example of aggressive attack: 13 ♗g5 a4 14 ♖e1 ♕e6 15 d5! ♕d6 (15...♕xe4 16 ♗b5 ♕f5 17 ♗xe7) 16 e5! *(D)*.

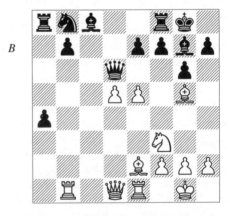

For a second pawn, White wins the dark squares and opens lines: every one of his pieces gains in terms of activity. Gelfand-Leko, Cap d'Agde (rapid) 1996 continued 16...♗xe5 17 ♘xe5 ♕xe5 18 ♕d2 ♕d6 19 ♗c4 ♖e8 20 ♗f4

♛d8 21 ♕c3! ♘d7 22 ♗b5 e5 23 dxe6 ♖xe6 24 ♗c4 ♕f6 (24...♖xe1+ 25 ♖xe1 threatens ♗h6) 25 ♕d2 ♘f8 26 ♗xe6 ♘xe6 27 ♗e5 ♕d8 28 ♕c3. White is clearly better and still owns the dark squares. It took him some time to win but he eventually did so.

We return to 12...♗g4 *(D)*:

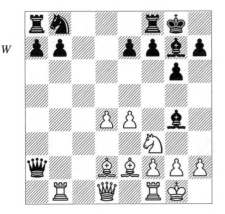

We'll now look briefly at two of the classic games from this position.

Kramnik – Svidler
Linares 1999

13 ♗e3

The obvious line 13 ♖xb7 ♗xf3 14 ♗xf3 ♗xd4 15 ♗b4, initially considered harmless, has recently been reappraised. Cox analyses 15...♖d8!? (15...♘c6 16 ♗xe7 ♖fe8 has the idea ...♗b6 and ...♘d4, although White must stand better) 16 ♕c1 e5 17 ♗e7 ♖e8 18 ♕h6 as winning for White. However, 18...♕e6! 19 ♗g4 ♕xe7 20 ♖xe7 ♖xe7 leaves Black with the powerful bishop on d4 and a dangerous a-pawn. A possible line is 21 ♕c1 ♖e8 22 ♕a3 a5 23 h4 h5 24 ♗h3 (24 ♗e2 ♖c8) 24...♘a6! 25 ♗d7 ♖eb8 26 ♕xa5 ♘c5 27 ♕c7 ♔g7!.

Our main game here is an eye-opener when it comes to the power of a mobile central majority in the hands of great masters.

13...♘c6 14 d5 ♘a5!?

Black can also try to simplify, and indeed may equalize by doing so. There have been several games with 14...♗xf3 15 ♗xf3 ♘e5 16 ♗e2 ♘c4; e.g., 17 ♗g5 ♖fe8!? (17...♖fb8! has also drawn games) 18 ♖xb7 ♘d6 19 ♖b4 a5 20 ♖a4 ♕b2 21 ♗c1 ½-½ Lorentzen-Krueger,

Chessfriend.com 2005. In the final position, White still seems to have a small advantage.

15 ♗g5 ♗xf3 16 ♗xf3 ♖fe8 17 e5! *(D)*

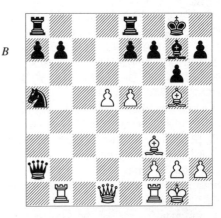

Another pawn sacrifice! The fun of this variation is in the reckless advance of White's centre.

17...♘c4

There are some very nice variations that are also typical of the kinds of tactics you get in this variation; for example, 17...♗xe5 18 d6! ♗xd6 (18...exd6 19 ♗d5 ♕a3 20 ♗d2!, threatening ♗b4) 19 ♖a1 ♕c4 20 ♖xa5 ♗xh2+ 21 ♔h1!.

18 d6 ♘xe5 19 ♗d5! ♕a3

Another pretty idea is 19...♕a5 20 ♗xe7 ♗f8 21 ♖e1! ♗xe7 22 ♖xe5 ♗xd6 23 ♗xf7+ ♔xf7 24 ♖xa5.

20 ♗xe7 ♗f8 21 ♖xb7 ♗xe7 22 ♗xa8 ♗xd6 23 ♗d5 ♖e7 24 ♔h1

Threatening f4-f5. White is ahead materially but it takes some technique to win.

24...h5 25 h3 ♔g7 26 ♕d2! ♗c7 27 ♖bd1 ♘d7 *(D)*

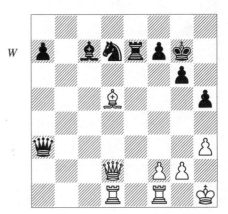

28 ♗xf7!

A wonderful finishing touch. White heads for a winning ending.

28...♖xf7

The very same idea follows 28...♔xf7 29 ♕xd7 ♖xd7 30 ♖xd7+ ♔f6 31 ♖xc7 a5 32 ♖cc1! a4 33 ♖a1 ♕b3 34 ♖fb1 ♕c2 35 ♔g1 a3 36 ♖b6+ ♔g7 37 ♖a6 and the pawn falls.

29 ♕xd7 ♖xd7 30 ♖xd7+ ♔h6 31 ♖xc7 ♕d3 32 ♔g1 ♕d4 33 ♖c2 1-0

If we know anything about lines like this we know that their theory will evolve, perhaps rapidly. Various innovations will leave the examples that I'm using marginally relevant if that. But I doubt if the nature of the play will be such as to invalidate the basic concepts we shall see.

The following is one of the most complicated and brilliant games in recent years. Again I won't delve into the details (which would fill a pamphlet!) but present a picture of White's space and centre battling Black's passed a-pawn.

Gelfand – Shirov
Polanica Zdroj 1998

13 ♗g5 h6 14 ♗h4

After 14 ♗e3 ♘c6 15 d5 another beautiful game went 15...♘a5?! 16 ♗c5 ♗f6 17 e5! (there's that sacrifice again, and White doesn't even get the bishop-pair) 17...♗xe5 18 ♖b4! (you get used to these ideas) 18...♗xf3 19 ♗xf3 ♗f6 20 ♖a4 ♕b3 21 ♖xa5 ♕xd1 22 ♖xd1 b6 *(D)*.

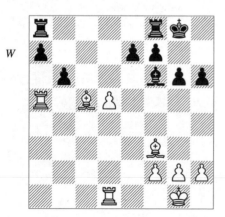

23 d6! ♖ac8 (23...exd6 24 ♗xb6; 23...bxa5 24 dxe7 ♖fc8 25 ♗xa8 ♖xa8 26 ♖d7) 24 d7

♖cd8 25 ♗xe7 ♗xe7 26 ♖xa7 ♖b8 27 ♖e1 ♗d8 (27...♗f6 28 ♗d5 b5 29 ♖e8!) 28 ♖e8 b5 29 ♖a8 ♖xa8 30 ♗xa8 b4 31 ♗d5 ♔g7 32 ♔f1 (zugzwang!) 1-0 Kramnik-Timman, Novgorod 1995.

But again, Black is hardly forced to go into this sort of defensive nightmare. He should play 15...♗xf3 16 ♗xf3 ♘e5 17 ♖xb7, and now both 17...a5 and 17...e6 give reasonable chances.

14...a5 15 ♖xb7 g5 16 ♗g3 a4 17 h4! a3 18 hxg5 hxg5 19 ♖c7!? ♘a6 20 ♖xe7 ♕b2 21 ♗c4 ♕b4 22 ♗xf7+! ♔h8 *(D)*

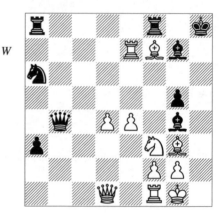

White's rook looks trapped.

23 ♖d7!! ♗xd7 24 ♘xg5

Threatening mate by ♕h5+.

24...♕b6 25 ♗e6! ♕xe6 26 ♘xe6 ♗xe6 27 ♗e5 ♖f7 28 ♕h5+ ♔g8 29 ♕g6 ♗d7 30 ♗xg7 ♖xg7 31 ♕d6 ♔h7

31...a2 32 ♕d5+.

32 ♕xa3 ♘c7 33 ♕e3 ♘e6 34 d5 ♘g5 35 f4 ♘h3+ 36 ♔h1 ♖a2 37 f5 ♘g5 38 f6 ♖g6 39 f7 1-0

White can promote to a knight!

Russian System

1 d4 ♘f6 2 c4 g6 3 ♘c3 d5 4 ♘f3 ♗g7 5 ♕b3

This is known as the Russian System. Now the vast majority of games continue as follows:

5...dxc4

Black prefers to play actively. 5...c6 is a rare alternative in master play (a sort of Grünfeld/Slav mix with a passive reputation).

6 ♕xc4 0-0 7 e4 *(D)*

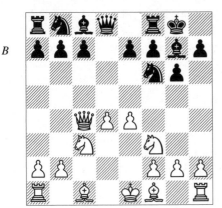

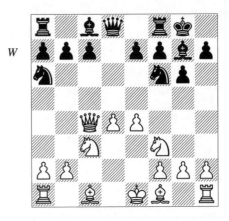

This position introduces all main lines of the Russian System. What are its features? First, White has established his ideal centre and the usual free development associated with it. Moreover he has a fair number of pieces out, and he can quickly bring a rook to d1 to shore up the centre after developing his dark-squared bishop. What can be wrong with that? Simply that one of those developed pieces is the queen on c4, and it is subject to attack with loss of time. Moreover, White is still two moves away from castling. Thus Black would like to combine the idea of rapid development with attacking White's centre. He can do this with pawns or pieces. Notice too that White's central majority is inherently more vulnerable than it is in the Exchange Systems, where it is supported by a pawn on c3. Thus White's advantage in space is extremely important so as to keep Black's pieces off aggressive squares. In the face of such restriction, Black needs a set-up which develops some of his pieces without blocking off the rest. Of the various eligible strategies, I've chosen to examine the Hungarian Variation 7...a6 and the traditional 7...♗g4, sometimes known as the Smyslov Variation.

Among other possibilities, 7...c6 doesn't challenge the centre, and Black is unlikely to equalize after the simple 8 ♕b3! with the idea 8...b5?! 9 a4!. Black has better moves than 8...b5, but White can ignore flank advances and gain a nice lead in development with his centre intact.

There are two major alternatives to 7...a6 and 7...♗g4. The Prins Variation 7...♘a6 *(D)* has been used by many of the great Grünfeld players and has devoted advocates.

Why would the knight move to the edge of the board? Simply to support the move ...c5 without getting in the way of Black's other pieces. That applies most obviously to the c8-bishop which would like to go to e6 or g4, but also to the knight on f6, which will appreciate having d7 free in case of White's e5. I won't give any examples, but the situation can be described in general terms. Assuming that ...c5 is played early on, White will usually respond with d5 and it will not surprise the reader that this potentially passed pawn can prove bothersome for Black. This d-pawn advance is usually better than dxc5, which invites Black to develop with tempo by ...♗e6, and can lead to tactical difficulties. After d5, Black counters with ...e6, and after the exchange of pawns on d5 we have the usual situation of White's passed, isolated d-pawn trying to advance down the board while Black attempts to render it harmless and work around it. White hopes to tie Black down to defence while he exploits his greater space to rush his pieces forward (♗f4 and ♘b5 are common, to escort the d-pawn if possible, or just attack), whereas Black will tend to stay active. Rather than rush to blockade by, say, ...♘c7-e8-d6, he can play aggressive moves such as ...♕b6, ...♘b4, ...♗f5 and ...♘e4 with a counterattack and/or simplification. The timing of all this is crucial and most authors warn of the degree of memorization that is required to play these lines well.

Obviously White needs to be ready for the Prins, and if this description of ideas appeals to you as Black you may wish to take up 7...♘a6. The ideas are relatively straightforward, and you can probably learn on the job.

Finally, the modern line 7...♞c6 *(D)* is a logical attack on the centre that entails some risk. It is often combined with ...♝g4.

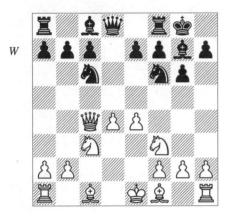

Most players find 7...♞c6 a little hard to believe at first, since it walks directly into d5 now or later. That was the conventional wisdom for some years until, armed with computer analysis, some players decided that a knight on a5 (for that is where it's headed after d5) would be in no great danger, and that its influence over the board will be significant if Black can open the c-file by means of ...c6. Such a modern view of flank knights is not so unusual. Black is saying: "I don't care where my pieces end up as long as I can break up your centre." Another consideration: Black is giving up the ...c5 break for a while, much as in the 7...♝g4 lines. If White isn't provoked to play d5 soon then Black may find himself without a meaningful central pawn-break. One reaction to this situation is to aim for ...♞d7-b6 (as in the Smyslov Variation below), when apart from ...e5 it may even be possible to use the move ...f5 effectively. Let's briefly examine how the respective strategies can collide:

a) Black's idea is shown by lines such as 8 d5?! ♞a5 9 ♕c5 c6! 10 dxc6 (10 b4? is beautifully refuted by 10...♞d7 11 ♕e3 ♕b6!) 10...♞xc6 11 ♗e2 ♝g4 12 ♗e3 ♞d7 13 ♕a3 ♝xf3 14 ♝xf3 ♞de5 (already with a real advantage) 15 ♗e2 ♕a5! 16 ♕xa5 ♞xa5 17 ♖d1 ♖fc8 with the powerful idea of ...♞ac4. Black grabbed the seventh rank after 18 ♞d5 ♖c2 19 ♗d2 ♞ec4 and eventually converted his clear advantage into victory in J.Richardson-S.Ernst, Lichfield 2000.

b) 8 ♗f4!? provokes the sequence 8...♞h5 9 ♗e3 ♝g4, when Black aims his forces at d4 and the dark squares in general. Things can get hot after 10 0-0-0 ♝xf3 11 gxf3 e5!? 12 d5!? (12 dxe5 ♕h4 13 e6 has to be considered) 12...♞d4 13 f4! and an aggressive course would be 13...♕h4 14 fxe5 ♞f3 15 ♗e2 ♞xe5 16 ♕xc7 ♖ac8 with an attack. But this line looks shaky and is the sort of thing that may leave players nervous about 7...♞c6.

c) Speaking of which, advocates of 7...♞c6 always said that one of the main points was that White's most natural plan with 8 ♗e3 and 9 0-0-0 could be ruined by the powerful 8...♞g4, and indeed, 9 0-0-0 ♞xe3 10 fxe3 e5! 11 dxe5 ♕e8 is at least equal, as is 9 ♖d1 ♞xe3 10 fxe3 e5!. But someone noticed that you can change orders by the simple 9 e5! *(D).*

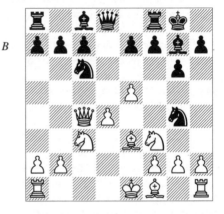

For example, 9...♞xe3!? (9...♝e6 10 ♕c5 a5 {10...♞xe3 11 fxe3 a5? 12 d5} 11 a3 a4 12 ♗b5; 9...♞a5!? 10 ♕d5! ♞c6 11 ♗f4!? ♞b4 12 ♕b3 a5 13 h3 ♝e6 14 ♕d1 ♞h6 15 ♗e2 favours White; these are just typical ideas – if White's basic central advantage goes untouched, Black's pieces usually can't do it on their own) 10 fxe3 a5 (10...♞a5!? 11 ♕d5!? ♞c6! 12 ♗b5 is another possibility) 11 a3 a4 12 ♖d1 ♖a5? 13 h4!? (13 ♞xa4!) 13...♝d7 14 h5 b5 (14...e6 15 ♞e4 with a clear advantage) 15 ♞xb5 ♕b8 16 hxg6 hxg6 17 ♞g5! e6 (17...♞xe5 18 dxe5 ♝xb5 19 ♖h8+!! ♝xh8 20 ♕h4 and wins) 18 ♞h7 ♖e8 19 ♞f6+ ♝xf6 20 exf6, Piket-S.Ernst, Dutch Ch (Leeuwarden) 2001. White is winning.

Of course, Black could settle for 8...♞d7 after all, abandoning one of the major points of

7...♘c6. This would be a sad but hardly fatal outcome.

The Hungarian Variation

7...a6 *(D)*

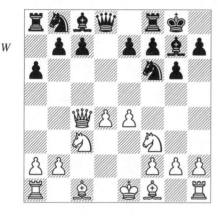

This little move is undoubtedly the most radical way to meet the Russian System. Black intends a direct attack by ...b5 and further disruption to regain the centre, ideally by ...c5. If White plays e5 Black can reply ...♘fd7 followed by moves such as ...♘b6 and ...♗e6 to control the d5- and c4-squares. Against slow moves such as ♗e2 and ♗e3, the idea of ...♗b7 and an early ...c5 is typical, even if it involves the sacrifice of the c-pawn. As usual, White would like to advance his central majority. If Black can lure White's pawn to d5 without playing ...c5, however, it can be attacked by both ...c6 and ...e6 (which is not the case in the Exchange Variation). In fact White will generally prefer e5 to d5. It gains a tempo and is sometimes followed by e6 with an attack. Barring that, the e5-pawn still serves to limit the scope of Black's Grünfeld bishop on g7. More than any other Russian System variation, the Hungarian tends to be forcing, tactical, and aggressive. As is the case with some such lines, I'll use a game and excerpts to illustrate important attacking and defending ideas.

Lautier – Leko
Tilburg 1997

8 ♕b3

a) As usual there are some move-order issues to be understood. 8 e5 can be met by 8...b5

9 ♕b3, transposing to the main line. However, 8...♘fd7!? is a serious alternative; for example, 9 ♗e3 (9 ♕b3 ♘b6 10 ♗e3 ♗e6 11 ♕c2 ♘c6 12 a3 ♘d5 with equality, Gershon-Kariakin, Moscow 2002, shows what Black is up to) 9...b5 10 ♕d5 (it's important to see that 10 ♕b3 c5! transposes into the 8...b5 9 ♕b3 ♘fd7 10 ♗e3 line without allowing White to play other 10th moves – a trick worth knowing for both sides!) 10...♘b6 11 ♕xd8 ♖xd8 12 ♗e2 ♗b7 13 0-0 b4 14 ♘d1 c5! 15 dxc5 ♘d5 16 ♖c1 ♘c6 17 ♗d2, Kožul-Mikhalevski, Bugojno 1999, and 17...♘xe5!? 18 ♘xe5 ♗xe5 19 c6 ♗c8 has been suggested with the assessment of 'unclear'.

b) 8 ♗e2 b5 9 ♕b3 transposes to the uninspiring 9 ♗e2 below, when Black plays 9...c5.

c) And how about 8 ♗f4? Especially after the slow move 7...a6 this would seem to be an excellent option because it develops with tempo. The problem is that Black sacrifices the c-pawn, which is customary in this dynamic variation: 8...b5! 9 ♕xc7 ♕xc7 10 ♗xc7 ♗b7 *(D)*.

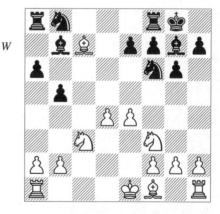

Black's bishops and initiative are quite sufficient to balance the play if not more. For starters, Black hits the e-pawn twice and threatens ...b4 as well. Thus: 11 e5 (11 ♗d3 b4 12 ♘a4 ♘xe4 and White is saddled with a fairly useless isolated queen's pawn) 11...♘d5 12 ♘xd5 ♗xd5 13 ♗e2 ♖c8 14 ♗b6 ♖c2 15 b3 ♘c6 16 ♗d1 ♖c3 17 0-0 ♖b8 18 ♗c5 ♖d8 (intending ...♗xf3 and ...♘xd4) 19 ♗b6 ♖b8 20 ♗c5 b4 (Black rejects the draw by repetition; 20...♗xf3 21 ♗xf3 ♘xe5 is another try) 21 ♖e1 f6 22 exf6 ♗xf6 with adequate compensation for the pawn, but no more than that.

8...b5

Continuing with the move-order discussion, Black can play 8...c5!? *(D)* here, which White could have avoided by 8 e5.

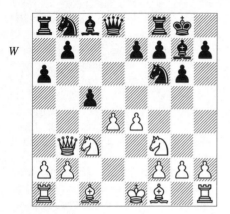

W

White seems to be on top after 9 dxc5 (9 e5 ♘g4!) 9...♕a5?! (9...♘bd7! 10 c6! bxc6 11 ♗e2 ♖b8 12 ♕c2 is only slight worse for Black) 10 ♕b6 ♕xb6 11 cxb6 ♘bd7 12 ♗e2 ♘xb6 13 ♗e3 ♘bd7 14 ♘d4 ♘c5 15 f3. This type of position arises fairly often in d-pawn play. Black's inferiority in the centre means that he has a hard time finding good squares for all of his pieces. Kasparov-Leko, Frankfurt (rapid) 2000 continued 15...e5 16 ♘c6 bxc6 17 ♗xc5 ♖d8 18 ♔f2.

9 e5 *(D)*

By far the most important move. White can play slowly by 9 ♗e2, but then 9...c5! 10 dxc5 ♗b7 gives good play. 9 a4 c5! 10 dxc5 ♗e6 also shows Black's teeth; e.g., 11 ♕a3 b4! 12 ♕xb4 ♘c6 13 ♕a3 ♖b8 14 ♗e3 ♖b3, etc.

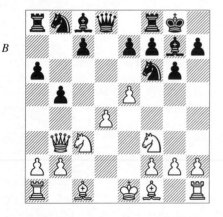

B

9...♘fd7

Two alternatives illustrate the aggressive nature of the play:

a) After 9...♗e6 10 exf6! ♗xb3 11 fxg7 ♔xg7 12 axb3 *(D)*, White has only three pieces for a queen and pawn, and he has doubled isolated b-pawns to boot. Yet he has more than enough compensation because of his better development, bishop-pair, and dark-square pressure.

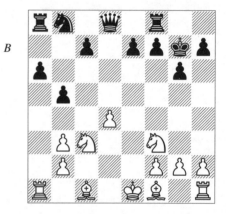

B

Several games have proven this, an early one being Bronstein-Poutiainen, Tallinn 1977: 12...♘c6 13 ♗e3 ♘b4 14 ♖c1 (the doubled b-pawns provide an excellent open file) 14...♕d7 15 ♗e2 c6 16 ♘e4 ♕f5 17 ♘fd2 ♘d5 18 0-0 ♕c8 19 ♘c5 ♕c7 20 ♘f3 ♖fd8 21 ♘e5 and White is controlling the queenside. Now Bronstein opens a second front: 21...♕b6 22 ♗d2 a5 23 ♗f3 ♖ac8 24 ♖a1 ♖a8 25 ♖fc1 ♖dc8 26 h4! ♔g8 27 h5 f6 28 ♘g4 g5 29 ♘h6+ ♔g7 30 ♘f5+ ♔f7 31 h6! ♖c7 32 ♗h5+ ♔g8 33 b4 a4 34 ♖e1 ♔h8 35 ♖e6 ♖aa7 36 ♖ae1 (total domination) 36...♕b8 37 g3 ♕f8 38 ♗f3 ♕f7 39 ♘d6 ♕f8 40 ♗xd5 cxd5 41 ♘xb5 1-0.

b) 9...♘g4 10 h3 ♘h6, attempting to force the dissolution of White's centre, runs into 11 ♗d3! ♘f5 12 ♗e4! ♖a7 13 g4! ♘h6 (13...♘xd4 14 ♘xd4 ♕xd4 15 ♗e3) 14 ♗e3 c6 15 0-0-0 with a substantial advantage, V.Milov-Svidler, Haifa 1995. In a variation like this in which White has so much space, it's unlikely that the loose squares resulting from a flank advance will hurt him.

We now return to 9...♘fd7 *(D)*:

10 h4!?

Going for broke. Other moves can lead to wild play; for example:

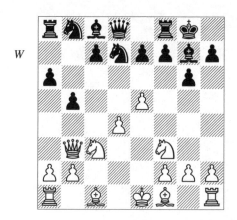

a) 10 e6 fxe6 11 ₩xe6+ ♔h8 12 ₩e4 (12 ♘g5 ♘e5!? 13 ₩d5 ₩xd5 14 ♘xd5 ♘ec6 15 ♘xc7 ♖a7 16 ♘ce6 ♘xd4! and the tactics favour Black) 12...♘b6 13 ₩h4 ♘c6 14 ♗d3 ♖xf3! 15 gxf3 ♘xd4 16 ♗e4 ♗f5 17 ♗e3 c5! 18 ♗xd4 cxd4 19 ♖d1 ♖c8 20 ♖g1 ♗f6 21 ₩h6 ♗g7 22 ₩h4 ♗f6 23 ₩h6 ♗g7 ½-½ Karpov-Kamsky, Elista FIDE Wch (5) 1996.

b) 10 ♗e3 c5 11 e6 cxd4 (11...c4!?) 12 ♗xd4 ♗xd4 13 ♘xd4 ♘c5 14 exf7+ ♖xf7 15 ₩d5 (15 ₩d1 ♖a7!? 16 ♘f3 ♖d7 with a slight edge) 15...₩xd5 16 ♘xd5 ♘bd7 17 b4!? ♗b7 18 ♘c3 e5! 19 ♘dxb5 axb5 20 bxc5 b4 21 ♘b5 ♖f4 22 ♖c1 ♖e4+ 23 ♔d1 ♗c6 24 f3 ♖f4 25 ♘d6 ♖xa2! 26 ♗c4+ ♖xc4 27 ♖xc4 b3! with multiple threats, Piket-Timman, Dutch Ch (Rotterdam) 1997.

10...c5! *(D)*

10...♘b6 11 h5 ♘c6 12 ♗e3 favours White.

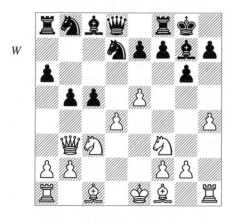

11 e6! fxe6!?

A safer and relatively 'positional' line is 11...c4! 12 exf7+ ♖xf7 13 ₩d1 ♘b6. This has held up for Black and may be described as unresolved but dynamically equal.

12 h5

12 ₩xe6+? ♔h8 leaves White's queen in poor shape.

12...cxd4 13 hxg6

The usual spectacular and chaotic play followed 13 ₩xe6+ ♔h8 14 hxg6 ♘f6! *(D)* in Bass-Larouche, New York 1985:

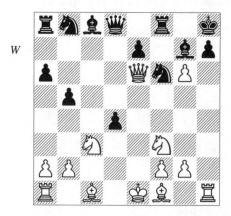

15 ₩e5 dxc3 16 ♖xh7+! ♔g8! 17 ₩h2 ₩d6 18 ♖xg7+ ♔xg7 19 ₩h6+ ♔g8 20 g7 ♖d8 21 ♗d3 ♗f5 22 ₩h8+ ♔f7 23 ♘g5+ ♔g6 24 ♗e2 ♘c6? (24...₩d5) 25 ♗h5+ ♘xh5 26 ₩h7+ ♔f6 27 ₩h6+ ♗g6 28 ♘e4+ ♔f7 29 ♘g5+ with a draw.

13...♘c5 *(D)*

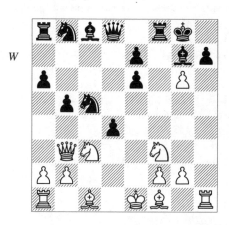

14 ₩c2!

14 gxh7+ ♔h8 15 ♘h4 threatens ♘g6#, but Black has the dynamic defence 15...♔xh7!! 16 ₩c2+ ♔g8! 17 ♘e4 ♘xe4 18 ₩xe4 ₩d5 19 ♗d3 ₩xe4+ 20 ♗xe4 ♖a7, etc.

14...♖xf3?!

This most aggressive move comes up short. Probably 14...d3 15 gxh7+ ♔h8 is the best try, but 16 ♕d1 followed by 17 ♗e3 also favours White.

15 gxh7+!?

Or 15 gxf3 d3 16 ♕d2!.

15...♔h8 16 gxf3 d3

Black tries to compensate for his material by dominating the centre. He has to avoid 16...dxc3 17 ♕g6!.

17 ♕d1 ♘c6 18 ♗h6?

18 ♗e3! is correct, when Black is in major trouble.

18...♗xh6 19 ♖xh6 ♗b7 20 ♗g2 ♘e5 *(D)*

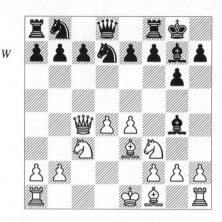

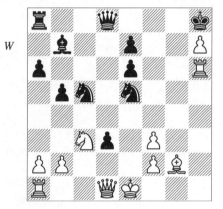

21 ♖h3?!

Losing the thread. White maintains the balance by 21 ♕d2.

21...♕d4!

Everything in the centre. The rest of the game isn't cleanly played, but eventually Black's d-pawn and pieces combine for victory:

22 ♖g3 ♘c4 23 ♔f1 ♖f8 24 ♔g1 ♖f4 25 ♕c1 e5! 26 ♘d1 ♗xh7 27 ♖b1 ♗c8 28 ♘e3 d2 29 ♕c2+ ♕d3 30 ♕xd3+ ♘xd3 31 ♗f1 ♘c1 32 ♗xc4 bxc4 33 ♖g5 ♗f5 34 ♖a1 ♖xf3 35 ♘d1 ♗c2 36 ♔g2 ♗xd1 37 ♖h5+ ♔g6 0-1

The Smyslov Variation

7...♗g4 8 ♗e3 ♘fd7 *(D)*

Whereas 7...a6 and 7...♘a6 tend to lead into disorderly channels, the Smyslov Variation (or 'System') is characterized by positional issues that can last throughout and beyond the opening stage. Black's plan is as yet undefined but can consist of a combination of ...♘fd7-b6 and ...♘c6. He has the flexibility of a change of plans if necessary, by, for example, ...♘bd7, ...c5 or ...e5. The logic is essentially that the bishop on g4 (usually exchanged on f3) and the knight on c6 combine to put pressure on d4, pressure which is increased when ...♘fd7-b6 unmasks the g7-bishop. Black will sometimes choose to restrain White's centre by ...e6. Against all this White will normally play d5 at some point. But then we have the ideal undermining situation for Black: as opposed to many other variations in which Black plays ...c5 and White plays d5, here Black has both the c7- and e7-pawns in reserve to challenge the pawn on d5 or at least prevent it from becoming a passed pawn.

That's not a bad collection of virtues. What does White have in return? Of course, the centre. In this case it's a centre that is reasonably easy to support with pieces and for the moment not attacked by any pawns. Furthermore, Black's ...♘fd7-b6 is slow, so White has the luxury of castling queenside or playing ♖d1, and/or 'wasting' a tempo on h3 in order to follow up ....♗xf3 with attack on the kingside along the open file. Some specifics are also of interest: when Black plays ...♘c6 and ...♘b6, White doesn't always have to retreat but can make the more aggressive move ♕c5. All this makes for intriguing play. Now let's explore these ideas by exemplary games:

Sosonko – Smejkal
Amsterdam 1979

9 0-0-0

Castling queenside isn't traditionally the main move here but has always been around and has attracted some attention in recent years. Previously, a majority of players may have felt that White's king was too exposed on c1, particularly to pawn and knight attacks on the queenside. Whether that is true or not, the play proceeds along lines that aren't much different from after 9 ♖d1.

9...♘b6

9...♘c6 10 h3 ♗xf3 11 gxf3 ♘b6 12 ♕c5 f5 yielded double-edged play in the game Smyslov-Botvinnik, Moscow Wch (6) 1957. The ...f5 break is relatively rare because of the weaknesses it creates. But if by threatening ...f4 Black can force White to exchange on f5, his e-file weakness are a reasonable trade-off for halving White's centre and gaining activity. In the game Botvinnik avoided this by means of 13 ♘e2.

10 ♕c5

Now Black can play the thematic 10...e5!?; for example, 11 d5 ♘8d7 12 ♕a3 ♖e8 13 ♔b1 a5 14 ♗b5 ♗f8, Sosonko-Liberzon, Amsterdam 1977. In the game he tries something more interesting:

10...e6 *(D)*

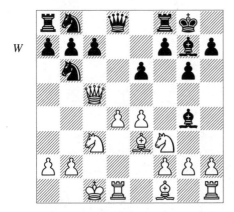

There are several ideas behind this flexible move. The obvious one is to restrain d5. Black also wants to see what White is doing before he commits to ...♘8d7 or ...♘a6, and he has the sly idea of ...♖e8 and ...♗f8. And then there's what happens in the game:

11 h3 ♗xf3 12 gxf3 ♘8d7 13 ♕a3 ♕h4!

Claiming the dark squares.

14 ♔b1 ♗h6

Simacek-Jansa, Brno 2006 saw Black mix it up with 14...♖fc8 15 ♖g1 ♗f8 16 ♕b3 c5 (a sign of belligerence) 17 ♗g5!? ♕xf2 18 ♘e2 c4 19 ♕c2 and the game slipped into obscure complications.

15 ♗xh6 ♕xh6 16 h4 ♘f6 17 ♘b5 ½-½

Black puts his queen on f4 and chases the knight back, achieving dynamic equality. This game and notes seem to offer a fair representation of 10...e6.

Vaganian – Hübner
Rio de Janeiro IZ 1979

9 ♕b3 *(D)*

White makes a useful move that attacks b7 and in some special cases prepares to develop White's f1-bishop to a more active square than e2. As a transpositional tool, it avoids 9 ♖d1 ♘c6 10 ♕b3 e5!? below, but at the cost of allowing 9...c5 as described in the next note.

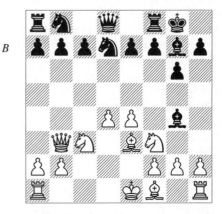

9...♘b6

As so often in the Grünfeld, Black has a stark choice between active play and solidity. The pseudo-sacrificial 9...c5!? exemplifies the former: 10 d5 (10 ♕xb7 ♗xf3 11 ♕xa8 cxd4 12 gxf3 dxc3; in spite of a nominal material advantage, few players would want to be White here) 10...♘a6 11 ♗e2 (there is probably a better move here) 11...♖b8! 12 ♗f4?! ♗xf3 13 ♗xf3 ♘e5, Bareev-Kasparov, Novgorod 1994. Here Black has ideas of exploiting White's weakness on d3 by 14...c4 and ...♘c5. Following 14 ♗e2, to prevent ...c4, 14...b5! reintroduced the idea to good effect.

10 ♖d1 e6!?

Black employs the strategy of restraining White's centre.

11 ♗e2 ♘c6 12 e5!? *(D)*

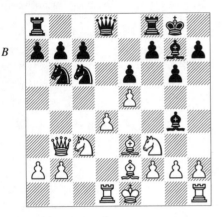

Remember that when Black plays ...e6 in this and the Exchange Variation, White's move e5, weakening in other variations, becomes more viable. First, White gains opportunities to control important dark squares around the king by means of ♗g5 and ♘e4. Moreover the advance ...f6, effective when there's still a pawn on e7, can simply weaken Black's e6, potentially on an open file following exf6.

12...♘e7!

On the flip side, d5 has become a natural outpost for Black's knights, and f5 has been freed for another, to put pressure on d4 or e3.

13 h3 ♗xf3 14 ♗xf3 ♘f5 15 0-0 *(D)*

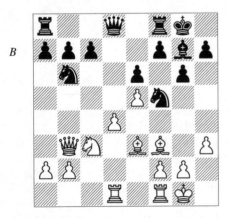

15...c6

Again, a choice: the ...c6/...e6 structure is seen here in an almost idealized form, forever preventing d5 and affording one of Black's

rooks a nice view of the backward d-pawn. The problem is that Black has no pawn-break, an example of the case where all of one's pieces are well-placed but there's little to do with them. By contrast, Black played dynamically in Hertneck-Birnboim, Munich Z 1987: 15...♕e7!? (to play ...c5) 16 ♗xb7 ♖ab8 17 ♗e4 ♘xe3 18 fxe3 ♕g5! 19 ♖f3 ♘d5 20 ♕c2 ♘xe3 with a terribly complex position.

16 ♘e4 ♘d5 17 ♗g5!? ♕b6 18 ♕xb6 axb6 19 g4 ♘xd4!? 20 ♖xd4 ♗xe5

This is a dynamic position that is difficult to assess, with Black's pawns apparently constituting sufficient compensation for the piece.

Mikhalevski – Dvoirys
Hoogeveen 2000

9 ♖d1 *(D)*

The time-honoured continuation, although 9 ♕b3 often leads to the same position.

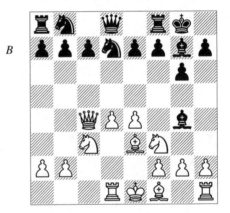

9...♘c6

9...♘b6 allows 10 ♕c5!, and Black would rather not deal with that option.

10 ♕b3

This is a sort of archetypal Grünfeld position. But the other approach also has a long history behind it: 10 ♗e2 ♘b6 11 ♕c5 (11 ♕d3 ♗xf3 12 gxf3 f5! is one of those cases in which ...f4 is a problem for White) 11...♕d6 12 e5! ♕xc5 13 dxc5 ♘c8 14 h3 ♗xf3 15 ♗xf3 ♗xe5 16 ♗xc6 bxc6 17 ♗d4 ♗f4 18 0-0 and after 18...a5? 19 ♖fe1 a4 20 ♘e4 ♗h6 21 ♗e5 a3 22 b3 ♘a7 23 ♖d7 ♗c1 24 ♖xc7 ♗b2 25 ♘a4! White won quickly in Karpov-Kasparov, London/Leningrad Wch (17) 1986. However, Black later improved in Karpov-Timman, Tilburg 1986 by 18...e5! 19 ♗e3 ♗xe3 20 fxe3 ♘e7! 21 ♖d7 ♘f5 22 ♖xc7 ♖fc8 23 ♖d7 ♖d8 with equality. Whether or not this line evolves further, you could do worse than to study those games.

10...♘b6

The older 10...e5!? strives for immediate freedom; for example, 11 dxe5 ♘cxe5 12 ♗e2 ♗e6 (or even 12...♕c8 13 ♘d5!? ♔h8 14 ♘xe5 ♘xe5 15 f4 ♗xe2 16 ♗xe2 c6) 13 ♕c2 ♘xf3+ 14 ♗xf3 c6 15 0-0 ♕a5 16 ♗e2 ♘e5 17 f4 ♘c4 18 ♗xc4 ♗xc4 19 ♖f2 ♖fd8 20 ♖fd2 ½-½ Sosonko-Smyslov, Biel IZ 1976.

Note that White can avoid this by 9 ♕b3, but at the cost of 9...c5!?. These trade-offs have to be understood in order to anticipate what can happen in any given position of the Russian System. You simply can't afford to be surprised.

11 d5 ♘e5 12 ♗e2 ♘xf3+ 13 gxf3 ♗h5 (D)

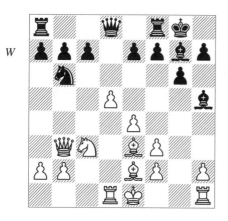

Black tries to tie White to f3 and prevent h4-h5. On the other hand that bishop could be far out of play in an ending.

14 ♖g1

White intends to play ♖g3 to protect h3 and f3, keeping Black's bishop in his role as a spectator. Of course, this is committing a big piece to a little role! Of the various other moves here the most direct one is 14 f4 ♗xe2 15 ♘xe2 c6!? (15...♕d7!) 16 h4 cxd5 17 h5 ♕c8! with equality, Forintos-Jansa, Budapest 1970.

14...♕d7 15 ♖g3

A common continuation is 15 a4!?, when 15...♕h3 16 f4 ♕xh2 17 ♔d2! ♗xe2 18 ♘xe2

c6 19 a5 ♘d7 20 ♘g3 cxd5! 21 ♖h1 ♕g2 22 ♔e2 dxe4 23 ♖xd7 e5 was utterly unclear in Ehlvest-Ernst, Tallinn 1989. You can see that the relative stability of the Smyslov Variation (compared to the anarchic nature of Black's other variations) begins to break down at about this point.

15...c6 (D)

There are ...f5 plans over the next moves. One is the immediate 15...f5!? 16 d6+ ♔h8 17 dxc7 ♕xc7, about equal.

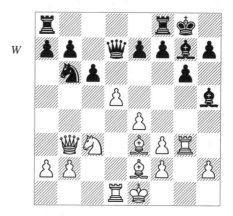

16 a4!?

A bold exchange sacrifice followed 16 dxc6 ♕xc6 17 ♘b5 ♖fc8! 18 ♘xa7 ♖xa7 19 ♗xb6 in Sosonko-Timman, Bergen (2) 1984: 19...♖xa2! 20 ♕xa2 ♕xb6 21 b3 ♗d4!? 22 ♗c4 ♗e5 23 ♔e2? (this ends up making the bishop on h5 relevant again) 23...♕f6 24 ♖d3 ♕h4 25 ♕d2 ♗xg3 26 hxg3 ♕xe4+ 27 ♕e3 ♗xf3+ 28 ♔d2 b5! with a winning game for Black.

16...♕c7 17 ♖c1 ♖fc8! 18 a5 ♘d7 19 a6 bxa6 20 ♗xa6 ♘e5!

Activating all of his pieces.

21 f4

21 ♗xc8 ♘d3+ 22 ♔d1 ♘xc1 23 ♔xc1 ♖xc8 leaves White struggling to defend.

21...♘f3+ 22 ♔f1 ♖cb8 23 ♕a4 ♖xb2!?

The accuracy of the play that follows isn't important, but suffice it to say that Black's opening was a strategic and tactical success.

24 ♗e2? ♘d2+?! 25 ♗xd2 ♖xd2 26 ♗xh5 ♕xf4! 27 ♗f3 ♗d4 28 ♖c2? ♗xf2 29 ♘e2 ♖xe2! 30 ♖xe2 ♗xg3 31 hxg3 ♕xf3+ 32 ♖f2 ♕h1+ 33 ♔e2 cxd5 0-1

9 Modern Benoni

1 d4 ♘f6 2 c4 c5 *(D)*

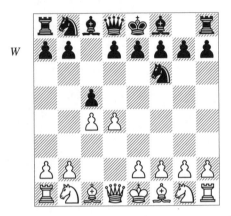

With this aggressive move Black strikes at the centre with the positional threat of 3...cxd4 4 ♕xd4 ♘c6, which would win time by attacking White's queen. The Benoni is one of very few defences to 1 d4 that counterattacks within the first few moves. Some of its other properties will become clear in a moment.

3 d5

White takes up the challenge and stakes out a large chunk of the centre. This is by far the most common move, and certainly the most interesting, because it sets up a classic imbalance. In view of move-order issues, it's important to see a few of the alternatives:

a) 3 e3 e6 (3...cxd4 4 exd4 d5 transposes to a Panov Caro-Kann; 3...g6 is also possible) 4 ♘c3 d5 (another transposition is 4...cxd4 5 exd4 d5 6 ♘f3 and again we have a Panov Caro-Kann; refer to Chapter 12 in Volume 1 for an analysis of these positions) 5 ♘f3 ♘c6 is a Semi-Tarrasch Queen's Gambit.

b) 3 dxc5 e6 4 ♘f3 ♗xc5 5 e3 (and not 5 ♗g5? ♘e4! 6 ♗e3 {6 ♗xd8?? ♗xf2#; 6 ♗h4?? ♕xh4!} 6...♗xe3 7 fxe3 0-0, when White's pawn-structure is awful and his development retarded) 5...0-0 6 ♘c3 ♘c6 (6...b6 7 ♗e2 ♗b7 is equal) 7 ♗e2 d5 with equality. This a sort of Queen's Gambit Accepted with colours reversed in which Black has no problems. As is true of so many colours-reversed openings, Black simply needs to hold back from playing the ambitious systems that White is able to get away with when he has a tempo more.

c) 3 ♘f3 is what most people play if they don't want to go into 3 d5. Then Black can play 3...cxd4 4 ♘xd4, which is a Symmetrical English Opening variation. Its theoretical status is quite satisfactory for Black, so most grandmasters won't play 3 ♘f3 unless they're particularly intent upon avoiding risk; however, the move is more popular among non-masters. Another option for Black after 3 ♘f3 is 3...e6, when 4 ♘c3 cxd4 5 ♘xd4 is another Symmetrical English line. The latter can even transpose into the Nimzo-Indian Defence after 5...♗b4 (a good move in any case) 6 g3, i.e., 1 d4 ♘f6 2 c4 e6 3 ♘c3 ♗b4 4 ♘f3 c5 5 g3 cxd4 6 ♘xd4.

We now return to 3 d5 *(D)*:

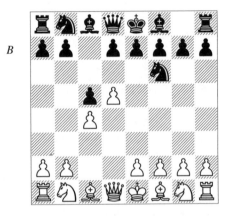

3...e6

This is the move-order associated with the Modern Benoni; it immediately attacks the centre. 3...e5 followed by ...d6 has been identified by several names, including the Czech Benoni. 3...b5!? is the Benko Gambit, not discussed here.

Black can also play 3...g6 (or 3...d6 4 ♘c3 g6) 4 ♘c3 ♗g7 5 e4 d6 (versus e5), but then it may be less productive to challenge White's centre later by means of ...e6 for a few reasons, among them the fact that after an eventual ...exd5 White has the additional option exd5. There may also be times at which White's dxe6 is a good move.

4 ♘c3

4 ♘f3 is an important continuation, although it will usually arrive from the popular move-order 1 d4 ♘f6 2 c4 e6 3 ♘f3 (to avoid the Nimzo-Indian Defence 3 ♘c3 ♗b4) 3...c5 4 d5. That move-order is particularly significant because White's choices are limited by the knight on f3, i.e., he can't play popular variations with the moves f4 and f3. See also the discussion of 1 d4 ♘f6 2 c4 e6 3 ♘f3 in the Queen's Indian chapter.

4...exd5 (D)

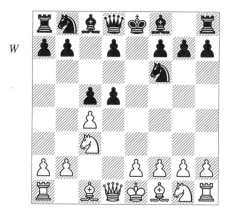

W

5 cxd5

Instead, White can play the rare move 5 ♘xd5, when 5...♘c6 6 ♗g5 ♗e7!? 7 ♘xe7 ♕xe7 gives up the bishop-pair but may be satisfactory for Black because of his faster development; e.g., 8 ♘f3 (versus ...♕e5) 8...0-0 9 e3 ♖d8!?, intending ...d5. The normal and reliable line is 5...♘xd5. Then Black equalizes after 6 ♕xd5 d6 (or 6...♘c6; also, 6...♗e7, to meet 7 b3 with 7...♗f6, is considered fine for Black) 7 ♘f3 ♘c6 8 e4 ♗e6 9 ♕d1 ♗e7 with equality. White has created the d5 outpost but a piece is a long way from occupying it (♘d2-f1-e3-d5) and a piece on d5 might be exchanged anyway.

White's rarely-chosen option 5 ♘xd5 ♘xd5 6 cxd5 (D) is rather instructive:

It turns out this particular simplification favours Black. White's knight is one of his best

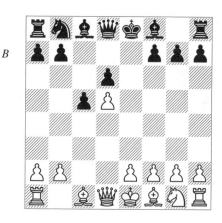

B

pieces and after Black plays ...g6 and ...♗g7 (or ...♗e7-f6), the exchange of the f6-knight will give Black's bishop an open view along the a1-h8 diagonal. Indeed, in the main lines with 5 cxd5 d6 (i.e., without 5 ♘xd5 ♘xd5) Black often has to move the knight from f6 to a mediocre square, precisely to increase the bishop's range and in order to hold up e4-e5.

5...d6 (D)

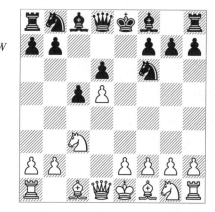

W

Black intends to play ...g6 and ...♗g7, but first he stops White's advance d6, and he also opens a diagonal for the c8-bishop. At this juncture, we'll look at the main moves, 6 e4 and 6 ♘f3 (with g3). It's also worthwhile to consider some of the lines involving the move ♗f4 as we go along. At this point 6 ♗f4 develops quickly and targets Black's weakest pawn on d6. A third-rank pawn that isn't on an open file is normally pretty easy to defend, but in the Benoni, Black's can be vulnerable, at least enough to disturb his development. A case in point is 6...g6 7 ♕a4+!? (the most forcing continuation, but probably not best; White can play into other lines by 7 ♘f3 or 7 e4) 7...♗d7 8 ♕b3 *(D)*.

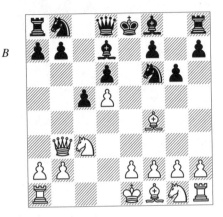

By attacking the pawn on b7, White is attempting to force Black to delay his development, since 8...♗g7 would lose the d-pawn to 9 ♗xd6. Thus Black would like to stay active, and a good way to do that is 8...b5! *(D)* (this is a typical dynamic pawn sacrifice for development and open lines; the alternative 8...♕c7 9 e4 ♗g7 10 ♘f3 leads to a main-line position but is not necessarily to everyone's taste as Black).

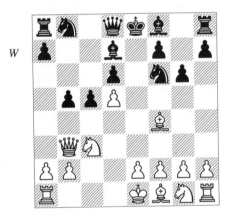

9 ♘xb5 (otherwise Black has expanded on the queenside for free, and remember that ...b5 is the move that Black strives so hard to achieve in the Benoni) 9...♗xb5 10 ♕xb5+ ♘bd7 11 ♕d3 (Black was threatening both ...♘xd5 and ...♖b8) 11...♕b6 12 b3 ♗g7 13 ♖d1 0-0 14 ♘f3; in Hausner-Belaska, Prague 1991 Black played 14...c4?! at this point, but 14...♖fe8 was very strong because of the cute tactic 15 e3?? ♕b4+! followed by ...♕xf4, winning a piece.

Black is able to employ this typical ...b5 sacrifice in similar situations throughout the Benoni. However, other versions of White playing an early ♗f4 were underestimated for years and are quite testing. See, for example, 7 ♗f4 in the section that follows.

We now move on to White's standard choice on move 6:

6 e4 *(D)*

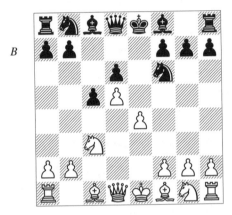

Although the move 6 e4 is by no means the only one, White plays it in most games for the obvious reasons of development (allowing the f1-bishop to move) and central control.

6...g6

Black prepares ...♗g7. At this point we again come to a major fork in the road. We shall look at 7 ♘f3, the Classical main line in which White develops normally and without delay; this generally leads to relatively quiet positional play. The resulting positions have been debated in more detail than any others in the Modern Benoni. Then we look at the pawn-storm systems that follow from the aggressive 7 f4, which itself leads to several distinct attacking formations.

These lines will get their own relatively detailed sections. I have made that decision based upon the desire to address the most fundamental issues inherent in the Benoni without cluttering the presentation. Keep in mind that the Modern Benoni is considerably less popular than the other 1 d4 openings that we deal with in this volume. Nevertheless, there are several other consequential variations that need to be addressed, if only in a selective manner:

7 ♗f4 is a complex move based upon the bishop's pressure on d6 and e5. Without going into a lot of detail, here are some lines that illustrate both White's development and Black's flexibility:

a) 7...♗g7 8 ♕a4+ ♗d7 9 ♕b3 is a controversial line that has served White well over the past decade, although with care Black should equalize or come very close to equalizing.

b) 7...a6 8 ♘f3 b5 *(D)* and now:

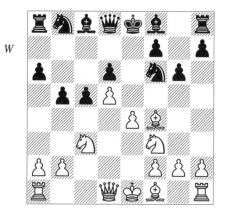

b1) 9 ♗d3 ♗g4!? – not necessarily best – is an example of Black's strategy to exchange his bishop for a knight in order to reduce White's control over e5. Palliser-Bates, British League (4NCL) 2003/4 went 10 h3 ♗xf3 11 ♕xf3 ♗g7 12 0-0 0-0 13 ♖fe1, and here Palliser recommends a manoeuvre that pops up in several Benoni variations: 13...♖a7!?, with the idea ...♖e7 and ...♖fe8. Although White looks better in that position, Black should always be on the lookout for the ...♖a7 resource.

b2) 9 ♕e2!? ♗e7! (not 9...♗g7 due to 10 e5) 10 e5 (10 ♕c2!? 0-0 11 a4 b4 12 ♘b1 b3!? is a typical Benoni device to ruin the coordination of White's pieces) 10...dxe5 11 ♗xe5 ♘bd7 12 0-0-0 ♘xe5 13 ♘xe5 *(D)*.

White's position looks powerful indeed; for example, d6 is threatened. Nevertheless, his kingside pieces are undeveloped, and 13...♕d6 14 ♘c6 ♔f8! blockades the d-pawn. This results in a surprisingly good position because that pawn can be weak and Black has an effective queenside majority. Naturally White has a lot of options (the move 9 ♗d3 above is promising), although Black has done well in this variation as a whole.

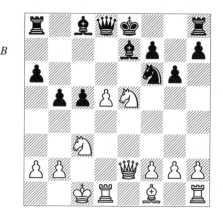

Although I won't be examining the 'Modern Main Line' with ♗d3 and h3, I'd like to take a quick look at it in terms of pawn-chains. There are numerous orders to get to the basic position; for example, 1 d4 ♘f6 2 c4 c5 3 d5 e6 4 ♘c3 exd5 5 cxd5 d6 6 e4 g6 7 ♘f3 ♗g7 8 h3 0-0 9 ♗d3 *(D)*.

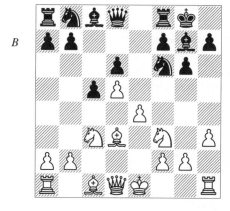

White has the mini-chain e4/d5, and Black has d6/c5. Let's talk about attacking these chains. White would like to get e5 in, attacking the base of the chain. Moves that might assist that are ♖e1 and ♗f4. The alternative f4 is weakening and hard to implement, but not out of the question in the long run. On the queenside, White has the option of b4 to attack the front of the chain, a favourite positional device, most appropriate after Black plays ...b5. For his part, Black can't legally make pawn contact with the front of White's e4/d5 chain, and ...f5 in such a position tends to be risky (the more so in this particular variation) because of the giant hole created on e6. Grabbing space by 9...a6 and ...b5 would be nice but White simply plays 10 a4. Black may therefore feel that he is restricted to 'counterplay by hook or by crook', which is why the move most often played is 9...b5!? (D).

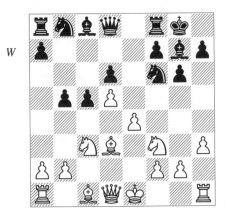

Black is counting upon the tactic 10 ♗xb5 ♘xe4 11 ♘xe4 ♕a5+, when 12 ♘fd2 ♕xb5 13 ♘xd6 ♕a6 gives Black compensation for his pawn, in large part based upon the weakness of White's d-pawn. An extraordinary amount of analysis has been devoted to 9...b5. For the record, Black needn't be so brash and there are other legitimate ways to approach the position, but this line says something about the nature of the opening as a whole. In many Modern Benoni variations, Black's main strategy is to hold up White's breaks such as e5 while using his pawn-mass in combination with an open file and powerful g7-bishop to create havoc on the queenside. This is often necessary because in terms of fundamental pawn-structure White has the advantage.

Classical Main Line

7 ♘f3 ♗g7 (D)

We're headed for the older but still worthwhile main line for White. Since White can get to one of the key positions via the move-order 6 ♘f3 g6 7 ♘d2 ♗g7 8 e4 0-0 9 ♗e2, Black can't easily avoid the whole variation, and he needs to understand the ideas.

Here we pause for a discussion of Modern Benoni strategies and themes, many of which apply to the pawn-storm systems (7 f4) as well.

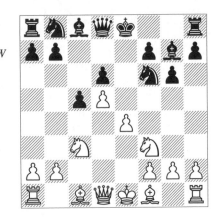

You can see right away from the pawn-structure that White has more space and that his main pawn-break in most cases will be e5. With the knight on f3, the move f4, which directly supports e5, is unlikely to happen soon; but by utilizing his greater command of territory White can reorganize his pieces so that eventually the e5 advance will be a real problem for Black. This can occur, for example, after ♗f4 with ♖e1, and/or the exotic-but-typical ♘d2-c4. The latter manoeuvre is difficult to answer because it attacks so many key squares like b6, d6, e5, and even a5 (if Black plays ...b5). White can also harass Black with the move ♗g5, which can be awkward to answer because Black may be reluctant to weaken himself with ...h6 (although to be fair, ...h6 is the correct response in most instances). Note that White has a central pawn-majority and, as usual, such a majority tends to assert itself in the long run. Therefore Black will want to upset the equilibrium at a fairly early stage of the game.

How is he going to do that? Black has a number of plans, but the larger story is that he must attend to the problem of limited space, which in turn means some problems with efficient development. In particular, his bishop on c8 can be a problem piece, even though it is a 'good' bishop. That's for several reasons:

a) ...♗f5 is either not on the cards because e4 is already in or will lose a tempo to that move;

b) ...♗g4 is sometimes not a good move, losing the bishop-pair. In situations where it would be desirable to exchange off that bishop (the timing can be delicate), White will often play a preemptive h3, denying it access to g4;

c) on b7, the bishop will run into White's well-guarded d5-pawn;

d) even on d7, it can obstruct Black's developmental scheme, in which ...♘bd7 is very often involved, and sometimes ...♘fd7 will be desirable to prevent White's e5 advance.

The good news for Black is that in any given opening situation, *one* of those squares tends to be both available and useful. For example, ...♗g4 is played in several main lines in order to release the pressure on e5. After an exchange on f3, it turns out that a combination of knights of d7 and f6 with a rook on e8 and bishop on g7 produces a harmonious set-up in which the knight-pair is often as good as the bishop-pair, and even better in terms of supporting Black's goals in the centre and on the queenside. And a bishop on d7 can be surprisingly useful in supporting ...b5 after Black's knight makes a typical journey from a6 to c7. Here's a common picture:

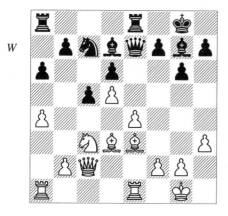

Black has been trying to enforce ...b5 and White to prevent it. Now that this advance is imminent, White will often play a5, after which Black can play ...♘b5 (supported by the bishop on d7), a good move that eyes d4 and even the exchange on c3. Alternatively, after a5, ...♗b5 is sometimes played to contest the c4-square.

8 ♗e2 0-0 9 0-0 (D)

We've made a couple more moves. There arises a crucial issue: will Black be able to mobilize his queenside majority? The move ...b5 is his most likely pawn-break, mainly to prepare ...c4 and/or ...b4, but also giving his pieces some space to work with. The less frequent move ...c4 (by itself, that is, without ...b5) can sometimes

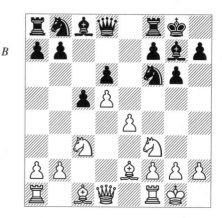

provide enough piece-play to compensate for the loss of the important d4-square. Then ...♘c5 attacks the e-pawn and puts pressure on the interior weaknesses on d3 and b3 (assuming that White has played a4).

Barring either ...b5 or ...c4, Black will suffer a cramped position on the queenside. Thus White will concentrate his efforts in this area and of course look to e5, with the emphasis depending upon the specifics of the position. White normally plays a4, which in conjunction with his light-squared bishop and knight on c3 is meant to hold down ...b5, at least until White implements his own goals. If White can suppress Black's principal freeing moves, he will have time to organize an attack of his own.

Assuming that White has control of the situation just described, then Black will have to look to the kingside. Remember that waiting around is usually bad for him since White has the best long-term weapon, the central majority. The other break against White's pawn-chain is ...f5, difficult to organize because it weakens the interior square e6 so badly. Nevertheless, Black does succeed in breaking up the centre with ...f5 in a minority of positions, mainly because White's move exf5 will activate Black's bishop to f5, from where it can create threats. Finally, Black can try to launch some kind of effective kingside attack by, for example, ...g5-g4 or by some combination of ...♘h5, ...♘e5, ...♗e5, ...♘g4 and/or ...♕h4. The latter attack arises surprisingly often because White is so concerned with the queenside and moves his pieces in that direction.

Thus in the Modern Benoni we are faced with a situation that arises in many d-pawn openings: Black's flank threats pitted against White's long-term advantages of space and central pawn-structure.

From the position after 9 0-0, we'll look at a few games that involve ...♞a6. In this situation play tends to be entirely on the queenside.

Kelečević – Burgermeister
Lenk 2000

9...♞a6

This may not be the most accurate move, because White can play 10 ♗f4 and the knight is perhaps not best-placed on a6. Nevertheless, numerous masters have played 9...♞a6, and this game introduces and illustrates the key ideas of the ...♞a6 strategy in general.

10 ♞d2 ♞c7 11 a4 ♜b8

To begin with, Black aims for ...b5 and White tries to prevent it.

12 f3

White feels that he can prevent ...a6 and ...b5 with a timely ♞c4 and ♗f4, sometimes in conjunction with a5. Black will have a hard time defending d6 and getting anything at all started on the queenside.

12...b6! *(D)*

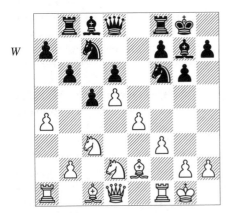

In response, Black introduces an alternate strategy. His c8-bishop can't find a good square in this position, so he simply trades it off and *then* expands on the queenside.

13 ♞c4

Why does White assent to Black's plan? For one thing, it may be that he will retain the advantage by doing so. Furthermore, a slow move like 13 ♔h1 might encourage Black to return to

the standard plan by 13...a6 14 ♞c4 b5 15 ♞a5 ♗d7 with quite an interesting position in which White needs to find a way to proceed.

13...♗a6

White's knight is awfully strong on c4, so it's worth giving up the bishop-pair to get rid of it.

14 ♗g5 h6?!

This has been played in many games, but will lose a critical tempo. See the next game for a similar position in which Black plays ...♕d7, a move which should probably be considered at this point.

15 ♗e3 ♕d7 16 ♕d2!

Even in a slow-looking positional line, every tempo counts. White attacks h6 and develops.

16...♗xc4 17 ♗xc4 ♔h7

Now how will White stop Black from expanding by ...a6 and ...b5, which is his main goal in most Benonis?

18 ♜ab1! *(D)*

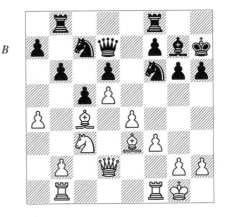

He won't, but he'll stop the black pawns cold by playing b4. The combination of ♜b1 and b4 is another manoeuvre that is characteristic of Benoni positions. Note that this attacks the front of the pawn-chain, a mode of play quite as common as attacking the base. In the meantime, White's queen protects the knight on c3, so all his pieces are safe and Black has no funny tactics along the a1-h8 diagonal.

18...a6 19 b4! b5 20 axb5 axb5 21 ♗d3 c4

White was threatening the c-pawn.

22 ♗c2 *(D)*

Let's take a tally of the opening and early middlegame: White has a space advantage and can use the d4-square for his pieces. He can also operate with the idea of e5. In return, Black

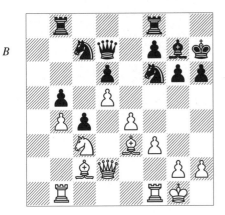

can brag about his passed pawn and great bishop on g7 compared to White's poor one on c2. This piece comparison is a bit of a wash, however, when we consider that Black's knight on c7 also has no good moves. Finally, the rooks are equally able to use the a-file if needed. Altogether, White has more advantages than Black and he will show how to use them.

22...罝a8 23 奧d4 罝fe8 24 f4

This isn't subtle: White is aiming for an eventual e5.

24...豐e7 25 罝bd1 罝a6 26 罝fe1 豐d7 27 h3 h5

To stop an attack by g4.

28 豐f2 豐e7 29 含h2 豐d7 *(D)*

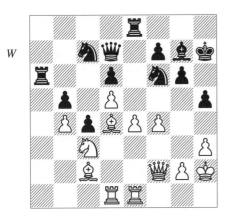

It's a bad sign when Black is shuffling back and forth.

30 豐f3

Slowly but surely, White prepares for the assault. He has a won game.

30...罝a3?

What can be wrong with a pin?

31 奧xf6! 奧xf6 32 e5! dxe5 33 ②e4!

It wasn't much of a pin after all! 34 豐xa3 is threatened and the fight is suddenly over.

33...罝xf3 34 ②xf6+ 含g7 35 ②xd7 罝f2 36 奧e4 f5 37 d6! ②a6 38 ②c5! fxe4 39 d7 1-0

The final blow is 39...罝d8 40 ②e6+.

Instead of 9...②a6, Black's more accurate order is:

9...罝e8

Then White defends his pawn and prepares to head to the queenside:

10 ②d2 *(D)*

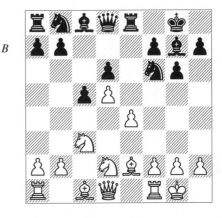

We have arrived at an important and thematic variation that for years was the main battleground for the Modern Benoni. As mentioned above, White can get to this position via the move-order 6 ②f3 g6 7 ②d2 奧g7 8 e4 0-0 9 奧e2 罝e8 10 0-0. In order to focus on explaining ideas rather than covering as many lines as possible, I shall continue to examine the ...②a6-c7 defensive scheme. It is probably the best of Black's options.

10...②a6 *(D)*

This is a stable variation, marked by manoeuvring rather than tactics. As in the last game, Black is aiming for ...b5 via the moves ...②c7, ...罝b8 and ...a6 in some order. If White plays a4-a5, the knight on c7 may move to b5, exerting influence over d4 and c3. By playing 10...②a6 only after 9...罝e8 10 ②d2, Black has avoided the move 奧f4 which might have disturbed his plans in the last game (9...②a6 10 奧f4). With the order played, however, White has permitted the move ...罝e8 in return for ②d2, speeding up his plan of playing f3, ②c4,

♗f4, and perhaps e5. He has an advantage in space and freer pieces, so he hopes that the resulting positions will force Black on the defensive. Neither side is consumed by the kind of tactics that characterize many main-line Benoni variations, so the underlying clash of ideas will be apparent throughout the opening stage.

W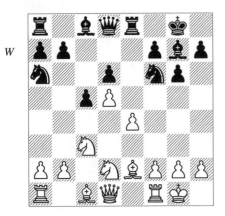

11 f3 ♘c7 12 a4 b6

Again, this is the distinguishing move. Preparing ...b5 by ...a6 would allow ♘c4 and ♗f4, attacking d6, and let White invade on b6 (perhaps with a5 first). To preface this with ...♖b8 and ...b6 is slow and invites the move ♗f4 followed by e5, when the bishop on f4 strikes at the core of Black's position, through to c7 and b8. Therefore, as above, Black switches to the idea of a quick ...♗a6, both to get rid of the bishop that he can't use and to eliminate White's powerful knight. Of course this costs time and the bishop-pair, so a kind of positional balance results. We follow two games:

Beliavsky – Portisch
Szirak IZ 1987

13 ♘c4 ♗a6 14 ♗g5 ♕d7! (D)

Black avoids ...h6, which only gives White a target.

15 ♖b1 ♗xc4 16 ♗xc4 a6 17 b4

This is White's standard idea that we explained above; its purpose is to immobilize Black's pawns.

17...b5 18 ♗d3

18 axb5 axb5 would open the a-file for Black, who could fight for the initiative by ...♖a3. Then the unprotected state of the knight on c3

W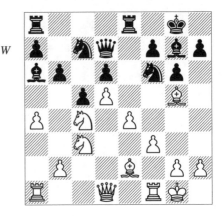

makes it impossible to contest the a-file by ♖a1, so Black could double or triple pieces on it.

18...c4 19 ♗c2

Here White has achieved his goal of limiting Black's pawn advance. As in the last game, his bishop on c2 is as bad as Black's knight on c7. The difference is that the latter piece isn't stuck where it is, and White's knight on c3 is unprotected.

19...bxa4! (D)

W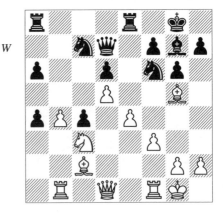

This is a common theme: if Black can't win the a-file (in the case where White plays axb5), then he can often play ...bxa4 himself and win the b5-square for his knight on c7.

20 ♗xa4

Instead, 20 ♘xa4!? ♖ab8 covers b6. There might follow 21 ♘c3 ♘b5 22 ♘xb5 axb5 23 ♗e3 ♖a8 24 ♗d4 ♕c7 (24...♘h5 25 ♗xg7 ♔xg7 26 ♕d4+ f6 and ...♖a2 is also good) 25 ♖a1 ♘d7, when Black's knight is better than White's light-squared bishop; for example, 26

♗xg7 ♔xg7 27 ♕d4+ f6 with a positional advantage.

20...♘b5 21 ♔h1

Nothing stands out here for White; e.g., 21 ♕d2 ♕a7+ (or 21...♕b7) 22 ♗e3 ♗h6! 23 ♗xa7 ♗xd2 24 ♗xb5 axb5 25 ♘xb5 ♖xa7! 26 ♘xa7 ♗e3+ wins material.

21...♕b7 22 ♗xb5!? axb5 *(D)*

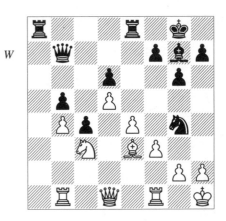

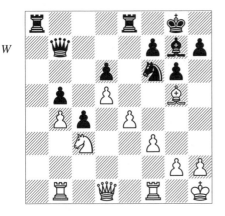

This kind of pawn-structure will often favour White if Black still has his light-squared bishop (on d7, for example). But here Black has no such bad pieces and he does have key advantages: he controls the a-file, has great pressure down the long diagonal, and his c-pawn has the potential to be mobile if White needs to rearrange his pieces in defence.

23 ♗e3

Black's g7-bishop finally shows its stuff after 23 ♕d2 ♖a3 24 ♗e3 ♖xc3! 25 ♕xc3 ♘xe4 26 ♕a3 ♘c3 27 ♖be1 ♘xd5 with two passed pawns for the exchange. This is close to winning already. Black also stands better after 23 ♕c1 ♘d7! with the idea ...♘e5-d3.

23...♘g4! *(D)*

24 ♗d4

White has major positional problems after 24 fxg4? ♗xc3 25 ♗d4 ♗xd4 26 ♕xd4 ♖e5 with a beautiful outpost in front of the backward pawn.

24...♘e3! 25 ♗xe3 ♗xc3 26 ♗d4 ♗xd4 27 ♕xd4 ♕a7!

Black shows that he has won the opening. The exchange of dark-squared bishops has revealed the superiority of Black's pawn-structure. White's pawn on b4 is a target and he is vulnerable to the break ...f5 because after exf5

his d-pawn will need tending. Those factors wouldn't be decisive but the passed c-pawn's power has grown with simplification.

28 ♕c3

a) After 28 ♕xa7 ♖xa7, Black not only controls the a-file but has ...f5 as a break in order to weaken White's e-pawn (after ...fxe4) or reach the seventh rank (after exf5).

b) The same trick works in seemingly less favourable circumstances following 28 ♕f6 ♕e7 29 ♕c3 ♕e5!? (29...♖a2 also favours Black) 30 ♕xe5 ♖xe5 31 ♖a1 ♖xa1 32 ♖xa1 f5! *(D)*.

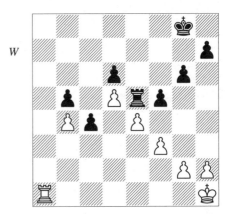

This is an instructive ending, so I'll take it a bit further: 33 ♖e1 (33 exf5 ♖xf5 34 ♖d1 c3 35 ♔g1 {35 ♖c1 ♖xd5 costs White a pawn due to 36 ♖xc3?? ♖d1#} 35...♖xd5! 36 ♖xd5 c2, etc.) 33...♔g7! and the king will take over e5: 34 ♔g1 fxe4 35 fxe4 ♔f6 36 ♔f2 (36 ♖f1+ ♔g5 37 ♖f7 ♖xe4 38 ♖xh7 c3 39 ♖c7 ♖c4 wins for Black) 36...♖h5 37 h3 ♔e5, threatening ...c3 and ...♔d4.

28...♕e7 29 ♖a1

After 29 ♖fe1 ♖a2 Black takes over the file.

29...♖xa1 30 ♕xa1

30 ♖xa1 f5! 31 ♖e1 ♕e5 and Black's advantage is growing.

30...♖c8 31 ♖c1 ♕c7 32 ♕c3 ♖a8 33 f4 ♕a7! 34 ♕d2

34 e5 ♕f2! 35 exd6 ♕xf4 36 d7 ♕f5 and Black picks up a pawn.

34...♕a2 35 ♕e1 ♕b2 36 ♖b1 c3! (D)

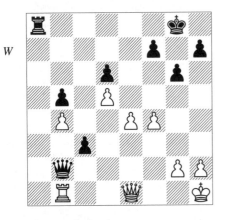

37 h3 ♖a2 38 ♕f1 c2! 39 ♖c1 ♕xb4 40 e5 ♖b2 41 ♕f2 ♕e4 42 ♔h2 ♕xd5 0-1

Pinter – Brynell
Elista OL 1998

13 ♔h1 (D)

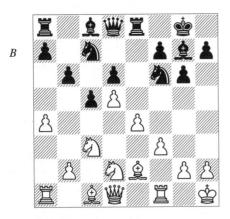

13...♖b8 14 ♘c4 ♗a6 15 ♗g5 ♕d7!

Again, this seems better than 15...h6.

16 ♖e1

16 ♕d2 would resemble Kelečević-Burgermeister above. Then 16...♗xc4 17 ♗xc4 a6 is

natural. The fact that White never gained time by forcing ...♔h7 would mean that he doesn't get time for ♖b1 and b4. Therefore he should leave his rook on the a-file and try to make progress on the kingside; for example, 18 ♗d3!? b5? (a mistake; 18...h5!? with the idea ...♘h7 is a good prelude to this queenside advance, and 18...♖b7!? to cover the 2nd rank is also useful) 19 axb5 axb5 20 ♖a7! b4 21 ♘a4 ♕d8 22 b3! and White has a strong grip on the queenside squares.

16...♗xc4 17 ♗xc4 a6 18 ♗f1 h6

18...♖b7 would prepare ...b5 without allowing White's rook to a7. Black plays this in two more moves, but by then White has prepared for the event. Timing is the essence of strategy!

19 ♗e3 ♔h7 20 ♕d2 ♖b7 21 ♖ab1! b5 22 b4! (D)

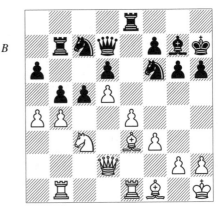

22...c4

Crucially, there's no time to keep things open by 22...bxa4? because of 23 bxc5 ♖xb1 24 ♖xb1 (24 c6?? ♖e1) 24...dxc5 25 ♗xc5 and Black has no centre to oppose White's pawns with.

23 a5! (D)

The difference between this and Beliavsky-Portisch is clear: with the queenside closed, White can play in the two areas where he has superiority, the centre and the kingside. At this point the respective opening strategies have been played out, and White's has been the successful one.

23...♕e7 24 ♗d4

It's always nice when this square is available. If Black is going to play ...c4 in the Benoni and give up d4, he needs to be able to put a piece on c5 or otherwise open up the game.

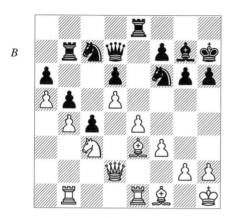

24...♘d7 25 ♗xg7 ♔xg7 26 ♖bd1 ♕f8 27 f4 ♔h7

27...f5 28 e5 dxe5 29 d6 ♘e6 30 fxe5 illustrates the dream position for White's centre. He even has a good bishop after g3 and ♗g2 (if necessary).

28 g3 ♖bb8 29 ♗h3

Normally White's worst piece in the Benoni, the bishop is now active and could even be exchanged to good effect.

29...♖bd8 30 ♖e3 ♕g7 31 ♖de1 h5 32 ♘e2!?

Coming to d4. In fact, 32 e5! was already strong due to 32...dxe5 33 d6! ♘e6 (33...♘a8 34 ♗xd7! ♖xd7 35 fxe5) 34 fxe5, when White dominates the position.

32...♘f6 33 ♘d4 ♘g4 34 ♗xg4 hxg4 *(D)*

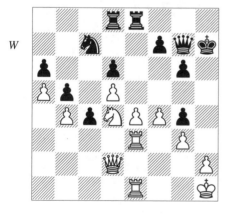

35 f5!?

A rather strange way of doing things, ceding an outpost to Black on e5. White feels that with his h3-bishop gone this will suffice, since it would take Black's knight five moves to get to e5! Instead, 35 ♘c6 ♖d7 36 ♕d1 f5! is not so

clear; e.g., 37 exf5 ♖xe3 38 fxg6+ ♕xg6 39 ♖xe3 ♕f7.

35...gxf5?

Giving away the f5-square is generally bad policy! He may as well make White prove that he has anything, by playing 35...♕h6, for instance.

36 ♘xf5 ♕g6 37 h3!

This threatens ♖e2-h2. Black has no good defence.

37...gxh3 38 g4 ♖e5 39 ♖xh3+ ♔g8 40 ♖h6 1-0

A model game for White.

Pawn-Storm Systems

7 f4 *(D)*

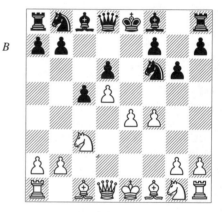

This move defines the basic starting position for pawn-storm variations. Like other Indian systems that permit White to construct a large centre, a fundamental test of the Benoni is whether White's centre pawns can be used simply to roll over Black's position or at least cramp him beyond acceptable bounds. For example, the King's Indian Defence essentially passes this test when confronted with the Four Pawns Attack. The Grünfeld Defence holds up well if, having established a d4/e4 centre, White plunges ahead with f4. In the Sämisch Nimzo-Indian, and in the 4 ♕c2 0-0 5 e4 variation, Black can defend against the blind advance of White's centre (with great care, to be sure). For all of these defences we find that White's ultra-ambitious play can produce no more than dynamic equality. But interestingly, the Modern

Benoni has real difficulties with White's most primitive attacks via e4 and f4. We can ascribe this to various reasons, one of which is his delay in castling. In the King's Indian, Black tends to castle on move 5, and in the Nimzo-Indian as early as move 4. In the Benoni, not only is Black unprepared to castle until move 8, but his king can be subject to harassment in some lines.

7...≗g7 (D)

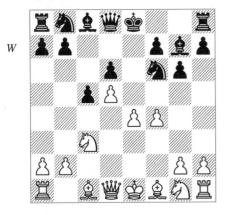

From this position, we're going to look at the Mikenas Attack, 8 e5, and the Taimanov Attack, 8 ≗b5+. 8 ♘f3 is the Four Pawns Attack of the King's Indian Defence; see that chapter. However, with this move-order Black is committed to a ...c5-based approach, and doesn't have option of an early ...♘a6 (and ...e5) as he did in the King's Indian Defence.

The Mikenas Attack

8 e5 (D)

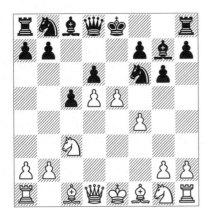

In the days when the Modern Benoni first gathered a steady following, this radical advance was used regularly. It comes very close to blowing Black's position apart. By investigating why it fails to do so, we can understand why the Benoni is possible at all.

Bozinović – Cebalo
Pula 2002

8...♘fd7

Black thinks that White's centre is overextended and takes care not to open things up. Indeed, e5 is attacked three times already, so White has to react. 8...dxe5 9 fxe5 ♘fd7 10 e6 is riskier.

9 ♘b5!

a) 9 exd6 0-0 results in a broken centre for White and a large lead in development for Black.

b) 9 ♘e4 dxe5 10 ♘d6+ transposes to the line we'll be looking at.

c) After 9 ♘f3 0-0 10 ≗e2 dxe5 11 0-0 ♘a6!? 12 ≗e3 ♖e8, Black threatens ...e4 and remains a pawn ahead.

d) 9 e6?! fxe6 10 dxe6 ♘b6 is a model of overextension! White's e-pawn is vulnerable and he trails in development.

9...dxe5 10 ♘d6+ ♔e7 (D)

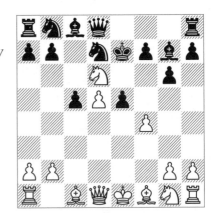

Black's king is stuck in the centre, which is a serious disadvantage, but this situation would be a lot more convincing if White had more developed pieces and he weren't a pawn down!

11 ♘xc8+

11 ♘b5 is the main alternative, with the idea 12 d6+ and ♘c7. After 11...♘a6 12 d6+ ♔f8,

White again lacks enough pieces out to cause Black's king any serious difficulties.

11...♕xc8 12 ♘f3 e4! *(D)*

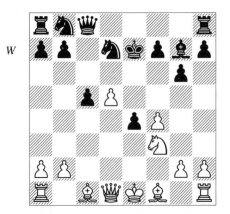

Not the only move, but an important one to remember in a number of fianchetto openings like the King's Indian, Pirc, and Modern. Black prevents the opening of lines by fxe5 with tempo and leaves the f4-pawn looking particularly stupid because it only gets in the way of the c1-bishop and a rook on f1 (after 0-0). Now Black would like to 'castle' in peace by means of ...♖e8 and ...♔f8. From White's point of view, however, ...e4 uses a tempo while Black's king is still exposed, and a pawn on d6 could be a powerful influence on the game. Finally, f7 presents itself as a target.

13 ♘g5

13 d6+ ♔f8 14 ♘g5 transposes.

13...♘b6 14 d6+ ♔f8 15 a4!? *(D)*

In the current position, 15 ♕b3 runs into 15...c4, so White tries to dislodge the troublesome knight on b6.

15...h6

15...a5?? is a blunder because Black loses a piece after 16 ♕b3.

16 ♘xf7?!

16 a5 hxg5 17 axb6 ♘c6 or 17...a6 is hard to assess; however, Black's pieces are active and White doesn't have any of his own in play yet.

16...♔xf7 17 a5 ♗d4!

Returning the piece to block everything off. Now it's *White* who can't castle!

18 axb6 ♘c6 19 bxa7 ♕e6!? 20 ♗e2 ♔g7 21 ♖a4 ♖hd8 22 ♗c4 ♕xd6 23 ♕b3 ♕c7

The alternative 23...♘b4 is also strong because ...♘d3+ will force open more lines. Black wins fairly easily from this point onwards:

24 ♕h3 ♖f8 25 f5 g5 26 ♕h5 ♖xf5 27 ♖a3 ♕d6 28 g4 ♖ff8 29 h4 ♗f2+ 30 ♔e2 ♗xh4 31 ♖xh4 gxh4 32 ♕xh4 ♘d4+ 33 ♔e1 e3 34 ♖xe3 ♘c2+ 35 ♔e2 ♘xe3 36 ♗xe3 ♖ad8 37 ♗xh6+ 0-1

Taimanov Attack

8 ♗b5+ *(D)*

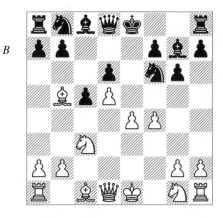

Here we have the contemporary main line of the Modern Benoni with 4 ♘c3 (i.e., without an early ♘f3). This simple check has proven to be a reliable weapon. Its point is that, by contrast with 8 e5, 8 ♗b5+ speeds White's development and assists in castling before over-committing White's centre. In fact, the move e5 may be greatly delayed or it might never even happen. But the constant threat of e5 can force Black into convoluted piece placements and passive play. Because of the Taimanov Attack, some players intending to use the Benoni wait for

White to commit to ♘f3, as in the line 1 d4 ♘f6 2 c4 e6 3 ♘f3, before playing 3...c5 4 d5 exd5, etc.

Nevertheless, the play resulting from 8 ♗b5+ is terribly double-edged and unresolved in theoretical terms. Although facing the difficulties just described, Black may be able to create play on the queenside, and White is also running some risks due to his exposed centre.

8...♘fd7

Apart from general considerations, there is a specific problem for Black: how to answer the check! 8...♘bd7 can be met by 9 e5, threatening the knight on f6 as well as e6. This leads to extreme complications following 9...dxe5 10 fxe5 ♘h5 11 e6 ♕h4+ 12 g3 ♘xg3 (a motif that you will see throughout the whole of chess practice) 13 hxg3! (13 ♘f3 ♗xc3+ 14 bxc3 ♕e4+ 15 ♗e2 has also been tried) 13...♕xh1 14 ♗e3 *(D)*.

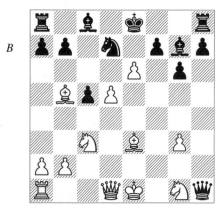

You need to be aware of this kind of thing if you play 7 f4 and 8 ♗b5+. White will end up with two pieces for a rook, but his king is exposed. This is something that you'll have to look up and/or study. But I shall say that existing theory begs for improvement. Likewise with the variation 8...♗d7 9 e5 dxe5 10 fxe5 ♘h5 11 ♘f3 0-0 12 ♗xd7 ♘xd7!? 13 g4 ♘xe5 14 gxh5 ♘xf3+ 15 ♕xf3 ♖e8+ 16 ♔d1 ♕h4 17 ♗d2 b5, and so on and so forth.

Fortunately, 8...♘fd7, to which we now return, is very likely better and more strategically-based than the alternatives.

9 a4 *(D)*

Having drawn the knight back to d7, White can return to a Four Pawns Attack set-up by 9

♗e2 (9 ♗d3 is also possible; note that both 9 ♗e2 and 9 ♗d3 run away from Black's planned ...a6 and ...b5 so that ...a6 can now be met by a4, quashing any notion of ...b5 for a long time to come) 9...0-0 10 ♘f3. Whether this is advantageous or disadvantageous is unclear, because a knight on d7 serves a prophylactic function versus e5 but doesn't attack the centre. You should definitely consult the King's Indian chapter in order to understand this one. Typical Benoni moves might follow, such as ...♖e8, ...♘a6-c7, ...a6, ...♖b8, etc., with ...b5 as the goal. White plays for the e5 break, typically prepared by moves such as a4, ♖e1, ♗f1 and h3.

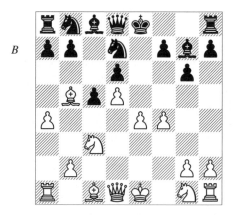

With 9 a4, White obviously wants to prevent Black from playing ...a6 and ...b5, but he also wants to see what his opponent is doing so that he can react accordingly. From this point we'll look at games with 9...0-0, 9...♘a6 and 9...♕h4+, beginning with two famous performances by Kasparov. They made 8 ♗b5+ the centre of attention, and it has remained so ever since.

Development by 9...0-0

Kasparov – Kuijpers
Dortmund jr Wch 1980

9...0-0 10 ♘f3 a6

10...♘a6 11 0-0 ♘c7 *(D)* is a common sequence:

12 ♖e1 (12 ♗e2 and 12 ♗c4 have also been played) 12...♖e8 13 ♗f1 ♖b8 14 ♕c2 a6 15 a5 b5 16 axb6 ♘xb6 17 ♗e3 ♘b5!? and here

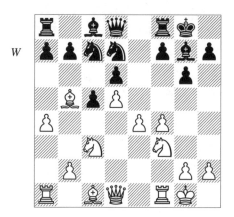

instead of 18 h3?!, played in Bermejo Marti-nez-Oleksienko, Peniscola 2002, Emms recommends 18 ♘xb5 axb5 19 ♗xb5. Nevertheless, he adds that 19...♖xe4!? 20 ♕xe4 ♗f5 21 ♕e8+! ♕xe8 22 ♗xe8 ♖xe8 provides unclear compensation. In fact, even the materialistic machines think that Black is equal in this position.

11 ♗e2!

11 ♗c4 is also possible. The idea is that after White plays e5 and Black responds with ...dxe5, then White's move d6 will open up a wonderful diagonal for the c4-bishop, aiming directly at f7. But after 11...♘b6!, Black has had no trouble holding his own because he gets ...♗g4 in. Compare other lines in this section.

11...♘f6?!

This has a bad feel to it. White gets a KID Four Pawns Attack a full tempo ahead with a4 and ...a6 inserted. This is a significant advantage in a violent attacking line.

12 0-0 (D)

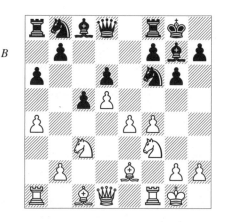

12...♕c7?!

This can't be best, but what is? It has been claimed that 12...♖e8 is better, but then 13 e5 dxe5 (13...♘fd7 14 e6 fxe6 15 dxe6 ♘f6 16 f5 gxf5 17 ♘g5 and the attack is worth much more than a pawn) 14 fxe5 ♘g4 15 ♗g5 (or 15 e6 fxe6 16 ♗c4) 15...f6 (15...♕b6 16 d6!) 16 exf6 ♗xf6 17 ♕d2 ♗xg5 18 ♘xg5 ♘e3 19 ♘ce4 yields a winning game.

13 e5 ♘e8 14 e6! fxe6 15 ♗c4! (D)

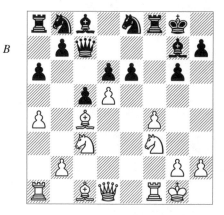

15...♕e7

Black still can't get developed (15...exd5? loses to 16 ♘xd5).

16 dxe6 ♘c7 17 f5! ♘c6 (D)

Some of White's characteristic tactics are shown by 17...♖xf5 18 ♗g5! ♗f6 19 ♗xf6 ♖xf6 and one fascinating winning line is 20 ♘e4 ♖f4 21 ♘fg5 ♖xf1+ 22 ♕xf1 d5 23 ♘f6+ ♔g7 24 ♘xd5 ♘xd5 25 ♗xd5 (threatening ♕f4) 25...h6 26 ♕f3! hxg5 27 ♖f1 ♘c6 28 ♕c3+ ♔h7 29 ♖f7+.

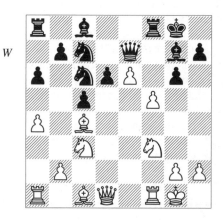

18 ♗g5 ♗f6 19 ♘e4! ♗xg5 20 ♘fxg5 gxf5

The main alternative would be 20...♖xf5 21
♖xf5 gxf5 22 ♕h5, which analysis will show to
give White a winning advantage.

21 ♘xd6 ♘d4 22 ♕h5 ♗xe6 23 ♖ae1 ♖f6
(D)

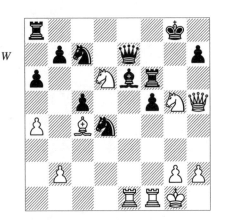

**24 ♘xf5! ♘xf5 25 ♘xe6 ♘xe6 26 ♖xe6
♖xe6 27 ♕xf5 ♖e8 28 ♖e1 1-0**

Development by 9...♘a6

Kasparov – Nunn
Lucerne OL 1982

9...♘a6

Black wants to move rapidly on the queenside. For a similar idea, see 9...0-0 10 ♘f3 ♘a6
above.

10 ♘f3 ♘b4!? 11 0-0 a6?

This move just doesn't work out due to an
unexpected idea by Kasparov. 11...0-0 is the
natural alternative, though then White has time
to provide the f1-square as a convenient spot for
his bishop to drop back to when hit by ...a6.

12 ♗xd7+! ♗xd7 13 f5! *(D)*

It's surprising but logical (with hindsight!)
to give up the bishop-pair, because White gives
up his bad bishop while extending the range of
his good one. In the meantime, although the
knight on b4 hits some good internal squares, it
doesn't manage to return to the centre, from
where it would protect his kingside.

13...0-0

After 13...gxf5, 14 exf5 0-0 15 ♘g5 sets up a
nice attack, while 14 ♗g5!? ♗f6 15 ♗f4 0-0 16
e5 dxe5 17 ♘xe5 is also possible.

14 ♗g5 f6

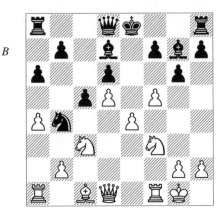

14...♗f6!? 15 ♗f4 (or 15 ♕d2) 15...gxf5 16
e5 dxe5 17 ♘xe5 gives White an obvious advantage.

15 ♗f4 gxf5?!

But 15...♕e7 is uninspiring: 16 fxg6 hxg6 17
♘h4 ♔h7 18 ♗g3!.

16 ♗xd6 ♗xa4

Kasparov offers the line 16...♖e8 17 ♗xc5
fxe4 18 ♘d4 ♘d3 19 ♘xe4!.

17 ♖xa4 ♕xd6 18 ♘h4!

The point. White captures f5 (Kasparov's favourite square), which can't be challenged by
Black's pieces. He also plays against an entombed bishop.

**18...fxe4 19 ♘f5 ♕d7 20 ♘xe4 ♔h8 21
♘xc5 1-0**

The finish might be 21...♕xd5 22 ♕xd5
♘xd5 23 ♘e6. This short game contains remarkably many positional and tactical themes.

The Queen Check Variation

9...♕h4+

This check has become one of Black's most
popular moves. 9...a6 is often played in order
to see where the bishop is going before deciding upon the desired set-up. That's a technical
move-order issue, however, and we want to get
a feel for the broader ideas. In this section some
of the games actually transposed from 9...a6.

10 g3 ♕d8 *(D)*

10...♕e7 is also frequently played, just as it
is in the lines 9 ♗e2 ♕h4+ and 9 ♗d3 ♕h4+.
From e7 the queen puts direct pressure on e4
but is somewhat more vulnerable to the e5 advance, because ...dxe5 might be answered by
d6.

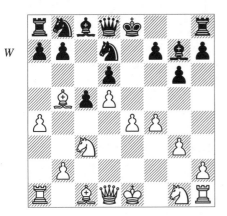

Black has had fair success from this position and similar ones with ...a6 in. What on earth is going on? He sacrifices two tempi to provoke the little move g3. This has several ideas behind it:

a) First, it asks White exactly what his plan is if Black doesn't expose his pieces to direct attack. Often the answer to that question in other lines is the manoeuvre ♗d2-e1-h4 (or ♗g3), but that is eliminated here.

b) The move g3 weakens White's kingside pawn-structure.

c) Black's light-squared bishop, his main problem in this variation, now has good chances to get to g4 (or h3). Once that occurs he can play ...♗xf3 and neutralize White's threat to advance by e5. White can only stop ...♗g4 by further weakening himself.

Or so the theory goes. Of course, White isn't crying over his fate and is glad to get the opportunity to use two extra tempi productively – especially in an attacking position!

11 ♘f3 0-0 12 0-0 a6 *(D)*

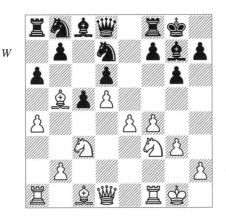

Now there are various bishop retreats. I'll give some sample games.

Van Beek – Gofshtein
Tel Aviv 2001

13 ♗e2 ♖e8 14 ♔g2!
Covering h3 against intrusion by a black bishop. Black did well after 14 ♕c2 ♘f6 15 e5 dxe5! 16 fxe5 ♘g4 17 ♗g5 ♕a5 18 ♗c4 ♘d7 19 ♘e4 ♘dxe5 20 ♘xe5 ♖xe5 21 ♗f4 ♗f5! with a pawn, two bishops and tremendous pieces, in Tikkanen-de Firmian, Swedish Cht 2001/2.

14...♘f6 15 e5!? dxe5 16 fxe5 ♘g4 17 e6
A good try to seize the initiative. 17 ♗g5 doesn't achieve enough after 17...♕xg5! 18 ♘xg5 ♘e3+ 19 ♔h1 ♘xd1 20 ♖axd1 ♗xe5. White has enough for his pawn, but no more than that. Theoretically, this line ends in equality.

17...fxe6 18 ♘g5 ♘f6?!
Probably best is 18...♘e5! 19 dxe6 ♕xd1 20 ♖xd1 b6 with equality.

19 ♗c4?!
19 ♘xe6! ♗xe6 20 dxe6 ♘c6 21 ♕xd8 ♖axd8 22 ♗g5 with some edge for White, Muir-E.Peicheva, Copenhagen 1990.

19...b5!
The h1-a8 diagonal is weak.

20 axb5 ♗b7 21 ♘ge4?
21 bxa6!? ♘xa6 isn't so clear.

21...♘xe4 22 ♘xe4 axb5 23 ♗g5 ♖xa1 24 ♕xa1 ♕b6 25 ♗b3 c4
With two extra pawns, Black went on to win.

Bareev – Gelfand
Khanty-Mansiisk (FIDE WCup) 2005

13 ♗c4 ♘b6 14 ♗e2 ♗g4 15 ♗e3 ♖e8 16 ♕c2 ♕e7 *(D)*

17 e5?!
White lashes out. The question is whether he has any better options. It's likely, but not with 17 a5?, when a typical trick followed: 17...♗xc3 18 ♕xc3 ♘xd5 19 exd5 ♕xe3+ 20 ♕xe3 ♖xe3 21 ♔f2 ♖b3 and Black was a pawn up for nothing in Laine-Paavilainen, Helsinki 1990.

17...dxe5 18 fxe5 ♗xf3 19 ♖xf3 ♘8d7 20 d6 ♕e6 21 ♖d1 ♘xe5 22 ♗xc5!? ♘bd7 23 ♗a3 ♘xf3+ 24 ♗xf3 ♖ab8 25 ♘d5 ♔h8
Or 25...♘e5 with advantage.

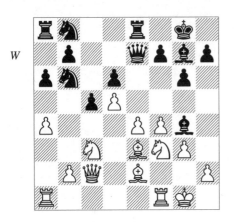

26 ♔g2 ♖ed8 27 ♘c7 ♕f6 28 ♖f1 ♕e5 29 ♖f2 h5! 30 ♕b3 ♖f8

Black stands better, even though these two world-class players eventually drew.

We conclude with two games of interest:

Palo – de Firmian
Copenhagen 2001

13 ♗d3

This third retreat is the most popular one.

13...♘f6 *(D)*

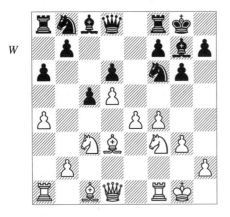

14 ♖e1

We shall see 14 f5 in the game that follows this one.

14 ♗d2 is another possibility, but 14...♗h3! 15 ♖e1 ♘bd7 16 ♗f1?! ♗xf1 17 ♖xf1 ♖e8 18 ♕c2 c4! 19 ♖ae1 ♘c5 gave Black an excellent game in Hammer-Bronznik, Rommelshausen 2002.

14...♗g4 15 ♗e2

I suspect that 15 ♗f1 ♘bd7 16 h3 ♗xf3 17 ♕xf3 is better, as in Brasoy-Vik Hansen, Alta 2003. Now Emms suggests that 17...♕a5 is best, when Black will aim to advance with ...b5 or, less often, with ...c4.

15...♘fd7!? 16 ♘d2 ♗xe2 17 ♖xe2 ♖e8 18 ♘c4 ♘b6 *(D)*

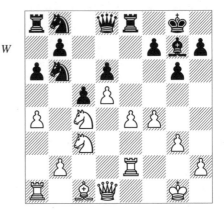

A knight on c4 tends to be so powerful that Black challenges it more often than not. The opposing knight on b6 is particularly well-placed to do so.

19 ♘a3 ♗d4+ 20 ♔h1 ♘8d7 21 ♕d3 ♘f6 22 a5 ♘bd7 23 ♘c2

Now, however, 23 ♘c4 ♕e7 threatens to capture on c3 and e4, and 24 e5 dxe5 25 fxe5 ♘xe5 26 ♘xe5 ♗xe5 27 ♗f4 ♕d6 doesn't give White anything for his pawn.

23...♗xc3! 24 bxc3 *(D)*

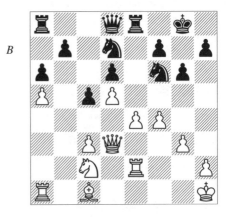

24...c4!

A characteristic sacrifice.

25 ♕xc4 ♖c8 26 ♕d3

26 ♕b4 ♘xd5 isn't exactly inspiring either in view of 27 ♕xd6 ♘xc3 28 ♖e1 ♘xe4.

26...♘c5

Black's pieces are in their ideal Benoni spots, and he is even getting his pawn back.

27 ♕f3 ♖xe4 28 ♗b2 ♖xe2 29 ♕xe2 ♘b3 30 ♖e1 ♘xa5 31 c4

Otherwise White's bishop remains passive.

31...♘xc4 32 ♗a1 ♘b6?!

32...♘xd5! is good, with three extra pawns; perhaps this didn't look safe enough. Now he gets only two doubled pawns but they are sufficient.

33 ♘e3 ♘bd7 34 ♕b2 ♕a5 35 ♖d1 ♕b5 36 ♕xb5 axb5

and Black went on to win.

M. Carlsen – K. Lie
Norwegian Ch (Molde) 2004

13 ♗d3 ♘f6 14 f5 ♘g4!?

The obvious 14...♘bd7 protects the outpost (which is in front of a backward pawn) and needs more tests. In Ragnarsson-H.Olafsson, Reykjavik 1998, Black got an excellent game after 15 ♗g5 ♕c7 16 ♘d2 ♖b8 17 a5 h6 18 ♗f4 g5! 19 ♗e3 ♘e5 20 ♘c4 ♘fg4! (refusing to concede the occupation of e5 by a knight!) 21 ♗c1 ♘xc4 22 ♗xc4 ♗d4+ 23 ♔g2 ♘e5. Black will close the kingside and then try to win on the queenside. Nevertheless, White can improve upon this play and we shall probably see some tests of this variation.

15 ♗g5!? ♕b6 16 a5! *(D)*

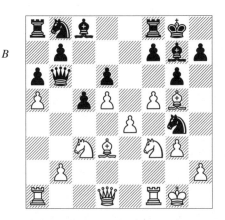

16...♕xb2 17 ♘a4 ♗d4+

17...♕xa1!? is an interesting alternative.

18 ♔h1 ♕xa1 19 ♕b3! ♘d7 20 ♖xa1 ♗xa1 21 ♗e7! ♖e8 22 ♗xd6 ♘f2+ 23 ♔g2 ♘xe4 24 ♗xe4 ♖xe4 25 ♘g5 ♖e2+ 26 ♔f1 ♖e8 27 ♕f3!? ♘e5!? 28 ♕d1 ♗d4 29 ♘b6?

29 fxg6! followed by 30 ♗xc5 is correct.

29...♗xf5!

Suddenly White's king is badly exposed.

30 ♘xa8?! ♘g4 31 ♗f4 ♖xa8??

Black overlooks 31...h6!, which effectively wins the game after 32 ♘c7 ♖e3! or 32 ♘f3 ♘xh2+!.

32 ♕b3 ♖e8 33 d6!

and White went on to win. Even taking into account Black's alternatives from move 14 onwards, 14 f5 poses an interesting challenge to the 9...♕h4+ variation.

Fianchetto System

6 ♘f3 *(D)*

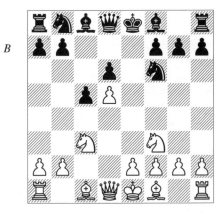

In the variations above White played e4. Here he denies Black a central target.

6...g6

Now we shall look at the fianchetto lines beginning with 7 g3. 7 ♗f4 may transpose into one of the ♗f4 systems mentioned above. Without entering into a serious discussion, independent play can come from such lines as 7...a6 8 a4 ♗g7 9 e4 (9 h3 0-0 10 e3 is safe and logical) 9...♗g4, inviting 10 ♕b3 (10 ♗e2 ♗xf3 11 ♗xf3 0-0 with the idea ...♕e7 and ...♘bd7 is considered fully equal) 10...♗xf3 11 ♕xb7 ♘bd7 12 gxf3 ♖b8 13 ♕a6 ♘h5 14 ♗c1 0-0 with plenty of compensation for a pawn.

7 g3 ♗g7 8 ♗g2 0-0 9 0-0 *(D)*

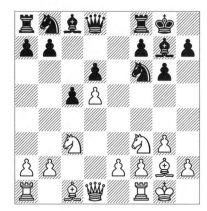

We haven't examined many fianchetto lines versus Indian systems in this book. With this variation we have a solid approach that defends d5, and to all appearances doesn't do much else. Of course that's not so. In the initial stages of the game, White proceeds along the principle of prophylaxis to counter Black's normal plans. Then he patiently reorganizes, implementing his own strategy of piece-play versus d6 and eventual expansion in the centre. This usually involves the manoeuvre ♘d2-c4, possibly in conjunction with ♗f4. Of a sudden Black can be helpless against the threats, frequently created by a delayed e4-e5. Remember that a central majority is often the last thing to be mobilized, but then it can prove deadly!

On the flip side, White's bishop on g2 runs right into its own pawn on d5. Furthermore, Black's efforts to realize ...b5 and ...c4 benefit from the absence of the bishop from the f1-a6 diagonal. His most popular plan involves ...a6 and ...♘bd7 and, once White's knight gets to c4, he can play ...♘b6 or ...♘e5 to challenge it. There's also nothing wrong with ...♘a6-c7 as long as Black is careful to watch the tactics. Finally, before White reorganizes his pieces Black can play for ...♖e8 and ...♘e4. All this should be done as quickly as possible before White's pawns assert themselves. If White can fend off short-term threats, as he often can, he will normally remain with some advantage.

Let's see games using these ideas.

Play Down the e-File

9...♖e8 *(D)*

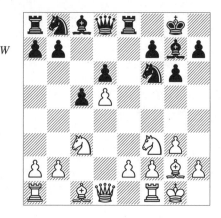

Black aims for ...♘e4. Here are two games that show different treatments:

Nikolić – Hraček
Batumi Echt 1999

10 ♗f4
White allows the following thematic intrusion because he wants to develop rapidly.
10...a6 11 a4 ♘e4! 12 ♘xe4 ♖xe4 13 ♘d2 ♖b4 *(D)*

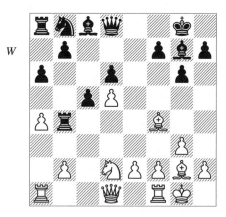

So far, so standard. Black takes up an active post and attacks b2. If he can develop his other pieces he should have the superior game. That's a big 'if'.

14 ♖a2! ♕e7
If Black doesn't capture the b2-pawn his whole idea is in danger of failing. So the critical line goes 14...♗xb2!? (taking an initiative by 14...g5 15 ♗e3 f5 is a reasonable idea; on the other hand, after 14...♖xb2? 15 ♖xb2 ♗xb2 16 ♘c4! White wins the pawn on d6, after which

his own d-pawn will roll forward, among other problems for Black) 15 ♕c2 ♗g7 16 ♘c4 b5! 17 axb5 ♖xc4! (the only chance; this is all Emms's analysis) 18 ♕xc4 axb5 19 ♕c2 ♖xa2 20 ♕xa2 b4 with a passed pawn and some play for the exchange.

15 b3 g5 16 ♗e3 ♗d4 17 ♗xd4 ♖xd4 18 e3 ♖b4 19 ♘c4 ♘d7 20 f4!

White keeps Black's knight out of e5. He has space and the centre, while Black's unchallengeable rook on b4 provides some definite compensation, but probably not enough.

20...♖b8 21 ♕d3 g4 22 ♖d1 ♘f8!?

Black still had 22...♘f6 with the idea 23 e4?! b5 24 axb5 axb5, which looks OK for him. Instead, however, 23 a5! ♗d7 24 e4 ♗b5 invites 25 ♖e2!, when the dream move e5 can't be stopped any more: 25...♗xc4 26 bxc4 ♘d7 27 e5! dxe5 28 ♕f5 f6 29 d6! (or 29 ♕xg4+) 29...♕g7 30 ♗d5+ ♔h8 31 ♗e6 ♖d8 32 ♗xd7 ♖xd7 33 fxe5 and wins.

23 ♕c3 ♗d7 24 e4 b5 25 axb5 axb5 26 ♘e3

With his centre pawns and a-file, White stands clearly better. A model positional effort by Nikolić.

Kalisvaart – Ballo
Van Gent 1998

10 ♘d2 b6!? 11 ♘c4!?

The prophylactic moves 11 h3 and 11 a4 are better tries for advantage.

11...♗a6 12 ♕b3 ♗xc4! 13 ♕xc4 a6 (D)

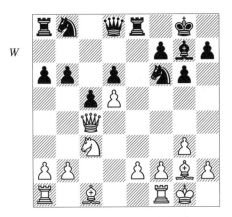

This is like the Old Main Line with ...♘a6. The move ...b5 can't be stopped, which means that at the very least Black has no problems

14 a4!? b5! 15 ♕d3

15 axb5?? loses outright to 15...axb5.

15...c4 16 ♕c2 b4 17 ♘d1 ♕c7 18 ♘e3 ♖c8 19 b3!? cxb3 20 ♕xc7?

20 ♕xb3 is best, but then 20...♘e4 21 ♖a2 ♘c3 is strong.

20...♖xc7 21 ♖b1 a5 22 ♖xb3 ♘bd7 23 ♖b1 ♘b6 (D)

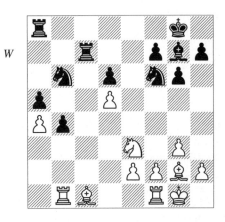

Black will end up with two advanced passed pawns and much the better game.

Direct Support of ...b5 by the Knight

Korchnoi – Tal
USSR Ch (Erevan) 1962

9...♘a6 (D)

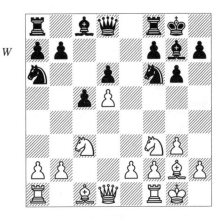

Black initiates his familiar plan of ...♘c7, ...a6, ...♖b8 and ...b5. In this old game the plan doesn't hold together, but with accurate play theory concludes that it's satisfactory.

**10 h3 ♘c7 11 e4 ♘d7 12 ♖e1 ♘e8 13 ♗g5!
♗f6 14 ♗e3 ♖b8 15 a4 a6 16 ♗f1! ♕e7 17
♘d2 ♘c7 18 f4** (D)

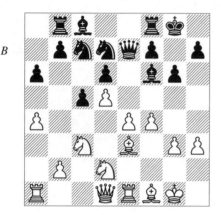

A terrific picture of the two majorities collid-
ing.

**18...b5 19 e5! dxe5 20 ♘de4 ♕d8 21 ♘xf6+!
♘xf6 22 d6!**

Korchnoi's treatment of the position has
been masterful.

**22...♘e6 23 fxe5 b4! 24 ♘d5 ♘xd5 25
♕xd5 ♗b7 26 ♕d2 ♕d7**

Tal has managed to scrape up some activity
by resourceful play, but White is clearly ahead.

**27 ♔h2 b3!? 28 ♖ac1!? ♕xa4 29 ♗c4 ♗c8
30 ♖f1 ♖b4 31 ♗xe6 ♗xe6 32 ♗h6 ♖e8 33
♕g5** (D)

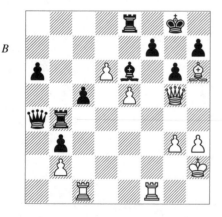

It's amazing that Black lasts 20 more moves!

33...♖e4! 34 ♖f2

34 ♕f6? ♖e2+ 35 ♖f2 ♖xf2+ 36 ♕xf2 ♕d4
37 ♕f6 ♕xb2+ 38 ♔g1 ♕d4+ 39 ♔h2 ♕b2+
with a draw.

**34...f5! 35 ♕f6 ♕d7 36 ♖xc5 ♖c4 37 ♖xc4
♗xc4 38 ♖d2 ♗e6 39 ♖d1 ♕a7 40 ♖d2 ♕d7
41 ♖d1 ♕a7 42 ♖d4! ♕d7 43 g4! a5! 44 ♔g3
♖b8 45 ♔h4?!**

White misses a way to break down Black's
defences by 45 gxf5 ♗xf5 46 ♖c4! ♕a7 47
♖c5! ♖e8 48 ♔h2 a4 49 e6! ♖xe6 50 ♖c7.

**45...♕f7 46 ♔g5! fxg4 47 hxg4 ♗d7! 48
♖c4 a4** (D)

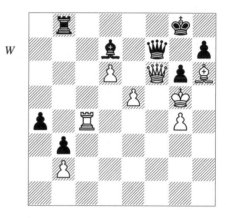

Amazingly, what seemed a slaughter has
turned into a race!

49 ♖c7 a3

49...♕xf6+ loses by a tempo: 50 ♔xf6 a3 51
e6 ♗xe6 52 ♔xe6 axb2 53 d7.

50 ♖xd7 ♕xd7 51 e6! ♕a7

The most fascinating defence is 51...♕b5+
52 ♔h4 ♕b7 53 ♔g3 ♕a7 54 ♔h2 axb2 55 d7
♕g1+ 56 ♔xg1 b1♕+ 57 ♔h2 ♕c2+ 58 ♔h3
♕d3+ 59 ♔h4 g5+ 60 ♕xg5+ ♕g6 61 ♕xg6+
hxg6 62 e7.

52 ♕e5 axb2 53 e7 ♔f7 54 d7 1-0

A wonderful game.

The Flexible 9...♘bd7

Ligterink – Nunn
Marbella Z 1982

9...♘bd7 (D)

Black plays traditionally, covering e5 before
committing to ...♖e8 or ...a6.

10 e4

10 h3 is more solid.

10...a6

There's nothing wrong with this, but later the
straightforward 10...b5! was discovered, with

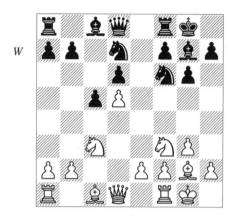

W

the idea of meeting 11 ♘xb5 ♘xe4 12 ♖e1 by 12...a6!.

11 ♗f4 ♕e7 12 ♖e1 ♘g4! 13 ♗g5 ♕e8

An instructive illustration of White fulfilling his ambitions in the Benoni is given by Nunn: 13...♗f6? 14 ♗xf6 ♕xf6 15 h3 ♘ge5 16 ♘xe5! ♘xe5 17 f4 ♘c4 18 e5!; e.g., 18...dxe5 19 ♕e2! ♘b6 20 fxe5 and White's centre is simply too powerful, especially in conjunction with weak squares like f6.

14 e5!? ♘dxe5

This prepares a lovely queen sacrifice. Ligterink may have expected 14...dxe5 15 d6 with the d5 outpost and good prospects. Black can expand on the kingside, but his pieces aren't well placed for defence.

15 ♘xe5 ♘xe5 16 f4 ♘g4! *(D)*

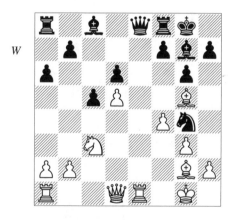

W

17 ♖xe8 ♖xe8 18 ♘e2

Black's ideas include ...♗d4+ and ...♘e3, so White attends to the former. Nunn gives a number of alternatives here, Black getting at least equality in all of them; e.g., 18 ♘e4 ♖xe4! 19

♗xe4 ♗d4+ 20 ♕xd4 (on all other moves Black will fork the king and queen!) 20...cxd4 21 ♗e7 ♗f5! 22 ♗xf5 gxf5 23 ♖d1 ♖e8 24 ♗xd6 ♖d8 with a level game.

18...♘e3 19 ♕d2 ♘c4 20 ♕c2 *(D)*

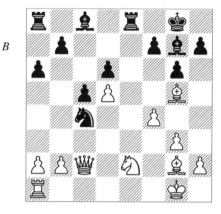

B

20...b5!?

Black daringly rejects the draw which was to be had by 20...♘e3. He only has a rook and pawn for the queen, but the bishops are a terror. This is more or less what the opening has led to(!), so I'll limit the remaining notes:

21 g4

An alternative is 21 ♘c3 ♗f5 22 ♗e4 b4 23 ♗xf5 bxc3 24 bxc3 ♘e3 25 ♕a4 ♘xf5. This is one of White's better lines, according to Nunn, but he'd still rather be Black.

21...♗xg4! 22 ♘g3 h6 23 ♗h4 ♗xb2 24 ♖c1 ♗d4+ 25 ♔h1 ♘e3! 26 ♕d2 ♘xg2 27 ♕xg2

27 ♔xg2!? ♗e3 28 ♕b2 ♗xf4 29 ♗f6 is Vegh's suggestion, and it may improve; nevertheless, I would rather play Black.

27...♖e3! 28 ♖f1

Or 28 ♘f1 ♗f3! 29 ♘xe3 ♗xg2+ 30 ♘xg2 c4 and the three pawns are much stronger than the piece.

28...♖ae8 29 f5?

Instead, 29 h3! offers more resistance.

29...g5 30 f6 ♔h8! 31 ♗xg5 hxg5 32 ♘f5 ♗xf5 33 ♖xf5 ♖e1+ 34 ♖f1 ♗xf6 35 ♕h3+ ♔g7 36 ♖xe1 ♖xe1+ 37 ♔g2 c4 0-1

Play on Both Wings

9...a6 *(D)*

Again aiming for ...b5, but delaying ...♘bd7.

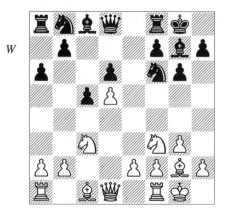

10 a4 ♖e8 11 ♘d2

In this line White prevents ...♘e4 and prepares to take over the queenside.

11...♘bd7

This time we have two games:

R. O'Kelly – Mariotti
Islington 1970

12 e4?!

This doesn't go with White's philosophy in this variation. The advance e4 should only be played after White reorganizes to control that square, starting with the moves ♘c4, h3 and ♗f4. Better is 12 h3!, with the idea that we shall see in Kovačević-Nemeth below.

12...♘e5

Attacking d3 but also eyeing g4. You can see the usefulness of h3.

13 ♕c2 ♘h5 (D)

Black prepares ...f5. He has achieved equality and more out of the opening.

14 f4?

An instructive error, because it demonstrates the extent to which the dynamic qualities of Black's position can dominate. That doesn't become clear for a few more moves. 14 h3 was again better.

14...♘g4 15 ♘f3 f5!

This is arguably the move of the game. It's what White must have missed, and without it the attack would have petered out.

16 ♘g5

A key variation is the advance 16 e5 dxe5 17 h3, which fails to 17...e4! 18 hxg4 exf3 19 gxh5 fxg2 20 ♕xg2 gxh5.

16...♗d4+ 17 ♔h1 fxe4 18 ♗xe4 ♖xe4!

This exchange sacrifice exploits White's light-squared weaknesses by eliminating their defender.

19 ♘cxe4 ♗f5 (D)

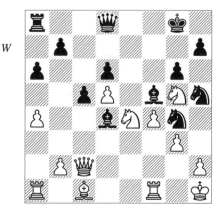

Black has one internal weakness on e6; White has four of them! This marks the end of the 'opening'.

20 ♔g2 ♕d7 21 ♗d2 h6 22 ♘e6

This terrific outpost never compensates for Black's attack, in particular because of White's exposed king position. According to analysts, the best alternative was 22 h3 ♘gf6 23 g4 ♘xg4! 24 hxg4 ♗xe4+ 25 ♘xe4?! (25 ♕xe4!?) 25...♕xg4+ 26 ♔h2 ♖e8! *(D).*

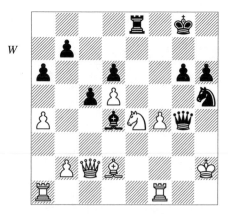

Even though he's temporarily a rook down, Black is close to winning on the spot.

22...♘gf6 23 ♖ae1 ♘xe4 24 g4!? ♘xd2 25 gxf5 ♘xf1 26 f6 ♔f7! 27 ♔xf1

Black's idea is 27 ♘xd4 cxd4 28 ♖e7+ ♕xe7 29 fxe7 ♘e3+. In a good position the tactics tend to work your way.

27...♗xf6 28 ♕e2 ♘g7 29 ♕g4 ♘f5 0-1

The knight on f5 occupies a great outpost that almost equals White's on e6. As Black is a piece and pawn ahead, there's really nothing for White to play for.

Kovačević – Nemeth
Karlovac 1979

12 h3 *(D)*

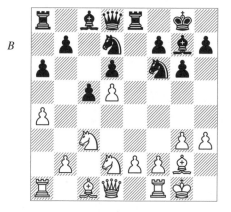

12...♖b8 13 ♘c4 ♘e5

This leads to chaos almost by force. The positional option 13...♘b6 leads to unbalanced, equal play.

14 ♘a3!

Getting ready for f4 followed by returning to c4 with the knight. In view of the overwhelming position that would then result, Black is virtually forced to sacrifice a piece. The tactics are important if we are to understand what each side's strengths are.

14...♘h5

Sriram-Antonio, Calcutta 2001 continued 14...♗d7!? 15 f4 ♘h5 16 fxe5 ♗xe5 17 ♗f4!? ♘xg3 18 ♗xg3 ♗xg3 19 e4! with the idea of ♕f3. White is better in this complex variation, although the last word may not have been spoken.

15 e4 *(D)*
15...f5?!

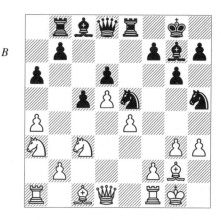

The classic game Korchnoi-Kasparov, Lucerne OL 1982 went 15...♖f8 16 ♔h2 f5 17 f4 b5 18 axb5 axb5 19 ♘axb5, and Black didn't really have enough for a pawn but won in the complications. 15...♗d7!? is considered unclear.

16 exf5 ♗xf5 17 g4 ♗xg4! 18 hxg4 ♕h4 19 gxh5 ♖f8 *(D)*

After 19...♘g4, 20 ♗f4 stops the attack.

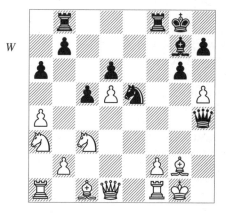

20 h6! ♗h8 21 ♘c4!!

An amazing defence. Black can't capture without losing the initiative.

21...♘g4! 22 ♕xg4 ♕xg4 23 ♘xd6 ♗e5 24 ♘de4 ♖f3 25 ♘g5! ♖bf8?!

25...♖d3 looks worth a try.

26 ♘xf3 ♖xf3 27 ♖e1

and White eventually won.

Index of Players

Numbers refer to pages. When a player's name appears in **bold**, that player had White. Otherwise the FIRST-NAMED PLAYER had White.

AKOPIAN – **Gurevich, M.** 58
ALTERMAN – Pigusov 40; Spassov, L. 109
ANAND – **Karpov** 111; **Khalifman** 79;
   Lputian 103; Morozevich 87; **Topalov**
   171, 172
ATALIK – Zheliandinov 33
AVRUKH – Lugovoi 62
BACROT – Gustafsson, J. 82
BALLO – **Kalisvaart** 311
BAREEV – Gelfand 307; Golubev 240; Polzin
   237
BELIAVSKY – **Epishin** 179; **Gligorić** 84;
   Kasparov 65; Portisch 298; **Yusupov** 95
BJARNASON – **Tisdall** 126
BLOKH – Feldman, A. 196
BOGDANOVSKI – Golubev 232
BOLOGAN – **Krush** 211
BORN – Tonneman 206
BOTVINNIK – **Keres** 152; Kotov 123;
   Petrosian 148; Tal 120
BOZINOVIĆ – Cebalo 302
BRONSTEIN – Najdorf 132
BROWNE – **Donaldson** 209
BRYNELL – **Pinter** 300
BUNZMANN – Golubev 233
BURGERMEISTER – **Kelečević** 296
CAMPORA – **Milov, V.** 128
CARLSEN – **Jobava** 93; Lie, K. 309
CEBALO – **Bozinović** 302
COSTAS VARELA – Ivanov, J. 216
DANAILOV – Kasparov 207
DE FIRMIAN – **Palo** 308
DEL RIO – Illescas 226
DJURIĆ – Pfleger 56
DOMINGUEZ, L. – **Illescas** 80
DONALDSON – Browne 209
DREEV – Short 147
DVOIRYS – **Mikhalevski** 288
EPISHIN – Beliavsky 179; **Kiselev** 259
EUWE – Keres 168
FELDMAN, A. – **Blokh** 196

FISCHER – **Gheorghiu** 129; **Spassky** 258
FTAČNIK – Sznapik 221; Topalov 234
GAGUNASHVILI – Pedersen, N. 147
GELFAND – **Bareev** 307; **Gunawan, Ro.** 246;
   Kantsler 219; **Neverov** 64; Shirov 280
GELLER – **Timman** 37
GEORGIEV, KI. – **Karpov** 41
GHEORGHIU – Fischer 129
GLIGORIĆ – Beliavsky 84; Plater 120;
   Smyslov 257
GOFSHTEIN – **Van Beek** 307
GOLUBEV – **Bareev** 240; **Bogdanovski** 232;
   Bunzmann 233
GULKO – **Platonov** 242
GUNAWAN, RO. – Gelfand 246
GUREVICH, M. – Akopian 58
GUSEINOV – Magomedov 49
GUSTAFSSON, J. – **Bacrot** 82
HECTOR – **Hillarp Persson** 106
HILLARP PERSSON – Hector 106; Rowson 265
HJARTARSON – Short 60
HRAČEK – **Nikolić** 310
HÜBNER – Müller, K. 102; **Vaganian** 287
IBRAHIMOV, R. – Mamedyarov 153
ILLESCAS – **del Rio** 226; Dominguez, L. 80;
   Topalov 97
IVANISEVIĆ – Nisipeanu 156
IVANOV, J. – **Costas Varela** 216
IVANOV, S. – Mikhalevski 274
IVKOV – **Petrosian** 140
JENNI – **Kacheishvili** 130
JOBAVA – Carlsen 93
JOHANNESSEN, L. – Shirov 90
KACHEISHVILI – Jenni 130
KALISVAART – Ballo 311
KAMSKY – Short 97
KANTSLER – **Gelfand** 219
KARPOV – Anand 111; Georgiev, Ki. 41;
   Kasparov 44; Kasparov 262, 272;
   Korchnoi 45; Ljubojević 54; **Short** 155;
   Yusupov 27; **Yusupov** 133

KASIMDZHANOV – Kasparov 105
KASPAROV – Beliavsky 65; **Danailov** 207;
Karpov 44; **Karpov** 262, 272;
Kasimdzhanov 105; Korchnoi 177;
Kramnik 28; Kuijpers 304; Morozevich
89; Nunn 306; Ponomariov 167; **Shirov**
241; Short 42, 51; **Timman** 59; Timman
160
KELEČEVIĆ – Burgermeister 296
KERES – Botvinnik 152; **Euwe** 168
KHALIFMAN – Anand 79; **Yusupov** 251
KHENKIN – Sulskis 34
KHUZMAN – **Olafsson, H.** 250
KINDERMANN – **Vaïsser** 199
KIRIAKÓV – Sowray 275
KISELEV – Epishin 259
KNAAK – Vaganian 141
KOPIONKIN – Ulko 196
KORCHNOI – Karpov 45; **Kasparov** 177;
Short 23; Tal 311
KOTOV – **Botvinnik** 123
KOTRONIAS – **Nielsen, P.H.** 229
KOVAČEVIĆ – Nemeth 315
KOVALEVSKAYA – **Lugovoi** 78
KOŽUL – Naiditsch 180; Nunn 200; Radjabov
222
KRAMNIK – Kasparov 28; Morozevich 92;
Shirov 245; Svidler 279
KRASENKOW – Navara 182
KRUSH – Bologan 211; Shirov 161
KUIJPERS – **Kasparov** 304
LAGOWSKI – Shishkin 270
LALIĆ – **Yusupov** 142
LARSEN – **Portisch** 57
LAUTIER – Leko 283
LEKO – **Lautier** 283; **Vallejo Pons** 158
LIE, K. – **Carlsen, M.** 309
LIGTERINK – Nunn 312
LJUBOJEVIĆ – **Karpov** 54
LPUTIAN – Anand 103; **Mamedyarov** 36
LUGOVOI – **Avrukh** 62; Kovalevskaya 78
LUKACS – Stohl 139
MACIEJA – **Wojtaszek** 169
MAGOMEDOV – **Guseinov** 49
MAMEDYAROV – **Ibrahimov, R.** 153; Lputian
36
MARIOTTI – **O'Kelly, R.** 314
MIKHALEVSKI – Dvoirys 288; **Ivanov, S.** 274
MILOV, V. – Campora 128; Polgar, J. 134
MOROZEVICH – **Anand** 87; **Kasparov** 89;
Kramnik 92

MÜLLER, K. – **Hubner** 102
NAIDITSCH – **Kožul** 180
NAJDORF – **Bronstein** 132
NAVARA – **Krasenkow** 182
NEMETH – **Kovačević** 315
NEVEROV – Gelfand 64
NIELSEN, P.H. – Kotronias 229
NIKOLIĆ – Hraček 310
NISIPEANU – **Ivanisević** 156
NOR – Peter 216
NUNN – **Kasparov** 306; **Kožul** 200;
Ligterink 312
O'KELLY, R. – Mariotti 314
OLAFSSON, H. – Khuzman 250
PALO – de Firmian 308; **Portisch** 178
PARMENTIER – **Piskov** 197
PEDERSEN, N. – **Gagunashvili** 147
PETER – **Nor** 216
PETROSIAN – Botvinnik 148; Ivkov 140
PFLEGER – **Djurić** 56
PIGUSOV – **Alterman** 40
PINTER – Brynell 300
PISKOV – Parmentier 197
PLATER – **Gligorić** 120
PLATONOV – Gulko 242
PLIESTER – Rosten 137
POLGAR, J. – **Milov, V.** 134; **Sokolov, I.** 181
POLZIN – **Bareev** 237
PONOMARIOV – **Kasparov** 167
PORTISCH – **Beliavsky** 298; Larsen 57; Palo
178; **Seirawan** 150
RADJABOV – **Kožul** 222
RAZUVAEV – Shirov 246; Stohl 253
ROSTEN – **Pliester** 137
ROWSON – **Hillarp Persson** 265
SAKAEV – Svidler 212
SCHANDORFF – **Vallejo Pons** 158
SEIRAWAN – Portisch 150
SHIROV – **Gelfand** 280; **Johannessen, L.** 90;
Kasparov 241; **Kramnik** 245; **Krush** 161;
Razuvaev 246; **Van Wely** 83
SHISHKIN – **Lagowski** 270
SHORT – **Dreev** 147; **Hjartarson** 60;
Kamsky 97; Karpov 155; **Kasparov** 42,
51; **Korchnoi** 23
SMEJKAL – **Sosonko** 286
SMYSLOV – **Gligorić** 257
SOKOLOV, I. – Polgar, J. 181
SOSONKO – Smejkal 286
SOWRAY – **Kiriakov** 275
SPASSKY – Fischer 258

SPASSOV, L. – **Alterman** 109
SPEELMAN – Uhlmann 228
STOHL – **Lukacs** 139; **Razuvaev** 253
SULSKIS – **Khenkin** 34
SUTOVSKY – **Van Wely** 267
SVIDLER – **Kramnik** 279; **Sakaev** 212
SZNAPIK – **Ftačnik** 221
TAL – **Botvinnik** 120; **Korchnoi** 311
TIMMAN – Geller 37; Kasparov 59; **Kasparov** 160
TISDALL – Bjarnason 126
TONNEMAN – **Born** 206
TOPALOV – Anand 171, 172; **Ftačnik** 234; **Illescas** 97; Yermolinsky 32
TORRE – Unzicker 136

UHLMANN – **Speelman** 228
ULKO – **Kopionkin** 196
UNZICKER – **Torre** 136
VAGANIAN – Hübner 287; **Knaak** 141
VAÏSSER – Kindermann 199
VALLEJO PONS – Leko 158; Schandorff 158
VAN BEEK – Gofshtein 307
VAN TILBURY – Zadrima 264
VAN WELY – Shirov 83; Sutovsky 267
WOJTASZEK – Macieja 169
YERMOLINSKY – **Topalov** 32
YUSUPOV – Beliavsky 95; **Karpov** 27; Karpov 133; Khalifman 251; Lalić 142
ZADRIMA – **Van Tilbury** 264
ZHELIANDINOV – **Atalik** 33

Index of Openings

Numbers refer to pages. Codes are ECO codes.

1 d4 Miscellaneous
A40 *9*; A45 *13, 183*; A50 *114*; A56 *290*

Modern Benoni
A60 *310*; A62 *311, 314*; A63 *312*; A64 *315*;
A65 *291*; A66 *301, 302*; A67 *304, 306, 307,
308, 309*; A68 *196, 199, 200*; A69 *196, 197*;
A70 *293, 296*; A77 *298*; A79 *300*

1 d4 d5 Miscellaneous
D00 *10*; D05 *101*

Queen's Gambit:
Unusual 2nd Moves
D06 *11, 12, 14*; D07 *17, 18, 19*; D08 *15*; D09 *16*

Slav
D10 *70, 95*; D13 *97*; D15 *74*; D17 *86, 87, 89,
90, 92, 93*; D18 *76, 78, 79, 80, 84*; D19 *82, 83*

Queen's Gambit Declined:
Exchange and Miscellaneous
D30 *12, 21*; D31 *20, 42, 44, 45, 66*; D35 *21,
22, 46, 51, 54*; D36 *49, 56, 57, 58, 59, 60, 62,
64, 65*

Semi-Slav
D43 *98*; D45 *111*; D47 *102, 103, 109*; D48 *104,
105, 106*

Queen's Gambit Declined:
Classical and Orthodox
D50 *23*; D55 *25*; D56 *27, 28*; D58 *35, 40, 41*;
D59 *36, 37*; D63 *29*; D67 *32, 33*; D68 *34*

Grünfeld
D80 *248*; D85 *249, 250, 251, 268, 270, 272,
274, 275, 279, 280*; D86 *253*; D87 *255, 257,
258, 259, 260, 262*; D88 *264*; D89 *265, 267*;
D97 *280, 283*; D98 *286, 288*; D99 *287*

Colle
E00 *67*

Queen's Indian
E10 *164*; E12 *173, 177, 178, 179, 180, 181,
182*; E15 *165, 167, 169, 171, 172*; E19 *168*

Nimzo-Indian: Sämisch and others
E20 *116*; E24 *120, 122, 123, 126*; E27 *120,
129*; E29 *132, 133, 134*

Nimzo-Indian: Classical
E32 *143, 155, 156, 158, 160, 161*; E34 *143,
147*; E35 *148, 150, 152, 153*

Nimzo-Indian: 4 e3
E41 *139, 140, 141, 142*; E43 *10*; E46 *135, 136*;
E49 *128*; E49 *130*; E50 *137*; E57 *135*

King's Indian: Averbakh, Four Pawns,
Sämisch and others
E61 *185*; E70 *186*; E73 *240*; E76 *188, 191, 201*;
E80 *241*; E81 *245, 246*; E87 *242*

King's Indian: Classical
E90 *184, 206*; E92 *207*; E94 *208, 209, 211, 216*;
E95 *212*; E97 *216, 231, 232, 233, 234, 237*; E98
218, 219; E99 *221, 222, 224, 226, 228, 229*

Other Books from Gambit Publications

Mastering the Chess Openings Volume 1
John Watson
Acclaimed author Watson presents a
wide-ranging view of the way in which
top-class players really handle the opening,
rather than an idealized and simplified model.
Volume 1, focusing on king's pawn openings,
offers both entertainment and challenging
material for study in openings such as the
Sicilian and Ruy Lopez.
336 pages, 248 x 172 mm; $29.95 / £19.99

101 Chess Endgame Tips
Steve Giddins
This is an ideal endgame study book to read
without using a chess set, as the abundant
diagrams guide you through the analysis and
illustrate the key points. All types of endings
are covered, including both simple technical
situations and more complex strategic battles.
112 pages, 248 x 172 mm; $19.95 / £11.99

Modern Chess Planning
Efstratios Grivas
Good planning is central to good chess. A plan
gives meaning to manoeuvres and tactical
devices, forming a coherent whole that brings
us closer to our goals. This challenging book
provides 75 superb practical examples where it
is important to choose the right plan.
144 pages, 248 x 172 mm; $24.95 / £14.99

Decision-Making at the Chessboard
Viacheslav Eingorn
Grandmaster Eingorn draws upon his vast
experience to show how to weigh the various
factors in positions, and decide on the best
course of action. The reader will gain a
greater understanding of decision-making and
develop an enhanced feel for the harmonious
use of intuition and calculation.
208 pages, 210 x 145 mm; $24.95 / £15.99

Fundamental Chess Endings
Karsten Müller & Frank Lamprecht
In a major event in chess publishing, two
German endgame experts have produced a
masterly one-volume encyclopaedia that
covers all major endgames. This is the first
truly modern one-volume endgame
encyclopaedia, and makes full use of endgame
tablebases and analytical engines.
416 pages, 248 x 172 mm; $29.95 / £19.99

Secrets of Modern Chess Strategy
John Watson
In a profound but thoroughly practical
manner, this classic work explores how chess
concepts have evolved over the past 70 years.
Acclaimed double-winner of the 1999 British
Chess Federation and 1999 United States
Chess Federation 'Book of the Year' awards.
272 pages, 248 x 172 mm; $24.95 / £19.99

Chess Strategy in Action
John Watson
Here Watson fleshes out the theory presented
to enormous acclaim in *Secrets of Modern
Chess Strategy*. He uses examples from
imaginative players such as Kasparov,
Kramnik, Anand, Ivanchuk and tempestuous
innovators such as Shirov and Morozevich.
288 pages, 248 x 172 mm; $24.95 / £19.99

Grandmaster Chess Move by Move
John Nunn
The King of chess writers provides another
irresistible mixture of instructive games,
opening novelties, entertaining anecdotes and
thought-provoking ideas. Throughout, the
emphasis is on what the reader can learn from
each game, so the book is ideal study material
for those seeking to progress to a higher level
of chess understanding.
288 pages, 248 x 172 mm; $24.95 / £15.99

About the Publisher: Gambit Publications Ltd is passionate about creating innovative and instructive chess books. Gambit specializes in chess, and the company is owned and run exclusively by chess masters and grandmasters.

www.gambitbooks.com